Praise for *The Edmund Wilson Reader*

"A generous assortment of the writing of the most versatile man of letters in our recent history. . . . An invaluable book." —*Christian Science Monitor*

"It is hard to see how the job could have been better done. All of Wilson's major interests are well represented; the material has been skillfully arranged to provide a clear view of his development over the years."
—John Gross, *New York Review of Books*

"[*The Edmund Wilson Reader*] offers an introduction to a marvellous mind playing over a range of vital cultural matters and everyone should rush to read it."
—*Times Literary Supplement*

"[This collection] indicates Wilson's wide-ranging interests and his ability to make complex ideas accessible to a large audience." —*Sewannee Review*

THE EDMUND WILSON READER

*Edited, with an Introduction
and Notes, by Lewis M. Dabney*

REVISED AND EXPANDED

DA CAPO PRESS
NEW YORK

Library of Congress Cataloging-in-Publication Data

Wilson, Edmund, 1895–1972.
  [Selections. 1997]
  The Edmund Wilson reader / edited, with an introduction and
notes, by Lewis M. Dabney.—Rev. and expanded, 1st Da Capo Press
ed.
    p.   cm.
  Rev. ed. of: The portable Edmund Wilson, 1983.
  Includes bibliographical references.
  ISBN 0-306-80809-9 (alk. paper)
  I. Dabney, Lewis M. II. Wilson, Edmund, 1895–1972. Portable
Edmund Wilson. III. Title.
PS3545.I6245A6   1997
818'.5209—DC21   97-22105
                                                             CIP

First Da Capo Press edition 1997

This Da Capo Press paperback edition of *The Edmund Wilson Reader* is
a revised and expanded republication of the edition first published
under the title *The Portable Edmund Wilson* in 1983 in New York. The
new material includes a revised preface, introduction, and notes; an
updated chronology and bibliography; essays on Trotsky, Jane Austen,
and detective fiction; two short stories, six poems, one drawing, and
excerpts from all of Wilson's journals. It is published by arrangement
with the Estate of Edmund Wilson, Farrar, Straus & Giroux, Inc., and
Viking Penguin, a division of Penguin Books USA, Inc.

Da Capo Press gratefully acknowledges the help and kindness of
Roger Straus and Michael Hathaway at Farrar, Straus & Giroux,
Lewis M. Dabney, Viking Penguin, Simon & Schuster, and Penguin
UK for making this new edition possible.

Published by Da Capo Press, Inc.
A Subsidiary of Plenum Publishing Corporation
233 Spring Street, New York, N.Y. 10013

CONTENTS

VI Credos and Characterizations

VII Fiction

PREFACE TO THE NEW EDITION

~~~~~~

The Edmund Wilson Reader is the successor to the *Portable Edmund Wilson*, which was produced almost fifteen years ago with the encouragement of Malcolm Cowley and Roger Straus. The format of Viking's Portables was well-suited to Wilson's writing, for he worked in units that could stand by themselves, as they first did in the magazines. Grouped thematically into a broadly historical pattern, they acquire a new resonance within the developing expression of the man's life in art. No complete book could be included, for *Patriotic Gore* and *To the Finland Station* were too long, while the major essays were scattered through collections such as *The Triple Thinkers* and *The Wound and the Bow*, but from these and other volumes I assembled work that had lasted as well as any literature of Wilson's generation. I also included a number of short pieces. Wilson, a master of the short, illuminates general issues when dealing with the particular, describing a writer or reporting a scene.

My aim in the *Portable* was to reveal his achievements as a critic of literature, history, and personality. Although he was widely celebrated as a man of letters, the gossip about his famous friends, connections, wives, and sex life had somewhat obscured the substance of his writing. Never fashionable in the academy, partly because his eclectic interests, historical vision, and reliance on his own judgment and experience made him difficult to teach, by 1983 Wilson was practically invisible in literary studies dominated by critical theory. Today, theory is less monolithic, and Wilson's readers include younger academic critics as well as literary journalists, who join the ranks of his admirers in *Edmund Wilson: Centennial Reflections*—soon to appear from Princeton University Press. His name and opinions are cited regularly in book reviews and quarterlies.

The increased authority of Wilson's criticism—which I have occasionally taken account of in revising the introduction and notes to this book—makes it appropriate to look more closely at his non-critical writing. With a premium on space, I settled in the *Portable* for token representations of his fiction and verse, and, except for a few pages from *Upstate*, passed over his journals (only two of which had then appeared). In addition to new examples of Wilson's criticism, Da Capo Press has made it possible in this collection to demonstrate how good his fiction and verse can be and to suggest the richness of the journals. Taken together, even as seen in these brief selections, the journals make an extraordinary chronicle of personal as well as social history.

Readers will continue to explore Wilson's work for themselves. This book is one man's approach to the essential Wilson, a complement to the shelfful that, with admirable grace, strength, and accuracy, tell us what he has to say about life and literature.

Lewis M. Dabney
Laramie, Wyoming
May 1997

INTRODUCTION

~~~~~~

Edmund Wilson's reputation continues to grow. The versatility and range, sound intelligence and taste, dramatic imagination, and lucid, vigorous style that were a force in the literary life of five decades retain their power many years after his death. Critic, portraitist, reporter, and historian, Wilson is a guide to the movements of the 1920s and '30s, which he helped to shape. He is an interpreter of the humanistic tradition, as well as the connections among personality, social history, politics, and literature. His fiction, poetry, and plays, his accounts of languages and traveling, his satire and his *jeux d'esprit* still instruct, amuse, and move. The last of the great journalists who wrote for the educated man-in-the-street, Wilson was the heir of the men of letters of Britain and France, and of American critics from Poe and Emerson to Henry Adams. Like his predecessors, he educated himself for the benefit of his readers. "If there is an American civilization," a writer in *The New York Times* observed when he died in 1972, "Mr. Wilson has helped us to find it, and is himself an important part of it."

No one book, however, conveys the weight of Wilson's work and influence, and the continuities among his books have not been easy to perceive. Conversations turn to his personality, to his relationships with Nabokov, Fitzgerald, or Mary McCarthy, and to the affairs chronicled in his journals, not only because this prickly, generous, eccentric, and determined man lived among famous names and wrote about his sex life, but because one reader's Wilson seldom corresponds to another's. In youth Wilson wanted "to learn something about all the main departments of human thought," as he rather grandly told his father after college. He learned "to pursue a line of thought through pieces on miscellaneous and more or less fortuitous subjects," first working up material for books in reviews and essays. In *Axel's Castle* he interpreted the modernist masters, in *To the Finland Station* the heroes of the Marxist intellectual tradition, subjects equally important to educated people between the two world wars. As he outlasted his literary generation and found himself on the margins of American life, he opened up new territories, exploring the languages, history, and culture of the Jews, the Russians, the Hungarians, and, on his own native ground, the struggle of the Iroquois to maintain their identity. He returned to British and European writers, and to nineteenth-century American statesmen, soldiers, and artists who could write and who mirrored social concerns. For his contemporary Malcolm Cowley he became a mixture "of Dr. Johnson, Carlyle, and Burton the traveler." One read *The New Yorker*, Cowley wrote, "to see what in God's name he would be doing next."

Patriotic Gore, a history of the consciousness of Civil War America, was Wilson's last important book and is considered by many his best. Portraying people through literary documents, he brought the old republic to life for new readers. He sought perspective upon Lincoln's war, as he had once identified with Lenin's revolution. To put *Patriotic Gore* and *Finland Station* side by side is to see how they supplement, complement, and argue with each other, mirroring the author's life and times. Posthumously published letters and journals fill out the picture composed by his earlier writings. Wilson's letters to friends illustrate what Fitzgerald meant by calling him an intellectual conscience, and they show him acquiring new interests without relinquishing old ones, just as the journals document his social experience over half a century. He has been the subject of a number of eloquent, discerning partial portraits; the centennial year saw the publication of a biography, a collection of short critical pieces largely of the early years, and two symposiums in his honor—themselves leading to *Edmund Wilson: Centennial Reflections.* Able now to see the whole work in its development, we can begin to give the man his place in the history of criticism.

In English departments Wilson's place has been a marginal one. He was never a critical theorist, and although he savored the intricacies of *Ulysses* and *Finnegans Wake,* he was bored by *explication de texte.* He evaluated books and tried to understand the life from which they came, yet left no formulation of his methods that others could adopt. "The Historical Interpretation of Literature" is not such an account, but instead a survey of the contributions of Marx and Engels, Taine and Freud, whose taste and moral conviction are as important to him as their deterministic ideas. Wilson can teach us how to adapt intellectual systems to literary ends. When criticism moved into the academy after World War II, however, he found himself an isolated figure. Cast as a popularizer in the era of the New Critics, he seemed elitist to the literary left of the sixties. His accounts of language and culture were too concrete, too personal for the structuralists, and none of these schools shared his novelistic interest in the writer's life or his historian's perspective on the times. For his part Wilson, who admired good scholarship, satirized the narrowness and pretension found in what his friend H. L. Mencken called the professorial. Wilson saw criticism as a service to artists and readers and, in his irritation with those who made it an end in itself, sometimes preferred to call himself a writer and a journalist. We can settle for describing him as Henry James described Sainte-Beuve: "He was the student, the inquirer, the observer, the active, indefatigable commentator, whose constant aim was to arrive at justness of characterization."

He was read by everyone, including writers, scholars, diplomats, and rock singers. From the days of *Partisan Review* to those of *The New York Review of Books*, the New York critics learned from him, valuing his ability to connect the spheres of art and politics, to mediate between modernism and the literature of the past. Lionel Trilling recalled how Wilson asked about his work on Arnold, at a Marxist political affair of the thirties. "He actually thought that a book on Matthew Arnold might be interesting and useful. He wanted to read it," Trilling wrote, still grateful for the "liberating effect that only Wilson could have had, with his involvement in the life of the present which was so clearly not at odds with his natural and highly developed feeling for scholarship." This same sense of the utility of learning and the community of those who write and read is available in Wilson's books. Most emerged from magazine articles, and even the books that were conceived as wholes have their ambivalences and contradictions, yet they communicate the vitality of the cultural moment, the issues, and the man, the pulse of Emerson's "man thinking." In each of his books Wilson is a scholar, an artist, and an activist.

This volume is a chronological selection from the best of Wilson's work, and in the first section are memoirs of important people and places from his youth. As he writes of the old stone house (a modest family estate in upstate New York), his father's extraordinarily divided personality, the benevolent authority of Christian Gauss, and the romantic intensity of Edna St. Vincent Millay, Wilson establishes his enduring values. Next come articles that span the interests of the twenties and thirties. These decades are all too easily contrasted, but his writing is an important continuity, for he was trying "to make something of America, to make an American culture," whether assimilating Proust and Joyce or investigating labor struggles after the stock market crash. *To the Finland Station* is represented by the portrait of Marx, which develops one of Wilson's great themes, the relationship of suffering and neurosis to creative power, a theme restated in the story of Philoctetes, the hero whose suppurating wound is the price of his magical bow. Other essays from this period illustrate the critic's methods and his range. After World War II, Wilson was often on the road, investigating minority civilizations and the religions that helped them to survive. Some of this work is included in "Credos and Characterizations." In the portraits from *Patriotic Gore*, including Harriet Beecher Stowe, General Grant, and Justice Holmes, he returns to his family's origins in Puritan New England.

1

Wilson derived his individualism and literary idealism from the nineteenth century, when the written word seemed humanity's natural language, and his sense of vocation from the professional class into which he was born in Red Bank, New Jersey in 1895. He was the only child of a brilliant trial lawyer, sometime attorney general of the state, whose dinner-table discourses affected his son's literary style, and who, in an age of robber barons and corrupt city bosses, passed on a patriotic allegiance to the republic of Lincoln. The boy grew up in a genteel enclave in suburban New Jersey, enjoying trips to Canada, the West, and Europe, and summer family reunions in upstate New York. His father's family was Presbyterian, and the senior Edmund Wilson—Wilson signed himself "Jr." until age 28—taught him to admire effort, energy, and commitment, to fear laziness and mediocrity. His mother's people, although descended from the New England Mathers, "had scrapped the old-time religion and still retained a certain animus toward it." Like other classic American writers, Wilson carried on the Puritan tradition by rebelling against it. Like other critics from the Romantics on, he transferred to literature the passion and piety of a faith increasingly undermined by science.

Readers of his autobiographical essays know that his boyhood was difficult, for his mother was deaf, and his father suffered from depression and hypochondria. Behind Wilson's "wounded" heroes lies this formidable figure who, in his bad spells, oppressed the household from behind a felt-lined study door. Wilson's portraiture owes something to pride in his father's mind and work as well as a need to comprehend his pain. The boy's pleasures were his numerous relatives and the books in the family libraries. At prep school he acquired the beginnings of a style by imitating British classics. Taine, who made the English writers interesting as personalities, was his first model as a critic. Shaw was his first intellectual hero; at sixteen Wilson lost his faith when reading the critique of religion in the preface to *Major Barbara.* The fine memoir of his Greek teacher, "Mr. Rolfe," shows him discovering the humanistic tradition in the evangelical milieu of the Hill School.

The education of the gentleman-amateur, which at its best fostered sound judgments and the ability to express oneself, to assimilate great figures of the past and find one's way around in new terrain, sustained Wilson as a professional journalist. In the Princeton setting of football and torchlight parades he became familiar with those English critics, from the age of Johnson on, to whom this American seems closer than modern British colleagues whose range and confidence inevitably reflect the shrinking away of the empire. Wilson found a cosmopolitan American ancestor in Henry James, and on a summer trip abroad he began the journal he would keep for half a century. Meanwhile, he went on from Homer and Plato to Dante and French literature. Wilson approaches literature as a student of languages, and, like so many major writers of the American twenties, he was deeply impressed by the Continental aesthetic, which gave him a perspective on English literature and a way to treat his native material. In Christian Gauss's courses he learned that great art could be polished, orderly, and impersonal, that the artist's morality was not the citizen's or the churchgoer's. He was soon infatuated with Flaubert's irony and *le mot juste*. Gauss also introduced Wilson to Voltaire, Michelet, Renan, and Sainte-Beuve, whom he would carry with him during World War I. He admired their formal versatility as well as the cause of the Enlightenment and the historical point of view. Like these French predecessors, as George Steiner has pointed out, Wilson wrote "dialogues, fables, political pamphlets, masses of criticism," and became a "seminal and powerful" presence between the two worlds of the university and journalism.

This was the great age of American reporter-writers, and Mencken and James Huneker drew Wilson to literary journalism by their success at promoting culture outside the genteel scene in which he had grown up. Restless in that milieu, after college he got a job on a New York newspaper. World War I broke the cocoon of privilege, thrusting the young man with all his humanistic baggage into the modern world. Wilson's friends stayed with their caste and became officers, but a summer in training camp persuaded him to enlist as a private in the hospital corps. He came to appreciate the variety of American cultures, and army life made him sceptical of rank and social privilege. He tasted the horror of war in the Vosges, and in his protest fiction and verse are seeds of the introduction to *Patriotic Gore* half a century later. His war experience bound the man to his literary generation. When he returned to take up a career in New York, memories of the tragic waste he had witnessed made him demand more of life and art.

2

Wilson came to think of himself as "a man of the twenties," and although he never jumped into the Plaza fountain, he was exuberant enough to surprise his friend Dos

Passos by doing a handstand in front of an elevator in his three-piece suit. His documentary, critical, and imaginative writings make up our best account of that scene of "drinks, animated conversation, gaiety, brilliant writing, uninhibited exchange of ideas," the scene in which he came of age. With Dorothy Parker's help he became an editor at *Vanity Fair*, and there he published most of his first reviews and essays, while covering plays for *The Dial* and the life of the metropolis in *The New Republic*. In a day when the popular arts were fresh and high art seemed secure, when people were less self-conscious about their tastes, he moved easily from Stravinsky's music, the paintings of Georgia O'Keeffe, or the latest production of the Moscow Art Theater, to vaudeville, burlesque, and—himself an amateur magician—the art of Houdini. Sensitive to personalities, in a few lines he could suggest the quality of a life, re-creating the murder trial of a young woman whose circumstances and character moved him, chronicling a drunken weekend against the backdrop of the imminent executions of Sacco and Vanzetti. Such pieces foreshadow the concern with social justice and responsibility evident in his reports on Depression America.

The aggressively liberated Cummings had called Wilson "the man in the iron necktie," but he was soon absorbing his share of Prohibition liquor, and the novel *I Thought of Daisy* conveys his excited response to the women of Greenwich Village and Broadway. His memoir of Edna Millay shows how eagerly he rushed into a hopeless grand passion for the poet. His subsequent marriage to the actress Mary Blair was not a happy one, and he began restlessly pursuing chorus girls, eventually settling into a long relationship with Frances Menihan, the dance-hall girl of his journals, called "Anna" in *Memoirs of Hecate County*. In 1930 he married a longtime friend, Margaret Canby, a marriage that ended before it could really begin, as we learn from the long passage in *The Thirties* written after her accidental death in California in 1932. Personal experience also provided him the material for plays and poems, and in *I Thought of Daisy* a "symphonic structure" out of Proust and Joyce is imposed on the conventional materials of a youth's attempt to find his way in life.

The important work of Wilson's youth was the reviewing collected in *The Shores of Light* and built upon in *Axel's Castle* and later essays in *The Triple Thinkers* and *The Wound and the Bow.* No other American critic has had such a role as he did when adjudicating the claims of his compatriots and interpreting the international modernist movement. He helped launch Hemingway, appreciating the writer's originality and power, and deserves partial credit for Fitzgerald's development to *The Great Gatsby.* Celebrating *Ulysses,* which made everything else, he said, "look brassy," he was an astute admirer of the early Eliot, and one of the first to see Yeats as the great modern poet, whose lyric voice kept the muse alive in a scientific, democratic world. When he commented on Stein's emulation of cubism or Lawrence's account of sexual experience, it was with an awareness of Freud's influence, the philosophy of Whitehead, the effects of World War I. From the first, he also mediated between the present and the past. Contrasting the modernists to such prewar heroes as Shaw and Anatole France, Wilson reminded his own American generation of its affinities and debts to Poe and the great New Englanders, its need for the solid craftsmanship of authors like Wharton and James.

As reviewer-critic, he held himself responsible to give the gist of a book or tell the story, acquiring the skill at plot summary that he would exercise on obscure novels with the same relish as on the work of Pushkin, Pasternak, and Proust. He turned to dialogues, dramatic monologues, and polemic, entertaining readers while instructing them about cultural issues, from the conflict of highbrow and lowbrow to the doctrinaire humanism of

Irving Babbitt and Paul Elmer More. In mid-decade Wilson left *Vanity Fair,* the most literate of fashion magazines, for Herbert Croly's *New Republic,* where the articles of *The Shores of Light* and *The American Earthquake* appeared along with the serial versions of *Axel's Castle* and *To the Finland Station.* There he could better carry on the work of Mencken and Van Wyck Brooks, those prophets of the renascence of the twenties who had never escaped the provincialism of the old America. While Mencken continued denouncing the philistines and Brooks continued describing our artistic failures, the younger man spoke for the generation that created an indigenous literature to match the European standard. His work captures the energy of a literate culture not yet hemmed in by mass taste, and of a nation emerging onto the world stage.

Axel's Castle (1931), which made his reputation, is both celebration and critique of the modern masters. Wilson saw that Proust, Joyce, Eliot, Yeats, Valery, and Stein, whom he termed collectively Symbolists, had common techniques and values and that, like the Romantics in their time, they had "disintegrated the old mechanism and revealed to the imagination a new flexibility and freedom." To Maxwell Perkins he wrote that he intended "to give popular accounts that will convince people of their importance and persuade people to read them." The result was a map of this artistic and intellectual terrain that remains useful after fifty years of specialized scholarship. As he lived with these writers, however, he grew skeptical of them as "guides to life," at any rate for Americans. If Joyce was a great life-affirmer—Wilson promoted *Finnegans Wake* as eagerly as *Ulysses*—the critic's activist temperament and Protestant heritage, his vision of literature as a moral force, rebelled against Eliot's spiritual weariness, the narcissism of Valery, the escapist strain in Yeats, and especially against Proust's hypochondria. His reservations were strengthened by the collapse of the stock market, and the Proust chapter breaks in two when a remarkable paraphrase of the novel, which captures its themes and power in thirty pages, is succeeded by an attack on the author's perversities. Unable as yet to reconcile these with Proust's moral insight, in the manner of *The Wound and the Bow*, Wilson found historical perspective in Marx. The thirties have begun in his famous summation of *Remembrance of Things Past* as "the Heartbreak House of capitalist culture."

His detractors are right in saying that he did not fully assimilate modernism. The split between the aesthetic and the moral values of *Axel's Castle* owes something to Wilson's derivation of the Symbolists from the *fin de siècle* and his failure to see their equal debt to the Victorians, to whom he would himself return not many years later. It reflects the conflict between the avant-garde and its bourgeois public, a creative tension that would not survive the Depression. His own literary idealism was now to be visited on the Marxist heroes, people who instead of retreating into themselves had imposed their ideals on the world. Yet he could compare the moral genius of Lenin to that of Proust for Soviet readers in 1935 and he made the politics of the left compatible with high culture for American intellectuals of the 1930s, as well as their heirs.

3

In the 1930s, a period of radical aspirations and severe disappointments, Wilson came into full possession of his powers. He did lasting work as a reporter and biographer-historian as well as a literary critic. Through the first half of the decade he was on the road. *The American Jitters*, his survey of the United States in 1931, is one of our best books about the Depression, while his journal of five months spent in the Soviet Union in 1935 captures the face of that country on the eve of the great purges. In these books, and in *To the Finland Station*, begun at about the same time, he sees Marxism as the child of the Enlightenment, bringing to it the special enthusiasm of literary Americans who have abandoned the cloister for a cause. Before *Finland Station*, published in 1940, was complete, however, the Moscow Trials had destroyed his belief in the revolution in Russia, dealing his assumptions about human progress a lasting blow. The book survived as a study of revolutionary personalities, and it remains the classic account of the heroic tradition of socialism. Freud had helped him come to terms with Marx's personality, and, when applying his Marxist experience to criticism, he also explored the place of neurosis and trauma in the lives of writers. The results were the major essays of *The Triple Thinkers* and *The Wound and the Bow.*

In the same week that *Axel's Castle* appeared, two years before the New Deal began, he was urging writers to help "take Communism away from the Communists and apply it to American conditions." Unlike the specialized, poetic accounts of Steinbeck, Agee, and others, his Depression reporting conveys the plight of the whole country, and his dramatic irony and ear for speech—the tape recorder did not exist—are sure instruments. In *The American Jitters* he sets the dedication of the Empire State Building off against the suicides of unemployed workers. He surveys the world of those who *do* have jobs, from the Detroit assembly lines, where a sudden silence means that someone has lost a finger, to the 110-degree heat at Hoover Dam, to the bleak winter streets of Lawrence, Massachusetts, where immigrant workers confront the power of the textile mills. The hopelessness of rural poverty, the impersonal pressures of New York, and the Southern California intellectual wasteland all underscore the bankruptcy of a system where "everybody is out for himself and devil take the hindmost, with no common purpose and little common culture to give life stability and sense." This had been the experience of his father's generation in the gilded age, and Wilson saw himself with a chance to redeem their frustration. In his literary articles he pressed the artist's case against a commercial society: "It gave us a new sense of power," he wrote many years later, "to find ourselves still carrying on while the bankers, for a change, were taking a beating."

Like other writers and artists on the left, he delivered food to striking miners, put out pamphlets, contributed to revolutionary magazines, and carefully followed Roosevelt's reforms. He also recorded the activities of himself and his friends, and the journals of *The Thirties* allow us to see his sexual life as part of "the disintegration of society." Communism, which he would come to consider a religious myth, at first seemed a scientific program through which humanity could direct its own fate, a secular alternative to the faiths of the churches. He conceived a book that would proceed from Marx's theories to Lenin's arrival in Russia in 1917 to carry them out, a study of the movement of history toward the Finland station in St. Petersburg. The book mirrored and was intended to complete his political evolution. Characteristically, however, Wilson went to Russia to see for himself, and he returned with grave doubts. Against the still-surviving Leninist idealism his Soviet journal sets the "Moscow tic," a compulsion to look over one's shoulder when discussing politics. Now he grasped the "absolute value" of republican American institutions. He tried to rationalize the dictatorship in Russian terms, blaming everything he distrusted on the heritage of the old regime—"These six-winged angels give me the willies," he writes of the icons in an ancient monastery. Yet as he warmed to the personal qualities of the Russian people, their spontaneity, idealism, and love of art, he grew warier of the Soviet state, and the show trials of 1937 turned him fiercely anti-Stalinist.

Because it ends as the Russian Revolution begins, *To the Finland Station* is not destroyed by this disillusionment. Although he dismisses the Marxist dialectic, he continues to admire the individuals who led lives of extraordinary self-denial for the sake of the socialist idea. He re-creates the intricate movement of socialist life, its assumptions and counterassumptions, its actions and stallings, from the aftermath of the French Revolution to 1917. *Finland Station* has been called the noblest of Wilson's books, and it is the most tightly unified, displaying a narrative momentum not found in *Patriotic Gore*. For the first time he integrates his abilities as a reporter, an interpreter of texts, a storyteller, and a dramatist. Michelet, the hero of the early chapters, has taught the American how to unite research with re-creation of the human struggle. The portrait of the French historian states Wilson's scholarly ideal from that moment on—the man who works up his own languages and knows the whole literature of his subject, who goes directly to the sources and reports on them for his readers, "without allowing either the journalistic or the academic formulas to come between first-hand knowledge and us." It is an ideal of writing as action. Michelet's *History of France* had handed on the spirit of 1789, and in his "revolutionary will" the strengths of Protestantism, Romanticism, and the Age of Reason asserted themselves against the bourgeois age, as Wilson now saw this embodied in the compromises of his old heroes, Renan, Taine, and Anatole France.

The portrait of Marx that dominates *Finland Station* captures the intellectual and moral power of the founder of Communism. It is the fullest, most intense of Wilson's characterizations, incorporating the history of the movement with a human life he shared to the point of breaking out in boils like those which had afflicted his hero. Wilson's Marx is a philosopher, a scientist, an artist—in *Das Kapital* "the poet of commodities"—who combats the dehumanization of society by the profit motive. He is also the paterfamilias of the family picnics in Soho, and "the great secular rabbi of the nineteenth century," who avowed that the bourgeoisie would have cause to remember his carbuncles. With a receptivity to unconscious motives derived from Freud, Wilson sees Marx's difficult life coloring his cruel account of the historical process. "Only so sore and angry a spirit, so ill at ease in the world," the critic concludes, "could have recognized and seen into the causes of the wholesale mutilation of humanity, the grim collisions, the uncomprehended convulsions, to which that age of great profits was doomed." Marx, then, not Dickens or Kipling, is the great embodiment of the wound and the bow. The agony of the artist—the romantic agony, as Wilson's friend Mario Praz calls it—is wedded to a Hegelian vision of historical necessity.

Wilson can also move us when he writes of men of action, but Lenin and Trotsky were less fully available in their writings than Marx and Engels, and their features were blurred by the ambiguities of the revolution in Russia. We are never quite sure of Wilson's sources, nor was he, as his introduction to the 1972 edition of the book admits, citing Soviet censorship. To have seen through Stalin made impossible for him to idealize Trotsky, despite the man's heroic qualities, but he never reconciled Lenin the selfless statesman, the benign headmaster of the Communists, with the creator of the Party dictatorship. In the preface to *Patriotic Gore* twenty years later, Wilson wrestles with the paradox that Lenin's attempt to free the Russian people resulted in a tightening of the bureaucratic net.

The intellectual experience of the thirties is applied to criticism in *The Triple Thinkers* and *The Wound and the Bow*, necessary reading for anyone concerned with the origins of imaginative literature in personality and social history. Life and art are better correlated in these essays than in *Axel's Castle*, for instead of introducing an avant-garde he is taking another look at writers, many of the nineteenth century, who had formed his taste in youth. The two collections illustrate the dialogue of the moderns with their elders, reminding us that, in America at any rate, the Victorian age did not really end till World War II. In *The Triple Thinkers* Shaw's political ideas are explored in the context of his dramatic art, "a music of ideas, or rather a music of moralities." Wilson's famous Freudian reading of *The Turn of the Screw* is joined to an analysis of James's double standard in judging European and American society. The portraits of Housman and John Jay Chapman resemble the work of a gifted painter whose empathy with his subjects enables him to project his own malaise while at the same time defining his code. In Chapman the critic discovers a heroic figure from the American 1890s, wounded in the same psychological and moral struggle as was Wilson's father. The other essay uses Housman's brilliant, bitter classical scholarship to underscore the frustrations of the poet of *The Shropshire Lad.* If the early Freudianism of the *Turn of the Screw* essay now seems naive—although Leon Edel does not share this judgment—Wilson's Chapman is definitive, and his portrait of Housman is as revealing as recent studies of the man's homosexuality. *The Triple Thinkers* has the suggestiveness, polish, and moral authority of criticism created by a man among his peers.

At the end of the book he calls art a victory of the intelligence over "some ache of disorder, some oppressive burden of uncomprehended events," and seven writers are viewed in this perspective in *The Wound and the Bow.* The influential monographs on Dickens and Kipling locate the abandonment each suffered in childhood as a source of the power of his fiction. Dickens's memory of fear and helplessness became a powerful instrument to expose the corruption of Victorian England, while Kipling's talent was partly thwarted, Wilson believes, by the nature of the man's adjustment to authority. Pointing out a comparable psychic strain in the work of Hemingway, Wilson shows how it could yield moral insight when artistically controlled. His long study of Turgenev, written many years later, relates the novelist's vision of Russian society to his struggles with a tyrannical mother who oppressed her sons as she did her serfs. Such work does not pretend to clarify the creative process, and it offers successor critics no formulas. Wilson's experience, imagination, and reading contribute as much as an acquaintance with Freud. He enables us to understand people of another time and place as though they were our contemporaries. He projects a conviction that the human spirit, though quick to bruise, is not easily crushed, that the artist-hero can make comprehensible and bearable a world which politics seems powerless to change.

4

It has been said that Wilson lost his subject as he came to critical maturity, and it is true that in the second half of his career he was no longer the interpreter of the literary and political avant-garde, itself now in retreat. He paid more attention to the younger writers than some of them believed—Berryman, Lowell, Updike were among his favorites—yet he did not identify with them as he did with his own generation, and he was something of an exile in the America of *Life* magazine, the Cold War, the academic ascendancy, and television. His curiosity, enthusiasm, and personal convictions carried him through the literatures of the past and into the corners of the modern world. Where his work had followed a line of development through the aestheticism of the twenties and the social commitment of the Depression years, now Wilson moved about, as he said, among "tables rotating interesting tasks," and at *The New Yorker* he acquired a forum that afforded more space and latitude than the tight columns of *The New Republic*. By the 1950s he was publishing ten-thousand-word reviews and book-length essays and travel journals, replete with anecdotes and quotations that conveyed the detail of his subject. The argument expanded, lapsed, was resumed, as the reporter-scholar digested his material. Wilson's literary personality was also expanding, lending weight to what he wrote about.

The 1940s were his dark period, a sort of mid-life crisis of morale. Wilson never believed in World War II, remembering the First World War and considering Stalin's Russia as bad as Hitler's Germany. He watched the literary community, already fragmented by politics, being bought out by Hollywood, the Luce magazines, and the big book clubs; the deaths of Fitzgerald, Sherwood Anderson, and John Peale Bishop brought home his role as a survivor in a darkened world. Collecting Fitzgerald's fragmentary work in *The Crack-Up* and editing *The Last Tycoon,* he turned to the American past in *The Shock of Recognition,* documenting a national tradition through the responses of our writers to one another. Meanwhile, he was writing *Memoirs of Hecate County,* a purge of his disappointments with the contemporary scene, including politics, the book business, art, romance, and social life. He had married Mary McCarthy, then beginning her career in New York, and they left the city to settle on Cape Cod. They had a son, Reuel, Wilson's second child—he had a daughter, Rosalind, by Mary Blair—and McCarthy produced her own volume of stories, *The Company She Keeps.* Their partnership became a collision of egos, ending in divorce in 1946, and these difficulties added to the gloom of *Hecate County.* With the heroic aspirations of *Finland Station* now badly undermined, he yielded to the old Puritan vision of the world going to hell in a hack.

Hecate County will never be popular as fiction, but is a better book than widely assumed. The notorious sexual frankness that caused it to be banned in New York has obscured his use of the philosophic and satiric tale. No longer crowding his material into a single plot, as in *I Thought of Daisy,* Wilson develops his themes in separate modes, moving from realism to macabre fantasy within a shadowy ex-urban background. Scenes and people as meticulously described as in his reportorial writing arbitrarily appear and disappear like the magical properties manipulated by one of his characters in a nightclub act. In "The Princess with the Golden Hair," a tale of illusion and reality, the pursuit of a sterile bourgeois goddess is counterpointed by the hot, doting affair with the "Anna" of the journals. If it is disturbing to see the author of *To the Finland Station* and *Patriotic Gore* taking notes on his encounters like a naturalist, as someone said, at the zoo of himself, and if his relationships with women are presented at their most exploitative, he successfully shows the narrator falling between classes like the hero of Flaubert's *Sentimental Education*. The mechanistic sex makes sense in terms of the novel, where such a rejection of Calvinistic inhibitions accentuates a sense of the corruption of the world. Our "man of the twenties" falls back on his heritage from Hawthorne and Twain. In the last tale the devil appears in the guise of an eighteenth-century *philosophe*, to boast, in French, of his triumphs in the age of Hitler and Stalin.

An ebullient temperament and strong loyalties helped Wilson regain his confidence, as did his marriage in 1946 to Elena Thornton, with whom he achieved a lasting domestic accord. While he exorcised his demons in *Memoirs of Hecate County*, he was beginning the affirming memoirs of teachers, family, and friends completed in the 1950s. Written after their subjects' deaths and scattered through various volumes, these portraits are truer to character than the composites in Wilson's fiction and more vivid than his diaries, owing more to memory than to notes. They express the warmth, generosity, and nurturing responsiveness implicit in his criticism. The writing is both polished and informal. The author appears at the side of the stage, a foil to those whose values he admires. What Alfred Kazin calls his gift "for articulating his life without telling it" gives this work a special place in American autobiography.

He chronicles his introduction to the life of art and thought. His grandparents' home, an oasis in his boyhood, embodies for him "the spirit that studies and understands" as opposed to "the spirit that acquires and consumes." The figure of his old Greek teacher, Mr. Rolfe, dramatizes the literary ideals that for Wilson had replaced the Christian faith, and in the portrait of Christian Gauss, he pays tribute to a humanist's influence in the classroom. The deaths of Edna Millay and Paul Rosenfeld move him to reassert the courage implicit in the high toll that art exacts. At the end these comrades of his youth had seemed defeated by illness and the world's neglect, but he takes Millay's work as a monument to her courageous spirit, and believes that "Paul's best writing bears on every page his triumph and his justification." The Protestant theme of the price of integrity returns in the critic's portrait of his father. In youth he had liked to speak of the senior Edmund Wilson's distinctions—Woodrow Wilson had wanted to put him on the Supreme Court—but remained silent about his morbid hypochondria. To confront this in "The Author at Sixty," giving it a context in the financial and moral insecurities of the gilded age, strengthens the son for his own later years, when one of his models was the independent lawyer, inquiring traveler, and first citizen of Red Bank, New Jersey, an old-fashioned republican unintimidated by the corporations or the government.

After World War II Wilson was both reviewer and travel writer for *The New Yorker,* roles that overlapped as he commented on the writers of countries he visited and on the societies from which his literary subjects came. The reviews of three decades are reprinted in the "literary chronicles," which Leon Edel considers part of his major work. In *Classics and Commercials* he addresses the American scene to object to detective stories, best-sellers, and the beginnings of the cult of fantasy literature. He finds relief in British comedy and satire, in Austen and Swift, Thackeray and Waugh. This amusing volume indulges Wilson's satirical gift, just as does the verse of his middle years, reprinted in *Night Thoughts*. There is more attention to new talent in his chronicle of the fifties and sixties, *The Bit Between My Teeth*, but the critic's account of his reading is no longer central to the period. Most of his space is devoted to the literary world of his youth, including the British *fin de siècle*. The charming essay "My Fifty Years with Dictionaries and Grammars" and two self-interviews complete what Wilson elsewhere calls the process of folding back upon himself. Yet the book also contains two fine essays on the Marquis de Sade, which do justice to the historical figure while putting the Sade cult in its place, alongside Wilson's passionate appreciation of *Doctor Zhivago*, one of his best pieces on a Russian writer.

Russian language and literature were a continuing interest from the thirties, when he began learning Russian in the Soviet Union and translated Pushkin's *Bronze Horseman*, through his attack, three decades later, on Nabokov's translation of *Eugene Onegin*. Reading the classics with his part-Russian wife Elena, Wilson believed he could see things those who grew up with them had missed; and as a foreigner he could comment on the national character in the mirror of art, balancing the Russians' admirable qualities against what he took to be their vices, among these a susceptibility to authoritarian rule. The essays collected in *A Window on Russia* illustrate Wilson's virtues and limitations as a generalist. He prefers Tolstoy to Dostoevsky, Pasternak to Solzenitsyn, and is irritated by the Russian religion of suffering. He knows little of the literature of the silver age, the revolutionary years, or the post-Stalinist period, but he can show how the exotic, impenetrable aspects of old Russia are mirrored in Gogol's prose and can clarify the relationships of Pushkin and Turgenev to their

Russian material. He identifies with these Westernizers, whose cosmopolitan perspective and command of style taught a nation how to know itself.

Travel was as much a part of his life as reading, and though he did not revisit the Soviet Union, he returned to Western Europe and explored a series of minority cultures on the margins of the United States and the Soviet Union. His journals record the decline of England, France, and Italy over the half century since he had watched London crowds celebrating the advent of World War I. The Old World and its snobberies brought out the chauvinist in Wilson, who once declared the American bathroom as much of a contribution to civilization as the Gothic cathedral. Yet in his own country he was politically isolated. He detested American expansionism as much as that of the Soviets and, unlike his liberal readers, had come to fear bureaucracy and big government. A lengthy, wearing battle with the Internal Revenue Service—he had not reported his small income for a number of years—made him angrier, and in *The Cold War and the Income Tax* he tries to turn his tax delinquency into a Thoreauvian attack upon the state.

This is the background of his reports on peoples struggling to maintain their independence in Israel, Hungary, Haiti, French Canada, and on American Indian reservations. Wilson described their languages and cultures with the same pleasure he took in telling friends about books they hadn't read, and he admired the cohesive role religion played in such societies. The place of the Catholic Church in the Polish workers' rebellion would have stirred him, and, if he had lived, he would have been learning Polish in 1980. There was more to this than the nostalgic politics of a literary man in a technological society. As progressivism failed Wilson, he took the long view of the human struggle and found he could renew himself through communal belief and ritual. This is what happens at the intense moments in his travel writing. When *Apologies to the Iroquois* turns from the life of the tribe in white America to the Little Water Ceremony, a reporting job becomes an artistic re-creation of a rite of rebirth, through which this secular individualist fortifies himself against intellectual isolation and old age.

He could only momentarily enter into a preliterate culture, but Judaism long engaged his imagination and intellect. The Jews were the people of the Book, and their God was not perverse and full of surprises like the God of Calvin; their ritual appealed to Wilson as Christian mythology did not. *A Piece of My Mind* and *Patriotic Gore* amusingly recall how Lowell, Chapman, and Calvin Stowe (Harriet Beecher's husband) identified themselves with the Chosen People to the point of imagining themselves of Hebrew descent. The "Judaizing" tendency that emerges in Wilson's portrait of Marx as a Hebrew prophet led him, in the early 1950s, to learn Hebrew and travel in Israel, where he observed a modern state being built on ancient religious foundations. In the Arnoldian tradition, he believed that the "transcendent principle" of the Hebrews should be corrected by a "practical worldliness" and "realistic observation" he associated with the Graeco-Roman heritage. Without the ability to anticipate Israeli military expansion, he drily noted that the Bible promises the Lord's chosen not only their own lands but also the houses and cities of others. Yet he admired the moral vitality of Jewish culture. Seeking this for his own work, in the 1960s he tacked up in his study the words *hazak, hazak, venithazayk* from the end of the Torah—"Be strong, be strong, let us make ourselves strong." He sometimes used the phrase as a grace over the orange juice at breakfast, assuring this writer that it helped him "jack up my waning powers."

Wilson's tour in Israel led him to the story of the Dead Sea scrolls, which resulted in one of his most popular books. His novelistic command of character and

scene involved readers in a quest for the meaning of
these ancient manuscripts. "Wilson's contribution to the
worldwide interest and popular understanding of the
Scrolls was immense," observed Yigael Yadin, "because
he sensed very early in the research proceedings that
perhaps one of the most important aspects is the relation
between the writings of the Essenes—the Dead Sea
scrolls people, that is to say—and the birth and beginning of Christianity." Yadin adds that "he influenced
some scholars in the way that they dealt with the scrolls,
because he was very provocative in his writings. He was
trying to define the views of some scholars more boldly
than they themselves dared, perhaps." In the tradition of
Voltaire and Renan, Wilson wanted to "iron out the
wrinkle in history," weakening the claims of Christianity
as revelation, striking a blow against the exclusiveness of
both Christians and Jews. The monastery of the Essenes
seemed to him "the cradle of a spirit that would range
through the whole ancient world, touching souls with
that gospel of purity and light to which the brotherhood
had consecrated itself." If he underestimated the power
of orthodoxy to absorb such a challenge, he once again
provided readers with testimony to "the power of the
spirit, the authority of the moral sense."

5

The perspective of his later years is focused on his own
country in *Patriotic Gore* (1962). Often called a classic, yet
by no means universally accepted or understood, Wilson's
Civil War book is composed of portraits of personalities
first tried out in *The New Yorker,* that he derived from the
letters, speeches, diaries, memoirs, reports, and apologet-
ics of people who experienced the war, and from novels
and poems that register its effects. "Everyone speaks in
character in such a way that one can almost hear their
voices," he states of these writers. What they say of one
another, of themselves, and what he can intuit from their

prose is distilled in the light of his own reading and experience. A Critic's Tour of Neglected Works becomes a moral history of nineteenth-century America, and something of an epic—the sort of national epic that our writers of fiction and poetry have not provided.

He discards the mythology of the war and the state found in classical epics. Wilson does not believe that the consolidation of the Union was a sacred cause, worth the deaths of five hundred thousand men, nor that slavery had much to do with the North's reasons for subduing the South. In his once notorious preface, written on the eve of our confused intervention in Vietnam, he rejects the moral justifications of American wars and, with a bitterness recalling the aging Mark Twain, likens warring nations to sea slugs devouring their own kind to the accompaniment of righteous noises. The imperial states of the U.S. and the U.S.S.R. confront each other, after gobbling up everyone from the Indians and the secessionist South to the Hungarian revolutionists. Lincoln and Lenin are the idealists who consolidated these empires and gave them new mythologies. This vision, challenging both the left and the right, incorporates history from Stalin's purges and Roosevelt's maneuvering before World War II to the crises of the Cold War, and reaches back to a soldier's experience in World War I. Commenting on the crusade to make the world safe for democracy, young Wilson had invoked the Gettysburg Address in an epitaph at the graves of American soldiers, ironically inverting its rhetoric:

> All stubborn and obscene, they toiled in pain.
> Go, countryman of theirs. They bought you pride.
> Look to it the Republic leave not vain
> The deaths of those who knew not why they died.

He had already raised questions about the Civil War and Lincoln, his father's hero. In trying to answer those questions in *Patriotic Gore*, he sustains the republican idealism of this youthful poem.

The preface simplifies to make its point, but the book itself is discursive and pluralistic, developing no exclusive thesis. Wilson traces the reverberations of the war in varied lives, pointing up the ways that people's stories and their values intertwine, interpreting the same events through different eyes. He moves from North to South and back, and from prophets of the crisis to statesmen, soldiers, observers, and the postwar writers who make up the chorus. Within this structure he distributes space as he likes, lingering with obscure figures to whom he would once have paid less attention than to the utopian socialists whose experiments are dispatched in a few pages of *Finland Station*. He indulges personal interests. All the New Englanders are projected onto a Calvinist screen, which figures differently for Harriet Beecher Stowe and Julia Ward Howe, author of the *Battle Hymn of the Republic*, for the postwar novelist De Forest and for Mr. Justice Holmes, who carries over the old culture into the twentieth century. Calvinism is also a factor in the bitter art of Ambrose Bierce, the bloody determination of John Brown, and the fatalism of Stonewall Jackson. Through the letters of Harriet and Calvin Stowe and the journals of Southern women, Wilson opens up the field of domestic history, and this is fused with psychohistory in the account of Sherman's strange son Tom. A Jesuit priest who wore a uniform and had military delusions, his life is perceived as a comment on the march through Georgia and the spirit of the *Battle Hymn*.

Some of these chapters, of course, have little to do with the war itself. Discovering *The Valley of Shadows*, Francis Grierson's remarkable evocation of the mood of the Middle West as the crisis approached in the 1850s, Wilson traces Grierson's career as a music critic and a pianist upon the European concert stage, a mystic who died an impoverished storekeeper in Los Angeles. "The appreciator of the modern French poets, the critic of Wagner and Nietzsche, proved, after all, to have more in common with Lincoln than any of these," he writes with the sense of self-discovery characteristic of this book. At an old-fashioned lecturer's leisurely pace he goes through the novels of Cable, Stowe, and De Forest, genre paintings that reveal the ambiance of the period. Bierce is another of Wilson's "wounded" artists, and this portrait could fit with the psychological studies in *The Triple Thinkers* and *The Wound and the Bow*. Wilson deduces that American prose was reshaped during the war by those who, like Lincoln and Grant, "had to convince and direct," who "had no time to waste words." Drawn to such men of action, he prefers this "war style" to the florid eloquence of prewar literature and oratory, and to the elaborate mannerisms that Adams and James, he believes, derived from being youthful spectators of the great conflict.

What makes *Patriotic Gore* an American Plutarch—as Robert Lowell first used the phrase—are the longer portraits of the Stowes, Lincoln, Sherman, Grant, the Confederate Vice President Alexander Stephens, and Justice Holmes. All but one are Northerners. His Sherman is a subtle characterization, for the fierce honesty, the contempt for cant, that kept the general from falling into the hands of the politicians after the war did not keep him from being intoxicated by killing. He lacked the sensitivity and discipline of Lee, who said, "It is good that war is so terrible. Otherwise we should grow to enjoy it." In contrast to Sherman, Wilson's Grant is a moral hero: modest, decent, staunch, a great man when he has Lincoln's will and purpose behind him, although hapless in the presidential years. While Grant is the democratic hero, Holmes is the aristocrat, surviving wounds and wartime disillusionment, dedicated to his career in a way that also served the nation. Wilson shows how the old Justice held himself to a higher standard than he did anyone else, how he brought to the law the perspective of "the great world of art and thought."

Wilson's political views shape two portraits, those of Lincoln, the Caesar of the book, and of Stephens, who is retrieved from obscurity to make the case against the imperial state. As a political prisoner after the war, the Southerner had a foretaste of modern despotism that intensified his defense of his principles. This staunch individualist sets off the man of destiny and molder of others. Stephens had written that "With Lincoln, the Union rose to the solemnity of a religious mysticism." Wilson contrasts the young freethinker of Herndon's portrait with the prophet who absorbed New England's secular faith as he presided over the consolidation of the state. The critic stresses Lincoln's ambition, precise intelligence, imagination, and command of language. This is a partial portrait, a corrective to the sentimentalizations of Sandburg. It reflects Wilson's disappointments with great men. He sees Lincoln creating a myth, one which still shapes our perception of events, that he did not fully control or comprehend, paying no heed to the explosion of technology and capital already beginning in the Union sanctified by blood.

Wilson, then, withholds from Lincoln the faith he grants to Lenin and Marx in *To the Finland Station*. His Lenin and Marx are versions of the Hegelian hero, as defined on pages 255–56 of "The Partnership of Marx and Engels." Wilson's Lincoln, as Robert Penn Warren pointed out in a discerning review of *Patriotic Gore*, is a failed Hegelian hero, not really in touch with the world spirit, perceiving the surface of the historical moment but not its depths. The perspective of *Patriotic Gore* is characteristic of our time, as that of *Finland Station* is of the thirties. Each book also mirrors a phase in a man's life, which is why they complement each other. *Finland Station* is a young man's book, impatient to change history, taking unity and momentum from the revolution toward which it moves. *Patriotic Gore* is less intent, less taut, more savoring of experience. The aging Wilson is concerned not with making but with enduring history, and his rejection of the centralized state leads naturally to a looser literary structure. The dialogue between these books is unique in an age of broken careers and cultural discontinuities. Each brings the individualism of the nineteenth century into the present, and heroic personality into the age of the antihero.

Patriotic Gore did not, as some hoped, help its author win a Nobel Prize, but it led to the presentation of a Freedom Medal by President Kennedy, an appropriate honor for someone whose "single aim," he once said, was "not art or science but the improvement of America." Financial awards followed, yet Wilson would not behave as a respectable monument. In the sixties his public personality grew more quarrelsome. He regularly attacked the users of cliches and jargon, equating the health of society and language as Orwell and Pound had done. He ridiculed the ostentatious pedantry of the editions of the American classics sponsored by the Modern Language Association, and promoted a series modeled on the French Pléiade of readable editions, which ten years after his death came into being as the Library of America. The same conviction that the classics should be accessible precipitated his public quarrel with Nabokov, whose translation of *Eugene Onegin,* Wilson thought, exercised the Russian's taste for the "perverse-pedantic-impossible." If it was amusing when each of these friends claimed a superior knowledge of the other's native tongue, it was sad to see them demolishing each other in the magazines, sacrificing the intellectual companionship and mutual admiration apparent in their long correspondence. For Wilson, however, anger was by then a tonic that kept him from relaxing too much, and sustained his vigor.

To visit him in the mid-sixties, when he was editing his journals of the twenties, was to hear of Dos Passos, Cummings, Fitzgerald, Hemingway, and Stein, as well as Walter Lippman (who had got Wilson his job on *The*

New Republic) and Croly, its devoted editor. Wilson kept returning to the contemporary scene, a moralist whose intense curiosity recalled Henry James's injunction to be one of those on whom nothing is lost. Kazin has pictured him among the intellectuals on the beach at Cape Cod, looking out of place, yet still the center of attention. He was more at home in upstate New York, where he spent some part of the summers of his last decades in the stone house he had inherited from his mother. He had friends etch their poems with a stylus on the glass of the old windows, and the Auden poem in the guest bedroom (a portion of which may be found on page 731) was lovely and a little frightening in the moonlight. The old place had become an emblem of life as a work of art, as well as a base of operations for forays into the Indian country and Canada. His journal in *Upstate* shows Wilson engaged by the landscapes and the village scene, in a round of country expeditions and visits to and from acquaintances. He sometimes succumbed to pessimism as he considered the danger of nuclear war and the decline of literate culture, or noted the deterioration of his body, worn out by a malaria acquired in Haiti, radical dentistry, and too much drinking. Yet he continued to write vigorously about books and travel, filling in the corners of the American literary landscape, completing his work on the Russians, exploring new interests. Although he acknowledged he was too old to start learning Chinese, during his last winter he dabbled at Welsh and began rereading Balzac in preparation for a long article.

6

What is one to make of such a career? What are the major values of Wilson's work, or its uses? His importance for the history of modern culture is clear. Emerging from the old American life, from a privileged, provincial scene, he absorbed the intellectual and moral experience of the twentieth century more thoroughly than any other writer.

Delmore Schwartz once likened Wilson to a son of one of the heroes of Henry James, who has his moral education among the literary modernists and Marxists rather than in the Italy of Milly Theale or the France of Lambert Strether. Schwartz was thinking of his journeys to Axel's castle and the Finland station, but there were other, equally powerful experiences in Wilson's youth, from piling bodies as a hospital orderly to being treated for gonorrhea, and his intellectual range broadened through the later years. He does not draw all this together in one work, as Adams unifies his life in the *Education*, but the important connections are there, and more instructively so than if he were referring everything to himself or attempting to force a synthesis. The multiplicity that Adams bemoans, Wilson negotiates as a reporter, a spokesman for the present with a historian's perspective, who can look to the past for models and allies.

The historical point of view transforms his journals into documentaries, his memoirs into cultural history, his reviews into literary chronicles. In the major portraits he sees people in terms of their origins while following their careers. *To the Finland Station* and *Patriotic Gore* are histories of consciousness. They put us in touch with the past through the minds of people who write, which is not the only way to do so, but is as useful as the study of material culture. In the subtitle of *Finland Station* Wilson joins the writers of history to the actors, and in *Patriotic Gore*, rephrasing Milton, he asserts, "They also serve who only stand and watch. The men of action make history, but the spectators make most of the histories, and these histories may influence the action." Wilson recurs to the art of Gibbon and Macaulay in his letters and journals, and his account of Francis Parkman in *O Canada* complements the portraits of Michelet and Marx in *Finland Station*. His work reminds students of literature and history that these have been the joint concerns of educated men, although now separated fields in the academy, just as Wilson reminds us that the artist and the social commentator may at their best be the same person.

His focus is biographical. He sees society through the individual, takes style as a mirror of personality, and has the nineteenth-century interest in authors as persons. This is one reason he was not a great man for the New Critics, but their taboos have long since faded. Wilson's work is an antidote to purely sociological or topical criticism, and to the pursuit of theoretical agendas that abstract literature from its human groundings. He could not have imagined cutting himself off from the past or trying somehow, in Geoffrey Hartman's words, "to liberate the critical activity from its positive or reviewing function." Instead of bypassing the author, Wilson turns directly to him, after the example of Taine, who "created the creators themselves as characters in a larger drama of cultural and social history." In this way he can write criticism as an art without attempting to take the artist's place.

Wilson's artistic instincts are more fully expressed in his portraiture than in his novels, poems, or plays. When young, he had hoped to make a name as a playwright or novelist, but he was already a brilliant critic and a good reporter. These roles shaded into one another in unequal fashion, the essayist sometimes turning Wilson's fiction into discourse, while the storyteller and dramatist enlivened his expository prose. By his middle years he had become an artist of the actual, whose imagination worked best on facts and documents, whose experience and values emerged in the practice of interpreting others. The critic continued commenting on the ideas and styles of writers, while the theme of the cost of art, derived from the Romantics and Freud, enabled him to enter into their lives. Wilson developed a vision of the hero as man of letters, which extended to public figures in *Finland Station* and

Patriotic Gore. Like Dickens, Marx and Holmes communicated and were accessible through print, and they too had wrung something from stress and pain.

That vision is a personal one, but it is derived from the material rather than imposed on it. Wilson is not a solipsist. He projects himself when he writes of Holmes's loss of faith and political disillusionment, his loyalty to his country and his work, but he is absolutely right about Holmes. He is right, too, about Lenin's self-denial and Lincoln's Caesarian ambition, though he exaggerates each of these, through both youthful idealism and a subsequent reaction in the other direction. Wilson's studies are saturated in detail, and his art of quotation conveys the person in his or her own words. He enters into his material in organizing it. The result is an imaginative construction strongly rooted in fact, which tells us something we did not know about the individual case, while dramatizing the larger struggle of human beings to create order, justice, truth.

For Wilson writers are antennae of the race, who help the rest of us negotiate experience. "By understanding things we make it easier to survive and get around among them," he writes, a pragmatism that kept him from doing justice to the despair of Kafka or the pure aestheticism of Stevens. This perspective is implicit in the critic's style, his voice, that conversational yet formal prose which with the years becomes less taut but is always recognizable. We can cite the force of his long paragraphs or (as he once did) his debt to the periodic sentence, but the essence of his prose is that it brings to complex subjects the lucidity, force, and ease which he had first admired at school. For Erasmus the chief goal of education was to write in a good style, yet the end of literature was not art but truth. Wilson would have agreed. "We have to take life—society and human relations—more or less as we find them—and there is no doubt they leave much to be desired," he writes to

Louise Bogan when she is recovering from a nervous breakdown. "The only thing that we can really make is our work. And deliberate work of the mind, imagination, and hand, done, as Nietzsche said, 'notwithstanding,' in the long run remakes the world."

This conviction ties Wilson to and bespeaks the Victorians, the high tide of confidence of the twenties, when a group of creative minds remade American literature. Wilson saw himself as a catalyst within this group, and to look back on their work and personalities, as the ever-expanding store of letters, papers, and biographies encourages us to do, is to find the man and his influence at many turnings. His later years were often discouraging, as his ambivalent interest in faiths and churches suggests—backsliding, he might have called it—but he did not take refuge in dogma. He remained an independent writer, a patriot but not a chauvinist, sustaining the responsibilities and range of the old educated class in what he was eager to see as a multinational culture. While others adapted themselves to the media or the universities, Wilson somewhat cantankerously went his own way, completing his career as he began it, an individual speaking for himself to readers. He continued to work when old age forced him to eat, sleep, and work in the same room, for writing was part of his definition of himself. *"Scribo ergo sum"* could have been his motto.

The notices of his death called him the last man of letters, on the premise that a technological age can no longer foster someone for whom literature, in all its forms, is the natural record of human experience and aspiration. It is easy to praise Wilson in this vein. Rather than be thus elevated into irrelevance, he would certainly have preferred the skepticism of those not yet willing to rank him among the great critics. Wilson may have been an anachronism, but he never saw himself as the last of his kind. He believed that new literary generations would demand and provide better work, as he and his friends had, that the life of "thought and creative instinct and fellowship" would survive, like the authority of the classics. Looking back to his college years, he remembered that "you read Shakespeare, Shelley, George Meredith, Dostoevsky, Ibsen, and you wanted, however imperfectly and on however infinitesimal a scale, to learn their trade and have the freedom of their company." Wilson learned their trade, and his work continues to make their company available to his readers.

CHRONOLOGY

~~~~~~

1895   Edmund Wilson born on May 8 in Red Bank, New Jersey.

1908   The first of many trips to Europe.

1909–12 Attends Hill School, Pottstown, Pennsylvania.

1912–16 Attends Princeton University.

1917–19 Serves in the U.S. Army in France, as a private at base hospital in the Vosges; as a sergeant at G.H.Q., Chaumont.

1920–21 Joins editorial staff of *Vanity Fair*. Criticism begins appearing there and in *The Dial*, *The New Republic*, and other journals.

1921   Travels in England, France, and Italy, June–October.

1922   *The Undertaker's Garland*, verse and prose (with John Peale Bishop). Managing editor of *Vanity Fair*. Essay on F. Scott Fitzgerald and reviews of *Ulysses* and *The Waste Land*.

1923   Marries Mary Blair. Father dies. Daughter is born—Rosalind Baker Wilson.

1924   *The Crime in the Whistler Room*, a play, produced by Provincetown Players in New York City, with Mary Blair in the lead.

1925   Becomes literary editor of *The New Republic*, responsible for weekly articles on books and the cultural scene.

1926   *Discordant Encounters: Plays and Dialogues.*

1929   *I Thought of Daisy.* Serial version of *Axel's Castle* in *The New Republic*. Suffers breakdown and spends month in sanitorium. *Poets, Farewell!*, a collection of verse.

1930   Is divorced from Mary Blair. Marries Margaret Canby. Begins reading Marx.

1931   *Axel's Castle: A Study in the Imaginative Literature of 1870–1930.* Leaves editor's desk to report on Depression America, while continuing to do literary articles.

1932   *The American Jitters: A Year of the Slump.* Takes part in protest expedition to Harlan County, Kentucky. Margaret Canby killed in a fall in Santa Barbara, California.

1934   First chapters of *To the Finland Station* in *The New Republic.*

1935   Travels in the Soviet Union, May–October. Begins learning Russian to read Pushkin.

1936   *Travels in Two Democracies.* Takes house in Stamford, Connecticut.

1937   Works on essays on James, Shaw, Flaubert, Housman, and Chapman and on *To the Finland Station.* Publishes a play, *This Room and This Gin and These Sandwiches.*

1938   *The Triple Thinkers: Ten Essays on Literature.* Marries Mary McCarthy. Son is born— Reuel Kimball Wilson.

1939   Teaches Dickens course at the University of Chicago. Essays on Hemingway and *Finnegans Wake.*

1940   *To the Finland Station: A Study in the Writing and Acting of History.* Severs connection with *The New Republic.* F. Scott Fitzgerald dies.

1941   *The Wound and the Bow: Seven Studies in Literature. The Boys in the Backroom: Notes on California Novelists.* Buys house at Wellfleet on Cape Cod, Massachusetts. Edits *The Last Tycoon.*

1942   *Note-books of Night.*

1943   Edits *The Shock of Recognition.* Becomes weekly book reviewer for *The New Yorker.*

1945   Edits *The Crack-Up.* Begins to publish his travel reporting in *The New Yorker.*

1946   *Memoirs of Hecate County.* Is divorced from Mary McCarthy and marries Elena Mumm Thornton. *Hecate County* banned in New York State.

1947   *Europe without Baedeker: Sketches in the Ruins of Italy, Greece, and England.* Visits Zuni pueblo.

1948   Daughter is born—Helen Miranda Wilson.

1949   Goes to Haiti for the *Reporter.*

1950   *Classics and Commercials: A Literary Chronicle of the Forties.* Edna St. Vincent Millay dies.

1951   Christian Gauss dies. Wilson's mother dies, leaving him the stone house in Talcottville, New York. *The Little Blue Light,* a play, produced in New York. Drafts of chapters of *Patriotic Gore* begin appearing in *The New Yorker.*

1952–53   *The Shores of Light: A Literary Chronicle of the Twenties and Thirties.* First summer in Talcottville. Winter in Princeton, where he conducts the Christian Gauss seminars and begins studying Hebrew.

1954   *Five Plays.* Travels in Europe, and is sent to Israel for *The New Yorker.*

1955   *The Scrolls from the Dead Sea.*

1956   *Red, Black, Blond and Olive: Studies in Four Civilizations. A Piece of My Mind: Reflections at Sixty.* First attempts to settle tax dispute with the Internal Revenue Service. Reading and writing on Turgenev.

1958   *The American Earthquake: A Documentary of the Twenties and Thirties.* Investigates New York State Indians, visiting Seneca and Iroquois reservations.

1959–60   Lowell professor at Harvard, lecturing from manuscript of *Patriotic Gore.*

1960   *Apologies to the Iroquois.* Borrows money and sells his papers to Yale. Takes up study of Hungarian.

1961   *Night Thoughts.*

1962   *Patriotic Gore: Studies in the Literature of the American Civil War.* Internal Revenue Service cuts off sources of income. Is awarded Medal of Freedom by President Kennedy. Goes to Canada to explore Canadian literature in September.

1963–64   *The Cold War and the Income Tax.* Winter in Cambridge complicated by illness. After summer in Talcottville spends six months in London, Paris, Rome, and Budapest.

1965   *O Canada: An American's Notes on Canadian Culture. The Bit Between My Teeth: A Literary Chronicle of 1960–65.*

1966   *Europe without Baedeker* reissued together with "Notes from a European Diary, 1963–1964." Is awarded National Medal for Literature.

1967–68   *A Prelude: Characters and Conversations from the Earlier Years of My Life.* Visits Israel and Jordan, April–May.

1969   *The Dead Sea Scrolls, 1947–1969. The Duke of Palermo and Other Plays,* with "An Open Letter to Mike Nichols."

1970   Has coronary in New York in March; slight stroke around Christmas.

1971   Finishes articles on Russian literature and writes another introduction to *To the Finland Station. Upstate: Records and Recollections of Northern New York.*

1972   Spends winter in Florida. Has another stroke in May. Dies in Talcottville, June 12; is buried at Wellfleet, June 15. *A Window on Russia* and new edition of *To the Finland Station* published posthumously.

1973   *The Devils and Canon Barham;* foreword by Leon Edel.

1975   *The Twenties: From Notebooks and Diaries of the Period;* edited, with an introduction, by Leon Edel.

1977   *Letters on Literature and Politics;* edited by Elena Wilson, with an introduction by Daniel Aaron.

1980   *The Thirties: From Notebooks and Diaries of the Period;* edited, with an introduction, by Leon Edel.

1983   *The Forties: From Notebooks and Diaries of the Period;* edited, with an introduction, by Leon Edel. The Viking *Portable Edmund Wilson;* edited with an introduction and notes by Lewis M. Dabney.

1986   *The Fifties: From Notebooks and Diaries of the Period;* edited, with an introduction, by Leon Edel.

1993   *The Sixties: The Last Journal;* edited, with an introduction, by Lewis M. Dabney.

1995   Edmund Wilson's centennial is celebrated in May. Symposiums are held at the Mercantile Library in Manhattan and at Princeton University. *The Uncollected Edmund Wilson;* edited, with an introduction, by Janet Groth and David Castronovo.

1997   *The Edmund Wilson Reader;* edited, with an introduction and notes, by Lewis M. Dabney.

I
Starting Point and Retrospect

~~~~~~

EDITOR'S NOTE

In these selections Wilson considers some important people, places, and ideas of his youth in the perspective of his middle years, reasserting his values as he makes his historical experience available to readers. In "The Old Stone House" he tells the story of the family place in upstate New York, from the time when his mother's Mather ancestors crossed the Berkshires to plant the civilization of New England on the Appalachian frontier. He evokes the experience of a nation that came into being as a succession of frontiers—the exhilaration of freedom as well as the cultural poverty that keeps him from wanting to turn back the clock. This essay was written in 1933, when he was reporting on Depression America, and the gloom of the deserted house reflects the state of the nation as well as Wilson's sense of his own place between two worlds.

His autobiographical writings stand comparison with the early chapters of *The Education of Henry Adams*, yet Wilson's is not an old man's reinterpretation of the past. He convincingly re-creates his father, his most important teacher Christian Gauss, and his first great love, Edna Millay, as he knew them in youth, while understanding them better than he had. The portrait of the senior Edmund Wilson is a fine study of the American character. The demands, the remoteness, the hypochondria that had oppressed the household seem to the historical and psychological critic the scars of a displaced person in the gilded age, the price of his integrity. Wilson's father was most at ease in the stone house in Talcottville, which the son had now restored to life, and in this essay the old house is a reassuring symbol of continuity. When he imagines it "crystallizing in the forests" of northern New York, Wilson suggests the paradox of a civilization in the wilderness, and the mystery of personality itself.

Christian Gauss and Edna Millay were the two people he most admired at the beginning of his career, as one learns from his early fiction, poetry, and plays, as well as from these memoirs, published in 1952. Gauss gave the young man almost the whole of his literary ideal, and their relationship became a quasi-filial one after Wilson's father's death. Visiting him in Princeton afforded perspective on New York in the jazz age. Wilson consulted Gauss when writing *Axel's Castle*, and dedicated the book to the professor, from whose lectures, he wrote, "I acquired my idea of what literary criticism ought to be—a history of man's ideas and imaginings in the setting of the conditions which have shaped them." Between the two there remained something of a generation gap, for Gauss never took the great modernists or Marxism as seriously as Wilson thought he should. His French background, however, was again useful to Wilson at the beginning of *To the Finland Station*. The correspondence between them is found in *The Papers of Christian Gauss* (1957). It illustrates the tradition of humanistic apprenticeship that is celebrated in the citation from Dante with which Wilson's memoir concludes.

Loyalty to a literary comrade is also a motive of his portrait of Millay, written when she was entirely out of fashion. He sees the vitality of the human spirit in Millay's poetry and measures the cost in pain and isolation, as in his critical essays. This memoir is one of Wilson's most frankly personal pieces of writing. "Edna ignited both my intellectual passion and my unsatisfied desire, which went up together in a blaze of ecstasy that remains for me one of

the high points of my life," he explains in *The Twenties.*
He had tried to do justice to her as the Rita of *I Thought
of Daisy,* when he was too much the wounded lover and
rationalizing young intellectual. In "Edna St. Vincent
Millay" something is recovered from the erosion of time,
the missed connections of their later years. Emotion is rec-
ollected, if not in tranquillity, by an artist who can use
the fragmentary materials of memories and diary notes to
put before us a relationship that exemplifies general
human experience.

In "Thoughts on Being Bibliographed," written at the
midpoint of his career, in 1943, Wilson describes his practice as a literary journalist while he sees the twenties and
thirties as history. Perceiving his work in a continuum
from the eighteenth and nineteenth centuries, he fears that
literature will *now* be absorbed by the academy and cor-
porate journalism, although he hopes that his methods
may be useful to others. The essay clarifies the relationship between Wilson's articles and his books, and defines
some of the values which this "literary worker of the
twenties" would sustain in his later years.

"The Old Stone House" was first published among the
Depression scenes of *Travels in Two Democracies,* while
"The Author at Sixty" concludes the collection of essays
A Piece of My Mind. "Christian Gauss as a Teacher of
Literature" is complemented by the fine essay in *The
Triple Thinkers* in which Gauss is a foil to the narrow but
formidable Paul Elmer More. Wilson's memoir was begun
as a tribute for *The Princeton Alumni Weekly,* while his
portrait of Millay was intended as a "counter-memoir" to
Vincent Sheean's biography, as he tells us in the paragraph with which the two essays are introduced in *The
Shores of Light,* the collection of his articles of the twenties and thirties published shortly after the deaths of these
friends. "Thoughts on Being Bibliographed" first appeared with a bibliography of his work in *The Princeton
University Library Chronicle.*

THE OLD STONE HOUSE

As I go north for the first time in years, in the slow, the constantly stopping, milk train—which carries passengers only in the back part of the hind car and has an old stove to heat it in winter—I look out through the dirt-yellowed double pane and remember how once, as a child, I used to feel thwarted in summer till I had got the windows open and there was nothing between me and the widening pastures, the great boulders, the black and white cattle, the rivers, stony and thin, the lone elms like feather-dusters, the high air which sharpens all outlines, makes all colors so breathtakingly vivid, in the clear light of late afternoon.

The little stations again: Barnevald, Stittville, Steuben—a tribute to the Prussian general who helped drill our troops for the Revolution. The woman behind me in the train talks to the conductor with a German accent. They came over here for land and freedom.

Boonville: that pale boxlike building, smooth gray, with three floors of slots that look in on darkness and a roof like a flat overlapping lid—cold dark clear air, fresh water. Like nothing else but upstate New York. Rivers that run quick among stones, or, deeper, stained dark with dead leaves. I used to love to follow them—should still. A fresh breath of water off the Black River, where the blue closed gentians grow. Those forests, those boulder-strewn pastures, those fabulous distant falls!

There was never any train to Talcottville. Our house was the center of the town. It is strange to get back to this now: it seems not quite like anything else that I have ever known. But is this merely the apparent uniqueness of places associated with childhood?

The settlers of this part of New York were a first westward migration from New England. At the end of the eighteenth century, they drove ox-teams from Connecti-

cut and Massachusetts over into the wild northern country below Lake Ontario and the St. Lawrence River, and
they established here an extension of New England.

Yet an extension that was already something new. I
happened last week to be in Ipswich, Massachusetts, the
town from which one branch of my family came; and, for
all the New England pride of white houses and green
blinds, I was oppressed by the ancient crampedness. Even
the House of the Seven Gables, which stimulated the
imagination of Hawthorne, though it is grim perhaps, is
not romantic. It, too, has the tightness and the self-
sufficiency of that little provincial merchant society,
which at its best produced an intense little culture, quite
English in its concreteness and practicality—as the block
letters of the signs along the docks make Boston look like
Liverpool. But life must have hit its head on those close
and low-ceilinged coops. That narrowness, that meagerness, that stinginess, still grips New England today: the
drab summer cottages along the shore seem almost as slit-
windowed and pinched as the gray twin-houses of a mill
town like Lawrence or Fall River. I can feel the relief myself of coming away from Boston to these first uplands of
the Adirondacks, where, discarding the New England religion but still speaking the language of New England, the
settlers found limitless space. They were a part of the new
America, now forever for a century on the move; and they
were to move on themselves before they would be able to
build here anything comparable to the New England civilization. The country, magnificent and vast, has never
really been humanized as New England has: the landscape
still overwhelms the people. But this house, one of the few
of its kind among later wooden houses and towns, was an
attempt to found a civilization. It blends in a peculiar fashion the amenities of the eastern seaboard with the rudeness and toughness of the new frontier.

It was built at the end of the eighteenth century: the
first event recorded in connection with it is a memorial
service for General Washington. It took four or five years

in the building. The stone had to be quarried and brought out of the river. The walls are a foot and a half thick, and the plaster was applied to the stone without any intervening lattice. The beams were secured by enormous nails, made by hand and some of them eighteen inches long. Solid and simple as a fortress, the place has also the charm of something which has been made to order. There is a front porch with white wooden columns which support a white wooden balcony that runs along the second floor. The roof comes down close over the balcony, and the balcony and the porch are draped with vines. Large ferns grow along the porch, and there are stone hitching-posts and curious stone ornaments, cut out of the quarry like the house: on one side, a round-bottomed bowl in which red geraniums bloom, and on the other, an unnamable object, crudely sculptured and vaguely pagoda-like. The front door is especially handsome: the door itself is dark green and equipped with a brass knocker, and the woodwork which frames it is white; it is crowned with a wide fan-light and flanked by two narrow panes of glass, in which a white filigree of ironwork makes a webbing like ice over winter ponds. On one of the broad sides of the building, where the mortar has come off the stone, there is a dappling of dark gray under pale gray like the dappling of light in shallow water, and the feathers of the elms make dapplings of sun among their shadows of large lace on the grass.

The lawn is ungraded and uneven like the pastures, and it merges eventually with the fields. Behind, there are great clotted masses of myrtle-beds, lilac-bushes, clumps of pink phlox and other things I cannot identify; pink and white hollyhocks, some of them leaning, fine blue and purple dye of larkspur; a considerable vegetable garden, with long rows of ripe gooseberries and currants, a patch of yellow pumpkin flowers, and bushes of raspberries, both white and red—among which are sprinkled like confetti the little flimsy California poppies, pink, orange, white and red. In an old dark red barn behind, where the hayloft is almost collapsing, I find spinning-wheels, a carder, candle-molds, a patent bootjack, obsolete implements of carpentry, little clusters of baskets for berry-picking and a gigantic pair of scales such as is nowadays only seen in the hands of allegorical figures.

The house was built by the Talcotts, after whom the town was named. They owned the large farm in front of the house, which stretches down to the river and beyond. They also had a profitable grist mill, but—I learn from the county history—were thought to have "adopted a policy adverse to the building up of the village at the point where natural advantages greatly favored," since they "refused to sell village lots to mechanics, and retained the water power on Sugar River, although parties offered to invest liberally in manufactures." In time, there were only two Talcotts left, an old maid and her widowed sister. My great-grandfather, Thomas Baker, who lived across the street and had been left by the death of his wife with a son and eight daughters, paid court to Miss Talcott and married her. She was kind to the children, and they remembered her with affection. My great-grandfather acquired in this way the house, the farm and the quarry.

All but two of my great-grandfather's daughters, of whom my grandmother was one—"six of them beauties," I understand—got married and went away. Only one of them was left in the house at the time when I first remember Talcottville: my great-aunt Rosalind, a more or less professional invalid and a figure of romantic melancholy, whose fiancé had been lost at sea. When I knew her, she was very old. It was impressive and rather frightening to call on her—you did it only by special arrangement, since she had to prepare herself to be seen. She would be beautifully dressed in a lace cap, a lavender dress and a white crocheted shawl, but she had become so bloodless and shrunken as dreadfully to resemble a mummy and reminded one uncomfortably of Miss Havisham in Dickens's *Great Expectations*. She had a certain high and formal coquetry and was the only person I ever knew who really talked like the characters in old novels. When she had been able to get about, she had habitually treated the townspeople with a condescension almost baronial. According to the family legend, the great-grandmother of Great-grandmother Baker had been a daughter of one of the Earls of Essex, who had eloped with a gardener to America.

Another of my Baker great-aunts, who was one of my favorite relatives, had married and lived in the town and had suffered tragic disappointments. Only her strong intellectual interests and a mind capable of philosophic pessimism had maintained her through the wreck of her domestic life. She used to tell me how, a young married woman, she had taught herself French by the dictionary and grammar, sitting up at night alone by the stove through one of their cold and dark winters. She had read a great deal of French, subscribed to French magazines, without ever having learned to pronounce it. She had rejected revealed religion and did not believe in immortality; and when she felt that she had been relieved of the last of her family obligations—though her hair was now turning gray—she came on to New York City and lived there alone for years, occupying herself with the theater, reading, visits to her nephews and nieces—with whom she was extremely popular—and all the spectacle and news of the larger world which she had always loved so much but from which she had spent most of her life removed.

When she died, only the youngest of the family was left, the sole brother, my great-uncle Tom. His mother must have been worn out with childbearing—she died after the birth of this ninth child—and he had not turned out so well as the others. He had been born with no roof to his mouth and was obliged to wear a false gold palate, and it was difficult to understand him. He was not really simple-minded—he had held a small political job under Cleveland, and he usually beat me at checkers—but he was childlike and ill-equipped to deal with life in any very effective way. He sold the farm to a German and the quarry to the town. Then he died, and the house was empty, except when my mother and father would come here to open it up for two or three months in the summer.

I have not been back here in years, and I have never before examined the place carefully. It has become for me something like a remembered dream—unearthly with the powerful impressions of childhood. Even now that I am here again, I find I have to shake off the dream. I keep walking from room to room, inside and outside, upstairs and down, with uneasy sensations of complacency that are always falling through to depression.

These rooms are very well proportioned; the white mantelpieces are elegant and chaste, and the carving on each one is different. The larger of the two living rooms now seems a little bare because the various members of the family have claimed and taken away so many things; and there are some disagreeable curtains and carpets, for which the wife of my great-uncle Tom is to blame. But here are all the things, I take note, that are nowadays sold in antique stores: red Bohemian-glass decanters; a rusty silver snuff-box; a mirror with the American eagle painted at the top of the glass. Little mahogany tables with slim legs; a set of curly-maple furniture, deep seasoned yellow like satin; a yellow comb-backed rocker, with a design of green conch-shells that look like snails. A small bust of Dante with the nose chipped, left behind as defective by one of my cousins when its companion piece, Beethoven, was taken away; a little mahogany melodeon on which my aunt "Lin" once played. Large engravings of the family of Washington and of the "Reformers Presenting Their Famous Protest before the Diet of Spires"; a later engraving of Dickens. Old tongs and poker, impossibly heavy. A brown mahogany desk inlaid with yellow birdwood, which contains a pair of steel-rimmed spectacles and a thing for shaking sand on wet ink. Daguerreotypes in fancy cases: they seem to last much better than photo-graphs—my grandmother looks fresh and cunning—I re-member that I used to hear that the first time my grandfather saw her, she was riding on a load of hay—he came back up here to marry her as soon as he had got out of medical school. An old wooden flute—originally brought over from New England, I remember my great-uncle's telling me, at the time when they traveled by ox-team—he used to get a lonely piping out of it—I try it but cannot make a sound. Two big oval paintings, in tarnished gilt frames, of landscapes romantic and mountainous: they came from the Utica house of my great-grandfather Baker's brother—he married a rich wife and invented ex-celsior—made out of the northern lumber—and was pre-sented with a solid-silver table service by the grateful city of Utica.

Wallpaper molded by the damp from the stone; unin-viting old black haircloth furniture. A bowl of those enor-mous upcountry sweet peas, incredibly fragrant and bright—they used to awe and trouble me—why?

In the dining room, a mahogany china closet, which originally—in the days when letters were few and Great-grandfather Baker was postmaster—was the whole of the village post office. My grandmother's pewter tea-service, with its design of oak-leaves and acorns, which I remem-ber from her house in New Jersey. Black iron cranes, pip-kins and kettles for cooking in the fireplace; a kind of flat iron pitchfork for lifting the bread in and out, when they baked at the back of the hearth. On the sideboard, a glass decanter with a gilt black-letter label: "J. Rum." If there were only some rum in the decanter!—if the life of the house were not now all past!—the kitchens that trail out behind are almost too old-smelling, too long deserted, to make them agreeable to visit—in spite of the delightful brown crocks with long-tailed blue birds painted on them, a different kind of bird on each crock.

In the ample hall with its staircase, two large colored pictures of trout, one rising to bait, one leaping. Upstairs, a wooden pestle and mortar; a perforated tin box for hot coals to keep the feet warm in church or on sleigh-rides; a stuffed heron; a horrible bust of my cousin Dorothy Read in her girlhood, which her mother had done of her in Germany. The hair-ribbon and the ruffles are faithfully reproduced in marble, and the eyes have engraved pupils. It stands on a high pedestal, and it used to be possible, by pressing a button, to make it turn around. My cousin Grace, Dorothy's mother, used to show it off and invite comparison with the original, especially calling attention to the nose; but what her mother had never known was that Dorothy had injured her nose in some rather disgraceful row with her sister. One day when the family were making an excursion, Dorothy pleaded indisposition and bribed a man with a truck to take the bust away and drop it into a pond. But Uncle Tom got this out of the man, dredged the statue up and replaced it on its pedestal. An ugly chair with a round rag back; an ugly bed with the head of Columbus sticking out above the pillows like a figurehead. Charming old bedquilts, with patterns of rhomboids in softened browns, greens and pinks, or of blue polka-dotted hearts that ray out on stiff phallic stalks. A footstool covered in white, which, however, when you step on a tab at the side, opens up into a cuspidor—some relic, no doubt, of the times when the house was used for local meetings. (There used to be a musical chair, also brought back from Germany, but it seems to have disappeared.) A jar of hardly odorous dried rose-leaves, and a jar of little pebbles and shells that keep their bright colors in alcohol.

The original old panes up here have wavy lines in the glass. There are cobweb-filthy books, which I try to examine: many religious works, the annals of the state legislature, a book called *The Young Wife, or Duties of Women in the Marriage Relation,* published in Boston in 1838 and containing a warning against tea and coffee, which "loosen the tongue, fire the eye, produce mirth and wit, excite the animal passions, and lead to remarks about ourselves and others, that we should not have made in other circumstances, and which it were better for us and the world, never to have made." But there is also, I noticed downstairs, Grant Allan's *The Woman Who Did* from 1893.

I come upon the *History of Lewis County* and read it with a certain pride. I am glad to say to myself that it is a creditable piece of work—admirably full in its information on geology, flora and fauna, on history and local politics; diversified with anecdotes and biographies never overflattering and often pungent; and written in a sound English style. Could anyone in the county today, I wonder, command such a sound English style? I note with gratification that the bone of a prehistoric cuttlefish, discovered in one of the limestone caves, is the largest of its kind on record, and that a flock of wild swans was seen here in 1821. In the eighties, there were still wolves and panthers. There are still bears and deer today.

I also look into the proceedings of the New York State Assembly. My great-grandfather Thomas Baker was primarily a politician and at that time a member of the Assembly. I have heard that he was a Jacksonian Democrat, and that he made a furious scene when my grandmother came back from New Jersey and announced that she had become a Republican: it "spoiled her whole visit." There is a photograph of Great-grandfather Baker in an oval gilt frame, with his hair sticking out in three spikes and a wide and declamatory mouth. I look through the Assembly record to see what sort of role he played. It is the forties; the Democrats are still angry over the Bank of the United States. But when I look up Thomas Baker in the index, it turns out that he figures solely as either not being present or as requesting leave of absence. They tell me he used to go West to buy cattle.

That sealed-up space on the second floor which my father had knocked out—who did they tell me was hidden in it? I have just learned from one of the new road-signs which explain historical associations that there are caves somewhere here in which slaves were hidden. Could this have been a part of the underground route for smuggling Negroes over the border into Canada? Is the attic, the "kitchen chamber," which is always so suffocating in summer, still full of those carpetbags and crinolines and bonnets and beaver-hats that we used to get out of the old cowhide trunks and use to dress up for charades?

It was the custom for the married Baker daughters to bring their children back in the summer; and their children in time brought their children. In those days, how I loved coming up here! It was a reunion with cousins from Boston and New York, Ohio and Wisconsin, as well as with the Talcottville and Utica ones: we fished and swam in the rivers, had all sorts of excursions and games. Later on, I got to dislike it: the older generation died, the younger did not much come. I wanted to be elsewhere, too. The very fullness with life of the past, the memory of those many families of cousins and uncles and aunts, made the emptiness of the present more oppressive. Isn't it still?—didn't my gloom come from that, the night of my first arrival? Wasn't it the dread of that that kept me away? I am aware, as I walk through the rooms, of the amplitude and completeness of the place—the home of a big old-fashioned family that had to be a city in itself. And not merely did it house a clan: the whole life of the community passed through it. And now for five sixths of the year it is nothing but an unheated shell, a storehouse of unused antiques, with no intimate relation to the county.

The community itself today is somewhat smaller than the community of those days, and its condition has very much changed. It must seem to the summer traveler merely one of the clusters of houses that he shoots through along the state highway; and there may presently be little left save our house confronting, across the road, the hot-dog stand and the gasoline station.

For years I have had a recurrent dream. I take a road that runs toward the west. It is summer; I pass by a strange summer forest, in which there are mysterious beings, though I know that, on the whole, they are shy and benign. If I am fortunate and find the way, I arrive at a wonderful river, which runs among boulders, with rapids, between alders and high spread trees, through a countryside fresh, green and wide. We go in swimming; it is miles away from anywhere. We plunge in the smooth flowing pools. We make our way to the middle of the stream and climb up on the pale round gray stones and sit naked in the sun and the air, while the river glides away below us. And I know that it is the place for which I have always longed, the place of wildness and freedom, to find which is the height of what one may hope for—the place of unalloyed delight.

As I walk about Talcottville now, I discover that the being-haunted forest is a big grove which even in daytime used to be lonely and dark and where great white Canadian violets used to grow out of the deep black leaf-mold. Today it is no longer dark, because half the trees have been cut down. The river of my dream, I see, is simply an idealized version of the farther and less frequented and more adventurous bank of Sugar River, which had to be reached by wading. Both river and forest are west of the road that runs through the village, which accounts for my always taking that direction in my dream. I remember how Sugar River—out of the stone of which our house is built—used, in my boyhood, so to fascinate me that I had an enlargement made of one of the photographs I had taken of it—a view of "the Big Falls"—and kept it in my room all winter. Today the nearer bank has been largely blasted away to get stone for the new state highway, and what we used to call "the Little Falls" is gone.

I visit the house of my favorite great-aunt, and my gloom returns and overwhelms me. The huge root of an elm has split the thick slabs of the pavement so that you have to walk over a hump; and one of the big square stone fence-posts is toppling. Her flowers, with no one to tend them, go on raggedly blooming in their seasons. There has been nobody in her house since she died. It is all too appropriate to her pessimism—that dead end she always foresaw. As I walk around the house, I remember how, once on the back porch there, she sang me old English ballads, including that gruesome one, "Oh, where have you been, Randall, my son?"—about the man who had gone to Pretty Peggy's house and been given snakes to eat:

"What had you for supper, Randall, my son?"
"Fresh fish fried in butter. Oh, make my bed soon!
For I'm sick at my heart and I fain would lie down!"

She was old then—round-shouldered and dumpy—after the years when she had looked so handsome, straight-backed and with the fashionable aigrette in her hair. And the song she sang seemed to have been drawn out of such barbarous reaches of the past, out of something so surprisingly different from the college-women's hotels in New York in which I had always known her as living: that England to which, far though she had come from it, she was yet so much nearer than I—that queer troubling world of legend which I knew from Percy's *Reliques* but with which she had maintained a real contact through centuries of women's voices—for she sang it without a smile, completely possessed by its spirit—that it made my flesh creep, disconcerted me.

My great-aunt is dead, and all her generation are dead—and the new generations of the family have long ago left Talcottville behind and have turned into something quite different. They were already headed for the cities by the middle of the last century, as can be seen by the dispersal of Great-grandfather Baker's daughters. Yet there were still, in my childhood, a few who stayed on in this country as farmers. They were very impressive people, the survivors of a sovereign race who had owned their own pastures and fields and governed their own community. Today the descendants of these are performing mainly minor functions in a machine which they do not control. They have most of them become thoroughly urbanized, and they are farther from Great-grandfather Baker than my grandmother, his daughter, was when she came back from New Jersey a Republican. One of her children, a retired importer in New York, was complaining to me the other day that the outrageous demands of the farmers were making business recovery impossible, and protesting that if the advocates of the income tax had their way, the best people would no longer be able to live up to their social positions. A cousin, who bears the name of one of his Ipswich ancestors, a mining engineer on the Coast and a classmate and admirer of Hoover, invested and has lost heavily in Mexican real estate and the industrial speculations of the boom. Another, with another of the old local names, is now at the head of an organization whose frankly avowed purpose is to rescue the New York manufacturers from taxation and social legislation. He has seen his native city of Utica decline as a textile center through the removal of its mills to the South, where taxes are lighter and labor is cheaper; and he is honestly convinced that his efforts are directed toward civil betterment.

Thus the family has come imperceptibly to identify its interests with those of what my great-grandfather Baker would have called the "money power." They work for it and acquiesce in it—they are no longer the sovereign race of the first settlers of Lewis County, and in the cities they have achieved no sovereignty. They are much too scrupulous and decent, and their tastes are too comparatively simple for them ever to have rolled up great fortunes during the years of expansion and plunder. They have still the frank accent and the friendly eye of the older American world, and they seem rather taken aback by the turn that things have been taking.

And what about me? As I come back in the train, I find that—other causes contributing—my depression of Talcottville deepens. I did not find the river and the forest of my dream—I did not find the magic of the past. I have been too close to the past: there in that house, in that remote little town which has never known industrial progress since the Talcotts first obstructed the development of the water power of Sugar River, you can see exactly how rural Americans were living a century and a half ago. And who would go back to it? Not I. Let people who have never known country life complain that the farmer has been spoiled by his radio and his Ford. Along with the memory of exaltation at the immensity and freedom of that countryside, I have memories of horror at its loneliness: houses burning down at night, sometimes with people in them, where there was no fire department to save them, and husbands or wives left alone by death—the dark nights and the prisoning winters. I do not grudge the sacrifice of the Sugar River falls for the building of the new state highway, and I do not resent the hot-dog stand. I am at first a little shocked at the sight of a transformer on the road between Talcottville and Boonville, but when I get to the Talcottville house, I am obliged to be thankful for it—no more oil-lamps in the evenings! And I would not go back to that old life if I could: that civilization of northern New York—why should I idealize it?—was too lonely, too poor, too provincial.

I look out across the Hudson and see Newburgh: with the neat-windowed cubes of its dwellings and docks, distinct as if cut by a burin, built so densely up the slope of the bank and pierced by an occasional steeple, undwarfed by tall modern buildings and with only the little old-fashioned ferry to connect it with the opposite bank, it might still be an eighteenth-century city. My father's mother came from there. She was the granddaughter of a carpet-importer from Rotterdam. From him came the thick Spanish coins which the children of my father's family were supposed to cut their teeth on. The business, which had been a considerable one, declined as the sea trade of the Hudson became concentrated in New York. My father and mother went once—a good many years ago—to visit the old store by the docks, and were amazed to find a solitary old clerk still scratching up orders and sales on a slate that hung behind the counter.

And the slate and the Spanish coins, though they symbolized a kind of life somewhat different from that evoked by Talcottville, associate themselves in my mind with such things as the old post office turned china closet. And as I happen to be reading Herndon's *Life of Lincoln*, that, too, goes to flood out the vision with its extension still farther west, still farther from the civilized seaboard, of the life of the early frontier. Through Herndon's extraordinary memoir, one of the few really great American books of its kind, which America has never accepted, preferring to it the sentimentalities of Sandburg and the ladies who write Christmas stories—the past confronts me even more plainly than through the bootjacks and daguerreotypes of Talcottville, and makes me even more uneasy.

Here you are back again amid the crudeness and the poverty of the American frontier, and here is a man of genius coming out of it and perfecting himself. The story is not merely moving, it becomes almost agonizing. The ungainly boorish boy from the settler's clearing, with nobody and nothing behind him, hoping that his grandfather had been a planter as my great-aunt Rosalind hoped that she was a descendant of the Earls of Essex, the morbid young man looking passionately toward the refinement and the training of the East but unable to bring himself to marry the women who represented it for him—rejoining across days in country stores, nights in godforsaken hotels, rejoining by heroic self-discipline the creative intelligence of the race, to find himself the conscious focus of its terrible unconscious parturition—his miseries burden his grandeur. At least they do for me at this moment.

> Old Abe Lincoln came out of the wilderness,
> Out of the wilderness, out of the wilderness—

The echo of the song in my mind inspires me with a kind of awe—I can hardly bear the thought of Lincoln.

Great-grandfather Baker's politics and the Talcottville general store, in which people sat around and talked before the new chain store took its place—Lincoln's school was not so very much different. And I would not go back to that.

Yet as I walk up the steps of my house in New York, I am forced to recognize, with a sinking, that I have never been able to leave it. This old wooden booth I have taken between First and Second Avenues—what is it but the same old provincial America? And as I open the door with its loose knob and breathe in the musty smell of the stair-carpet, it seems to me that I have not merely stuck in the world where my fathers lived but have actually, in some ways, lost ground in it. This gray paintless clapboarded front, these lumpy and rubbed yellow walls—they were probably once respectable, but they must always have been commonplace. They have never had even the dignity of the house in Lewis County. But I have rented them because, in my youth, I had been used to living in houses and have grown to loathe city apartments.

So here, it seems, is where I must live: in an old cramped and sour frame-house—having failed even worse than my relatives at getting out of the American big-business era the luxuries and the prestige that I unquestionably should very much have enjoyed. Here is where I end by living—among the worst instead of the best of this city that took the trade away from Newburgh—the sordid and unhealthy children of my sordid and unhealthy neighbors, who howl outside my windows night and day. It is this, in the last analysis—there is no doubt about it now!—which has been rankling and causing my gloom: to have left that early world behind yet never to have really succeeded in what was till yesterday the new.

1933

THE AUTHOR AT SIXTY

I have lately been coming to feel that, as an American, I am more or less in the eighteenth century—or, at any rate, not much later than the early nineteenth. I do not drive a car and rather dislike this form of travel—I have not progressed further than the bicycle. I cannot abide the radio—though I regularly play the phonograph, which gives me, as the radio cannot, exactly what music I want at exactly the moment I want it. I have rarely watched a television program, and I almost never go to the movies (a word that I still detest as I did the first time I heard it). I have ceased to try to see at first hand what is happening in the United States, and my movements are all along a regular beat, which enables me to avoid things that bore or annoy me. I live mainly in two old-fashioned country towns: Wellfleet, Massachusetts, and Talcottville, New York, with visits of days, weeks or months to New York City and Boston, where I see my old friends and transact my business, and occasional excursions to Washington, Charlottesville and Princeton. I do not want any more to be bothered with the kind of contemporary conflicts that I used to go out to explore. I make no attempt to keep up with the younger American writers; and I only hope to have the time to get through some of the classics I have never read. Old fogeyism is comfortably closing in.

Life in the United States is much subject to disruptions and frustrations, catastrophic collapses and gradual peterings-out. I have felt myself at times, when younger, threatened by some such fate; but now, in my sixty-first year, I find that one of the things that most gratifies me is the sense of my continuity. It seems to me at moments extraordinary that I should still be sitting here in the country—having grown up in country houses, I have always, after spells in the city, come back to the country again—surrounded by the books of my boyhood and furniture that belonged to my parents. I see, on the tops of the bookcases, among my other animals and my Mexican gods, a plaster reproduction of a gargoyle that I bought at Notre Dame at the age of thirteen and a yellow stuffed bird of cloth, most elaborately embroidered with blue and orange beads, that a cousin and I, at an earlier age, bought from an Indian woman on a steamer-trip up the St. Lawrence River, as a present for our grandmother Kimball, who pleased us by thinking it amusing and hanging it on the gas-jet in her bedroom, to which she was then confined. The bird held a cluster of cherries, also adorned with beads, and one of these cherries has been lost; the gargoyle has lost part of a wing. But it reassures and rather surprises me to find them still with me here, and to know that through all my experiences, different interests, different women, different homes, I can still recognize myself as authentically the same individual who climbed the steep spiral of Notre Dame and who took that trip through the Thousand Islands.

This book was begun in Talcottville in the middle of last August, and I am finishing it here in June. The house in which I am living, which belonged to my family and which now belongs to me, was built out of the local limestone at the end of the eighteenth century. We used to spend the summer in Talcottville. The family reunion in the old town in summer was still at that time a feature of American life in the East, particularly perhaps in New York State. With the further opening up of the West, the families of New York State became widely dispersed, and such places were *points de repères,* they had a unifying and stabilizing function. As my own generation grew up and the older generations died off, we did not return to Talcottville so often. It was dull for us, we wanted to circulate; yet I sometimes came up here alone, when I found nothing better to do, spending weeks of unbroken reading and taking a long walk or a swim in the river every afternoon. I had always the highest regard for my Lewis County relatives. I had grown up in Red Bank, New Jer-

sey, in a town about four miles from the ocean, at a time
when that part of the Jersey coast was a resort of, in general, the second-rate rich, and I had passed my prep school
years in Pottstown in the midst of the Pennsylvania steel
mills. I knew that the Lewis County people—with their
dairy farms and big tracts of land in the foothills of the
Adirondacks—had a dignity and a self-assurance that
many Americans lacked. They were amiable, calm, independent. I have been fortified by this place and its people
to withstand many fakes and distractions. And now that I
have seen the world, I no longer find them dull.

The period after the Civil War—both banal in a bourgeois way and fantastic with gigantic fortunes—was a difficult one for Americans brought up in the old tradition:
the generation of my father and uncles. They had been
educated at Exeter and Andover and at eighteenth-
century Princeton, and had afterwards been trained, like
their fathers, for what had once been called the learned
professions; but they had then had to deal with a world in
which this kind of education and the kinds of ideals it
served no longer really counted for much. Such people,
from the moment they left their schools, were subjected to
dizzying temptations, overpowering pressures, insidious
diversions of purpose, and the casualties among them
were terrible. Of my father's close friends at college, but a
single one was left by the time he was in his thirties: all
the rest were dead—some had committed suicide. My father, though highly successful, cared nothing about making a fortune or keeping up with current standards of
luxury, which in our part of the world were extravagant.
Like many Americans who studied law, he had in his
youth aimed at public life, and a letter to my mother from
Exeter, written in 1880—when she was a student at Abbot
Academy—encloses a newspaper clipping which reports
the visit to the school of a Republican candidate for governor: "Those Phillips Academy boys," the reporter declares, "looked just splendid; there must be several future

governors among the lot and good stock for a President."
At Princeton he was famous as an orator, in the days of an
active Whig Hall. But the political career he had hoped for
was conceived in the classical republican terms. After law
school, he went as a delegate to one of the Republican
conventions, and he continued to follow politics, to advise
the Republican Party and sometimes to make campaign
speeches; but—though he did not lack encouragement to
run for office—he could not beyond this be induced to
take any active part in the kind of political life that he
knew at the end of the century. By the time he was
thirty-five, he was subject to neurotic eclipses, which
came to last longer and longer and prove more and more
difficult to cope with. He suffered from hypochondria—
the only neurosis which, according to Freud, the analyst
cannot touch; and there were in those days no analysts:
the system of Weir Mitchell prevailed. Such conditions
were called neurasthenia. Dr. Mitchell had grasped the
fact that the speeded-up pace of American life, the constant changing-hands of money which produced social insecurity in a society where social position was coming
more and more to depend on money, were driving Americans to overwork and to anxieties that became obsessive—
obsession was one of the words that loomed large in my father's vocabulary. Weir Mitchell invented the "rest cure,"
where people got away from their worries. My father
spent all of his later years in and out of these sanitariums.
But before he had got to this point, he had been sent to a
"neurologist" in London by one of my mother's physician
brothers, who had made him go abroad, I think, in order
to get him away from his work. My mother, as a young
woman—so her maid of over fifty years tells me—did not
seem to "have a nerve in her body"; but the effect on her
of my father's derangement must have been deeply shocking. On the boat she became deaf—literally overnight—
and never regained her hearing. When the doctor in London had examined my father, he saw my mother alone and
said, "Your husband is mad." This upset my mother but

made her indignant, since she knew he was not really mad. The next device tried by my uncle was himself to take my father to Carlsbad and to have him sit at outdoor cafés, listening to Lehar waltzes and consuming much Pilsner beer. The effect of this treatment was excellent. My father became quite cheerful and no longer imagined he was dying of one illness after the other. I believe that his hypochondria may partly have been a form of the Calvinist fear of damnation. I have spoken of my formidable grandmother, who had also, my mother told me, a "queer" and morbid side. And my father had undoubtedly been frightened as well as severely taxed by the fate of his only brother, who—a milder personality, much loved, rather more on the literary side, with less energy and authority than my father—had not survived his thirty-eighth year. My uncle John had studied law at the University of Virginia and had married the daughter of the head of the school, a delightful Virginian woman, full of humor and charm, with no grasp of practical life and—aside from a trip to Europe and occasional visits in the East—with little experience of any society outside the old-fashioned Virginian one. My uncle John took her to Pittsburgh, where he had a few friends from college and where he supposed there were great opportunities. They had three handsome children there. But Pittsburgh was too much for my uncle and aunt. I remember a description of them by someone who had seen them then: the young husband lying on his back on a couch, so ill that he could not practice, the young wife—so I imagine, though I am told she would never hear a word against Pittsburgh—quite out of her element with the Pittsburghers and the cold Western winter. He was found to have Bright's disease, and they could not go on any longer. She returned to her family in Charlottesville, taking the three children. He went to stay with his parents, who were then at Spring Lake, New Jersey. That was the winter and the blizzard of 1899. My uncle grew rapidly worse, and my father came on to Spring Lake, but could not get a doctor on account of the snow.

My aunt Susan had been summoned from Charlottesville. She found a "stage" at the station that would take her to the house, and on the way she heard one of the passengers say, "Such a sad thing about that young man, the son of Dr. Wilson. He's left a wife and three little children, and she wasn't even with him when he died." My father had been there alone with him, unable to do anything for him—the experience was to leave with him a kind of "trauma." And thereafter, only just established, he was obliged to meet the expenses of his brother's family as well as support his own. He was admirable in all this. He was fond of my aunt Susan, and I never heard him complain of her carelessness in spending money or her tendency to run up debts. He would descend periodically on Charlottesville, sometimes taking me, and straighten out her affairs. She would entertain him lavishly, with relays of "hot bread," Southern fashion, and she would always make him laugh a good deal—undoubtedly one of the most beneficent things that it was possible for anybody to do for him.

Another factor, however, which laid him open to neurotic depressions was his lack of objectives in life. He had given up political ambitions; he had had every possible success at law, and law in the long run bored him. More and more he would drop his practice and retire to a sanitarium or to a plantation in North Carolina or shut himself up at home in a room with a felt-covered door. When he felt that the money was running low, he would emerge from his shadow or exile and take on a couple of cases, enough work to retrieve the situation. He was a crack trial lawyer, and, in the latter part of his life, was much sought after by other lawyers to try their less easy cases. He had only lost one case in his life, very early in his legal career. He sometimes worked for corporations, who paid him substantial fees; but all kinds of local people would come to him with their troubles, and if he thought that they had been badly treated and had a good case, he would rescue them from their difficulties for little or nothing. He had got his clients acquitted in several much-publicized murder cases, and I once drove with him to the prison in Freehold, to which he went at the request of a tailor indicted for killing his wife. I could not get him to talk about this interview except to tell me, as we were driving back, that he could not do anything for the man. He had prosecuted only one murderer. The reason for his success was undoubtedly that he never undertook a case which he did not think he could win, and that his judgment about this was infallible. In court, he attacked the jury with a mixture of learning, logic, dramatic imagination and eloquence which he knew would prove irresistible. He would cause them to live through the events of the crime or supposed crime, he would take them through the steps of the transaction, whatever this was, and he would lodge in their heads a picture that it was difficult for his opponent to expel. I was impressed by the intense concentration that these feats of persuasion cost him—they could not be allowed to fail—on the occasions when he prepared a brief at home. He would pace back and forth through the rooms, go nervously up and down stairs, and all other operations would have to be suspended. The atmosphere became insupportable.

Edmund Wilson—I was a Junior—had always been an active Republican but had never held any kind of office till, in 1908, he was appointed Attorney General by a Republican governor of New Jersey. The Democrat Woodrow Wilson, however, succeeded this governor in office before the end of my father's term. My father did not much like Wilson, but to me he was then a great hero. I arrived as a freshman at Princeton when he was still in residence there, and when the college was still divided into passionate adherents and venomous foes. My father took no sides in this controversy, for he did not like Andrew West, the antagonist of Wilson, either. But I read and listened to Wilson's speeches and accepted him as a shining champion in the war against sordid business, a reformer-intellectual in politics. I did not find his literary style quite so excellent as some people thought—it was better to hear him than to read him—but he did have a literary style, which was hardly possible to say of any other recent candidate for the presidency. I would, therefore, when my father at dinner would mention that he had been to see the governor that day, express an extreme interest. "What is he like?" I would ask, and would receive some such dampening reply as, "He was like an animated corpse." It was only years later that I saw the point of my father's adverse comments on the bigotry and suspiciousness of Wilson. I remember his telling me with amusement of the plaints of the machine politicians who had put Woodrow Wilson in power and had then been repudiated by him with accents of reprobation. No political betrayal of the kind had ever occurred in New Jersey. "I p-picked him," had said one of them, stuttering, "I p-picked him, and I p-picked a lemon!"

Woodrow Wilson had assumed characteristically that my father—allied with his political opponents—was also a member of the Republican machine, and he tried to embarrass my father by demanding that he investigate Atlantic City, a huge Republican racket, which he imagined my father would not dare to touch. Edmund Wilson had no inhibitions, having given no political hostages, and he at once came to grips with the problem, which proved to be tough indeed. The city was run by a boss, who kept his apparatus in power by every species of corruption at the polls; but it seemed at first out of the question to get anyone convicted of anything, since everyone in Atlantic City was either in on the racket or intimidated by the machine. My father then hit upon a brilliant device. He dug out a very ancient New Jersey law that no one else had ever heard of, which—the converse of a change of venue—made it possible for the prosecutor, in cases where a fair trial could not be obtained, to bring in jurors—called elisors—from another county. He thus secured his elisors and tried before them, I think, several hundred men, all or most of whom were sent to jail. He even got a verdict against the boss. He did not dislike this man, and told me that he had behaved with dignity, calmly going off to jail in a fur coat and limousine. My father pointed out to me at this time that—though Wilson undoubtedly did not know it—most of the cities in the United States were controlled by a boss and by methods exactly like those in Atlantic City, and that Atlantic City itself would be back, before very long, in the same situation as before. In the course of these proceedings, the local powers had laid all sorts of traps for my father in the hope of getting something on him, and he had had to fight off several beautiful blondes whose mission was to compromise him. Woodrow Wilson, when the clean-up was accomplished, was so much impressed by this feat—which my father regarded as futile—that when he very soon moved up to the presidency, he kept offering my father appointments. Edmund Wilson, who had never in his life voted anything but the Republican ticket, departed for once from his principles when Wilson ran for President the second time, and voted for the Democratic candidate, for the reason that Wilson, in his speeches, had pledged himself to "keep us out of war"—an act which he afterwards regretted when the President immediately plunged us in. My father did some war work, at Wilson's request, in straightening out the affairs of the sequestrated North German Lloyd, but he would not accept any appointment. Moving to Washington seemed too much trouble, and it would upset his independent habits, for he chose his own tasks and times, and sometimes, as I have said, fell into complete inertia. He would never, for similar reasons, accept offers of partnerships in New York firms. He did not like to specialize; he practiced a variety of kinds of law; and he liked to be able to choose his cases. He had had eight years of partnership with an older man and had then, on the latter's death, established himself alone on the floor above a liquor dealer—which was always rather pleasantly permeated by a casky vinous smell—from which he continued to operate all the rest of his life. But one day when we were taking a walk he told me, with an injunction of secrecy, that the President had sounded him out as to whether he would fill the next Supreme Court vacancy. This, he felt, would be interesting enough to reconcile him to living in Washington, and he had said that he would accept. But no vacancy occurred during Wilson's term. My father died not long after this—in 1923, in his sixty-first year.

He followed the eccentric—perhaps unique—course, for a public man in New Jersey, of never investing in anything. He regarded the Stock Exchange as a gambling house, and he did not approve of gambling. This gave him a tremendous advantage in a state that was dominated by corporations. Since he did not have a stake in anything, he was quite free to act as he pleased. At the memorial unveiling of a portrait of him in the courthouse of the county seat, Freehold, it happened that the eulogy of him was read by the lawyer brother of a great public utility family, and he frankly confessed his perplexity at sometimes having found my father on the opposite side from himself in cases that involved corporations. My father was at one time attorney for the Pennsylvania Railroad, as well as later on a member of the New Jersey Board of Railroad Commissioners, and he had grown to loathe the P.R.R. Once when I was away at school, my mother sent me a box which contained a few clothes, a cake and several volumes of Shakespeare. It arrived with the package broken open, the clothes and the *Hamlet* gone, and the chocolate cake considerably battered. My father proceeded with glee to bring a suit against the Pennsylvania Railroad, and compelled them to pay him damages, regretting that these had to be small. The sole speculation of his life was a shrewd deal in Florida real estate, the future of which he early foresaw.

When I ran down big business, he would answer—as a Republican, he could hardly do less—that the business men had done a good deal to develop our national resources. But business men bored him; and when his classmate Rodman Wanamaker attempted to muster support for his project of a business school at Princeton, he was strongly opposed by my father. He had few companions in Red Bank, none on his own level. He amused himself mainly by traveling. From the moment he arrived in a city, he began asking people questions, beginning with the driver of his cab. It was characteristic of him that he took me once to Salt Lake City. We read up the history of Mormonism and even tried the Book of Mormon, which turned out to be dreadful stuff. He was completely without snobbery of race or class—which was not the case with my mother, who would not allow him to bring some of his friends to the house. He was on very good terms with the Negroes and often spoke to Negro audiences. There was a very large Negro population in Red Bank, with several Negro papers, and it is true that it was important for the Republicans to get out the Negro vote; but his sympathy with them was quite sincere, and he liked to read books about Negro self-advancement, such as those of Booker T. Washington. His closest ally in Red Bank was a Jew from Czechoslovakia, who had come into New Jersey as a peddler and had built up entirely by himself the sole industry in Red Bank: a uniform factory. This man sent his sons to Harvard, and he and my father were the only people in town who were seriously interested in education. Together, and without much encouragement, they attempted to give Red Bank a first-class school system. They were also, I learn from an obituary, "associated in a number of private and personal charities." My father's benefactions were many and sometimes rather odd. One day I discovered in his library a group of books by a poet of whom I had never heard—old-fashioned Victorian verse of a very insipid kind. This puzzled me, for he never read poetry, and I asked him what on earth they were, expressing my opinion of their quality. I saw that he was rather abashed, since he thought I had some competence in these matters. He murmured that Mr. R. was a very refined old gentleman. I found out later, by asking my mother, that my father had financed all these volumes. He

also financed a young man, who had been working as a
sign-painter in Red Bank but who wanted to become an
actor. He got more pleasure out of this investment than he
did from the works of the poet. The young man, in a certain field, turned out to be a great success. He built up a
traveling stock company that was one of the most popular
in the East. Yet it always remained something of a mystery why this man should have wanted to go on the stage.
It would be wrong to call him a ham, since he had no theatrical abilities of even the coarser kind. He stood about on
the stage like a cigar-store Indian, and he had never improved his English to the point of being able to deliver
grammatical lines correctly. But the rest of the company
were not so bad: it consistently improved with time and
included one or two at least respectable actors. Whenever
C.K.C. came to Red Bank, my father would go two or
three nights a week. He always sat in the front row at the
theater, and there under the nose of his protégé, he would
chuckle with delight at the absurdities of the dramas and
the ineptitudes of the leading man. He was pleased by the
latter's success, and he regarded the whole thing a little as
a show he had arranged for his own entertainment. He
loved to quote lines from these plays. One of his favorite
scenes occurred in some melodrama of London high life.
Sir Charles is saying something that agitates the hero
deeply; he manifests this agitation by a few stiff and jerky
gestures. "Why, what is the matter?" asks Sir Charles; he
has been swinging a pince-nez on a ribbon. "Sir Charles,"
replies C.K.C., concealing the true reason, "them glasses
make me nervous." This actor was much too stupid to be
aware of my father's attitude, and he always adored my
father, on the occasion of a birthday sending him an enormous framed photograph of himself (my father), with a
tribute in gold lettering. After my father's death, when
my mother bought a new house, this actor purchased our
old one.

I have found among my father's papers a speech on the
Homestead strike, in which he sharply takes the strikers to

task. This, in the early nineties, was of course the correct Republican line. Having read the Fabian essays and other socialist writings, I always assumed through my college days that my father was as reactionary as I was advanced, and I did not dare discuss my ideas with him; but I had failed, as I realized later, to understand his real point of view. One of his favorite cronies in Red Bank was the socialist editor of a local paper, and, since my mother would not allow him to invite this man to dinner—she objected to his deliberately unmodish clothes and asserted that he did not wash—they were obliged to take long walks together. It was only after the war when I came back from France, and felt quite independent, that I ventured to talk to my father about socialism in Europe and Russia. To my surprise he was not disapproving, but spoke of it with moderation as something they went in for abroad which had no relevance to the United States. "The main merit of socialism," he said—he was thinking of our local variety—"is to emphasize the brotherhood of man." I was by that time no longer afraid of him, and only then did I get to know him. My first meeting with him on my return unexpectedly made me feel proud of him. I had been waiting for my discharge all too many days in a Long Island army camp, and he came to see me there. He was always impatient of delay, and he complained with his usual peremptoriness to a bureaucratic officer who had failed to produce me at once. The officer had retorted that he'd better be careful, he couldn't talk to the army like that, there were penalties for that kind of talk. "You're no doubt thinking," my father replied, "of the Espionage Act and the Sedition Act. Neither of them has any application to what I've been saying to you nor to what I'm about to say. The inefficiency of you army people is an outrage against the tax-paying citizens." I was gratified when—still fuming—he told me about this interview: I had had almost two years of the army, and a story I had written in France about the dismal side of army life had recently been held up by the censor when I had tried to send it to the United States, and had brought upon me a bawling-out. When I got home, I was rather surprised—knowing how little my father could sympathize with the aims of the Communists and Anarchists—to find that he was indignant over the arrests without warrant and the indiscriminate expulsion of radicals. I had been so full of Wells and Shaw and Barbusse and the Russian Revolution that I was only learning now from my father what the principles of American justice were.

He enormously admired Lincoln—his allegiance to the Republican Party had undoubtedly been partly inspired by this. He collected a whole library of Lincolniana, and he liked to deliver a popular speech called "Lincoln the Great Commoner." I made, automatically, a point of knowing as little as possible about Lincoln. I could see that my father in some way identified himself with the Great Commoner, and this seemed to me purely a pose, which verged upon demagoguery. I have said that he was quite without snobbery, but though he dealt with people strictly on their merits, it was always to some extent *de haut en bas*. When he died, I was struck by the criticism in one of the local papers that, in spite of his distinguished qualities, he had either not the desire or the ability to meet people on a democratic level. Both at home and in his office, he was constantly sought by persons who wanted to ask his advice on every conceivable subject, and when he died, many people we had never seen—sometimes poor farmers, and their wives—came from miles around to his funeral; yet it was true, I remembered, when I read this obituary, that he had always told people what to do in a dictatorial tone and with a certain restrained impatience, for which, however, he would later try to compensate by dismissing them at the end of the interview with an exaggerated courtesy and sweetness. Where, I wondered, was the kinship with Lincoln? It was only after his death that I understood. Now for the first time I read up Lincoln, and I realized that the biographies he had recommended were always the least sentimental ones. I remembered his saying at a time when he was reading one of the books about Lincoln by Nathaniel Wright Stephenson that it was more realistic than most; and he was always trying to get me to read Herndon—which I never did till after his death. Then, in Herndon's portrait of Lincoln, I at last found the explanation of my father's great interest in him: a great lawyer who was deeply neurotic, who had to struggle through spells of depression, and who—as it followed from this portrait—had managed, in spite of this handicap, to bring through his own nightmares and the crisis of society—somewhat battered—the American Republic.

I assumed, as I have said, that my father and I were at opposite poles in everything, and—since he usually appeared so opinionated—I was always surprised by the sympathy, or rather, perhaps, by the judicial detachment, with which, in important decisions, he treated my point of view. After college, before I enlisted, I told him I should like to go to Washington to try my hand at political journalism. "At Princeton," he answered, "you specialized in literature; then you went to Columbia Summer School to study sociology and labor. Now you want to do political journalism. Don't you think you ought to concentrate on something?" "Father," I replied, "what I want to do is to try to get to know something about all the main departments of human thought. I don't know anything about politics yet, and I'd like to see something of it at first hand." He did not even smile at this. "That's a possible ambition," he said. "Go ahead if you're really serious." He had, however, a horror of my not making something of myself—I think he had been appalled by the frivolities of that moneyed era—and he told me from time to time that I was not to be "a rich man's son"—by the standards of that period, we were not very rich—and that he would send me through school and college and give me an allowance for study and travel up to the time I got out of Princeton; but that I would then have to shift for myself. This hung over me all through college as a menace, but he never allowed me to get into serious straits—though, when he died, he did not leave me a penny. Of course, living was easier then. I was almost able to cover my expenses—in an apartment on East Eighth Street, which I occupied with three friends—on the fifteen dollars a week that I drew as a cub reporter; and we were able to keep a Chinese servant and constantly entertained. When my father was sure I was working, he would supplement my pay a little.

My father and my mother had different tastes and temperaments that thwarted one another. My mother was "extroverted," liked bridge-playing, gardening, horses and dogs; she was lively and very shrewd, had no intellectual interests. My father became more and more neurotic; his eclipses, by the time he was fifty, were lasting for months and years, and it was wearing my mother down to try to talk him out of his "symptoms," to amuse him, to arrange for him distractions. His few friends had, in this phase, come to dread him, and he resorted more and more to nurses, who were likely to be a nuisance to my mother, or to the retreats into sanitariums which completely cut him off from his family. He did not come to my college graduation, and when I went to his sanitarium to see him, he could find nothing whatever to say to me. Through all this I sided with my mother, though I had, I believe, really less in common with her than with my father. It was a case of the only child monopolized by the lonely mother. She had also the impulse to dominate, to manage the people she loved—an instinct of which my father had nothing. He simply gave people advice, did not otherwise try to control them. And I suffered like her from the burden of a chronic depressive in the household. I, too, had to act as companion—to go with him for desolating drives and walks, in the course of which he talked about nothing but his ailments. He studied medical books and, the moment one terror was banished, would discover something even more gruesome. He had already had two operations—which I assume to have been really needed—and the difficulty now was to prevent him from having all his internal organs removed. My mother at one point was on the verge of leaving him. He no longer paid any attention to her, seemed hardly aware of her presence; and she almost convinced herself that he could not be any worse off in the hands of his nurses and doctors. I encouraged her to get away, but she never could take this step. Instead, she had herself a collapse, a slight blood clot which left no bad consequences—she lived to be eighty-six—and which jolted him back for a moment. I remember how touched she was that he was kind to her, solicitous about her. For a moment he forgot his obsessions. I overheard her from my bedroom next to hers ask him whether he no longer loved her, calling him by a nickname that she must have used in their youth—the only time I ever knew her to speak to him in this way; but I do not remember his reply, and, indeed, find it difficult to imagine him answering such a question. Yet he was supposed to have been originally more in love with her than she with him: somebody once told me of his pacing the floor, at a time when her consent was doubtful, and swearing that if she would not have him, he could never marry anyone else.

But, aside from this crisis, which took place at a time when he hardly seemed with us at all, they had serious conflicts of interest even when my father was normal. I remember two major crises, though I cannot remember which came first. They could never agree about travel. My mother wanted to go to places that would be fashionable, lively and gay—the sort of thing that bored my father. Once when she demanded that he take her to the kind of place she liked—I think Florida was in her mind—he planned a trip to Europe that was irrelevant to her own desires. He had gone ahead and bought passages without asking her approval or, so far as I know, consulting her. One evening, at dinner, she rebelled. She said that she had been traveling with him on his own terms for years, and that there was nothing more in it for her; he simply visited cities, systematically informed himself about their populations, politics and products, inspected their public buildings and looked in on the proceedings of their legislatures, and paid no attention to her. Through his illnesses, he had made it impossible for her to enjoy, even at home, much social life, and when they were traveling, she had no friends at all. His way of taking this surprised me: he resorted to forensic eloquence, reproaching her, in a somewhat grandiloquent way, for having allowed him to go to so much trouble and then capriciously destroying his work. It was as if she had demolished some masterwork, capsized his whole career. I had never before heard him take this line in any situation of private life, and I thought it was due to a conviction of guilt: she had upset a furtive plot. It was the other way around on the other occasion: it was he who sabotaged her plan. When my father and mother were married and first bought the house that we lived in, the eventual prolongation of the Rumson Road was supposed to run past our property; but actually, when the road was completed, it was put through on the other side of the hill at the base of which we lived. Our neighborhood grew up as a slum. My father made a joke of the slum, but he continually bought more land in order to stave off its encroachment. Our house had been built in the eighties, a bad architectural period, when, for some reason, the rooms of the bottom floor were given enormous doorways and all opened into one another, and when my mother complained of its inconvenience, its inadequacy for the needs of the family, my father would have it enlarged in some way. She decided at last to move and to build another house. We were just off the highways with the big estates, where the rich people were rolling in their shiny black cars, hidden behind our hill, and the capillary attraction to range ourselves with them was strong. My mother had laughed at her sister-in-law, who, in Rumson, had an establishment of the fashionable kind, for her multiplication of servants: she had once taken on an extra maid to answer the telephone; and our household contrasted with hers: no fräuleins and mademoiselles, no

turnover of maids and chauffeurs. Most of the members of
our staff were permanent. The coachman was the illegitimate mulatto son of a local white judge, so serious and so
responsible that he might have been a judge himself.
When automobiles came in and we gave up keeping
horses, he quietly declined to learn to drive but assumed
that he was still in our employ and went on taking care of
our single cow, some chickens and a flock of guinea fowl.
His wife was part Indian and part Negro—a very handsome woman, proud, taciturn and sometimes fierce; she
was our cook, and when anything went wrong in the
kitchen, everybody kept away. The main pillar of the
household was an Irish girl, who came to work for my parents at the age of sixteen, a few years after they were married. She taught me to walk, and she became indispensible
to everyone in the family. She was sensitive, intelligent,
affectionate. At one point she decided to leave us and run a
boarding house. My father financed her in this, but we got
along so badly without her that, at the end of a year or
two, he coaxed her into coming back. She was an integral
part of the family, knew everything about everybody and
everything, and, after my father's death, she continued to
stay with my mother and herself handled all the transactions which the deafness of my mother made difficult.
This household satisfied my father, but, in spite of her attitude toward my aunt, my mother took on another maid
and gave the Irishwoman the title of "housekeeper." We
now had to have a chauffeur as well as the non-functioning
coachman, and there was also the problem of a gardener.
My mother had tried to offset the ugliness and gloom of
our house by a blazing and enormous garden, which became more and more of an operation and eventually won
first prize in a Monmouth County garden competition.
She decided at last that she could not expand any further
in our present location, that she must have a new house
and new grounds, and she may have persuaded herself
that my father had consented to this. She selected an at-

tractive piece of land on one of the transverse roads between the Ridge Road and the Rumson, and she consulted for months with an architect, planning a new habitation in which everything would be exactly as she wanted it. I heartily approved of this—I had no place to work at home where I was not likely to be disturbed by something going on in some other room, and I was not insensible to the luxuries of the Ridge and Rumson roads—I looked forward to our new demesne. Then one evening, just after dinner, my mother confronted my father with blueprints. He told her in a positive way that he could not afford a new house, that his illness made his income uncertain, and that she would have to put it out of her mind. She knew that he meant it, and in bitter chagrin, she tore up the blueprints in front of him. "The ambition of your grandmother Kimball," he explained to me a day or two later, "burdened the doctor's last years. She made him build that new house in Lakewood, and then, when he was old and ill, it was hard for him to keep it up." He added, or implied, that he had made a note not to let that happen to him.

He cared nothing about his surroundings—hence his alcohol-flavored office, hence the awkwardness of our house. When, after his death, I sometimes slept in his bedroom, I was chilled by its bareness and bleakness: there was nothing but the necessary furniture and photographs of his mother and father. Yet he liked to travel in style and paid a good deal of attention to his clothes. He was tall and good-looking and rather vain, and women were supposed to adore him. He was undoubtedly a very self-centered man, and, when sunk in his neurotic periods, would be shut in some inner prison where he was quite beyond communication. He died of pneumonia; just before he died, he murmured the pathetic question that he had put to us so often about illnesses that were wholly imaginary: "What does the doctor say about my condition?" My mother gave a little cry, but as soon as we had gone downstairs she astounded me by saying immediately, "Now I'm going to have a new house!" She did, not long afterwards, though not on the scale of the one she had originally planned, and when I saw it, I realized fully, and realized for the first time, how much my father had suppressed in her life. Everything about her was suddenly bright. The mahogany and silver shone; the armchairs had flowery covers; there was a sun-parlor full of plants, and large birds with large winged insects fluttering in their beaks appeared on the shades of this sun-parlor. I was reminded of the color and the smell of my grandmother's house in Lakewood, which was supposed to have been a burden to my grandfather. But my mother then became very sad: she seemed to suffer from the loss of my father as if from an amputation. She would not go near the old house, in which nobody wanted to live and which was soon in a run-down condition; and did not like me to tell her about it when I went there to see what had happened to it.

I had never thought she understood what my father's real point of view was and why, in his professional life, he behaved in the way he did. Her respect for him was partly derived from the respect that other people had for him. Her values were worldly, it seemed to me, to a degree that I sometimes found disheartening: she admired social prestige, and she also admired money. She had had two able brothers with weaknesses of an order somewhat different from my father's—though they were partly due, like his, I believe, to a fundamental lack of adjustment to the American life of the period. She said to me once that "these brilliant men always had something wrong with them." I do not think she was pleased with a destiny that had made her spend her life with such men. And I was another one: she had hoped I would be an athlete, a change from my cerebral father—something more like her sportsman brother who had played on the football team. She was an enthusiastic follower of collegiate sport, and even in her old age, she continued as long as she was able to go to football and baseball games at Princeton, and in the off season attended basketball for want of anything better. I was sure that she understood my activities even less well than she did my father's. In the radicalizing thirties, for example, my old friend John Dos Passos took part in a visit of protest to the terrorized Kentucky coal miners and was indicted by a local grand jury under the Kentucky criminal syndicalism law. This had been in the New York papers, and I remember how jarred I was when the next time I saw my mother, she remarked, "I see they've caught Dos Passos." She was sure that Sacco and Vanzetti were "perfectly awful men," who deserved to be executed—though I felt, since she was very kind-hearted, that this was due to her not being able to bear to imagine they had been executed unjustly. Yet I remember, in all this connection, her giving me one touching piece of testimony—entirely unexpected on my part—to her real appreciation of my father. I did not often talk to her about my work, but I did speak to her on one occasion of my fear that I might be outvoted on what I considered some important policy of the liberal weekly for which I wrote. "Your father," she promptly told me, "would go into court when he knew that the judge and the jury were prejudiced, and public sentiment was all against him, and try his case and win it."

My father's career had its tragic side—he died in his sixty-first year. I have been in some ways more fortunate—I am writing this in my sixty-second. And yet to have got through with honor that period from 1880 to 1920!—even at the expense of the felt-muted door, the lack of first-class companionship, the retreats into sanitariums. I have never been obliged to do anything so difficult. Yet my own generation in America has not had so gay a journey as we expected when we first started out. In repudiating the materialism and the priggishness of the period in which we were born, we thought we should have a free hand to refashion American life as well as to have more fun than our fathers. But we, too, have had our casualties. Too many of my friends are insane or dead or Roman Catholic converts—and some of these among the most gifted; two have committed suicide. I myself had an unexpected breakdown when I was in my middle thirties. It was pointed out to me then that I had reached exactly the age at which my father had first passed into the shadow. I must have inherited from him some strain of his neurotic distemper, and it may be that I was influenced by unconscious fear lest I might be doomed to a similar fate. I did not recover wholly for years, and there were times when I was glad to reflect that I had covered more than half of my threescore and ten—"on the home stretch," I used to phrase it in reassuring myself. But now that I am farther along, I find I want to keep on living.

My father was undoubtedly an exceptional case. This house where I am writing in Talcottville is, I realize, a complete anomaly. In my childhood, it seemed so enchanting, so unlike the rest of my life, that, even in later years, I could hardly, when I was not actually here, believe that it really existed. Now I understand something of the reasons for its seeming so much to belong to a magical world of its own. It was built when this part of the country was only just being opened up for settlement, after a treaty with the Oneida Indians had made it possible for white people to live here. But the first pioneers had so trying a time, with the cold and the lack of supplies, that the government made a temporary ruling that no further land should be sold unless the prospective settler agreed to take in newcomers who had not yet had time to build, and to provide grist for their cattle. The Talcotts were thus engaged in a kind of land speculation. They sold people grist from their mill and building materials from their quarry. The size of the house is accounted for as well as its internal architecture by the necessity of housing a great many people. There used to be outbuildings which have disappeared: a ballroom, a dairy, a quilting room. They made their own candles and nails, and they spun the cloth for their clothes. The place was a town in itself: it was hostelry, town hall and post office, social center and source of supplies. The line between Lewis and Oneida Counties and a good many other matters were decided beneath this roof. But the speculation did not pan out. The Talcottville pioneers expected to have a railroad run through here, but the railroad passed Talcottville by. The town was supposed to center about a New England green, on one side of which our house would have stood; but this project was never developed: the "green" is an unused field. The village has remained a small settlement, strung along a relatively unfrequented road. Many members of the family went West; some who stayed here drank far too much and kept on selling pieces of their immense estates. Yet it perfectly pleased my father. It belonged to my mother's family, but he bought it in her name from her uncle and, in his later and darker years, spent as much time as possible here. It was Talcottville he gave her, not Rumson, and at that time she did not want it. The place became, queerly enough, one of the things about which they disagreed. Though it was *her* family who came from here—his own were from central New York (with another stone house in the family background, by that time, I believe, a museum)—it was my father who enjoyed it most. The family reunions of the summer had dwindled to an occasional cousin, and the relatives my mother had liked best were dead. It was depressing for my mother and bored her: she still wanted my father to take her to some place where she could meet new people, where there would be a good deal going on. But he loved the wild country and the solitude; ‸nd he had here a devoted friend—one of my mother's connections, a quiet good-humored man of such imperturbable placidity that one felt it would be difficult for anyone to try to impress him with neurotic complaints— with whom he made countless fishing-trips, sometimes lasting for days, to the cascading rivers and the forested lakes. He liked to talk to the people in the blacksmith shop and the general store, and would sometimes stay an hour while they came and went. When sitting on the vine-screened porch of our house, he would sometimes fall silent when people passed, attentive to what they were saying. He seemed somehow to have made closer connections with the microscopic community of Talcottville than he had ever been able to do in New Jersey. He was elected to the local Grange as an honorary member and enjoyed attending their meetings. He sometimes came up here alone, and, I am told, would give splendid picnics for my mother's remaining relations. Indoors he would occupy himself with the inspection of his fishing tackle or whittle sticks into slender canes that were always finely tapering—I sometimes carry one that he made—or carpenter wooden boxes that were beautifully joined and finished and that he would stain and equip with brass catches—there are several about the house. He would relax here, as I can relax—at home with his own singularity as well as with the village life, at home with the strangeness of this isolated house as well as with the old America that it still represents so solidly.

For the house does today seem strange, and it must always have been rather exceptional. When Washington Irving, at twenty, first visited this part of the country, in the summer of 1803, it was all a romantic wilderness, in which, "at the head of Long Falls [now Carthage]," the best places he could find to lodge was what he called the "Temple of Dirt" of "a little squat Frenchwoman, with a red face, a black wool hat stuck on her head, her hair greasy and her dress and person in similar style. We were heartily glad to make an escape." Yet not many miles from there, this house had been built or was building. It is curious, in reading Irving, to imagine its excellent proportions, its elegance of windows and doorways, its carved fireplaces and branching columns, crystallizing in the forests that the traveler describes. It still seems curious to find it here. In a sense, it has always been stranded. And am I, too, I wonder, stranded? Am I, too, an exceptional case? When, for example, I look through *Life* magazine, I feel that I do not belong to the country depicted there, that I do not even live in that country. Am I, then, in a pocket of the past? I do not necessarily believe it. I may find myself here at the center of things—since the center can be only in one's head—and my feelings and thoughts may be shared by many.

[1956]

CHRISTIAN GAUSS AS A TEACHER OF LITERATURE

I have been asked to write about Christian Gauss as an influence on my generation at Princeton. Since we knew him as a teacher of literature only—I was in the class of 1916, and he did not become dean of the college till 1925—I shall speak mainly of this side of his activity.

As a professor of French and Italian, then, one of the qualities that distinguished Gauss was the unusual fluidity of mind that he preserved through his whole career. A teacher like Irving Babbitt was a dogmatist who either imposed his dogma or provoked a strong opposition. Christian Gauss was a teacher of a different kind—the kind who starts trains of thought that he does not himself guide to conclusions but leaves in the hands of his students to be carried on by themselves. The student might develop, extend them, transpose them into different terms, build out of them constructions of his own. Gauss never imposed, he suggested; and his own ideas on any subject were always taking new turns: the light in which he saw it would be shifted, it would range itself in some new context. It bored him, in his course on French Romanticism, to teach the same texts year after year; and with the writers that he could not get away from, he would vary the works read. With the less indispensable ones, he would change the repertory altogether. If Alfred de Vigny, for example, had been featured in the course when you took it, you might come back a few years later and find that he had been pushed into the background by Stendhal. Christian would have been reading up Stendhal, and his interest in him would seem almost as fresh as if he had never read him before. He would have some new insights about him, and he would pass these on to you when you came to see him, as he was doing to his students in class. I know from my own experience how the lightly dropped seeds from his lectures could take root and unfold in another's mind; and, while occupied in writing this memoir, I have happened to find striking evidence of the persistence of this vital gift in the testimony of a student of Romance languages who sat under Gauss twenty years later, and who has told me that, in preparing his doctor's thesis, he had at first been exhilarated by an illusion of developing original ideas, only to find the whole thing in germ in his old notes on Gauss's lectures. But though his influence on his students was so penetrating, Gauss founded no school of teaching—not even, I suppose, an academic tradition—because, as one of his colleagues pointed out to me, he had no communicable body of doctrine and no pedagogical method that other teachers could learn to apply. If one went back to Princeton to see him, as I more or less regularly did, after one had got out of college, one's memory of his old preceptorials (relatively informal discussions with groups of five or six students) would seem prolonged, without interruptions, into one's more recent conversations, as if it had all been a long conversation that had extended, off and on, through the years: a commentary that, on Christian's part, never seemed to be trying to prove anything in any overwhelming way, a voyage of speculation that aimed rather to survey the world than to fix a convincing vision. In his role of the least didactic of sages, the most accessible of talkers, he seemed a part of that good eighteenth-century Princeton which has always managed to flourish between the pressures of a narrow Presbyterianism and a rich man's suburbanism. It is prob-

able that Christian was at home in Princeton as he would
not have been anywhere else. He was delightful in the
days of his deanship, in the solid and compact and ample
yellow-and-white Joseph Henry house, built in 1837,
where there was always, during the weekends, a constant
going and coming of visitors, who could pick up with him
any topic, literary, historical or collegiate, and pursue it
till someone else came and the thread was left suspended.
Though by this time so important a local figure, he
seemed always, also, international. He had been born of
German parents in Michigan, and German had been his
first language. In his youth he had spent a good deal of
time in France. He had no foreign accent in English, and,
so far as I was able to judge, spoke all his languages correctly and fluently; but French, Italian and English, at any
rate, with a deliberate articulation, never running the
words together, as if they were not native to him. One did
not learn a bad accent from him, but one did not learn to
speak the Romance languages as they are spoken in their
own countries. On the other hand, the very uniformity of
his candid tone, his unhurried pace and his scrupulous
precision, with his slightly drawling intonations, made a
kind of neutral medium in which everything in the world
seemed soluble. I have never known anyone like him in
any academic community. He gave the impression of
keeping in touch, without the slightest effort—he must
have examined all the printed matter that came into the
university library—with everything that was going on
everywhere, as well as everything that had ever gone on.
It used to amuse me sometimes to try him out on unlikely
subjects. If one asked him a question about the Middle
Ages, one absolutely got the impression that he had lived
in Europe then and knew it at firsthand.

This extreme flexibility and enormous range were, of
course, a feature of his lectures. He was able to explain
and appreciate almost any kind of work of literature from
almost any period. He would show you what the author
was aiming at and the methods he had adopted to achieve

his ends. He was wonderful at comparative literature, for his reading had covered the whole of the West, ancient, medieval and modern, and his memory was truly Macaulayan (an adjective sometimes assigned too cheaply). He seemed to be able to summon almost anything he wanted in prose or verse, as if he were taking down the book from the shelf. (He told me once that, in his younger days, he had set out to write something about Rabelais and had presently begun to grow suspicious of what he saw coming out. On looking up Taine's essay on Rabelais, he found that he had been transcribing whole paragraphs from it, his unconscious doing the work of translation.) He was brilliant at revealing the assumptions, social, aesthetic and moral, implicit in, say, a scene from a romantic play as contrasted with a scene from a Greek tragedy, or in the significance of a character in Dante as distinguished from the significance of a character in Shakespeare. I remember his later quoting with approval A. N. Whitehead's statement, in *Science and the Modern World*, that, "when you are criticizing the philosophy of an epoch," you should "not chiefly direct your attention to those intellectual positions which its exponents feel it necessary explicitly to defend. There will be some fundamental assumptions which adherents of all the variant systems within the epoch unconsciously presuppose. Such assumptions appear so obvious that people do not know what they are assuming because no other way of putting things has ever occurred to them." Gauss had always had a special sense of this. But he was interested also in individuals and liked to bring out the traits of a literary personality. His commentary on a poem of Victor Hugo's—*Le Mendiant* from *Les Contemplations*—would run along something like this: "A poor man is passing in the frost and rain, and Victor Hugo asks him in. He opens the door '*d'une façon civile*'—he is always democratic, of course. '*Entrez, brave homme,*' he says, and he tells the man to warm himself and has a bowl of milk brought him—as anybody, of course, would do. He makes him

take off his cloak—'*tout mangé des vers, et jadis bleu*'—
and he hangs it on a nail, where the fire shines through its
holes, so that it looks like a night illumined by stars.

"*Et, pendant qu'il séchait ce haillon désolé*
D'où ruisselaient le pluie et l'eau des fondrières,
Je songeais que cet homme était plein de prières.
Et je regardais, sourd à ce que nous disions,
Sa bure où je voyais des constellations.

"This sounds impressive, but what does it mean? Not a
thing. We have not been told anything that would indicate
that the old man is full of prayers. It is a gratuitous assumption on the part of Hugo. That the cloak with its
holes reminded him of a heaven with constellations has no
moral significance whatever. Yet with his mastery of verse
and his rhetoric, Victor Hugo manages to carry it off. —I
don't mean," he would add, "that he was insincere. Rather
than live under Louis Napoleon, he went into voluntary
exile—at considerable personal inconvenience—for almost
twenty years. He lived up to his democratic principles,
but he was always a bit theatrical, and he was not very
profound."

I include such reminiscences of the classroom in the
hope that they may be of interest in putting on record
Gauss's methods as a teacher, for the work of a great
teacher who is not, as Gauss was not, a great writer is almost as likely to be irrecoverable as the work of a great
actor. Not that Christian was ever in the least histrionic,
as some of the popular professors of the time were. On the
contrary, for all the friendliness of one's relations with
him outside class when one eventually got to know him,
his tone was sober and quiet, his attitude detached and
impersonal. This was partly due to shyness, no doubt; but
the impression he made was formidable. He would come
into the classroom without looking at us, and immediately
begin to lecture, with his eyes dropped to his notes, presenting a mask that was almost Dantesque and leveling on

us only occasionally the clear gaze that came through his eyeglasses. When he made us recite in Dante, he would sometimes pace to and fro between the desk and the window, with his hands behind his back, rarely consulting the text, which he apparently knew by heart. In the case of some appalling error, he would turn with a stare of ironic amazement and remonstrate in a tone of mock grief: "You thought that barretry was the same as banditry? O-o-oh, Mr. X, that's too-oo ba-a-ad!" This last exclamation, drawled out, was his only way of indicating disapproval. His voice was always low and even, except at those moments when he became aware that the class was falling asleep, when he would turn on another voice, loud, nasal, declamatory and pitilessly distinct, which would be likely to begin in the middle of a sentence for the sake of the shock-value, I think, and in order to dissociate this special effect from whatever he happened to be saying—which might be something no more blood-curdling than a statement that André Chénier had brought to the classical forms a nuance of romantic feeling. When this voice would be heard in the class next door—for it penetrated the partition like a fire-siren—it always made people laugh; but for the students in Gauss's own room, it seemed to saw right through the base of the spine and made them sit forward intently. When it had had this effect, it would cease. He was never sarcastic and never bullied; but the discipline he maintained was perfect. Any signs of disorder were silenced by one straight and stern look.

Nevertheless, though Christian's methods were nondramatic, he had a knack of fixing in one's mind key passages and key facts. His handling of Rousseau, for example, was most effective in building up the importance of a writer whom we might otherwise find boring. (In this case, he *has* left something that can be used by his successors in his volume of *Selections* from Rousseau, published by the Princeton University Press—though, as usual with Gauss's writing, the introduction and notes have little of the peculiar effectiveness of his lecture-room presentation.) He would start off by planting, as it were, in our vision of the panorama of history that critical moment of Rousseau's life which, since he did not include it in the *Confessions,* having already described it in the first of his letters to M. de Malesherbes, is likely to be overlooked or insufficiently emphasized (compare Saintsbury's slurring-over of this incident and its consequences for Western thought, in his *Encyclopaedia Britannica* article): the moment, almost as momentous as that of Paul's conversion on the road to Damascus, when Jean-Jacques, then thirty-seven, was walking from Paris to Vincennes, where he was going to see Diderot in prison, and happened to read the announcement that the Academy of Dijon was offering a prize for the best essay on the question "Has the progress of the arts and sciences contributed to corrupt or to purify society?" Such an incident Gauss made memorable, invested with reverberating significance, by a series of incisive strokes that involved no embroidery or dramatics. It was, in fact, as if the glamor of legend, the grandeur of history, had evaporated and left him exposed to our passing gaze, the dusty and sunstruck Jean-Jacques—the clockmaker's son of Geneva, the ill-used apprentice, the thieving lackey, the vagabond of the roads—sinking down under a tree and dazzled by the revelation that all the shames and misfortunes of his life had been the fault of the society that had bred him—that "man is naturally good and that it is only through institutions that men have become wicked." In the same way, he made us feel the pathos and the psychological importance of the moment when the sixteen-year-old apprentice, returning from a walk in the country, found for the third time the gates of Geneva locked against him, and decided that he would never go back.

Christian admired the romantics and expounded them with the liveliest appreciation; but the romantic ideal in literature was not his own ideal. In spite of his imaginative gift for entering into other people's points of view, he was

devoted to a certain conception of art that inevitably asserted itself and that had a tremendous influence on the
students with literary interests who were exposed to
Gauss's teaching. Let me try to define this ideal. Christian
had first known Europe at firsthand as a foreign correspondent in the Paris of the late nineties, and he had always kept a certain loyalty to the "aestheticism" of the
end of the century. There was a legend that seemed almost incredible of a young Christian Gauss with long yellow hair—in our time he was almost completely
bald—who had worn a green velvet jacket;* and he would
surprise you from time to time by telling you of some
conversation he had had with Oscar Wilde or describing
some such bohemian character as Bibi-La-Purée. It was
rumored—though I never dared ask him about this—that
he had once set out to experiment one by one with all the
drugs mentioned in Baudelaire's *Les Paradis Artificiels.*
He rather admired Wilde, with whom he had talked in
cafés, where the latter was sitting alone and running up
high piles of saucers. He had given Christian copies of his
books, inscribed; and Christian used to tell me, with evident respect, that Wilde in his last days had kept only
three volumes: a copy of Walter Pater's *The Renaissance*
that had been given him by Pater, Flaubert's *La Tenta-
tion de Saint Antoine* and Swinburne's *Atalanta in Caly-
don.* And it was always Gauss's great advantage over the
school of Babbitt and More that he understood the artist's
morality as something that expressed itself in different
terms than the churchgoer's or the citizen's morality; the
fidelity to a kind of truth that is rendered by the discipline
of aesthetic form, as distinct from that of the professional
moralist: the explicit communication of a "message." But
there was nothing in his attitude of the truculent pose, the
defiance of the bourgeoisie, that had been characteristic of

---

* I learn from Mrs. Gauss, who has shown me a photograph, that the
realities behind this legend were a head of blond bushy hair and a
jacket which, though green, was not velvet. [E.W.]

the *fin de siècle* and that that other professor of the Romance languages, Gauss's near-contemporary, Ezra Pound, was to sustain through his whole career. How fundamental to his point of view, how much a thing to be taken for granted, this attitude had become, was shown clearly in a conversation I had with him, on some occasion when I had come back after college, when, in reply to some antinomian attitude of mine, or one that he imputed to me, he said, "But you were saying just now that you would have to rewrite something before it could be published. That implies a moral obligation." And his sense of the world and the scope of art was, of course, something very much bigger than was common among the aesthetes and the Symbolists.

Partly perhaps as a heritage from the age of Wilde but, more deeply, as a logical consequence of his continental origin and culture, he showed a pronounced though discreet *parti pris* against the literature of the Anglo-Saxon countries. In our time, he carried on a continual feud—partly humorous, yet basically serious—with the canons of the English Department. I remember his telling me, with sly satisfaction, about a visiting French professor, who had asked, when it was explained to him that someone was an authority on Chaucer, "*Il est intelligent tout de même?*" Certain classical English writers he patronized—in some cases, rightly, I think. Robert Browning, in particular, he abominated. The author of "Pippa Passes" was one of the very few writers about whom I thought his opinions intemperate. "That Philistine beef-eating Englishman," he would bait his colleagues in English, "—what did he know about art? He writes lines like 'Irks care the crop-full bird? Frets doubt the maw-crammed beast?'" When I tried to find out once why Browning moved Christian to such special indignation, he told me, a little darkly, that he had greatly admired him in boyhood and had learned from him "a lot of bad doctrine." He said that the irregular love affairs in Browning were made to

seem too jolly and simple, and insisted that the situation of
the self-frustrated lovers of "The Statue and the Bust"
had never been faced by Browning: If "the end in sight
was a vice," the poet should not have wanted to have them
get together; if he wanted them to get together, he ought
not to have described it as a vice, but, on the other hand,
he ought to have foreseen a mess. "He is one of the most
immoral poets because he makes moral problems seem
easy. He tells you that the good is sure to triumph." He
would suggest to you an embarrassing picture of a
Browning offensively hearty—"not robust," he would say
slyly, "but robustious"—bouncing and booming in Italy,
while the shades of Leopardi and Dante looked on, as
Boccaccio said of the latter, *"con isdegnoso occhio."* The
kind of thing he especially hated was such a poem as the
one, in *James Lee's Wife*, that begins, "O good gigantic
smile o' the brown old earth." . . . Of Byron—though
Byron's writing was certainly more careless than Browning's—he had a much better opinion, because, no doubt,
of Byron's fondness for the Continent as well as his freer
intelligence and his experience of the ills of the world. He
accepted Byron's love affairs—he had nothing of the prig
or the Puritan—because Byron knew what he was doing
and was not misleading about it. As for Shakespeare,
though Christian was, of course, very far from the point of
view of Voltaire, there was always just a suggestion of
something of the kind in the background. He knew
Shakespeare well and quoted him often, but Shakespeare
was not one of the authors whom Christian had lived in or
on; and he always made us feel that that sort of thing
could never come up to literature that was polished and
carefully planned and that knew how to make its points
and the meaning of the points it was making. He was certainly unfair to Shakespeare in insisting that the Shakespearean characters all talk the same language, whereas
Dante's all express themselves differently. For Christian,
the great poet was Dante, and he gradually convinced you
of this in his remarkable Dante course. He made us see the

objectivity of Dante and the significance of his every stroke, so that even the geographical references have a moral and emotional force (the Po that finds peace with its tributaries in the Paolo and Francesca episode, the mountain in the Ugolino canto that prevents the Pisans from seeing their neighbors of Lucca); the vividness of the scenes and the characters (he liked to point out how Farinata's arrogant poise was thrown into dramatic relief by the passionate interruption of Cavalcanti); and the tremendous intellectual power by which all sorts of men and women exhibiting all sorts of passions have been organized in an orderly vision that implies, also, a reasoned morality. No Englishman, he made us feel, could ever have achieved this; it would never have occurred to Shakespeare. Nor could any English novelist have even attempted what Gustave Flaubert had achieved—a personal conception of the world, put together, without a visible seam, from apparently impersonal descriptions, in which, as in Dante, not a stroke was wasted. He admired the Russians, also, for their sober art of implication. I remember his calling our attention to one of the church scenes in Tolstoy's *Resurrection*, in which, as he pointed out, Tolstoy made no overt comment, yet caused you to loathe the whole thing by describing the ceremony step by step. This non-English, this classical and Latin ideal, became indissolubly associated in our minds with the summits of literature. We got from Gauss a good many things, but the most important things we got were probably Flaubert and Dante. John Peale Bishop, who came to Princeton intoxicated with Swinburne and Shelley, was concentrating, by the time he graduated, on hard images and pregnant phrases. Ezra Pound and the imagists, to be sure, had a good deal to do with this, but Gauss's courses were important, too, and such an early poem of Bishop's as "Losses," which contrasts Verlaine with Dante, was directly inspired by them. Less directly, perhaps, but no less certainly, the development of F. Scott Fitzgerald from *This Side of Paradise* to *The Great Gatsby*, from a loose and subjective conception of the novel to an organized impersonal one, was also due to Christian's influence. He made us all want to write something in which every word, every cadence, every detail, should perform a definite function in producing an intense effect.

Gauss's special understanding of the techniques of art was combined, as is not always the case, with a highly developed sense of history, as well as a sense of morality (he admirably prepared us for Joyce and Proust). If he played down—as I shall show in a moment—the Thomist side of Dante to make us see him as a great artist, he brought out in Flaubert the moralist and the bitter critic of history. And so much, at that period, was all his thought pervaded by the *Divine Comedy* that even his own version of history had at moments a Dantesque touch. It would not have been difficult, for example, to transpose such a presentation as the one of Rousseau that I have mentioned above into the sharp concise self-description of a character in the *Divina Commedia:* "I am the clockmaker's son of Geneva who said that man has made man perverse. When for the third time the cruel captain closed the gates, I made the sky my roof, and found in Annecy the love Geneva had denied" . . .

With this sense of history of Christian's was involved another strain in his nature that had nothing to do with the aestheticism of the nineties and yet that lived in his mind with it quite comfortably. His father, who came from Baden—he was a relative of the physicist Karl Friedrich Gauss—had taken part in the unsuccessful German revolution of 1848 and come to the United States with the emigration that followed it. The spirit of '48 was still alive in Christian, and at the time of the First World War an hereditary hatred of the Prussians roused him to a passionate championship of the anti-German cause even before the United States declared war. Later on, when Prohibition was imposed on the nation, the elder Gauss, as Christian told me, was so much infuriated by what he regarded as an interference nothing short of Prussian with the rights of a free people that he could not talk calmly about it, and, even when dean of the college and obliged to uphold the law, the American-born Christian continued in public to advocate its repeal, which required a certain courage in Presbyterian Princeton. It was this old-fashioned devotion to liberty that led him to admire Hugo for his refusal to live under the Second Empire, and Byron for his willingness to fight for Italian and Greek liberation. "Everywhere he goes in Europe," Christian would say of Byron, "it is the places, such as the prison of Chillon, where men have been oppressed, that arouse him." When he lectured on Anatole France, he would point out the stimulating contrast between the early France of *Sylvestre Bonnard,* who always wrote, as he said, like a kindly and bookish old man, and the France who defended Dreyfus, made a tour of the provinces to speak for him and remained for the rest of his life a social satirist and a radical publicist. In the years when I was first at Princeton, Gauss called himself, I believe, a socialist; and during the years of depression in the thirties, he gravitated again toward the Left and, in *A Primer for Tomorrow* (1934), he made some serious attempt to criticize the financial-industrial system. In an inscription in the copy he sent me, he said that my stimulation had counted for something in his writing the book. But I was never able to persuade him to read Marx and Engels at first hand: he read Werner Sombart instead; and I noted this, like the similar reluctance of Maynard Keynes to look into Marx, as a curious confirmation of the theory of the Marxists that the "bourgeois intellectuals" instinctively shy away from Marxist thought to the extent of even refusing to find out what it really is. Yet Christian had read Spengler with excitement—it was from him that I first heard of *The Decline of the West*—immediately after the war; and he never, in these later years, hesitated, in conversation, to indulge the boldest speculations as to the destiny of contemporary society.

He was a member of the National Committee of the American Civil Liberties Union, and he made a point, after the second war, of speaking to Negro audiences in the South. On my last visit to Princeton when I saw him, in the spring of 1951, he talked to me at length about his adventures in the color-discrimination states—how the representatives of some Negro organization under whose auspices he had been speaking had been unable to come to see him in his white hotel, and how, as he told me with pride, he had succeeded, for the first time in the history of Richmond, in assembling—in a white church, to which, however, he found the Negroes were only admitted on condition of their sitting in the back pews—a mixed black and white audience. As he grew older, he became more internationalist. He foresaw, and he often insisted, at the end of the First World War, that nothing but trouble could come of creating more small European states, and, at the end of the second war, he was bitterly opposed to what he regarded as the development of American nationalism. He complained much, in this connection, of the intensive cultivation, in the colleges, of American literature, which had been carried on since sometime in the middle thirties with a zeal that he thought more and more menacing to sound international values. I did not, on the whole, agree with him in disapproving of the growth of American studies; but I could see that, with his relative indifference to English literature, he must have conceived, at the end of the century, an extremely low opinion of American. He took no interest in Henry James and not very much in Walt Whitman. He told me once that Henry Ford had said, "Cut your own wood and it will warm you twice," not knowing that Ford had been quoting Thoreau. For Christian, the level of American writing was more or less represented by William Dean Howells, the presiding spirit of the years of his youth, for whom he felt hardly the barest respect. It was absolutely incredible to him— and in this I did agree with him—that *The Rise of Silas Lapham* should ever have been thought an important novel. "It wasn't much of a rise," he would say. Yet the "renaissance" of the twenties—unlike Paul Elmer More— he followed with sympathetic, if critical, interest.

Christian Gauss was a complex personality as well as a subtle mind, and one finds it in some ways difficult to sort out one's impressions of him. I want to try to deal now with the moral qualities which, combined with his un- usual intellectual powers, gave him something of the stat- ure of greatness. In some sense, he was a moral teacher as well as a literary one; but his teaching, in the same way as his criticism, was conveyed by throwing out suggestions and dropping incidental comments. In this connection, I want to quote here the tribute of Mr. Harold R. Medina, the distinguished federal judge, from the symposium in the *Alumni Weekly*. It expresses a good deal better than anything I was able to write myself, when I drafted this memoir for the first time, the penetrating quality of Gauss's power, and is interesting to me in describing an experience that closely parallels my own on the part of an alumnus of an earlier class—1909—who was to work in a different field yet who had known Christian Gauss, as I had, not as dean of the college, but as teacher of literature.

"Of all the men whom I have met," Mr. Medina writes, "only four have significantly influenced my life. Dean Gauss was the second of these; the first, my father. From freshman year on I had many courses and precepts with Dean Gauss and during my senior year I was with him al- most daily. He attracted me as he did everyone else; and I sensed that he had something to impart which was of infi- nitely greater importance than the mere content of the courses in French Literature. It was many years after I left Princeton before I realized that it was he who first taught me how to think. How strange it is that so many people have the notion that they are thinking when they are merely repeating the thoughts of others. He dealt in ideas without seeming to do so; he led and guided with so gentle a touch that one began to think almost despite oneself. The process once started, he continued in such fashion as to instil into my very soul the determination to be a seeker after truth, the elusive, perhaps never to be attained, complete and utter truth, no matter where it led or whom it hurt. How he did it I shall never know; but that it was he I have not the slightest doubt. His own intellectual integrity was a constant example for me to follow. And to this precious element he added another. He gave me the vision of language and literature as something representing the continuous and never-ending flow of man's struggle to think the thoughts which, when put into action, constitute in the aggregate the advance of civilization. Whatever I may be today or may ever hope to be is largely the result of the germination of the seeds he planted. The phenomena of cause and effect are not to be denied. With Dean Gauss there were so many hundreds of persons, like myself, whom he influenced and whose innate talents he developed that the ripples he started in motion were multiplied again and again. In critical times I always wondered whether he approved or would approve of things I said and did. And this went on for over forty years."

"To instil into my very soul the determination to be a seeker after truth . . . no matter where it led or whom it hurt." I remember my own thrilled response when, in taking us through the seventeenth canto of the *Paradiso*, Christian read without special emphasis yet in a way that brought out their conviction some lines that remained from that moment engraved, as they say, on my mind:

> *E s'io al vero son timido amico,*
> *Temo di perder viver tra coloro*
> *Che questo tempo chiameranno antico.*

—"If to the truth I prove a timid friend, I fear to lose my life [to fail of survival] among those who will call this time ancient." The truth about which Dante is speaking is his opinion of certain powerful persons, who will, as he has just been forewarned in Heaven, retaliate by sending him into exile—a truth which, as Heaven approves, he will not be deterred from uttering. Another moment in the classroom comes back to me from one of Christian's preceptorials. He had put up to us the issue created by the self-assertive type of romantic, who followed his own impulse in defiance of conventional morality and with indifference to social consequences; and he called upon me to supply him with an instance of moral conflict between social or personal duty and the duty of self-realization. I gave him the case of a problem with which I had had lately to deal as editor of the *Nassau Lit*, when I had not been able to bring myself to tell a friend who had set his heart upon contributing that the manuscripts he brought me were hopeless. "That's not an impulse," said Christian, "to do a humane thing: it's a temptation to do a weak thing." I was struck also by what seemed to me the unusual line that he took one day in class when one of his students complained that he hadn't been able to find out the meaning of a word. "What did you call it?" asked Christian. "Didn't you call it something?" The boy confessed that he hadn't. "That's bad intellectual form," said Christian. "Like going out in the morning with your face unwashed. In reading a foreign language, you must never leave a gap or a blur. If you can't find out what something means, make the best supposition you can. If it's wrong, the chances are that the context will show it in a moment or that you'll see, when the word occurs again, that it couldn't have meant that." This made such an impression on me that—just as Mr. Medina says he has been asking himself all his life whether Christian would approve of his actions—I still make an effort to live up to it.

I love to remember, too, how Christian began one of his lectures as follows: "There are several fundamental philosophies that one can bring to one's life in the world—or rather, there are several ways of taking life. One of these ways of taking the world is not to have any philosophy at all—that is the way that most people take it. Another is to regard the world as unreal and God as the only reality; Buddhism is an example of this. Another may be summed up in the words *Sic transit gloria mundi*—that is the point of view you find in Shakespeare." He then went on to an explanation of the eighteenth-century philosophy which assumed that the world was real and that we ourselves may find some sense in it and make ourselves happy in it. On another occasion, in preceptorial, Christian asked me, "Where do you think our ideals come from—justice, righteousness, beauty and so on?" I replied, "Out of the imaginations of men"; and he surprised me by answering, "That is correct." This made an impression on me, because he usually confined himself to a purely Socratic questioning, in which he did not often allow himself to express his own opinions. I felt that I had caught him off guard: what he had evidently been expecting to elicit was either Platonic idealism or Christian revelation.

It was only outside class and at second hand that I learned that he said of himself at this time that his only religion was Dante; yet it could not escape us in the long run that the Dante we were studying was a secular Dante—or rather, perhaps, a Dante of the Reformation— the validity of whose art and morality did not in the least depend on one's acceptance or non-acceptance of the faith of the Catholic Church. Christian would remind us from time to time of Dante's statement, in his letter to Can Grande, that his poem, though it purported to describe a journey to the other world, really dealt with men's life in this, and we were shown that the conditions of the souls in Hell, Purgatory and Heaven were metaphors for our moral situation here. The principle of salvation that we learned from Dante was not the Catholic surrender to Jesus—who plays in the *Divine Comedy* so significantly small a role—but the vigilant cultivation of *"il ben del intelletto."*

Some of those who had known Christian Gauss in his great days as a teacher of literature were sorry, after the war, to see him becoming involved in the administrative side of the University. I remember his saying to me one day, in the early stages of this, "I've just sent off a lot of letters, and I said to myself as I mailed them, 'There are seventeen letters to people who don't interest me in the least.' " But the job of the dean's office did interest him—though it seemed to us that it did not take a Gauss to rule on remiss or refractory students. He had never liked repeating routine, and I suppose that his department was coming to bore him. He made, by all accounts, a remarkable dean—for his card-catalogue memory kept all names and faces on file even for decades after the students had left, and the sensitive feeling for character that had been hidden behind his classroom mask must have equipped him with a special tact in dealing with the difficult cases. His genius for moral values had also a new field now in which it could exercise itself in an immediate and practical way, and the responsibilities of his office—especially in the years just after the war, when students were committing suicide and getting into all sorts of messes—sometimes put upon him an obvious strain. Looking back since his death, it has seemed to me that the Gauss who was dean of Princeton must have differed almost as much from the Gauss with whom I read French and Italian as this austere teacher had done from the young correspondent in Paris, who had paid for Oscar Wilde's drinks. The Gauss I had known in my student days, with his pale cheeks and shuttered gaze, his old raincoat and soft flat hat, and a shabby mongrel dog named Baudelaire which had been left with him by the Jesse Lynch Williamses and which sometimes accompanied him into class—the Gauss who would pass one on the campus without speaking, unless you attracted his attention, in an abstraction like that of

Dante in Hell and who seemed to meet the academic world with a slightly constrained self-consciousness at not having much in common with it—this figure warmed up and filled out, became recognizably Princetonian in his neckties and shirts and a touch of that tone that combines a country-club self-assurance with a boyish country-town homeliness. He now met the college world, unscreened, with his humorous and lucid green eyes. He wore golf stockings and even played golf. He interested himself in the football team and made speeches at alumni banquets. Though I know that his influence as dean was exerted in favor of scholarships, higher admission requirements and the salvaging of the Humanities—I cannot do justice here to this whole important phase of his career—the only moments of our long friendship when I was ever at all out of sympathy with him occurred during these years of officialdom; for I felt that he had picked up a little the conventional local prejudices when I would find him protesting against the advent in Princeton of the Institute for Advanced Study or, on one occasion, censoring the *Lit* for publishing a "blasphemous" story. One was always impressed, however, by the way in which he seemed to have absorbed the whole business of the University.

We used to hope that he would eventually be president; but, with the domination of business in the boards of trustees of the larger American colleges, it was almost as improbable that Christian would be asked to be president of Princeton as it would have been that Santayana should be asked to be president of Harvard. Not, of course, that it would ever have occurred to anyone to propose such a post for Santayana, but it was somehow characteristic of Christian's career that the idea should have entered the minds of his friends and that nothing should ever have come of it. There appeared in the whole line of Christian's life a certain diversion of purpose, an unpredictable ambiguity of aim, that corresponded to the fluid indeterminate element in his teaching and conversation. He had originally been a newspaper correspondent and a writer of reviews for the literary journals, who hoped to become a poet. He was later a college professor who had developed into a brilliant critic—by far the best, so far as I know, in our academic world of that period—and who still looked forward to writing books; I once found him, in one of his rare moments of leisure, beginning an historical novel. Then, as dean, in the late twenties and thirties, he came to occupy a position of intercollegiate distinction rather incongruous with that usually prosaic office. Was he a "power" in American education? I do not believe he was. That kind of role is possible only for a theorist like John Dewey or an administrator like Charles W. Eliot. Though he was offered the presidency of another college, he continued at Princeton as dean and simply awaited the age of retirement. When that came, he seemed at first depressed, but later readjusted himself. I enjoyed him in these post-official years. He was no longer overworked and he no longer had to worry about the alumni. He returned to literature and started an autobiography, with which, however, he said he was unsatisfied. In October of 1951, he had been writing an introduction for a new edition of Machiavelli's *Prince*, and he was pleased with it when he had finished. He took Mrs. Gauss for a drive in the car, and they talked about a trip to Florida. He had seemed in good spirits and health, though he had complained the Saturday before, after going to the Cornell game, where he had climbed to one of the top tiers of seats, that he was feeling the effects of age—he was now seventy-three. The day after finishing his introduction, he took the manuscript to his publisher in New York and attended there a memorial service for the Austrian novelist Hermann Broch, whom he had known when the latter lived in Princeton. While waiting outside the gates for the train to take him back to Princeton, with the evening paper in his pocket, his heart failed and he suddenly fell dead.

One had always still expected something further from Christian, had hoped that his character and talents would arrive at some final fruition. But—what seems to one still incredible—one's long conversation with him was simply forever suspended. And one sees now that the career was complete, the achievement is all there. He has left no solid body of writing; he did not remake Princeton (as Wood-row Wilson in some sense was able to do); he was not really a public man. He was a spiritual and intellectual force—one does not know how else to put it—of a kind that it may be possible for a man to do any of those other things without in the least becoming. His great work in his generation was unorganized and unobtrusive; and *Who's Who* will tell you nothing about it; but his influence was vital for those who felt it.

> *Chè in la mente m'è fitta, ed or m'accora,*
>   *La cara e buona imagine paterna*
>   *Di voi, quando nel mondo ad ora ad ora*
> *M'insegnavate come l'uom s'eterna. . . .*

[1952]

EDNA ST. VINCENT MILLAY

1

I first met Edna Millay sometime early in 1920, but I had already known about her a long time. A cousin of mine, also a poet, Carolyn Crosby Wilson (now Carolyn Wilson Link), had been in Edna's class at Vassar, 1917, and when I had visited her at college in the spring of 1916, she had given me the April number of the *Vassar Miscellany Monthly*, of which she was one of the editors. I had read it coming back on the train and had been rather impressed by the leading feature, a dramatic dialogue in blank verse called "The Suicide," by Edna St. Vincent Millay. Sometime later in 1916, my cousin sent me a copy of *A Book of Vassar Verse*, an anthology of poems from the *Miscellany*, in which I found "The Suicide" and another similar poem by Miss Millay called "Interim." I was then a fifteen-dollar reporter on the New York *Evening Sun* and was sometimes allowed to do book reviews. I tried to give the Vassar girls a little publicity—it must have been sometime in December—by the following two-paragraph notice, which, in view of later developments, has a certain ironic interest:

"The imaginative development exhibited in *A Book of Vassar Verse*, published by the *Vassar Miscellany Monthly*, bears out the editors' prefatory boast that the book has 'a certain significance of symbolism,' which makes apparent 'the widening range of the college girl's emotional and intellectual interest and the quickening of her contact with reality.' The poems which represent the last six years of the last century and the first six of this one seem a little pale and diffident, even when they are ecstatic, but the contemporary verse sounds a new note of frankness, intensity and dramatic feeling. Such things as "The Suicide," "The Dragon Lamp" and Miss Ruth Pickering's fresh songs are original poems not unworthy of the American generation which has produced Miss Reese and Miss Teasdale.

"But it is, perhaps, still on the side of paleness and shyness that these lyrics err. It is of moonlight and the sound of the wind that they are fondest of singing, and of the wistful moods of sadness or joy which evaporate before we can examine them. That the Vassar poets have succeeded in giving some of these beautiful expression is not the least merit of a fine collection."

In 1917, when Miss Millay's book *Renascence* came out, I was in France with the A.E.F., and my cousin sent me a copy of the book, which impressed me much more than the Vassar poems. In 1920, when I was back in America again, I read in the March issue of the new literary magazine, *The Dial*, a sonnet called "To Love Impuissant," which I immediately got by heart and found myself declaiming in the shower:

Love, though for this you riddle me with darts,
And drag me at your chariot till I die,—
Oh, heavy prince! Oh, panderer of hearts!—
Yet hear me tell how in their throats they lie
Who shout you mighty: thick about my hair,
Day in, day out, your ominous arrows purr,
Who still am free, unto no querulous care
A fool, and in no temple worshiper!
I, that have bared me to your quiver's fire,
Lifted my face into its puny rain,
Do wreathe you Impotent to Evoke Desire
As you are Powerless to Elicit Pain!
(Now will the god, for blasphemy so brave,
Punish me, surely, with the shaft I crave!)

The fascination that this poem had for me was due partly to its ringing defiance—at that time we were all defiant—but partly also to my liking to think that one who appreciated the poet as splendidly as I felt I did might be worthy to deal her the longed-for dart. This was a different, a bolder voice than the brooding girl of *Renascence*. How I hoped I might someday meet her!

This was finally brought about—sometime in the spring of that year—by Hardwick Nevin (the nephew of Ethelbert Nevin, the composer), whom my friend John Peale Bishop had known at Princeton. He had further excited my interest by his description of Edna's enchanting personality, and he had invited John and me to an evening party at his apartment in Greenwich Village, to which Edna came, late, from the theater, where she was acting with the Provincetown Players. I think it was just before this that I had seen the double bill there: a play of Floyd Dell's, in which she had acted, and her own *Aria da Capo*, in which her sister Norma played Columbine. I was thrilled and troubled by this little play: it was the first time I had felt Edna's peculiar power. There was a bitter treatment of war, and we were all ironic about war; but there was also a less common sense of the incongruity and the cruelty of life, of the precariousness of love perched on a table above the corpses that had been hastily shoved out of sight, and renewing its eternal twitter in the silence that succeeded the battle. In any case, it was after the theater that Edna came to Hardwick Nevin's. She complained of being exhausted, but was persuaded to recite some of her poems. She was dressed in some bright batik, and her face lit up with a flush that seemed to burn also in the bronze reflections of her not yet bobbed reddish hair. She was one of those women whose features are not perfect and who in their moments of dimness may not seem even pretty, but who, excited by the blood or the spirit, become almost supernaturally beautiful. She was small, but her figure was full, though she did not appear plump. She had a lovely and very long throat that gave her the look of a muse, and her reading of her poetry was thrilling. She pronounced every syllable distinctly; she gave every sound its value. She seemed sometimes rather British than American—in her quick way of talking to people as well as in her reading of her poems, and I have never understood how her accent was formed. I suppose it was partly the product of the English tradition in New England, and no doubt—since she had acted from childhood—of her having been taught to read Shakespeare by a college or school elocutionist. She had probably also been influenced by the English Mitchell Kennerleys—Kennerley had been her first publisher—who had taken her up when she was still a girl, and, in a more important way, by the English dramatist Charles Rann Kennedy, who, with his wife Edith Wynn Matthison, the actress, had also been interested in her and had tried to persuade her to go on the stage. In any case, the trueness of her ear made it possible for her to write verse which was really in the English tradition. I believe that our failure in the United States to produce much first-rate lyric poetry is partly due to our flattening and drawling of the vowels and our slovenly slurring of the consonants; and Edna spoke with perfect purity. It may have been partly her musical training, which came out also in her handling of her voice. Among poets whose phonograph recordings I have heard, it seems to me that Edna Millay and E. E. Cummings and James Joyce gave conspicuously the best performances. Joyce, like Edna Millay, is a musician with a well-trained voice; Cummings has, like Edna, the New England precision in enunciating every syllable. All three are masters of tempo and tone. If you play the recording of *Renascence,* you will hear how the *r* in the first line gets just the right little twist—so different from the harsh or the slighted *r*'s of the American regional accents; and how the vowels in *long* and *wood* are correctly made, respectively, short and long. If you play *Elegy,* you will hear in the closing lines her characteristic cadences that are almost like song. I do not remember whether she recited this poem the night that I met her first. If she did not, I heard it soon after. It was one of a series she had written for a girl-friend at Vassar who had died, which I thought among the finest of the things that she showed me then. What was impressive and rather unsettling when she read such poems aloud was her power of imposing herself on others through a medium that unburdened the emotions of solitude. The company hushed and listened as people do to music—her authority was always complete; but her voice, though dramatic, was lonely.

My next move was to cultivate her acquaintance by way of *Vanity Fair,* in the editorial department of which magazine John Bishop and I were both working then. She had at that time no real market for her poems; she sold a lyric only now and then to the highbrow *Dial,* on the one hand, or to the trashy *Ainslie's,* on the other. She was hard-up and lived with her mother and sisters at the very end of West Nineteenth Street. When I would go to get her there or take her home in a cab, the children that were playing in the street would run up and crowd around her. It was partly that she gave them pennies and sometimes taxi-rides, just as she later put out food for the birds, but it was also, I think, the magnetism that Vincent Sheean felt.* We published in *Vanity Fair* a good deal of Edna's poetry and thus brought her to the attention of a larger public. This was the beginning of her immense popularity. Frank Crowninshield, the editor of *Vanity Fair*—a clever and extremely entertaining man—was in some ways rather shallow as well as unreliable, but he did have—as it were, as a heritage from his distinguished Boston family—a true instinct about painting and writing and a confidence in his own taste. He deserves a good deal of credit for featuring Edna Millay's poetry and for enabling her later to go abroad. There was nobody else in the publishing world who was both qualified to appreciate her work and in a position to do something to help her in a financial and practical way. As for John Bishop and me, the more we saw of her poetry, the more our admiration grew, and we both, before very long, had fallen irretrievably in love with her. This latter was so common an experience, so almost inevitable a consequence of knowing her in those days, that it is possible, without being guilty of personal irrelevancies, to introduce it into a memoir of this kind. One cannot really write about Edna Millay without bringing into the foreground of the picture her intoxicating effect on people, because this so much created the atmosphere in which she lived and composed. The spell that she exercised on many, of the most various professions and temperaments, of all ages and both sexes, was at that time exactly that which Vincent Sheean imagines she cast on the birds. I should say here that I do not believe that my estimate of Edna Millay's work has ever been much affected by my personal emotions about her. I admired her poetry before I knew her, and my most exalted feeling for her did not, I think, ever prevent me from recognizing or criticizing what was weak or second-rate in her work. Today, thirty years later, though I see her in a different "context," my opinion has hardly changed. Let me regis-

---

* In his biography of Edna St. Vincent Millay, *The Indigo Bunting.* [L.M.D.]

ter this unfashionable opinion here, and explain that Edna Millay seems to me one of the only poets writing in English in our time who have attained to anything like the stature of great literary figures in an age in which prose has predominated. It is hard to know how to compare her to Eliot or Auden or Yeats—it would be even harder to compare her to Pound. There is always a certain incommensurability between men and women writers. But she does have it in common with the first three of these that, in giving supreme expression to profoundly felt personal experience, she was able to identify herself with more general human experience and stand forth as a spokesman for the human spirit, announcing its predicaments, its vicissitudes, but, as a master of human expresson, by the splendor of expression itself, putting herself beyond common embarrassments, common oppressions and panics. This is man who surveys himself and the world in which he moves, not the beast that scurries and suffers; and the name of the poet comes no longer to indicate a mere individual with a birthplace and a legal residence, but to figure as one of the pseudonyms assumed by that spirit itself.

This spirit so made itself felt, in all one's relations with Edna, that it towered above the clever college girl, the Greenwich Village gamine and, later, the neurotic invalid. There was something of awful drama about everything one did with Edna, and yet something that steadied one, too. Those who fell in love with the woman did not, I think, seriously quarrel with her or find themselves at one another's throat and they were not, except in very small ways, demoralized or led to commit excesses, because the other thing was always there, and her genius, for those who could value it, was not something that one could be jealous of. Her poetry, you soon found out, was her real overmastering passion. She gave it to all the world, but she also gave it to you. As in "The Poet and His Book"— at that time, one of my favorites of her poems—with its homely but magical images, its urgent and hurried movement—she addressed herself, not to her lover, by whom, except momentarily, she had never had the illusion that she lived or died, but to everyone whose pulse could throb quicker at catching the beat of her poetry. This made it possible during the first days we knew her for John and me to see a good deal of her together on the basis of our common love of poetry. Our parties were in the nature of a sojourn in Pieria—to which, in one of her sonnets, she complains that an unworthy lover is trying to keep her from returning—where it was most delightful to feel at home. I remember particularly an April night in 1920, when we called on Richard Bennett, the actor, who had been brought by Hardwick Nevin to the Provincetown Players, in the cheerful little house halfway downtown where he lived with his attractive wife and his so soon to be attractive daughters. I sat on the floor with Edna, which seemed to me very Bohemian. On some other occasion, we all undertook to write portraits in verse of ourselves. John's, under the title "Self-Portrait," appeared in *Vanity Fair*, and we wanted to publish Edna's, but one of her sisters intervened and persuaded her that it wouldn't do. There was also a trip on a Fifth Avenue bus—we were going to the Claremont for dinner, I think—in the course of which Edna recited to us a sonnet she had just written: "Here is a wound that never will heal, I know." For me, even rolling up Fifth Avenue, this poem plucked the strings of chagrin, for not only did it refer to some other man, someone I did not know, but it suggested that Edna could not be consoled, that such grief was in the nature of things.

I used to take her to plays, concerts and operas. We saw Bernard Shaw's *Heartbreak House* together, when it was first done in New York, in the November of 1920. I had not liked it much when I read it and had told her that it was a dreary piece on the model of *Misalliance*. But the play absorbed and excited her, as it gradually did me, and I saw that I had been quite wrong: *Heartbreak House* was, on the contrary, the first piece of Shaw's in which he had fully realized the possibilities of the country-house

conversation with which he had been experimenting in
Getting Married and *Misalliance*. At the end of the second act, Edna became very tense and was rather upset by
the scene in which Ariadne—who had just said, "I get my
whole life messed up with people falling in love with
me"—plays cat-and-mouse with the jealous Randell; and
when the curtain went down on it, she said: "I hate
women who do that, you know." She must have had, in
the course of those crowded years, a good many Randells
on her hands, but her method of dealing with them was
different from that of Bernard Shaw's aggressive Ariadne.
She was capable of being mockingly or sternly sharp with
an admirer who proved a nuisance, but she did not like to
torture people or to play them off against one another.
With the dignity of her genius went, not, as is sometimes
the case, a coldness or a hatefulness or a touchiness in intimate human relations, but an invincible magnanimity,
and the effects of her transitory feminine malice would be
canceled by an impartiality which was amiably humorous or sympathetic. It is characteristic of her that, in her
sonnet "On Hearing a Symphony of Beethoven," she
would write of the effect of the music,

> The spiteful and the stingy and the rude
> Sleep like the scullions in the fairy-tale.

Spitefulness and stinginess and rudeness were among the
qualities she most disliked and of which she was least
willing to be guilty.

Between John Bishop and me relations were, nevertheless, by this time, becoming a little strained. Frank Crowninshield was complaining that it was difficult to have
both his assistants in love with one of his most brilliant
contributors. There was a time when, from the point of
view of taking her out, I was more or less monopolizing
Edna, and John, who, between the office and his perfec-
tionist concentration on his poetry—which he recited in
the bathroom in the morning and to which he returned at

night—had collapsed and come down with the flu. I went to see him, and afterwards told Edna—no doubt with a touch of smugness—that I thought he was suffering, also, from his frustrated passion for her. The result of this— which I saw with mixed feelings—was that she paid him a visit at once and did her best to redress the balance. I knew that he had some pretty good poetry to read her, and this did not improve the situation.

But her relations with us and with her other admirers had, as I say, a disarming impartiality. Though she reacted to the traits of the men she knew—a face or a voice or a manner—or to their special qualifications—what they sang or had read or collected—with the same intensely perceptive interest that she brought to anything else—a bird or a shell or a weed—that had attracted her burning attention; though she was quick to feel weakness or strength—she did not, however, give the impression that personality much mattered for her or that, aside from her mother and sisters, her personal relations were important except as subjects for poems; and when she came to write about her lovers, she gave them so little individuality that it was usually, in any given case, impossible to tell which man she was writing about. What interests her is seldom the people themselves, but her own emotions about them; and the sonnets that she published in sequences differed basically from Mrs. Browning's in that they dealt with a miscellany of men without—since they are all about *her*—the reader's feeling the slightest discontinuity. In all this, she was not egotistic in any boring or ridiculous or oppressive way, because it was not the personal, but the impersonal Edna Millay—that is, the poet—that preoccupied her so incessantly. But she was sometimes rather a strain, because nothing could be casual for her; I do not think I ever saw her relaxed, even when she was tired or ill. I used to suppose that this strain of being with her must be due to my own anxieties, but I later discovered that others who had never been emotionally involved with her were affected in the same way. She could be very amusing in company, but the wit of her conversation was as sharp as the pathos of her poetry. She was not at all a social person. She did not gossip; did not like to talk current events; did not like to talk personalities. It was partly that she was really noble, partly that she was rather neurotic, and the two things (bound up together) made it difficult for her to meet the world easily. When Mr. Sheean met her, late in her life, she at first, he tells us, seemed tongue-tied; then puzzled him extremely by thanking him, as if it had happened yesterday, for his having, in some official connection about which he had completely forgotten, sent her some flowers five years before; then analyzed, with a closeness he could hardly follow, a poem by Gerard Manley Hopkins, the sense of which she insisted, with bitterness and an "animation" that brought out "her very extraordinary beauty—not the beauty of every day but apart," had been spoiled by Hopkins's editor Robert Bridges's having put in a comma in the wrong place. But although Edna sometimes fatigued one, she was never, as even the most gifted sometimes are, tyrannical, fatuous or vain. She was either like the most condensed literature or music, the demands of which one cannot meet protractedly, or like a serious nervous case— though this side of her was more in evidence later—whom one finds that one cannot soothe.

What was the cause of this strain? From what was the pressure derived that Edna Millay seemed always to be under? At that time I was too young and too much in love to be able to understand her well, and I afterwards saw her only at intervals and in a much less intimate way. But I had found, when I had come into contact with the formidable strength of character that lay behind her attractiveness and brilliance, something as different as possible from the legend of her Greenwich Village reputation, something austere and even grim. She had been born in Rockland, Maine, and had grown up in small Maine towns. I heard her speak of her father only once. He and her mother had not lived together since the children were quite small, and her mother, who had studied to be a singer, supported them by district nursing without ceasing—as I learn from Mr. Sheean—to train the local orchestra and write out their scores. They were poor; the mother was away all day, and the three girls were thrown much on themselves. To Edna, her sisters and her poetry and music must have been almost the whole of life. Such suitors as she had had in Maine she did not seem to have taken seriously. By her precocious and remarkable poem, *Renascence,* written when she was hardly nineteen, she had attracted, at a summer entertainment, the attention of a visitor, Miss Caroline B. Dow, the New York head of the National Training School of the YWCA, who raised the money to send her to college. She did not graduate, therefore, till she was twenty-five, when she at last emerged into the freedom of a world where her genius and beauty were soon to make her famous, to bring all sorts of people about her, with an intellect and a character that had been developed in solitude and under the discipline of hard conditions. Her human emotional life had, it seemed to me, in her girlhood been rather cramped, but she had herself given her emotions their satisfaction through the objects—the poems—she was able to create, and this life of the mind, this life of art, by which she had triumphed in a little Maine town that offered few other triumphs, was to remain for her the great reality that made everything else unimportant. It is all in the astonishing *Renascence,* which is a study of claustrophobia (as well as, of course, a great affirmation of the stature of the human spirit). Hemmed in between the mountains and the sea of Camden on Penobscot Bay, the girl is beginning to suffocate; she looks up, and the sky seems to offer escape, but when she puts up her hand, she screams, for she finds it so low that she can touch it, and Infinity settles down on her—she can hear the ticking of Eternity; she is beset by a new ordeal, for she begins to feel all human guilt, experience all human suffering, and this, too, becomes an oppression which is killing her; she now sinks six feet into the ground, and she feels the weight roll from her breast; her tortured soul breaks away, and the comforting rain begins to fall; but she is dead now and she wants to escape from the grave, which itself has become a prison, for she imagines how beautiful the world will be as soon as the rain is over; she prays to God for the rain to wash away the grave, and a storm comes and sets her free to those beauties of the world she has longed for; she springs up, embraces the trees, hugs the ground, feels that nothing can ever hide her from God again; the world, she now knows, is as wide as the heart, the heavens as high as the soul, but East and West will close in and crush you if you do not keep them apart, and the sky will cave in on you if your soul is flat. This poem gives the central theme of Edna Millay's whole work: she is alone; she is afraid that the world will crush her; she must summon the strength to assert herself, to draw herself up to her full stature, to embrace the world with love; and the storm—which stands evidently for sexual love—comes to effect a liberation. Her real sexual experience, which came rather late, was to play in her poetry the role of this storm, for it gives her the world to embrace, yet it always leaves her alone again, alone and afraid of death. Withdrawal is her natural condition: she was always, as Mr. Sheean indicates—and this made itself felt as a part of the strain—extremely shy of meeting people; and she was terrified by New York, of which I do not think she saw much, for she would not cross a street alone. She feels that she is "caught beneath great buildings," and she longs to be back in Maine—though the Maine she is homesick for is never in the least idealized, but, on the contrary, a meager country with threadbare interiors, wizened apples and weedy mussels on rotting hulls. One of her poems of this time that impressed me most was the long "Ode to Silence," in which she celebrates an inner sanctuary that is like the grave of *Renascence*—a garden which lies "in a lull," like it, "between the mountains and the mountainous sea."

Of the household in which Edna grew up I had a glimpse, in the summer of 1920, when I went at her invitation—she had John Bishop and me on different weekends—to visit her at Truro, near the tip of Cape Cod. It was already dark when I got there—there was in those days a train that went all the way to Provincetown, shuffling along so slowly that it might have been plodding through the sand—and though I was met by a man with a cart, he did not, for some curmudgeonly Cape Cod reason, drive me all the way to the house, but dropped me some distance away from it, so that I somehow got lost in a field and dragged my suitcase through scrub-oak and sweetfern in the breathless hot August night. At last I saw a gleam—a small house—which I approached from the fields behind it, and there I found the Millays: Edna, with her mother and her two sisters, none of whom I had met. The little house had been lent them for the summer by George Cram Cook (always known as "Jig"), the organizer of the Provincetown Players, who with Susan Glaspell lived across the road. It was bare, with no decoration and only a few pieces of furniture; a windmill that pumped water and no plumbing. Norma has told me since that, when it rained the first night they got there, before they knew they had neighbors who could see them, they had all taken a shower under the spout from the roof. They gave me a dinner on a plain board table by the light of an oil-lamp. I had never seen anything like this household, nor have I ever seen anything like it since. Edna tried to reassure me by telling me that I mustn't be overpowered by all those girls, and one of the others added, "And *what* girls!" Norma, the second sister, was a blonde, who looked a little like Edna; Kathleen, the youngest, was different, a dark Irish type. Edna was now very freckled. All were extremely pretty. But it was the mother who was

most extraordinary. She was a little old woman with
spectacles, who, although she had evidently been through
a good deal, had managed to remain very brisk and bright.
She sat up straight and smoked cigarettes and quizzically
followed the conversation. She looked not unlike a New
England schoolteacher, yet there was something almost
raffish about her. She had anticipated the Bohemianism of
her daughters; and she sometimes made remarks that were
startling from the lips of a little old lady. But there was
nothing sordid about her: you felt even more than with
Edna that she had passed beyond good and evil, beyond
the power of hardship to worry her, and that she had attained there a certain gaiety. The daughters entertained
me with humorous songs—they sang parts very well
together—which they had concocted in their girlhood in
Maine. Here are the words of one that I remember, of
which Norma has supplied me with an accurate version:

SONG TO MEN
Kathleen, soprano; Vincent, baritone; Norma, tenor

Let us sing a little song
To the men we've loved so long—
And to those we've only loved
A little while

Tenor solo: A lit-tle while.
Ti de dee and ta dee da,
We must take them as they are—
Let them spoof us
For they love so
To beguile.

Baritone solo: Let them beguile.

Chorus

Oh, darling men!
Baritone: Oh, men, men, men.
Oh, men alluring,
Waste not the hours—

Tenor:	Sweet idle hours—
	In vain assuring,
	For love, though sweet,
Tenor:	Love though tho thweet—
	Is not enduring.
	Ti de da! Ti da dee da!
	Shall we have a smoke? We can—
	Oh, a man is just a man
	But a little old Fatima
	Burns so snug.
Baritone:	She burns so snug.
	Should we have another drink,
	Do you think? (*Spoken*) Oh, let's
	not think!
	Pour another
	From the little
	Earthen jug—(*Sound of cork*)
	gug-gug-gug
	gug-gug-gug-gug-gug.

Chorus

Oh, darling men!
Oh, men, men, men, etc.
(*Ending*)
Ti de da! Ti da dee da!
So there you are.

Edna had been turning into verse, for a collection called *Folk Songs of Many Peoples*, prose translations of some European peasant songs, and she sang me her versions, which enchanted me—especially one from Esthonia, with a merry and poignant tune:

Piper, pipe a tune, call the dancers out!
Oh, the happy bag-pipes, the laughing shout!
Now the merry step we are treading!
Health to all, and joy bless this wedding!
Tra la la! Tra la la! Youth is all pleasure!
Let the beating foot strike the time of the measure!

Now the master's son, riches spurning,
Weds the farmer maid of his yearning;
Now the girl the rose garland covers,
Leaves her father's house for her lover's.
Tra la la! Lonely my heart, dream laden.
Would that I the bridegroom were, of so sweet a
    maiden.

The word *lonely* in the second stanza was given a dramatic emphasis by being put in the place of the second *tra la la*, in such a way that the first syllable was prolonged in the two drooping notes.

Since there were only two rooms on the first floor, with no partition between them, the only way for Edna and me to get away by ourselves was to sit in a swing on the porch; but the mosquitoes were so tormenting—there being then no mosquito control—that we soon had to go in again. I did, however, ask her formally to marry me, and she did not reject my proposal but said that she would think about it. I am not sure that she actually said, "That might be the solution," but it haunts me that she conveyed that idea. In any case, it was plain to me that proposals of marriage were not a source of great excitement.

The next morning she sat on the floor and recited a lot of new poems—she rarely read her poetry, she knew it by heart. The Millays were rather vague about meals and only really concentrated on dinner, but they never apologized for anything. We played the Fifth Symphony on a primitive old phonograph that had been left with them by Allan Ross Macdougall. She was committing the whole thing to memory, as she liked to do with music and poems; and, raspy and blurred though it sounded, the power of its bold or mysterious motifs came through to me—surcharged with her power—as it never had done before. Jig Cook and Hutchins Hapgood dropped by and sat on the edge of the porch. The conversation was light but learned, and I was rather astonished when Jig quoted a poem in Sanskrit: I did not know at that time that he was a lib-

erated Greek professor. But the things that remain with
me most vividly—because she called my attention to
them—are the vision of Jig Cook's daughter, Nilla, a
handsome and sturdy little girl in a bright red bathing-suit
walking along the beach, as we looked down from the cliff
above; and a gull's egg we found on the sand—gulls do not
build nests—which made Edna stop and stare. It came
back to me seven years later when, going up to Cape Cod
in the early summer, I found myself alone in Provincetown:

PROVINCETOWN

We never from the barren down,
    Beneath the silver-lucid breast
Of drifting plume, gazed out to drown
    Where daylight whitens to the west.

Here never in this place I knew
    Such beauty by your side, such peace—
These skies that, brightening, imbue
    With dawn's delight the day's release.

Only, upon the barren beach,
    Beside the gray egg of a gull,
With that fixed look and fervent speech,
    You stopped and called it beautiful.

Lone as the voice that sped the word!—
    Gray-green as eyes that ate its round!—
The desert dropping of a bird,
    Bare-bedded in the sandy ground.

Tonight, where clouds like foam are blown,
    I ride alone the surf of light,
As—even by my side—alone
    That stony beauty burned your sight.

For I was not "the solution," nor was anyone else she
knew; and she had come to a crisis in her life. "I'll be
thirty in a minute!" she said to me one day. She moved
from the apartment she had shared with her family and
where, she complained, the sewing-machine had inter-

fered with her writing, and took two rooms and a bath on West Twelfth Street, where Kathleen eventually joined her. But this made her more accessible and exposed her to the importunities of her suitors, who really besieged her door. She did not want to marry any of them, and, having tried two Greenwich Village ménages, she no longer had any illusions about extramarital arrangements that were supposed to leave the parties free but, since somebody was always jealous, actually made their relations intolerable. And even with her literary career, she had lately been running into difficulties of a most discouraging kind. Her new book, *Second April*, had been set up a long time before—she showed me the proofs when I first knew her—but Mitchell Kennerley, who was having financial troubles, did not bring the book out and would not even communicate with her. Besides this, her benefactress, Miss Dow, to whom she had dedicated *Second April*, did not approve of her recent work—just as James Joyce's patron, Miss Harriet Weaver, was scandalized by *Ulysses*—and this worried her very much, for she could not write differently to please Miss Dow, and did not know how to answer her letters. She had one or two depressing illnesses. Her apartment was poorly heated, and I brought her an electric heater. I remember how miserable she seemed—though she never lost a certain liveliness—wrapped up in an old flannel bathrobe and bundled in shabby covers. Above the bed was a modern painting, all fractured geometrical planes that vaguely delineated a female figure, which the Millay girls called *Directions for Using the Empress.**

---

* This, I learn from Norma Millay (Mrs. Charles Ellis) was the painter's own name for the picture, which was painted by Charles Ellis. "It was shown," she writes me, "at the Independent Artists' Show and was reviewed under this startling title." The picture, she says, was "an abstract portrait of Vincent's mechanical dressform, the Empress, which gained and lost weight by an intricate system of adjusting nuts and screws. When we later learned that the inventor of the Empress had killed himself, we understood it perfectly."

It was decided she should go abroad. She had never been in Europe, and she wanted to get away from the Village. She had begun to do for *Vanity Fair* the satirical dialogues and sketches which were published under the pseudonym "Nancy Boyd," and this made it possible for Crowninshield to pay her a regular allowance. He did his best to induce Edna to sign these pieces with her own name—he offered her, in fact, more money; but she never would compromise about her work. No matter how confused her life became, she was always clear about this. If one compares the contents of *Figs from Thistles*, written in the same year as the poems in *Second April*, with the contents of the other book, one can see that she imposed on herself a pretty rigorous critical standard. She would not mix with her serious work any of the merely cute feminine pieces that had something in common with the songs that the sisters made up for their own amusement, nor any of the easier lyrics that reflected the tone of the women's magazines. This serious work, never loosely written, was tragic, almost pessimistic (though the best of her lighter verse had the same sort of implications). It was natural that Hardy and Housman should have been among her admirers. From Housman she partly derived (Mr. Sheean, in asserting that Edna Millay owed nothing to any other poet since Shakespeare, has neglected this important exception), and she was closer to this masculine stoicism than to the heartbreak of Sara Teasdale. It was this tough intellectual side combined with her feminine attraction that made her such a satisfactory companion, and that persuaded so many men that they had found their ideal mate. She was quite free from the bluestocking's showing-off, but she did have a rather schoolmarmish side—which rapped Mr. Sheean's knuckles when he put out a cigarette in his coffee-cup. In just this way I have heard her complain of the vandalisms of Greenwich Villagers who made a point of scorning bourgeois sanctions. And so she reprimanded me once when I tried to fulfill my editorial function by urging her to sign her name to her Nancy Boyd articles. Her attitude was: "Don't you know it's impolite to the teacher and reflects on the home you come from to throw chalk around in class?"

I tried to help her get on with these sketches, at the time when she was not yet well, by typing to her dictation, but she was anything but a facile writer and she insisted on putting in as comic lines remarks I had just made in earnest. We had at this time some wonderful conversations, at which quite a lot of bootleg gin was drunk, and, even in that dreadful form, this exhilarating bitter liquor has always kept for me a certain glamor that others have not acquired. On one of these occasions, she recited to me the fragments of a long poem she had started, called "Epitaph for the Race of Man." This was something quite different from the sonnet sequence that she published in 1934. It was written, like *Renascence,* in iambic tetrameter; but it was equally evolutionary: there were monkeys, though not yet, I think, dinosaurs. It surprised me, for it was purely philosophical, and it gave me a new idea of her range. One evening we set out to talk French in preparation for her coming trip. I remarked that her ex-admirers ought to organize an alumni association—to which she answered with promptness and point: *"On en parle toujours, mais on ne le fait jamais."* John Bishop and I, who had realized that we were both quite out of the running without, however, we thought, having yet been superseded by a serious rival, had renewed our good relations and spent an evening with her together, just before she left, on our old high and festive basis. But neither of us saw her off. I think that we were both afraid of the possible unknown others we might have to confront on the pier.

That I missed her may be seen from the following poem. I had read the *Georgics* of Virgil in the summer of 1922, and the phrase *in luminis oras*—which he uses in connection with the sprouting plants that reach upwards

to "the shores of light"—though a conventional Latin formula that had appeared in the older poets, had echoed in
my head with the accent of pathos that haunts even fertility in Virgil, and eventually gave me a motif.

Shut out the Square!
Though not for grayness and the rainy path—
For that intolerable aching air
Of meetings long resolved to silences
And absences like death—
For the throat a moment lifted, the wide brow shaken
    free,
Where there was neither leaf nor wind
A dryad by her tree—
Against the narrow door that closed the narrow hall,
Blank then but for a night that now for all
With blankness wounds the mind.

Gaze out with steady glare!
Present the tough unbroken glove!
For suddenly you heard to-night
Your voice that speaks and saw your hands that
    write,
Yet never speak nor write the name they love—
And knew the hours were waves that wash away
Farther each day to sea the summer sound
Of children shrill and late, of summer hours that run
Late, late, yet never sleep and never tire
Before they meet the sun.

We spoke the sudden words, the words already
    known—
We spoke, and spoke no more, for tongues were fire.
Now, watching from this shore at last, alone
I seem to wait the turning of that tide
That ebbs for ever.
             Children, waking to the day,
Cry out for joy.
           My stubborn heart to-night
Divines the fate of souls who have not died,
Buried in sullen shadows underground—
That reach for ever toward the shores of light.

2

I saw her in Paris in the summer of 1921. She had made new friends and, both there and in England, was having, I think, a very good time. I had the impression that Europe frightened her less than New York, but she must have continued to live with considerable recklessness, for, at the end of two years abroad, she was in very bad shape again. Returned home at the beginning of 1923, she married, in July, Eugen Boissevain, just before she went to the hospital for a serious operation. She had met him at Croton since she had come back from Europe, and had first got to know him in a round of charades. He was a Dutchman with an Irish mother, the son of the editor of the largest Dutch newspaper and himself a coffee importer, with offices in New York. He had been married to Inez Milholland, a Vassar girl who had practiced law and become a famous public champion of labor causes and women's rights, who had died in 1916. He was a gentleman and had once been quite well-to-do. Max Eastman, in his autobiographical *Enjoyment of Living,* describes him at the time of his first marriage as "handsome and muscular and bold, boisterous in conversation, noisy in laughter, yet redeemed by a strain of something feminine that most men except the creative geniuses lack." With no particular talent or bent of his own, it was possible for him only vicariously to express this imaginative and sensitive side, and he was led, as it were, to the special vocation of assisting the careers of gifted women. He was twelve years older than Edna, and, although, as Max Eastman says, he had "the genius, the audacity and the uncompromising determination to enjoy the adventure of life," he made one feel that he had always behind him a stout background of Dutch burgher stability. She had made a very sound choice. He took her on a trip to the Orient and then bought a large farm at Austerlitz, New York, where they settled in 1925 and lived for the rest of their lives.

I used to see and correspond with her occasionally. I

have a memory of calling on her once in January, 1924, in the tiny little house in Bedford Street, 75½, where they lived before they went to the country. I found her absorbed in a paint catalogue, of which she made the special shades of color and their often delightful names start into a relief that seemed almost as vivid as the voices of the Fifth Symphony when she had played it on the phonograph in Truro. From a note-book of 1928—it must have been early in the year, since *The Buck in the Snow* had not yet come out—I learn that she "summoned me to the Vanderbilt to talk about her bobolink poem," about which I seem to have been only moderately enthusiastic. "You mean you think it sounds like Mary Carolyn Davies!" I find she replied to my criticisms. "I said," my record continues, "that, when she had written *Second April*, she had been under so many kinds of pressure that the people who read her poems hardly thought about them as literature at all: there had been an element of panic about them. She said, 'Yes, and I still want to knock 'em cold!' For two cents she would tear up the bobolink proof and not let the *Delineator* have it.... She looked quite beautiful, very high pink flush, and brown dress that brought out her color." I noted, also, Boissevain's "protective attitude" and his saying that her recent work was "more objective." He was right, and the volume of lyrics called *The Buck in the Snow*—the first she had published since *The Harp-Weaver* of 1923—which came out later that year, contained work of a much less desperate, a more contemplative kind, which included, along with the bobolink, several of her finest poems: "Dawn," "The Cameo," "Sonnet to Gath," "On Hearing a Symphony of Beethoven."

This book contained also a piece that I read with both pleasure and embarrassment, for I recognized it—she afterwards confirmed this—as an account of an evening we had spent together (it must have been sometime that same winter), when I had been living in a little room on West Thirteenth Street opposite a taxi-garage and just around the corner from Greenwich Avenue. I had read her the

Latin elegiacs that A. E. Housman had prefixed to his
Manilius and a translation of them I had made; some of
Yeats's latest poems, which she had not seen; James
Joyce's *Pomes Penyeach*, as to which I thought her rather
old-fashioned for objecting that the title cheapened them,
as if he had let them go as the work of some "Nancy
Boyd." I do not remember behaving as she describes (as
people seem so often to say). I think she must have combined this occasion with some memory from our earlier
phase, but it is painful to me to reread this poem today
and to feel again, in retrospect, how much I must have
hated to part from her.

PORTRAIT

Over and over I have heard,
As now I hear it,
Your voice harsh and light as the scratching of dry
    leaves over the hard ground,
Your voice forever assailed and shaken by the wind
    from the island
Of illustrious living and dead, that never dies down,
And bending at moments under the terrible weight of
    the perfect word,
Here in this room without fire, without comfort of
    any kind,
Reading aloud to me immortal page after page con-
    ceived in a mortal mind.
Beauty at such moments before me like a wild bright
    bird
Has been in the room, and eyed me, and let me come
    near it.

I could not ever nor can I to this day
Acquaint you with the triumph and the sweet rest
These hours have brought to me and always bring,—
Rapture, coloured like the wild bird's neck and wing,
Comfort, softer than the feathers of its breast.
Always, and even now, when I rise to go,
Your eyes blaze out from a face gone wickedly pale;

I try to tell you what I would have you know,—
What peace it was; you cry me down; you scourge me
  with a salty flail;
You will not have it so.

She had said to me in the course of this evening that the
only bad feature of Austerlitz was its not being near the
sea, of which she had a permanent need, that the hills and
the woods walled her in and sometimes made her feel imprisoned (this was, as I now can see, one of the phases of
her recurrent claustrophobia). I suppose it was to remedy
this that they later bought their island in Maine. In the
May of 1928, I had a wire from her inviting me to Austerlitz for a weekend. I went, and it was pleasant, as I learn
from my notes—the prospect of seeing her again must, as
usual, have stimulated my perceptions—to find myself on
the train, in the widening landscape of upstate New York,
with its dark and thick-bristling hills, today blurred with
mist at the tops and misted at the bases with fruit-
blossoms; and, in intervals of reading Proust's letters to
Mme. Sheikévitch, I looked out on the long roads leading
over these hills, the white houses and little red cabins and
large-looming tarnished barns, the stone fences that lay in
loose meshes, the small faded rural hotels that so often
stood opposite the stations—with the soddenly wet gray
day superimposed rather queerly on the freshest green-
ness of spring. There were desolate yellow freightcars
trailing along the route, and the timbery marshes were
studded with the rank green of skunk-cabbage leaves. The
ponds and the streams had a dark smooth luster even
under the rain, but the foam of the apple-blossoms, like
some dirty sheep in a pasture, seemed yellowed by the
turbid weather. A growth of squarish whitish houses in
the bowl of one of the valleys seemed almost a product of
the damp like the skunk-cabbage in the swamp. At Austerlitz—hirsute hills—the overcast sultry weather seemed
brooding like a mother-bird over the not yet quite opening
beauties of spring, the little pink fruit-tree buds that were

just on the point of bursting. The birds themselves seemed subdued, and Edna, when I reached the Boissevains' place, said that she imagined the farmhands—"ominously silent," also—perched somewhere with their heads under their wings. I had, on my side, been saving for her a simile and remarked that on one of the lawns I had passed the dandelions had looked like grated egg on spinach. We were neither of us, perhaps, at our best, but we always made a certain effort. Above the Boissevains' house—called Steepletop—a big densely green tree-grown hill, with the flat effect of a tapestry, was stitched with distinct white birch.

Gene Boissevain, when I arrived, was planting a border of pansies with a gardener's intent application; but his attention seemed soon to flag, for he began singing cockney songs at the top of his voice. Then he addressed himself to oiling the lawn-mower; then suddenly dropped it and proposed a drink. There was a comfortable living room, in which, as one first came into it, one was startled at being confronted by a dark human head staring fixedly and almost fiercely from eyes that had black irises and glowing whites: a bronze bust of Sappho, painted black, on an immense marble pedestal, which an admirer had sent Edna from Italy. There were also hangings from India, golden birds on a background of green, that she had brought back from her first trip to London. We did a good deal of leisurely drinking, all in the gamut of apple products, on which people who lived in the country much depended under Prohibition: apple brandies and apple wines that ranged in color from citron to amber. Edna was interesting herself in the local animals and birds and trees, which were beginning to turn up in *The Buck in the Snow;* but we decided not to go for a walk, as it had been earlier proposed to do. They had a sensitive German police-dog, who, when Boissevain had given her a scolding, would drag herself into the room, bumping against the chairs, as if her hind legs were paralyzed. They thought she was a case for Freud.

There was a piano in the living room, and the next morning I asked her to play. I had not heard her since years before, when she had taken off her rings and left them on the piano in my apartment in Sixteenth Street, and I had found in my mailbox the next morning a note dated "Three p.m. (out to get food)"—since she lived only a few blocks away—asking me to bring them back. She had now, she told me, taken up music again and was trying to work regularly at it. She was studying a sonata of Beethoven and played parts of it with her bright alive touch, dropping them, however, with impatience at the raggedness of her own performance. Then she got out a lot of new poems, over which we had a long session. It brought her back to her old intensity. She was desperately, feverishly anxious not to let her standard down. She sometimes kept a poem for decades before she got it into satisfactory form. I remember one ambitious piece called "Pittsburgh Rose," on which she had been working that summer, that impressed me very much at the time but that she never got to the point of publishing—also "Menses," which was not printed till *Huntsman, What Quarry?* in 1937. I would try to relieve the strain that was inevitably set up between us by talking about current ideas and books—to which at that time she paid little attention—and by telling her a gag of Joe Cook's, which I had also been saving for her, because it was a little in her own vein. Cook, in his latest show, had exhibited to the audience two shower-baths and explained they were his own invention: the remarkable thing about them was that you could have a complete shower without taking off your clothes and without getting them wet. He introduced to the audience two men in full evening-dress, wearing silk hats. They stepped into the showers and pulled the curtains—the sound of water was heard. Joe Cook then jerked open the curtains, and the gentlemen emerged drenched. Cook turned to the audience and said, "I have never been more embarrassed in my life!" But even as I was telling this and Edna was laughing at it, I was chilled by the awful seriousness of the implications it was taking on.

The next summer I was visiting near Austerlitz and called on the Boissevains one afternoon. While we were talking, it began to grow dark, and the living room was half in shadow. There were a number of people there, and the conversation was general. I had a curious and touching impression, as Edna sat quiet in a big chair, that—torn and distracted by winds that had swept her through many seas—she had been towed into harbor and moored, that she was floating at anchor there.

It was difficult for the romantics of the twenties to slow down and slough off their youth, when everything had seemed to be possible and they had been able to treat their genius as an unlimited checking account. One could always still resort to liquor to keep up the old excitement, it was a kind of way of getting back there; the old habit of recklessness was hard to drop, the scorn for safe living and expediency, the need to heighten the sensations of life. Edna had now been led back to something like the rural isolation of her girlhood, and in her retreat she had no children to occupy her, to compel her to outgrow her girlhood. Though I did not see much of her through all these years, I got the impression that she was alternating between vigorously creative periods when she produced the firm-based strong-molded work that represented her full artistic maturity—*Fatal Interview* and "Epitaph for the Race of Man"—and dreadful lapses into depression and helplessness that sometimes lasted for months. I did not encourage her to talk about these; but I remember her telling me on one occasion, not very long after her marriage, when she had apparently spent weeks in bed, that she had done nothing but weep all the time; and on another, she startled me by saying, in the midst of showing me her poetry: "I'm *not* a pathetic character!" This must have been in 1928, at the time when she was still a romantic figure and a fabulously popular poet, imitated, adored and envied all over the United States, who was able to make large fees by reading her poems in public. Through all this, Eugen Boissevain must have been inexhaustibly patient, considerate and comprehending. He had given his whole life to Edna. He dropped his business and seriously worked the farm. He accompanied her on the triumphs of her reading tours and saw her through the ordeals of her hospitals. He arranged for her a social life—it is reflected, I supposed, to some extent, in *Conversation at Midnight*—of a kind that she could never have made for herself, which afforded her more "human" contacts than were possible in the exhausting relationships that were natural to her passionate spirit. Yet she continued, from time to time, to follow her old pattern of escape by breaking away from her domestic arrangements. The sequence of sonnets called *Fatal Interview*—certainly one of her most successful works and one of the great poems of our day—was evidently the product of such an episode. It is, I think, unique among her poems in representing the lover as wanting to end the affair before the poet is willing to let him go.

I did not see her for nineteen years after my call of 1929. It was not till 1944 that I seem even to have written her again. I had been astonished and worried by the poetry she had been publishing during the war, on a level of wartime journalism of which I had not imagined her capable. I tried to explain it as partly due to the natural anxieties of Eugen when Holland was seized by Hitler, and I remembered Henry James's description, in his life of William Wetmore Story, of Mrs. Browning's "feverish obsession" with the Italian Risorgimento. "It is impossible," says James, "not to feel, as we read, that to 'care,' in the common phrase, as she is caring is to entertain one's convictions as a malady and a doom.... We wonder why so much disinterested passion ... should not leave us in a less disturbed degree the benefit of the moral beauty. We ... end by asking ourselves if it be not because her admirable mind, otherwise splendidly exhibited, has inclined us to look in her for that saving and sacred sense of proportion, of the free and blessed *general,* that great poets, that genius and the high range of genius, give us the impression of even in emotion and passion, even in pleading a cause and calling on the gods." I concluded that when women of genius got carried away by a cause, this was the kind of thing that deplorably sometimes happened. But I thought that, since she had come to that pass, she probably needed artistic encouragement; the reviewers were giving her plenty of scolding. So I wrote her a letter in which I refrained from mentioning her war-verse at all but congratulated her on the album of her recordings, which, although it had been made some time before, in 1941, I had only recently bought. One of the poems she had recorded was "The Harp-Weaver," for which I had not much cared when it first appeared. I had told her that it was one of her poems that belonged in a woman's magazine, and was surprised when she defended it strongly, as she did not always do with her work when it verged on the sentimental. I had known that it was about her own mother, and the volume was dedicated to Cora Millay. During the years when Edna had been living in Europe, she had arranged to bring her mother over—which, with her own meager resources at that time, could not have been easy to manage; and I knew how devoted she was to the debonair hard-bitten old lady who had worked for her and educated her. But I did not know with how much effectiveness she had put it into the "Harp-Weaver" poem—or, at least, into her reading of it, for it is better to hear than to read: the loneliness, the poverty, the unvalued Irish heritage, the Spartan New England self-discipline, the gift of artistic creation and intellectual distinction—she had taught her to write verse at four and to play the piano at seven—that the mother had been able to transmit. She had made of it something dramatic and almost unbearably moving, a record of the closest relationship that Edna, up to then, I suppose—that is, up to her marriage—had ever known. I wrote her something of this, and I told her that John Bishop had died that spring. I heard nothing from her for two years; then, in the summer of 1946, I received from her this strange letter:

Steepletop,
August, 1946.
... It is two years now since I received your letter. You had bad news to tell me: the death of John Bishop. Even now, that seems unlikely. How you must have missed him that summer, and how you still must miss him, is something that I would rather not go into in my mind. For it would make me ache, only to think of it, and I don't like aching, any more than anybody else.

You told me also, in that letter, that you liked my recorded readings from my poems. That pleased me enormously. I had felt pretty sure, myself, that they were good, but your verdict was like an Imprimatur to me.

Your letter reached me at a time when I was very ill indeed, in the Doctors Hospital in New York. I was enjoying there a very handsome—and, as I afterwards was told, an all but life-size—nervous breakdown. For five years I had been writing almost nothing but propaganda. And I can tell you from my own experience, that there is nothing on this earth which can so much get on the nerves of a good poet, as the writing of bad poetry. Anyway, finally I cracked up under it. I was in the hospital a long time.

This does not explain, of course, why, when I got out and came home, after I got well and strong again, still I did not write you. But here, happily for me, and for you, I can save ourselves the cumbersome explaining, by reminding you of a letter of Gerard Hopkins. In this letter he makes apology—I forget to whom; possibly to Robert Bridges, although, somehow, I think not—for having been so slow in answering. And he states—not in these words at all, but this is the meaning of it—: that the driving of himself by himself to make the beginning of a letter, is almost more than his strength can support. When once he has forced himself to begin the letter, he says, the going is not so bad. Well, I, too, suffer from that disease. For it is a disease. It is as real, and its outlines are quite as clear, as in a case of claustrophobia, or agoraphobia. I have named it, just in order to comfort myself, and to dignify this pitiful horror with a name, epistolaphobia. I say, "I, too, suffer from that disease." But I think I have it very much worse than he had. For after all, he did write many letters. And I don't. It is sheer desperation and pure panic—lest, through my continued silence, I lose your friendship, which I prize— that whips me to the typewriter now. I don't know where you are. But I think, and I think it often, "Wherever he is, there he still is, and perhaps some day I shall see him again, and we shall talk about poetry, as we used to do."

I have just finished learning by heart Matthew Arnold's "Scholar Gypsy,"—such a lovely poem. I had wanted for years to know it by heart, but it had always looked a bit long to me. It is not at all difficult, however, to learn by heart, stanza by stanza; it is so reasonable. I have also learned by heart "The Eve of St. Agnes" and "Lamia." "Lamia," let me tell you, is a very long poem. And Keats, in both these poems, makes it as tricky as possible for you, by shifting all the time from "thou" to "you," and by whisking you suddenly from the past tense into the present tense. To get these passages into your memory, and exact, is really quite a chore. I have learned by heart, of Shelley, not only "To the West Wind"—and surely the second stanza of that poem is as fine a thing as ever was written in English—but also the "Hymn to Intellectual Beauty"—a devil to learn by heart. Anyway, I have them all now. And what evil thing can ever again even brush me with its wings?

> With love, as ever,
> Edna

... I am sending you, here—enclosed, three new poems of my own.* I hope, of course I hope very much, that you will like them. But don't—oh, for God's sake, don't for one moment—feel that you must write me something about them, or, indeed, in any way acknowledge this letter at all. I would not put so great a burden upon the shoulders and upon the brain of the person that in all the world I hated the most. I do not need your answer. I am happy enough as it is. For I have at last, after two years of recurring spiritual torment, been able to flog myself into writing a very simple letter to a dear and trusted friend.

E.

I forgot to tell you, even though I was speaking of Father Hopkins, that I have also learned by heart at least one third of his published poetry. Have you ever tried to learn him by heart?—It is great fun, very exciting, difficult.

In the August of 1948, I was attending the Berkshire Music Festival and, discovering that Austerlitz was not far away, I called up the Boissevains and went over with my wife to see them. I had not seen them for nineteen years, and when I had inquired about them of such friends of theirs as I happened to meet, they had not seemed to know much about them either. As we drove through the long tunnel of greenery that led to the Steepletop house, I felt, as I had not done before, that Edna had been buried out there. Gene Boissevain came out in his working-clothes. He shuffled in his leather moccasins, he had aged: he was graying and stooped. It seemed to me that he was low in morale. "I'll go and get my child," he said. I did not realize at first that this meant Edna. I found in the living room

---

* These were "Ragged Island," "To a Snake" and a sonnet beginning "Tranquillity at length, when Autumn comes . . .", which have since appeared in periodicals, but have not yet been collected in a book.

most of the things that had been there in 1929: the scaring
Ethiopian Sappho, the golden birds on the "Tree of Life."
But the birds were paler, their background was gray; the
couches looked badly worn; the whole place seemed
shabby and dim. I had the feeling that it was so long ago
that they had set up keeping house together that they had
ceased to notice the room, that they never did anything to
freshen it up. One saw, standing outside the window,
three rusty old tin oil-barrels, on which Edna could put
food for birds without having it stolen by the squirrels. In
one corner, a litter of copy-books covered table, couch,
chair and floor.

In a few minutes, Edna came in, wearing slacks and a
white working shirt, open at the neck. It was a moment
before I recognized her. She had so changed in the nineteen years that, if I had met her unexpectedly somewhere,
I am sure I should not have known her. She had become
somewhat heavy and dumpy, and her cheeks were a little
florid. Her eyes had a bird-lidded look that I recognized
as typically Irish, and I noticed for the first time a certain
resemblance to her mother. She was terribly nervous;
her hands shook; there was a look of fright in her bright
green eyes. Eugen brought us martinis. Very quietly he
watched her and managed her. At moments he would
baby her in a way that I had not seen him use before but
that had evidently become habitual, when she showed
signs of bursting into tears over not being able to find a
poem or something of the kind. My wife said afterwards
that Gene gave the impression of shaking me at her as if I
had been a new toy with which he hoped to divert her.
She said that she had been writing in the last two months
and was very much excited about it, because, for two
years before that, she had not been able to work. She
talked about her wartime poetry as an error that she
frankly confessed to. She knew that she had deserved the
reviews she got, but had been hurt by them, nevertheless.
She said that she had been dismayed when this handful
of political verses—under the title *Make Bright the*

Arrows—had been issued in the same format as her other books, as if she meant it to stand beside them, for she had intended a paperbound pamphlet that could circulate quickly and be thrown away. I was confirmed in my supposition that these poems had been inspired by loyalty to Eugen, when he talked about his family in Holland. One of his cousins had been tortured and killed; others had had hairbreadth escapes. Edna now constantly sent them packages. She always spoke of "our relatives," and one could see that she was very much attached to them. She had visited them in Holland and had even learned the language. My wife knows Holland and understands Dutch, and Edna, for her benefit, produced and read a poem she had written in Dutch. She showed us a good deal of her poetry, much of it in an unfinished state. It was of an almost unrelieved blackness. I could see that she was just emerging from some terrible eclipse of the spirit. I had difficulty in adjusting myself to Edna in her present phase. There was something more distressing than the old anxiety that she had shown before in discussing her verse: a pressure that she now put upon you for assurance, approval, praise, and, even in those moments when she sounded like a good-natured healthily laughing elderly woman, this, too, was a person I did not know, and these moments, as it were interpolated, seemed to leave her more nervous still. But the nervousness wore off with the drinks, as did my feeling of strangeness about her. This was, after all, the girl, the great poet, I knew, groping back *in luminis oras* from the night of the underworld. She had tackled Catullus's bitter poem, "*Si qua recordanti benefacta priora voluptas...*"; and I could see that the last lines,

Ipse valere, opto et taetrum nunc deponere morbum.
O di, reddite mi hoc pro pietate mea!

had for her a special and desperate meaning. She was afraid that the translation she had sketched would not do the poem justice; and she told us that, when she had sat on the judges' committee for the Guggenheim fellowships, she had not been able to bring herself to vote for Horace Gregory, in spite of his list of distinguished supporters, on account of the badness of his translations of Catullus. But she had had some misgivings since—wasn't it better, perhaps, that the Latinless public should be able to get Catullus, even in an imperfect version? Eugen pulled her up: "Remember," he said, "that was the kind of thing you thought about your war poetry—that it was important to rouse the country." I thought this was very shrewd of him. We talked about John Bishop's poetry, of which I had sent her the collected volume, brought out after his death. She said that his poems had "more overtones" than those of any other contemporary poet: "It's like a row of poplars on a river, with another row reflected in the river." I told her how impossible it had been for me, though John had talked about his illness, to realize that the gloom of his poetry had a real and serious cause or to guess that it announced the approach of death. "Yes: he was despairing," she said.

I was reminded of the little Esthonian folk-song that I had loved so when she sang it in Truro, and I asked her about the anthology in which it had appeared. She didn't know where to find it, but, after reflecting a moment, she was able to recover the song, with its sweet little plaintive tune and her own bittersweet words. I inquired about the original version of the "Epitaph for the Race of Man"—I had been surprised by its coming out in such a different form from that of the version I had heard in 1920; and she told me that she had lost her first draft, of which she could now recall only scraps. Wanting Elena to hear her read, I asked her to recite "The Poet and His Book." As she did so, the room became so charged with emotion that I began to find it difficult to bear. I could not weep, I did not want her to weep, and, though Elena thought we ought to have stayed, I soon insisted on leaving.

I told myself that Edna was even more fatiguing than

she had been in her younger days, and I reasserted my middle-aged indifference. It was too much for me, at fifty-three, to go back to that old state of mind, so demandingly, imprisoningly personal. The whole thing was like one of those dreams that I had never quite ceased to have, in which I found myself with Edna again—though in these dreams she had sometimes seemed faded and shrunken, never ruddy and overblown as I saw her now. The gap of the almost two decades was something that, encountering the real woman, I could not accept or take in. I had found them there, Edna and Eugen, just as I had left them in 1929, and this latest visit connected itself with my glimpses of that summer long past, not with anything that had happened between. It became like the fears and desires, the revived emotions, of sleep; and the changes in her were like the old images of dreams that come to us exaggerated, distorted, swollen with longing or horror. So she was still, although now in a different way, almost as disturbing to me as she had ever been in the twenties, to which she had so completely belonged—for she could not be a part of my present, and to see her exerted on me a painful pull, as if to drag me up by the roots, to gouge me out of my present personality and to annihilate all that had made it. My own life was now organized and grounded, I had children to worry and divert me; and from my present point of view, besides, it disturbed me to find Edna and Eugen haunting like deteriorated ghosts their own comfortable old house in the country. I tried to imagine their lives. They were evidently very hard-up—a certain income that Gene had from Java had ceased at the time of the war, and Edna could no longer give readings; they never seemed to see anyone or go anywhere. When we asked them to come to Tanglewood—an hour's drive away—and go with us to one of the concerts, I was astonished to find that Edna, who loved music so, had no idea at all of what the festival had become and assumed that the concerts were still held under canvas as they had not been since the very first years. We could not persuade her to go. Gene had said that he would ask us to dinner, but "I'm the only thing in the house—I'm the cook and bottlewasher and maid,"—so I assumed that he attended to the house as well as—with little help nowadays—the farm, and cooked all the meals for Edna. But I could not conceive what their daily existence, month after month, had been like or what it would be like in the future. It did not occur to me, as it had not done in connection with John Bishop, that they were both very soon to die. What had desolated and frightened me there was death, to which Eugen was wearily resigned but against which Edna, when I saw her, with the drafts of her unfinished Erebean poems, was making her last fierce struggle.

Eugen Boissevain died in the autumn of 1949. I had wondered already, at the time of our visit, what would happen to Edna if he should die first. All I was able to learn about her was that she was still living out at Steepletop. The night of October 20, 1950, I had a long dream about Edna. It began with a kind of revival of the longing I had had for her in the twenties, and she came to me in her old dream-shape, which was so much more familiar to me than that in which I had seen her last; but then it turned into a conversation that was taking place in the present. I was telling her about John Bishop's relations with another contemporary poet, who had sat at his feet and learned from him, then later had become better known than John and treated him, I had thought, rather shabbily. The next evening I heard of her death, which had taken place the day before, apparently very early on the morning of the nineteenth (Mr. Sheean gives the erroneous impression that she died the morning of the twenty-first). She had been living alone in the house and had evidently sat up all night reading the proofs of Rolfe Humphries's translation of the *Aeneid*, which were found in the living room on the floor around the chair in which she worked, with her notes on the table beside it. She must have been going upstairs at dawn and have felt faint and sat down on a step. She had set down on the step just above her a glass of wine she was carrying. A man who came in to do the chores found her there the next afternoon.* My dream was probably prompted by Sartre's book on Baudelaire, which I had been reading that night in bed and which must have led me to Edna by way of the translation of the *Fleurs du Mal* that she and George Dillon had made, which I had recently reread and thought better of than at the time of my review of *Conversation at Midnight.* My dream was partly motivated, no doubt, by my wanting, in my sleep, to have somebody to listen to my literary gossip and somebody from old times to talk to, but partly, I believe, also, by the impulse to console her in this vicarious way for the neglect that she, too, had been suffering. And I may have had some sort of intuition about what had happened the morning before. I do not mean anything supernatural, but the kind of sympathetic sense of the rhythms of another's life that may sometimes persist in absence, as I had had, in 1944, the feeling that she needed support, at the time of her nervous breakdown.

And she was to speak to me after her death, for the writing of this memoir had a curious sequel. Edna's sister has sent me two letters which Edna had written to me but which I had never seen. The first was dated March 5, 1929, and discussed a novel of mine that I had given her in manuscript. She had not said much about the book the last time I had seen her before she had written, but had promised to send me some notes on it. The letter with these notes had been sent to an address I had already left and

---

* She had at first, I learn, collapsed, after Eugen's death; then had sent away the friends who had come to be with her and insisted on living at Steepletop alone. Her letters show that, as autumn arrived, she had dreaded the winter there. Her sister writes me that when she came there after Edna's death, she found the house "in perfect and beautiful order: the floors were waxed; furniture polished; couches and chairs newly and brightly recovered."

was forwarded to a wrong address, so that it came back to Steepletop when Edna and Gene were abroad and was never sent again. If I had had it, I should have answered it as she asked me to do and might not so completely have lost touch with her for almost twenty years. I thought that she had been offended by a character that was partly derived from her or had so much disliked the book that she had not wanted to write me about it. I now find that she had made careful and copious notes and had good-naturedly undertaken to rewrite in what she thought a more appropriate vein the speeches assigned to the character partly based on herself.

The second letter was an earlier unfinished draft of the one I have given above, which she had written, apparently, the year before and which was in some ways quite different from the one she eventually sent:

... I miss you very much. I wish I could see you and talk with you. Not see you just once, and pour out my heart to you, nothing like that. I wish I could see you every once in a while and talk with you, not about war and peace and depressing things like that, but about poetry, which is never depressing, because no matter how many people have done it badly, a few have done it well, and you can't get around that.

Your letter reached me a year ago last summer in Doctors Hospital in New York, where, after years of Painstaking and Pious Prostitution of Poetry to Propaganda, I was relaxing in a complete and handsome nervous breakdown.

("O di, reddite mi hoc pro pietate mea!")

You said in your letter that you liked the recordings of my poems which I had made for Victor. That came at just the right time ...; it helped me get well.

I wish I could see you. But if I can't see you, I wish I could write letters. It's too bad you haven't known all this time how much your letter meant to me. That is, if you would have cared, and I think you would have. But I can't write letters. Only when the moon is in perigee and the sun is in at least partial eclipse, can I seem to write a letter. But perhaps you're like that, too. After all, I haven't been hearing from *you* so very often, either, now that I come to think of it.—It's a real sickness, though, and no joking, this dread of writing letters, "Hard for the non-elect to understand," and the fact that one has, infrequently, a lucid interval, makes it no less a mania. Or rather, a phobia: *Epistolaphobia*—quite as real as *agora*, and much more of a nuisance—much more of a public nuisance, anyway.

Did you know that the line I just quoted ("Hard for the non-elect to understand") is from "Lamia"?—I would never have known it, except that I have just finished learning "Lamia" by heart. I am letter-perfect in it now; you can't fault me. It is something of a job, learning "Lamia" by heart; not because it is a long poem, although it is really a rather long poem, nor because Keats is difficult to memorize, for he isn't, except in the few places—and it is astonishing how few those places are, in a poem like "Lamia"—where obviously he could not make up his mind just how to say it, and so you can't make up your mind just how to remember it—but because Keats, like all the other boys then, had such an off-hand inconsequential, irritating way of changing from *thee* to *you* in the flicker of a lid-lash, and of swapping tenses mid-phrase.

> And I neglect the holy rite for thee.
> Even as you list, invite your many guests.
> > "Lamia"

> ... Meantime, across the moors,
> Had come young Porphyro, with heart on fire
> For Madeline; beside the portal doors,
> Buttressed from moonlight stands he, and implores—
> > "The Eve of St. Agnes"

... The stately music no more breathes,
The myrtle sickened in a thousand wreaths.
"Lamia"

Nor suffer thy pale forehead to be kissed
By nightshade, ruby grape of Proserpine,
Weave not your rosary of yewberries
"Ode to Melancholy"

Go, for they call you, shepherd, from the hill,
Go, shepherd, and untie the wattled cotes;
No longer leave thy wistful flock unfed
"The Scholar Gypsy"

The quotation from Catullus shows that the poem I found her translating in 1948 was already much in her mind. The first of the quotations from Keats at the end illustrates the shift from *thou* to *you*. The third, fourth and fifth quotations evidently apply to her own state of mind. She has written them all down from memory, with variations on the original punctuation, and in the fourth has unconsciously changed *make* to *weave*.

At the time I was writing this memoir, I happened one day, in the country, at Wellfleet on Cape Cod, where I live, to meet my neighbor from Truro, Phyllis Duganne. We talked about Edna Millay, and she told me of a memory she had of seeing her years ago in Greenwich Village running around the corner of Macdougal Street, flushed and laughing "like a nymph," with her hair swinging. Floyd Dell, also laughing, pursued her. Phyllis said she had always remembered it; and I leave this image here at the end to supplement my first hand impressions—a glimpse of Edna as the fleeing and challenging Daphne of her "Figs from Thistles" poem—from the time when I did not yet know her, when she had first come from Vassar to the Village.

[1952]

THOUGHTS ON BEING BIBLIOGRAPHED

There has come a sort of break in the literary movement that was beginning to feel its first strength in the years 1912–1916, at the time I was in college at Princeton: the movement on which I grew up and with which I afterwards worked. The first prophets of that movement are patriarchs now—classics or pseudo-classics. Of the writers in their late forties or their fifties, some go on rather somniferously bringing out just the same kind of books that they were writing with more energy twenty years ago; and others, who have practiced an intenser art and seemed to promise self-renewal, are in a state of suspended animation. Two of the best of our poets of fiction, Sherwood Anderson and F. Scott Fitzgerald, have died prematurely, depriving us of a freshening and an exhilarating influence that had been felt by us as principles of life, and leaving a sad sense of work uncompleted (though Anderson was in his sixties, it was impossible to think of him as aging, and though he had published a score of books, he seemed always still making his way toward some further self-realization). Certain others of our top rank of writers have disconcertingly abandoned their own standards and published work so outrageously awful that it suggests premature senility. Others yet, whom we might have been regarding as men of still-maturing abilities, on the verge of more important things, have turned up suddenly in the role of old masters with the best of their achievement behind them, and are attempting to pass on the torch, with paternal and hieratic gestures, to a war-driven younger generation which has obviously no idea what to do with it.

These "classes" who have come on since the Depression—it is a better word here than the vague "generations"—have found themselves involved in very different conditions from the ones into which we emerged at the end of the last war. For us, a variety of elements seemed to contribute to produce an atmosphere that was liberating and stimulating. The shadow of Big Business that had oppressed American culture in our childhood seemed finally to be passing away. Woodrow Wilson, for all his shortcomings, had something of the qualities of the Presidents of the earlier years of the Republic: he was a writer and thinker of a kind, and, though most of his reforms were aborted, he did succeed, on the plane of ideas at least, in dissociating the government of the United States from financial and industrial interests, and presided with some moral dignity over the entry of the United States out of its complacent provinciality on to the larger stage of the world. Later, a livid spark seemed to flash from the American labor movement in the direction of the Russian Revolution. And then the period of "prosperity" began, and there was no end of money around, which publishers and editors and foundations could dispose of as well as brokers. The American writer at this moment seemed at last to be getting all the breaks, and it was not always obvious to him that he was in danger of becoming debauched by an atmosphere of fantastic speculation. In the last years of the century before, a "straight" writer like Stephen Crane or Dreiser had found that it demanded all his stubbornness and courage even to get his novels published, and that he then had to be prepared to face public suppression and private slander, while the quieter kind of artist was left simply to die of chill. In that era, it was possible for Theodore Roosevelt to acquire a reputation as a great patron of the national letters by procuring for E. A. Robinson a job in the custom-house. But now in our day it was altogether different. The young man or young woman was scarcely out of college when his first novel was seized on by a publisher who exploited instead of censoring whatever in it was improper or disturbing, and he soon found himself a figure of glamour in the world between the Algonquin and Greenwich Village, at a kind of fancy-dress party of frantic self-advertisement. Even the older and more sober writers who had survived the inhospitable period suffered sometimes from the dazzling Klieg lights and the forcing of immediate profits—as Anderson was persuaded, I feel, to write a spurious bestseller in *Dark Laughter* before his always reliable instincts led him back to his small towns and obscurity. The less mature writers, in that period, often gambled, without quite being aware of it, on values that had been overinflated, like those of the boom days of the stock market.

In any case, at the end of the twenties, a kind of demoralization set in, and this was followed by a shrinkage of those values, and for the writer the conditions became different again. There was suddenly very little money around, and the literary delirium seemed clearing. The sexual taboos of the age before had been dismissed both from books and from life, and there was no need to be feverish about them; liquor was legal again, and the stock market lay gasping its last. The new "classes" of intellectuals—it was a feature of the post-boom period that they tended to think of themselves as "intellectuals" rather than as "writers"—were in general sober and poor, and they applied the analysis of Marxism to the scene of wreckage they faced. This at least offered a discipline for the mind, gave a coherent picture of history and promised not only employment but the triumph of the constructive intellect. But then, within the decade that followed, the young journalists and novelists and poets who had tried to base their dreams on bedrock, had the spectacle, not of the advent of "the first truly human culture," the ideal of Lenin and Trotsky, but of the rapid domination of Europe by the state socialism of Hitler and Stalin, with its strangling of political discussion and its contemptuous extermination of art; and they no longer knew what to think. In some cases, under the illusion that the bureaucracy that ran Russia was still Lenin and that they were serving the cause of a better world by calling themselves Communists in secret, they fell a pathetically easy prey to the two great enemies of literary talent in our time: Hollywood and

Henry Luce, who reduced them to a condition where they appeared to have been subjected to druggings and secret operations and converted into creatures so radically deprived of any kind of personal self-confidence that they had hardly the moral conviction that gives a dignity to genuine unhappiness. Those who have not lent themselves to this fate have for the most part fallen back on teaching, a profession where they are at least in a position to keep in touch with the great work of the past instead of degrading the taste of the present. Though we are left now with very little journalism of the literary and liberal kind that flourished just after the last war, we are witnessing the curious phenomenon—which would have been quite inconceivable in my college days—of young men teaching English or French in the most venerable schools and universities at the same time that they hold radical political opinions and contribute to "advanced" magazines. The youngest classes of all, the ones not yet out of or just out of school, emerge into manhood on the contemporary stage at the moment when the curtain is down and the scenery is being shifted, and find themselves dispatched into the services with no chance to think seriously of literary careers.

It is thus, ás I have said, rather difficult for the veteran of letters of the earlier crop who is retiring a little before his time, to find an appropriate young master on whom to bestow the accolade. On their side, the younger people want precisely to thrust him onto a throne and have him available as an object of veneration. The literary worker of the twenties who had recently thought of himself as merely—to change the figure—attempting to keep alive a small fire while the cold night was closing down, is surprised and even further disquieted to find himself surrounded by animals, attracted or amazed by the light, some of which want to get into the warmth but others of which are afraid of him and would feel safer if they could eat him. What is wonderful to both these groups is that the man should have fire at all. What is strange is that he should seem to belong to a kind of professional group, now becoming extinct and a legend, in which the practice of letters was a common craft and the belief in its value a common motivation. The journalist of the later era is troubled at the thought of a writer who works up his own notions and signs his own name; and for the literary man in a college, incorporated in that quite different organism, the academic profession, with its quite other hierarchies of value and competitions for status, the literary man of the twenties presents himself as the distant inhabitant of another intellectual world; and he figures as the final installment of the body of material to be studied. The young men of our earlier classes saw in literature a sphere of activity in which they hoped themselves to play a part. You read Shakespeare, Shelley, George Meredith, Dostoevsky, Ibsen, and you wanted, however imperfectly and on however infinitesimal a scale, to learn their trade and have the freedom of their company. I remember Scott Fitzgerald's saying to me, not long after we had got out of college: "I want to be one of the greatest writers who have ever lived, don't you?" I had not myself quite entertained this fantasy because I had been reading Plato and Dante. Scott had been reading Booth Tarkington, Compton Mackenzie, H. G. Wells and Swinburne; but when he later got to better writers, his standards and his achievement went sharply up, and he would always have pitted himself against the best in his own line that he knew. I thought his remark rather foolish at the time, yet it was one of the things that made me respect him; and I am sure that his intoxicated ardor represented a healthy way for a young man of talent to feel. The young men of the later classes have too often seemed inhibited from these impulses. The good fortune of the college faculties in acquiring some of the ablest of them has, I fear, been offset by the curbs thus imposed on the writers themselves. But it had been true from the beginning of many of these men that they were resigned to classify and to analyze: it was the case with the Marxist critics as well as with the teachers who read Eliot.

Marxism, as Trotsky said, had produced a new political culture but no distinctive artistic culture. The young intellectuals of the thirties *did* want to join Marx and Lenin in their great field of intellectual historical action; but when the problems of historical action seemed to have been removed in Europe to a less intellectual plane, they could only take sanctuary in learned research. The scholarship of Marxism in some cases shaded easily into the scholarship of the English Department; and the inquest on literary culture from the social-economic point of view was contracted to a simple ambition to get the whole thing under glass. And this is where this bibliography comes in.

I visited Princeton last spring, and one evening, at the house of a professor, I uneasily became aware that this all-absorbing scholarship was after me. I had already been slightly troubled by the efforts of the Princeton librarian to collect the letters of Mencken and by his project of bringing out a volume of them while the writer was still alive. I still thought of Mencken as a contemporary, whose faculties showed no signs of failing; I still looked forward to reading what he should write. That the librarian should have been able to induce him to accept this semi-posthumous status seemed to me an ominous sign that the movement was folding back on itself before having finished its work. And now they were creeping up on me, who was fifteen years younger than Mencken and had arrived at middle age under the illusion that I had not yet really begun to write. I had even a chilling impression that the forces of bibliography would prefer me already to be dead, since the record could then be completed.

I have lent myself, however, to their dubious design under the persuasion of Arthur Mizener (who of course ought to be writing his own essays and poems instead of cataloguing Archibald MacLeish's and mine). My scholarly instincts were tempted as well as my literary vanity, and I have ended by scraping up items of nauseating puerilia and insignificant reviews and paragraphs which

the Library might never have found for itself and
which might better perhaps have been left unidentified.
Having thus, to this extent, fallen a victim to the folding-
back process myself, I may as well complete my lapse by
playing the patriarch, too, and performing a brief obituary
on my work as it is bibliographed here—a process which
will lead me again to the general questions with which I
began.

This list, then, is the record of a journalist, and the only
real interest it can have is that of showing how a journalist
works. When I speak of myself as a journalist, I do not of
course mean that I have always dealt with current events
or that I have not put into my books something more than
can be found in my articles; I mean that I have made my
living mainly by writing in periodicals. There is a serious
profession of journalism, and it involves its own special
problems. To write what you are interested in writing and
to succeed in getting editors to pay for it, is a feat that may
require pretty close calculation and a good deal of ingenuity. You have to learn to load solid matter into notices of
ephemeral happenings; you have to develop a resourcefulness at pursuing a line of thought through pieces on miscellaneous and more or less fortuitous subjects; and you
have to acquire a technique of slipping over on the routine
of editors the deeper independent work which their over-
anxious intentness on the fashions of the month or the
week have conditioned them automatically to reject, as
the machines that make motor parts automatically reject
outsizes. My principal heroes among journalists in
English have been De Quincey, Poe and Shaw, and they
have all, in their various manners, shown themselves masters of these arts. Poe in particular—though at the cost of
an effort which was one of the pressures that shattered
him—succeeded in selling almost all he wrote to the insipid periodicals of his day, studying the forms that were
effective with the public, passing off his most anguished
visions in the guise of mystery stories, and by getting the
editors, in some cases, to print pieces that had been pub-

lished before but of which he had prepared new versions, scoring the triumph of thus making them pay him for the gratuitous labor of rewriting demanded by his artistic conscience. The masterpieces excreted like precious stones by the subterranean chemistry of his mind were sprinkled into a rapid stream of news letters and daily reviewing that was itself made to feed his interests and contribute to his higher aims. And Bernard Shaw, when he was doing for the *Saturday Review* the weekly chronicle of the London theaters, succeeded, without ever being dull, in gradually impressing on his readers his artistic and moral principles. My own strategy—to make an anticlimax—has usually been, first to get books for review or reporting assignments to cover on subjects in which I happened to be interested; then, later, to use the scattered articles for writing general studies of these subjects; then, finally, to bring out a book in which groups of these essays were revised and combined. There are usually to be distinguished in the writings listed here at least two or three stages; and it is of course by the books that I want to stand, since the preliminary sketches quite often show my subjects in a different light and in some cases, perhaps, are contradicted by my final conclusions about them. This method of working out in print one's treatment of something one is studying involves a certain amount of extra writing and consequently of energy wasted; but it does have the advantage of allowing one's ideas first to appear in a tentative form, so that they are exposed to correction and criticism. My non-critical and non-reportorial productions I have also to some extent smuggled in, and their forms may have been sometimes affected by the importunate consideration of the usefulness of detachable units of the right size for magazines.

As for the content of all these articles, I see that I was more or less consciously trying to follow a definite tradition. I had been stimulated at boarding-school and college by the examples of Shaw and Mencken, and, to a lesser extent, by that of James Huneker. All these men were exciting in their day because they had news to bring and unconventional causes to serve. In Huneker's case, it was simply a matter of communicating to the United States, then backward to what seems an incredible degree in its assimilation of cultural movements abroad, the musical and literary happenings of the preceding half-century in Europe. But Mencken and Shaw were the prophets of new eras in their national cultures to which they were also important contributors; and, though their conceptions of their social aims differed, both were carrying on that work of "Enlightenment" of which the flame had been so fanned by Voltaire. I suppose that I, too, wanted to prove myself a "soldier in the Liberation War of humanity" and to speak for the "younger generation" who were "knocking at the door": such phrases were often in my head. But for American writing, when I came upon the scene, the battle had mostly been won: I was myself a beneficiary of the work that had been done by Mencken and others. There remained for the young journalist, however, two roads that had still to be broken: the road to the understanding of the most recent literary events in the larger international world—Joyce, Eliot, Proust, etc.—which were already out of the range of readers the limits of whose taste had been fixed by *Egoists* and *The Quintessence of Ibsenism;* and to bring home to the "bourgeois" intellectual world the most recent developments of Marxism in connection with the Russian Revolution. I was of course far from being either alone or first in popularizing either of these subjects; but they were the matters with which I was mostly concerned, and I felt that what I was doing had some logical connection with the work of the older men I admired.

And now what is the next logical step? I am today past the age for this kind of activity; but I have been wondering in the last few years, and especially going back over my work in this list, what the next phase of literature will be and what is to become of the "Enlightenment." Well, in

the literary field, it does look as if the movements for
which people have been fighting had, if not actually run
their courses, at least completed certain phases of their development. Two of the tendencies that have stimulated
most controversy, both *vis-à-vis* traditional methods and
in conflict with one another: naturalism and symbolism—
culminated and fused in the work of Joyce at the time that
he wrote *Ulysses*. And there was also embodied in *Ulysses*
an exploitation or a parallel exploration of the Freudian
tendencies in psychology which had themselves had to
fight for their lives and which could still seem sensational
in fiction. *The Waste Land* came out the same year as
Ulysses: 1922; and the result was one of those blood-
heating crises that have been occurring periodically in literature since the first night of *Hernani* in 1830: howls of
denunciation, defiant applause and defense, final vindica-
tion and triumph. But when the successor to *Ulysses* arrived, even more daring and equally great though it was,
its reception was completely different; and the difference
is significant and perhaps marks the drop of a trajectory in
modern literature. Such occasions had never been deprived in the past either of evening clothes to hiss from the
boxes or of young men to wear the red vest of Gautier; but
the appearance of *Finnegans Wake*, instead of detonating
a battle, was received with incurious calm. No exalted
young journalists defined it; no old fogeys attacked it with
fury. The reviewers spoke respectfully of Joyce while deprecating an aberration, and detoured around the book
without giving it the smallest attention; and among the
older writers who had been interested in *Ulysses*, now
comfortably ensconced in their niches, a few read it, but
most ignored. The only group of intellectuals that gave a
serious hearing to this work turned out, by a curious reversal of the traditional situation, to be made up, precisely, of members of the profession which had become
proverbial as the enemies of anything new. *Finnegans
Wake* went straight from the hands of Joyce into the
hands of the college professors, and is today not a literary

issue but a subject of academic research. Nor is this, in my opinion, entirely due to the complex erudition of the book itself or to the abstruseness of some of its meanings: *Finnegans Wake* gives a scope to Joyce's *lyric* gift in a way that *Ulysses* did not, and it makes a new departure in the merging of the techniques of the novel and verse that ought to be of special interest to poets and fiction-writers both. The fate of *Finnegans Wake* is partly, I believe, the result of the process which I have mentioned above: the inevitable gravitation toward teaching jobs of able young literary men who can find no decent work outside them. In the twenties, Mr. Harry Levin, who has written so brilliantly on Joyce, would undoubtedly have been editing the *Dial* and going to bat for *Ulysses* in its pages: today he teaches English at Harvard, while an old-red-waistcoat-wearer like me who made a move to get the garment out of moth-balls at the time *Finnegans Wake* was published, is being treated to a quiet bibliography under the auspices of the Princeton Library, where, as I remember, in 1912, Ernest Dowson and Oscar Wilde were the latest sensational writers who had got in past the stained-glass windows.

As for the Marxist or social-economic branch of the naturalistic school—John Dos Passos and André Malraux—it has definitely passed into eclipse, either perplexed or suppressed by the war. The reaction against all forms of naturalism in the direction of universalizing mythologies which had already been a vital element in Yeats and Eliot and Joyce and Mann, and which has lately taken the form of a cult for the psychological fantasies of Kafka, natural and useful though this shift may be, hardly constitutes, as some of its partisans insist, a great renovating subversive movement for which its champions must still contend. An attempt to get back to the pure fairy-tale would certainly be retrograde if it ever became formidable; and in the meantime, what, from the artistic point of view, have Kafka and his emulators done—though they reflect a different moral atmosphere—that had not already been done in the nightmares of Gogol and Melville and Poe?

In the case of political journalism, something similar has taken place. The exponents of the various traditions of radical and liberal writing have mostly been stunned or flattened out by Hitler's bombs and tanks. The socialists are now for the most part simply patriots, as they inevitably become in time of war; the Communists are Russian nationalists who would not recognize a thought of Lenin's if they happened by some mistake to see one; the liberal weeklies are not merely dull shades of the luminous spirits they once were, but false phantoms whose non-incandescence is partly due to an alien mixture of the gases of propaganda injected by the Stalinists and the British. All this press of the Left has been losing its best talent, through its own mediocrity and timidity, to the Curtis and Luce organizations. But *The Saturday Evening Post*, our old enemy, seems itself to have passed into a decline, and to have abandoned the talent-wrecking field to *Fortune* and *Time* and *Life*, whose success during the last fifteen years has been one of the main events of our journalism. The method of summarizing the news which has been characteristic of these magazines has had of course its considerable value. It is a logical result of the need to survey and to articulate the happenings which wireless and airplane can bring us so much quicker and in so much greater abundance than was possible in the past. The kind of reports that you find in *Time*, factual, lucid and terse, give you something that you cannot get from the newspapers or the liberal weeklies; and they compensate by compactness and relative perspective for the shredding and dilution of the radio. But the competence of presentation tends to mask the ineptitude and the cynicism of the mentality behind the report; and the effect on the public consciousness may be almost as demoralizing in its more noncommittal way as the tirades of the old Yellow Press. For you cannot have a presentation of facts without implying also an attitude; and the attitude of the Luce publications has been infectious though it is mainly negative. The occasional statements of policy signed by Mr. Luce and others which appear in these magazines are on the level of Sixth Form orations or themes: they confirm the impression one gets from the rest of a complete absence of serious interpretation on the part of the editorial director; and the various points of view of the men who put *Time* together, appear to have been mashed down and to figure in what they print only as blurred streaks of coloration that blot the machine-finished surface. Their picture of the world gives us sometimes simply the effect of school-boy mentalities in a position to avail themselves of a gigantic research equipment; but it is almost always tinged with a peculiar kind of jeering rancor. There is a tendency to exhibit the persons whose activities are chronicled, not as more or less able or noble or amusing or intelligent human beings, who have various ways of being right or wrong, but—because they are presented by writers who are allowed no points of view themselves—as manikins, sometimes cocky, sometimes busy, sometimes zealous, sometimes silly, sometimes gruesome, but in most cases quite infra-human, who make speeches before guinea-pig parliaments, issue commands and move armies of beetles back and forth on bas-relief battle-maps, indulge themselves maniacally in queer little games of sport, science, art, beer-bottle-top collecting or what-not, squeak absurd little boasts and complaints, and pop up their absurd little faces in front of the lenses of the Luce photographers—adding up to a general impression that the pursuits, past and present, of the human race are rather an absurd little scandal about which you might find out some even nastier details if you met the editors of *Time* over cocktails. This habit of mind must have been prompted in the beginning by a natural reaction from the habit of the period just before, when Charley Schwab, Charley Mitchell and Herbert Hoover had all been celebrated as great public figures; but it has turned into purely gratuitous caricature—that is, caricature without a purpose. The journalism of the age of Voltaire was a journalism that was mainly purpose with a selection of relevant facts, and its inadequacies have often been noted; but a journalism which aims merely at facts, with no political or moral intent, ends by dispensing with even the conviction that the human race ought to go on, and so cannot help making it hateful. Who would drive a plane or man a ship or write a sentence or perform an experiment, or even build a factory or organize a business, to perpetuate the race shown in *Time*? It is the part of an educated man—and the employees of Henry Luce are far from the old-fashioned illiterate reporters—to try to give life some value and point; but these papers which were started on the assumption, to quote an early statement of Luce's "that most people are not well-informed, and that something ought to be done," have ended by having nothing to tell them that appears to be worth the telling.

In all this, it is very hard to know whether tendencies are coming or going, whether movements are running down or merely being interrupted. But certainly, as I said at the beginning, a definite break has occurred. It is the moment, perhaps, failing anything better, for an innocent bibliography. Tomorrow the cessation of the war will be turning loose again those forces that are in conflict within all our nations, and setting free, with the end of the slaughter, the creative instincts again. We must hope that the men who will come out of the services will do again as they did in 1919: both demand and provide better work. But, in the meantime, in spite of bibliographies and their effect of well-ordered finality, we must apply ourselves to bridging a gap; and the risks of the civilian writer which he is bound to accept in war-time are poor remuneration or complete lack of market, public disapproval, self-doubt.

1943

II
The Young Critic: The 1920s

~~~~~~

EDITOR'S NOTE

The full range of his intelligence is brought to bear in Wilson's review-criticism, with its still useful judgments and characterizations, its lucid conversational style. His reviews of the twenties have the vitality of a time and place in which first-rate writers commanded an audience. He had covered the whole scene of European and American writing, winning the respect of Mencken, Hemingway, and Joyce by his discussion of their work, before he moved to *The New Republic*, where these selections first appeared. His critique of Van Wyck Brooks's biography of James is a declaration of independence from a critic with whom he is sometimes linked, as well as an expert introduction to James's development and moral themes. He would later draw closer to Brooks—two volumes of the latter's history of American literary life are favorably reviewed in *Classics and Commercials*—but could never sacrifice art to sociology or prophecy. Aesthetic criticism was not enough for Wilson, however. In "The Critic Who Does Not Exist" he sets out to assess the various schools of literary opinion, aiming to make his trade a central force in the culture. He is carrying out this program when he rejects the opposed ideologies of Dos Passos and Eliot during consecutive weeks in the spring of 1929. Wilson had been a shrewd, sympathetic observer of Eliot since

The Waste Land, and would soon be praising the aesthetic and moral power of *U.S.A.;* yet he finds these writers and others too liable to mythologies of the left and
right. With a critical detachment that would no longer be
so tenable after the stock market crash, he cites the difficulty of confronting the realities of modern American life
head-on.

These selections from *Axel's Castle,* published in January 1931, show why the book remains a valuable account
of modernist literature. Expounding the modern classics
when they were fresh, new, and strange, he gives them a
context in the work of the past and current philosophical
ideas as well as the personalities of the writers. He celebrates Joyce's union of Symbolist with Naturalist technique, of mind and spirit with the flesh they struggle to
transcend, yet he is irreverent enough to find parts of
Ulysses overelaborated. In "Axel and Rimbaud" Wilson
rejects the obscurantism and what he termed the "resigna-
tionism" of the avant-garde, while insisting on its relevance to the general life of society. The poets, for him, are
still in some sense legislators of mankind. If there is little
close reading in these chapters, written before the New
Criticism, they have the confidence of an elite culture not
yet isolated in the academy, still able to contend against
specialization and mass taste. At the end of the twenties,
moving now to the left, Wilson is master of the scene between the acts.

The first four pieces in this section are reprinted from
The Shores of Light, with the stylistic improvements he
made there. The discussion of *Ulysses* in *Axel's Castle* is
framed by a summary of the Homeric parallel and a comment on the beginnings of *Finnegans Wake,* which are
omitted here. Readers are also referred to the accounts of
Viliers de L'Isle Adam's play *Axel* and of Rimbaud's life
and work, through which, in his concluding chapter, Wilson dramatizes what he considered the alternatives of
modern writers.

THE PILGRIMAGE OF
HENRY JAMES

It is becoming a commonplace to say of Mr. Van Wyck
Brooks that he is really a social historian rather than a literary critic, but one cannot avoid raising the question in
connection with his new book. *The Pilgrimage of Henry
James*, like *The Ordeal of Mark Twain*, is a page of
American social history: in it, Henry James figures as the
type of sensitive and imaginative American who, in the
later nineteenth century, found the United States too barren and too crude for him and sought a more congenial
environment in Europe. Mr. Brooks points out James's
original isolation as the son of the elder Henry James, that
well-to-do wandering philosopher who traveled back and
forth between Boston and New York, between the United
States and Europe, without finding himself quite at home
anywhere; and he traces James's first saturation with European impressions during the formative years of his
teens; his attempt at the beginning of his career to establish himself in America as an American novelist working
with native material; his discouragement, his longing for
Europe, his experiments with France and Italy and his
dissatisfaction with his life there; his decision to live permanently in England and to find a field for his art in the
depiction of English society; his failure, after years of living among them, to establish intimate relations with the
English and his disillusioned reaction against them; the
bankruptcy of his imagination, his homesickness and his
visit to the United States; his consternation and despair at
the spectacle of modern America, and his final return to
England. In short, Henry James's tragedy, according to
Mr. Brooks, was that of the literary artist who has lost
contact with his own society without having been able to
strike roots in any other. And of all this aspect of James's
career he has given the most intelligent and the most ex-

haustive account that we have yet had; in fact, it may be said that James's social significance and the part that his social situation plays in his work have here been properly appreciated for the first time. Mr. Brooks has made a contribution of permanent value toward the criticism of Henry James. He has interpreted the complex subject with all his incomparable instinct for divining the feelings and motives of Americans, for getting under their skins; and he has presented his logical theory with the consummate orderliness, neatness and point that he always brings to making out a case. When, for example, he disentangles James's reasons for turning playwright at one period of his career, he generates a kind of excitement in the process of demonstration that seems almost to be independent of the interest of what is being demonstrated. And he has reduced the whole to an entertaining narrative colored by imagination and written with grace. From the point of view of literary form, Mr. Brooks's *Henry James* is, in fact, probably the best of his books.

Where the book is unsatisfactory is in its failure to recognize the real nature and development of James's art. Mr. Brooks has completely subordinated Henry James the artist to Henry James the social symbol, with the result that James's literary work, instead of being considered in its integrity on its own merits, has undergone a process of lopping and distortion to make it fit the Procrustes bed of a thesis. According to Mr. Brooks's simplification, Henry James was at first a very good novelist and then, later on, a very bad one. Mr. Brooks admires James's earlier fiction as a Turgenev-like social document and writes a warm appreciation of it—that is, he admires James in direct proportion as James performs the same sort of function as Mr. Brooks himself. But what he says, in effect, is that, after the publication of *The Bostonians* in 1886, James's artistic record is an almost total blank: when James had settled in England and had used up his American impressions, his failure to make anything of his English material was virtually complete. Mr. Brooks here lumps together the work of thirty years and, in the interest of an a priori theory, refuses to admit distinctions among some thirty volumes of fiction of widely differing character and merit. The truth is that the work of James's English residence falls into three distinct periods. During the second of these—after *The Bostonians* and while he is already dealing chiefly with English material—he reaches what seems to me indisputably his completest artistic maturity: he has got over a certain stiffness, a certain naïveté, which characterized his earlier work and he has acquired a new flexibility and a personal idiom. He has come for the first time into the full possession of his language and form, and he has not yet lost any of the vividness of his youthful imagination. He has ten years ahead of him still before that imagination will begin to show signs of flagging in such books as *The Awkward Age,* and longer still before the style runs to seed in the thickets of the later novels. In the meantime, in the fiction of this period—particularly, perhaps, in the shorter novels which were characteristic of it: *What Maisie Knew, The Aspern Papers,* etc.—he is to produce what seems to the present writer his most satisfactory and distinguished work. As for the deterioration which afterwards sets in, it is to be ascribed chiefly to advancing age. An important thing to remember in connection with James's latest novels—which Mr. Brooks treats with such severity—is that *The Ambassadors, The Wings of the Dove* and *The Golden Bowl* were all written when James was in his late fifties. Their abstraction, their comparative dimness and their exaggerated mannerisms are such as not infrequently appear in the work of an artist's later years. George Meredith and Robert Browning, who did not labor under the handicap of being expatriated Americans, developed somewhat similar traits. These later novels of James are, in any case, not as Mr. Brooks asserts, fundamentally unreal and weak. Intellectually, they are perhaps the most vigorous, the most heroically conceived, of his fictions; but they are like tapestries from which, though the design and the figures still remain masterfully outlined, the colors are fading out.

When all this has been said, however, there still confronts us, in connection with James, the question of a lack in his work of direct emotional experience—a lack which is naturally felt more disconcertingly in his later than in his earlier books, since it is less easily comprehensible in a mature than in a callow man. One can agree here with Mr. Brooks that this insufficient experience of personal relations may be partly accounted for by James's isolation among the English. Yet to throw all the emphasis thus on James's social situation, as Mr. Brooks seems to do, is surely to proceed from the wrong direction. James's solitude, his emotional starvation, his inhibitions against entering into life, were evidently the result of his fundamental moral character, not merely an accident of his social maladjustment; and with the problem of that fundamental character Mr. Brooks never adequately deals. "An immortal symbol," he sums James up, "the embodiment of that impossible yearning of which Hawthorne somewhere speaks—the yearning of the American in the Old World" for the past from which he has been separated. But this theory that a man's whole career may hinge on his yearning for the European past is humanly unconvincing.

It is precisely because Mr. Brooks's interest is all social and never moral that he has missed the point of James's art. It is possible for him to find James's work so empty and disappointing only because he insists on comparing it with that of writers with whom James has little in common: Hardy, Dickens, Tolstoy and Balzac. One would be in a position to appreciate James better if one compared him with the dramatists of the seventeenth century— Racine and Molière, whom he resembles in form as well as in point of view, and even Shakespeare, when allowance has been made for the most extreme differences in subject and form. These poets are not, like Dickens and Hardy, writers of melodrama—either humorous or pessimistic, nor secretaries of society like Balzac, nor prophets like

Tolstoy: they are occupied simply with the presentation of conflicts of moral character, which they do not concern themselves about softening or averting. They do not indict society for these situations: they regard them as universal and inevitable. They do not even blame God for allowing them: they accept them as the conditions of life. Titus and Bérénice, Alceste and Célimène, Antony and Octavius—these are forces which, once set in motion, are doomed to irreconcilable opposition. The dramatist makes no attempt to decide between competing interests: he is content to understand his characters and to put their behavior before us.

Now, it was James's immense distinction to have brought to contemporary life something of this "classical" point of view. The conflicts in his early novels are likely to be presented in terms of European manners and morals at odds with American ones—with a predisposition in favor of the latter. But later on, James's contrasts tend to take on a different aspect: they represent, not merely national divergences, but antagonisms of ideals and temperaments of a kind that may occur anywhere. I cannot agree with Mr. Brooks when he says that in James's later novels "the 'low sneaks' have it all their own way . . . the subtle are always the prey of the gross . . . the pure in heart are always at the mercy of those that work iniquity." On the contrary, the leaning toward melodrama that allowed James in his earlier novels to play virtuous Americans off against scoundrelly Europeans has almost entirely disappeared. *The Ambassadors* is obviously a sort of attempt to re-do the theme of *The American*, as *The Wings of the Dove* is to re-do that of *The Portrait of a Lady*; but one has only to compare the two pairs of books to realize that James no longer sees life in terms of the innocent and the guilty. The Bellegarde family in the earlier novel are cold-blooded and impenitent villains, whereas Mme. de Vionnet, who plays a somewhat similar role in *The Ambassadors*, is shown in as attractive a light as the American to whom she is morally opposed; in the same way Gilbert

Osmond and his mistress, who make Isabel Archer miserable, are a good deal more theatrical than Kate Croy and her lover, who try to exploit Milly Theale. Mr. Brooks's account of *The Wings of the Dove* seems almost perversely unintelligent. He melodramatically describes Milly Theale as the "victim of the basest plot that ever a mind conceived"; yet one of the most remarkable things about *The Wings of the Dove* is the way in which, from the very first pages, Henry James succeeds in making us sympathize with the author of this unquestionably ignoble plot, in making us feel that what she does is inevitable. Kate Croy, though hard and crass, is striving for the highest aspirations she is capable of understanding, just as the more fastidious Milly is.

It is thus, in James's later novels, not a case of the pure in heart invariably falling a prey to the guilty, of the low snakes having it their own way. It is simply a struggle between different kinds of people with different kinds of needs. I do not know what Mr. Brooks means when he writes of "the constant abrogation of James's moral judgment, in these years of an enchanted exile in a museum-world" nor when he says that James "had seen life, in his own way, as all the great novelists have seen it, *sub specie aeternitatis;* he was to see it henceforth, increasingly, *sub specie mundi.*" On the contrary, James, in his later works, is just as much concerned with moral problems, and he is able to see all around them as he has not been able to do before. He has come to be occupied here even more than in his earlier work with what seem to him the irremediable antagonisms of interest between people who enjoy themselves without inhibitions, who take all they can get from life, and people who are curbed by scruples of aesthetic taste as well as of morality from following all their impulses and satisfying all their appetites—between the worldly, the selfish, the "splendid," and the dutiful, the sensitive, the humble. This humility, this moral rectitude takes on in Henry James the aspect of a moral beauty which he opposes, as it were, to the worldly kind; both kinds of beauty attract him, he understands the points of view of the devotees of both, but it is one of his deepest convictions that you cannot have both at the same time. The point of *What Maisie Knew*, for example, lies in the contrast between Maisie's other guardians—the vivid, the charming or the bold—who live only for their own pleasure and advantage and refuse to be bothered with her, and Mrs. Wix, the ridiculous old governess, who, by reason of her possession of a "moral sense," is left with the responsibility of Maisie, "to work her fingers to the bone." So, in *The Golden Bowl*, the brilliant figures of Charlotte and the Prince are contrasted with the unselfishness and the comparative dreariness of Maggie Verver and her father. Almost all Henry James's later novels, in one way or another, illustrate this theme. Surely this, and not, as Mr. Brooks suggests, any mere technical pattern, is that "figure in the carpet" that is hinted at in the famous short story; and in this tendency to oppose the idea of a good conscience to the idea of doing what one likes—wearing, as it does so often in James, the aspect of American versus European—there is evidently a Puritan survival that Mr. Brooks, in his capacity as specialist in American habits of thought, might have been expected to treat more prominently. As it is, he only touches upon it by way of a different route.

Of Mr. Brooks's queer use of his documents for the purpose of proving the artistic nullity of the latter half of James's career, many instances might be given. We sometimes get a little the impression that, instead of reading James's novels with a sense of them as artistic wholes, he has been combing them intently for passages that would seem to bear out his thesis even in cases where, taken in context, they clearly have a different meaning. The extreme abuse of this method is to be found in the chapter in which Mr. Brooks attempts to prove the inadmissible assertion that none of James's later novels is "the fruit of an artistic impulse that is at once spontaneous and sus-

tained," that they "are all—given in each case the tenuity
of the idea—stories of the 'eight to ten thousand words'
blown out to the dimensions of novels." One would ask
oneself at once: In what way can the "ideas" of *The Ambassadors* and *The Wings of the Dove* be described as
being any more "tenuous" than those of their predecessors? How could either of them conceivably be a short
story? They cover as long a period as the early novels,
they contain just as many important characters, they deal
with themes of just the same nature and they are worked
out on just as elaborate a scale. But Mr. Brooks does not
even pretend to go to the novels themselves in order to
justify his critical conclusions about them: he bases his
whole case on three passages which he has found in
James's correspondence. When we come to examine these,
we discover that two of them are references, respectively,
to the "long-windedness" of *The Wings of the Dove* and
the "vague verbosity" of *The Golden Bowl*—which certainly does not prove in the least that the author thought
their *ideas* tenuous. It is in the third of these references
that the phrase about "the tenuity of the idea" occurs, in
an entirely different connection. James writes apologeti-
cally to Howells in regard to *The Sacred Fount* that it had
been "planned, like *The Spoils of Poynton*, *What Maisie
Knew*, *The Turn of the Screw* and various others, as a
story of the 'eight to ten thousand words' " and had then
spun itself out much longer. He goes on to explain that he
might, perhaps, have "chucked" *The Sacred Fount* in the
middle if he had not had a superstition about not finishing
things. He does not, however, say that he considers these
other novels as unsatisfactory as *The Sacred Fount* nor
that he had any impulse to chuck them. In the only part of
this passage, moreover, that Mr. Brooks omits to quote, he
gives a quite different explanation from Mr. Brooks's one
for his practice, at this particular time, of projecting short
stories instead of novels: "*The Sacred Fount*," writes
James, "is one of several things of mine, in these last years,
that have paid the penalty of having been conceived only

as the 'short story' that (alone apparently) I could hope to work off somewhere (which I mainly failed of)." That is, he planned short stories rather than novels, because he thought that short stories were more salable. That, against this intention, he should have found the short stories growing uncontrollably into novels would seem to prove, not, as Mr. Brooks says, that James's "artistic impulse" was not "spontaneous and sustained," but, on the contrary, precisely that it was.

Mr. Brooks's misrepresentation of the obvious sense of this passage, his readiness to found upon such meager evidence so sweeping and damning a case, throws rather an unreassuring light on the spirit of his recent criticism. That spirit is one of intense zeal at the service of intense resentment. What Mr. Brooks resents and desires to protest against is the spiritual poverty of America and our discouragement of the creative artist. But, in preaching this doctrine, Mr. Brooks has finally allowed his bitterness to far overshoot its mark and to castigate the victims of American conditions along with the conditions themselves. In the latter part of *The Pilgrimage of Henry James*, we have the feeling that he has set out to show James up, just as, in his earlier one, he set out to show up Mark Twain. The story of Henry James, like that of Mark Twain, might have excited both our pity and our admiration; but in Mr. Brooks's hands, it gives rise to little but irony. Like Mr. Sinclair Lewis, that other exposer of the spiritual poverty of America, Mr. Brooks has little charity for the poor, and his enthusiasm for creative genius is not today sufficiently generous to prevent him, one is coming to feel, from deriving a certain satisfaction from describing its despair and decay.

There are, however, in any case, two reasons why Henry James is not a very happy subject for Mr. Van Wyck Brooks. In the first place, for all the sobriety of Mr. Brooks's tone, he is in reality a romantic and a preacher, who has little actual sympathy or comprehension for the impersonal and equanimous writer like James. One remembers in this connection a curious passage about Shakespeare in *America's Coming-of-Age*: "Why is it," asked Mr. Brooks, "that Shakespeare is never the master of originating minds? Plato may be, or Dante, or Tolstoy . . . but not Shakespeare . . . certainly anyone who requires a lesson of Shakespeare comes away with nothing but grace and good humor." The truth is that Mr. Brooks cannot help expecting a really great writer to be a stimulating social prophet. He can understand the lessons conveyed by a Plato or a Tolstoy, but he seems not much more responsive to Shakespeare than he is to Henry James. From Shakespeare he comes away with "nothing but grace and good humor," and from James with almost nothing at all. In the second place, Henry James lends himself to Mr. Brooks's treatment a good deal less satisfactorily than, say, Mark Twain, because the latter was admittedly a remarkable figure who wrote a few very fine things but the bulk of whose books, partly hack-work, have very little literary interest. In this case, it may be said that the man is more impressive than his work, and Mr. Brooks is in a position to tell us something important about him which is not to be found in his writings. But, in the case of Henry James, the work he accomplished in his lifetime is infinitely more interesting than the man. Henry James was not an intimidated and sidetracked artist, but a writer who understood both himself and the society in which he was living and who was able to say just what he meant about nations and human beings. It is difficult for Mr. Brooks to tell us anything about Henry James that James has not told us himself. *The Pilgrimage of Henry James*, which is shorter than its predecessor, falls short of it, also, in life and force. The *Mark Twain* was driven along by the author's passion of discovery and his fury of indignation to a conclusion which is, I suppose, so far Mr. Brooks's highest point of eloquence; but it is perhaps, in the later book, a sign of the critic's failure to be fully possessed by his subject, of his comparatively feeble reaction to it, that the last page, instead of leaving us, as its predecessor did, with a dramatic and significant image, should be evidently an unconscious imitation of the last page of Lytton Strachey's *Queen Victoria*.

May 6, 1925

THE CRITIC WHO DOES NOT EXIST

In Paul Valéry's address to the Académie Française on the occasion of his succeeding Anatole France, there is a passage in which he describes the literary situation in Paris as he found it in his youth. There were, he says, a number of different parties, each with its own definite set of policies and each with an eminent writer, or group of eminent writers, at its head. There were Zola and the naturalists; Leconte de Lisle and the Parnassians; Renan and Taine and the *"idéologues"*; Mallarmé and the Symbolists. These parties stated their programs and defended them against each other: they played roles in a literary politics equally exciting and equally important with politics of the other sort. When five of Zola's followers seceded from his party over the publication of *La Terre*, the event was profoundly significant: it was the first attack in a great campaign. When Valéry, received by the Academy, reasserts the claims of symbolism, at one time a literary minority, in a speech on the career of his predecessor, one of the leaders of a different camp—that is, again, an historic event and marks the success of a revolution. The French writers whom we read most today—France, Gourmont, Proust, Valéry, Gide—all came to intellectual maturity in this atmosphere of debate; and this gives them a kind of interest—the interest of the intelligence fully awakened to the implications of what the artist is doing, that is to say, to his responsibility—very rare in the literature of English-speaking countries, and nowadays perhaps nowhere to be found in any very intense degree save, on a smaller scale, in Dublin. For there is one language which all French writers, no matter how divergent their aims, always possess in common: the language of criticism.

When we come to survey the literary landscape of contemporary America, it seems to us at first that nothing could resemble less the clear political alignments that are nearly always to be found in France. But then, as we examine the prospect more closely, we are surprised to become aware of the presence both of able leaders and of powerful parties, each professing more or less explicitly a point of view and acting more or less consistently on a set of principles. There is, in the first place, H. L. Mencken, with his satellite George Jean Nathan, his disciple Sinclair Lewis, and his literary nursery, the *Mercury*. Then there is T. S. Eliot, who, despite the fact that he lives in England and has recently become a British citizen, exerts a tremendous influence in America and is always regarded by his American readers as still an American writer. It may be said that Mencken and Eliot between them rule the students of the Eastern universities: when the college magazines do not sound like Mencken's *Mercury*, they sound like Eliot's *Criterion*. Then there is the group of writers—it is a group that does not have any unity and is almost entirely without critical self-consciousness—of what may be called the neo-romantics, of which Edna Millay and Scott Fitzgerald, with their respective imitators and followers, are the leaders in the present generation, and which had for precursors such writers as Sara Teasdale, Joseph Hergesheimer and perhaps also James Branch Cabell. Then there is the more or less organized and highly self-conscious group of the social revolutionary writers: John Dos Passos, John Howard Lawson, Michael Gold, etc. Their organs are *The New Masses* and the Playwright's Theater. One should mention also—though they constitute a school rather than a group—the psychologico-sociological critics: Van Wyck Brooks, Lewis Mumford (whom I take to be a disciple of Brooks), Joseph Wood Krutch and a number of others.

What we lack, then, in the United States, is not writers or even literary parties, but simply serious literary criticism (the school of critics I have mentioned last, though they set forth their own ideas, do not occupy themselves much with the art or ideas of the writers with whom they deal). Each of these groups does produce, to be sure, a certain amount of criticism to justify or explain what it is doing, but it may, I believe, be said in general that they do not communicate with one another; their opinions do not really circulate. It is astonishing to observe, in America, in spite of our floods of literary journalism, to what extent the literary atmosphere is a non-conductor of criticism. What actually happens, in our literary world, is that each leader or group of leaders is allowed to intimidate his disciples, either ignoring all the other leaders or taking cognizance of their existence only by distant and contemptuous sneers. H. L. Mencken and T. S. Eliot present themselves, as I have said, from the critical point of view, as the most formidable figures on the scene; yet Mencken's discussion of his principal rival has, so far as my memory goes, been confined to an inclusion of the latter's works among the items of one of those lists of idiotic current crazes in which the editor of the *Mercury* usually includes also the recall of judges and paper-bag cookery. And Eliot, established in London, does not, of course, consider himself under the necessity of dealing with Mencken at all. Similarly, George Jean Nathan scoffs at the plays of Lawson and has never been willing to take seriously the movement he represents; and *The New Masses* has never gone further than an occasional gibe at Mencken. Van Wyck Brooks, in spite of considerable baiting, has never been induced to defend his position (though Krutch has recently take up some challenges). And the romantics have been belabored by the spokesmen of several different camps without making any attempt to strike back. It, furthermore, seems unfortunate that some of our most important writers—Sherwood Anderson and Eugene O'Neill, for example—should work, as they apparently do, in almost complete intellectual isolation, receiving from the outside but little intelligent criticism and developing, in their solitary labors, little capacity for supplying it themselves.

Now, it is no doubt impossible for an English-speaking country to hope for a literary criticism comparable to that of the French: like cookery, it is one of their specialties. But when one considers the number of reviews, the immense amount of literary journalism that is now being published in New York, one asks oneself how it is possible for our reviewing to remain so puerile. Works on history are commonly reviewed by historians, and books on physics by physicists; but when a new book of American poetry or a novel or other work of belles lettres appears, one gets the impression that it is simply given to almost any well-intentioned (and not even necessarily literate) person who happens to present himself; and this person then describes in a review his emotions upon reading the book. How many works of general literature are ever officially discussed in New York by people with any special knowledge of the subjects on which they are invited to write? Since the death of Stuart P. Sherman, who was second-rate at best, there has not been a single American critic who regularly occupied himself in any authoritative way with contemporary literature. Yet what might not have been the effect on Sinclair Lewis, for example, and on the great army of Mencken's younger followers, if Mencken had been systematically and periodically overhauled by a critic of equal vigor? What might not have been the effect on all that new crop of poets who have been made prematurely senile by imitating Eliot's "Gerontion," if a critic as intelligent as the people who ridiculed *The Waste Land* were stupid had, while doing full justice to Eliot, made fun of this tendency in time? Do not the champions of proletarian literature deserve the hard-hitting polemics which their appetite for controversy invites? And might not a critic who enjoyed Lawson's wit and valued his technical inventions have been of some service in discouraging his bathos and his bad rhetoric? And those scattered contemporary romantics who, since the war, have been repeating over here all the poses, the philosophy and the methods of the Europe of 1830—instead of finding themselves stalled, bewildered, out of date almost as soon as they were famous, if their situation had in time been a little cleared up by a competent criticism, might they not have already readjusted themselves and applied their brilliant abilities to the production of something more durable? Finally, with the advent of a new generation, there has emerged from our literature of the past a number of important names, a number of writers whom we are all agreed in regarding as of first-rate quality: Emerson, Hawthorne, Thoreau, Whitman, Melville, Poe, Stephen Crane, Henry James. Yet so far the studies by American hands which have dealt with these American classics have been almost exclusively biographical. We have been eager to expose the weaknesses and curious to probe the neuroses of these ranking American writers, but have found little to say that was interesting as to why we should consider them so. Have we not been unfortunate in the lack of a criticism which should have undertaken, for example, to show how Hawthorne, Melville and Poe, besides becoming excessively eccentric persons, anticipated, in the middle of the last century, the temperament of our own day and invented methods for rendering it?

I do not of course mean to assert that, except on the lower levels, any criticism, however able, could make or unmake artists. A work of art is not a set of ideas or an exercise of technique, or even a combination of both. But I am strongly disposed to believe that our contemporary writing would benefit by a genuine literary criticism that should deal expertly with ideas and art, not merely tell us whether the reviewer "let out a whoop" for the book or threw it out the window. In a sense, it can probably be said that no such creature exists as a full-time literary critic—that is, a writer who is at once first-rate and nothing but a literary critic: there are writers of poetry, drama or fiction who also write criticism, like most of the French writers mentioned above and like Coleridge, Dryden, Poe and Henry James; and there are historians like Renan, Taine, Saint-Beuve, Leslie Stephen and Brandes whose literary criticism is a part of their history. In America, neither kind of criticism has been very highly developed; and I fear that we must take this as a sign of the rudimentary condition of our literature in general. The poets, the dramatists and the novelists too often lack the learning and the cultivated intelligence to give us in works of art the full benefit of the promising material supplied by experience and imagination; and it may in general be said that where our writers of biography and history fail is precisely in their inability to deal adequately with works of literature.

February 1, 1928

DOS PASSOS AND THE
SOCIAL REVOLUTION

John Dos Passos's *Airways, Inc.*, was produced in March as the last play of the second season of the New Playwrights' Theater, and almost entirely failed to attract attention. This was due, principally, I believe, to the fact that by that time the critics had become rather discouraged with the revolutionary drama of Grove Street and that the New Playwrights themselves were so low in funds that they could not afford proper publicity. None the less, *Airways, Inc.* was a remarkable play, perhaps the best that the New Playwrights have done; and though this is not the place to speak of the merits of the Grove Street production, which I thought were considerable, the published text of the play demands attention as a work of literature.

Airways is, like the group's other plays, a social-political-economic fable; but Dos Passos is more intelligent than most of his associates—he is able to enter into more points of view—and he is a much better artist. His play is neither a naturalistic study nor a vaudeville in the manner of John Howard Lawson, though it has some of the elements of both; it is rather a sort of dramatic poem of contemporary America. With great ingenuity, Dos Passos had assembled on a single suburban street-corner representatives of most of the classes and groups that go to make up our society. We concentrate upon the life of a single middle-class household, but this is submerged in a larger world: its fate is inextricably bound up with a current real-estate boom; a strike that eventually gives rise to a Sacco-Vanzetti incident; and the promotion of a commercial aviation company. Nor, as is likely to be the case in this kind of play, are the social types merely abstractions which never persuade the imagination. Dos Passos has succeeded in producing the illusion that behind the little suburban street-corner of the Turners lies all the life of a great American city—all the confusion of America itself; and *Airways* made the meager stage of the bleak little Grove Street Theater seem as big as any stage I have ever seen. Dos Passos has also given the household of the Turners an extension in time as well as in space: he has provided a chorus of two old men, an American inventor and a Hungarian revolutionist, whose role is to relate what we see to what has gone before in history and to what may be expected to come after.

It is in the construction of this sort of sociological fable that Dos Passos particularly excels. The strength of his novel, *Manhattan Transfer*, lay in the thoroughness and the steady hand with which he executed a similar anatomy on the city of New York as a whole. As a dramatist he is less expert; and *Airways* suffers in certain ways from

comparison with *Manhattan Transfer*. Dos Passos sometimes interrupts his action with long passages of monologue, which, though they might go down easily in a
novel, discourage our attention in the theater; and his last
act, though the two separate scenes are excellent in themselves, fails to draw the different strands together as we
expect a third act to do. But, on the other hand, *Airways*,
at its best, has an eloquence and a spirit that *Manhattan
Transfer* largely lacked. It is one of the best-written
things that Dos Passos has so far done—perhaps freer than
any other of his productions both from rhetoric doing
duty for feeling and from descriptions too relentlessly
piled up. Dos Passos is probably only now arriving at his
mature prose style.

So much for the purely artistic aspect of *Airways*. It is
impossible to discuss it further without taking into account Dos Passos's political philosophy. Dos Passos is,
one gathers from his work, a social revolutionist: he believes that, in the United States as elsewhere, the present
capitalistic regime is destined to be overthrown by a
class-conscious proletariat. And his disapproval of capitalist society seems to imply a distaste for all the beings
who go to compose it. In *Manhattan Transfer*, it was not
merely New York, but humanity that came off badly. Dos
Passos, in exposing the disease organism, had the effect,
though not, I believe, the intention, of condemning the
sufferers along with the disease; and even when he seemed
to desire to make certain of his characters sympathetic, he
had a way of putting them down.

Now, in *Airways*, there are several characters whom
Dos Passos has succeeded in making either admirable or
attractive, but there are, in every case, either radicals or
their sympathizers. His bias against the economic system
is so strong that it extends beyond its official representatives to all those human beings whose only fault is to have
been born where such a system prevails and to be so lacking in courage or perspicacity as not to have allied themselves with the forces that are trying to fight it. In Dos

Passos, not only must the policeman not fail to steal the money with which the street-kids have been playing craps; but even the young people of *Airways* who, however irresponsible and immoral, might be expected to exhibit something of the charm of youth—become uglier and uglier as the play proceeds, till they finally go completely to pieces in a drunken restaurant scene which is one of Dos Passos's masterpieces of corrosive vulgarity. It is especially curious to note the treatment which the American aviators receive at the hands of both Dos Passos and Lawson. The aviator is one of the authentic heroes that our American civilization now produces. But for Lawson or Dos Passos, an aviator cannot be an authentic hero, or even, apparently, a genius, because he is not on the side of the revolution. The truth is, of course, that the aviator of the type of Lindbergh or Byrd never troubles himself with these questions at all and, even when, as in the case of Lindbergh, he is exploited for a time by the government, he exists and performs his achievements in a world independent of politics. But to a Lawson or a Dos Passos, he is suspect: they cannot let him get away with anything, and eventually, in what they write, they succeed in destroying or degrading him. In Lawson's play, *The International,* another New Playwrights production, the Lindbergh character appears as a drunken taxi-driver—or perhaps as a drunken bum in a taxi—amid the debacle of the capitalist state; and in *Airways,* the young aviator is sent up by the agents of his capitalist employers to scatter leaflets on a strikers' meeting. He is drunk, and falls and breaks his back.

Now, the life of middle-class America, even under capitalism and even in a city like New York, is not so unattractive as Dos Passos makes it—no human life under any conditions can ever have been so unattractive. Under however an unequal distribution of wealth, human beings are still capable of enjoyment, affection and enthusiasm— even of integrity and courage. Nor are these qualities and emotions entirely confined to class-conscious workers and their leaders. There are moments in reading a novel or seeing a play by Dos Passos when one finds oneself ready to rush to the defense of even the American bathroom, even the Ford car—which, after all, one begins to reflect, have perhaps done as much to rescue us from helplessness, ignorance and squalor as the prophets of revolution. We may begin to reflect upon the relation, in Dos Passos, of political opinions to artistic effects. Might it not, we ask ourselves, be possible—have we not, in fact, seen it occur—for a writer to hold Dos Passos's political opinions and yet not depict our middle-class republic as a place where no birds sing, no flowers bloom and where the very air is almost unbreathable? For, in the novels and plays of Dos Passos, everybody loses out: if he is on the right side of the social question, he has to suffer, if he is not snuffed out; if he is on the oppressors' side, his pleasures are made repulsive. When a man as intelligent as Dos Passos—that is, a man a good deal more intelligent than, say, Michael Gold or Upton Sinclair, who hold similar political views—when so intelligent a man and so good an artist allows his bias so to falsify his picture of life that, in spite of all the accurate observation and all the imaginative insight, its values are partly those of melodrama—we begin to guess some stubborn sentimentalism at the bottom of the whole thing—some deeply buried streak of hysteria of which his misapplied resentments represent the aggressive side. And from the moment we suspect the processes by which he has arrived at his political ideas, the ideas themselves become suspect.

In the meantime, whatever diagnosis we may make of Dos Passos's infatuation with the social revolution, he remains one of the few first-rate figures among our writers of his generation, and the only one of these who has made a systematic effort to study all the aspects of America and to take account of all its elements, to compose them into a picture which makes some general sense. Most of the first-rate men of Dos Passos's age—Hemingway, Wilder, Fitzgerald—cultivate their own little corners and do not confront the situation as a whole. Only Dos Passos has tried to take hold of it. In the fine last speech of *Airways*, he allows the moral of his play to rise very close to the surface. The spinster sister of the Turner household has just received the news that the strike leader, with whom she has been in love and who has been made the victim of a frame-up, has finally been electrocuted: "Now I'm beginning to feel it," she says, "the house without Walter, the street without him, the city without him, the future that we lived in instead of a honeymoon without him, everything stark without him. Street where I've lived all these years shut up in a matchwood house full of bitterness. City where I've lived walled up in old dead fear. America, where I've scurried from store to subway to church to home, America that I've never known. World where I've lived without knowing. What can I do now that he is gone and that he has left me full of scalding wants, what can I do with the lack of him inside me like a cold stone? The house I lived in wrecked, the people I loved wrecked, around me there's nothing but words stinging like wasps. Where can I go down the dark street, where can I find a lover in the sleeping city? At what speed of the wind can I fly away, to escape these words that burn and sting, to escape the lack that is in me like a stone?"

It is true that the lack of real leadership is felt by us today as a stone. It is Dos Passos's recognition of this—his relentless reiteration of his conviction that there is something lacking, something wrong, in America—as well as his insistence on the importance of America—that gives his work its validity and power. It is equally true, of course, of H. L. Mencken that he finds something lacking and something wrong; but the effect of Mencken on his admirers is to make them wash their hands of social questions. Mencken has made it the fashion to speak of politics as an obscene farce. And Dos Passos is now almost alone among the writers of his generation in continuing to take the social organism seriously.

April 17, 1929

T. S. ELIOT AND THE CHURCH OF ENGLAND

For Lancelot Andrewes by T. S. Eliot contains essays on Lancelot Andrewes and John Bramhall, two seventeenth-century English divines, and on Machiavelli, F. H. Bradley, Baudelaire, Thomas Middleton, Crashaw and Irving Babbitt. They all display the author's unique combination of subtle and original thinking with simple and precise statement, and will be read by everybody interested in literature. T. S. Eliot has now become perhaps the most important literary critic in the English-speaking world. His writings have been brief and few, and it is almost incredible that they should have been enough to establish him as an intellectual leader; but when one tries to trace the causes of the change from the point of view of the English criticism of the period before the war to the point of view of our own day, one can find no figure of comparable authority. And we must recognize that Eliot's opinions, so cool and even casual in appearance, yet sped with the force of so intense a seriousness and weighted with so wide a learning, have stuck oftener and sunk deeper in the minds of the post-war generation of both England and the United States than those of any other critic.

For Lancelot Andrewes, however, is not, like *The Sacred Wood,* a book merely of literary criticism. The essays which it contains have been selected by Eliot for the purpose of indicating a general position in literature, politics and religion. This position, he tells us in his preface, "may be described as classicist in literature, royalist in politics, and Anglo-Catholic in religion"; and it is further to be expounded in "three small books," called respectively *The School of Donne, The Outline of Royalism* and *The Principles of Modern Heresy.*

Mr. Eliot's ideas, in *For Lancelot Andrewes,* appear chiefly by implication; and we run the risk of misrepresenting them in attempting to discuss them on the basis of this book. Still, Eliot has invited us to read this slender collection of essays as a prelude to the trilogy mentioned above, and it is difficult to know how else to deal with it. The clearest and most explicit statement on the subject of religion I can find is the following from the essay in which Eliot points out the deficiencies of Irving Babbitt's humanism: "Unless by civilization you mean material progress, cleanliness, etc. . . . if you mean a spiritual and intellectual coordination on a high level, then it is doubtful whether civilization can endure without religion, and religion without a church." One recognizes a point of view which is by way of becoming fashionable among certain sorts of literary people, yet this usually presents itself merely as a sentiment that it would be a good thing to believe rather than as a real and living belief. And, though Eliot lets us know that he does believe, his faith, in so far as we find it expressed in these essays and in his recent poems, seems entirely uninspired by hope, entirely unequipped with force—a faith which, to quote his own epigraph, is merely "ready to die."

Now, no one will dispute that, at the present time, our society is in need of the kind of ideals which the churches were once able to supply; but the objection to Eliot's position is simply that the churches are now out of the question as a solution to our present difficulties, because it is so difficult to get educated people to accept their fundamental doctrines—and that, even if a few first-rate ones can convince themselves that they do, one does not see how they can possibly hope for a revival general enough to make religion intellectually important again. I agree that, without a church, you cannot have a real religion; and I sympathize with Mr. Eliot's criticism of certain substitute religions, like that of H. G. Wells, which try to retain the benefits of faith while doing away with the necessity of believing. You cannot have real Christianity without a cult of Jesus as the son of God. But since it has plainly become anachronistic to accept the prophet Jesus in this role, it seems that we must reconcile ourselves to doing without both the churches and religion. The answer to Mr. Eliot's assertion that "it is doubtful whether civilization can endure without religion" is that we have got to make it endure. Nobody will pretend that this is going to be easy; but it can hardly be any more difficult than persuading oneself that the leadership of the future will be supplied by the Church of England or by the Roman Catholic Church or by any church whatsoever.

Nothing seems to me more sadly symptomatic of the feeble intellectual condition of a good many literary people, of their unwillingness or incapacity to come to terms with the world they live in, than the movement back to Thomas Aquinas—or, in Eliot's case, back to Bishop Andrewes. It is not, of course, a question of the wisdom or the spiritual authority of Aquinas or Andrewes in his own day, when it was still possible for a first-rate mind to accept the supernatural basis of religion. But to argue, as in the literary world one sometimes finds people doing, that, because our society at the present time is badly off without religion, we should make an heroic effort to swallow medieval theology, seems to me utterly futile as well as fundamentally dishonest. If the salvation of our civilization depends on such religious fervor as our writers are capable of kindling—if it depends on the edifying example of the conversion of Jean Cocteau and the low blue flame of the later Eliot—then I fear that we must give up hope.

I was writing last week of John Dos Passos and his mirage of a social revolution. It seems to me that T. S. Eliot is a case of much the same kind: Eliot, like Dos Passos, is a highly cultivated American who does not care for contemporary America; but, instead of escaping from the American situation by way of Greenwich Village radicalism and the myth of a serious-minded and clear-eyed proletariat, as Dos Passos attempts to do, Eliot has gone to England and evolved for himself an aristocratic myth out of English literature and history. Eliot's classicism, royalism and Anglo-Catholicism, from the notion I get of them in his recent writings, seem to me as much academic attitudes, as much lacking in plausibility, as Dos Passos's cult of the class-conscious proletariat: it is as hard to imagine royalty and the Church becoming more instead of less important, even in England, as it is to imagine the American employees becoming less instead of more middle-class. Most Americans of the type of Dos Passos and Eliot—that is, sensitive and widely read literary people—have some such agreeable fantasy in which they can allow their minds to take refuge from the perplexities and oppressions about them. In the case of H. L. Mencken, it is a sort of German university town, where people drink a great deal of beer and devour a great many books, and where they respect the local nobility—if only the Germany of the Empire had not been destroyed by the war! In the case of certain American writers from the top layer of the old South, it is the old-fashioned Southern plantation, where men are high-spirited and punctilious and women gracious and lovely, where affectionate and loyal Negroes are happy to keep in their place—if only the feudal South had not perished in 1865! With Ezra Pound, it is a medieval Provence, where poor but accomplished troubadours enjoy the favors of noble ladies—if only the troubadours were not deader than Provençal! With Dos Passos, it is an army of workers, disinterested, industrious and sturdy, but full of the good-fellowship and gaiety in which the Webster Hall balls nowadays are usually so dismally lacking—if only the American workers were not preoccupied with buying Ford cars and radios, instead of organizing themselves to overthrow the civilization of the bourgeoisie! And in T. S. Eliot's case, it is a world of seventeenth-century churchmen, who combine the most scrupulous conscience with the ability to write good prose—if it were only not so difficult nowadays for men who are capable of becoming good writers to accept the Apostolic Succession!

Among these, the writers like Dos Passos and Mencken stay at home and denounce America, while the writers like Eliot and Pound go abroad and try to forget it. It is peculiarly hard for such men to get an intellectual foothold in our world: New York, in particular, just now, is like the great glass mountain of the *Arabian Nights*, against which the barques of young writers are continually coming to grief. And this is true not merely of the United States, but more or less of the whole Western world. Industrially, politically and socially, Europe itself is becoming more and more like America every day; and the catastrophe of the war has demoralized America, too. It is up to American writers to try to make some sense of their American world—for their world is now everybody's world, and, if they fail to find a way to make possible in it what T. S. Eliot desiderates: "a spiritual and intellectual coordination on a high level," it is improbable that any one else will be able to do it for them. That world is a world with a number of religions, but not amenable to the leadership of a single church—and it is a world in which, whatever reorganization one may prophesy for the democratic state, the restoration of the monarchic principle seems improbable to the last degree. It is a world in which Eliot's program would not appear very helpful. We shall certainly not be able to lean upon the authority of either Church or King, and we shall have to depend for our new ideals on a study of contemporary reality and the power of our own imaginations.

April 24, 1929

JAMES JOYCE'S *ULYSSES*

Ulysses is, I suppose, the most completely "written" novel since Flaubert. The example of the great prose poet of Naturalism has profoundly influenced Joyce—in his attitude toward the modern bourgeois world and in the contrast implied by the Homeric parallel of "Ulysses" between our own and the ancient world, as well as in an ideal of rigorous objectivity and of adaptation of style to subject—as the influence of that other great Naturalistic poet, Ibsen, is obvious in Joyce's single play, *Exiles.* But Flaubert had, in general, confined himself to fitting the cadence and the phrase precisely to the mood or object described; and even then it was the phrase rather than the cadence, and the object rather than the mood, with which he was occupied—for mood and cadence in Flaubert do not really vary much: he never embodies himself in his characters nor identifies his voice with theirs, and as a result, Flaubert's own characteristic tone of the somber-pompous-ironic becomes, in the long run, a little monotonous. But Joyce has undertaken in *Ulysses* not merely to render, with the last accuracy and beauty, the actual sights and sounds among which his people move, but, showing us the world as his characters perceive it, to find the unique vocabulary and rhythm which will represent the thoughts of each. If Flaubert taught Maupassant to look for the definitive adjectives which would distinguish a given cab-driver from every other cab-driver at the Rouen station, so Joyce has set himself the task of finding the precise dialect which will distinguish the thoughts of a given Dubliner from those of every other Dubliner. Thus the mind of Stephen Dedalus is represented by a weaving of bright poetic images and fragmentary abstractions, of things remembered from books, on a rhythm sober, melancholy and proud; that of Bloom by a rapid staccato notation, prosaic but vivid and alert, jetting out in all directions in little ideas growing out of ideas; the thoughts of Father Conmee, the Rector of the Jesuit college, by a precise prose, perfectly colorless and orderly; those of Gerty-Nausicaä by a combination of schoolgirl colloquialisms with the jargon of cheap romance; and the ruminations of Mrs. Bloom by a long, unbroken rhythm of brogue, like the swell of some profound sea.

Joyce takes us thus directly into the consciousness of his characters, and in order to do so, he has availed himself of methods of which Flaubert never dreamed—of the methods of Symbolism. He has, in *Ulysses*, exploited together, as no writer had thought to do before, the resources both of Symbolism and of Naturalism. Proust's novel, masterly as it is, does perhaps represent a falling over into decadence of psychological fiction: the subjective element is finally allowed to invade and to deteriorate even those aspects of the story which really ought to be kept strictly objective if one is to believe that it is actually happening. But Joyce's grasp on his objective world never slips: his work is unshakably established on Naturalistic foundations. Where *A la Recherche du Temps Perdu* leaves many things vague—the ages of the characters and sometimes the actual circumstances of their lives, and—what is worse—whether they may not be merely bad dreams that the hero has had; *Ulysses* has been logically thought out and accurately documented to the last detail: everything that happens is perfectly consistent, and we know precisely what the characters wore, how much they paid for things, where they were at different times of the day, what popular songs they sang and what events they read of in the papers, on June 16, 1904. Yet when we are admitted to the mind of any one of them, we are in a world as complex and special, a world sometimes as fantastic or obscure, as that of a Symbolist poet—and a world rendered by similar devices of language. We are more at home in the minds of Joyce's characters than we are likely to be, except after some study, in the mind of a Mallarmé or an Eliot, because we know more about the circumstances in which they find themselves; but we are confronted with the same sort of confusion between emotions, perceptions and reasonings, and we are likely to be disconcerted by the same sort of hiatuses of thought, when certain links in the association of ideas are dropped down into the unconscious mind so that we are obliged to divine them for ourselves.

But Joyce has carried the methods of Symbolism further than merely to set a Naturalistic scene and then, in that frame, to represent directly the minds of his different characters in Symbolistic monologues like "Mr. Prufrock" or "L'Après-midi d'un Faune." And it is the fact that he has not always stopped here which makes parts of *Ulysses* so puzzling when we read them for the first time. So long as we are dealing with internal monologues in realistic settings, we are dealing with familiar elements merely combined in a novel way—that is, instead of reading, "Bloom said to himself, 'I might manage to write a story to illustrate some proverb or other. I could sign it, Mr. and Mrs. L. M. Bloom,'" we read, "Might manage a sketch. By Mr. and Mrs. L. M. Bloom. Invent a story for some proverb which?" But as we get further along in *Ulysses*, we find the realistic setting oddly distorting itself and deliquescing, and we are astonished at the introduction of voices which seem to belong neither to the characters nor to the author.

The point is that of each of his episodes Joyce has tried to make an independent unit which shall blend the different sets of elements of each—the minds of the characters, the place where they are, the atmosphere about them, the feeling of the time of day. Joyce had already, in *A Portrait of the Artist*, experimented, as Proust had done, in varying the form and style of the different sections to fit the different ages and phases of his hero—from the infantile fragments of childhood impressions, through the ecstatic revelations and the terrifying nightmares of adolescence, to the self-possessed notations of young manhood. But in *A Portrait of the Artist*, Joyce was presenting everything from the point of view of a single particular character, Dedalus; whereas in *Ulysses* he is occupied with a number of different personalities, of whom Dedalus is no longer the center, and his method, furthermore, of enabling us to live in their world is not always merely a matter of making us shift from the point of view of one to the point of view of another. In order to understand what Joyce is doing here, one must conceive a set of Symbolistic poems, themselves involving characters whose minds are represented Symbolistically, depending not from the sensibility of the poet speaking in his own person, but from the poet's imagination playing a role absolutely impersonal and always imposing upon itself all the Naturalistic restrictions in regard to the story it is telling at the same time that it allows itself to exercise all the Symbolistic privileges in regard to the way it tells it. We are not likely to be prepared for this by the early episodes of *Ulysses*: they are as sober and as clear as the morning light of the Irish coast in which they take place: the characters' perceptions of the external world are usually distinct from their thoughts and feelings about them. But in the newspaper office, for the first time, a general atmosphere begins to be created, beyond the specific minds of the characters, by a punctuation of the text with newspaper heads which announce the incidents in the narrative. And in the library scene, which takes place in the early afternoon, the setting and people external to Stephen begin to dissolve in his apprehension of them, heightened and blurred by some drinks at lunch-time and by the intellectual excitement of the conversation amid the dimness and tameness of the library—"Eglintoneyes, quick with pleasure, looked up shybrightly. Gladly glancing, a merry puritan, through the twisted eglantine." Here, however, we still see all through Stephen's eyes—through the eyes of a single character; but in the scene in the Ormond Hotel, which takes place a couple of hours later—our reveries absorb the world about us progressively as daylight fades and as the impressions of the day accumulate—the sights and sounds and the emotional vibrations and the appetites for food and drink of the late afternoon, the laughter, the gold-and-bronze hair of the barmaids, the jingling of Blazes Boylan's car on his way to visit Molly Bloom, the ringing of the hoofs of the horses of the viceregal cavalcade clanging in through the open window, the ballad sung by Simon Dedalus, the sound of the piano accompaniment and the comfortable supper of Bloom—though they are not all, from beginning to end, perceived by

Bloom himself—all mingle quite un-Naturalistically in a harmony of bright sound, ringing color, poignant indistinct feeling and declining light. The scene in the brothel, where it is night and where Dedalus and Bloom are drunk, is like a slowed-up moving-picture, in which the intensified vision of reality is continually lapsing into phantasmagoric visions; and the let-down after the excitement of this, the lassitude and staleness of the cabmen's shelter where Bloom takes Stephen to get him some coffee, is rendered by a prose as flavorless, as weary and as banal as the incidents which it reports. Joyce has achieved here, by different methods, a relativism like that of Proust: he is reproducing in literature the different aspects, the different proportions and textures, which things and people take on at different times and under different circumstances.

I do not think that Joyce has been equally successful with all these technical devices in *Ulysses,* but before it will be possible to discuss them further, we must approach the book from another point of view.

It has always been characteristic of Joyce to neglect action, narrative, drama, of the usual kind, even the direct impact on one another of the characters as we get it in the ordinary novel, for a sort of psychological portraiture. There is tremendous vitality in Joyce, but very little movement. Like Proust, he is symphonic rather than narrative. His fiction has its progressions, its developments, but they are musical rather than dramatic. The most elaborate and interesting piece in *Dubliners*—the story called "The Dead"—is simply a record of the modification brought about during a single evening in the relations of a husband and wife by the man's becoming aware, from the effect produced on the woman by a song which she has heard at a family party, that she has once been loved by another man; *A Portrait of the Artist as a Young Man* is simply a series of pictures of the author at successive stages of his development; the theme of *Exiles* is, like that of "The Dead," the modification in the relations of a husband and wife which follows the reappearance of a man who has been the wife's lover. And *Ulysses,* again, for all its vast scale, is simply the story of another small but significant change in the relations of yet another married couple as a result of the impingement on their household of the personality of an only slightly known young man. Most of these stories cover a period of only a few hours, and they are never carried any further. When Joyce has explored one of these situations, when he has established the small gradual readjustment, he has done all that interests him.

All, that is, from the point of view of ordinary incident. But though Joyce almost entirely lacks appetite for violent conflict or vigorous action, his work is prodigiously rich and alive. His force, instead of following a line, expands itself in every dimension (including that of Time) about a single point. The world of *Ulysses* is animated by a complex inexhaustible life: we revisit it as we do a city, where we come more and more to recognize faces, to understand personalities, to grasp relations, currents and interests. Joyce has exercised considerable technical ingenuity in introducing us to the elements of his story in an order which will enable us to find our bearings: yet I doubt whether any human memory is capable, on a first reading, of meeting the demands of *Ulysses.* And when we reread it, we start in at any point, as if it were indeed something solid like a city which actually existed in space and which could be entered from any direction—as Joyce is said, in composing his books, to work on the different parts simultaneously. More than any other work of fiction, unless perhaps the *Comédie Humaine, Ulysses* creates the illusion of a living social organism. We see it only for twenty hours, yet we know its past as well as its present. We possess Dublin, seen, heard, smelt and felt, brooded over, imagined, remembered.

Joyce's handling of this immense material, his method of giving his book a shape, resembles nothing else in modern fiction. The first critics of *Ulysses* mistook the novel for a "slice of life" and objected that it was too fluid or too chaotic. They did not recognize a plot because they could not recognize a progression; and the title told them nothing. They could not even discover a pattern. It is now apparent, however, that *Ulysses* suffers from an excess of design rather than from a lack of it. Joyce has drawn up an outline of his novel, of which he has allowed certain of his commentators to avail themselves, but which he has not allowed them to publish in its entirety (though it is to be presumed that the book on *Ulysses* which Mr. Stuart Gilbert has announced will include all the information contained in it); and from this outline it appears that Joyce has set himself the task of fulfilling the requirements of a most complicated scheme—a scheme which we could scarcely have divined except in its more obvious features. For even if we had known about the Homeric parallel and had identified certain of the correspondences—if we had had no difficulty in recognizing the Cyclops in the ferocious professional Fenian or Circe in the brothel-keeper or Hades in the cemetery—we should never have suspected how closely and how subtly the parallel had been followed—we should never have guessed, for example, that when Bloom passes through the National Library while Stephen is having his discussion with the literary men, he is escaping, on the one hand, a Scylla—that is, Aristotle, the rock of Dogma; and, on the other, a Charybdis—Plato, the whirlpool of Mysticism; nor that, when Stephen walks on the seashore, he is reenacting the combat with Proteus—in this case, primal matter, of whose continual transformations Stephen is reminded by the objects absorbed or washed up by the sea, but whose forms he is able to hold and fix, as the Homeric Proteus was held and vanquished, by power of the words which give him images for them. Nor should we have known that the series of phrases and onomatopoetic syllables placed at the beginning of the Sirens episode—the singing in the Or-

mond Hotel—and selected from the narrative which follows, are supposed to be musical themes and that the episode itself is a fugue; and though we may have felt the
ironic effect of the specimens of inflated Irish journalism
introduced at regular intervals in the conversation with
the patriot in the pub—we should hardly have understood
that these had been produced by a deliberate technique of
"gigantism"—for, since the Citizen represents the Cyclops, and since the Cyclops was a giant, he must be rendered formidable by a parade of all the banalities of
his patriotic claptrap swollen to gigantic proportions.
We should probably never have guessed all this, and we
should certainly never have guessed at the ingenuity
which Joyce has expended in other ways. Not only, we
learn from the outline, is there an elaborate Homeric
parallel in *Ulysses*, but there is also an organ of the human
body and a human science or art featured in every episode. We look these up, a little incredulously, but there,
we find, they all actually are—buried and disguised beneath the realistic surface, but carefully planted, unmistakably dwelt upon. And if we are tipped off, we are able
further to discover all sorts of concealed ornaments and
emblems: in the chaper of the Lotos-Eaters, for example,
countless references to flowers; in the Laestrygonians, to
eating; in the Sirens, puns on musical terms; and in
Aeolus, the newspaper office, not merely many references
to wind but, according to Mr. Gilbert—the art featured in
this episode being Rhetoric—some hundred different figures of speech.

Now the Homeric parallel in *Ulysses* is in general point-
edly and charmingly carried out and justifies itself: it does
help to give the story a universal significance and it enables Joyce to show us in the actions and the relations of
his characters meanings which he perhaps could not easily
have indicated in any other way—since the characters
themselves must be largely unaware of these meanings
and since Joyce has adopted the strict objective method, in
which the author must not comment on the action. And

we may even accept the arts and sciences and the organs of the human body as making the book complete and comprehensive, if a little laboriously systematic—the whole of man's experience in a day. But when we get all these things together and further complicated by the virtuosity of the technical devices, the result is sometimes baffling or confusing. We become aware, as we examine the outline, that when we went through *Ulysses* for the first time, it was these organs and arts and sciences and Homeric correspondences which sometimes so discouraged our interest. We had been climbing over these obstacles without knowing it, in our attempts to follow Dedalus and Bloom. The trouble was that, beyond the ostensible subject and, as it were, beneath the surface of the narrative, too many other subjects and too many different orders of subjects were being proposed to our attention.

It seems to me difficult, then, not to conclude that Joyce elaborated *Ulysses* too much—that he tried to put too many things into it. What is the value of all the references to flowers in the Lotos-Eaters chapter, for example? They do not create in the Dublin streets an atmosphere of lotus-eating—we are merely puzzled, if we have not been told to look for them, as to why Joyce has chosen to have Bloom think and see certain things, of which the final explanation is that they are pretexts for mentioning flowers. And do not the gigantic interpolations of the Cyclops episode defeat their object by making it impossible for us to follow the narrative? The interpolations are funny in themselves, the incident related is a masterpiece of language and humor, the idea of combining them seems happy, yet the effect is mechanical and annoying: in the end we have to read the whole thing through, skipping the interpolations, in order to find out what has happened. The worst example of the capacities for failure of this too synthetic, too systematic, method seems to me the scene in the maternity hospital. I have described above what actually takes place there as I have worked it out, after several readings and in the light of Joyce's outline. The Oxen of the Sun are "Fertility"—the crime committed against them is "Fraud." But, not content with this, Joyce has been at pains to fill the episode with references to real cattle and to include a long conversation about bulls. As for the special technique, it seems to me in this case not to have any real appropriateness to the situation, but to have been dictated by sheer fantastic pedantry: Joyce describes his method here as "embryonic," in conformity to the subject, maternity, and the chapter is written as a series of parodies of English literary styles from the bad Latin of the early chronicles up through Huxley and Carlyle, the development of the language corresponding to the growth of the child in the womb. Now something important takes place in this episode—the meeting between Dedalus and Bloom—and an important point is being made about it. But we miss the point because it is all we can do to follow what is happening at the drinking-party, itself rather a confused affair, through the medium of the language of the *Morte d'Arthur*, the seventeenth-century diaries, the eighteenth-century novels, and a great many other kinds of literature in which we are not prepared at the moment to be interested. If we pay attention to the parodies, we miss the story; and if we try to follow the story, we are unable to appreciate the parodies. The parodies have spoiled the story; and the necessity of telling the story through them has taken most of the life out of the parodies.

Joyce has as little respect as Proust for the capacities of the reader's attention; and one feels, in Joyce's case as in Proust's, that the *longueurs* which break our backs, the mechanical combinations of elements which fail to coalesce, are partly a result of the effort of a supernormally energetic mind to compensate by piling things up for an inability to make them move.

We have now arrived, in the maternity hospital, at the climactic scenes of the story, and Joyce has bogged us as he has never bogged us before. We shall forget the Oxen of the Sun in the wonderful night-town scene which follows it—but we shall be bogged afterwards worse than ever in the interminable let-down of the cabman's shelter and in the scientific question-and-answer chapter which undertakes to communicate to us through the most opaque and uninviting medium possible Dedalus's conversation with Bloom. The night-town episode itself and Mrs. Bloom's soliloquy, which closes the book, are, of course, among the best things in it—but the relative proportions of the other three latter chapters and the jarring effect of the pastiche style sandwiched in with the straight Naturalistic seem to me artistically absolutely indefensible. One can understand that Joyce may have intended the colorless and tiresome episodes to set off the rich and vivid ones, and also that it is of the essence of his point of view to represent the profoundest changes of our lives as beginning naturally between night and morning without the parties' appreciating their importance at the time; but a hundred and sixty-one more or less deliberately tedious pages are too heavy a dead weight for even the brilliant flights of the other hundred and ninety-nine pages to carry. Furthermore, Joyce has here half-buried his story under the virtuosity of his technical devices. It is almost as if he had elaborated it so much and worked over it so long that he had forgotten, in the amusement of writing parodies, the drama which he had originally intended to stage; or as if he were trying to divert and overwhelm us by irrelevant entertainments and feats in order that we might not be dissatisfied with the flatness—except for the drunken scene—of Dedalus's final meeting with Bloom; or even perhaps as if he did not, after all, quite want us to understand his story, as if he had, not quite conscious of what he was doing, ended by throwing up between us and it a fortification of solemn burlesque prose—as if he were shy and solicitous about it, and wanted to protect it from us.

Yet even these episodes to which I have objected contribute something valuable to *Ulysses*. In the chapter of parodies, for example, Joyce seems to be saying to us:

"Here are specimens of the sort of thing that man has written about himself in the past—how naïve or pretentious they seem! I have broken through these assumptions and pretenses and shown you how he must recognize himself today." And in the question-and-answer chapter, which is written entirely from the conventional point of view of science and where we are supplied with every possible physical, statistical, biographical and astronomical fact about Stephen's visit to Bloom: "This is all that the twentieth-century man thinks he knows about himself and his universe. Yet how mechanical and rigid this reasoning seems when we apply it to Molly and Bloom—how inadequate to explain them!"

For one of the most remarkable features of *Ulysses* is its interest as an investigation into the nature of human consciousness and behavior. Its importance from the point of view of psychology has never, it seems to me, been properly appreciated—though its influence on other books and, in consequence, upon our ideas about ourselves, has already been profound. Joyce has attempted in *Ulysses* to render as exhaustively, as precisely and as directly as it is possible in words to do, what our participation in life is like—or rather, what it seems to us like as from moment to moment we live. In order to make this record complete, he has been obliged to disregard a number of conventions of taste which, especially in English-speaking countries, have in modern times been pretty strictly observed, even by the writers who have aimed to be most scrupulously truthful. Joyce has studied what we are accustomed to consider the dirty, the trivial and the base elements in our lives with the relentlessness of a modern psychologist; and he has also—what the contemporary Naturalist has seldom been poet enough for—done justice to all those elements in our lives which we have been in the habit of describing by such names as love, nobility, truth and beauty. It is curious to reflect that a number of critics—including, curiously enough, Arnold Bennett—should have found Joyce misanthropic. Flaubert is misanthropic, if you like—and in reproducing his technique, Joyce sometimes suggests his acrid tone. But Stephen, Bloom and Mrs. Bloom are certainly not either unamiable or unattractive—and for all their misfortunes and shortcomings, they inspire us with considerable respect. Stephen and Bloom are played off a little against the duller and meaner people about them; but even these people can scarcely be said to be treated with bitterness, even when, as in the case of Buck Mulligan or the elder Dedalus, Stephen's feeling about them is bitter. Joyce is remarkable, rather, for equanimity: in spite of the nervous intensity of *Ulysses,* there is a real serenity and detachment behind it—we are in the presence of a mind which has much in common with that of a certain type of philosopher, who in his effort to understand the causes of things, to interrelate the different elements of the universe, has reached a point where the ordinary values of good and bad, beautiful and ugly, have been lost in the excellence and beauty of transcendent understanding itself.

I believe that the first readers of *Ulysses* were shocked, not merely by Joyce's use of certain words ordinarily excluded today from English literature, but by his way of representing those aspects of human nature which we tend to consider incongruous as intimately, inextricably mingled. Yet the more we read *Ulysses,* the more we are convinced of its psychological truth, and the more we are amazed at Joyce's genius in mastering and in presenting, not through analysis or generalization, but by the complete re-creation of life in the process of being lived, the relations of human beings to their environment and to each other; the nature of their perception of what goes on about them and of what goes on within themselves; and the interdependence of their intellectual, their physical, their professional and their emotional lives. To have traced all these interdependences, to have given each of these elements its value, yet never to have lost sight of the moral through preoccupation with the physical, nor to have forgotten the general in the particular; to have exhibited ordinary humanity without either satirizing it or sentimentalizing it—this would already have been sufficiently remarkable; but to have subdued all this material to the uses of a supremely finished and disciplined work of art is a feat which has hardly been equaled in the literature of our time.

In Stephen's diary in *A Portrait of the Artist*, we find this significant entry apropos of a poem by Yeats: "Michael Robartes remembers forgotten beauty and, when his arms wrap her round, he presses in his arms the loveliness which has long faded from the world. Not this. Not at all. I desire to press in my arms the loveliness which has not yet come into the world."

And with *Ulysses*, Joyce has brought into literature a new and unknown beauty. Some readers have regretted the extinction in the later Joyce of the charming lyric poet of his two little books of poems and the *fin de siècle* prose writer of the *fin de siècle* phases of *A Portrait of the Artist as a Young Man* (both the prose and verse of the early Joyce showed the influence of Yeats). This poet is still present in *Ulysses:* "Kind air defined the coigns of houses in Kildare Street. No birds. Frail from the housetops two plumes of smoke ascended, pluming, and in a flaw of softness softly were blown." But the conventions of the romantic lyric, of "aesthetic" *fin de siècle* prose, even of the aesthetic Naturalism of Flaubert, can no longer, for Joyce, be made to accommodate the reality of experience. The diverse elements of experience are perceived in different relations and they must be differently represented. Joyce has found for this new vision a new language, but a language which, instead of diluting or doing violence to his poetic genius, enables it to assimilate more materials, to readjust itself more completely and successfully than that of perhaps any other poet of our age to the new self-consciousness of the modern world. But in achieving this, Joyce has ceased to write verse. I have suggested, in connection with Valéry and Eliot, that verse itself as a literary medium is coming to be used for fewer and fewer and for more and more special purposes, and that it may be destined to fall into disuse. And it seems to me that Joyce's literary development is a striking corroboration of this view. His prose works have an artistic intensity, a definitive beauty of surface and of form, which make him comparable to the great poets rather than to most of the great novelists.

Joyce is indeed really the great poet of a new phase of the human consciousness. Like Proust's or Whitehead's or Einstein's world, Joyce's world is always changing as it is perceived by different observers and by them at different times. It is an organism made up of "events," which may be taken as infinitely inclusive or infinitely small and each of which involves all the others; and each of these events is unique. Such a world cannot be presented in terms of such artificial abstractions as have been conventional in the past: solid institutions, groups, individuals, which play the parts of distinct durable entities—or even of solid psychological factors: dualisms of good and evil, mind and matter, flesh and spirit, instinct and reason; clear conflicts between passion and duty, between conscience and interest. Not that these conceptions are left out of Joyce's world: they are all there in the minds of the characters; and the realities they represent are there, too. But everything is reduced to terms of "events" like those of modern physics and philosophy—events which make up a "continuum," but which may be taken as infinitely small. Joyce has built out of these events a picture, amazingly lifelike and living, of the everyday world we know—and a picture which seems to allow us to see into it, to follow its variations and intricacies, as we have never been able to do before.

Nor are Joyce's characters merely the sum of the particles into which their experience has been dissociated: we come to imagine them as solidly, to feel their personalities as unmistakably, as we do with any characters in fiction; and we realize finally that they are also symbols. Bloom himself is in one of his aspects the typical modern man:

Joyce has made him a Jew, one supposes, partly in order that he may be conceived equally well as an inhabitant of any provincial city of the European or Europeanized world. He makes a living by petty business, he leads the ordinary middle-class life—and he holds the conventional enlightened opinions of the time: he believes in science, social reform and internationalism. But Bloom is surpassed and illuminated from above by Stephen, who represents the intellect, the creative imagination; and he is upheld by Mrs. Bloom, who represents the body, the earth. Bloom leaves with us in the long run the impression that he is something both better and worse than either of them; for Stephen sins through pride, the sin of the intellect; and Molly is at the mercy of the flesh; but Bloom, though a less powerful personality than either, has the strength of humility. It is difficult to describe the character of Bloom as Joyce finally makes us feel it: it takes precisely the whole of *Ulysses* to put him before us. It is not merely that Bloom is mediocre, that he is clever, that he is commonplace—that he is comic, that he is pathetic—that he is, as Rebecca West says, a figure of abject "squatting" vulgarity, that he is at moments, as Foster Damon says, the Christ—he is all of these, he is all the possibilities of that ordinary humanity which is somehow not so ordinary after all; and it is the proof of Joyce's greatness that, though we recognize Bloom's perfect truth and typical character, we cannot pigeonhole him in any familiar category, racial, social, moral, literary or even—because he does really have, after all, a good deal in common with the Greek Ulysses—historical.

Both Stephen and Molly are more easily describable because they represent extremes. Both are capable of rising to heights which Bloom can never reach. In Stephen's rhapsody on the seashore, when he first realizes his artist's vocation, in *A Portrait of the Artist as a Young Man,* we have had the ecstasy of the creative mind. In the soliloquy of Mrs. Bloom, Joyce has given us another ecstasy of creation, the rhapsody of the flesh. Stephen's dream was conceived in loneliness, by a drawing apart from his fellows. But Mrs. Bloom is like the earth, which gives the same life to all: she feels a maternal kinship with all living creatures. She pities the "poor donkeys slipping half asleep" in the steep street of Gibraltar, as she does "the sentry in front of the governor's house . . . half roasted" in the sun; and she gives herself to the bootblack at the General Post Office as readily as to Professor Goodwin. But, none the less, she will tend to breed from the highest type of life she knows: she turns to Bloom, and, beyond him, toward Stephen. This gross body, the body of humanity, upon which the whole structure of *Ulysses* rests—still throbbing with so strong a rhythm amid obscenity, commonness and squalor—is laboring to throw up some knowledge and beauty by which it may transcend itself.

These two great flights of the mind carry off all the ignominies and trivialities through which Joyce has made us pass: they seem to me—the soaring silver prose of the one, the deep embedded pulse of the other—among the supreme expressions in literature of the creative powers of humanity: they are, respectively, the justifications of the woman and the man.

[1931]

AXEL AND RIMBAUD

What then is to be the future of this literature? Will the poets become more and more esoteric as the world becomes more and more difficult for them, diverging further and further from the methods and the language of popular literature in proportion as popular literature approximates more and more closely to journalism? Will the sciences dominate the future, as Pierre de Massot has suggested in a book which traces the development of Symbolism from Mallarmé to Dadaism, "smothering the last works of the past, until the day when literature, music and painting have become the three principal branches of neurology"? Paul Valéry has recently predicted that as radio, moving picture and television come to take the place of books as means of affecting people's feelings and ideas, literature, as we have known it in the past, may become "as obsolete and as far removed from life and practice as geomancy, the heraldic art and the science of falconry." Literature, according to Valéry, has become "an art which is based on the *abuse of language*—that is, it is based on language as a creator of illusions, and not on language as a means of transmitting realities. Everything which makes a language more precise, everything which emphasizes its practical character, all the changes which it undergoes in the interests of a more rapid transmission and an easier diffusion, are contrary to its function as a poetic instrument." As language becomes more international and more technical, it will become also less capable of supplying the symbols of literature; and then, just as the development of mechanical devices has compelled us to resort to sports in order to exercise our muscles, so literature will survive as a game—as a series of specialized experiments in the domain of "symbolic expression and imaginative values attained through the free combination of the elements of language."

I agree with Valéry that "the development in Europe, since 1852, of literary works which are extremely difficult, subtle and refined, which are written in a complicated style, and which, for that reason, are forbidden to most readers, bears some relation to the increase in number of literates," and to the consequent "intensive production of mediocre or average works." But I am by no means sure that the future destiny of this difficult and subtle art is to be practiced only as a sort of game and with no relation to other intellectual activities. The truth is, I believe, that Valéry's pessimism arises itself from the special point of view which, as I have said, has been associated from the beginning with the school of literature that Valéry represents.

The disillusion and weariness which we recognize as characteristic of the eighties and nineties were in reality the aspects of a philosophy which, implicit in the writings of the Symbolists, was to come to its full growth and exert its widest influence during the period that followed the War. I do not mean that Symbolism as an organized movement went on becoming more and more powerful until it triumphed over all rival movements: the eminence at this particular time of a set of writers—such writers as I have discussed in this book—all stemming more or less directly from Symbolism, was unexpected and rather sudden, and it was due largely to extra-literary accidents. The period immediately before the War had been characterized, on the whole, by a predominance of Naturalistic and social-idealistic literature—the great reputations in England and France had been those of writers like Shaw, Wells, and Bennett, Romain Rolland and Anatole France. But when the prodigious concerted efforts of the War had ended only in impoverishment and exhaustion for all the European peoples concerned, and in a general feeling of hopelessness about politics, about all attempts to organize men into social units—armies, parties, nations—in the service of some common ideal, for the accomplishment of some particular purpose, the Western mind became peculiarly hospitable to a literature indifferent to action and unconcerned with the group. Many of the socially minded writers, besides, had been intellectually demoralized by the War and had irreparably lost credit in consequence; whereas these others—Yeats, Valéry, Joyce, Proust—had maintained an unassailable integrity and now fell heir to the prestige which had been sacrificed by other poets and novelists who had abandoned the detached study of human motives and the expression of those universal emotions which make all classes and peoples one, to become intolerant partisans. It had required a determined

independence and an overmastering absorption in literature to remain unshaken by the passions and fears of that
time—and in the masterpieces which these scattered and
special writers had been producing in isolation, and, as it
were, secretly, while pandemonium raged without, their
justification was plain. These books revealed new discoveries, artistic, metaphysical, psychological: they mapped
the labyrinths of human consciousness as they seemed
never to have been mapped before, they made one conceive the world in a new way. What wonder that for those
who survived the War these writers should have become
heroes and leaders?

There are, as I have said, in our contemporary society,
for writers who are unable to interest themselves in it
either by studying it scientifically, by attempting to reform it or by satirizing it, only two alternative courses to
follow—Axel's or Rimbaud's. If one chooses the first of
these, the way of Axel, one shuts oneself up in one's own
private world, cultivating one's private fantasies, encouraging one's private manias, ultimately preferring
one's absurdest chimeras to the most astonishing contemporary realities, ultimately mistaking one's chimeras for
realities. If one chooses the second, the way of Rimbaud,
one tries to leave the twentieth century behind—to find
the good life in some country where modern manufactur-
ing methods and modern democratic institutions do not
present any problems to the artist because they haven't
yet arrived. In this book, I have been occupied with writers who have, in general, taken Axel's course; but the period since the War has furnished almost as many examples
of writers who have gone the way of Rimbaud—without
usually, however, like him, getting to the point of giving
up literature altogether. All our cult, which Wyndham
Lewis has denounced, of more primitive places and peoples is really the manifestation of an impulse similar to
Rimbaud's—D. H. Lawrence's mornings in Mexico and
his explorations of Santa Fe and Australia; Blaise Cen-
drars's Negro anthology, the Negro masks which bring

such high prices in Paris, André Gide's lifelong passion for Africa which has finally led him to navigate the Congo, Sherwood Anderson's exhilaration at the "dark laughter" of the American South, and the fascination for white New Yorkers of Harlem; and even that strange infatuation with the infantile—because our children are more barbarous than we—which has allowed the term Expressionism to be applied at once to drawings done by the pupils in German schools and to the dramas of German playwrights, which caused Nathalia Crane to be taken seriously and made Daisy Ashford all the rage; that hysterical excitement over modern "primitives" which has led the generation of Jean Cocteau to talk about the Douanier Rousseau as their fathers did about Degas—all this has followed in the wake of Rimbaud.

Yet Lawrence, for all his rovings, must come back to the collieries again; and for Anderson, though he may seek in New Orleans the leisure and ease of the old South, it is the factories of Ohio which still stick in his crop. The Congo masks in Paris are buried in galleries or in the houses of private collectors almost as completely as if they were sunk among the ruins of their vanished dynasties in the African wilderness; and when white New Yorkers, obstreperous and drunken, visit the Harlem cabarets at night, they find the Negroes in American business suits, attempting modestly and drearily to conform to the requirements of Western civilization. Our shocking children soon grow up into adults as docile as their mothers and fathers. And as for those that choose Axel's course, the price paid by the man of imagination who, while remaining in the modern world, declines to participate in its activities and tries to keep his mind off its plight, is usually to succumb to some monstrosity or absurdity. We feel it in Proust's hypochondriac ailments and his fretting self-centered prolixities; in Yeats's astrology and spirit-tappings and in the seventeenth-century cadence which half puts to sleep his livest prose; in the meagerness of the poetic output of Paul Valéry and T. S. Eliot contrasted with their incessant speculations as to precisely what constitutes poetry, precisely what function it performs and whether there is any point in writing it; even in the mystifications by which Joyce, "forging," just behind that screen, "the uncreated consciousness" not merely of the Irish but of the Western man of our time, has made his books rather difficult of access to a public for whom a few chapter headings or a word of explanation might have enabled them to recognize more readily a mirror for the study of their own minds. (The philosophical mathematicians and physicists whose work these novelists and poets parallel seem to have developed, no doubt from the same social and political causes, a similar metaphysical hypertrophy: consider the disproportionate size of the shadow-structure of speculation which such a writer as Eddington tries to base on some new modification of physical theory, itself suggested on most uncertain evidence.)

It is true of these later writers that they have not dissociated themselves from society so completely as the original group of Symbolists: they have supplied us, as a matter of fact, with a good deal of interesting social criticism; but it is usually a criticism which does not aim at anything, it is an exercise—Proust is the great example—of the pure intelligence playing luminously all about but not driven by the motor power of any hope and not directed by any creative imagination for the possibilities of human life. If these writers ever indicate a preference for any social order different from the present one, it is invariably for some society of the past as they have read of it in its most attractive authors—as Yeats likes to imagine himself in the role of some great lord and patron of arts of the Renaissance, or as Eliot dedicates his credo to a seventeenth-century Anglican bishop. And this tendency to look to the past, in spite of the revolutionary character of some of their methods, has sometimes given even to their most original work an odd Alexandrian aspect: the productions of Eliot, Proust and Joyce, for example, are sometimes veritable literary museums. It is not merely that

these modern novelists and poets build upon their predecessors, as the greatest writers have done in all times, but
that they have developed a weakness for recapitulating
them in parodies.

When these writers do turn their attention to the contemporary world and its future, it is usually with strange,
and even eerie, results. Eliot has recently—explaining by
the way, in regard to causes in general, that "we fight
rather to keep something alive than in the expectation that
anything will triumph"—put forward, or announced his
intention of putting forward, a program of classicism,
royalism and Anglo-Catholicism; and Yeats, in his astro-
logical "Vision," has predicted the future of Europe as
follows:

"A decadence will descend, by perpetual moral improvement, upon a community which may seem like some
woman of New York or Paris who has renounced her
rouge pot to lose her figure and grow coarse of skin and
dull of brain, feeding her calves and babies somewhere
upon the edge of the wilderness. The decadence of the
Greco-Roman world with its violent soldiers and its mahogany dark young athletes was as great, but that suggested the bubbles of life turned into marbles, whereas
what awaits us, being democratic and *primary*, may suggest bubbles in a frozen pond—mathematical Babylonian
starlight. . . .

"It is possible that the ever increasing separation from
the community as a whole of the cultivated classes, their
increasing certainty, and that falling in two of the human
mind which I have seen in certain works of art is preparation. During the period said to commence in 1927, with
the 11th gyre, must arise a form of philosophy which will
become religious and ethical in the 12th gyre and be in all
things opposite of that vast plaster Herculean image, final
primary thought. It will be concrete in expression, establish itself by immediate experience, seek no general agreement, make little of God or any exterior unity, and it will
call that good which a man can contemplate himself as

doing always and no other doing at all. It will make a cardinal truth of man's immortality that its virtue may not lack sanction, and of the soul's reëmbodiment that it may restore to virtue that long preparation none can give and hold death an interruption. The supreme experience, Plotinus's ecstasy of the Saint, will recede, for men—finding it difficult—sustituted dogma and idol, abstractions of all sorts of things beyond experience; and man may be long content with those more trivial supernatural benedictions as when Athena took Achilles by his yellow hair. Men will no longer separate the idea of God from that of human genius, human productivity in all its forms."

I believe therefore that the time is at hand when these writers, who have largely dominated the literary world of the decade 1920–30, though we shall continue to admire them as masters, will no longer serve us as guides. Axel's world of the private imagination in isolation from the life of society seems to have been exploited and explored as far as for the present is possible. Who can imagine this sort of thing being carried further than Valéry and Proust have done? And who hereafter will be content to inhabit a corner, though fitted out with some choice things of one's own, in the shuttered house of one of these writers— where we find ourselves, also, becoming conscious of a lack of ventilation? On the other hand, it seems equally unsatisfactory, equally impossible, to imitate Rimbaud: we carry with us in our own minds and habits the civilization of machinery, trade, democratic education and standardization to the Africas and Asias to which we flee, even if we do not find them there before us. Nor can we keep ourselves up very long at home by any of the current substitutes for Rimbaud's solution—by occupying ourselves exclusively with prize-fighters or with thugs or by simply remaining drunk or making love all the time. In the meantime, Western Europe has been recovering from the exhaustion and despair of the War; and in America the comfortable enjoyment of what was supposed to be American prosperity, which since the War has made it

possible for Americans to accept with a certain complacency the despondency as well as the resignation of European books, has given way to a sudden disquiet. And
Americans and Europeans are both becoming more and
more conscious of Russia, a country where a central
social-political idealism has been able to use and to inspire
the artist as well as the engineer. The question begins to
press us again as to whether it is possible to make a practical success of human society, and whether, if we continue
to fail, a few masterpieces, however profound or noble,
will be able to make life worth living even for the few
people in a position to enjoy them.

The reaction against nineteenth-century Naturalism
which Symbolism originally represented has probably
now run its full course, and the oscillation which for at
least three centuries has been taking place between the
poles of objectivity and subjectivity may return toward
objectivity again: we may live to see Valéry, Eliot and
Proust displaced and treated with as much intolerance as
those writers—Wells, France and Shaw—whom they
have themselves displaced. Yet as surely as Ibsen and
Flaubert brought to their Naturalistic plays and novels
the sensibility and language of Romanticism, the writers
of a new reaction in the direction of the study of man in
his relation to his neighbor and to society will profit by
the new intelligence and technique of Symbolism. Or—
what would be preferable and is perhaps more likely—this
oscillation may finally cease. Our conceptions of objective
and subjective have unquestionably been based on false
dualisms; our materialisms and idealisms alike have been
derived from mistaken conceptions of what the researches
of science implied—Classicism and Romanticism, Naturalism and Symbolism are, in reality, therefore false alternatives. And so we may see Naturalism and Symbolism
combine to provide us with a vision of human life and its
universe, richer, more subtle, more complex and more
complete than any that man has yet known—indeed, they
have already so combined, Symbolism has already re-

joined Naturalism, in one great work of literature, *Ulysses.*

I cannot believe, then, with Paul Valéry, that Symbolism is doomed to become more and more highly specialized until it has been reduced to the status of an intellectual pastime like anagrams or chess. It seems to me far more likely that it will be absorbed and assimilated by the general literature and thought. All the exponents of Symbolism have insisted that they were attempting to meet a need for a new language. "To find a tongue!" Rimbaud had cried. "One has to be an academician—deader than a fossil—to make a dictionary of any language at all." And Valéry himself had followed Mallarmé in an effort to push to a kind of algebra the classical language of French poetry; Gertrude Stein has explained that her later writings are intended to "restore its intrinsic meaning to literature"; and Joyce, in his new novel, has been attempting to create a tongue which shall go deeper than conscious spoken speech and follow the processes of the unconscious. It is probably true, as Pater has suggested, that there is something akin to the scientific instinct in the efforts of modern literature to render the transitory phases of "a world of fine gradations and subtly linked conditions, shifting intricately as we ourselves change." In any case, the experiments of men who in their lifetimes have been either received with complete indifference or denounced as practical jokers or lunatics may perhaps prove of equal importance with those scattered researches in mathematics and physics which seemed at first merely whimsical exercises on the margins of their subjects, but which have been laid under contribution by the great modern physical systems—without which these could scarcely have been constructed. Mallarmé's poetry, in its time, seemed no more gratuitous and abstruse than Gauss's fourth-dimensional coordinates—yet it has been built upon by writers as considerable in their own field as Einstein is in his.

As I have pointed out in connection with Gertrude Stein, our ideas about the "logic" of language are likely to

be superficial. The relation of words to what they convey—that is, to the processes behind them and the processes to which they give rise in those who listen to or
read them—is still a very mysterious one. We tend to assume that being *convinced* of things is something quite
different from having them *suggested* to us; but the suggestive language of the Symbolist poet is really performing the same sort of function as the reasonable language of
the realistic novelist or even the severe technical languages
of science. The most, apparently, we can say of language
is that it indicates relations, and a Symbolist poem does
this just as much as a mathematical formula: both suggest
imaginary worlds made up of elements abstracted from
our experience of the real world and revealing relations
which we acknowledge to be valid within those fields of
experience. The only difference between the language of
Symbolism and the literary languages to which we are
more accustomed is that the former indicates relations
which, recently perceived for the first time, cut through or
underlie those in terms of which we have been in the habit
of thinking; and that it deals with them by means of what
amounts, in comparison with conventional language, to a
literary shorthand which makes complex ideas more easily
manageable. This new language may actually have the effect of revolutionizing our ideas of syntax, as modern philosophy seems to be tending to discard the notion of cause
and effect. It is evidently working, like modern scientific
theory, toward a totally new conception of reality. This
conception, as we find it today in much Symbolist literature, seems, it is true, rather formidably complicated and
sometimes even rather mystical; but this complexity may
presently give rise to some new and radical simplification,
when the new ideas which really lie behind these more
and more elaborate attempts to recombine and adapt the
old have finally begun to be plain. And the result may be,
not, as Valéry predicts, an infinite specialization and di-
vergence of the sciences and arts, but their finally falling
all into one system. He himself suggests such a possibility

by constantly reminding us of the single "method" common to all departments of thought. And who can say that, as science and art look more and more deeply into experience and achieve a wider and wider range, and as they come to apply themselves more and more directly and expertly to the needs of human life, they may not arrive at a way of thinking, a technique of dealing with our perceptions, which will make art and science one?

The writers with whom I have here been concerned have not only, then, given us works of literature which, for intensity, brilliance and boldness as well as for an architectural genius, an intellectual mastery of their materials, rare among their Romantic predecessors, are probably comparable to the work of any time. Though it is true that they have tended to overemphasize the importance of the individual, that they have been preoccupied with introspection sometimes almost to the point of insanity, that they have endeavored to discourage their readers, not only with politics, but with action of any kind—they have yet succeeded in effecting in literature a revolution analogous to that which has taken place in science and philosophy: they have broken out of the old mechanistic routine, they have disintegrated the old materialism, and they have revealed to the imagination a new flexibility and freedom. And though we are aware in them of things that are dying—the whole belle-lettristic tradition of Renaissance culture perhaps, compelled to specialize more and more, more and more driven in on itself, as industrialism and democratic education have come to press it closer and closer—they none the less break down the walls of the present and wake us to the hope and exaltation of the untried, unsuspected possibilities of human thought and art.

[1931]

III
Capitalism and
Communism

~~~~~~~~~~~~~~~~~~~~~~~~~~~~~~~~~~~~

EDITOR'S NOTE

The young critic was also a chronicler, and his chronicle
takes us from the jazz age through the crisis of society in
the Depression. If Wilson's perspective on the later,
wilder years of the boom scarcely prepares us for his political activism in the early thirties, it sometimes recalls John
Peale Bishop's remark that the ghost of Cotton Mather
(Wilson's remote ancestor) was "burrowing under his
conscience like a mole." His account of a weekend with
the Fitzgeralds was written a quarter of a century later,
but as he re-creates this glittering occasion he does not
forget his own eagerness to get away before Saturday
night, his sense that the party had already gone on too
long. The stock market crash, which Wilson once likened
to "a rending of the earth in preparation for the Day of
Judgment," brought home to him the writer's political and
moral responsibilities. He took a road that led from Axel's
Castle, that ivory tower of the artist, to the Finland station
in Leningrad, where an intellectual tradition had, he
thought, been vindicated in action.

"Frank Keeney's Coal Diggers" shows Wilson's outrage
at the conditions he found when traveling in his own
country in the early thirties. Independent radical movements were then a feature of the labor scene. In some-

what the tone that Steinbeck would take in *The Grapes of Wrath*, Wilson expresses his solidarity with the miners, led by an old socialist and fighting on their own ground. In "Detroit Motors" his methods anticipate those of the new journalism. Conveying the pressures of the assembly line, he interviews workers to let them tell their stories in their own words, and he explores the contradictions in Henry Ford's personality, where idealism and mechanical genius were matched with egotism, stinginess, and ignorance. What Marx called the contradictions of capitalism helped Wilson account for such anomalies, as well as the problems of the automobile industry. Crossing the continent to San Diego, Wilson contemplated the end of the westward movement and the exhaustion of the national ideal, as he read the coroner's record of suicides and, in the lovely Coronado Beach Hotel, heard the rousing rhythms of the "Battle Hymn of the Republic" applied to fund raising by people who had no idea what to do with the money. "Twenty-thousand dollars by 1934," these ladies chanted, the Depression equivalent of Eliot's "In the room the women come and go / Talking of Michaelangelo." The emptiness of "Prufrock" and *The Waste Land* acquires a local habitation and a name in "The Jumping-Off Place."

One could still go east, and when a Guggenheim Fellowship enabled him to travel to Russia in 1935, after he had written the first chapters of *To the Finland Station*, he set out eagerly for the new society. In the version of Wilson's journal published after his return, the pilgrim fights off a skepticism more fully documented in *Red, Black, Blond and Olive* twenty years later. Both contain the comic scenes in the Odessa hospital, which illustrate the primitive conditions inherited by the new Russia from the old. In the account of Soviet Moscow in *Travels in Two Democracies* (1936), however, there is no mention of the critic D. S. Mirsky. Although Wilson could not fully appreciate the danger in which his friend lived, he saw that Mirsky's position was insecure. His memoir, which appeared in 1956, captures the predicament of the Russian intellectual elite, with their international culture and their dedication to a society in which they were swept away, as Mirsky was soon swept away to his death in the Siberian goldfields.

Wilson had rejected Russian Communism when he finished *To the Finland Station*; yet his revolutionary aspirations survive in the portrait of Marx which is the centerpiece of these selections. Wilson's Marx is a Promethean hero whose labor seems to promise the liberation of humanity. His intellectual energy and dedication, his searching curiosity and ability to learn from experience, outweigh the limitations of the dialectic or the labor theory of value. With the psychological focus Wilson tried on interpreting writers, he correlates Marx's cruel vision of the historical struggle, his sado-masochistic metaphors, his excoriation of the bourgeoisie for behaving as he said it must, with the man's neglect of his wife Jenny and his exploitation of Engels. The latter is a foil to Marx, a warmly human figure who relieves the darkness and the abstraction of the vision on which he depends. Wilson's imagination shapes these characters from the documentary record, with an art of quotation that complements his ability to tell a story while filling in the intellectual and historical background.

"Trotsky and History," which closes this section, examines the cause of revolutionary socialism through the career and thoughts of a leader whose strengths and limitations were easier for Wilson to assess than Lenin's. Trotsky's gifts as a historian were matched to a theatrical flair and brilliant administrative abilities, and he had exemplified the writing and acting of history Wilson set out to celebrate in *Finland Station*. But Wilson had seen through Stalin and, unlike some of his contemporaries, could no longer romanticize the dictator's exiled opponent. In *Their Morals and Ours* Trotsky justified, in the name of progress, the behavior—in this case lying and killing—he denounced in conservatives. Wilson attacks this double standard just as Orwell would in *Animal Farm* and *1984*. Trotsky's appeal to History masked the old assumption that God and Providence are on one's side. He thus becomes a self-deluded "hero of the faith in Reason" to which Wilson himself subscribed.

* * *

The pieces on the American scene in this section appeared in *The New Republic* and are reprinted in *The American Earthquake*, except for "A Weekend at Ellerslie," first published in *The Shores of Light* in 1952. In *The Shores of Light* Wilson recalls the background of his visit to the Fitzgeralds in several paragraphs not included here. *The American Earthquake* contains a metaphorical description of the assembly line and other materials I have had to omit from the long essay "Detroit Motors," as well as a second installment of "Frank Keeney's Coal Diggers." An account of Mirsky's criticism complements the portrait of Mirsky in *Red, Black, Blond and Olive*. Wilson's original notes on his five months in the U.S.S.R. as well as on Depression America are found in *The Thirties*.

"The Partnership of Marx and Engels" is not the chapter of *To the Finland Station* by that name, but consists of parts of five chapters out of the ten chapters and nearly 250 pages on Marx and Engels in the 1972 edition of the book. Line spaces indicate breaks between the sections of Wilson's text, as in the case of "Detroit Motors." "Trotsky and History," also occasionally cut, appeared as "Trotsky Identifies History with Himself" in *To the Finland Station*, following on "The Young Eagle," which chronicles Trotsky's exploits as a revolutionary leader.

THE FOLLIES AS AN INSTITUTION

It may seem rather late at this time to be writing about the current Ziegfeld Follies—almost now at the end of its season—but the Follies is a permanent institution and comments on it are always in order. Mr. Ziegfeld has now "Glorified the American Girl" in a very real sense. He has studied, with shrewd intelligence, the American ideal of womanhood and succeeded in putting it on the stage. In general, Ziegfeld's girls have not only the Ango-Saxon straightness—straight backs, straight brows and straight noses—but also the peculiar frigidity and purity, the frank high-school-girlishness which Americans like. He does not aim to make them, from the moment they appear, as sexually attractive as possible, as the Folies Bergères, for example, does. He appeals to American idealism, and then, when the male is intent on his chaste and dewy-eyed vision, he gratifies him on this plane by discreetly disrobing his goddess. He tries, furthermore, to represent, in the maneuvers of his well-trained choruses, not the movement and abandon of emotion, but what the American male really regards as beautiful: the efficiency of mechnical movement. The ballet at the Ziegfeld Follies is becoming more and more like military drill: to watch a row of well-grown girls descend a high flight of stairs in a deliberate and rigid goose-step is far from my idea of what ballet ought to be; it is too much like watching setting-up exercises.

Yet there is still something wonderful about the Follies. It exhibits the persistent vitality as well as the stupidity of an institution. Among those green peacocks and gilded panels, in the luxurious haze of the New Amsterdam, there is realized a glittering vision which rises straight out of the soul of New York. The Follies is such fantasy, such harlequinade as the busy well-to-do New Yorker has been able to make of his life. Expensive, punctual, stiff, it moves with the speed of an express train. It has in it something of Riverside Drive, of the Plaza, of Scott Fitzgerald's novels—though it radically differs from these latter in being almost devoid of wit. In spite of the by no means mediocre efforts of Will Rogers and Ring Lardner, in spite of Mr. Tynan's impersonation of Belasco, there is still something formal about the jokes in the Follies: a signal is given from the stage, and the audience responds like a shot. The actor who made the joke is as cold as the American Beauties drilling on the Grand Staircase, and there is no trace of mirth in the metallic laughter set in motion by the stimulus from the stage. I personally was much entertained, a couple of weeks ago, by a skit called *Koo-Koo Nell, the Pride of the Depot,* but the last time I saw the show, it turned out that *Koo-Koo Nell* had been discontinued. There had been substituted a deafening farce of the Jarr Family school—one of those domestic scenes in which husband, wife and children break dishes and bawl at one another. As each cartridge of abuse is exploded, the audience lets off its automatic roar. I am told that *Koo-Koo Nell* was taken off because there were "no laughs in it."

Yet, as I say, there is a splendor about the Follies. It has, in its way, both distinction and intensity. At the New Amsterdam, the girls are always young—the *mise en scène* nearly always beautiful. And there is always one first-rate performer. Just now it is Gilda Gray. She is not the official American Girl; she embodies a different ideal: an ideal which was probably created by the vibrant and abandoned Eva Tanguay and which has produced the jazz baby of the years since the war who now rivals the magazine cover. She is the obverse of Mary Eaton—she is the semi-bacchante of Main Street.

April, 1923

THE LEXICON OF PROHIBITION

The following is a partial list of words denoting drunkenness now in common use in the United States. They have been arranged, as far as possible, in order of the degrees of intensity of the conditions which they represent, beginning with the mildest stages and progressing to the more disastrous.

lit
squiffy
oiled
lubricated
owled
edged
jingled
piffed
piped
sloppy
woozy
happy
half-screwed
half-cocked
half-shot
half seas over
fried
stewed
boiled
zozzled
sprung
scrooched
jazzed
jagged
pie-eyed
cock-eyed
wall-eyed
glassy-eyed

bleary-eyed
hoary-eyed
over the Bay
four sheets in the wind
crocked
loaded
leaping
screeching
lathered
plastered
soused
bloated
polluted
saturated
full as a tick
loaded for bear
loaded to the muzzle
loaded to the plimsoll
    mark
wapsed down
paralyzed
ossified
out like a light
passed out cold
embalmed
buried
blotto
canned

corked
corned
potted
hooted
slopped
tanked
stinko
blind
stiff
under the table
tight
full
wet
high
horseback
liquored
pickled
ginned
shicker (Yiddish)
spifflicated
primed
organized
featured
lit up like the sky
lit up like the Common-
   wealth
lit up like a Christmas
   tree

lit up like a store window
lit up like a church
fried to the hat
slopped to the ears
stewed to the gills
boiled as an owl
to have a bun on
to have a slant on
to have a skate on
to have a snootful
to have a skinful
to draw a blank
to pull a shut-eye
to pull a Daniel Boone
to have a rubber drink
to have a hangover
to have a head
to have the jumps
to have the shakes
to have the zings
to have the heeby-jeebies
to have the screaming-
   meemies
to have the whoops and
   jingles
to burn with a low blue
   flame

Some of these, such as *loaded* and *full*, are a little old-fashioned now; but they are still understood. Others, such as *cock-eyed* and *oiled*, which are included in the *Drinker's Dictionary* compiled by Benjamin Franklin (and containing two hundred and twenty-eight terms) seem to be enjoying a new popularity. It is interesting to note that one hears nowadays less often of people going on *sprees, toots, tears, jags, bats, brannigans* or *benders*. All these terms suggest, not merely extreme drunkenness, but also an exceptional occurrence, a breaking away by the drinker from the conditions of his normal life. It is possible that their partial disappearance is mainly to be accounted for by the fact that this kind of fierce protracted drinking has now become universal, an accepted feature of social life instead of a disreputable escapade. On the other hand, the vocabulary of social drinking, as exemplified by this list, seems to have become especially rich: one gets the impression that more nuances are nowadays discriminated than was the case before Prohibition. Thus, *fried, stewed* and *boiled* all convey distinctly different ideas; and *cock-eyed, plastered, owled, embalmed* and *ossified* evoke quite different images. *Wapsed down* is a rural expression originally applied to crops that have been laid low by a storm; *featured* is a theatrical word, which here refers to a stage at which the social drinker is inspired to believe strongly in his ability to sing a song, to tell a funny story or to execute a dance; *organized* is properly applied to a condition of thorough preparation for a more or less formidable evening; and *blotto*, of English origin, denotes a state of blank bedazement.

March 9, 1927

A WEEKEND AT ELLERSLIE

I had never yet visited the Fitzgeralds in the house just outside Wilmington that they had taken on their return from Europe at the end of 1927, but rumors had reached me of festivities on a more elaborate scale than their old weekends at Westport or Great Neck. Dos Passos had attended a party that Scott had given for his thirtieth birthday, which he described to me as "a regular wake"—Scott had been lamenting the passing of youth ever since his twenty-first birthday, and he had apparently commemorated his twenties with veritable funeral games. I had certainly never seen Scott and Zelda in such a magnificent setting. Ellerslie, Edgemoor, turned out to be a handsome old big square white house, with Greek columns and high-ceilinged rooms. It had been built in the early eighteen-forties and had always up to then been occupied by the managers of the Edgemoor Iron Company. I arrived there* with Thornton Wilder, whom I had not known before and whose books I had not read. Scott had had us met at the station, and, in the course of the drive to Ellerslie, we had talked about Marcel Proust. I had just read the final instalment of *A la Recherche du Temps Perdu*, which had reached New York not long before, and was about to describe it to Wilder. There are few things I enjoy so much as talking to people about books which I have read but they haven't, and making them wish they had—preferably a book that is hard to get or in a language that they do not know. But in this case my expectation was disappointed, for it turned out that Wilder had been following Proust just as attentively as I had and had read *Le Temps Retrouvé* as promptly. I had had the impression that his novels were rather on the fragile and precious side, and was surprised to find him a person of such positive and even peppery opinions. He had his doubts about *Le Temps Retrouvé;* he declared that too many of the characters turned out to be homosexual. Charlus was all right, he said; but in the case of Saint-Loup, for example, some further explanation was needed: there was a psychological problem there that Proust had simply shirked. I called his attention to the fact that the novel ended with the phrase *"dans le temps,"* as it had begun with the key sentence, *"Longtemps, je me suis couché de bonne heure,"* and he said he had noticed this.

Scott met his guests at the door and, the moment their hats and coats were off, took them for a tour of the house, of which he was extremely proud and which he was doing

---

* This was in November 1928. [L.M.D.]

his best to live up to. He would stop in one of the corridors and say mysteriously, "Don't you hear something? Don't you hear something strange?— It's the old Ellerslie ghost." He had posted the butler behind a door to groan and rattle a chain. But at a time when the whole house was buzzing with life and everybody looking forward to cocktails, these sounds did not even attract attention, and the clanking of a chain would, in any case, hardly have meant anything to anyone not fresh from a Gothic novel. We were next taken into a room, where we were given, for our entertainment, a choice of listening to records—which were still a novelty then—of *Le Sacre du Printemps* or of looking at an album of photographs of horribly mutilated soldiers. Scott had discovered the War, and this explained the antiquated allusions of his letter, as well as his just having pointed out to me, hanging on the wall of his study, the trench-helmet which, not having been sent overseas, he had never worn in action. At the time when he had been in the army, he must have been exclusively occupied with the first version of *This Side of Paradise* and his romance with Zelda in Alabama, for it was as if the unpleasant events of 1914–18 were now touching his imagination for the first time. They must have been brought to his notice by his friend Ernest Hemingway, of whom he had seen a good deal in Europe and who was then writing *A Farewell to Arms.* Preliminary drinks were served, but we had not got far with Stravinsky before we were taken outside and involved in a chaotic interlude, of which I can remember—on the darkening lawn—only playing diabolo while carrying on a conversation about Ford Madox Ford.

The crescendo of the evening was well under way when we had our pre-dinner drinks in a large and splendid salon. Gilbert and "Amanda" Seldes were there, and Esther Strachey, the sister of Scott's great friend Gerald Murphy. In a conversation with Seldes and me, Scott somehow got around to inviting us frankly to criticize his character. Gilbert told him that if he had a fault, it was making life seem rather dull; and this quite put him out of countenance till we both began to laugh. John and Anna Biggs arrived. John Biggs was an old friend of Scott's and mine, who had roomed with Scott in college. He practiced law in Wilmington—though he was just about to publish his second novel—and it was he who had got Scott established at Ellerslie. I had not seen John since his marriage, and Scott explained Anna to me: "She was one of the famous Rupert girls—don't you remember the beautiful Rupert sisters that were such a sensation at the proms?" In the atmosphere of exhilaration that the Fitzgeralds always generated on these occasions, I was called upon to give them an act that I had sometimes performed years before—after the summer of 1916 at Plattsburg—at convivial college gatherings. This was an impersonation of a Regular Army officer giving a hoarse-voiced lecture on Scouting and Patrolling. Major Waldron, red-faced and bespectacled, standing with his heels together and his arms held stiff at his sides, would bark out, without a gesture or a flicker of expression, such instructions as: "Places of concealment: trees and roofs of houses. If you climb on roof of house, be sure to keep on side that's hidden—side that's away from enemy. Don't get on side exposed to enemy. Scout that gets on side exposed to enemy can be seen by enemy and shot. Scout must keep from getting shot. Scout's no good if he's dead." I had completely forgotten this, but John Biggs fed it back to me, and I did my best to oblige, though I was really not up to it any more. At some point either just before or just after this, Scott took me aside in another room and told me that he had been harboring a grievance against me. It was something that had happened a long time before—he felt that I had behaved with him and Zelda in a way that he ought to resent. I thought it was all nonsense—especially as coming from him; but since Scott, like Dr. Johnson, considered himself an authority on manners, I tried to explain my offense away, and something like our good relations seemed to be reestablished.

Then a drove of new people arrived. A play of Zoë Akins's—*The Furies*—was being tried out in Wilmington, and the Fitzgeralds had invited her to dinner, with the designer of the sets and costumes and three or four other men who were also involved in the production. At dinner, we were floating divinely on good wine and gay conversation, in which I noted, however, that Wilder, though extremely responsive, remained sharply and firmly nonsoluble. He was talking with Esther Strachey about Colette, and saying that there were some of the Claudine books that he thought were pretty good. I sat next to Zelda, who was at her iridescent best. Some of Scott's friends were irritated, others were enchanted, by her. I was one of the ones who were charmed. She had the waywardness of a Southern belle and the lack of inhibitions of a child. She talked with so spontaneous a color and wit— almost exactly in the way she wrote—that I very soon ceased to be troubled by the fact that the conversation was in the nature of a "free association" of ideas and one could never follow up anything. I have rarely known a woman who expressed herself so delightfully and so freshly: she had no readymade phrases on the one hand and made no straining for effect on the other. It evaporated easily, however, and I remember only one thing she said that night: that the writing of Galsworthy was a shade of blue for which she did not care. But as the dinner went on, Miss Akins began to dominate the conversation. She was herself an accomplished performer in a more grandiose tradition than that of the unceremonious twenties, and she was presently holding the table with resounding speeches from Shakespeare. This rather threw out the Fitzgeralds, who were used to the center of the stage and preferred a more playful tone, and when Miss Akins and her companions had left in order to get to the theater, Scott, who had been charming at the beginning of dinner, now grumbled:

"All that memorized Shakespeare!" This was followed by a complete anticlimax. Scarcely had we left the table when the Fitzgeralds announced they were going to bed and left the guests to shift for themselves. I soon went to bed myself.

But this, though I saw nothing more, was by no means the end of the evening. The party from Miss Akins's play had been invited to come back when the performance was over, and, with the exception of Miss Akins herself, they did. Zelda, having had her sleep, decided to emerge again, and, coming into one of the spacious rooms, discovered the little designer, alone, leaning moodily on the marble mantel. "Please go away," he said. "I'm thinking, and I don't want to be disturbed." "Oh, you're not really thinking," said Zelda, for whom, as for all Southern women, any highhanded tone on the part of a man stimulated immediate insolence. "You're just homogeneous!" This could hardly have been due to ignorance: it must have been a species of euphemism intended to soften the remark; but, in any case, its effect was terrible. The young man stalked out of the room and complained to his companions of an insult, and, demanding the Fitzgeralds' car, they all huffily left.

I do not think that Scott, who had slept all night, heard anything about this incident till Zelda got up late the next morning. I remember his sitting around in his bathrobe and reading to Gilbert Seldes and me what must have been one of the early Riviera chapters from his novel then in progress, which was to turn into *Tender Is the Night*. There was especially one dazzling passage with which he had evidently taken much pains and on which he must have counted to stun us. It presented a group of attractive girls—on a beach or in a room, I can't remember—but in any case floating and glowing in richest Fitzgerald glamor. "What do you think of that description?" he asked. We told him we thought it was splendid. "I read this chapter to Dos Passos, when he was here," he said, "and afterwards he said that he liked it 'all except that part,' he said, 'that's so wonderful.' I asked him what he meant, and he said, 'Oh, you know: that part that's so wonderful—that part that's so perfectly marvellous.' " This may have led him to leave it out, or he may have had to scrap it with his original subject, for I cannot now find this passage, in any form I can recognize, in *Tender Is the Night*. Thornton Wilder, who had left early that morning, was, I found, Scott's most recent enthusiasm. He told me that *The Cabala* was the very best thing that had come out, I think, since Hemingway—he did not care so much for *The Bridge of San Luis Rey*. I must absolutely read it—he would send it to me.

But the news of the incident of the night before, when Scott heard of it, profoundly disturbed him. It had been a breach of hospitality, and he must do what he could to repair it. He would look up the offended guests and try to smooth the incident over. He set out in his car after lunch, taking along Esther Strachey and me to talk to him and support his morale. On the way, he questioned the driver—of whom he seemed to have made a trusted familiar—as to what the guests had said while he was taking them home. "Why, the little fellow said, 'Fitzgerald thinks he's got a swell place there, but an uncle of mine's got a house that makes that house look like a dump!' " This visibly depressed Scott, and Esther and I tried to dissuade him from pursuing the matter further; but, "It's only very seldom," he insisted, "that you get a real opportunity to hear what people say about you behind your back. — Didn't anybody," he turned to the driver, "have anything good to say about me?" "There was one that tried to speak up for you," the man replied, "but they had him down on the bottom, with their feet on him." Scott found out in Wilmington that the theater people were not all at the hotel with Miss Akins, and since it looked as if it might take him some time to run them down and to deal with the problem properly, he sent us back to the house. He wanted to make them come back, so that Zelda and he could be nice to them.

The aftermath of a Fitzgerald evening was notoriously a painful experience. I suddenly became terribly irritable and said something sarcastic to Esther about what seemed to me certain chi-chi attitudes that she had recently picked up in Paris. She replied—with great moderation in view of what must have been on my part a very disagreeable tone: "You have an intellectual arrogance that is sometimes very trying." I was somewhat piqued by this—let me say that my friendship of many years with this brilliant and most amiable woman has otherwise been quite unclouded—and I made up my mind that I would leave late in the afternoon. I did not want to see the theater people again; I could not face another evening. It seemed to me the party was slipping, and I knew that when these parties of the Fitzgeralds slipped they were likely to end in disaster. I knew that if I stayed through another night, I should be no good Monday. I was getting too old for this kind of thing. I found that I did not, however, have money for the railroad fare, so I asked Scott, when he came back, to cash a check. He had no money either and tried to persuade me to stay. When I insisted, he went away with the check and then came back to let me know that Esther Strachey was the only person in the house who had ten dollars to spare. This was very embarrassing to me, but Esther was neither embarrassed nor embittered, and the whole thing became a joke.

I later heard that Scott had waked up in the night and decided that he had not done justice to the possibilities of the Ellerslie ghost. He put a sheet over his head and invaded the Seldeses' room. Standing beside their bed, he began to groan in a way that he hoped was an improvement on the butler. But Gilbert started up from his sleep and gave a swipe with his arm at the sheet, which caught fire from a cigarette that the ghost was smoking inside his shroud. In the turmoil, something else caught fire, and everybody was rather alarmed.

1952

FRANK KEENEY'S COAL DIGGERS

The people who work at Ward, West Virginia, live in little flat yellow houses on stilts that look like chicken-
houses. They seem mean and flimsy on the sides of the
hills and at the bottom of the hollow, in contrast to
the magnificent mountains, wooded now with the forests
of mid-June. Between those round and rich-foliaged hills,
through the middle of the mining settlement, runs a road
which has, on one side of it, a long row of obsolete coal-
cars, turned upside down and, on the other, a trickle of a
creek, with bare yellow banks, half-dry yellow stones,
yellowing rusty tin cans and the axles and wheels of old
coal-cars. There are eight hundred or so families at Ward,
two or three in most of the houses, and eight or ten children in most of the families. And these families are just as
much prisoners, just as much at the mercy of the owners
of their dwellings as if they did live in a chicken-yard with
a high wire fence around it.

This settlement is situated in a long narrow valley
which runs back among the West Virginia hills. The walls
rise steep on either side, and the end of the hollow is a
blind alley. The Kelley's Creek Colliery Company owns
Ward, and the Paisley interests own Mammoth, another
settlement further back in the hollow, where the houses
are not even painted yellow and where the standard of
living is lower than at Ward. The people who live in these
houses mine coal from the surrounding hills. They work
from eight to twelve hours a day, and they get from $2.60
to $3 for it. They are paid not in United States currency,
but in chicken-feed specially coined by the companies—
crude aluminum coins, thin and light and some of them
with holes in the middle, like the debased French and
German currency that was issued at the end of the War.
Even Andrew Mellon, Secretary of the Treasury, who
owns one of the mines in this field, pays his men in this

imitation money. The company "scrip" is worth, on the average, about sixty cents on the dollar. The company forces the miners to trade at the company store—the only store, of course, on its property—and goods are sold there at so much higher prices than at the non-company stores only three miles away that the miners never come any nearer than sixty percent to their money's worth. The local movie houses have established two prices for admission: one for regular money and one for company scrip. Compelling the miners to trade at the commissary is very important for the company: it is actually true at the present time that some of these West Virginia coal companies which are getting no profit from their mines are making a profit on the commissaries. So if a miner has the temerity to go to an outside store and cash in his company scrip at a loss, he finds himself immediately fired.

Nor are the people who work at Ward ever able to get ahead, to save up money and try to do better elsewhere. When they are paid at the end of every fortnight, it is not for the work of that fortnight, but only for the work of the fortnight before. From this pay—say $40—the company deducts its charges—say $6 for rent, $5 for gas, $1 for electricity, $1 as contribution to a compulsory funeral fund, $3 or more as compulsory fee for hospital and medical treatment (whether they need a doctor or not). This leaves only about $24, and the bill at the company store always turns out either to equal or a little to exceed the balance. It is only very rarely that the miner manages to come out fifty or sixty cents ahead. If he does, it is likely to be shown that, during the last two weeks, he has run behind, and the fifty or sixty cents is held back to make up the deficit; or it may be that his father or his son is in debt, and the gain is transferred to the other account. If, however, the company can find no pretext for withholding the fifty or sixty cents, the miner receives it in regular currency. This is the only regular currency he ever sees. Since he is only getting paid for his work of the fortnight before the last, he is always in debt to the company and

must always be borrowing money to get through the fortnight ahead; and the money which the company advances
him is always the company's imitation money.

When times are hard, as they are at present, and the
coal business, which never does well, is doing particularly
badly, the operators cut their rates and make up the difference to themselves and their stockholders by getting more
work for less pay out of the miners. They put in mechanical cutters and loaders, and lay off as many men as they
can. According to their practice, the first to go are the men
over forty-five and the men who have been crippled in the
mines (at Andrew Mellon's mine, they never keep a man
who has been injured). And a medical examination weeds
out other classes of workmen. If it is found, for example,
that you are unable to read the bottom line of type on an
oculist's chart—as comparatively few people can—you are
likely to be eliminated. And the result is that the children
at Ward sometimes go without food for days and that they
have so little to wear that they are sometimes more or less
naked and cannot even be sent to the union for clothes.
Even at the time when their fathers were working, they
had no shoes to go to school, had hardly ever eaten fresh
meat or vegetables and had never known milk since they
were weaned from their mothers. Their dish consists of
sow belly, potatoes and pinto beans. If they had been living in certain of the other camps, they would probably already have died from drinking water polluted by the
outhouse and so escaped the pains of starvation.

About a month ago,* a hundred and fifty miners, with
their women and children, decided to appeal to the Governor. They set out to march to Charleston, more than
twenty miles away. They camped at night on the road
near a bridge on the outskirts of the city, and Governor
Conley, hearing about them—in order to avoid a scandal—came out and met them there the next morning. The
Governor received a delegation in front of a filling station,

---

* I was writing in June.

and a benevolent minister spoke for them. The minister told the Governor that the miners had had no work for weeks and now had nothing to eat. The Governor replied that he sympathized, that he had once been a miner himself—that he had even been a miner in the days when you still had to use a pick. "Whatever may be the shortcomings of our government," he said, "whatever conditions may be now, we have the best government on earth. We have eliminated all class distinctions, and any man, no matter how humble, may sometimes hold high office. It means something to live in a government like this, and your demeanor this morning shows"—the marches of striking miners had sometimes ended in shootings—"that you appreciate the advantages of our government." He went on to point out, however, that the mines were to re-open the next Monday: the company, becoming alarmed, had posted a notice to this effect after the marchers had left the camp. The miners wanted to know what they were going to live on in the meantime and how they were going to buy their powder (the miners have to pay for their own explosives), when they did start working again. The Governor then read them the Constitution and explained that it did not authorize him to do anything for them: the legislature had appropriated no funds for the purpose, and he was strictly forbidden by the law to divert funds from other purposes. He said that "the government was a business institution, and that its business had to be conducted along lines that safeguarded the interests of all citizens." "I am," he concluded in a munificent gesture, "turning over $10 of my own money to your presiding officers." The marchers went on to the courthouse, where they met with better success: the county raised some truckfuls of food.

The next Monday the mines did reopen, but not everybody was taken back. And, soon after, evictions began. Just at present, two dozen families are in process of being turned out at Ward. You can see the men from the company store dangling their legs from the back of the

company truck, as they wait for the arrival of the constable who is to see that the families go; and one finds, a little
further on, another evicted family, sitting on the ground
by the road, in the inadequate shade of a small tree—the
mother has an umbrella up—beside a pile of tables, bu-
reaus, chairs and beds which has been very carefully
stacked. They have been brought a safe distance from the
settlement so that they cannot move back into their
houses—as families have been known to do—as soon as
the constable goes, or move into the house of a neighbor.
In not only, thus, evicting its tenants but actually carrying
them away, the company, as a matter of fact, has gone beyond its rights. The road is supposed to be public—it is
supposed to belong to the county, and the company has no
authority to drive other people's furniture off. Yesterday
some of the younger men got sore and stopped the truck
and brought a load of furniture back. It belonged to a
young married man who had been one of the leaders of the
hunger march and who had been laid off and turned out
on that account.

This resistance frightened the constable: he was afraid
something worse might happen. So he had a warrant
served the next morning and arrested five of the miners,
on the charge of interfering with an officer in the performance of his duty. They were sent to the Charleston jail,
and their people are now angrier than before. Many of
them have lived here all their lives, and they are dismayed
at being treated like poultry to be casually dumped out of
their coops. They know they are human beings. They
have nailed possum-skins to their doors, trained pink and
crimson ramblers over their houses, grown gray Columbia
poplars in their yards. The women, in white slips, and
with thin bare legs, sit in swings on the porches of their
houses, like other women on hot afternoons. The girls put
on fresh pink and yellow dresses and walk along the railroad track, which runs beside the road through the hollow
and belongs to the company, too. They have learned, over
their radios, the popular songs that all the other American

girls have learned, and they amuse themselves by singing duets of "You—You're Drivin' Me Crazy!" and the ambitious "I Want to Be Bad!"

As for the men, they seem easygoing, good-humored and straightforward Southerners, so much in the old tradition of American backwoods independence that it is almost impossible to realize that they have actually been reduced to the condition of serfs. They themselves, in spite of much harsh experience, seem surprised at their position today. Some of them were Knights of Labor in the eighties of the last century, when labor had some reverberating victories. "I've lived in this hollow forty-two years," says one man, with wide serious eyes. "This country's gittin' corrupt! Under conditions, the President's agin' us and everybody!" "If it wasn't for conditions," says another—the young man who has been put out of his house—"Ward would be a right good place to live."

But they are not without leadership. Recently men who came originally from their own hollows and were trained in their strikes of ten years ago, have again become active among them. These leaders have had a good deal of difficulty in getting them organized: they are not allowed to hold meetings on the company property, and even the church is controlled by the company. So the organizers have had to go out to the blind-alley end of the hollow, where there is some land which is owned by an oil company. The oil company does not seem to care whether the coal workers organize or not. The miners have come out with enthusiasm to meet their old leaders in the midst of the oil derricks, to build bonfires and sign up for the union. Now they hold "speakin's" there every Sunday; but only in the afternoon, and, if possible—for fear of bullets from behind—with the speaker's truck backed up against something solid.

The coal miners have hailed these organizers as wrecked sailors would a ship. They are men, and the organizers are men. And the operators—who are they? They are corporations, holding companies, interests; vice-presidents, stockholders, boards of directors; a controversy with Pittsburgh, in the newspapers, over rates for freight to the Great Lakes, a franchise guaranteeing a monopoly of the Minneapolis docks; an office staff in a Charleston office building. The miners never see an operator—there is only a dubious legend that one of them once visited a mine on the occasion of a troublesome strike. But, in general, they merely send out orders from Pittsburgh or Chicago or Cleveland that wages have got to be cut, and they leave the rest to the superintendent (the superintendent at Ward is reputed to be a former detective). And since the operators have to make good with the stockholders, the superintendent tries to make good with the operators by paring down the payroll even further—if necessary, by shortweighting the men.

People hear that the operators are desperate. The coal industry is worse off than any other, because there is no future for coal as a fuel. The companies are all trying to undercut one another but, even at that, they can't sell their product. There are great mounds of coal lying around at Ward. According to the superintendent, there are now nearly 500 carloads of coal standing on the tracks unconsigned, and 400 carloads dumped on the ground. A few of the more intelligent operators want to stabilize prices and wages; but the competitive tradition is too strong for them. They keep on fighting one another and eventually going bankrupt.

Another organizer has come from New York—a young man trained at A. J. Muste's Brookwood—he holds night classes in the Negro schoolhouse—the only building which does not belong to the company. In Ward, the blacks and whites do not mix, but they live in neighboring houses, bathe side by side in the same creek, hold office together in the union and are now taking lessons in economics together. The speaker tonight is a Jewish girl from Vassar, an assistant to the Brookwood organizer, who seems to tower very tall in the low dimly gaslit room. The women sit at the desks with their babies; the men sit on the floor and stand up against the wall. The schoolchildren's cut-outs of flowers and figures make little ghosts on the windows.

The speaker explains to the miners that the reason they are now starving and being thrown out of their homes is that business is run for private profit. They are shy about answering questions, but they listen to her eagerly and with something like awe. One of the boys on a windowsill has heard a rumor that in Russia the government is run by the workin' people. The most loquacious person present is a round black Negro, who has thought the thing out with some intricacy and believes that the government "ought to be changed." At the end, the girl from Brookwood chalks up on the board the words of "Solidarity Forever" and has them sing it to the familiar tune that serves both for "John Brown's Body" and "The Battle Hymn of the Republic."

An hour ago—as I saw from the train—along the beautiful shores of the Kanawha and New Rivers, where paddlewheel steamboats still ply, the small independent farmers were hoeing their cabbage patches, while the sun brought out vivid light green on the inside bank of a bend and the shadows spread purple stains on the chocolate of the muddy water.

Here, at the end of the Southern day, a deliciously welcome coolness has welled up and filled the valley, and the darkness seems richer than daytime. Large fireflies look big as stars, floating among the mountains. And the miners, coming home from work, with their lanterns strapped to their foreheads, look rather like fireflies, too. Outside, in the summer dark, the boys are playing mandolins and singing ballads. And, at the bottom of the black valley, in the little Negro schoolhouse, the natives of the camp and the forest, not a roof or a tree of which they own and where their only condition of survival is to spend the hours of daylight grubbing in a hole in the hill, are hoping to find out from the speaker why it is they have to fight the constable, the Governor and even—as we shall see— the President for the right to work and to live.

[1932]

DETROIT MOTORS

Assembly Line

"It's not human—I could just bust when I talk about it— break the spirit of an elephant, it 'ud. I'd starve before I'd go back! They don't give ye no warnin'. Pick up your tools and get a clearance, the boss says—then they inspect your toolbox to see you're not takin' any of the company's tools—then ye report to the employment office with your time card and they give ye a clearance that says they 'cahn't use ye to further advahntage'—then ye're done. I've been laid off since last July. Sometimes they leave ye your badge, and then ye can't get a job anywhere else, be- cause if ye try to, they call up Ford's and they tell 'em ye're still on the payroll, though ye're not workin' and not gettin' a cent. Then they can say they've still got so many men on the payroll. He's a wonder at the publicity, is Ford.

"In England they do things more leisurely-like. I was an auto and tool worker in Manchester from fourteen years old. I got six shillin's a week for seven years—till the War, then I went into the Royal Air Force—but I failed in the nerve test—I was a second-clahss air mechanic durin' the War. An ahnt of mine had been in the States and had seen the pawssibilities, and when she came back, she said, 'Bert, you're wastin' your time!'—so I came over in September, '23. They're ridin' for a fall in England—they've got their back to the wall—the vital industries are bein' bled away from 'em, and they cahn't do away with the dole, but if they stop it, they've got to face the music. There's young chaps there that have grown up on the dole, and now you cahn't make 'em work—when they're given a job they get fired on purpose. The government's between the devil and the deep sea. Take the bread away from the animals and they'll bite. The way they do things in England, it's a miracle how they ever come through!

"When I first came over, I worked at Fisher Bodies for three months. I took a three-shift job on production at the start rather than be walkin' around. But then I went to Ford's—like everybody else, I'd 'eard about Ford's wages. And you do get the wages. I got $5 a day for the first two months and $6 ahfter, for a year or so—then I ahsked for a raise and got forty cents more a day for two and a hahlf years—I never saw this $7 a day. But the wages are the only redeemin' feature. If he cut wages, they'd walk out on 'im. Ye get the wages, but ye sell your soul at Ford's— ye're worked like a slave all day, and when ye get out ye're too tired to do anything—ye go to sleep on the car comin' home. But as it is, once a Ford worker, always a Ford worker. Ye get lackadaisical, as they say in Lancashire— ye haven't got the guts to go. There's people who come to Ford's from the country, thinkin' they're going to make a little money—that they'll only work there a few years and then go back and be independent. And then they stay there forever—unless they get laid off. Ye've never got any security in your job. Finally they moved us out to the Rouge—we were the first people down there—we pioneered there when the machinery wasn't hardly nailed down. But when they began gettin' ready for Model A, production shut down and we were out of a job. I'd tried to get transferred, but they laid me off. Then I 'eard they were wantin' some die-makers—I'd never worked at die-makin', but I said I'd 'ad five years at it and got a job, and I was in that department three years till I got laid off last July. I ahsked to be transferred and they laid me off. They'll lay ye off now for any reason or no reason.

"It's worse than the army, I tell ye—ye're badgered and victimized all the time. You get wise to the army after a while, but at Ford's ye never know where ye're at. One day ye can go down the aisle and the next day they'll tell ye to get the hell out of it. In one department, they'll ahsk ye why the hell ye haven't got gloves on and in another why the hell ye're wearin' them. If ye're wearin' a clean apron, they'll throw oil on it, and if a machinist takes pride in 'is tools, they'll throw 'em on the floor while he's out. The bosses are thick as treacle and they're always on your neck, because the man above is on their neck and Sorenson's on the neck of the whole lot—he's the man that pours the boiling oil down that old Henry makes. There's a man born a hundred years too late, a regular slave driver—the men tremble when they see Sorenson comin'. He used to be very brutal—he'd come through and slug the men. One day when they were movin' the plant he came through and found a man sittin' workin' on a box. 'Get up!' says Sorenson. 'Don't ye know ye can't sit down in here?' The man never moved and Sorenson kicked the box out from under 'im—and the man got up and bashed Sorenson one in the jaw. 'Go to hell!' he says. 'I don't work here—I'm workin' for the Edison Company!'

"Then ye only get fifteen minutes for lunch. The lunch wagon comes around—the ptomaine wagon, we call it. Ye pay fifteen cents for a damn big pile o' sawdust. And they let you buy some wonderful water that hasn't seen milk for a month. Sorenson owns stock in one of the lunch companies, I'm told. A man's food is in 'is neck when he starts workin'—it 'asn't got time to reach 'is stomach.

"A man checks 'is brains and 'is freedom at the door when he goes to work at Ford's. Some of those wops with their feet wet and no soles to their shoes are glad to get under a dry roof—but not for me! I'm tryin' to forget about it—it even makes me sick now every time I get on a car goin' west!"

"I wouldn't mind having my job at L——back—I quit last November to get married.

"First I worked at R——; that's the worst place of all to work. The presses are awfully close together, and there are no stools, you have to stand. There's an awful ringing in your ears from the noise of the presses, but I used to hum tunes to the rhythm—I used to hum the *Miserere.*

"But I didn't stay there long—I got a job at L——, which is a much better place to work. They made interior parts—ash-receivers and dome-light rims and escutch-eons—those are the little brass plates behind the doorknob that holds it in. You have a strip of brass and run it through the press—you step on a pedal, and the die comes down and cuts it out. We were working with small No. 4 presses and we were supposed to turn out 1,624 pieces an hour. Most of the girls couldn't make it, and if they couldn't enough times, they'd get their base rate lowered.

"For instance, if you were a dome-rim-maker, say, and couldn't do 512 pieces an hour, you'd be cut from thirty-two to twenty-eight cents. If you made a misstep on the pedal, you were liable to lose a finger—I always had some kind of a cut. When an accident happens nobody ever tells about it, and sometimes you don't know definitely till a week later—but I could always tell if something had happened as soon as I came into the room: the place always seems very clean and everybody's very quiet. Once when I was there, a girl lost her finger and gave a terrible shriek—and another time when the same thing happened to another girl, she just put a rag around her hand and quietly walked out. One day a girl got two fingers cut off, and they sent everybody home. A man in the hinge department lost three fingers once the same week. People often don't make use of the safety devices because they can work faster without them. Then your chest would get cut up from the trimmings—mine was all red. And the oil gives you an itch—your arms get itchy and you just about go crazy—they gave you some white stuff to put on it, but it didn't do any good.

"But I got so I had a certain amount of skill—I used to take satisfaction in turning out so many pieces a day, and I got to be known as a fast worker. I liked it better than the telegraph company. I liked the girls at L—— much better than the telegraph girls; the telegraph girls are always talking about the men who are going to take them out and how much money they spend on them. The girls at L—— were mostly married, and you could have a much better time with them. The telegraph girls are thin and nervous as a rule. They're always breaking down. The turnover is terribly high—it's supposed to be one hundred percent every three years. The machine that you punch out the messages on is speeded up to sixty words a minute—3,600 words an hour. No stenographer has to work that fast. And you've got the supervisor over you all the time. You have to join the company union—if you refuse, you're fired. Ever since the telephone and telegraph strike, the company has been scared of the CTU.

"I only make $75 a month now—less than at L——: I never earned less than $40 for two weeks when I was there. And they're going to put in eighty-word-a-minute machines now, it seems—they've got them in Chicago already. When we get them here, I'm going to quit.

"There was a freedom at L——; you could go in a gingham dress. And I could bully the foreman and everybody. At the telegraph company, the supervisors aren't supposed to fraternize with the girls. And I enjoyed wearing a clean cap on Fridays—on Fridays we all wore a clean cap, and I used to get a kick out of it."

"I came over from Glasgow in 1923, when I was sixteen—they pretty near had a revolution over there in 1919 after the War. My father had a barbershop—when he first came over here, he was out of work for three months—our sole piece of furniture was a trunk—we'd brought bed-

ding from the old country. My father finally went to worruk as a check-strap-maker and got $8 a day. I went to
high school—I won a couple of prizes while I was there. I
was on the debating team, and I won a prize in an oratori-
cal contest held by the Better America Federation—that's
a bunch of patriots in Los Angeles. I was on the committee on the class-day program the year that I graduated and
I had a tiff with one of the teachers: she said to me, 'James
McRae, you'll either die on the gallows or become a socialist!'

"Then I went to City College. In the meantime, I carried papers for the *Free Press*—then I checked accounts
for a news company. I also worruked in a department
store for $5 a week and as bookkeeper in a savings bank.
One summer I worruked at Packard. I was assistant treasurer at college—but we had Weisbord and Scott Nearing
come and speak under the auspices of the YMCA, and as a
result they kicked us out of it. Then we forrumed a Liberal Club and became more neurotic and radical than before. We got out a paper and we asked an organizer of the
Auto Worrukers' Union to speak before our club, and as a
result of that our club was forbidden to meet in the college. We had three sessions with the Dean, and he finally
threw us out of the office. He told me to shut up or get
kicked out. We were very nervous and hysterical at that
time. But then Forrest Bailey hearrud about it and wrote
it up in the Scripps-Howard papers, and the Dean backed
down and took me back as assistant treasurer.

"In the meantime, my father'd had an accident—he was
blown up in a shack where he was worruking and the
company fought the case. My mother tried to go to worruk at R——, but, what with the noise and the fear of losing a finger, she collapsed after two days. There are more
accidents at R—— than anywhere else—they have no
safety devices. They used to say R—— supported the
Checker cabs carrying people to the infirmary. Then
the paint room blew up out there in the spring of
'27—the paint wasn't properly stored. The papers said

there were twenty-nine killed, but there were a couple of hundred actually—lots of them were foreign-born with families in the old country, and they just said nothing about them. You couldn't get into the hospital that day for stepping over bodies from the R—— blast.

"We lost our house because we couldn't keep up the payments—then the first big lay-off came, and they've been laying off ever since. I'd worruked at the Kelsey Wheel Company—I worruked twelve hours a night on the night shift and got $30 a week. I carried rims from one section to another section on the Chevrolet line. Then I got a job at Ford's as a pushrod-grinder at $5 a day—I was raised to $6 at the end of sixty days, and when the wage raise came in, I got seven bucks—but by that time we were only worruking two days a week, so I only got $14 a week. Finally I quit—I wanted to go to Brookwood Labor College. I didn't mind factory worruk in itself—for two or three hours it used to stimulate my mind. But eight or ten hours of it deadens you—you're too tired to do much when you're through.

"I was disappointed in Brookwood. Muste asked me to be a delegate to the Conference for Progressive Labor Action, but I didn't have much faith in progressivism. I expect nothing from students and middle-class movements. When I used to go around and make speeches, I found the college audiences the worst of all.

"When I left Ford's, I was idle for three weeks, then I got a job as adding-machine operator in a bank. I stuck on by hook or by crook, till I was laid off the other day. I was laid off while I was eating lunch—they said, 'Here's your pink slip—you're a fine worruker and so forth, but we've got to cut down expenses.' Now I'm looking for worruk. I'd like to go to Russia and worruk in a factory over there, if I could raise the transportation. At one time, I thought I wanted to be a college instructor—but when I saw the colleges and the teachers and the restrictions they were under, I gave up the idea—I'd rather be free.

"What we want here is a revolutionary movement

geared into the peculiar needs of the American worrukers, and I'll say quite frankly that if it isn't the Communist Party, I don't see any other elements in the country who will supply it. The Communists have done a lot—they've practically stopped evictions. When there's an eviction about to take place, the people notify the Unemployed Council and the Communists go around and wait till the sheriff has gone and then move all the furniture back into the house. Then the landlord has to notify the authorities again, and the sheriff has to get a new warrant, and the result is that they usually never get around to evicting the people again. They've got the landlords so buffaloed that the other day a woman called up the Unemployed Council and asked whether she could put her tenants out yet. The Unemployed Council said no.

"The Communists led the Flint strike last summer. It started as a spontaneous walk-out by the trimmers and was taken up by the Auto Worrukers' Union, where the Communists were dominant. They were striking against a wage-cut of 33⅓ percent and certain foremen they didn't like and the speed-up and worruking conditions. The whole force of the state was mobilized against them. They broke up the strike meetings and the six leaders were taken out by dicks and beaten up in the woods. Finally they broke the strike by rounding up the leaders and locking them up—they couldn't get a lawyer in Flint to defend them. But the company took back the wage-cut and got rid of the foremen and granted their other demands. The union was wiped out, however. *The Auto Worrukers' News*, that had a circulation of twenty thousand, went out of existence after the strike.

"It's a weakness of the Communists just at present that they don't talk the language of the American worruker. Take the leaflets they pass out at these demonstrations— they're all stereotyped radical phrases. Your American worruker wants something concrete. I could wish, too, that they had more interest here in the discussion of their ideas. I went around one day with a book by Plekhanov on the philosophical problems of Marxism, a very illuminating book—but they wouldn't take any interest in it.

"There's a small IWW group, too—I went around there and tried to see them, but they're so suspicious that you can't get to them at all.

"What we need are democratic organs of education to educate the worrukers along Marxist lines."

The Master of the Scene

Henry Ford is, of course, a remarkable man: he is a mechanical and industrial genius. It is true that he has made few important inventions, that he has usually been a mere exploiter of principles discovered by other people; yet the boy who ran away at night against his father's orders and swam across a creek in order to fix the engine of a neighbor's threshing machine, whose hands, he says, "just itched to get hold of the throttle," who repaired his first watch with an old nail sharpened on a grindstone, who built a "farm locomotive" before he was twenty by mounting a steam engine on mowing-machine wheels—this boy exhibited already the capacity for concentration and the instinctive affinity for a medium by which one recognizes the vocation of a master. From the improvised screwdriver and the farm locomotive, Henry Ford, in spite of formidable difficulties, has gone straight to the River Rouge plant, with all its sources of raw material and its auxiliaries, that self-sufficing industrial cosmos, a masterpiece of ingenuity and efficiency. Few people in any field are capable of following their line with the intense singlemindedness of Ford; few people have a passion for their work of a kind that so completely shuts out other interests. ("I don't like to read books," says Ford. "They muss up my mind.") And it is a passion that has bred no ambition to do anything but satisfy itself. There is no evidence that Henry Ford has ever cared much about money. He has not applied himself systematically to acquiring a fortune for pleasure or show: his financial sense has been developed under the pressure of meeting emergencies. He needs money to expand his plant, and figuring in terms of the last fraction of a cent he has found to be one of the rules of the game he has set himself. This game is the direct expression of Henry Ford's personal character: to make cars which, though as homely as he is, shall be at once the cheapest, the most energetic and the most indestructible possible. When in 1921 the bankers almost had Ford on his back, he checkmated them by the unexpected and quite non-professional financial move of unloading all his stock on the dealers and making them pay him by borrowing from the banks (thus inaugurating, according to some, the era of high-pressure salesmanship).

Nor is there evidence that, except for a brief period, Henry Ford has ever cared very much about the welfare of the people who work for him. His immunity to social ambitions and to the luxuries of the rich has evidently been the result rather of an obstinate will to assert himself for what he is than of a feeling of solidarity with the common man. It has already been too difficult for Henry Ford to survive and to produce the Ford car and the River Rouge plant for him to worry about making things easy for other people, who, whatever disadvantages they may start with, can get along very well, he is certain, if they really have the stuff in them as he did. Has he not helped to create a new industry and made himself one of its masters—a boy from a Western farm, with no education or training, and in the teeth of general ridicule, merciless competition and diabolical conspiracies of bankers? Let others work as hard as he has. What right have the men in his factories to complain of the short eight hours that they are paid good money to spend there?

Yet to take good care of one's workers is a policy that saves money and that safeguards against rebellions, and a reputation for being humane is also good advertizing. In the volume called *My Life and Work*, Ford allows Samuel Crowther to write for him the following account of the establishment, at the beginning of 1914, of the eight-hour day, the six-day week and the five-dollar minimum wage. "It was to our way of thinking an act of social justice, and in the last analysis we did it for our own satisfaction of mind. There is a pleasure in feeling that you have made others happy—that you have lessened in some degree the burdens of your fellow men—that you have provided a margin out of which may be had pleasure and saving. Good will is one of the few really important assets of life. A determined man can will almost anything that he goes after, but unless, in his getting, he gains good will he has not profited much."

Here, however, is Mr. Pipp's* account: "I . . . have heard of disputes as to who was responsible for the five-dollar wage. I have put the question directly to Ford, who said he worked many a night on it and concluded that machinery was playing such an important part in production that if men could be induced to speed up the machinery, there would be more profit at the high wage than at the low wage. He figured out a plan of doubling the wage of the lowest paid men and others accordingly, the wage to apply after they had been with the company six months and complied with other conditions. As I recall the figures he gave me, they were $4.84 a day for the lowest paid man of six months' standing. He said he put the figures up to Couzens,† who said: 'Why not make it a straight five-dollar wage and it will be the greatest advertizement an automobile ever had,' or words to that effect. Couzens didn't have to say it twice to Ford. When the information came out, it was real news for the public and of high advertizing value to the company, from which Ford still benefits."

One does not need to doubt that for Ford certain genuinely benevolent emotions were released by the unusual direction which the profit motive had taken. With so

---

* E. G. Pipp, author of *Henry Ford: Both Sides of Him* (1926). [L.M.D.]
† James Couzens, an adviser to Ford. [L.M.D.]

much imagination for machinery, he is not without imagination for life. Here is a third explanation of the $5 minimum, as made by Ford to Dr. Marquis:* "I asked him why he had fixed upon $5 as the minimum pay for unskilled labor. His reply was, 'Because that is about the least a man with a family can live on in these days. We have been looking into the housing and home conditions of our employees, and we find that the skilled man is able to provide for his family, not only the necessities, but some of the luxuries of life. He is able to educate his children, to rear them in a decent home in a desirable neighborhood. But with the unskilled man it is different. He's not getting enough. He isn't getting all that's coming to him. And we must not forget that he is just as necessary to industry as the skilled man. Take the sweeper out of the shop and it would become in a short time an unfit place in which to work. We can't get along without him. And we have no right to take advantage of him because he must sell his labor in an open market. We must not pay him a wage on which he cannot possibly maintain himself and his family under proper physical and moral conditions, just because he is not in a position to demand more.'

" 'But suppose the earnings of a business are so small that it cannot afford to pay that which, in your opinion, is a living wage; what then?' I asked.

" 'Then there is something wrong with the man who is trying to run the business. He may be honest. He may mean to do the square thing. But clearly he isn't competent to conduct a business for himself, for a man who cannot make a business pay a living wage to his employees has no right to be in business. He should be working for someone who knows how to do things. On the other hand, a man who can pay a living wage and refuses to do so is simply storing up trouble for himself and others. By un-

---

* Rev. Samuel S. Marquis, author of *Henry Ford: An Interpretation* (1923). [L.M.D.]

derpaying men we are bringing on a generation of children undernourished and underdeveloped, morally as well as physically: we are breeding a generation of workingmen weak in body and in mind, and for that reason bound to prove inefficient when they come to take their places in industry. Industry will, therefore, pay the bill in the end. In my opinion it is better to pay as we go along and save the interest on the bill, to say nothing of being human in our industrial relations. For this reason we have arranged to distribute a fair portion of the profits of the company in such a way that the bulk of them will go to the man who needs them most.'"

But what actually happened was that, in spite of these benevolent intentions, between 1914 and 1927 the cost of living nearly doubled in Detroit, and although in 1919 Ford raised his minimum rate to $6, his workers were actually less well off getting $30 a week than they had been before the $5 minimum was established. In December, 1929, the rate was raised to $7. Ford announced this latter event, in a spectacular manner, at the White House, before an industrial conference called by Hoover after the first stock market crash, and it produced the usual effect of reinforcing his reputation for boldness and generosity. Yet Ford was not only giving much less employment, he was distributing much less money than formerly, and he was saving on production. In 1925, he had been employing 200,000 men at $6, an aggregate of $300,000,000, but by the fall of 1929, there were only about 145,000 men working at Ford's, who at $7 a day would get an aggregate of only $253,750,000. By December, 1929, then, when Ford was turning out more motorcars, he was employing many fewer men. This was due partly to the technological innovations which have been throwing people out of work ever since the Nottingham weavers broke their mechanical looms; but it meant also that the men still employed were considerably speeded up and that the fat bait of $7 a day made it possible for the manufacturer to recruit the quickest and most vigorous workers at the expense of the less able ones. Since the fall of 1929, the number of men employed at Ford's has shrunk from 145,000 to something like 25,000, and at the present time the plant is shut down for all but the first three days of the week.

The whole of the Ford plant seems stamped with its creator's qualities as few great industries are. You are aware of a queer combination of imaginative grandeur with cheapness, of meanness with magnificent will, of a North Western plainness and bleakness with a serviceable kind of distinction—the reflection of a personality that is itself a product of the cold winds, flat banks and monotony of those northern straits. The enormous motor plant which has overgrown the little town of Dearborn where Henry Ford was born, truly original creation though it is and wild dream though it would have seemed to the earlier inhabitants of Michigan, has in certain ways never transcended the primitive limitations of that crude and meager American life. Beside the tight River Rouge, in February mutton-jade and as dead and insignificant as ditchwater, between its willow thickets and the dry yellow grass of its banks, the office buildings of brick and concrete rise block-shaped and monstrous before us, like the monuments of some barbarian king approached after a journey in the wilderness. But the taste of this king is the same as that of the American five-and-ten-cent store, which is indulged here on a scale almost stupefying. The platitudes over the doors about industry and agriculture, though they are actually cut in stone, give the impression of common cement.

Inside, the reception rooms—in which men that look like police-court detectives check up grimly on everyone that enters—are equipped with yellow gumwood panels and window sills of white-grained black marble. The offices themselves are furnished with rubber-black white-veined linoleum and golden-oak furniture of flypaper yellow. Even the office workers and attendants at Ford's seem to present certain qualities in common, as if Ford had succeeded in developing a special human race of his own. There is a masculine type in Detroit which, though lumpish, is robust and dynamic, with the genial hard-boiled bluffness of a Chicagoan. But the subordinates at Ford's seem to run to an unappetizing pastiness and baldness, an avoidance or a disregard of any kind of smartness of dress. Some of them have sharp brown eyes, others are gooseberry-eyed; but the preference seems to be for pale keen blue eyes like Ford's, and like Ford, they part their hair in the middle. The army of "servicemen" give the impression of a last dilution of the lusterless middle-class power which dominates the workers at Ford's. Openly jeered at by these, upon whom they are set to spy, not particularly beloved by the lower white-collars, whom they are supposed to have an eye on, too, they must keep to the right side of the middle-class line, and they prowl in the plant and the offices like sallow and hollow trolls, dreaming no doubt of executive desks.

Just outside the steel-and-concrete offices of Ford's engineering laboratory stands his early-American museum. This covers an immense area, and its main entrance—a complete reproduction of Independence Hall (according to Ford, an improvement on the original because it has the advantage of a concrete foundation)—is only a single façade in a whole series of colonial reproductions, which differ but little from one another and are limited to two or three types, very much like the sedans and tudors that one sees on the double-track conveyor, as if Ford had undertaken a mass production of Independence Halls. He likes to give old-fashioned balls, reviving the schottische and the polka, on a polished hardwood floor in these laboratories. The dancers disport themselves in a space between an antique collection of lusters and girandoles and a glossy gleaming row of new car models, and the host instructs the new generation of those older pre-motor families who twenty years ago, in Detroit, were still laughing at him as an upstart and a yokel.

One approaches the plant itself through the not yet salvaged materials of ancient discarded projects: a line of croquet-wickets that traces the now extinct electrified freightline of the Detroit, Toledo and Ironton, a rusty junk-heap of still-tough steel vertebrae from old merchant-marine hulls bought by Ford from the government after the war. The water-covered thawing road lies before us a dull gray-blue, like Ford fenders beaten flat, like the eyes of Ford office workers. The buildings of the plant have a certain beauty, though still a little on the dime-store size: black-tipped silver cigarette chimneys rise above elongated factories of the dull green of pale pea soup, with large darker rows of little rectangular windows. The green cement has not been tinted, this is its natural color: it is a salvage from the blast-furnace slag. Beyond a level yellowish stretch, cinder-gritty on the hither side of tracks, where dark workmen's figures move stolidly coming or going on the afternoon shift, there looms a by-products plant, a set of black silo-shaped towers, with white smoke pouring low in front of them, and a blast furnace with silver cylinders and angular black cranes.

And there are parking-places densely packed with dingy dirt-colored Ford cars. Ford workers are said to be more or less blackmailed into buying these cars—whether they want them or can afford them or not—in instalments stopped out of their wages. When it was discovered a few years ago that a number of Ford workers had acquired cars of other makes, they were ordered to park them outside so as not to cause a scandal to the company; but then it was reported that the contraband cars were exciting the derision of the passers-by, and their owners were ordered to bring them in. It is doubtful whether any Ford worker has ever dared to buy a Chevrolet: Henry Ford—who once answered complacently, when asked what color a new model should be, "I don't care what color you make it so long as it's black!"—is being pressed hard by Chevrolet, who have succeeded in producing a six-cylinder car for a price almost as low as that of Ford's four-cylinder car and with a smartness which Ford cars lack.

At any rate, these Fords that are waiting today inside the Ford parking-yards have a dismal unalive look as if they were under discipline and dumbly enduring the shift. The market for Fords is poor, but these Fords have been driven here in order that their owners may make more of them. There are already far too many Ford cars, it would be well to cut down their numbers: future Fords should be sure of good homes; but the fate of their race was decided by a process of perpetual motion which was also supposed to accelerate. For years they brought their masters to the plant in order that the latter might earn money to buy more and more of the new cars which their life was occupied in fabricating. And now the old cars can feel it in their screws that the perpetual motion process, so far from accelerating, is rapidly running down—that even after they themselves have been scrapped and their bodies have been melted up to make crankshafts and connecting rods for new cars, those new cars may find no one to keep them. So, hitched, they wait here without hope.

For though Ford has fought the capitalist system according to his own lights, keeping out of the clutches of the bankers and refusing to issue inflated stock—standing out as best he could against all the attempts of big business to absorb or disintegrate his unique and intense personality, so inseparable from the thing it is making, he finds himself at last overwhelmed, helpless in the collapse of that system. Yet until we have succeeded, in the United States, in producing statesmen, organizers or engineers with the ability and the will to prevent the periodical impoverishment of the people who work for Ford and the wrecking of their energies in his factories, we cannot afford to be too critical of the old-fashioned self-made American so ignorant and short-sighted that he still believes that any poor boy in America can make good if he only has the gumption and, at a time when thousands of men, who have sometimes spent their last nickel to get there, are besieging his employment offices, can smugly assure the newspapers that "the average man won't really do a day's work unless he is caught and can't get out of it"—the man of genius so little dependable that he can break the careers of his closest associates with the petulance of a prima donna.

[1932]

THE JUMPING-OFF PLACE

The Coronado Beach Hotel* was built by the California millionaire John Spreckels and opened in 1887. Spreckels had made his money in Hawaiian sugar, and in 1887 the United States signed a treaty with the Hawaiian king—a treaty which guaranteed to the Americans the exclusive use of the harbor at Honolulu.

In the same year, the first vestibule train was put on the tracks by George Pullman, and the revolt of the Apaches under the formidable Geronimo, the last attempt of the Indians to assert their independence, had been put down by the government and the Apaches penned up in a reservation; the American Federation of Labor had just been founded, Kansas and Nebraska were parching with a drought, and Henry George had just run for mayor of New York and had been beaten only with difficulty by a coalition against him of the other parties; Grover Cleveland was in the middle of his first term of office and threw the capitalists into consternation by denouncing the protective tariff, and an Interstate Commerce Act designed to curb the rapacity of the railroads was in process of being

---

* The fashionable watering place in San Diego. [L.M.D.]

put through by the small businessmen and farmers; inquiries into the practices of the trusts were being got under way in Congress, while the Standard Oil Company, entering the drilling and pumping field, was already well embarked on the final stage of its progress; and Edward Bellamy had a huge and unexpected success with his socialist novel, *Looking Backward*, which prefigures an industrial utopia.

The Coronado Beach Hotel must represent the ultimate triumph of the dreams of the architects of the eighties. It is the most magnificent specimen extant of the American seaside hotel as it flourished on both coasts in that era; and it still has its real beauty as well as its immense magnificence. Snowy white and ornate as a wedding cake, clean, polished and trim as a ship, it is a monument by no means unworthy to dominate this last blue concave dent in the shoreline of the United States before it gives way to Mexico.

The bottom layer of an enormous rotunda is slit all around with long windows that remind one of those old-fashioned spinning toys that made strips of silhouettes seem to move, and surmounted, somewhat muffled, almost smothered by a sort of tremendous bonnet. This bonnet involves a red roof, a second layer of smaller windows and an elaborate broad red cone that resembles an inverted peg-top and itself includes two little rows of blinking dormer windows and an observation tower with a white railing around it, capped in turn by a red cone of its own, from which, on a tall white flagpole, flies an American flag. Behind this amusing rotunda extends the main body of the great hotel: a delirium, a lovely delirium, of superb red conical cupolas, of red roofs with white-lace crenellations, of a fine clothlike texture of shingles, of little steep flights of stairs that run up the outside of the building and little outside galleries with pillars that drip like wedding-cake icing, and of a wealth of felicitous dormers, irregular and protrusive, that seem organic like the budding of a sea-hydra. In the pavement of the principal entrance have been inlaid brass compass-points, and brass edges mark the broad white stairs which, between turned banister-rungs, lead up to the white doors of bedrooms embellished with bright brass knobs.

The whole building surrounds a large quadrangle, admirably planted and gardened. The grass is kept vivid and tender by slowly revolving sprays, and against it blooms a well-conceived harmony of the magenta and vermilion and crimson of begonia and salvia and coxcomb, bouquet-like bushes of rose-red hibiscus and immense clumps of purple bougainvillea that climbs on the stems of palms, tall-grown and carefully trimmed, in mounds of green fern or myrtle. The trees are all labeled with Latin names, as in a botanical garden. In the middle stands a low polygonal summerhouse, vine-embowered and covered with bark, inside which a boy is chalking up on a blackboard the latest stock-market quotations, while interested male guests sit and watch them in silence.

This courtyard has real dignity and brilliance. With its five tiers of white-railinged porches like decks, its long steep flights of steps like companionways, its red ladders and brass-tipped fire hose kept on hand on red-wheeled carts around corners, the slight endearing list of its warped floors and the thin wooden pillars that rise, at the bottom, from flagstones flush with the ground, it manages to suggest both an ocean liner and the portico of a colonial mansion. As you look out from one of the higher galleries at the tops of the exotic tame palms and at the little red ventilators spinning in the sun, you feel that you can still enjoy here a taste of the last luscious moment just before the power of American money, swollen with sudden growth, had turned its back altogether on the more human comforts and ornaments of the old non-mechanical world.

In the lobby, you walk as on turf across carpeting of the thickest and softest. There are wicker chairs; soft plush couches; panels of greenish-bluish tapestries on which ladies with round pulpy faces take their pleasance in Elysian boskage; sheets of stock market quotations on hooks at the head of the stairs going down to the barbershop; and a masterpiece of interior decorating, elaborate and not easily named, but combining a set of mirrors covered with yellow curlicues, yellow-varnished rows of banister-rungs and an ambitious stained-glass window representing red poinsettias.

In the spacious, round and many-windowed dining room, where yellow-shaded candles light white tables, old respectable ladies and gentlemen eat interminable American-plan meals. After dinner, they sit on couches and talk quietly or quietly play cards in the card room.

You can wander through long suites of apartments— passing from time to time through darkish in-between chambers, made unlivable by closed-up grates, glossy mahogany mantels and sometimes a pair of twin vases cold as funeral urns.

Eventually reaching the rotunda, you come upon a swarming convention of the California Federation of Business and Professional Women's Clubs. (The General Federation of Women's Clubs was organized about two years after the opening of the Coronado Beach Hotel.) The business and professional women are fussing on the outskirts of the ballroom: "I've just seen Mildred, and she hasn't done anything about the corsages yet! Do you think we ought to give them to all the officers or just to the incoming ones?" And in a conclave under hanging electric lamps in the shape of enormous coronets, they are solemnly reading aloud and debating, one by one, the amendments proposed to their innumerable by-laws.

From time to time the chambers of the vast hotel resound to a chorus of feminine voices, deliberate, schoolgirlish, insipid. They have composed an anthem of their own, to the tune of "John Brown's Body," in connection with a fund they are trying to raise:

Twenty thousand dollars by nineteen thirty-four!
Twenty thousand dollars by nineteen thirty-four!
Twenty thousand dollars by nineteen thirty-four!
    Our fund is marching on!
Glory, Glory, Hallelujah!
Glory, Glory, Hallelujah!
Glory, Glory, Hallelujah!
    Our fund is marching on!

These business and professional women are not altogether sure about what they are going to do with this money after they have succeeded in raising it; but they have arranged for a speaking contest at which a speaker from each district will be given three minutes to offer suggestions on "How can the income of $20,000 be used to the greatest advantage of the Federation?"

The new hotel at Agua Caliente across the border, where people go to see the Mexican races, has taken a good deal of the trade away from the Coronado Beach Hotel; but people still come from all over the country to San Diego across the bay.

The Americans still tend to move westward, and many drift southward toward the sun. San Diego is situated in the extreme southwestern corner of the United States; and since our real westward expansion has come to a standstill, it has become a kind of jumping-off place. On the West Coast today, the suicide rate is twice that of the Middle Atlantic coast, and the suicide rate of San Diego has become since 1911 the highest in the United States. Between January, 1911, and January, 1927, over five hundred people have killed themselves here. The population in 1930 was only about 148,000, having doubled since 1920.

For one thing, a great many sick people come to live in San Diego. The rate of illness in San Diego is twenty-four percent of the population, whereas for the population of the United States the sick rate is only six percent. The climate of Southern California, so widely advertised by Chambers of Commerce and Southern California Clubs, but probably rather unhealthy with its tepid enervating days and its nights that get suddenly chill, brings invalids to San Diego by the thousand. If they have money to move about and have failed to improve in the other health centers, the doctors, as a last resort, send them to San Diego, and it is not uncommon for patients to die just after being unloaded from the train. In the case of "ideational" diseases like asthma—diseases which are partly psychological—the sufferers have a tendency to keep moving away from places, under the illusion that they are leaving the disease behind. And when they have moved to San Diego, they find they are finally cornered, there is nowhere farther to go. According to the psychoanalysts, the idea of the setting sun suggests the idea of death. At any rate, of the five-hundred-odd suicides during the period of fifteen years mentioned above, seventy percent were put down to "despondency and depression over chronic ill health."

But there are also the individuals who do not fit in in the conventional communities from which they come and who have heard that life in San Diego is freer and more relaxed. There at last their psychological bents or their peculiar sexual tastes will be recognized, allowed some latitude. It is certain that many such people find here what they are seeking; but if they fail to, if they feel themselves too different from other people and are unable to accept life on the same terms, they may get discouraged and decide to resign. And then there are the people who are fleeing from something in their pasts they are ashamed of or something which would disgrace them in the eyes of their friends in the places where they previously lived. San Diego is not quite big enough so that the members of the middle-class groups do not all know one another and follow one another's doings with the most attentive interest. If your scandal overtakes you and breaks, your whole circle will hear about it; and if you are sensitive, you may prefer death. And then there are settlers in San Diego who are actually wanted by the law. This September the city is being searched for a gangster escaped from New York, who, in a beer-war, turned a machine-gun on some children. California has been a hideaway for gangsters in trouble elsewhere ever since Al Capone came here. And there are also the people with slender means who have been told that San Diego is cheap, but who find that it is less cheap than they thought; and the girls (married young in this part of the world) deserted by husbands or lovers; and the sailors and naval officers who have had enough of the service.

Since the Depression, the rate has increased. In 1926, there were fifty-seven suicides in San Diego. During nine months of 1930, there were seventy-one; and between the beginning of January and the end of July of 1931, there have already been thirty-six. Three of these latter are set down in the coroner's record as due to "no work or money"; two to "no work"; one to "ill health, family troubles and no work"; two to "despondency over financial worries"; one to "financial worry and illness"; one to "health and failure to collect"; and one to "rent due him from tenants." The doctors say that some of the old people who were sent out to San Diego by their relatives but whose income has been recently cut off, have been killing themselves from pride rather than go to the poorhouse.

These coroner's records in San Diego are melancholy reading, indeed. You seem to see the last futile effervescence of the burst of the American adventure. Here our people, so long told to "go West" to escape from ill health and poverty, maladjustment and industrial oppression, are discovering that, having come West, their problems and diseases remain and that the ocean bars further flight. Among the sand-colored hotels and power plants, the naval outfitters and waterside cafés, the old spread-roofed California houses with their fine grain of gray or yellow clapboards—they come to the end of their resources in the empty California sun. In San Diego, brokers and bankers, architects and citrus ranchers, farmers, housewives, building contractors, salesmen of groceries and real estate, proprietors of poolrooms and music stores, marines and supply-corps lieutenants, machinists, auto mechanics, oil-well drillers, molders, tailors, carpenters, cooks and barbers, soft-drink merchants, teamsters, stage-drivers, longshoremen, laborers—mostly Anglo-Saxon whites, though with a certain number of Danes, Swedes and Germans and a sprinkling of Chinese, Japanese, Mexicans, Negroes, Indians and Filipinos—ill, retired or down on their luck— they stuff up the cracks of their doors and quietly turn on the gas; they go into their back sheds or back kitchens and eat ant-paste or swallow Lysol; they drive their cars into dark alleys, get into the back seat and shoot themselves; they hang themselves in hotel bedrooms, take overdoses of sulphonal or barbital; they slip off to the municipal golf-links and there stab themselves with carving-knives; or they throw themselves into the bay, blue and placid, where gray battleships and cruisers guard the limits of their broad-belting nation—already reaching out in the eighties for the sugar plantations of Honolulu.

[1932]

SOVIET RUSSIA:
SCARLET FEVER IN ODESSA

I was received at the Hospital for Contagious Diseases by [a young doctor] of the modernized generation, not unlike a young American Southerner, and by a competent blond girl, one of the most beautiful I had yet seen. With expedition, I was registered by the blond girl, given a shower and a scrubbing by an old woman, neatly done up like a mummy in a blanket so that only my head stuck out, and laid out on a stretcher on the floor. Rather impressed by the good job that they seemed to have made of this and reassured by the appearance of the doctor, I was beginning to have hopes that the hospital might be one of their more up-to-date institutions. I lay there a long time on the stretcher regarding the blond girl's feet; she had thick ankles and wore no stockings, and she had unbuttoned the straps of her shoes. Then it turned out they had swathed me too soon, that I should have to burst out of my cocoon to count my money and sign receipts for my things. There were two Jewish helpers hanging around, who looked like old Weber-and-Fields comedians; they had whiskers that went all around their chins, reaching from ear to ear. At the time we were counting the money, one of them peered through the door just behind the blond girl's shoulder and, grinning, extended a clawlike hand. With one vigorous push, she slammed the door. I wound myself up in the shroud again, and the two comics carried me out. After taking me a little way, they grew weary and set me down in a courtyard. I lay looking up at the Euxine night, still, blue, starry and clear, while my bearers discussed at some length whether or not I had been given a receipt for my money. Then they carried me into a stale-smelling building with high ceilings and dirty blue-gray walls. Everybody was terribly nice and anxious to meet the emergency. A bed was set up for me in a doctor's room. When I had been put in it, I called attention to a bed-bug that was crawling on the tablecloth of the little table beside the bed. The nurse at once changed the tablecloth, but did nothing about the bug. I asked whether I could have a window open. "Certainly," said the young doctor and told the nurse to open one. "Don't you want them both open?" he asked. It was hot: I said yes. But the nurse seemed to demur. "Open the other one, too," said the doctor. Here was a man who had "culture"!

As soon as the lights were turned out, I was made unmistakably aware of the myriad teeming bed-life. They were swarming out of the pillows and the mattress. I got up and went out into the hall, and there I found two old women. They were two opposite types, but both very Russian; one was always cheerful and the other was always sad, but both had that deep resignation, that inca-pacity for being surprised. They brought in another bed, put me in it, and proceeded to treat the infested one with a roaring kerosene torch. I suggested that bugs sometimes lurked in the mattress, but they scouted this idea. In ar-ranging the new bed, the sad old woman knocked over a big wine bottle filled with gargle, which inundated the floor and had to be mopped up; and, in mopping, the cheerful one knocked over the medicine glass and broke it.

Then, when everything seemed to be set for the night, I was confronted by two more *klópy*—which was what the old woman called them—reconnoitering on the tablecloth of the night-table and evidently getting ready to drop on me. I pointed them out to the sad old woman, who immediately caught and killed them, making half-stifled grief-stricken sounds, as of one who had seen many little children die and who knew that there was nothing to be done. Then she strapped onto her foot a polisher like the one that the orderly uses in the Soviet film *Chapáev*, and began rubbing it back and forth on the floor. It was a sort of dolorous dance, evidently hard on her back. She would stop and rest, and then go on, and then, after a time, stop and rest again. I felt rather sorry for her, because she had been so sweet about everything, and I had noticed that the nurses tended to pick on her; but I should probably have felt more sorry if she had not seemed so terribly resigned. Her eyes looked as if she were always crying, or rather as if she had cried so much that they had gone dry a long time ago.

I fell asleep and went into my fever-dreams. I thought that a play I had written and had titled *A Bit of the New* was being produced at home by some serious theater group. But the producers had kept it so long that it had finally been found necessary to change the title to *Quite a Lot of the Old*. Seeing a poster in the lobby of the theater, I was suddenly seized with disgust. I resolved to go on in the second act—which took place on an old-

fashioned American porch—made up as an unknown
stranger with a derby hat, side-whiskers and a watch-
chain, and deliver a long speech bearing vitally on the plot
of the play, but unconnected with what was to follow. I
hoped that this would break up the show. I woke up—it
was morning now. Repressing hysterical laughter, I said
to myself: "I mustn't let Russia get me! That was a Russian dream!"

A figure now appeared before me, who might have been
part of the dream: a man in a straw cap, spectacles, a black
coat, a white vest and a pair of striped trousers, who carried an umbrella hooked over one arm. He was a very old
man, as I later found out; but, in spite of the gray bristles
of his shaved scalp, he did not give the impression of being
old. He had broad shoulders and dark heavy arched eyebrows. As soon as his attention was directed to me, he was
energized into extraordinary activity. First he made somebody give him a spoon and, after nervously scratching his
bristles with the handle, he thrust it down my throat and
peered in; then, nervously and heavily coughing down my
chest, he applied a stethoscope to my heart.

Then, in a deep loud theatrical voice, he told the attendants to clear out the furniture, addressing them as
"továrishchy," but in the magistral peremptory tones of
one who has always commanded. They stood, of course,
without doing anything, as Russians are likely to do when
confronted with a demand for immediate action: the room
was the doctor's office, and there was quite a lot of equipment to be removed. He ordered them again to start at
once. They reluctantly carried out a few pieces. Then the
doctor drove everybody out, and, closing the great, old,
high double doors, he first stood for a moment with his
back to them, then marched over to me in the manner of
an operatic bass about to impart a secret or vow a revenge,
and announced in thundering accents that he was putting
his office at my disposal in order that I might have a room
to myself. He then went on to declare that he would have
me well in no time, emphasizing the climax of his solo by

clapping his palms together and holding up his right hand with all five fingers extended. Then, unexpectedly, cocking his head, he lapsed into a whimsical smile that had something almost childishly appealing; and ended with a little aria, based upon the phrase "All right!", the only words of English he knew, and its Russian equivalent, "*Khoroshó.*" At last he summoned the attendants back and directed them to go on with the dismantling. This took hours: they accomplished it by stages, with long intervals between their appearances. When the old doctor made his rounds the next morning, he brought me a small volume o̲f Tennyson. It had belonged, he said, to his daughter, who knew English and was living in Paris.

I spent six weeks in that Odessa hospital. I recovered very quickly from my original attack, but had to stay on account of the quarantine; then, just as I seemed to be cured and they were going to let me out, I had a relapse and had to spend another week.

The life was pretty monotonous: it was a little like living in a monastery. At the end of a few days, they moved me out of the doctor's room into a ward with other patients; and my world was contracted to that ward, the corridor and the operating room, which they let me use at night for a study. I would read Marx and Engels during the daytime and Gibbon in the evening. An old Jewish doctor who knew some English brought me a volume of Sir Alfred Lyall's poems and a small book of selections from *Little Women*, edited for German readers. The only thing to be seen out the window was the Bacteriological Institute across the street, and one of the events of my stay was when it was repainted.

Yet it was interesting to watch day by day, from inside, the working of a Soviet institution, and I got in some ways a much clearer idea of the processes and relations of Russian life than I had been able to do in Moscow.

The hospital itself was old and dirty. It had been built about 1795—one of the oldest public buildings in

Odessa—and it seemed to have remained practically untouched. Those high-ceilinged high-windowed rooms had been harboring contagious diseases since years before the exile of Pushkin, when he had come to live in Odessa, almost ever since the days when the town had been only a Turkish fort. Odessa, which has very few factories and little value now as a port, has been neglected in the Soviet programs. There is, I understand, one fine new hospital, but efforts on the part of the Odessans to get a new contagious hospital have so far been unsuccessful; and what I saw was a bit of old Russia with very few of the cobwebs knocked off. I was subjected, for example, to treatments which I had supposed were entirely obsolete: at one time they "cupped" me daily with a set of twenty heavy brass cups which must have been a part of the original equipment, and they dosed me continually with valerian, an old-fashioned bitter drug, of which, according to the modern pharmacopoeia, the effects are "largely psychic."

There was evidently a scarlatina epidemic: the cases were coming in by the dozen—women, children and men. At one time there were three hundred cases, out of a city of half a million. One woman died while I was there. They would allow them to accumulate in the corridor, in their lazy Russian fashion, putting off as long as possible the necessity of opening another room, which would involve the displacement of furniture. Everybody, as far as I could see, got exactly the same care and the same food, and everybody was treated with kindness. The *besprizórnye,* little homeless tramps, and the children of Communist officials were put to bed just as they came, and all the rooms were crowded—though the little waifs, to be sure, had nobody to bring them toys, fruit and books, as the children of well-to-do parents did.

It was a public service, of course, and nobody paid a kopek. I was not even allowed to pay for telegrams or cables: they told me that there was money set aside for such things. The food, although greasy like all Russian food and tiresome like all hospital diet—I got terribly fed up with potatoes—was good of its kind, and there was plenty of it: the vegetables and fruit of the Ukraine. Only the milk did not seem to me what it ought to be, and they did not have any real coffee.

The hospital, as I have said, was terribly dirty. I never realized how extremely low the Russian standard of cleanliness had been till I saw the conditions which were tolerated in one of the places where sanitation was most necessary but where the new broom had not yet swept clean. The washbasin in our room, for example, though it did have running water, was used for face-washing, dish-washing, gargling and emptying urine; and I once saw one of the older doctors spit into it without bothering to turn on the faucet. The toilet had no seat and no way of fastening the door, and, though the hospital people tried to keep it in order, the patients, as is usual in Russia, generally left it in a mess. The glass panes in the door could not have been cleaned up since at least 1915, for that was the earliest date which had been scratched in the paint, or whatever it was, with which they were partly coated. When you went to take a bath, you were likely to find garbage in the bathroom (just as in Chekhov's story of a provincial hospital, "Ward Number Six," the potatoes are kept in the bathtub). I never understood why they put it there unless they used it for fuel for the stove that heated the water. The flies were frightful, and nothing was done in the way of screening the windows, except for a single piece of netting nailed over one of the windows in the doctor's room, which did not, of course, prevent the flies from entering through the other window. Nor was anything done to prevent them from breeding in the long grass outside, which was allowed to grow rank with weeds.

Periodically there was a bug crisis. The only thing they knew to do about them was to apply the torch to the iron bedsteads, and I never could convince them that bugs also lived in the cracks of the wood. Finally one day, however, a fastidious woman doctor, who always smelled of lavender water, discovered some *klópy* on the old horsehair chair in which I used to read every day, and insisted that action be taken. The sensible thing to do would have been to burn the chair, but it is hard for them to take summary measures in Russia. At first they would go only so far as to peel off the strips of ribbon that were tacked along the back and arms, and then when, a few days later, the doctor was still able to show bugs walking in and out of the cracks, they took to spraying it with something or other.

The nurses were almost entirely untrained. They were generally middle-aged women, with children and no husbands, who had been forced to earn their livings. They would make wrong entries on the temperature charts (I was once given a rise for the following day) and lose the papers out of the dossiers for the cases. One nurse smoked continual cigarettes and made the patients cough. One, whose husband had left her, frankly disliked the whole thing and paid as little attention to it as possible. One got sick at the operations. The ward, to be sure, was under-staffed: ten nurses to a hundred patients; and they had to do all the things which in our hospitals are done by order-lies. Visiting mothers and grandmothers were permitted to sleep in the ward and take care of their own children. The nurses had no control over the little boys, who kept climbing in and out of bed, went to sleep at any hour they pleased and engaged in hilarious roughhousing when they were running high temperatures. The way of handling the hospital nightgowns was typical of nurses and patients alike: I used to wonder at first why so many of the night-gowns had the strings about the neck left tied but one of them always torn off. Then I noticed that when they re-moved them, they would never go to the trouble of unty-ing the knot, but simply rip them apart. What the nurses did best was amuse the children, reading to them, telling them stories and acting out little plays. They had for themselves, the nurses, two principal sources of diversion: a shabby geranium plant, which they would water from time to time but which never flowered; and an old volume of Lérmontov's *A Hero of Our Time*, which they would read in moments of leisure, each one, apparently, taking it up where the last one had left off.

The Head Nurse was quite a different matter. She was a much more energetic and positive person, and she was also much bulkier and taller. She looked a little like the Ugly Duchess, but her expression of haughtiness or indignation would melt into tenderness or humor when the slightest appeal was made to her. She had that ready humanity of Russians which, when character backs the generous impulse, may take such heroic forms; and she worked exceedingly hard, wrestling with the hospital arrangements, seeing to it that the nurses gave the treatments on time and did not lose the records, banging the hands of the neophytes when they tried to fool with the surgical instruments and, in the moments when she had nothing else to do, reading to the children herself. One day she showed me her Communist card and told me that she had formerly done more active work, but that her heart was bad and that they had put her here where the work was not so exhausting.

In the hospital, as I gradually came to find out who were and who were not Communists, I got a much clearer notion than I had had before of the relations between the Communists and their followers, on the one hand, and the rest of the Russian community on the other. The Communists, it was plain to me in Odessa, were the people who took all the responsibility. And though I sometimes resented in Moscow the constraining and intimidating effect which their presence had on other Russians, I was grateful to them when I got into the hospital, because they seemed to be the only people who were sensible, efficient and up-to-date. If you really wanted to get anything done, you had to go to a Communist about it. I came to sympathize with their constant trials in making the other Russians get things done.

One day, for example, not long after I had come, I gave some letters to one of the nurses and asked her to mail them for me. She told me that I would have to ask the doctor, which puzzled me, as I had had letters mailed before. When the old man, the one who had received me so dramatically and who was supposed to be in charge of the ward, came in on his rounds the next morning, I told him that I wanted to mail some letters. In his resounding basso profondo, first in Russian and then in German, he tried to impress upon me, with terrible emphasis on all the grave consequences, that it was prohibited for scarlet fever patients to send letters out of the hospital: the letters would transmit the germs and the recipients would catch the disease. I became indignant at this, for I knew that they had had all my telegrams translated in order to find out what was in them, and I dreaded their devious methods of censorship. I demanded to see the director. He was a young man, a Communist, I suppose, at any rate the new type of Russian whom, despairing more or less of the older generations, they are training as fast as they can to take command of Soviet institutions. He and the older doctor discussed the situation in my presence. The director was for letting me send the letters. "But," the old man insisted, drooping but throwing out his hands, "the people who get them will catch scarlatina! *Bolshóy skandál!*" "Ilyá Petróvich," replied the director, "that's nothing but *pedantízm*. People don't get diseases from letters." And he took my mail, explaining, to save Ilyá Petróvich's face, that he would disinfect them before he mailed them. Afterwards the Head Nurse came in. "All that fuss about a few letters!" she said. "Don't you remember that you gave me some and that I mailed them the other day? You can't give people scarlet fever through your hands."

On another day, the Workers' Inspection came round. The delegation sent to the hospital turned out to be an old man and an elderly woman, who behaved very much like simple workers in any other country. The old man held his hat in his hand and was very respectful toward the nurses. The woman looked around her, eyes shining, deeply gratified that this was their hospital, that she herself had been appointed to approve it. They asked me how things were, and I told them that everything was fine. When they were gone, the Head Nurse said to me, "Why did you tell them that everything was all right? You know that plenty of things are wrong." It was plain that the Workers' Inspection would never have known for themselves whether things were wrong or right.

Ilyá Petróvich and the Communist Head Nurse used to have terrific altercations. There was one that seemed to go on all morning and to surge back and forth like a battle. Suddenly the door of our room flew open and Ilyá Petróvich burst in with the Ugly Duchess in full pursuit. He dropped down in our buggy armchair and went on protesting about something while the big woman stood over him, insisting. Neither paid the slightest attention to the people already in the room. But very soon Ilyá Petróvich sprang up again and rushed out, and the Head Nurse rushed out after him. I laughed about it to the green-eyed nurse. "What's the matter?" I asked. She took my dictionary and showed me a word which was defined as meaning "hurly-burly." "But what's it all about?" I asked. "Old!" she answered, smiling serenely. "He's seventy-five and she's fifty-five."

Not long after my conversation with this nurse in which she had talked about Russia under the Tsar, I was gazing at Ilyá Petróvich, as he stood in the doorway with his back to me. He was evidently brooding about his cases, wondering what he ought to do next or trying to remember something. His enormous shoulders were rounded, his head drooped forward on his chest, so that from behind one saw only his shoulders and the gray bristling stubble of his crown. I had always thought of his slumped-over carriage as being due to his age and his social demotion; but now I reflected that he was one of the men who *had* "had science" at the time when, as the nurse had told me, the Tsar had kept science from the people. He had been a man of science in a feudal country, where the implications of science for society were dangerous to pursue and impossible to apply; he seemed a crippled man. They had all been crippled men, even the greatest of them, the old intellectuals and technicians who had lived and worked in Russia. They had always had to keep their heads down, and their position was always ambiguous. Now, with the new regime, they were still compelled to keep them down, and they were still not always sure which side they were on. A big man with small hands, a sensitive face and an habitually bent spine, Ilyá Petróvich was typical, I suppose, of a class who had lost all and suffered much. Yet today he was devoting to these thin little children, the race of the new Russia, as much gentleness and care and solicitude as he could ever have done for the patients for whom, so many years ago, he had assumed his white vest and striped trousers. His daughter was in Paris, but he was here.

Getting out of the hospital was very curious—probably something like getting out of jail. I had been in bed for most of six weeks and had been living on a vegetarian diet, and, toward the end, when I had my relapse and the fever had taken my appetite away, I had not eaten much of that. The result was that all my senses had been rendered abnormally acute; and going out into the world again was attended by something of the painfulness of what the psychologists call the birth trauma. Having for so long had nothing to smell but the stale unvaried air of the hospital, the odor of the carpets and upholstery in the lobby of the Hotel London, which I had not even noticed when I had been there before, now tormented me almost unendurably with a blending of pleasure and distress; and when I went into the barbershop for a shave, the perfumes of the shaving-soap and toilet water and the emanations from the various bottles caused me a series of poignant sensations of a kind which I had read about in Huysmans and other *fin de siècle* literature, but had never experienced before. Later, when I went up to my room, I was obliged to steady myself to get accustomed to a new set of odors. I pulled the long curtains aside and looked out on the deserted courtyard, which in August had been an out-of-doors restaurant. The tourists who had been there were gone and the place had been dismantled for winter. The night was coming early now. There were trees that were shaking dark leaves in the darkening autumn light, and their shape and their shuddering movement both fascinated me and compelled me to turn away. Alone in the silence of the room, I suddenly dropped into a depression of a kind that I had never known all the time I was in the hospital. It was loneliness: I was missing the children and the nurses who had bothered me when I was trying to work and from whom I had looked forward to escaping. I walked back and forth across the room a few times, then began declaiming aloud some old poems of my own composition. I found that a need was relieved: my loneliness disappeared. It was the assertion of my own personality against those weeks of collective living.

[1936]

D. S. MIRSKY*

I found Mirsky, when I first went to call on him, in antique and rather shabby surroundings at the extreme other end of Moscow from the Nóvo-Moskóvskaya and the other hotels, the main shops and the government buildings. When Moscow was not brand new, it had nothing in common with anything as disciplined and

---

* A prince by birth, who had fought with the Whites in the civil wars, D. S. Mirsky had converted to Communism in exile in Great Britain, where he wrote his books. Wilson admired his *Pushkin* and his two-volume *History of Russian Literature*. Anxious to meet Mirsky, he sought him out in the Soviet Union in 1935, where Mirsky had returned under the protection of Maxim Gorky. [L.M.D.]

modern as Communism was supposed to be. Almost anything might lurk in those neglected old houses, and a good
many queer things did. I heard stories of outlandish religious cults, spiritualistic séances, dens of gangsters and
houses of prostitution. This seemed to me the kind of
quarter where such things could be expected. The address
I had took me, I found, through a dark and narrow passage
that was cluttered by a secondhand bookstall. I came out
into a cobbled court where the walls had once been
painted pink, and had to penetrate beyond that to a second
one, in which they had been painted white. I located
Mirsky's door on the stairway of one of the entrances. It
was covered—I supposed, for warmth—by what I took to
be a piece of old carpet. This muted my attempt to knock,
so I tried turning the bell, which did not seem to ring.
Though he had made an appointment with me, I decided
he had not yet come in, so went away to kill time for an
hour by visiting the Museum of the Revolution, which
was not very far away. When I returned, I worked the bell
in the other direction, and this time I heard it ring. The
door was opened, and I saw before me, standing immobile
and very erect, a tall, bearded, bald and bespectacled man
who stared at me without shaking hands. He invited me
in, however, and apologized for receiving me in his dressing gown, in which he said he always worked. In appearance, he had something of Kropótkin, something of
Edward Lear. His large and glowing brown eyes had a
pronounced Oriental slant that was particularly notice-
able in profile, and he would knit his dark bushy eyebrows, when vexed or perplexed about something, in a
way that suggested the frown of a Tsar; but his gaze was
more often quite friendly and straight. He had a high intellectual forehead, with a large brown mole on one side of
the crown. As in the case of many Russian émigrés, his
teeth were in hideous condition. He was stiff and seemed
rather shy, but I guessed that the constraint of our conversation as due to the difficulty of adapting himself to a
visitor from the outside world, and one whom he did not

know. He invited me to dinner for the following night,
and, this arranged—since our talk seemed so halting and I
supposed that he wanted to go back to his work—I got up
to take my leave; but he checked me and made me sit
down. He said he was in no hurry, inquired whether I was
in a hurry, and apologized again for his dressing gown.
There was an unmade bed in the background, and a door
stood open on a bathtub which was also made to serve as a
washstand. When I came there the next evening, he complained that the soap smelt badly. I learned later that, returning to Russia, he had insisted on only one thing: that
he should have a room of his own. He told me now that he
had been revising an old translation of Milton, and that
the speeches of God the Father were "an awful bore." A
flat and explicit atheism was a part of his Marxist stand,
and when I mentioned T. S. Eliot, whom I knew he had
known in London, he made fun of Eliot's play *The Rock*,
written to raise funds for the London churches, and of his
having said, in some connection, that family prayers were
important because they were good for the servants. I tried
talking about the Museum of the Revolution, but this
brought little response, except for his asking me whether I
was able to read "the letterpress"—and we were stalled in
one of our silences. I said that I had come by way of Leningrad, and he asked me whom I had seen there. It was always very important in the Soviet Union in those days to
know whom people had seen, since everybody had to be
identified with something—some movement or milieu or
group—other than his own individuality. I mentioned a
number of names, but he made, I think, no comment on
any of them. I told him about the accomplished young
man in Leningrad, who had spoken so highly of a poem in
which the raising of Lazarus had been invested with a
novel implication, and showed him a list of names which
this young man had written down for me when I had
asked him who were the best recent Russian poets. Mirsky
looked at the list and handed it back, announcing with a
certain sternness as he contracted his heavy eyebrows.

"Almost every one of those poets is homosexual." I knew that there had just been promulgated an edict against homosexuality, imposing severe penalties, and I resolved to destroy the list; but this again stopped the conversation. I made, however, a last effort to stimulate it by telling him about seeing in Leningrad Alexéy Tolstóy's *Peter the First.* "Ah, you saw that?" he said with some interest. "I suppose it will be done here," I ventured. "I don't think so," he answered laconically, but looked at me with a gravity that seemed just to stop short of the quizzical. He volunteered, however, no explanation; and I still do not know what the point was. Every novel, play and poem in Russia seemed to have some political significance. We were stalled again, and I left.

The next evening, when I went to dinner, I found a professional linguist, who had had his head shaved in the Soviet style, and a Jewish woman, who did translating. We had pressed caviare—cheaper than the regular kind— black bread and the little Russian cucumbers that you peel and dip in salt. (A friend who knew Mirsky in Paris has told me that he was then a gourmet, who delighted in the best restaurants.) A Russian girl who spoke French and was writing an article on "*Poètes de café,*" came in later to take tea. In the course of the conversation, Mirsky, talking of Gorky, said that he had become in the Soviet Union "*une manière de personnage,*" and, turning to the French specialist, quizzed her: "Who said that of whom?" It had been said of Voltaire by Saint-Simon: "Arouet, the son of a notary who was employed by my father and me up to the time of his death, was exiled and sent to Tulle for verses that were satirical and extremely impudent. It would not amuse me to record such a trifle were it not that this same Arouet, today, under the name of Voltaire, a great poet and academician, has become, after many tragic misadventures, a kind of personage in the republic of letters, and has even acquired a certain importance among a certain set." The allusion was characteristic of Mirsky's systematic practice of deprecating the aristocracy of birth by playing off against them the aristocracy of talent. The young woman now put a problem. She had been trying to look up something in connection with the history of the Communist Party, but the books she had so far consulted had seemed to her strangely baffling. She asked Mirsky where she could find something more satisfactory. He replied, *"Vous êtes terrible, ma petite,"* and diverted the conversation.

I began to be aware of the dislocation in Mirsky's whole intellectual life that had been caused by his conversion to Marxism. When he spoke of *The Waste Land* as a document on the decadence of capitalist society, I said that that did not prevent it from being also a very fine poem. He surprised me by answering with enthusiasm that Eliot was the greatest living poet. On another occasion, he was praising Belínsky, the early nineteenth-century critic who had written of Pushkin and Gogol in terms of their social content in so relentlessly moralistic a way, and had thus become the patron saint of the dogmatic Soviet criticism which made of every work of literature a move in the game of propaganda and tried to rule on the attitude of the author as "correct" or "incorrect." I remembered having read in Mirsky's *Pushkin* a characterization of Belínsky's Russian as "long-winded, vulgar and untidy," and the assertion that "the man who could write such insipid and vulgar journalese about Pushkin cannot be believed to have had any real understanding of literary art." When I reminded him of this, he murmured, "Ah, that was *von einem anderen Standpunkt."* I admired his way of disposing of this by stepping over into another language. When he spoke to us that evening of Mayakóvsky, I felt that he was very much pleased at believing himself to have found a thoroughly Soviet writer who satisfied his literary taste. "I've just been reading Mayakóvsky," he said, "and you know he is a really great love poet—I mean, *really* great." It was as if he were dealing with our doubts as to whether Mayakóvsky's poems of love might not be mere declamation. I have been told that Mirsky himself was always in love in the most romantic fashion, and that an unwise affair in Moscow supplied one of the pretexts for banishing him.

These people I met at his house—all remnants, it was obvious, of the old intelligentsia—admired him and came to consult him; but my friend G. believed that his life was lonely. His relations with the rest of the Soviet world could not have been at all easy. On the part of the typical intellectual of Moscow, he inspired, I think, a mixture of jealousy, annoyance and awe. His learning and his information were enormous, exact and wide-ranging. He had nothing of the dilettante: his reading had been systematic; nor had he anything, on the other hand, of the academic scholar, who specializes minutely in a single field. He wrote effectively in English and French; and his unusual historical range, when he had once got the hang of the Marxist method, enabled him to make novel interpretations. He was conspicuous, also, in public, not merely, as my friend G. was, by his being so much taller than the people on the street that he towered above them like Gulliver among the Lilliputians, but also by reason of his British clothes: Oxonian gray flannel trousers, a jacket that did not match, and a flat English cap with a visor—all shabby to the point of trampishness. I have told about the Black Hundreds Cossack who pursued and abused him in public—denouncing him as a renegade aristocrat; and on another occasion a man that Mirsky said he had never seen came over and spoke to him in a restaurant. Dining out with him was always liable to queer or uncomfortable incidents.

On the other hand, even people who had something in common with Mirsky could not afford to know him. I had once heard an intelligent Englishwoman married to a commissar make fun of him as "Comrade Prince." He had been famous for his arrogance and his irascibility among his own social world, and I used to shudder to think of the effort of self-restraint that his relations with his Soviet colleagues must cost him, and of the consequences when it inevitably broke down. My relations with him at first were a little uneven, because, not being involved as he was, in spite of my then Soviet sympathies, I would tend to base my conversation on our common love of literature, and he would have to pull himself up by remembering his new orientation. He was not naturally a pedantic or fanatical man, and the wobblings, the abrupt shifts of mood, that were apt to result from this had sometimes their comic side. His wavering over the cognac [on a previous occasion] was characteristic of him, as was his giving money to beggars, which was not considered correct. He usually started out by maintaining his attitude with a certain rigidity and tartness, but I soon found that he would readily relax under the influence of a bottle of Caucasian wine followed by several cognacs, begin quoting favorite poems—he seemed to know yards of poetry in half a dozen languages; and on one occasion, for some reason I cannot remember, he sang the Greek national anthem. He would offset the bristling and slanteyed mask that recalled the Muscovite Tsars by a giggle that suggested Edward Lear and was not always the proper accompaniment for the conventional Communist sneer. Or Kropótkin would come to the fore, and, warmed by the good cheer (of which he did not get much: he was not, and made a point of not being, a member of the privileged groups), his dark eyes would melt and glow with an emotional sensibility and idealism that had something quite guileless and touching. On the subject of the United States, at that time much admired in Russia, he combined the condescension of the official line toward a bankrupt capitalist society with an anti-Americanism which had evidently been stimulated by his residence in England. He had once done a lecture tour in Canada and the United States, and was equipped with the usual anecdotes about the impossible people one met there. Once I described to him my state of mind when I had made a prolonged sojourn in Italy: my surfeit with the furniture of the past, my restlessness at feeling that the big parade was going by in another street;

and he told me that he had never felt like that in the least, that such a reaction was possible only for an American tourist—an inappropriate attitude, I thought, for one who was under the impression that he had just proved the insufficiency of two or three centuries of Western art, and was ready to kick them downstairs. In the course of our evening at the Sokólniki Gardens, I became a little nettled by this attitude. I had asked him whether I could send him any books when I was back in the United States, and he replied without enthusiasm that he would be glad to have the Beards' *The Rise of American Civilization* and Vachel Lindsay's collected poems, adding scrupulously, with an accent of Soviet disdain, "Those are the only American books that interest me." A little later, when we were sitting on a bench and well out of earshot of anyone, he asked me what the Ford plant in Dearborn was like. I replied that it was a whole domain in itself, completely walled off from the rest of Detroit; that one could only gain admittance with difficulty, and that, once one was inside, one became aware of being checked on at every point; that the workers could never escape from the demands of industrial discipline, and that they were spied upon every moment. "In fact," I concluded, "it's rather like here." He was silent for a little while, then got up from the bench and said, "Shall we be moving?" In spite of some provocation, I at once regretted this dig, for, though I was quite free to criticize my country, he was not so to criticize his.

One day I attended a meeting especially held for the enlightenment of a delegation of American schoolteachers. Mirsky, who was usually produced when fluent English was needed, was there on the platform to answer their questions. One woman wanted to know whether modern writers like Joyce didn't have a bad influence. "I'd say," he equivocated, "that a book like *Ulysses* could only have been produced by a perfectly putrid society." He came over to me after the meeting and asked what I had thought of his answer. Feeling that he was rather ashamed of it, I told him, non-committally, that the question had been stupid. "But it had to be answered," he said. I did not know then that *Ulysses* was, for Mirsky, a delicate subject. There was actually a good deal of interest in Joyce— *Ulysses* was being translated (in a curiously literal word-by-word way), and coming out in one of the literary magazines, and there had just been a controversy about it. I learn from Mr. Gleb Struve's book *Soviet Russian Literature* that Mirsky had written, two years before, some articles condemning the influence of Joyce, and that one of the writers he had criticized, a playwright named Vsévolod Vishnévsky (later, in 1949, the winner of a Stalin prize for a drama that glorified Stalin as a hero of the Civil Wars) had vigorously defended himself on the grounds that *Ulysses* constituted "a perfectly outspoken portrayal of men in the capitalistic era," and that Eisenstein had known Joyce in Paris and learned from him some of his methods. The discussion reached such a pitch that it had to be adjudicated by Rádek at the Congress of Soviet Writers which took place the following year. He— so soon to be liquidated himself—declared on this occasion that "Joyce stands on the other side of the barricades ... Our road lies not through Joyce, but along the highway of Socialist realism." This justified Mirsky, no doubt, but at that moment he was taking a beating over his criticism of a novel by Alexander Fadéyev. Though Mirsky, Mr. Struve informs us, had written "from the ultra-left standpoint and shown himself *plus royaliste que le roi même*," he was given an indignant blast by the "proletarian" critics, who declared that an ex-White Guardist had no right to find fault with a Communist writer, and he was henceforth excluded from the *Literary Gazette* till Gorky came to his rescue in January, 1935, declaring that "everybody knew" that Fadéyev's novel was bad, and that Mirsky should not be disqualified for having been, through no fault of his, born a prince. The attack on him had been renewed with a certain official sanction, since an article denouncing him was published simultaneously in both *Izvestia* and *Pravda*. This had happened not long before I saw him, but Mirsky still had Gorky's backing.

I did not find him at home one day when I called at his flat to return some books, and did not see him for weeks. At last, just before I left Moscow, he turned up at my own apartment, having walked the whole distance across the city. We dined at the Nóvo-Moskóvskaya. He was quite frank in falling in with a proposal that, rather than sit down for a drink in the new Moskóvskaya bar which was advertising *koktéyli*, where we should have had people close around us, we go up to the outskirts of the dining room—that this would "perhaps be more to the point" was Mirsky's way of putting it—where we could have our drinks in relative privacy. He explained that he had been out of Moscow: they had sent him out somewhere beyond Tashként, a journey of many days, traveling "hard" all the time, so that he had had to sit up for nights. I had already had the impression that he was purposely given hackwork, and I suspected now that this mission had been meant to humiliate him. But, if so, it had affected him in the opposite way. I had never seen him so stimulated and cheerful. To get away from Moscow on his own must in itself have been a great relief. "You know, there are place-names out there," he told me, with the relish of the traveler discovering unexpected things, "that have no vowels at all—they consist of just three or four consonants!" He had been lecturing to the local officials about Russian literature—"rather elderly men, you know—very much interested, they're very keen to learn." Instead of proving a hardship and bore, the trip was the kind of thing he was ready and glad to do, for it gave him the satisfaction of feeling that he was performing, at the cost of inconvenience, a service to the national culture and a service to the new Russia. After dinner, when I suggested a second cognac, he answered, *"Je ne dis que non."* When he left, I told him I was going away and thanked him for all his kindness. "No kindness on my part!" he answered, with a beaming benevolent glow.

That was the end of July. Struve says that Mirsky was arrested "in the summer of 1935"—if this is true, it must have been in August—and that he was released a few months later, but forced to live outside Moscow. I have been told, however, by Mr. E. H. Carr, the historian and biographer, that he saw Mirsky once on a visit to Russia which took place sometime after my visit. Though he and Mirsky had been formerly on very good terms, he found now, he said, that Mirsky could no longer talk to him when other people were present, and it had been only by stopping in the men's room together that they had been able to exchange a few words. And a Russian friend of Mirsky's, Mrs. Vera Traill, has written me as follows: "I arrived in Moscow in August, 1936, and saw Dim nearly every day. He was arrested in the very first days of June, 1937. (I think it was on the third.) He had never been arrested before. Though he might have been through some kind of interrogation—I cannot vouch for that." This final disappearance, then, took place during the purges of 1937. Gorky, reputedly murdered, had died a year before in June, 1936, and Mirsky had been left at the mercy of the sycophants and jailors of Stalin. The pressure of mediocrity, of avid inferiority, cannot be overestimated in any field; but in the department of literature, it is likely to be particularly rampant. The arts of music and painting, the discipline of learned subjects, the technical domain of the sciences, require a minimum of training; but anyone who can read and write—and even the partly illiterate—are at liberty to occupy themselves with literature. In a dictatorship, this is fatal, for the hacks can then rule the roost. Maxim Gorky had been doing his best to prevent the ascendancy of the second-rate, but when he died, he left the literary world to the type of vindictive journalist who, elsewhere as well as in Russia, attached themselves to the

Communist movement and beside whom the Salieri who murders Mozart in Pushkin's terrible little play is a man of respectable talent. The aristocracy of letters was going by the board as well as the old nobility. Not, of course, that one needed this animus to account for the suppression of Mirsky at the time of Stalin's gigantic purges. In any case, I do not like to think of Mirsky opening his door in his spectacles and dressing gown, and being dragged from his pressed caviare and bad-smelling soap, from those almost Dostoevskian lodgings, in which he had had momentarily the illusion that he was serving Russia in lecturing to provincial officials and revising a translation of *Paradise Lost*.

There were at first various rumors as to what had become of him—that he was confined in a monastery and allowed to do nothing but translating, that he was editing a local paper in a remote Siberian town. Since nothing certain was heard, it was assumed, as time went on, that he was dead; and this supposition has been confirmed by a letter (dated May 1, 1952) written to one of Mirsky's friends by a Russian D.P. in Europe. I here translate this document, which has never been published before. It is obviously not written by a person of very much education, and I have had to straighten out some bad grammar.

Gracious Lady
Much-esteemed —— ——,
    Most willingly and with sorrowful heartfelt pain, I am complying with your request. I had unfortunately few meetings with Prince Svyátopolk-Mirsky—the dates are rather uncertain, since everything then was rather confused—we felt like flies in autumn.
    Like many other political prisoners, I was sent, at the end of September, 1937, from the Ussurískaya Taigá to a transit camp on our way to the city of Vladivostók. Two or three days after my arrival there—on October 3, 1937—there arrived in that transit camp a detachment of prisoners from Moscow, who had been condemned under the political

statutes. In this transit camp were concentrated political prisoners to be sent to Kolymá. About a hundred and fifty had been assigned to our barracks, "brandnew" prisoners from the Moscow detachment. Finding myself in the same barracks with them, I made the acquaintance of Zhénya, the son of Professor Alexander Alexándrovich Florénsky, who in time made me acquainted with the people in his section, among whom was Dr. Svyátopolk-Mirsky. They were interested, on our first meeting, when they learned that I had already done about a year in the camp, whereas they had only arrived from Gigorkhána. He questioned me about the conditions of life, the food and the work in the concentration camps. Then Zhénya, the son of Professor Florénsky, told me about each of the people in his section. And from him I learned that Prince Svyátopolk-Mirsky had been in England and that he had been persuaded by Maxim Gorky to return to the U.S.S.R., that the Prince had worked at the Academy of Sciences in the Literary Division. He was arrested in 1937 in I do not remember what month and condemned without a hearing, not in court but at a special council of a special N.K.V.D. *troíka,* to ten years' imprisonment. We had arrived in Vladivostók by October 27, 1937, and during those three weeks we were in the same barracks. At the time of our conversations, the Prince was not very communicative, but he did not refrain from expressing his opinion on the subject of Maxim Gorky. He said that Maxim Gorky ought to be removed if he had planned to spread such a mass terror through the whole country, and that he could not be an indifferent observer of this bloody despotism.*

On October 27, 1937, four hundred and fifty men, as well as four hundred women, were loaded on the steamer *Kuku,* and on November 4, 1937, we arrived at the town of Magadán, four kilometers from the Bay of Nagáev, in the [name illegible] Point No.

---

* There is clearly something wrong here. The writer must have reported Mirsky incorrectly. The latter can hardly have imagined that Gorky was responsible for the purges.

I. There I landed in another barracks; we met seldom, and I only rarely dropped in on their barracks. On November 16 or 17, they were sent to the "Five Year Plan" gold field, but I to the "Unexpected" gold field. The winter of 1937–38 was terrible for the prisoners in Kolymá. In some of the camps, up to 75 percent perished.*

In 1938, in the month of December, after getting my feet frozen, I was sent as an invalid to the invalid camp, which was twenty-three kilometers from the town of Magadán, where I met some of the people from the Moscow group, and they told me that Prince Svyátopolk-Mirsky was then in that camp in the hospital barracks. He was violently insane. I several times asked for permission to go to the hospital barracks, but this was always refused. At the end of several weeks, I was notified by the orderly that Prince Svyátopolk-Mirsky was dead. I suppose that this was at the end of January, 1939—the exact date I do not remember.

Out of this group of prisoners only Florénsky's son Zhénya survived. A. A. Florénsky himself had died a long time before D. Svyátopolk-Mirsky's death at the "Five Year Plan" gold field at the beginning of 1938.

This is all, much-esteemed —— ——, that I know about the sad story of Prince Svyátopolk-Mirsky.

Accept the assurances of my perfect respect.

[1956]

---

* Kolymá in northeast Siberia is almost uninhabitable. The rivers are frozen up for eight or nine months of the year, and the polar night lasts from six to ten weeks. In a snow-storm the natives will not venture out without a rope tied to the izbá, since it is possible to be buried in the snow and die a few yards from one's own doorstep. It was the decision of Nicholas II that conditions in Kolymá were too severe for human beings to be made to live there. Stalin had no such scruples.

THE PARTNERSHIP OF MARX AND ENGELS

Early in 1844 there came under [the young Marx's] eye an essay which Engels had written from England for the *Deutsch-Französische Jahrbücher,* to which Karl Marx was also contributing. It was an original and brilliant discussion of the "political economy" of the British, which Engels on his side had been reading up. Engels held that the theories of Adam Smith and Ricardo, of MacCulloch and James Mill, were fundamentally hypocritical rationalizations of the greedy motives behind the system of private property which was destroying the British peoples: the Wealth of Nations made most people poor; Free Trade and Competition left the people still enslaved, and consolidated the monopoly of the bourgeoisie on everything that was worth having—all the philosophies of trade themselves only sanctified the huckster's fraud; the discussions of abstract value were kept abstract on purpose to avoid taking cognizance of the actual conditions under which all commercial transactions took place: the exploitation and destruction of the working class, the alternation of prosperity with crisis. Marx at once began to correspond with Engels, and he set himself to master as much of the British economists as he could find translated into French.

Engels arrived back from Lancashire about the end of August and stopped in Paris on his way home to Barmen. He immediately looked up Marx, and they found that they had so much to say to one another that they spent ten days together. Their literary as well as their intellectual collaboration began from that first moment of their meeting. They had been working toward similar conclusions, and now they were able to supplement one another. Like the copper and zinc electrodes of the voltaic cell of which they used to debate the mystery—the conductor liquid would be Hegel diluted in the political atmosphere of the eve of 1848—the two young Germans between them were able to generate a current that was to give energy to new social motors. The setting-up of this Marxist current is the central event of our chronicle and one of the great intellectual events of the century; and even this electrical image is inadequate to render the organic vitality with which the Marx-Engels system in its growth was able to absorb such a variety of elements—the philosophies of three great countries, the ideas of both the working class and the cultured, the fruits of many departments of thought. Marx and Engels performed the feat of all great thinkers in summing up immense accumulations of knowledge, in combining many streams of speculation, and in endowing a new point of view with more vivid and compelling life.

It would not be worth while here to attempt to trace in detail the influence of all the thinkers that Marx and Engels laid under contribution. In a sense, such attempts are futile. The spotlighting method that I have used in this book must not be allowed to mislead the reader into assuming that great ideas are the creations of a special race of great men. I have discussed some of the conspicuous figures who gave currency to socialist ideas; and Professor Sidney Hook in his admirable *From Hegel to Marx* has indicated with exactitude the relation of Marx to his background of German philosophy. But behind these conspicuous figures were certainly sources less well known or quite obscure: all the agitators, the politicians, the newspaper writers; the pamphlets, the conversations, the intimations; the implications of conduct deriving from inarticulate or half-unconscious thoughts, the implications of unthinking instincts.

It is appropriate, nevertheless, to point this out at this particular moment, because it was precisely the conception of intellectual movements as representative of social situations which Marx and Engels were to do so much to implant; and it may be interesting to fill in a little more completely the background of early nineteenth-century thought out of which Marx and Engels grew as well as to understand the relation of these two thinkers to one another.

The great thing that Marx and Engels and their contemporaries had gotten out of the philosophy of Hegel was the conception of historical change. Hegel had delivered his lectures on the *Philosophy of History* at Berlin University during the winter of 1822–23 (Michelet, it may be remembered, had first come in contact with Vico the next year); and, for all his abstract and mystical way of talking, he had shown a very firm grasp on the idea that the great revolutionary figures of history were not simply remarkable individuals, who moved mountains by their single wills, but the agents through which the forces of the societies behind them accomplished their unconscious purposes. Julius Caesar, says Hegel, for example, did of course fight and conquer his rivals, and destroy the constitution of Rome in order to win his own position of supremacy, but what gave him his importance for the world was the fact that he was performing the necessary feat— only possible through autocratic control—of unifying the Roman Empire.

"It was not then merely his private gain but an unconscious impulse," writes Hegel, "that occasioned the accomplishment of that for which the time was ripe. Such are all great historical men—whose own particular aims involve those large issues which are the will of the World-Spirit. They may be called Heroes, inasmuch as they have derived their purposes and their vocation, not from the calm, regular course of things, sanctioned by the existing order; but from a concealed fount—one which has not attained to phenomenal, present existence—from that inner Spirit, still hidden beneath the surface, which, impinging on the outer world as on a shell, bursts it in pieces, because it is another kernel than that which belonged to the shell in question. They present themselves, therefore, as men who appear to draw the impulse of their life from themselves; and whose deeds have produced a condition of things and a complex of historical relations which appear to be only *their* interest, and *their* work.

"Such individuals have had no consciousness of the general Idea they were unfolding, while prosecuting those aims of theirs; on the contrary, they were practical, political men. But at the same time they were thinking men, who had an insight into the requirements of the time— *what was ripe for development.* This was the very Truth for their age, for their world; the species next in order, so to speak, and which was already formed in the womb of time. It was theirs to know this nascent principle; the necessary, directly sequent step in progress, which their world was to take; to make this their aim, and to expend their energy in promoting it. World-historical men—the Heroes of an epoch—must, therefore, be recognized as its clear-sighted ones; *their* deeds, *their* words are the best of that time. Great men have formed their purposes to satisfy themselves, not others. Whatever prudent designs and counsels they might have learned from others, would be the more limited and inconsistent features in their career; for it was they who best understood affairs; it was they from whom *others* learned and approved—or at least acquiesced in—their policy. For that Spirit which had taken this fresh step in history is the inmost soul of all individuals; but abides in a state of unconsciousness from which the great men in question aroused it. Their fellows, therefore, follow these soul-leaders; for they feel the irresistible power of their own inner spirit thus embodied."

In the December of 1843, Marx had written for the *Deutsch-Französische Jahrbücher* a *Critique of the Hegelian Philosophy of Law,* in which he had postulated the proletariat as the class which was to play the new Hegelian role in effecting the emancipation of Germany: "A class in *radical chains,* one of the classes of bourgeois society which does not belong to bourgeois society, an order which brings the break-up of all orders, a sphere which has a universal character by virtue of its universal suffering and lays claim to no *particular right*, because no *particular wrong*, but complete wrong, is being perpetrated against it, which can no longer invoke an *historical* title but only a *human* title, which stands not in a one-sided antagonism to the consequences of the German state but in an absolute antagonism to its assumptions, a sphere, finally, which cannot emancipate itself without freeing itself from all the other spheres of society and thereby freeing all these other spheres themselves, which in a word, as it represents the *complete forfeiting* of humanity itself, can only redeem itself through the *redemption of the whole of humanity.* The *proletariat* represents the dissolution of society as a special order."

Yet even though Marx has got so far, the proletariat remains for him still something in the nature of a philosophical abstraction. The primary emotional motivation in the role which he assigns to the proletariat seems to have been borrowed from his own position as a Jew. "The social emancipation of the Jew is the emancipation of society from Judaism"; "a sphere, finally, which cannot emancipate itself without emancipating all the other spheres in society"—these are the conclusions in almost identical words of two essays written one after the other and published, as it were, side by side. Marx, on the one hand, knew nothing of the industrial proletariat and, on the other hand, refused to take Judaism seriously or to participate in current discussions of the Jewish problem from the point of view of the special case of Jewish culture, holding that the special position of the Jew was vitally involved with his money-lending and banking, and that it would be impossible for him to dissociate himself from these until the system of which they were part should be abolished. The result was that the animus and rebellion which were due to the social disabilities of the Jew as well as the moral insight and the world vision which were derived from his religious tradition were transferred in all their formidable power to an imaginary proletariat.

Perhaps the most important service that Engels performed for Marx at this period was to fill in the blank face and figure of Marx's abstract proletarian and to place him in a real house and real factory. Engels had brought back from England the materials for his book on *The Condition of the Working Class in England in 1844*, and he now sat down at once to get it written. Here was the social background which would make Marx's vision authentic; and here were cycles of industrial prosperity which always collapsed into industrial depressions—due, as Engels could see, to the blind appetites of the competing manufacturers—and which could only result in a general crash: that millennial catastrophe that for Marx was ultimately to dethrone the gods and set the wise spirit of man in their place.

And for Engels, on his side, here in Marx was the backing of moral conviction and of intellectual strength which was to enable him to keep his compass straight in his relation to that contemporary society whose crimes he understood so well, but out of which he himself had grown, and to which he was still organically bound as Marx was not. Besides, Marx had more weight and more will. Engels wrote with lucidity and ease; he had sensibility and measure and humor. He is so much more like a French writer of the Enlightenment—something between a Condorcet and a Diderot—than a philosopher of the German school that one is inclined to accept the tradition that his family had French Protestant blood. This young man without academic training was an immensely accomplished fellow: he had already learned to write English so well that he was able to contribute to Robert Owen's paper; and his French was as good as his English. He had a facility in acquiring information and a journalist's sense of how things were going; his collaborator Marx used to say that Engels was always ahead of him. But Engels had not Marx's drive; it is what we miss in his writing. From the beginning Marx is able to find such quarrel in matters like the wood-theft debates that he can shake us with indignation against all violators of human relations; while Engels, with his larger experience of the cruelties and degradations of industrial life, does not—even in *The Condition of the Working Class in England*—rouse us to protest or to fight but tends rather to resolve the conflict in an optimistic feeling about the outcome. "Marx was a genius," wrote Engels later. "The rest of us were talented at best."

It is perhaps not indulging too far the current tendency toward this kind of speculation to suggest that Marx took over for Engels something of the prestige of paternal authority which the younger man had rejected in his own father. There was always something boyish about Engels: he writes Marx in the September of 1847, when he is twenty-seven, that he does not want to accept the vice-presidency of one of their communist committees, because he looks "so frightfully youthful." Young Friedrich had been rebelling since his teens against old Caspar Engels's combination of the serious crassness of business with the intolerance of religion; but old Engels's decisions for his son had hitherto determined his practical career. And, in spite of Friedrich's final enfranchisement from theology, some of the fervor of his father's faith had nevertheless been communicated to him. He had grown up in Elberfeld-Barmen under the pulpit of the great Calvinist preacher Friedrich Wilhelm Krummacher, who with an eloquence that Engels had found impressive had used to alternate the legends of the Bible and a majestic oratory drawn from its language with illustrations from ordinary life and who had harrowed and subdued his congregations with the terrible Calvinist logic which led them either to damnation or grace. Karl Marx was a great moralist, too, and, on occasion, a formidable preacher. He seems to have provided the young apostate from Pietism with a new spiritual center of gravity.

The discovery of economic motivation had equipped Marx and Engels with an instrument which was to enable them to write a new kind of history as with a biting pyrographic needle.

They were entering upon a phase of their lives in which they were to suffer a relative political eclipse; and now, in their journalism, their pamphlets, their books, and in that extraordinary correspondence which plays for the nineteenth century a role somewhat similar to that of those of Voltaire and the Encyclopaedists for the eighteenth, they were to apply their new method of analysis to the events of the past and the present. Karl Marx inaugurated this work with a product of his mature genius at its most brilliant, the study called *The Class Struggles in France* (*1848–50*), written in London during the first year of his exile and printed in a magazine called *Revue der Neuen Rheinischen Zeitung,* which he and Engels published and wrote. It was followed in 1852 by *The Eighteenth Brumaire of Louis Bonaparte,* dealing with the *coup d'état* of December, 1851; and later, in 1871, by *The Civil War in France,* which analyzed the episode of the Commune.

This whole series, which aims at a profounder interpretation and is sustained on a higher level of expression than the run of Marx's newspaper commentary, is in fact one of the great cardinal productions of the modern art-science of history.

Let us look back again at the French historians who have been serving as our point of reference in situating the positions of Marxism. It is obvious that these men were perplexed by the confused and complex series of changes which had been taking place in France during their time and in the course of which republic, monarchy, proletarian uprising and empire had been alternating, existing simultaneously, exchanging one another's masks. Now Marx knocks away the masks, and he provides a chart of the currents that have been running below the surface of French politics—a chart which has thrown overboard completely the traditional revolutionary language made up of general slogans and abstract concepts and which has been worked out exclusively in terms of the propulsions deriving from such interests as the bread and wine wrung by the peasants out of their tight little plots of land, and as

the Parisian security and luxury obtainable through speculation in office. In Michelet's work of this period, it is, to
be sure, becoming possible for him to see that what, for
example, had been at the bottom of the imbroglio in the
industrial city of Lyons in 1793, when the Convention had
played the game of the rich against Joseph Chalier, the
revolutionary leader, had been the struggle between the
exploited and the exploiters; but this, as he says, he has
learned from the socialists, and he fails to follow the clue.

But now Marx, in *The Eighteenth Brumaire*, never relinquishing this economic thread, is able to penetrate all
the pageantry of Legitimists and Orleanists and Bona-
partists and Republicans and Party of Order, and to show
what had really happened in France after the abdication of
Louis-Philippe: The great industrials, the great landlords
and the financiers had combined against the small bourgeoisie and the workers; all the political parties had found
themselves frustrated in their efforts to achieve their ends
through the medium of parliamentary government; and it
had then been possible for Louis Bonaparte to take over,
not through sheer force of Napoleonic magic, but through
the support of a class of farm-holding peasants, who had
not been able to organize politically but who wanted a
father-protector to stand between them and the bourgeoisie—together with the interested backing of a group of
professional bureaucrats, created by the centralization of
the government. For a moment, says Marx, Louis Bonaparte will be able to hold all groups in equilibrium; but as
it will be impossible for him to do anything for one group
without discriminating somehow against the others, he
will in time arouse them all against him. And in the
meantime, the so-called democrats, who had been trying
to unite in a Social Democratic Party the socialist working
class with the republican petty bourgeoisie, had, although
they had "arrogated to themselves a position of superiority to class conflicts," been defeated between bourgeoisie
and workers, as a result of their inability to rise above the
intellectual limitations of the petty bourgeoisie and to do

as Marx himself is doing here: grasp the class interests actually involved. Never, after we have read *The Eighteenth Brumaire,* can the language, the conventions, the combinations, the pretensions, of parliamentary bodies, if we have had any illusions about them, seem the same to us again. They lose their consistency and color—evaporate before our eyes. The old sport of competition for office, the old game of political debate, look foolish and obsolete, for now we can see for the first time through the shadow-play to the conflict of appetites and needs which, partly unknown to the actors themselves, throw these thin silhouettes on the screen.

These writings of Marx are electrical. Nowhere perhaps in the history of thought is the reader so made to feel the excitement of a new intellectual discovery. Marx is here at his most vivid and his most vigorous—in the closeness and the exactitude of political observation; in the energy of the faculty that combines, articulating at the same time that it compresses; in the wit and the metaphorical phantasmagoria that transfigures the prosaic phenomena of politics, and in the pulse of the tragic invective—we have heard its echo in Bernard Shaw—which can turn the collapse of an incompetent parliament, divided between contradictory tendencies, into the downfall of a damned soul of Shakespeare.

Marx, when he first came to England, had taken furnished lodgings for his family in the fashionable suburb of Camberwell; but they were evicted in the spring of 1850 for inability to pay the rent, and had resorted to a poor street in Soho. There the whole family lived in two small dark unventilated rooms: there were six of them now, with the children, and with the maid, Helene Demuth, called Lenchen, whom Jenny's mother had given her as a wedding present and who, though they rarely had the money to pay her, was to stay with them to the end of their lives. The boy that Jenny had borne a few days after coming to England died in this place that November. They had been turned out while she was still nursing the baby; and she has left a vivid record of the incident in a letter to the wife of a comrade.

"I shall describe to you a day of this life just as it is, and you will see that perhaps few other refugees have gone through anything like it. Since wet-nurses are here much too expensive for us, I decided, in spite of continual and terrible pains in my breasts and back, to nurse the child myself. But the poor little angel drank in from me so much secret sorrow and grief with the milk that he was constantly unwell, lay in violent pain night and day. He has not slept a single night since he came into the world—two or three hours at most. Now lately he has been having violent cramps, so that the poor child is always hovering between life and death. In this pain he used to suck so hard that my nipple got sore and bled; often the blood would stream into his little quivering mouth. As I was sitting like this one day, our landlady suddenly appeared. We have paid her in the course of the winter over two hundred and fifty thalers, and we had made an arrangement with her that in future we were not to pay her but the landlord, who had put in an execution. Now she denied this agreement and demanded five pounds, which we still owed her; and as we were unable to produce this sum at once, two bailiffs entered the house, took possession of all my little belongings: beds, linen, clothes, everything, even my poor baby's cradle, and the best of the toys that belonged to the little girls, who were standing by in bitter tears. They threatened to take everything away in two hours' time—in which case I should have had to lie flat on the floor with my freezing children and my sore breast. Our friend Schramm hurried to town to get help. He got into a cab, and the horses bolted. He jumped out and was brought bleeding into the house, where I was in misery with my poor shivering children.

"The next day we had to leave the house. It was cold and rainy and dreary. My husband tried to find a place for us to live, but no one was willing to have us when we

mentioned the four children. At last a friend came to our
rescue, we paid, and I quickly sold all my beds, in order to
settle with the chemist, the baker, the butcher and the
milkman, who had been alarmed by the scandal of the
bailiffs' arrival and who had come wildly to present their
bills. The beds which I had sold were taken out of doors
and loaded onto a cart—and do you know what happened
then? It was long after sunset by this time, and it is illegal
in England to move furniture so late. The landlord produced the police and said that there might be some of his
things among them, we might be escaping to a foreign
country. In less than five minutes, there were two or three
hundred people standing in front of our door, the whole
Chelsea mob. The beds came back again—they could not
be delivered to the purchasers till after sunrise the next
day. . . ."

She apologizes for talking so much about her troubles,
but says that she feels the need of pouring out her heart
for once to a friend. "Don't imagine that these petty sufferings have bent me. I know only too well that our struggle is no isolated one, and that I in particular belong to the
specially fortunate and favored, for my dear husband, the
mainstay of my life, is still by my side. The only thing
that really crushes me and makes my heart bleed is that he
is obliged to endure so much pettiness, that there should
be so few to come to his aid, and that he who has so willingly and gladly come to the aid of so many, should find
himself so helpless here."

They were to remain in Dean Street, Soho, six years.
As Jenny said, few would help her husband; and it turned
out, as time went on, that he would not do much to help
himself. And now we must confront a curious fact. Karl
Marx was neurotic about money. It was one of the most
striking "contradictions" of Marx's whole career that the
man who had done more than any other to call attention to
economic motivation should have been incapable of doing
anything for gain. For difficult though it may have been
for an émigré to find regular work, it can hardly have been

impossible. Liebknecht, Willich and Kossuth managed to support themselves in London. Yet on only one recorded occasion during the whole of Marx's thirty years' stay did he attempt to find regular employment.

This resistance to the idea of earning a livelihood may, at least partly, have been due to an impulse to lean over backwards in order to forestall the imputation of commercialism which was always being brought against the Jews. Certainly the animus of those of his writings which are sometimes characterized as anti-Semitic is mainly directed against the Jew as moneychanger or as truckler to bourgeois society. Take the passage in *Herr Vogt*, for example, in which he so remorselessly rubs it in that a certain newspaper editor in London has taken to spelling his name "Levy" instead of "Levi" and made a practice of publishing attacks on Disraeli, in order to be accepted as an Englishman, and elaborates with more stridency than taste on the salience of Levy's nose and its uses in sniffing the sewers of gossip. The point is that this man—who has libeled Marx—is a toady and a purveyor of scandal. And Marx's charge against another Jew, who has been profiteering out of the Second Empire, is that he has "augmented the nine Greek muses with a tenth Hebraic muse, the 'Muse of the Age,' which is what he calls the Stock Exchange." If Marx is contemptuous of his race, it is primarily perhaps with the anger of Moses at finding the Children of Israel dancing before the Golden Calf.

In any case, there is no question at all that Marx's antipathy to writing for money was bound up with an almost maniacal idealism. "The writer," he had insisted in his youth in the article already quoted, "must earn money in order to be able to live and write, but he must by no means live and write for the purpose of making money. . . . The writer in no wise considers his works a means. They are *ends in themselves*; so little are they a means either for himself or for others that, if necessary, he sacrifices *his own* existence to *their* existence and, in his own way, like the preacher of religion, takes for his principle, 'Obey God rather than man,' in relation to those human beings among whom he himself is confined by his human desires and needs." This was written, of course, before Marx had developed his Dialectical Materialism; but he was to act on this principle all his life. "I must follow my goal through thick and thin," he writes in a letter of 1859, "and I shall not allow bourgeois society to turn me into a money-making machine." Note Marx's curious language: the writer is "confined" (*"eingeschlossen"*) among men. Instinctively Marx thinks of himself as a being set above their world.

Yet he *is* confined in this world by his "human needs and desires"; and if he will not allow himself to be turned into a money-making machine, somebody else will have to turn himself into one in order to make money for him.

Engels had written in *The Peasant War in Germany* of the ascetism indispensable to proletarian movements both in the Middle Ages and modern times: "This ascetic austerity of behavior, this insistence on the renunciation of all the amenities and pleasures of life, on the one hand sets up in contrast to the ruling classes the principle of Spartan equality, and on the other hand constitutes a necessary transitional stage, without which the lowest stratum of society would never be able to launch a movement. In order to develop their revolutionary energy, in order to feel clearly their hostile position in relation to all the other elements of society, in order to concentrate themselves as a class, they must begin by stripping themselves of everything that could reconcile them to the existing social order, must deny themselves even the smallest enjoyment which could make their oppressed position tolerable for a moment and of which even the severest pressure cannot deprive them." Karl Marx, as the proletariat's Münzer, exemplified something of the sort; and Engels had made a resolute effort to dissociate himself from his bourgeois origins. But the miseries of the Marxes in London weighed upon Engels's mind. From almost the beginning of the Marx-Engels correspondence, when Engels writes to his friend about hunting for a lodging for him in Ostend, with details about the *déjeuners* and cigars, and gives him specific instructions about trains in a tone which suggests that Marx could not be depended upon to catch them, there is apparent a sort of loving solicitude in which the protector is combined with the disciple; and now, by the autumn of 1850, that terrible year for the Marxes, Engels has decided that there is nothing for it but to return to the "filthy trade" against which he had so rebelled in Barmen. After all, the revolution had been adjourned; and Marx had to have the leisure to accomplish his own work.

One of the most striking features of all [the] commentary of Marx and Engels, if we return to it after the journalism and the political "theses" of the later phases of Marxism, is precisely its flexibility, its readiness to take account of new facts. Though the mainspring of the Dialectic was conceived as a very simple mechanism, the day-by-day phenomena of society were regarded by Marx and Engels as infinitely varied and complex. If they were mystical about the goal, they were realistic about the means of getting there. Certain assumptions—we shall examine them later—they had carried over from the more idealistic era of the *Communist Manifesto;* but these never blocked their realization that their hypothesis must fit actual facts. There are many respects in which Marx and Engels may be contrasted with the crude pedants and fanatics who have pretended to speak for the movement which Marx and Engels started; but none is more obvious than the honesty of these innovators in recognizing and respecting events and their willingness to learn from experience.

With this went an omnivorous interest in all kinds of intellectual activity and an appreciation of the work of others. This last may not seem easily reconcilable with the tendency we have noticed in Marx to split off from and to shut out other thinkers or with his habitual tone of scornful superiority and the earnest imitation of it by Engels.

There are many passages in the Marx-Engels correspondence in which these two masters, who, like Dante (much quoted for such utterances by Marx), have decided to make a party by themselves, seem perversely, even insanely, determined to grant no merit to the ideas of anyone else. Yet it is as if this relentless exclusion of others were an indispensable condition for preserving their own sharply-angled point of view. It is as if they had developed their special cutting comic tone, their detached and implacable attitude, their personal polyglot language ("Apropos! Einige Portwein und Claret wird mir sehr wohl tun under present circumstances"; "Die verfluchte vestry hat mich bon gré mal gré zum 'constable of the vestry of St. Pancras' erwählt") in proportion as they have come to realize that they can take in more and more of the world, that they can comprehend it better and better, while other men, vulgarly addicted to the conviviality of political rhetoric, have never caught the sense of history at all, have no idea what is happening about them. Inside that reciprocal relationship, limited to the interchange of two men, all is clarity, coolness, intellectual exhilaration, self-confidence. The secret conspiracy and the practical joke conceal a watch-tower and a laboratory.

And here, in the general field of thought, if not always in that of practical politics, Marx and Engels are candidly alert for anything in science or literature that can help them to understand man and society. The timid man who seizes a formula because he wants above everything certainty, the snob who accepts a doctrine because it will make him feel superior to his fellows, the second-rate man who is looking for an excuse that will allow him to disparage the first-rate—all these have an interest in ruling out, in discrediting, in ridiculing, in slandering; and the truculence of Marx and Engels, which has come down as a part of the tradition, is the only part of their equipment they can imitate. But to the real pioneers of the frontiers of thought, to those who have accepted the responsibility for directing the ideas of mankind, to supply the right answer to every problem is far from appearing so easy. Such pioneers are painfully aware how little men already know, how few human beings can be counted on even to try to find out anything new, to construct a fresh picture of experience. Though Marx and Engels trusted the Dialectic, they did not believe it would do everything for them without initiative or research on their part nor did they imagine that it relieved them of the necessity of acquainting themselves with the ideas of other men. Hypercritical and harsh though Marx is in his strictures on such competitors as Proudhon, his sense of intellectual reality did compel him to do them justice—though it must be admitted that he was likely, as in the cases of Lassalle and Ernest Jones, to wait until after they were dead; and he was punctilious to the point of pedantry in making acknowledgments not merely to such predecessors as Ricardo and Adam Smith, but even to the author of an anonymous pamphlet published in 1740, in which he had found the first suggestion of the Labor Theory of Value.

Also, the Marxism of the founders themselves never developed into that further phase, where it was to be felt by the noblest of those working-class leaders who had accepted Dialectical Materialism, that all their thought should be strictly functional—that is, agitational and strategic; that they must turn their backs on non-political interests, not because these were lacking in value but because they were irrelevant to what had to be done. The tradition of the Renaissance still hung about Marx and Engels: they had only partly emerged from its matrix. They wanted to act on the course of history, but they also loved learning for its own sake—or perhaps it would be more correct to say that they believed that learning gave power; and for all the intensity of Marx's desire to defeat the antagonist in the class struggle, he declared that his favorite maxim was *"Nihil humanum alienum puto"*; and he and Engels approached the past with a respect that had nothing in common with the impulse which, justified on Marxist grounds, figured in one phase of the Russian Revolution and which was imitated by Marxists in other countries: the impulse to make a clean slate of culture.

Engels's championship of the Humanities in *Anti-Dühring* might indeed be cordially approved by any defender of the "Liberal Arts" education. "The people's school of the future" projected by Herr Dühring, says Engels, is to be "merely a somewhat 'ennobled' Prussian grammar school in which Greek and Latin are replaced by a little more pure and applied Mathematics and in particular by the elements of the philosophy of reality, and the teaching of German brought back to Becker, that is, to about a Third Form level." Dühring "wants to do away with the two levers that in the world as it is today give at least the opportunity of rising above the narrow national standpoint: knowledge of the ancient languages, which opens a wider common horizon at least to those who have had a classical education; and knowledge of modern languages, through the medium of which alone the people of different nations can make themselves understood by one another and acquaint themselves with what is happening beyond their own frontiers." "As for the aesthetic side of education, Herr Dühring will have to fashion it all anew. The poetry of the past is worthless. Where all religion is prohibited, it goes without saying that the 'mythological or other religious trimmings' characteristic of poets in the past cannot be tolerated in this school. 'Poetic mysticism,' too, 'such as, for example, Goethe practised so extensively' is to be condemned. Well, Herr Dühring will have to make up his mind to produce for us those poetic masterpieces which 'are in accord with the higher claims of an imagination reconciled to reason,' and which represent the pure ideal that 'denotes the perfection of the world.' Let him lose no time about it! The conquest of the world will be achieved by the economic commune [proposed by Herr Dühring] only on that day when the latter, reconciled with reason, comes in at double time in Alexandrines."

And Marx and Engels had always before them—something which the later Marxists have sometimes quite lost sight of—the ideal man of the Renaissance of the type of Leonardo or Machiavelli, who had a head for both the sciences and the arts, who was both thinker and man of action. It was, in fact, one of their chief objections to the stratified industrial society that it specialized people in occupations in such a way as to make it impossible for them to develop more than a single aptitude; and it was one of their great arguments for Communism that it would produce "complete" men again. They themselves had shied desperately away from the pundits of idealist Germany, whom they regarded as just as fatally deformed through a specialization in intellectual activity as the proletarian who worked in the factory through his concentration on mechanical operations; and they desired themselves, insofar as it was possible, to lead the lives of "complete" men. Something of the kind Engels certainly achieved, with his business, his conviviality, his sport, his languages, his natural sciences, his economics, his military studies, his article-writing, his books, his drawings and verses, and his politics; and what Marx lacked in practical ability and athletic skill he made up for by the immense range of his mind. It is true that the work of Marx himself, merging into and almost swamping that of Engels, had to become, under the pressure of the age, more exclusively economic; that the effects of the advance of machinery, which we have noted in the methods of Taine, are seen also in the later phases of Marxism, where it grows grimmer, more technical, more abstract. But there is still in Marx and Engels to the end that sense of a rich and various world, that comprehension of the many kinds of mastery possible for human beings, all interesting and all good in their kinds.

Engels's visits to London were always great events for the Marxes. Karl would become so much excited the day he was expecting his friend that he would be unable to do any work; and he and Engels would sit up all night, smoking and drinking and talking. But the life of the Marxes in England continued to be dismal and hard.

Marx had characteristically neglected to talk terms when he had been invited to write for *The* [New York] *Tribune,* and was taken aback when he learned that he was to get only five dollars an article. He supplied Dana with sixty articles during the first year that he was writing them himself. Dana liked them so well that he began running the best parts of them as leaders and leaving the remains to appear over Marx's name. Marx protested, but the best he could do was to get Dana to run the whole article anonymously in this way. Marx found himself reduced to two articles a week; and then—when the war was over and the boom of the early fifties collapsing, so that *The Tribune* began to retrench—to one; though Dana tried to make up for this by offering Marx supplementary work for *The American Encyclopaedia* and certain American magazines. In any case, Marx found that his income had now been cut down by two-thirds.

There is extant an apparently veracious account of the Marx household at the time when they were living in Soho, by a police agent who got to see them in 1853:

"[Marx] lives in one of the worst, therefore one of the cheapest neighborhoods in London. He occupies two rooms. The room looking out on the street is the parlor, and the bedroom is at the back. There is not one clean or decent piece of furniture in either room, but everything is broken, tattered and torn, with thick dust over everything and the greatest untidiness everywhere. In the middle of the parlor there is a large old-fashioned table covered with oilcloth. On it there are manuscripts, books and newspapers, as well as the children's toys, odds and ends from his wife's sewing-basket, cups with broken rims, dirty spoons, knives and forks, lamps, an ink-pot, tumblers, some Dutch clay-pipes, tobacco ashes—all in a pile on the same table.

"When you go into Marx's room, smoke and tobacco

fumes make your eyes water to such an extent that for the first moment you seem to be groping about in a cavern, until you get used to it and manage to pick out certain objects in the haze. Everything is dirty and covered with dust, and sitting down is quite a dangerous business. Here is a chair with only three legs, then another, which happens to be whole, on which the children are playing at cooking. That is the one that is offered to the visitor, but the children's cooking is not removed, and if you sit down, you risk a pair of trousers. But all these things do not in the least embarrass Marx or his wife. You are received in the most friendly way and cordially offered pipes, tobacco and whatever else there may happen to be. Eventually a clever and interesting conversation arises which makes amends for all the domestic deficiencies, so that you find the discomfort bearable. You actually get used to the company, and find it interesting and original."

Sometimes they lived on bread and potatoes for days. Once when the baker had given them notice and asked for Marx when he brought the bread, the little boy, then seven and a half, had saved the situation by answering, "No, he ain't upstairs," and grabbing the bread and rushing off to deliver it to his father. They pawned everything at one time or another, including the children's shoes and Marx's coat—which prevented them from going out of doors. Jenny's family silver went to the pawnshop piece by piece. On one occasion, the pawnbroker, seeing the crest of the Duke of Argyll, sent for the police and had Marx locked up. It was Saturday night, and his respectable friends had all gone out of town for the weekend, so that he had to stay in jail till Monday morning. Sometimes Jenny would cry all night, and Karl would lose his temper; he was trying to write his book on economics.

The neighborhood was full of infections. They survived a cholera epidemic; but one winter they all had grippe at the same time. "My wife is sick. Jennychen is sick," Marx wrote Engels in the fall of '52. "Lenchen has a sort of nervous fever. I can't and haven't been able to call the doctor, because I haven't any money for medicine." Marx was visited with piles and boils, which made it impossible for him to sit down and prevented his frequenting the library. In the March of 1851 another little girl was born, but she died of bronchitis a year later. She had never had a cradle, and Jenny had to go to a French refugee to borrow two pounds for a coffin: *"Quoique de dure complexion,"* Marx wrote Engels on this occasion, *"griff mich diesmal die Scheisse bedeutend an."* In January, 1855, another girl was born; but in April the surviving boy died. Liebknecht says that he had "magnificent eyes and a promising head, which was, however, much too heavy for his body"; and he had shown signs of inheriting his father's brilliance; it was he who had outwitted the baker. But he was delicate, and they had no way of taking care of him. Marx was more affected by the death of this boy than by that of any of his other children. "The house seems deserted and empty," he writes Engels, "since the death of the child who was its living soul. It is impossible to describe how much we constantly miss him. I have suffered all sorts of bad luck, but now I know for the first time what a genuine misfortune is. I feel myself broken down [the last phrase is in English in the original].... Among all the frightful miseries that I've been through in these last days, the thought of you and your friendship has always kept me up, and the hope that we still have something useful to accomplish in the world together." Two years later Jenny gave birth to a still-born child under circumstances so painful that Karl tells Engels he cannot bring himself to write about them.

Jenny does not seem to have been a very good housekeeper; the strong-minded Lenchen ran the household. But she had much humor: her daughter Eleanor remembered her mother and father as always laughing together; and she brought to her unexpected role a dignity and loyalty that endured. To the orphan Wilhelm Liebknecht, still in his twenties, another socialist refugee from Germany, she appeared "now Iphigenia, softening and educating the barbarian, now Eleonore, giving peace to one who is slipping and doubts himself. She was mother, friend, confidante, counselor. She was and she remains for me still my ideal of what a woman should be. ... If I did not go under in London, body and soul, I owe it in a great measure to her, who, at the time when I thought I should be drowned in fighting the heavy sea of exile, appeared to me like Leucothea to the ship-wrecked Odysseus and gave me the courage to swim."

The police agent who has been quoted above said that Marx "as a husband and father, in spite of his wild and restless character, was the gentlest and mildest of men"; and everybody else bears him out. With his family Karl Marx was a patriarch, and where he dominated, he was able to love. He always turned off his cynical jokes and his bad language when there were women or children present; and if anybody said anything off-color, he would become nervous and even blush. He liked to play games with his children and is said to have written several of the biting pages of *The Eighteenth Brumaire of Louis Bonaparte* while they were sitting behind him playing horse, and whipping him to giddap. He used to tell them a long continued story about an imaginary character named Hans Röckle, who kept an enchanting toy-shop but who never had money in his pocket. He had men and women, dwarfs and giants, kings and queens, masters and journeymen, birds and four-footed beasts, as many as there were in Noah's Ark, tables and chairs, boxes and carriages, big and little, and all made out of wood. But in spite of the fact that he was a magician, he had debts to the butcher and the Devil, which he was never able to pay, and so he was forced to his great distress to sell all his beautiful things piece by piece to the Devil. And yet, after many adventures, some frightening and some funny, every one of them came back to him again.

Liebknecht, who called on the Marxes almost every day, gives a very genial picture of the family. They had Sunday outings on Hampstead Heath, with bread and cheese and beer and roast veal, which they carried along in a basket. The children were crazy for green things, and once they found some hyacinths in a corner of a field which had No Trespass signs but which they had had the temerity to invade. The walk home would be very gay: they would sing popular nigger songs and—"I assure you it's true," says Liebknecht—patriotic songs of the fatherland, such as *"O Strassburg, O Strassburg, Du Wunderschöne Stadt,"* which had been one of the pieces that Karl had copied out in a collection of folk-songs from different lands which he had made, when he was a student, for Jenny; and Marx would recite *Faust* and *The Divine Comedy,* and he and Jenny would take turns at Shakespeare, which they had learned so to love from her father. They made it a rule on these occasions that nobody was to talk about politics or to complain about the miseries of exile.

Sometimes little Jenny, who had the black eyes and big forehead of her father, would burst out in what Liebknecht describes as a "prophetic Pythian rapture." On one of these walks one day she seemed to go into a trance and improvised a kind of poem about another life on the stars. Her mother became worried, and her father gave her a scolding and made her stop.

Karl Marx's great book *Das Kapital* is a unique and complex work, which demands a different kind of analysis from that which it usually gets. At the time when Marx was working on the first volume, he wrote Engels (July 31, 1865) that whatever the shortcomings of his writings might be, they had "the merit of making an artistic whole"; and in his next letter to Engels (August 5) he speaks of the book as a " 'work of art,' " and mentions "artistic considerations" in connection with his delay in getting it finished. Certainly there went into the creation of *Das Kapital* as much of art as of science. The book is a welding-together of several quite diverse points of view, of several quite distinct techniques of thought. It contains a treatise on economics, a history of industrial development and an inspired tract for the times; and the morality, which is part of the time suspended in the interests of scientific objectivity, is no more self-consistent than the economics is consistently scientific or the history undistracted by the exaltation of apocalyptic vision. And outside the whole immense structure, dark and strong like the old Trier basilica, built by the Romans with brick walls and granite columns, swim the mists and the septentrional lights of German metaphysics and mysticism, always ready to leak in through the crevices.

But it is after all the poet in Marx who makes of all these things a whole—that same poet who had already shown his strength in the verses he had written as a student but whose equipment had not been appropriate to the art of romantic verse. Marx's subject is now human history; and that bleak inhuman side of his mind which disconcerts us in his earlier writings has been filled in with mathematics and logic. But it is the power of imagination as well as the cogency of argument which makes *Das Kapital* so compelling.

Let us, then, before we go behind *Das Kapital*, take into account the tremendous effect which it produces on us the first time we read it.

It is characteristic of Marx's work in general that there is more of the Hegelian interplay between opposites than of the Hegelian progression from the lower to the higher about his use of the dialectical method. His writings tend to lack formal development; we find it hard to get hold of a beginning or an end. But this is less true of the first volume of *Das Kapital*, as Marx finally got it into shape, than perhaps of any other of his productions. Once we have worked through the abstractions of the opening, the book has the momentum of an epic.

It is a vision which fascinates and appals us, which strikes us with a kind of awe, this evolution of mechanical production and of the magnetic accumulation of capital, rising out of the feudal world, with its more primitive but more human handicrafts; wrecking it and overspreading it; accelerating, reorganizing, reassembling, in ever more ingenious complexity, ever more formidable proportions; breaking out of the old boundaries of nations; sending out the tracks and cranes of its commerce across countries and oceans and continents and bringing the people of distant cultures, at diverse stages of civilization, into its system, as it lays hold on the destinies of races, knocks new shapes out of their bodies and their minds, their personalities and their aspirations, without their really grasping what has happened to them and independently of any individual's will. Yet all this development is not merely technological; it is not actually the result of the operation on humanity of a remorseless non-human force. There is also a human principle at work—"those passions which are," as Marx says, "at once the most violent, the basest and the most abominable of which the human breast is capable: the furies of personal interest." For another element of Marx's genius is a peculiar psychological insight: no one has ever had so deadly a sense of the infinite capacity of human nature for remaining oblivious or indifferent to the pains we inflict on others when we have a chance to get something out of them for ourselves.

In dealing with this theme, Karl Marx became one of the great masters of satire. Marx is certainly the greatest ironist since Swift, and he has a good deal in common with him. Compare the logic of Swift's "modest proposal" for curing the misery of Ireland by inducing the starving people to eat their surplus babies with the argument in defense of crime which Marx urges on the bourgeois philosophers (in the so-called fourth volume of *Das Kapital*): crime, he suggests, is produced by the criminal just as "the philosopher produces ideas, the poet verses, the professor manuals," and practising it is useful to society because it takes care of the superfluous population at the same time that putting it down gives employment to many worthy citizens.

Marx has furthermore in common with Swift that he is

able to get a certain poetry out of money. There is in Swift a kind of intellectual appetite for computations and accounts and a feeling almost sensuous for currency. In the *Drapier's Letters*, for example, we seem to see the coins, hear them, finger them. But with Marx the idea of money leads to something more philosophic. We have seen how, in writing of the wood-theft laws, he had personified the trees on the landowner's estate as higher beings to which the peasants had to be sacrificed. Now— improving on Sir Thomas More, who, at an earlier stage of capitalist development, at the time when the great estates were being depopulated and turned into sheep-runs, had said that the sheep were eating the people—Marx presents us with a picture of a world in which the commodities command the human beings.

These commodities have their own laws of movement; they seem to revolve in their orbits like electrons. Thus they keep the machinery moving, and they keep the people tending the machines. And the greatest of the commodities is money, because it represents all the others. Marx shows us the metal counters and the bank-notes, mere conventions for facilitating exchange, taking on the fetishistic character which is to make them appear ends in themselves, possessed of a value of their own, then acquiring a potency of their own, which seems to substitute itself for human potency. Marx had stated the whole theme in a sentence of an English speech of 1856: "All our invention and progress seem to result in endowing material forces with intellectual life, and in stultifying human life into a material force." Mankind is caught helpless in a web of wages and profits and credit. Marx's readiness to conjure up these visions of independent and unpetitionable fetishes, which, though inanimate, usurp the rights of the living, is evidently primarily derived from his own deficiency in personal feeling, which he projected into the outside world. Like other great satirists, he punished in others the faults he felt to be dangerous in himself; and it was precisely this blinded and paralyzed side of Karl

Marx's peculiar personality which had made it possible for the active and perceptive side to grasp and to explain and to excoriate, as no one else had been able to do, that negation of personal relations, of the responsibility of man to man, that abstract and half-unconscious cruelty, which had afflicted the life of the age.

Marx, to be sure, loves his abstractions, too; he elaborates them at inordinate length. A good deal of this part of *Das Kapital* is gratuitous and simply for show; and one's interest in it is naturally proportionate to one's capacity for enjoying exercises in pure logic. Marx's method does possess a certain beauty: it enables him, as Mehring has said, to make distinctions infinitely subtle—though, if one looks at it the other way round, he may appear to be almost perversely turning concrete industrial processes into the elusive definitions of metaphysics. (Engels used to complain that it was difficult to recognize the historical processes behind the steps of the dialectical argument.) But the chief value of these abstract chapters which alternate with the chapters of history is—in the first volume, at any rate—an ironic one. It is a great trick of Marx's first to hypnotize us by the shuttling back and forth of his syllogisms, to elevate us to the contemplation of what appear to be metaphysical laws; and then, by dropping a single phrase, to sting us back to the realization that these pure economic principles that lend themselves to such elegant demonstration are derived simply from the laws of human selfishness, and that if they may be assumed to operate with such sureness, it is only because the acquisitive instinct is as unfailing as the force of gravitation. The meaning of the impersonal-looking formulas which Marx produces with so scientific an air is, he reminds us from time to time as if casually, pennies withheld from the worker's pocket, sweat squeezed out of his body, and natural enjoyments denied his soul. In competing with the pundits of economics, Marx has written something in the nature of a parody; and, once we have read *Das Kapital*, the conventional works on economics never seem the same to us again: we can always see through their arguments and figures the realities of the crude human relations which it is their purpose or effect to mask.

For in Marx the exposition of the theory—the dance of commodities, the cross-stitch of logic—is always followed by a documented picture of the capitalist laws at work; and these chapters, with their piling-up of factory reports, their prosaic descriptions of misery and filth, their remorseless enumeration of the abnormal conditions to which the men and women and children of the working class have had to try to adjust themselves, their chronicle of the sordid expedients by which the employers had almost invariably won back, minute by minute and penny by penny, the profits that legislation, itself always inadequate and belated, had tried to shave down a little, and with their specimens of the complacent appeals to morality, religion and reason by which the employers and their economist apologists had had the hypocrisy to justify their practice—these at last become almost intolerable. We feel that we have been taken for the first time through the real structure of our civilization, and that it is the ugliest that has ever existed—a state of things where there is very little to choose between the physical degradation of the workers and the moral degradation of the masters.

From time to time, with telling effect, Marx will light up for a moment the memory of other societies which have been fired by other ideals. The disgrace of the institution of slavery on which the Greek system had been founded had at least, in debasing one set of persons, made possible the development of an aristocracy of marvelous taste and many-sided accomplishment, whereas the masses of the people in the industrial world had been enslaved to no more impressive purpose than "to transform a few vulgar and half-educated upstarts into 'eminent cotton spinners,' 'extensive sausage makers' and 'influential blacking dealers.' " The feudal system of the Middle Ages, before it had been thrown into disorder by the rebellion of the nobles against the king, had at least guaranteed certain rights in return for the discharge of certain duties. Everybody had in some sense been somebody; whereas when the industrial depression occurred and the mill closed its door on the factory worker, neither his employer nor the State was responsible for him. Where the baron had blown in his plunder in such a way as to give his dependents a good time, the great new virtue of the bourgeois was thrift, the saving of money in order to reinvest it. And though Marx has always kept our nose so close to the counting-house and the spindle and the steam hammer and the scutching-mill and the clay-pit and the mine, he always carries with him through the caverns and wastes of the modern industrial world, cold as those abysses of the sea which the mariner of his ballad spurned as godless, the commands of that "eternal God" who equips him with his undeviating standard for judging earthly things.

Something like this is our first impression of *Das Kapital.* It is only later, when we come to think about it coolly and after some further acquaintance with Marx's writings, that its basic inconsistencies become plain.

The most obvious of these is the discrepancy between the scientific point of view of the historian and the moral point of view of the prophet. "What astonished me most in Marx," writes the Russian sociologist Maxím Kovalévsky, "was his passionate partisanship in political questions, which did not jibe with the calm objective method which he recommended to his disciples and which was supposed to be intended as an instrument for investigating economic principles." And H. M. Hyndman was also struck by "the contrast between [Marx's] manner and utterance when thus deeply stirred to anger [over the policy of the Liberal Party] and his attitude when giving his views on the economic events of the period."

On the one hand, Marx is telling you in *Das Kapital* that a certain "historic" development, indispensable for the progress of the race, could only have been carried out by capitalism; and, on the other hand, he is filling you with fury against the wickedness of the people who have performed it. It is as if Darwin had been a kind of Luther Burbank and had caused the blood of his readers to boil over the inadequacies, in the sight of the ideal, of the species produced by evolution and the wrongs of those animals and plants which had been eliminated in the struggle for life. Marx, the scientific historian, declares that the centralization required for socialism could have been provided in no other way than by the competitive processes of capitalism. In a striking passage in the second volume, he accepts the very horrors of the system as an aspect of its beneficent development: "Looking upon capitalist production in its details . . . we find that it is very economical with materialized labor incorporated in commodities. But it is more than any other mode of production prodigal with human lives, with living labor, wasting not only flesh and blood, but also nerves and brains. Indeed, it is only by dint of the most extravagant waste of individual development that human development is safeguarded and advanced in that epoch of history which immediately precedes the conscious reorganization of society. Since all the economies here mentioned [on the part of the operators of coal mines] arise from the social nature of labor, it is just this social character of labor which causes this waste of the life and health of the laborer." The capitalist forces, then, could not have operated otherwise: even in their destruction of human beings, they are somehow the agents of human salvation; and yet every individual manufacturer must be blasted as either a cold-blooded slave-driver or a canting and rationalizing fraud.

Now where does the animus behind *Das Kapital* come from? It is the bitterest of all Marx's bitter books. It has hardly a trace of the exhilaration which gives his earlier work a kind of fire. "Reading your book again," he wrote Engels, April 9, 1863—the book was *The Condition of the English Working Class in 1844*—"has sadly made me feel my age. With what freshness and passion and boldness of vision and freedom from learned and scientific scruples you have handled the subject here! And the illusion that tomorrow or the day after tomorrow the result will spring to life as an historical reality before our eyes gives the whole a warm and spirited humor—with which the later 'gray on gray' makes a damnable unpleasant contrast."

But it is not only age which makes the difference between Engels's book and Marx's. It is impossible to read *Das Kapital* in the light of Marx's life during this period without concluding that the emotional motivation, partly or totally unconscious no doubt, behind Marx's excoriation of the capitalists and his grim parading of the affliction of the poor is at once his outraged conviction of the indignity and injustice of his own fate and his bad conscience at having inflicted that fate on others. Marx himself is not only the victim, the dispossessed proletariat; he is also the exploiting employer. For has he not exploited Jenny and Engels? Is he himself not responsible, not merely for the being of his beloved daughters, but for the handicaps and hardships they have been born to? In a letter to Siegfried Meyer, written April 30, 1867, when he has finally got *Das Kapital* off to the printer, he speaks of it as "the task to which I have sacrificed my health, my happiness in life and my family."

True—as he goes on to say—it has all been done for the ideal and for mankind: "I laugh at the so-called 'practical' men and their wisdom. If one had the hide of an ox, one could naturally turn one's back on the sufferings of humanity and look after one's own skin; but, as it is, I should have considered myself very unpractical if I had died without completing my book, at least in manuscript form." "To work for humanity," says Lafargue, "was one of his favorite phrases." For that science to which one sacrifices others "should not be," as Marx writes elsewhere, "an egoistic pleasure: those who are in a position to devote themselves to scientific studies should be also the first to put their knowledge at the service of humanity."

Yet if you choose to work for humanity, if you will not write for money, why then you must make other people earn it for you or suffer and let others suffer, because you haven't got it.

If it was true, as I have suggested, that Marx and Engels in relation to one another were like the electrodes of the voltaic cell, it became more and more obvious as time went on that Marx was to play the part of the metal of the positive electrode, which gives out hydrogen and remains unchanged, while Engels was to be the negative electrode, which gradually gets used up. "There's nothing I long for more," Engels wrote Marx, April 27, 1867, just after the last pages of the first volume of *Das Kapital* had finally been got off to the printer, "than to escape from this miserable commerce, which is demoralizing me completely by reason of the time it makes me waste. So long as I remain in it, I can't accomplish anything—especially since I've been one of the bosses, it's got to be a great deal worse on account of the increased responsibility." He is going to give it up, he says; but then his income will be very much reduced, "and what I always have on my mind is what are we going to do about you?" Marx replies on a note of contrition: "I confidently hope and believe that I shall be within a year's time enough of a made man so that I can fundamentally reform my economic situation and stand finally on my own feet again. If it had not been for you, I should never have been able to bring this work to completion, and I assure you that it has always weighed like an incubus on my conscience that it should have been principally on account of me that you have been allowing your splendid abilities to be wasted and rusted in business and have had, besides, to live through all my *petites misères* with me."

But, he adds, he cannot conceal from himself that he has "a year of trial" still ahead of him; and he intimates, without explicitly asking for it, that an immediate advance of money would be helpful. "What—aside from the uncertainty—frightens me most is the prospect of going back to London [he was in Germany arranging the publication of his book], as I must do in six or eight days. The debts there are considerable, and the Manichees [the creditors] are eagerly awaiting my return. That means family worries again, domestic collisions, a hunted life, instead of going freely and freshly to work."

We have seen what the situation at home was. The next year Laura Marx was to succumb to the fate which her parents had been trying to stave off and take a position as governess. Poor Marx, more in torment than ever, with on the one hand the needs of his family and on the other the exactions of his book, had been suffering from a chronic insomnia. He had been visited by a succession of plagues which were none the less physically agonizing because they were probably partly due to the strain of the domestic situation, as Marx himself suggested, combined, as Engels thought, with his difficulties over his book. For years he was tormented almost incessantly by outbreaks of carbuncles and boils—an ailment of which only those who have had it can appreciate the exasperating character, with its malignant and nagging inflammations always coming out in new places, often inaccessible and sometimes crippling, as if a host of indestructible little devils were hatching under one's skin. And these were diversified with influenza, rheumatism, ophthalmia, toothache and headache. But his most serious complaint was an enlarged liver. He had had trouble with his liver all his life: his father had died of cancer of the liver; and the fear of it had always hung over Karl. During the sixties his trouble became acute; later on, he was to be forced to take a cure. In the meantime, during the years when he is in labor with *Das Kapital*, he passes through a Valley of the Shadow of Death. He will write Engels that his arm is so sore with rheumatism that he cries out without being aware of it every time he moves it in his sleep, that his liver attacks have stupefied his brain, paralyzed all his limbs. We have seen how, unable to read or write, he had given himself up at one period, to "psychological reveries as to what it would be like to be blind or mad." And he extends his afflictions to all about him in a way which betrays a conviction that he is doomed to be a bringer of grief. When Jenny takes a trip to Paris to arrange about a French translation of *Das Kapital*, she finds that the man she has gone to interview has just had a paralytic stroke; and on her way back in the train something goes wrong with the locomotive so that she arrives two hours late; then the omnibus in which she is riding upsets; and when she finally gets back to London, the cab in which she is driving home has a collision with another cab and she is obliged to walk the rest of the way. In the meantime, Lenchen's sister, who had been staying at the Marxes', had suddenly fallen ill and, just before Jenny's arrival, had died. When Marx's mother, upon whose demise he had, as we have seen, been counting, does finally die, he writes strangely to Engels that Fate has been demanding some member of his family: "I myself have one foot in the grave (*unter der Erde*)." And in one of his letters to Engels during his visit to Lassalle in Berlin, he reveals by another fantasy the symbolic significance which he attaches to illness: "*Apropos* Lassalle-Lazarus! Lepsius has proved in his big work on Egypt that the exodus of the Jews from Egypt is nothing more or less than the story that Manetho tells about the expulsion from Egypt 'of the race of lepers,' led by an Egyptian priest called Moses. Lazarus the leper is thus the prototype of the Jews and Lazarus-Lassalle. Only in the case of our Lazarus, the leprosy has gone to his brain. The disease from which he is suffering was originally secondary syphilis, imperfectly cured. He developed a caries of the bone from it ... and something has still remained in one of his legs ... neuralgia or *something of the sort*. To the detriment of his physique, our Lazarus now lives as luxuriously as his antithesis, the rich man, and this I regard as one of the main obstacles to his cure."

And the better times to which Marx looked forward when the first volume of *Das Kapital* was finished, were never really to come. Engels had hoped, as he told him, that his outlook would now become less gloomy. But

Marx's poverty and his dependence on others were permanent features of his life; and as their consequences had become more painful, he could only grow more bitter.
Hyndman tells us that, unlike certain other aging men, he
grew less tolerant instead of more. *Das Kapital* is the reflection of this period. He said that he had written the terrible chapter on the "Working Day" at a time when, as a
result of his illness, his head had been too weak for theoretical work; and when he had finally finished his book, he
wrote Engels: "I hope that the bourgeoisie as long as they
live will have cause to remember my carbuncles." Thus,
in attacking the industrial system, he is at the same time
declaring his own tribulations, calling the Heavens—that
is, History—to witness that he is a just man wronged, and
damning the hypocritical scoundrel who compels others
to slave and suffer for him, who persists in remaining indifferent to the agony for which he is responsible, who
even keeps himself in ignorance of it. The book has behind
it the exalted purpose, it is a part of the noble accomplishment, of Karl Marx's devoted life; but the wrong and the
hurt of that life have made the whole picture hateful or
grievous. The lofty devotion and the wrong are inextricably involved with one another; and the more he asserts
the will of his highest impulses, the blacker the situation
becomes.

Marx may appear to have kept the two things apart
when he has set the bad capitalist on one side and the good
Communist of the future on the other; but, after all, to arrive at that future, the Communist must be cruel and re-
pressive just as the capitalist has been; he, too, must do
violence to that common humanity in whose service the
prophet is supposed to be preaching. It is a serious misrepresentation of Marx to minimize the sadistic element in his
writing. In his address to the Communist League of April,
1850, he had declared to the revolutionary working class
that, "far from opposing so-called excesses, the vengeance
of the people on hated individuals or attacks by the masses

on buildings which arouse hateful memories, we must not only tolerate them, but even take the lead in them." Nor was this, as we have seen from his correspondence, a tendency which he reserved for politics. In the letter to Engels just quoted, for example, there is a passage in which Marx tells his friend that the publisher who had let them down twenty years before by being afraid to bring out *The German Ideology* and who had unloaded "that young fellow Kriege on our necks" had recently fallen out of a window and "if you please (*gefälligst*), broken his own neck."

If we isolate the images in Marx—which are so powerful and vivid in themselves that they can sometimes persuade us to forget his lack of realistic observation and almost produce the illusion of a visible and tangible experience—if we isolate and examine these images, we can see through to the inner obsessions at the heart of the world-vision of Marx.

Here all is cruel discomfort, rape, repression, mutilation and massacre, premature burial, the stalking of corpses, the vampire that lives on another's blood, life in death and death in life: "The Abbé Bonawita Blank . . . operated on magpies and starlings in such a way that, though they were free to fly about as they pleased, they would always come back to him again. He cut off the lower part of their beaks so that they were not able to get their food themselves and so were obliged to eat from his hand. The good little bourgeois who looked on from a distance and saw the birds perched on the shoulders of the good priest and apparently dining with him in a friendly fashion, admired his culture and his science. His biographer says that the birds loved him as their benefactor. And the Poles, enchained, mutilated, branded, refuse to love their Prussian benefactors!" "But capital not only lives upon labor. Like a magnificent and barbarous master, it drags with it into its grave the corpses of its slaves, whole hecatombs of workers, who perish in the crises." "If the silkworm's object in spinning were to prolong its existence as caterpillar, it would be a perfect example of the wage-worker" (both are condemned, thus, to living graves). "This miserable Assembly left the stage, after it had given itself the pleasure, two days before the anniversary of its birthday, May 4, of rejecting the notion of amnesty for the June insurgents. Its power shattered, held in deadly hatred by the people, repulsed, maltreated, contemptuously thrown aside by the bourgeoisie, whose tool it was, forced in the second half of its life to disavow the first, robbed of its republican illusions, with no great creations in the past, with no hope for the future, and with its living body dying bit by bit, it was able to galvanize its own corpse only by continually recalling the June victory and living it over again, substantiating itself by constantly repeated damnation of the damned. Vampire, that lives on the blood of the June insurgents!" "But from 1848 to 1851 there was nothing more than a walking of the ghost of the old revolution—now in the form of Marrast, *'le républicain en gants jaunes,'* dressed up as Bailly; and now in the form of the adventurer who hid his commonplace and unpleasing physiognomy behind the iron death-mask of Napoleon." "Universal suffrage seems to have survived only for a moment, in order that it might before all men's eyes draw up a holograph will, declaring in the name of the people: 'Everything that exists is fit for the scrap-heap.' " "Neither a nation nor a woman can be forgiven for the unguarded hour in which a chance comer has seized the opportunity for an act of rape." "Thetis, the sea-goddess, had foretold to her son Achilles that he would perish in the heyday of his youth. Like Achilles, the constitution has its weak spot; and, like Achilles, it has a foreboding of premature death." "If, subsequently, the constitution was bayoneted out of existence, we must not forget that while in the womb it had been guarded by bayonets directed against the people, and that by bayonets it had been brought into the world." "The champions of the Party of Order were still seated upon the shoulders of armed force, when they realized, one fine morning, that the seat had become prickly, for the shoulders had turned into bayonets." "The bourgeois order, which at the beginning of the century had stationed the state as a sentry before the newly created petty land-holdings and dunged them with laurels, has now turned into a vampire, which sucks out their heart's blood and brain-marrow and casts it into the alchemist's retort of capital." (This last has been pointed out by Max Eastman as an example of Marx's bad taste. The metaphor is certainly mixed; yet the style is not so very much different from the apocalyptic parts of the Bible. It may be noted that Marx himself was always pitiless to the mixed metaphors of his opponents.)

These images have been excerpted almost as they come from the Marx of the most brilliant period: from his writings in the *Neue Rheinische Zeitung* and from *The Class Struggles in France* and *The Eighteenth Brumaire;* and they might be multiplied by countless examples from his more unrelievedly saturnine works. Here is his description of the worker from *Das Kapital.* We have seen, says Marx, "that within the capitalist system all the methods for increasing the social productivity of labor are carried out at the cost of the individual worker: that all the means for developing production are transformed into means of domination over and exploitation of the producer; that they mutilate the worker into a fragment of a human being, degrade him to become a mere appurtenance of the machine, make his work such a torment that its essential meaning is destroyed; cut him off from the intellectual potentialities of the labor process in exact proportion to the extent to which science is incorporated into it as an independent power; that they distort the conditions under which he works, subjecting him, during the labor process, to a despotism which is all the more hateful because of its pettiness; that they transform his whole life into working time, and drag his wife and children beneath the Juggernaut wheels of capital's car."

There is a German expression *"lasten wie ein Alp,"*

which means something like "weigh like an incubus," to which Marx was very much addicted. We find it on the first page of *The Eighteenth Brumaire*, where he says that "The tradition of all the dead generations weighs like an incubus on the brain of the living." We have seen it in the letter already quoted, in which he tells Engels that the injury to his friend's career for which he feels himself responsible has weighed like an incubus on his conscience; and he had written to the Countess Hatzfeldt after Lassalle's death that this event—in a similar phrase—had weighed upon him "like a hideous and evil dream." In writing about *Das Kapital* to Engels, he says that the task weighs upon him like an incubus; and he complains that the Workers' International "and everything that it involves . . . weighs like an incubus on me, and I'd be glad to be able to shake it off." It is always the same oppression, whether Marx has objectified it and generalized it as the oppression of the living by the dead or felt it personally as his own oppression under the conviction of his own guilt or under the greatest of his own achievements. It is always the same wound, as to which it is never quite clear—as in the case of the Dialectic, which is now a fundamental truth of nature, now an action performed by human agents, as in the case of the development of the capitalist economy, which is now an inevitable and non-moral process, now the blackest of human crimes—whether the gods have inflicted it on man or man has inflicted it on himself. It is always the same burial alive, whether it is the past trying to stifle the present or the future putting away the past. The French constitution of 1848, which, according to Marx in one of the passages just quoted, has been guarded in the womb by bayonets, is brought out of the womb by bayonets only to be bayoneted to death.

"You see," he had once written Engels, "that I'm the object of plagues just like Job, though I'm not so godfearing as he was." No: he is not so godfearing. He sees himself also as "Old Nick," the Goethean spirit that denies. Yet Old Nick is not the right symbol either: this Devil has been twisted and racked. Though he is capable of satanic mockery of the publisher who had sent Kriege on their necks and then fallen and broken his own, the mocker cannot jeer at such a doom without breaking, by a dialectical joke, his own neck as well; and, after all, had not the publisher buried Marx's book alive? It is Prometheus who remains his favorite hero; for Prometheus is a Satan who suffers, a Job who never assents; and, unlike either Job or Satan, he brings liberation to mankind. Prometheus turns up in *Das Kapital* (in Chapter 23) to represent the proletariat chained to capital. The Light-Bringer was tortured, we remember, by Zeus's eagle's tearing, precisely, his liver; as Karl Marx himself—who is said to have reread Aeschylus every year—was obsessed by the fear that his liver would be eaten like his father's by cancer. And yet, if it is a devouring bird which Father Zeus has sent against the rebel, it is also a devourer, a destroyer, fire, which Prometheus has brought to man. And in the meantime the deliverer is never delivered; the slayer never rises from the grave. The resurrection, although certain, is not yet; for the expropriators are yet to be expropriated.

Such is the trauma of which the anguish and the defiance reverberate through *Das Kapital*. To point it out is not to detract from the authority of Marx's work. On the contrary, in history as in other fields of writing, the importance of a book depends, not merely on the breadth of the view and the amount of information that has gone into it, but on the depths from which it has been drawn. The great crucial books of human thought—outside what are called the exact sciences, and perhaps something of the sort is true even here—always render articulate the results of fundamental new experiences to which human beings have had to adjust themselves. *Das Kapital* is such a book. Marx has found in his personal experience the key to the larger experience of society, and identifies himself with that society. His trauma reflects itself in *Das Kapital* as the trauma of mankind under industrialism; and only so sore and angry a spirit, so ill at ease in the world, could have recognized and seen into the causes of the wholesale mutilation of humanity, the grim collisions, the uncomprehended convulsions, to which that age of great profits was doomed.

The closing ten years of [Marx's] life did bring him certain consolations: Engels was living in London; he was able to take trips for his health. But all these years he is helplessly sinking, forced to relinquish his work at sixty—succumbing to that mortal wound which he had brought with him into the world. He had banished the International when he had felt it slipping out of his hands; now he was losing his grip on *Das Kapital*, the first volume of which had failed to bring him the public recognition he had expected. He had had the humiliation of seeing a review of his book, which Engels had written for the *Fortnightly Review* and which the historian Beesly had promised to publish, sent back by John Morley on the ground that it was too dry for the *Fortnightly*'s readers; and was to see his friend and disciple Hyndman bring out a book called *England For All*, based partly on Marx's ideas, in which, for fear of antagonizing *his* readers, he respectfully acknowledged his debt "to the work of a great thinker and original writer" without mentioning Marx's name.

Jenny Longuet, who was living in France with her husband, had a baby in the spring of 1881, and her parents went over to see her that summer. But Jenny Marx came back ill. She had developed an incurable cancer, and her nerves had pretty badly given way. She had had herself on occasion to write begging letters to Engels, and she had eventually become rather jealous of him and bitter about their obligations to him. When Marx had gone back to Trier at the time of his mother's death, he had written to the wife he had met there: "I have been making a daily pilgrimage to the old Westphalen house (in the Rosnerstrasse), which has interested me more than all the Roman ruins, because it reminds me of happy youth and used to shelter my sweetheart. And every day people ask me right and left about the quondam 'most beautiful girl' in Trier, the 'Queen of the ball.' It's damned agreeable for a man to find that his wife lives on as an 'enchanted princess' in the imagination of a whole town." He had indeed made her drink the poisoned cup, which the lover had proffered his beloved in that ominous poem of his youth; and he, like the lover of the poem, was growing cold from the poison, too.

By December Jenny was dying; and Marx himself was in bed with pleurisy. "I shall never forget the morning," their daughter Eleanor writes, "when he felt strong enough to go into Mother's room. It was as if they were young again—she a loving girl and he a loving young man, embarking on life together, and not an old man shattered by illness and a dying old lady taking leave of one another forever." Liebknecht says that she followed with the eagerness of a child the first elections held in Germany after the enactment of the anti-Socialist law, and was delighted when the results showed a gain for the outlawed Social Democrats; and Marx wrote Sorge that it was a source of gratification that she should have been cheered up just before she died by the appearance, with a certain amount of publicity, of an article on him by Belfort Bax. The last thing she said that was understood was, "Karl, my strength is broken." He was too ill to attend her funeral. When Engels arrived, he said: "The Moor is dead, too."

He was right: Marx went the next year to Algiers, to Monte Carlo, to Enghien, to the Lake of Geneva, but the pleurisy went with him all the way. Back in England, he took refuge in the Isle of Wight to escape from the London fogs, but there he caught cold again. The death of Jenny Longuet, about whose health he had worried so when he had had no money to send her to the seaside, followed her mother's in January, 1883. Marx by March had an abscess of the lung. When Engels came to call on him on the afternoon of the fourteenth, he found the household in tears: they told him that his friend had had a hemorrhage. Lenchen went up and found her master in his study, half asleep, as she thought. He had gotten up from his bed, and gone to his study and sat down at his worktable. Engels went in, and felt his pulse and listened for his breath, and found they had both stopped.

Marx's collaborator outlived him twelve years. Lizzy Burns had died in '78, and Engels had married her to please her on her deathbed. When the Marx ladies had come to call on him, he had had to send Lizzy out marketing, giving her money for a drink at a pub and a ride home through the park in a hansom. He hoped and searched to the end of his days to prove that Lizzy and her sister were the descendants of Robert Burns. After Lizzy's death, a young niece of hers named Mary Ellen, who had been brought up in Engels's household, made an attempt to keep house for him. But she got into trouble with the son of a well-to-do business contractor, and Engels compelled him to marry her, to the indignation of the young man's family. He had been surprised to find out that this young fellow was neither a revolutionist nor a man of any intellectual ability. He tried to help the young couple get started, but Mary Ellen's husband failed in business, and Engels had to take them in. "The family is very numerous," he wrote Regina Bernstein. "Two dogs, three cats, a canary, a rabbit, two guinea-pigs, fourteen hens and a rooster." When the baby also arrived, Engels used to like to play with him. He advanced a great deal of money to Mary Ellen's husband, but the young man was never able to make a go of it. After the deaths of both the Marxes, Lenchen came to take care of Engels.

He seems to have enjoyed these last years. In the streets of that London of which the atomized population had so shocked him when he had come there in his twenties, he still walked erect and slender, almost with the energy of youth. He was living, as Marx had done, in one of those monotonous rows of houses—with so much soot, as Liebknecht says, on the back gardens that it was impossible to tell the gravel from the grass—where the fronts were so much alike that his near-sighted friend had not infrequently attempted to unlock the wrong door when he had been coming back home after dark. But in London he had more interesting companionship and the leisure to pursue his studies and pleasures. Eleanor Marx, who had been staying with him in Manchester at the time he finally quitted the office, tells how he shouted "For the last time!" when he drew on his top-boots in the morning, and how, at the end of the day, "when we stood waiting for him in the doorway, we saw him coming across the little field . . . flourishing his stick in the air and singing and laughing all over his face." In London, he gave convivial Sunday evenings, to which he invited men of all social classes who had either distinguished themselves intellectually or done some service to the socialist cause. He did not insist on their professing the correct doctrine and even entertained Prussian conservatives. His cellar was always full of good Bordeaux, great quantities of which he had sent to Marx. The conversation was unrestrained, and the host, when things had reached a certain point, used to start up old students' songs. He was so delighted with "The Vicar of Bray"—from which he said it was also possible to learn a good deal of English history—that he translated it into German. A fortnight before Christmas he would have the ladies of his acquaintance come in and chop great heaps of apples, nuts, raisins, almonds and orange peel, which were put into an enormous tub. "Later in the evening," says Bernstein, "the male friends of the house would arrive, and each of them was required to lay hold of a ladle that stood upright in the tub, and stir the paste three times round—a by no means easy task, which required a great deal of muscular strength. But its importance was mainly symbolical, and those whose strength was inadequate were mercifully exempted. The concluding touch was given by Engels himself, who descended into the wine-cellar and brought up champagne, in which," sitting round the great kitchen, "we drank to a merry Christmas and to many other things as well." At Christmas he sent everyone a pudding out of the enormous tub, and gave an enormous dinner at his house, at which the pudding came in flaming.

When the goading of Marx was removed, the natural bonhomie of Engels tended to reassert itself. He stuck loyally to Marx's old feuds: he would not have anything to do with H. M. Hyndman or with anyone whom he thought to have injured Marx; and he continued to fight the Lassalleans and to hold it against Wilhelm Liebknecht that he had disregarded Marx's criticisms of the Gotha program. But his advice to the various groups, which he gave only when people asked him for it, was full of good sense and moderation. He adopted, as Mehring has remarked, very much the same realistic policy which Lassalle had pursued in Germany in supporting the agitation for the franchise: Let the working class formulate their own demands; there will be time for doctrine later. He wrote to Sorge that he need be in no hurry to publish Marx's criticism of Henry George, who ran for mayor in New York on the ticket of a United Labor Party in 1886: George would compromise himself in the long run, and in the meantime "the masses must be set in motion along the road that corresponds to each country and to the prevailing circumstances, which is usually a roundabout road. Everything else is of secondary importance if only they are really aroused."

With the whole field now to himself, falling heir to the Marxist glory, he became more modest than ever. He insisted in reply to praise that if perhaps he had been a little underrated at the time when Marx was alive, he was now being overrated. In the summer of '93, he appeared for the first time in person at a congress of the Second International, which had been founded by the Social Democrats in 1889. The repeal of the anti-Socialist law had made it possible for him to go back to Germany, and the socialists had begged him to come. When he saw the towers of Cologne cathedral from the train that took him through the Rhineland, tears came into his eyes, and he said: "What a lovely land, if only one could live in it!" When he appeared at the congress in Zürich, he was amazed at the ovation given him and passed it all back to Marx. At the house of the Russian socialist Axelrod, he was delighted to meet and to kiss a group of pretty little Russian comrades, who, he said, had wonderful eyes; "but my real darling," he wrote his brother, "is a delicious little factory girl from Vienna, with the sort of alluring face and charming manners that are really very rare." "The people were all very nice," he afterwards wrote to Sorge, "but it isn't for me—I'm glad it's over." The next time he would write them beforehand, so that he shouldn't "have to parade before the public." He would leave all that to the parliamentarians and the spell-binders: "that sort of thing belongs to their role, but it hardly fits in with my kind of work."

He had counted on elaborating the *Peasant War* into a really considerable book, which should present his whole theory of German history; but the confused and illegible manuscripts, the brain-racking subtleties of *Das Kapital*, consumed all the rest of his life. He only succeeded in bringing out the third volume—in which the Labor Theory of Value is discussed—in October, 1894, the year before he died; and he had to bequeath the remaining material to Kautsky.

It is ironic and characteristic that Engels should in the end have been left by Marx holding the bag, as we say, for the two most questionable features of Marxism: the Dialectic and the Labor Theory of Value—those two dogmas on our acceptance of which the whole philosophy as a system depends. Engels had written at Marx's request a polemic against the Berlin philosopher Dühring, who, in default of any systematic exposition by Marx and Engels of their own fundamental ideas, was getting a hold on the younger German socialists. Engels tried to defend the Dialectic and he did not make a very convincing job of it, though his book had the approval of Marx. Later, after Marx's death, he had to answer the questions of young socialists who were having difficulties with Marxist theory. Marx himself had with telling effect and with acrid satisfaction to himself brought into play the materialistic aspect of Marxo-Hegelian Dialectical Materialism to blight the shimmering mirages of the utopians and to make the blood of the bourgeois run cold. Conscientiously, almost morbidly, reluctant to put himself on record about anything which he had not completely excogitated, Marx had never far pursued the inquiries which would have led him down to dialectical first principles. It is significant that in the preface to *Das Kapital* he should, instead of expounding himself the materialistic view of history, be content to quote with approval a rather inadequate attempt to state it, but a version which made it seem extremely grim, volunteered by a Russian admirer. Engels with his readier fluency and his relative superficiality now tried to explain everything plausibly; and as he did so the old German idealism which he had drunk in with his first Rhine wine began to flow back into the Dialectic. We have already discussed the varying emphasis which Marx and Engels gave to their doctrines at different moments of history and different periods of their own careers; but it ought to be added here that the widely diverging interpretations which have been put upon Dialectical Materialism have also been partly due to certain fundamental divergences betwen the temperaments of the two different men.

And now Engels had on his hands the Labor Theory of Value, against which a great outcry went up. He died earnestly trying to defend it, leaving the last of his polemics unfinished. He was suffering from cancer of the esophagus and was no longer able to speak, but could write. He carried on conversations with his friends by chalking his remarks on a slate, and they could see from them that he was bearing his pain "with stoicism and even with humor."

He left legacies to both the Marx daughters and to the niece of Mary and Lizzy Burns (who nevertheless made trouble about the will in an effort to get more then he had left her), and twenty thousand marks to the Party. He wrote Bebel to "take care above everything that . . . it doesn't fall into the hands of the Prussians. And when you feel sure on that score, then drink a bottle of good wine on it. Do this in memory of me." He left directions for the disposal of his body, which were carried out by his friends. They had him cremated, and on a windy autumn day threw his ashes out to the sea off Beachy Head.

TROTSKY AND HISTORY

It will be seen that the Marxist movement had arrived by the beginning of the century at a point where it could provide a base and frame for an ambitious and gifted young man. Trotsky is not, like Marx, a great original thinker; he is not a great original statesman, like Lenin; he was perhaps not even inevitably a great rebel: the revolution was, as it were, the world in which he found himself living. He is one of those men of the first rank who flourish inside a school, neither creating, nor breaking out of, its system.

The young student who had impressed his fellows by the eloquence and force of his reasoning at a time when he did not yet know what he was talking about, because he had at any cost to play a role, found his place in the army of Marxism—in the drama of progress, on the stage of the earth, conceived in a certain way. This is not, of course, to imply that there has been anything insincere or specious about the relation of Trotsky to this role. On the contrary, he has staked upon it not only such things as comfort and peace of mind, but his own life and the lives of his followers and family, and that enjoyment of political power itself which is the only worldly satisfaction that Marxism allows to its true priesthood; and he has learned in the Marxist academy a certain perfection of revolutionary form and standards of revolutionary honor.

There is a passage in which Trotsky tells of the effect on him of reading the Marx-Engels correspondence which is worth quoting as a description of the tradition that Marx and Engels had founded. "The correspondence between Marx and Engels was for me not a theoretical, but a psychological revelation. *Toutes proportions gardées*, I found proof on every page that I was bound to these two by a direct psychological affinity. Their attitude to men and ideas was mine. I guessed what they did not express, shared their sympathies, was indignant and hated as they did. Marx and Engels were revolutionaries through and through. But they had not the slightest trace of sectarianism or asceticism. Both of them, and especially Engels, could at any time say of themselves that nothing human was strange to them. But their revolutionary outlook lifted them always above the hazards of fate and the works of men. What philistines and vulgarians considered aristocratic in them was really only their revolutionary superiority. Its most important characteristic is a complete and ingrained independence of official public opinion at all times and under all conditions."

But even here we can see that it is the attitude itself, rather than what is to be accomplished through the attitude, that appeals to the imagination of Trotsky: he sees himself as the aristocrat of revolution. Lunachársky tells of Trotsky's exclaiming of the Social revolutionary leader Chernóv, who had accepted a place in the coalition government before the October Revolution: "What contemptible ambitiousness!—to abandon his historic position for a portfolio." But the position of honor is only removed to the end of a longer perspective. "Trotsky," Lunachársky adds, "treasures his historic role, and would undoubtedly be willing to make any personal sacrifice, not by any means excluding that of his life, in order to remain in the memory of mankind with the halo of a genuine revolutionary leader." Bruce Lockhart wrote in his diary in February, 1918, after his first interview with Trotsky: "He strikes me as a man who would willingly die fighting for Russia provided there was a big enough audience to see him do it." And there is somehow the impression created that the cause of human progress stands or falls with Trotsky: Truth's quarrel is Trotsky's quarrel. He tells in his autobiography of his judgment on the boys at his school when he went back after having been suspended over the demonstration against the French teacher. He divided them into three distinct groups: those who had "betrayed" him, those who had "defended" him, and those who had "remained neutral." The first group he "cut completely"; the second group he cultivated. "Such, one might say," he goes on, "was the first political test I underwent. These were the groups that resulted from that episode: the tale-bearers and the envious at one pole, the frank courageous boys at the other, and the neutral vacillating mass in the middle. These three groups never quite disappeared even during the years that followed. I met them again and again in my life, in the most varied circumstances." So even the reader of Trotsky inevitably finds himself involved in something in the nature of an issue of personal allegiance to the author. Trotsky is not content, as Lenin was, to present the course of events, which he or another in this or that case may have interpreted more or less correctly: he must justify himself in connection with them.

We who of recent years have seen the State that Trotsky helped to build in a phase combining the butcheries of the Robespierre Terror with the corruption and reaction of the Directory, and Trotsky himself figuring dramatically in the role of Gracchus Babeuf, may be tempted to endow him with qualities which actually he does not possess and with principles which he has expressly repudiated. We have seen the successor of Lenin undertake a fantastic rewriting of the whole history of the Revolution in order to cancel out Trotsky's part; pursue Trotsky from country to country, persecuting even his children and hounding them to their deaths; finally blame him, in staged scenes of vilification, hysterical, oriental and vulgar, and more degrading to the human spirit than the frank fiendishness of Ivan the Terrible, for all the treacheries, mistakes and disasters that have been the fate of his own administration—till he has made the world conscious of Trotsky as the accuser of Stalin's own bad conscience, as if the Soviet careerists of the thirties were unable to deny the socialist ideal without trying to annihilate the moral authority of this one homeless and hunted man. It is not Trotsky alone who has created his role: his enemies have given it a reality that no mere self-dramatization could have compassed. And as the fires of the Revolution have died down in the Soviet Union at a time when the systems of thought of the West were already in an advanced state of decadence, he has shone forth like a veritable pharos, rotating a long shaft of light on the seas and the reefs all around.

But we must try to see the man inside the role and to examine his real tendencies and doctrines.

The boy who came back to the farm from Odessa with his book learning and his new glasses, his new habits of cleanliness and his new city clothes, found himself cut off from his kindred, a creature of another order, who felt that he was superior to them; and the relationship established here seems to have persisted all Trotsky's life in connection with human beings in general. He tells us in *My Life* with that candor that sets him off sharply from the ordinary public figure, that his first emotions of "social protest" consisted of "indignation over injustice" rather than of "sympathy for the downtrodden," and "even when my revolutionary ideas were already taking shape, I would catch myself in an attitude of mistrust of action by the masses, taking a bookish, abstract and therefore skeptical view of the revolution. I had to combat all this within myself, by my thinking, my reading, but mainly by means of experience, until the elements of psychic inertia had been conquered within me." It is characteristic of Trotsky that—in an article on a book by Céline—he should argue, as no other of the great Marxists would have done, in favor of the revolutionary movement on the ground that it "leads humanity from out the dark night of the circumscribed I."

Possessing neither Lenin's gift for establishing personal relations of confidence nor the cunning political sense which has made it possible for Stalin to build up his machine and manipulate public opinion, Trotsky has ended by finding himself today in essentially the same position that he occupied between the split of 1903 and the revolution of 1905, and then again after 1905 up to the time of his return to Russia in 1917: that of an independent Marxist with a few devoted followers but no real popular constituency behind him. It is when he has been brought by a moment of crisis to a position of unquestioned authority and is free to act for himself that he becomes powerful as a political force, for he has the genius of making people do things. As Commissar for War in 1918 and 19, he managed, traveling in his armored train, to speed so fast from front to front, to appeal to the soldiers with such passion, to telegraph so promptly for supplies, to write and despatch so many resonant press stories, to put pressure so effectively on the military experts who had been trained under the old regime to lend their skill to the Revolution, and to catch and shoot so many disaffected officers, that the sixteen Soviet armies, feeling behind them this demon of will, held their fronts against the Kolcháks and Deníkins and saved the Revolution; and when Yudénich was advancing on Petrograd and Lenin was in favor of abandoning it, when the regimental commander had given his men the order to fall back and his troops were running away and had already reached division headquarters, Trotsky mounted the first

horse he could find and, chasing one soldier after another with his orderly behind him brandishing a pistol
and shouting, "Courage, boys: Comrade Trotsky is leading you!", compelled the whole regiment to turn and recover the positions it had left; the commander now appeared at the most dangerous points and was wounded
in both legs; the men attacked the tanks with bayonets.
And in politics itself it is evidently true, as Bruce Lockhart said years ago, that Trotsky is never so formidable
as when he has been driven into a tight place. Certainly
his stature never appeared so imposing as at the time
when, denied asylum by all the nations of Europe, he
was forced to defend himself against the murderous persecution of Moscow.

And so the drive of the ideal behind all this is less the
desire for human happiness than the enthusiasm for human culture, for that "first truly human culture," as he
says in *Literature and Revolution*, which socialism is eventually to make possible, that blazes out from the shut-in
man to illuminate this twilight of society. And so it is
the theory of Marxism, the diagram of social development, rather than the immediate vicissitudes of the lives
of his fellow creatures, that is present to Trotsky's mind.
The Marxist must act, of course, but he cannot consent
to do so unless he can understand the situation and explain his own intervention in terms of Marxist theory.
"The feeling," he writes, "of the supremacy of general
over particular, of law over fact, of theory over personal
experience, took root in my mind at an early age and
gained increasing strength as the years advanced. . . .
[This feeling] became an integral part of my literary and
political work. The dull empiricism, the unashamed
cringing worship of the fact which is so often only
imaginary, and falsely interpreted at that, were odious to
me. Beyond the facts, I looked for laws. . . . In every
sphere, barring none, I felt that I could move and act
only when I held in my hand the thread of the general."

At its worst, this results in the substitution of a kind of logical demonstration—recalling his mathematical aptitude—for the appreciation of men in their milieux, as is likely to be the case particularly with certain of his political predictions, written remote from the seat of operations. At its best—when he is examining events that have already taken place, so that the foundation of reality is given—it produces historical studies of extraordinary subtlety and solidity. Trotsky differs from the typical Marxist pedant, with his spinning of abstract "theses," in that the dominance in his mind of Marxist theory still leaves the play of his intelligence pretty free: one finds in his writings not only the Marxist analysis of mass behavior but a realistic observation—in regard to personality particularly—in the tradition of the great Russian writers; and not only a sense of development and form which gives dignity to the least of his articles but also a vein of apt imagery which lends beauty to even his polemics and makes some passages in his books unforgettable. *1905*, *The History of the Russian Revolution*, *My Life*, the biography of Lenin, and *Literature and Revolution* are probably a part of our permanent literature.

It has been the burden of all Trotsky's later writings and the chief basis of his self-justification that from the beginning of the Revolution, he has been orientated toward Lenin (he admits, of course, his conflicts with Lenin, but the fact that he should attempt to minimize them shows his need for a fixed "pivot" of authority); and since Lenin's death, toward the memory of Lenin. And Trotsky's Marxism is as dogmatic as Lenin's. He is as far from the exploratory spirit that distinguished Marx and Engels, and, being essentially a writer and a doctrinaire rather than like Lenin an inspired worker in the immediate materials of humanity, the implications of this dogmatic Marxism are all the more clearly exposed in his work.

Let us see what these implications are. First of all: there has been so far as I know, no other first-rate Marxist for whom the Marxist conception of History, derived from the Hegelian Idea, plays so frankly teleological a role as it does in the work of Trotsky. Here are some references from his book on the 1905 revolution, written soon after the events it describes. "If the prince was not succeeding in peacefully regenerating the country, he was accomplishing with remarkable effectiveness the task of a more general order for which history had placed him at the head of the government: the destruction of the political illusions and the prejudices of the middle class." "History used the fantastic plan of Gapón for the purpose of arriving at its ends, and it only remained for the priest to sanction with the priestly authority its [history's] revolutionary conclusions." History, with its dialectical Trinity, had chosen Prince Svyatopólk-Mirsky to disillusion the middle class, had propounded revolutionary conclusions which it had compelled Father Gapón to bless, and will cruelly discredit and destroy certain Pharisees and Sadducees of Marxism before it summons the boiling lava of the Judgment. These statements make no sense whatever unless one substitutes for the words *history* and the *dialectic of history* the words *Providence* and *God*. And this Providential power of history is present in all the writing of Trotsky. John Jay Chapman said of Browning that God did duty in his work as noun, verb, adjective, adverb, interjection and preposition; and the same is true of History with Trotsky. Of late, in his solitude and exile, this History, an austere spirit, has seemed actually to stand behind his chair as he writes, encouraging, admonishing, approving, giving him the courage to confound his accusers, who have never seen History's face.

What it may mean in moments of action to feel History towering at one's elbow with her avenging sword in her hand is shown in the remarkable scene at the first congress of the Soviet dictatorship after the success of the October insurrection of 1917, when Trotsky, with the contempt and indignation of a prophet, read Mártov and his followers out of meeting. "You are pitiful isolated individuals," he cried at the height of the Bolshevik triumph. "You are bankrupt; your role is played out. Go where you belong from now on—into the rubbish-can of history!" These words are worth pondering for the light they throw on the course of Marxist politics and thought. Observe that the merging of oneself with the onrush of the current of history is to save you from the ignoble fate of being a "pitiful isolated individual"; and that the failure so to merge yourself will relegate you to the rubbish-can of history, where you can presumably be of no more use. Today, though we may agree with the Bolsheviks that Mártov was no man of action, his croakings over the course they had adopted seem to us full of farsighted intelligence. He pointed out that proclaiming a socialist regime in conditions different from those contemplated by Marx would not realize the results that Marx expected; that Marx and Engels had usually described the dictatorship of the proletariat as having the form, for the new dominant class, of a democratic republic, with universal suffrage and the popular recall of officials; that the slogan "All power to the Soviets" had never really meant what it said and that it had soon been exchanged by Lenin for "All power to the Bolshevik Party." There sometimes turn out to be valuable objects cast away in the rubbish-can of history—things that have to be retrieved later on.

Two years later, after the Moscow trials of March, 1938, he wrote a long article called *Their Morals and Ours* (*New International*, June, 1938) against persons who had been asserting that the systematic falsehoods of the Kremlin and its remorseless extermination of the old Bolsheviks had grown quite logically out of the Jesuitical policy pursued by the Bolsheviks themselves. This article must be regarded as the *locus classicus* of Trotsky's ideas on this subject. What do we find in it? We find first of all that the Jesuits have been maligned. The notion that they ever believed that the end could justify *any* means is a malicious invention of their opponents: what they did hold was that a given means may be neither bad nor good in itself, but may become either through the purpose it serves. Thus it is a criminal act to shoot a man "with the aim of violation or murder," but an act of virtue to shoot a mad dog which is about to attack a child. "The Jesuits represented a militant organization, strictly centralized, aggressive, and dangerous not only to their enemies, but to their allies as well." They were superior to the other Catholic priests of their day because they were "more consistent, bolder and more perspicacious." It was only in so far as they became less Jesuits, less "warriors of the Church," that is, in so far as they were perverted into "bureaucrats," that their order degenerated.

Thus such means as lying and killing are morally indifferent in themselves. Both are necessary in time of war, and it depends on which side we want to win whether we approve them or reprobate them. Trotsky illustrates this phenomenon strikingly, and evidently without being aware of it, in the very essay under discussion, by bitterly complaining of the "hypocrisy" and the "official cult of mendacity" of the Kremlin and denouncing one of his calumniators of the GPU as a "bourgeois without honor or conscience." When the Bolsheviks calumniated the Mensheviks, then, the reader is moved to inquire, did this not imply anything derogatory to their conscience or their honor? One finds the answer in another passage: "The question does not even lie in which of the warring camps caused or itself suffered the greatest number of victims. History has different yardsticks for the cruelty of the Northerners and the cruelty of the Southerners in the [American] Civil War. A slave-owner who through cunning and violence shackles a slave in chains, and a slave who through cunning and violence breaks the chains—let not the contemptible eunuchs tell us that they are equals before a court of morality!" There is, then, a court of morality above the warring classes, and this court is presided over by, precisely again, the Goddess History. For anyone but a Marxist it would appear as if history in the ordinary sense of the description or study of past events might well approach without moral animus the casualties of both North and South in the American Civil War. Should the historian, even in assuming that one side in a given conflict represents a progressive force and the other a retrograde one, have "different yardsticks" for the heroism or cruelty of the one and of the other? In using the word cruelty itself, Trotsky implies a moral judgment which is independent of partisan feelings and belongs to the common language. (It is, however, worth noting that the Russian word for *cruelly*, used in a generalized sense, as in the passage quoted from Lenin on page 467, is likely to be translated into English as "severely." *Severely* has no moral connotations, whereas *cruelly* has; but the element of cruelty in life had been, as it still is, in Russia so much a matter of course that it almost loses its moral implications. Where the conflict becomes so acute, it is difficult for either side to admit common concepts of morality. What is true here is also true of the other "means" with which Trotsky is dealing. A foreigner who has been lied to by Russian officials over a long enough period of time will end by losing his native candor.)

It would be possible to work out a point of view which would take care of these contradictions, which would explain in what proportion our notions of good and evil are universal and in what proportion they are determined by class, much more adequately than Trotsky has done here; I have tried to suggest how it might be put at the end of my chapter on the Dialectic. But it could perhaps never really be developed by anyone who, as Trotsky is, was trying to fight the class struggle himself. The shell of party polemics, that convention which is in itself an abrogation of peacetime relations and an obstacle to serious discussion, interposes itself here between Trotsky and the real problems at issue. There is a good deal of the mere argument *ad hominem*—or rather, argument to social class—of the kind exploited first by Marx and Engels in the *Communist Manifesto*. In reply to the objection that communism "repudiates, instead of refashioning them, religion and morality," the "eternal truths . . . that are common to all social systems," the founders of Marxism retort that since these social systems are all built on exploitation, they may well arrive at similar values; and in answer to such complaints as that communism destroys marriage and the family, throw back into the teeth of their opponents the disintegration of family relations produced by industrial work. In this way the question of whether, and if so, to what degree, certain qualities and types of behavior may be agreed to be desirable in themselves by human beings of different classes—this question never gets discussed at all; and Trotsky meets it here even less squarely than the *Communist Manifesto*: Who are these creatures who dare to probe our morality? They are the "petty pick-pockets of history," etc. The very title *Their Morals and Ours* attempts to divert attention by putting the debate on a polemical plane.

But again he invokes Lenin: "The 'amoralism' of Lenin," he says, "that is, his rejection of super-class morals, did not hinder him from remaining faithful to one and the same ideal throughout his whole life; from devoting his whole being to the cause of the oppressed; from displaying the highest conscientiousness in the sphere of ideas and the highest fearlessness in the sphere of action, from maintaining an attitude untainted by the least superiority to the 'ordinary' worker, to a defenseless woman, to a child. Does it not seem that 'amoralism' in the given case is only a pseudonym for higher human morality?" It is true, of course, that Lenin followed a moral logic of his own; but he lived it, and we can see how he was torn in feeling, if not perplexed in decision, by its difficulty. Even less than Trotsky did Lenin examine it or try to formulate it; yet today the best that Trotsky can do is to point into the past toward Lenin—that is, to show that there was once a great Bolshevik who was a humane and dedicated person.

It cannot be said that Trotsky has shown himself particularly humane. It seems to have been principally the planning side of socialism, the opportunity for increasing efficiency, and the ruthless side of Marxism, that attracted him when he was actually in power. The whole Bolshevik dictatorship, of course, was fundamentally undemocratic. With a people quite untrained in political democracy, it was inevitable that a revolutionary government should itself have to resort to despotism. And it is true that during the years of civil war the brutal methods of war-time imposed themselves as a matter of life or death for the Revolution itself. It is true that the first impulses of the Bolsheviks to be generous with their political enemies brought extremely disillusioning results: when they had released the monarchist general Krásnov, after his raid on Petrograd, in return for his word of honor that he would cease to fight the Bolshevik regime, he immediately returned to the attack. But through this crisis, which called forth Trotsky's best, he did not respond in any very sensitive way to the feelings and needs of the people. Read the pamphlet, *The Defense of Terrorism*, published in 1920, in reply to a pamphlet by Kautsky that attacked the Bolshevik regime, in which he defends both the Bolshevik shooting of military and political enemies and his own project for a compulsory labor army. True it was written "in the car of a military train and amid the flames of civil war" and Trotsky begs us to bear this in mind; but what we feel in it is the terrific force of a will to domination and regimentation with no evidence of any sympathy for the hardships of the dominated and regimented.

For when he had whipped the Red Army into shape at the cost of many drumhead executions and definitely routed the Whites, he proceeded, against Lenin's advice, to turn his admirable military machine into a conscript army of labor. But the soldiers, who had stuck it out against the enemies of the Revolution, began to vanish when they were put on public works. So also, the Commissar of War was opposed to allowing trade unions, insisting that since trade unions were by definition class weapons against the employees and since they were living in a workers' republic, they had no longer any need for such instruments. Lenin pointed out to him that the Bolshevik regime was not yet really wholly a workers' republic, but rather—since the workers were to a considerable extent directed by officials not of working-class origin—a "workers' republic with bureaucratic distortions."

The inauguration of the New Economic Policy (at the beginning of 1921), which allowed a certain amount of private exchange and let up on the requisitions from the peasants, relieved the whole situation by restoring the old motive of personal gain in place of the ideal of communist discipline. It is to the credit of Trotsky's sagacity that he had advocated the adoption of such measures in February, 1920, at a time when they were rejected by Lenin. But there had in the meantime taken place an incident which, instead of being eventually forgotten, has come to take on a more sinister significance in view of subsequent developments in Russia. In February, 1921, the sailors of the Kronstack fortress, who had played an heroic part in the 1917 revolution, rebelled in behalf of the peasants, and troops were sent against them by the

Bolsheviks and the mutiny was ruthlessly extinguished. Trotsky has recently defended his action on the ground that the personnel at Kronstadt were no longer the heroes of October and that the mutiny meant counter-revolution. But, after all, it was thought proper immediately afterwards to accede to the mutineers' demands by the establishment of the N.E.P, and in the meantime—as we learn from other sources—the men's families had been taken as hostages, and the sailors themselves, with such women as were with them, including the prostitutes of the barracks, had been massacred with every circumstance of ferocity by the child of the Tsar's Okhrána and the father of Stalin's GPU, the Cheká. One remembers Trotsky's satisfaction at the time of the 1905 revolution when the action of the St. Petersburg Soviet in connection with a similar mutiny on the part of the Kronstadt sailors prevented their execution by the Tsar; and one realizes that Trotsky's enthusiasm for freedom is less a positive than a negative affair, that it is expressed mainly in indignation against other people who will not let his side be free. Even in *Literature and Revolution* (of 1924), where Trotsky is dealing with a field that is more or less his own, and despite the range of his appreciation and his opposition to the more vulgar kind of attempt to break literature to the yoke of party doctrine, he is trying to bring the other Soviet writers inside his Marxist intellectual circle or chiding them when they stray.

Lenin was moved to rebuke Trotsky during the period of which I have spoken and which was the occasion of their only serious falling out, for his addiction to "intellectualistic formulas that fail to take into account the practical side of the question"; and in his "testament," Lenin's notes to the Central Committee written down not long before his death, in indicating Trotsky as "the ablest man" on the Central Committee, he criticizes his "too far-reaching confidence and a disposition to be far too much attracted by the purely administrative side of affairs." And it is as a hero of the faith in Reason that Trotsky must figure for us. He tells us in his autobiography how he used to be driven mad at school by hearing boys who were studying science talk about "'unlucky' Monday or about meeting a priest crossing the road," and how he would "get all excited and use hard words" (as he was to do in the above case, with Kautsky) when he could not convince the people at Yanóvka that the measure of the area of a trapezoidal field which he got quickly by applying Euclid was more accurate than the different one which they arrived at after "many weary hours" of measuring it bit by bit. But Marx, after all, is not Euclid; you may be able to calculate to some extent in moments of revolution what Trotsky is so fond of describing as the parallelogram of social forces; but to mold the living growth of a society you must be aware of what people want. Trotsky has illustrated by his whole career in a very instructive way what is valid and what is blind in this rationalistic aspect of Marxism.

IV
Literary Essays

~~~~~~~~~~~~~~~~~~~~~~~~~~~~~~~~~~~~~

EDITOR'S NOTE

This sampling of Wilson's literary essays shows the range of his interests and abilities. Written when he was also finishing *To the Finland Station* and first published in *The Triple Thinkers* and *The Wound and the Bow,* they involve biography and social history as well as texts from English, American, Russian, and Greek literature. "My purpose has always been to try to create something new," he writes in the preface to the second edition of *The Triple Thinkers.* "I have aimed either to present some writer who was not well enough known or, in the case of a familiar writer, to call attention to some neglected aspect of his work or career." The essay on *Eugene Onegin* shows how he conveys the qualities of an unfamiliar writer and makes us want to read him. Wilson specializes in characterizing works in a foreign language, and he places Pushkin's poetry in relation to eighteenth-century and Romantic literature in the West. He then retells the story in a way that establishes both its universality and its Russian resonances. His responsiveness to life and art, his sympathies and moral seriousness, enable him to make good use of the humble form of paraphrase. This was the beginning of three decades of interpreting the Russian literary tradition for Americans.

"The Historical Interpretation of Literature," which was delivered as a university lecture, is not a description of a system but an informal survey of those thinkers who laid the basis for historical and psychological criticism. For Wilson, as for Eliot and the New Critics, such work cannot replace aesthetic judgment (see also his review of Brooks's biography of James on page 125), but he differs from these contemporaries in seeing art in a broadly historical context, as an expression of the lives and characters of writers. His most influential study of a writer was "Dickens: The Two Scrooges" (1940), which replaced the sentimental comedian of the British middle class with the dark, symbolic novelist of modern critics and readers. The first half of this monograph, separately published as "Dickens and the Marshalsea Prison," remains one of our best accounts of an artist's use of traumatic experience, and editors have sometimes sought to reprint it alone. Wilson rereads the novels through *Little Dorrit* in the light of Dickens's boyhood suffering when his family went to prison and he was apprenticed to the blacking factory. His own isolated childhood helps the critic see how Dickens's sense of abandonment conditioned his work, giving him a lifelong sympathy with the criminal and the rebel, a conviction of the duplicity of Victorian England. In the Hemingway essay, on the other hand, an artist's use of psychic pain is approached, not biographically, but by contrasting his failures with the work in which his feelings are successfully controlled in art. When Hemingway is not brilliantly probing the moral condition of his time, he is seen succumbing to personal fears, political illusions, or unconscious self-parody. Wilson's earlier reviews of *In Our Time* and *The Sun Also Rises* had helped establish Hemingway in the twenties. The essay included here shows the man as he appeared to his generation in mid-passage.

The metaphor of the wound and the bow, derived from the Philoctetes myth, helps Wilson point up the relationship between neurosis and artistic or intellectual power, and in the title essay of the collection that includes his studies of Dickens and Hemingway he retells the story of

Sophocles's *Philoctetes* and interprets its meaning. Looking at a classical play with the insights made available by Freud, he leads us to speculate about the conflict of artist and society, along with the connections between genius and disease. His account of the mediating role of Neoptolemus reflects the modesty and pride of a great critic.

The companion piece to "The Historical Interpretation of Literature" is "Marxism and Literature," which contrasts the value of art for Marx and Engels, and in lesser degree for Lenin and Trotsky, with its reduction to a weapon in the 1930s. Both essays appear in *The Triple Thinkers.* Wilson's later studies of Pushkin's poems and their background are found in *A Window on Russia,* his reviews of Hemingway in *The Shores of Light* and *The Devils and Canon Barham.* The journals and reminiscences offer vivid glimpses of this man whom he never personally liked, yet whose death was for him the loss of "one of the foundation stones of my generation" (see page 639). Wilson developed his interpretation of Dickens when teaching at the University of Chicago, in 1939. The second half of his monograph leads from Dickens's two ménages, which had just been revealed by Foster's *Life,* to the critic's personal solution to *The Mystery of Edwin Drood.* "Dickens and the Marshalsea Prison" first appeared in *The Atlantic Monthly,* while the present text is from *The Wound and the Bow,* pages 3–59.

IN HONOR OF PUSHKIN:
*EVGENI ONEGIN**

Anyone who has read criticism by foreigners, even well-informed criticism, of the literature of his own country knows what a large part of it is likely to be made up of either banalities or errors. In the case of a novice at Russian like the writer, this danger is particularly great; and I shall probably be guilty of many sins in the eyes of Russian readers who should happen to see this essay. But Pushkin, the hundredth anniversary of whose death is being celebrated this year by the Soviets, has in general been so little appreciated in the English-speaking countries that I may, perhaps, be pardoned for however imperfect an attempt to bring his importance home to English-speaking readers. And Evgeni Onegin, who has played such a role for the Russian imagination, really belongs among those figures of fiction who have a meaning beyond their national frontiers for a whole age of Western society. The English Hamlet was as real, and as Russian, to the Russians of the generations that preceded the Revolution as any character in Russian literature. Let us receive Evgeni Onegin as a creation equally real for us.

It has always been difficult for Westerners—except perhaps for the Germans, who seem to have translated him more successfully than anyone else—to believe in the greatness of Pushkin. We have always left him out of account. George Borrow, who visited Russia in the course of his work for the Bible Society, published some translations of Pushkin in 1835; but the conventional world of literature knew little or nothing about him. Three years after Pushkin's death (and when Lermontov's career was nearly over), Carlyle, in *Heroes and Hero Worship*, described Russia as a "great dumb monster," not yet ma-

---

* Written for the centenary of Pushkin's death, January 29, 1937.

tured to the point where it finds utterance through the "voice of genius." Turgenev struggled vainly with Flaubert to make him recognize Pushkin's excellence; and even Renan was so ignorant of Russian literature that it was possible for him to declare on Turgenev's death that Russia had at last found her voice. Matthew Arnold, in writing about Tolstoy, remarked complacently that "the crown of literature is poetry" and that the Russians had not yet had a great poet; and T. S. Eliot, not long ago, in a discussion of the importance of Greek and Latin, was insisting on the inferior educational value of what he regarded as a merely modern literature like Russian, because "half a dozen great novelists"—I quote from memory— "do not make a culture." Even today we tend to say to ourselves, "If Pushkin is really as good as the Russians think he is, why has he never taken his place in world literature as Dante and Goethe have, and as Tolstoy and Dostoevsky have?"

The truth is that Pushkin *has* come through into world literature—he has come through by way of the Russian novel. Unlike most of the poets of his period, he had the real dramatic imagination, and his influence permeates Russian fiction—and theater and opera as well. Reading Pushkin for the first time, for a foreigner who has already read later Russian writers, is like coming for the first time to Voltaire after an acquaintance with later French literature: he feels that he is tasting the pure essence of something which he has found before only in combination with other elements. It is a spirit whose presence he has felt and with whom in a sense he is already familiar, but whom he now first confronts in person.

For the rest, it is true that the poetry of Pushkin is particularly difficult to translate. It is difficult for the same reason that Dante is difficult: because it says so much in so few words, so clearly and yet so concisely, and the words themselves and their place in the line have become so much more important than in the case of more facile or rhetorical writers. It would require a translator himself a poet of the first order to reproduce Pushkin's peculiar combination of intensity, compression and perfect ease. A writer like Pushkin may easily sound "flat," as he did to Flaubert in French, just as Cary's translation of Dante sounds flat. Furthermore, the Russian language, which is highly inflected and able to dispense with pronouns and prepositions in many cases where we have to use them and which does without the article altogether, makes it possible for Pushkin to pack his lines (separating modifiers from substantives, if need be) in a way which renders the problem of translating him closer to that of translating a tightly articulated Latin poet like Horace than any modern poet that we know. Such a poet in translation may sound trivial just as many of the translations of Horace sound trivial—because the weight of the words and the force of their relation have been lost with the inflections and the syntax.

So that, failing any adequate translation, we have tended, if we have thought about Pushkin at all, to associate him vaguely with Byronism: we have heard that *Evgeni Onegin* is an imitation of *Don Juan*. But this comparison is very misleading. Pushkin was a great artist: he derived as much from André Chénier as from Byron. *Don Juan* is diffuse and incoherent, sometimes brilliant, sometimes silly; it has its unique excellence, but it is the excellence of an improvisation. Byron said of some of the cantos that he wrote them on gin, and essentially it is a drunken monologue by a desperately restless, uncomfortable man, who does not know what is the matter with him or what he ought to do with himself, who wants to tell stories about other things or to talk about himself in such a way as to be able to laugh and curse and grieve without looking into anything too closely. Byron's achievement, certainly quite remarkable, is to have raised the drunken monologue to the dignity of a literary form. But the achievement of Pushkin is quite different. He had, to be sure, learned certain things from Byron—for example, the tone of easy negligence with which *Evgeni Onegin* begins and the habit of personal digression; but both of these devices in Pushkin are made to contribute to a general design. *Evgeni Onegin* is the opposite of *Don Juan* in being a work of unwavering concentration. Pushkin's "novel in verse" came out of Pushkin's deepest self-knowledge and was given form by a long and exacting discipline. The poet had adopted a compact speech and a complicated stanza-form as different as possible from Byron's doggerel; and he worked over the three hundred and eighty-nine stanzas which fill about two hundred pages through a period of eight years (1823–31) and was still, with every successive edition, revising them and cutting them down up to the time of his death.

One can convey a much more accurate impression of what Pushkin's actual writing is like by comparing him to Keats than to Byron. There are passages in *Evgeni Onegin*, such as those that introduce the seasons, which have a felicity and a fullness of detail not unlike Keats's "Ode to Autumn"—or, better perhaps, the opening of "The Eve of St. Agnes," which resembles them more closely in form:

> St. Agnes' Eve—Ah, bitter chill it was!
> The owl, for all his feathers, was a-cold;
> The hare limp'd trembling through the frozen grass,
> And silent was the flock in woolly fold:
> Numb were the Beadsman's fingers while he told
> His rosary, and while his frosted breath,
> Like pious incense from a censer old,
> Seem'd taking flight for heaven without a death,
> Past the sweet Virgin's picture, while his prayer he
>   saith.

Here is Pushkin's description of the coming of winter:

> Already now the sky was breathing autumn, already the dear sun more seldom gleamed, shorter grew the day, the forest's secret shadow was stripped away with sighing sound, mist lay upon the fields, the caravan of loud-tongued geese stretched to-

ward the south: drew near the duller season; November stood already at the door.

Rises the dawn in cold murk; in the fields the sound of work is still; the wolf with his hungry mate comes out upon the road; sniffing, the road-horse snorts—and the traveler who is wise makes full speed up the hill; the herdsman now at last by morning light no longer drives his cattle from the byre; at mid-day to their huddle his horn no longer calls them; inside her hut, the farm girl, singing, spins, while—friend of winter nights—her little flare of kindling snaps beside her.

And now the heavy frosts are snapping and spread their silver through the fields ... smoother than a smart parquet glistens the ice-bound stream. The merry mob of little boys with skates cut ringingly the ice; on small red feet the lumbering goose, hoping to float on the water's breast, steps carefully but slips and topples; gaily the first snow flashes and whirls about, falling in stars on the bank.

If you can imagine this sort of thing, which I have translated more or less literally, done in something like Keats's marrowy line, you will get some idea of what Pushkin is like. He can make us see and hear things as Keats can, but his range is very much greater: he can give us the effect in a few lines of anything from the opening of a bottle of champagne or the loading and cocking of pistols for a duel to the spinning and skipping of a ballet girl— who "flies like fluff from Aeolus' breath"—or the falling of the first flakes of snow. And as soon as we put "The Eve of St. Agnes" (published in 1820) beside *Evgeni Onegin*, it seems to us that Keats is weakened by an element of the conventionally romantic, of the mere storybook picturesque. But Pushkin can dispense with all that: here everything is sharp and real. No detail of country life is too homely, no phrase of city life too worldly, for him to master it by the beauty of his verse. Artistically, he has outstripped his time; and neither Tennyson in "In Memoriam" nor Baudelaire in *Les Fleurs du Mal* was ever to surpass Pushkin in making poetry of classical precision and firmness out of a world realistically observed.

I should note also—what I have never seen mentioned—that the passages of social description often sound a good deal more like Praed than like Byron. It is not likely that Pushkin was influenced by Praed, since Praed's peoms began to appear in *Knight's Quarterly* only in 1823, the year that *Onegin* was begun, and his characteristic vein of *vers de société* seems to date only from 1826, in which year Pushkin completed his sixth chapter. But the stanza in Chapter 2, with its epitaph on the death of Tatyana's father, might have been imitated from Praed's poem *The Vicar*, and if you can imagine Praed's talent raised to a higher power and telling a long story in his characteristically terse and witty stanzas (Pushkin's measure is shorter than Byron's, a rapid tetrameter like Praed's), you will be closer to Pushkin than *Don Juan* will take you:

> Good night to the Season!—the dances,
>   The fillings of hot little rooms,
> The glancings of rapturous glances,
>   The fancyings of fancy costumes;
> The pleasures which Fashion makes duties,
>   The praisings of fiddles and flutes,
> The luxury of looking at Beauties,
>   The tedium of talking to Mutes;
> The female diplomatists, planners
>   Of matches for Laura and Jane;
> The ice of her Ladyship's manners,
>   The ice of his Lordship's champagne.

To have written a novel in verse, and a novel of contemporary manners, which was also a great poem was Pushkin's unprecedented feat—a feat which, though anticipated on a smaller scale by the tales in verse of Crabbe and several times later attempted by nineteenth-century poets, was never to be repeated. And when we think of *Evgeni One-*

gin in connection with *Don Juan* or *The Ring and the Book* or *Aurora Leigh* or *Evangeline*, we find that it refuses to be classed with them. Pushkin's genius, as Maurice Baring has said, has more in common with the genius of Jane Austen than with the general tradition of the nineteenth-century novel. It is classical in its even tone of comedy which is at the same time so much more serious than the tragedies of Byron ever are, in its polishing of the clear and rounded lens which focuses the complex of human relations.

But Pushkin is much more vigorous than Jane Austen: the compression and rigor of the verse cause the characters to seem to start out of the stanzas. And he deals with more violent emotions. *Evgeni Onegin* is occupied with Byronism in a different way than that of deriving from Byron: it is among other things an objective study of Byronism. Both in the poem itself and in a letter that Pushkin wrote while he was working on it, he makes significant criticisms of Byron. "What a man this Shakespeare is!" he exclaims. "I can't get over it. How small the tragic Bryon seems beside him!—that Byron who has been able to imagine but a single character: his own ... Byron simply allots to each of his characters some characteristic of his own: his pride to one, his hatred to another, his melancholy to a third, etc., and thus out of a character which is in itself rich, somber and energetic, he makes several insignificant characters; but that is not tragedy." And in *Evgeni Onegin*, he speaks of Bryon's "hopeless egoism." Pushkin has been working away from his early romantic lyricism toward a Shakespearean dramatization of life, and now he is to embody in objective creations, to show involved in a balanced conflict, the currents of the age which have passed through him. Evgeni Onegin is presented quite differently from any of the romantic heroes of Bryon or Chateaubriand or Musset: when Byron dropped the attitudes of Childe Harold, the best he could do with Don Juan was to give him the innocence of Candide. Evgeni differs even from his immediate successor and kinsman, Lermontov's

Hero of Our Time—because Lermontov, though he tells his story with the distinctive Russian realism absent in the other romantic writers, is really involved to a considerable degree with the attitudes of his hero; whereas Pushkin, in showing us Evgeni, neither exalts him in the perverse romantic way nor yet, in exposing his weakness, hands him over to conventional morality. There is, I think, but one creation of the early nineteenth century who is comparable to Evgeni Onegin: Stendhal's Julien Sorel; and the poem is less akin to anything produced by the romantic poets than it is to *Le Rouge et le Noir* and *Madame Bovary*.

Our first glimpse of Pushkin's hero is not an ingratiating one: he has just been summoned to the bedside of a dying uncle, whose estate he is going to inherit, and he is cursing at the tiresome prospect of sitting around till the old man dies. But the scene is shifted at once to his previous life in St. Petersburg. He has been a young man about town, who has had everything society can give him. We see him at the restaurant, the opera, the ball; in one masterly passage we are shown him falling asleep after a round of the pleasures of the capital while the Petersburg of the merchants and cabmen and peddlers is just waking up for the day. But Evgeni is intelligent: he gets tired of his friends, tired of his love affairs. He is infected with the "English spleen" and grows languid and morose like Childe Harold. He shuts himself up to write, but he finds it terribly hard and gives it up. Then his uncle dies, and he inherits the estate and goes to live in the country.

The country bores him, too. Being a man of liberal ideas, he tries to lighten the lot of his serfs, and the neighbors decide he is a dangerous fellow. Then there appears in the neighborhood a young man named Lensky with whom Evgeni finds he has something in common. Lensky has just come back from Göttingen and is saturated with German idealism; and he is a poet in the German-romantic vein. Evgeni thinks him callow and naïve, but tries not to throw cold water on his illusions. He likes Lensky, and they go riding and have long arguments together.

Lensky is in love in the most idealistic fashion with a girl whom he has known since childhood and to whom he has always been faithful. She is pretty but entirely uninteresting: Pushkin tells us that she is just like the heroines of all the popular love stories of the day. Lensky goes to see her every evening—she lives with her sister and her widowed mother on a nearby estate—and one day takes Evgeni with him. Evgeni has sarcastically told Lensky in advance what the refreshments and the conversation will be like—the Larins will be just a "simple Russian family"; and on the drive back home he remarks that the face of Lensky's worshipped sweetheart is lifeless, red, and round "like this silly moon over this silly horizon," and remarks that if *he* were a poet like Lensky, he would have preferred the older sister, who had sat sadly by the window and said nothing.

This older sister, Tatyana, is "wild, melancholy, silent, and shy" and not so pretty as Olga. As a child, she hadn't liked games and hadn't been fond of dolls; she had thought it was funny to mimic her mother by lecturing her doll on how young ladies ought to comport themselves. Now her head is full of Richardson and Rousseau, and she likes to get up before dawn and watch the stars fade and the distance grow bright and feel the morning wind. And now, from the first moment she sees him, she falls furiously in love with Evgeni. She waits for a time in silence; then, as Evgeni does not come to call again, she sits down and writes him a letter, in which, painfully, uncontrollably, innocently, she confesses to him her love. This chapter, which deals with Tatyana's letter, is one of the great descriptions of first love in literature. Pushkin renews for us as we read all the poignancy and violence of those moments when for the first time the emotional forces of youth are released by another human being and try to find their realization through him. All the banal and deluded things that young people say and feel—that Evgeni is the one man in the world for her, the man for whom she has been waiting all her life, that he has been appointed by God to be her protector, that she is all alone and that no one understands her—poor Tatyana believes them all and puts them all into her letter; and Pushkin has succeeded in giving them to us in all their banality and deludedness, with no romantic sentimentalization, and yet making them move us profoundly. We enter into the emotions of Tatyana as we do into those of Juliet, yet at the same time Pushkin has set the whole picture in a perspective of pathetic irony which is not in that early play of Shakespeare's: there is nothing to indicate that Shakespeare's lovers might not have been ideally happy if it had not been for the family feud; but, in the case of Tatyana, we know from the first moment that her love is hopelessly misplaced in Evgeni. And the whole thing is set off and rooted in life by a series of marvelous touches—Tatyana's conversation with the nurse, the song she hears the serf-girls singing—and saturated with the atmosphere of the country estate where Tatyana has spent her whole life and where—so amazing is Pushkin's skill at evoking a complete picture through suggestion, needing only a few hundred lines where a novelist would take as many pages—we feel by the time she leaves it that we have lived as long as she.

Evgeni does not answer the letter, but two days afterwards he comes to see her. The role of the seducer is passé: it went out with periwigs and red heels; and for Evgeni the time for great passions is past: it is too much trouble to do anything about Tatyana. He conducts himself honorably, he talks to her kindly. He tells her that, if he had any desire for family life, she would certainly be the woman he would choose for a wife. But he was not created for happiness, such satisfactions are foreign to his soul. As a husband, he would be gloomy and disagreeable, and he would eventually cease to love her. He makes quite a long speech about it. And he tells her that she ought to

learn to control herself: another man might not understand as he does. Tatyana listens silently, in tears. He
gives her his arm and leads her back to the house.

But now Evgeni takes an unexpected turn. The Larins
give a big evening party to celebrate Tatyana's Saint's
Day. Evgeni goes and sits opposite Tatyana and realizes
that she is still in love with him and frightened to death in
his presence. He thinks that he is angry with Lensky because the party has turned out a bore and Lensky has
brought him there on false pretenses. He has for months
been watching Lensky moon over Olga with his eternal
romantic devotion which treats the beloved object with a
reverence almost religious and never makes any practical
advances; and he sets out now to annoy the young poet by
getting Olga away from him for the evening. Evgeni
makes Olga dance with him repeatedly, pays her animated
attentions—to which, as she is incapable of saying no, she
almost automatically responds. Lensky is deeply hurt and
furious; he leaves the party and goes straight home
and writes Evgeni a note calling him out.

Evgeni's first impulse, when he receives the challenge,
is to set things right with Lensky, not to let the young man
make a fool of himself. But then he is moved, as he tells himself, by the fear of public opinion: the second by whom
Lensky has sent the challenge, though a thoroughly disreputable individual, is an old-fashioned fancier and promoter
of duels. The night before they are to meet, Lensky sits
up till morning writing poetry. Evgeni sleeps sound and
late; he arrives on the field with his French valet, whom
he insolently presents as his second. The adversaries are
stationed by their seconds and take their paces toward
one another. Evgeni, as he is still approaching, quietly
raises his pistol, and he shoots while Lensky is aiming.*

---

* This is Wilson's description of the duel as corrected in the British
edition of *The Triple Thinkers*, after he had been enlightened by
Nabokov. Wilson had first thought that the duelists walked away
from each other before they turned and fired, this being the less brutal French version of dueling. [L.M.D.]

Lensky falls: in a remarkable simile, characteristically realistic and exact, Pushkin tells us how the young man's
heart, in which a moment before all the human passions
were dwelling, becomes suddenly like an abandoned
house blinded and dark and silent, with the windows covered with chalk and the owner gone away. Evgeni has
killed in the most cowardly fashion a man whose friend he
had believed himself to be and whom he had thought he
did not want to kill. Now at last we are sure of what
Pushkin, who has always given us Evgeni's version of his
own motives, has only so far in various ways suggested:
that, for all Lensky's obtuseness and immaturity, Evgeni
has been jealous of him, because Lensky has been able to
feel for Olga an all-absorbing emotion whereas Evgeni,
loved so passionately by Tatyana, has been unable to feel
anything at all. Lensky, the author now tells us, might or
might not have become a good poet; but the point is, as he
lets us know without telling us, that it is the poet in
Lensky whom Evgeni has hated. Evgeni had wanted to
write; but when he had sat down with the paper before
him, he had found it was too much trouble.

After the duel, Evgeni leaves the countryside. Lensky is
soon forgotten by Olga. She says yes to an uhlan, who
takes her off when he goes to join his regiment. Tatyana is
left alone. She walks over to Evgeni's house and gets the
caretaker to let her in; and there she returns day after day
and reads the books—so much more up to date than Richardson and Rousseau—which she has found in Evgeni's
library. There are a picture of Byron on the wall and a little iron statue of Napoleon; and, for the first time, Tatyana reads Byron, as well as several fashionable novels
which reflect the fashionable attitudes of the day. Evgeni
has marked them and made notes in the margin: and now
his lecture to her after her letter begins to have the sound
of an echo of all the things he has read.

But Tatyana continues to languish, doesn't get married.
Her mother decides to take her to Moscow. There follows
a wonderful description of the Larin family traveling to

Moscow. Pushkin, with his infinite sympathy and his
equally universal detachment, puts on record characteristics and customs of the Russians which are still striking to
a foreigner today. The Larins set several dates to get off,
but they never get off on those dates. Then at last they
do get off and get there. Now the leafy and mazy and
timeless estate is far behind Tatyana, and she sees the gold
crosses of the churches and then the people and shops and
palaces of Moscow. The shift from country to town is
beautifully handled by Pushkin; and there is nothing in
fiction more remarkable in its way than the account of
Tatyana's first days in Moscow. It is the forerunner of the
social scenes in *War and Peace*, and Natasha Rostova and
her family seem related to Tatyana and hers, just as Tolstoy's Moscow originals must have been to Pushkin's. The
Moscow cousin, to whose house Tatyana and her mother
first go and where an old Kalmuck in a ragged caftan and
spectacles lets them in, had been in love before she was
married with a dandy whom she had thought another Sir
Charles Grandison; and now the first thing she says to
Tatyana's mother, in whom she had used to confide, is,
"Cousin, do you remember Grandison?" "What Grandison? Oh, Grandison!—of course, I remember: where is
he?" "He's living in Moscow now; he came to see me at
Christmas; he married off his son not long ago."—But the
fashion of the younger generation—we are not told
whether or not Tatyana makes this reflection—is for
Byron instead of Grandison.

Tatyana cannot at first take her place in this world. Her
cousins, though urban, are nice; they look her over and
decide she is nice. They confide in her, but she cannot return their confidences: she moves among them detached,
distracted. She goes to dinner to be shown to her grandparents: " 'How Tanya has grown!' they say. 'Wasn't it
just the other day I christened you? and *I* used to carry
you in my arms! And *I* boxed your ears! And *I* used to
feed you gingerbread!' And the old ladies in chorus would
keep repeating: 'How our years fly by!'—But they—in

them she could see no change; it was all on the same old pattern: her aunt, the Princess Helena, still had the same tulle bonnet, Lukerya Lvovna still powdered herself just as much, Lyubov Petrovna still told the same lies, Ivan Petrovich was still just as silly, Semen Petrovich was still just as stingy, Pelagya Nikolavna still had the same friend, M. Finemouche, and the same Pomeranian and the same husband; and her husband was just as punctual at his club and just as meek and just as deaf as ever, and still ate and drank enough for two." One night at a ball, her solicitous aunt whispers to her to look to the left. An important-looking general is staring at her. "Who?" she asks. "That fat general?"

When Evgeni returns from his travels and goes into society again, he sees at a ball an extraordinarily smart lady who combines perfect naturalness with great dignity, whom everybody wants to speak to and to whom everybody defers; and he gasps at her resemblance to Tatyana. He inquires who she is of a man he knows. "My wife," the friend replies. It is Tatyana, now a princess; the man is the pompous general. Tatyana meets Evgeni without batting an eyelash: she asks him whether he has been long in St. Petersburg and whether he doesn't come from her part of the world.

Evgeni pays her court, follows her everywhere; but she refuses to recognize him. He writes her a letter, which is the counterpart of hers: now the roles are reversed—it is he who is putting himself at her mercy. She doesn't answer: he writes again and again. Then he shuts himself up in his house, cuts himself off from society and gives himself up to serious reading: history and moral philosophy. But Lensky gets between him and the page, and he hears a voice that says, "What, killed?" and he sees all the malicious gossips and the mean cowards and the young jilts and bitches whom he has known in Petersburg society and whom he has wanted to get away from and forget, and he sees Tatyana in the country house, sitting silent beside the window, as on the day when he first called.

Suddenly, one day when the winter snow is melting, he gets into his sleigh and drives off to her house. There is no one in the hall: he walks in. He finds her reading his letters. He throws himself at her feet. She looks at him without anger or surprise; she sees how sick and pitiful he is; the girl who loved him so in the country wakens again in her heart; she does not take her hand from his lips. Then, after a moment, she makes him get up. "I must be frank with you," she tells him. "Do you remember in the orchard how submissively I listened to your rebuke? Now it's my turn. I was younger then, and better. I loved you, and you were severe with me. The love of a humble country girl was not exciting for you. Good heavens! my blood still chills when I remember the cold look and the sermon you gave me. You didn't like me then in the country, and why do you run after me now? Because I'm rich and well known? because my husband has been wounded on the battlefield? because we're in favor at court? Isn't it because my shame would now be known to everybody, and would give you a reputation as a rake? Don't you think I would a thousand times rather be back with the orchard and my books and the places where I first saw you and the graveyard with my nurse's grave, than play this role in this noisy masquerade? But it's too late to do anything now. From the moment when you wouldn't have me, what did it matter to me what became of me? And now you're a man of honor; and although I love you still—why should I pretend?—I've given myself to another and I shall always be faithful to him."

She goes; and Evgeni stands thunderstruck, and then he hears the clank of the general's spurs. And there Pushkin leaves him.

The truth about Evgeni's fatal weakness has for the first time been fully driven home in Tatyana's speech: he has never been able to judge for himself of the intrinsic value of anything; all his values are social values; he has had enough independence, he has been enough superior to his associates, to be dissatisfied with the life of society, but, even in his disaffection, he has only been able to react into the disaffected attitude that is fashionable; his misanthropy itself has been developed in terms of what people will think of him, and, even trying to escape to the country, he has brought with him the standards of society. He had had enough sense of real values to know that there was something in Tatyana, something noble about her passion for him, to recognize in his heart that it was she who was the true unquiet brooding spirit, the true rebel against the conventions, where his quarrel with the world had been half a pose; but he had not had quite enough to love her just as she was: he had only been able to shoot Lensky.

Pushkin has put into the relations between his three central characters a number of implications. In one sense, they may be said to represent three intellectual currents of the time: Evgeni is Byronism turning worldly and dry; Lensky, with his Schiller and Kant, German romantic idealism; Tatyana, that Rousseauist Nature which was making itself heard in romantic poetry, speaking a new language and asserting a new kind of rights. And from another point of view they represent different tendencies in Russia itself: both Evgeni and Lensky are half foreigners, they think in terms of the cultures of the West, whereas Tatyana, who has spent her whole life on the wild old feudal estate, is for Pushkin the real Russia. Tatyana, like Pushkin, who said he owed so much to the stories of his Russian nurse, has always loved old wives' tales and is full of country superstitions. Before the fatal Saint's Day party and after her conversation with Onegin, she has an ominous dream, which is recounted at length. Tatyana's subconscious insight, going to the bottom of the situation and clothing it with the imagery of folk-tales, reveals to her a number of things which the others do not yet know about themselves: that there is something bad about Evgeni and that there is an antagonism between him and Lensky; in her dream, she sees Onegin stab Lensky. It is the sensitive though naïve Russian spirit, always aware of the hidden realities, with which Tolstoy and Dostoevsky were later on still attempting to make contact in their reaction against Western civilization. Yet with Pushkin, as Gide says of Dostoevsky, the symbols are perfectly embodied in the characters; they never deform the human being or convert him into an uninteresting abstraction. *Evgeni Onegin* has been popular because it has for generations been read by young Russians as a story—a story in which the eternal reasoning male is brought up against the eternal instinctive woman—like Elizabeth Bennet and Mr. Darcy; and in which the modest heroine—who, besides, is Cinderella and will end up expensively dressed and with the highest social position—gets morally all the best of it.

But there is still another aspect which the characters in *Evgeni Onegin* present. Pushkin speaks, at the end, of the years which have elapsed since he first saw Evgeni dimly, before the "free novel" which was to shape itself could be discerned "through the magic crystal." This magic crystal was Pushkin's own mind, which figures in the poem in a peculiar way. The poet, when he talks about himself, is not willful and egoistic like Byron; his digressions, unlike Byron's or Sterne's, always contribute to the story: they will begin by sounding like asides, in which the author is merely growing garrulous on the subject of some personal experience, but they will eventually turn out to merge into the experience of one of his characters, which he has been filling-in in this indirect way. Yet the crystal sphere is always there: it is inside it that we see the drama. Pushkin, throughout this period, had been tending to get away from his early subjective lyricism and to produce a more objective kind of art. After *Evgeni Onegin,* he was to write principally stories in prose. And in *Evgeni Onegin* it is almost as if we had watched the process—as we can see in the life-cell the nucleus splitting up into its separate nuclei and each concentrating its filaments and particles about it—by which the several elements of his character, the several strands of his experience, have taken symmetry about the foci of distinct characters. Pushkin had finally transfused himself into a dramatic work of art as none other of his romantic generation had done—for his serenity, his perfect balance of tenderness for human beings with unrelenting respect for reality, show a rarer quality of mind than Stendhal's.

Yet *Evgeni Onegin*, for all its lucidity, all its objectification, has behind it a conflict no less desperate than those which the other romantics were presenting so much more hysterically. Though Pushkin had triumphed as an artist as Byron was never able to do, he is otherwise a figure more tragic than the man who died at Missolonghi. For, after all, the chief disaster of *Evgeni Onegin* is not Evgeni's chagrin or Lensky's death: it is that Tatyana should have been caught up irrevocably by that empty and tyrannical social world from which Evgeni had tried to escape and which she had felt and still feels so alien. Pushkin married, the same year the *Onegin* was finished, a young and pleasure-loving wife who submerged him in the expenses of social life; and before he was out of his thirties, he got himself killed in a duel by a man whom he suspected of paying her attentions. It was as if in those generations where Byron, Shelley, Keats, Leopardi and Poe were dead in their twenties or thirties or barely reached forty, where Coleridge and Wordsworth and Beddoes and Musset burned out while still alive, where Lermontov, like Pushkin, was killed in a duel, before he was twenty-seven—it was as if in that great age of the bourgeois ascendancy—and even in still feudal Russia—it were impossible for a poet to survive. There was for the man of imagination and moral passion a basic maladjustment to society in which only the student of society—the social philosopher, the historian, the novelist—could find himself and learn to function. And to deal with the affairs of society, he had to learn to speak its language: that is, giving up the old noble language, he had—as Goethe and Hugo did, and as Pushkin did just before he died—to train himself to write in prose.

Yet Pushkin, who had done for the Russian language what Dante had done for Italian and who had laid the foundations of Russian fiction, had, in opposing the natural humanity of Tatyana to the social values of Evgeni, set a theme which was to be developed through the whole of Russian art and thought, and to give it its peculiar power. Lenin, like Tolstoy, could only have been possible in a world where this contrast was acutely felt. Tatyana, left by Pushkin with the last word, was actually to remain triumphant.

[1938]

THE HISTORICAL INTERPRETATION OF LITERATURE

I want to talk about the historical interpretation of literature—that is, about the interpretation of literature in its social, economic and political aspects.

To begin with, it will be worth while to say something about the kind of criticism which seems to be furthest removed from this. There is a kind of comparative criticism which tends to be non-historical. The essays of T. S. Eliot, which have had such an immense influence in our time, are, for example, fundamentally non-historical. Eliot sees, or tries to see, the whole of literature, so far as he is acquainted with it, spread out before him under the aspect of eternity. He then compares the work of different periods and countries, and tries to draw from it general conclusions about what literature ought to be. He understands, of course, that our point of view in connection with literature changes, and he has what seems to me a very sound conception of the whole body of writing of the past as something to which new works are continually being added, and which is not thereby merely increased in bulk but modified as a whole—so that Sophocles is no longer precisely what he was for Aristotle, or Shakespeare what he was for Ben Jonson or for Dryden or for Dr. Johnson, on account of all the later literature that has intervened between them and us. Yet at every point of this continual accretion, the whole field may be surveyed, as it were, spread out before the critic. The critic tries to see it as God might; he calls the books to a Day of Judgment. And, looking at things in this way, he may arrive at interesting and valuable conclusions which could hardly be reached by approaching them in any other way. Eliot was able to see, for example—what I believe had never been noticed before—that the French Symbolist poetry of the nineteenth century had certain fundamental resemblances to the English poetry of the age of Donne. Another kind of critic would draw certain historical conclusions from these purely aesthetic findings, as the Russian D. S. Mirsky did; but Eliot does not draw them.

Another example of this kind of non-historical criticism, in a somewhat different way and on a somewhat different plane, is the work of the late George Saintsbury. Saintsbury was a connoisseur of wines; he wrote an entertaining book on the subject. And his attitude toward literature, too, was that of the connoisseur. He tastes the authors and tells you about the vintages; he distinguishes the qualities of the various wines. His palate was fine as could be, and he possessed the great qualification that he knew how to take each book on its own terms without expecting it to be some other book and was thus in a position to appreciate a great variety of kinds of writing. He was a man of strong social prejudices and peculiarly intransigent political views, but, so far as it is humanly possible, he kept them out of his literary criticism. The result is one of the most agreeable and most comprehensive commentaries on literature that have ever been written in English. Most scholars who have read as much as Saintsbury do not have Saintsbury's discriminating taste. Here is a critic who has covered the whole ground like any academic historian, yet whose account of it is not merely a chronology but a record of fastidious enjoyment. Since enjoyment is the only thing he is looking for, he does not need to know the causes of things, and the historical background of literature does not interest him very much.

There is, however, another tradition of criticism which dates from the beginning of the eighteenth century. In the year 1725, the Neapolitan philosopher Vico published *La Scienza Nuova*, a revolutionary work on the philosophy of history, in which he asserted for the first time that the social world was certainly the work of man, and attempted what is, so far as I know, the first social interpretation of a work of literature. This is what Vico says about Homer: "Homer composed the *Iliad* when Greece was young and consequently burning with sublime passions such as pride, anger and vengeance—passions which cannot allow dissimulation and which consort with generosity; so that she then admired Achilles, the hero of force. But, grown old, he composed the *Odyssey*, at a time when the passions of Greece were already somewhat cooled by reflection, which is the mother of prudence—so that she now admired Ulysses, the hero of wisdom. Thus also, in Homer's youth, the Greek people liked cruelty, vituperation, savagery, fierceness, ferocity; whereas, when Homer was old, they were already enjoying the luxuries of Alcinoüs, the delights of Calypso, the pleasures of Circe, the songs of the sirens and the pastimes of the suitors, who went no further in aggression and combat than laying siege to the chaste Penelope—all of which practices would appear incompatible with the spirit of the earlier time. The divine Plato is so struck by this difficulty that, in order to solve it, he tells us that Homer had foreseen in inspired vision these dissolute, sickly and disgusting customs. But in this way he makes Homer out to have been but a foolish instructor for Greek civilization, since, however much he may condemn them, he is displaying for imitation these corrupt and decadent habits which were not to be adopted till long after the foundation of the nations of Greece, and accelerating the natural course which human events would take by spurring the Greeks on to corruption. Thus it is plain that the Homer of the *Iliad* must have preceded by many years the Homer who wrote the *Odyssey;* and it is plain that the former must belong to the northeastern part of Greece, since he celebrates the Trojan War, which took place in his part of the country, whereas the latter belongs to the southeastern part, since he celebrates Ulysses, who reigned there."

You see that Vico has here explained Homer in terms both of historical period and of geographical origin. The idea that human arts and institutions were to be studied and elucidated as the products of the geographical and climatic conditions in which the people who created them lived, and of the phase of their social development through which they were passing at the moment, made great progress during the eighteenth century. There are traces of it even in Dr. Johnson, that most orthodox and classical of critics—as, for example, when he accounts for certain characteristics of Shakespeare by the relative barbarity of the age in which he lived, pointing out, just as Vico had done, that "nations, like individuals, have their infancy." And by the eighties of the eighteenth century Herder, in his *Ideas on the Philosophy of History*, was writing of poetry that it was a kind of "Proteus among the people, which is always changing its form in response to the languages, manners, and habits, to the temperaments and climates, nay even to the accents of different nations." He said—what could still seem startling even so late as that— that "language was not a divine communication, but something men had produced themselves." In the lectures on the philosophy of history that Hegel delivered in Berlin in 1822–23, he discussed the national literatures as expressions of the societies which had produced them— societies which he conceived as great organisms continually transforming themselves under the influence of a succession of dominant ideas.

In the field of literary criticism, this historical point of view came to its first complete flower in the work of the French critic Taine, in the middle of the nineteenth century. The whole school of historian-critics to which Taine belonged—Michelet, Renan, Sainte-Beuve—had been occupied in interpreting books in terms of their historical origins. But Taine was the first of these to attempt to apply such principles systematically and on a large scale in a work devoted exclusively to literature. In the Introduction to his *History of English Literature,* published in 1863, he made his famous pronouncement that works of literature were to be understood as the upshot of three interfusing factors: *the moment, the race and the milieu.* Taine thought he was a scientist and a mechanist, who was examining works of literature from the same point of view as the chemist's in experimenting with chemical compounds. But the difference between the critic and the chemist is that the critic cannot first combine his elements and then watch to see what they will do: he can only examine phenomena which have already taken place. The procedure that Taine actually follows is to pretend to set the stage for the experiment by describing the moment, the race and the milieu, and then to say: "Such a situation demands such and such a kind of writer." He now goes on to describe the kind of writer that the situation demands, and the reader finds himself at the end confronted with Shakespeare or Milton or Byron or whoever the great figure is—who turns out to prove the accuracy of Taine's prognosis by precisely living up to this description.

There was thus a certain element of imposture in Taine; but it was the rabbits he pulled out that saved him. If he had really been the mechanist that he thought he was, his work on literature would have had little value. The truth was that Taine loved literature for its own sake—he was at his best himself a brilliant artist—and he had very strong moral convictions which give his writing emotional power. His mind, to be sure, was an analytic one, and his analysis, though terribly oversimplified, does have an explanatory value. Yet his work was what we call creative. Whatever he may say about chemical experiments, it is evident when he writes of a great writer that the moment, the race and the milieu have combined, like the three sounds of the chord in Browning's poem about Abt Vogler, to produce not a fourth sound but a star.

To Taine's set of elements was added, dating from the middle of the century, a new element, the economic, which was introduced into the discussion of historical phenomena mainly by Marx and Engels. The non-Marxist critics themselves were at the time already taking into account the influence of the social classes. In his chapters on the Norman conquest of England, Taine shows that the difference between the literatures produced respectively by the Normans and by the Saxons was partly the difference between a ruling class, on the one hand, and a vanquished and repressed class, on the other. And Michelet, in his volume on the Regency, which was finished the same year that the *History of English Literature* appeared, studies the *Manon Lescaut* of the Abbé Prévost as a document representing the point of view of the small gentry before the French Revolution. But Marx and Engels derived the social classes from the way that people made or got their living—from what they called the *methods of production;* and they tended to regard these economic processes as fundamental to civilization.

The Dialectical Materialism of Marx and Engels was not really so materialistic as it sounds. There was in it a large element of the Hegelian idealism that Marx and Engels thought they had got rid of. At no time did these two famous materialists take so mechanistic a view of things as Taine began by professing; and their theory of the relation of works of literature to what they called the *economic base* was a good deal less simple than Taine's theory of the moment, the race and the milieu.

They thought that art, politics, religion, philosophy and literature belonged to what they called the *superstructure* of human activity; but they saw that the practitioners of these various professions tended also to constitute social groups, and that they were always pulling away from the kind of solidarity based on economic classes in order to establish a professional solidarity of their own. Furthermore, the activities of the superstructure could influence one another, and they could influence the economic base. It may be said of Marx and Engels in general that, contrary to the popular impression, they were tentative, confused and modest when it came down to philosophical first principles, where a materialist like Taine was cocksure. Marx once made an attempt to explain why the poems of Homer were so good when the society that produced them was from his point of view—that is, from the point of view of its industrial development—so primitive; and this gave him a good deal of trouble. If we compare his discussion of this problem with Vico's discussion of Homer, we see that the explanation of literature in terms of a philosophy of social history is becoming, instead of simpler and easier, more difficult and more complex.

Marx and Engels were deeply imbued, moreover, with the German admiration for literature, which they had learned from the age of Goethe. It would never have occurred to either of them that *der Dichter* was not one of the noblest and most beneficent of humankind. When Engels writes about Goethe, he presents him as a man equipped for "practical life," whose career was frustrated by the "misery" of the historical situation in Germany in his time, and reproaches him for allowing himself to lapse into the "cautious, smug and narrow" philistinism of the class from which he came; but Engels regrets this, because it interfered with the development of the "mocking, defiant, world-despising genius," "der geniale Dichter," "der gewaltige Poet," of whom Engels would not even, he says, have asked that he should have been a political liberal if Goethe had not sacrificed to his bourgeois shrinkings his truer aesthetic sense. And the great critics who were trained on Marx—Franz Mehring and Bernard Shaw—had all this reverence for the priesthood of literature. Shaw deplores the absence of political philosophy and what he regards as the middle-class snobbery in Shakespeare; but he celebrates Shakespeare's poetry and his dramatic imagination almost as enthusiastically as Swinburne does, describing even those potboiling comedies, *Twelfth Night* and *As You Like It*—the themes of which seem to him most trashy—as "the Crown Jewels of English dramatic poetry." Such a critic may do more for a writer by showing him as a real man dealing with a real world at a definite moment of time than the impressionist critic of Swinburne's type who flourished in the same period of the late nineteenth century. The purely impressionist critic approaches the whole of literature as an exhibit of belletristic jewels, and he can only write a rhapsodic catalogue. But when Shaw turned his spotlight on Shakespeare as a figure in the Shavian drama of history, he invested him with a new interest as no other English critic had done.

The insistence that the man of letters should play a political role, the disparagement of works of art in comparison with political action, were thus originally no part of Marxism. They only became associated with it later. This happened by way of Russia, and it was due to special tendencies in that country that date from long before the Revolution or the promulgation of Marxism itself. In Russia there have been very good reasons why the political implications of literature should particularly occupy the critics. The art of Pushkin itself, with its marvelous power of implication, had certainly been partly created by the censorship of Nicholas I, and Pushkin set the tradition for most of the great Russian writers that followed him. Every play, every poem, every story, must be a parable of which the moral is *implied*. If it were stated, the censor would suppress the book as he tried to do with Pushkin's

Bronze Horseman, where it was merely a question of the packed implications protruding a little too plainly. Right down through the writings of Chekhov and up almost to the Revolution, the imaginative literature of Russia presents the peculiar paradox of an art that is technically objective and yet charged with social messages. In Russia under the Tsar, it was inevitable that social criticism should lead to political conclusions, because the most urgent need from the point of view of any kind of improvement was to get rid of the tsarist regime. Even the neo-Christian moralist Tolstoy, who pretended to be non-political, was to exert a subversive influence, because his independent preaching was bound to embroil him with the Church, and the Church was an integral part of the tsardom. Tolstoy's pamphlet called *What Is Art?*, in which he throws overboard Shakespeare and a large part of modern literature, including his own novels, in the interest of his intransigent morality, is the example which is most familiar to us of the moralizing Russian criticism; but it was only the most sensational expression of a kind of approach which had been prevalent since Belinsky and Chernyshevsky in the early part of the century. The critics, who were usually journalists writing in exile or in a contraband press, were always tending to demand of the imaginative writers that they should dramatize bolder morals.

Even after the Revolution had destroyed the tsarist government, this state of things did not change. The old habits of censorship persisted in the new socialist society of the Soviets, which was necessarily made up of people who had been stamped by the die of the despotism. We meet here the peculiar phenomenon of a series of literary groups that attempt, one after the other, to obtain official recognition or to make themselves sufficiently powerful to establish themselves as arbiters of literature. Lenin and Trotsky and Lunacharsky had the sense to oppose these attempts: the comrade-dictators of Proletcult or Lev or Rapp would certainly have been just as bad as the Count

Benckendorff who made Pushkin miserable, and when the Stalin bureaucracy, after the death of Gorky, got control of this department as of everything else, they instituted a system of repression that made Benckendorff and Nicholas I look like Lorenzo de' Medici. In the meantime, Trotsky, who was Commissar of War but himself a great political writer with an interest in belles-lettres, attempted, in 1924, apropos of one of these movements, to clarify the situation. He wrote a brilliant and valuable book called *Literature and Revolution,* in which he explained the aims of the government, analyzed the work of the Russian writers, and praised or rebuked the latter as they seemed to him in harmony or at odds with the former. Trotsky is intelligent, sympathetic; it is evident that he is really fond of literature and that he knows that a work of art does not fulfill its function in terms of the formulas of party propaganda. But Mayakovsky, the Soviet poet, whom Trotsky had praised with reservations, expressed himself in a famous joke when he was asked what he thought of Trotsky's book—a pun which implied that a commissar turned critic was inevitably a commissar still;* and what a foreigner cannot accept in Trotsky is his assumption that it is the duty of the government to take a hand in the direction of literature.

This point of view, indigenous to Russia, has been imported to other countries through the permeation of Communist influence. The Communist press and its literary followers have reflected the control of the Kremlin in all the phases through which it has passed, down to the wholesale imprisonment of Soviet writers which has been taking place since 1935. But it has never been a part of the American system that our Republican or Democratic administration should lay down a political line for the guidance of the national literature. A recent gesture in this

---

*Первый бдин дег наркомом, *The first pancake lies like a narkom* (people's commissar)—a parody of the Russian saying, Первый бдин дег комом, *The first pancake lies like a lump.*

direction on the part of Archibald MacLeish, who seems a little carried away by his position as Librarian of Congress, was anything but cordially received by serious American writers. So long as the United States remains happily a non-totalitarian country, we can very well do without this aspect of the historical criticism of literature.

Another element of a different order has, however, since Marx's time been added to the historical study of the origins of works of literature. I mean the psychoanalysis of Freud. This appears as an extension of something which had already got well started before, which had figured even in Johnson's *Lives of the Poets,* and of which the great exponent had been Sainte-Beuve: the interpretation of works of literature in the light of the personalities behind them. But the Freudians made this interpretation more exact and more systematic. The great example of the psychoanalysis of an artist is Freud's own essay on Leonardo da Vinci; but this has little critical interest: it is an attempt to construct a case history. One of the best examples I know of the application of Freudian analysis to literature is in Van Wyck Brooks's book *The Ordeal of Mark Twain,* in which Mr. Brooks uses an incident of Mark Twain's boyhood as a key to his whole career. Mr. Brooks has since repudiated the method he resorted to here, on the ground that no one but an analyst can ever know enough about a writer to make a valid psychoanalytic diagnosis. This is true, and it is true of the method that it has led to bad results where the critic has built a Freudian mechanism out of very slender evidence, and then given us what is really merely a romance exploiting the supposed working of this mechanism, in place of an actual study that sticks close to the facts and the documents of the writer's life and work. But I believe that Van Wyck Brooks really had hold of something important when he fixed upon that childhood incident of which Mark Twain gave so vivid an account to his biographer—that scene at the deathbed of his father when his mother had made him promise that he would not break her heart. If it was not one of those crucial happenings that are supposed to determine the complexes of Freud, it has certainly a typical significance in relation to Mark Twain's whole psychology. The stories that people tell about their childhood are likely to be profoundly symbolic even when they have been partly or wholly made up in the light of later experience. And the attitudes, the compulsions, the emotional "patterns" that recur in the work of a writer are of great interest to the historical critic.

These attitudes and patterns are embedded in the community and the historical moment, and they may indicate its ideals and its diseases as the cell shows the condition of the tissue. The recent scientific experimentation in the combining of Freudian with Marxist method, and of psychoanalysis with anthropology, has had its parallel development in criticism. And there is thus another element added to our equipment for analyzing literary works, and the problem grows still more complex.

The analyst, however, is of course not concerned with the comparative values of his patients any more than the surgeon is. He cannot tell you why the neurotic Dostoevsky produces work of immense value to his fellows while another man with the same neurotic pattern would become a public menace. Freud himself emphatically states in his study of Leonardo that his method can make no attempt to account for Leonardo's genius. The problems of comparative artistic value still remain after we have given attention to the Freudian psychological factor just as they do after we have given attention to the Marxist economic factor and to the racial and geographical factors. No matter how thoroughly and searchingly we may have scrutinized works of literature from the historical and biographical points of view, we must be ready to attempt to estimate, in some such way as Saintsbury and Eliot do, the relative degrees of success attained by the products of the various periods and the various personalities. We must be able to tell good from bad, the first-rate from the second-rate. We shall not otherwise write literary criticism at all, but merely social or political history as reflected in literary texts, or psychological case histories from past eras, or, to take the historical point of view in its simplest and most academic form, merely chronologies of books that have been published.

And now how, in these matters of literary art, do we tell the good art from the bad? Norman Kemp Smith, the Kantian philosopher, whose courses I was fortunate enough to take at Princeton twenty-five years ago, used to tell us that this recognition was based primarily on an emotional reaction. For purposes of practical criticism this is a safe assumption on which to proceed. It is possible to discriminate in a variety of ways the elements that in any given department go to make a successful work of literature. Different schools have at different times demanded different things of literature: *unity, symmetry, universality, originality, vision, inspiration, strangeness, suggestiveness, improving morality, socialist realism,* etc. But you could have any set of these qualities that any school of writing has called for and still not have a good play, a good novel, a good poem, a good history. If you identify the essence of good literature with any one of these elements or with any combination of them, you simply shift the emotional reaction to the recognition of the element or elements. Or if you add to your other demands the demand that the writer must have *talent,* you simply shift this recognition to the talent. Once people find some grounds of agreement in the coincidence of their emotional reactions to books, they may be able to discuss these elements profitably; but if they do not have this basic agreement, the discussion will make no sense.

But how, you may ask, can we identify this elite who know what they are talking about? Well, it can only be said of them that they are self-appointed and self-perpetuating, and that they will compel you to accept their authority. Imposters may try to put themselves over, but these quacks will not last. The implied position of the people who know about literature (as is also the case in every other art) is simply that they know what they know, and that they are determined to impose their opinions by main force of eloquence or assertion on the people who do not know. This is not a question, of course, of professional workers in literature—such as editors, professors and critics, who very often have no real understanding of the products with which they deal—but of readers of all kinds in all walks of life. There are moments when a first-rate writer, unrecognized or out of fashion with the official chalkers-up for the market, may find his support in the demand for his work of an appreciative cultivated public.

But what is the cause of this emotional reaction which is the critic's divining rod? This question has long been a subject of study by the branch of philosophy called aesthetics, and it has recently been made a subject of scientific experimentation. Both these lines of inquiry are likely to be prejudiced in the eyes of the literary critic by the fact that the inquiries are sometimes conducted by persons who are obviously deficient in literary feeling or taste. Yet one should not deny the possibility that something of value might result from the speculations and explorations of men of acute minds who take as their given data the aesthetic emotions of other men.

Almost everybody interested in literature has tried to explain to himself the nature of these emotions that register our approval of artistic works; and I of course have my own explanation.

In my view, all our intellectual activity, in whatever field it takes place, is an attempt to give a meaning to our experience—that is, to make life more practicable; for by understanding things we make it easier to survive and get around among them. The mathematician Euclid, working in a convention of abstractions, shows us relations between the distances of our unwieldy and cluttered-up en-

vironment upon which we are able to count. A drama of
Sophocles also indicates relations between the various
human impulses, which appear so confused and dangerous, and it brings out a certain justice of Fate—that is to
say, of the way in which the interaction of these impulses
is seen in the long run to work out—upon which we can
also depend. The kinship, from this point of view, of the
purposes of science and art appears very clearly in the
case of the Greeks, because not only do both Euclid and
Sophocles satisfy us by making patterns, but they make
much the same kind of patterns. Euclid's *Elements* takes
simple theorems and by a series of logical operations
builds them up to a climax in the square of the hypote-
nuse. A typical drama of Sophocles develops in a similar
way.

Some writers (as well as some scientists) have a different kind of explicit message beyond the reassurance implicit in the mere feat of understanding life or of molding
the harmony of artistic form. Not content with such an
achievement as that of Sophocles—who has one of his
choruses tell us that it is better not to be born, but who,
by representing life as noble and based on law, makes its
tragedy easier to bear—such writers attempt, like Plato, to
think out and recommend a procedure for turning it into
something better. But other departments of literature—
lyric poetry such as Sappho's, for example—have *less*
philosophical content than Sophocles. A lyric gives us
nothing but a pattern imposed on the expression of a feeling; but this pattern of metrical quantities and of consonants and vowels that balance has the effect of reducing
the feeling, however unruly or painful it may seem when
we experience it in the course of our lives, to something
orderly, symmetrical and pleasing; and it also relates this
feeling to the more impressive scheme, works it into the
larger texture, of the body of poetic art. The discord has
been resolved, the anomaly subjected to discipline. And
this control of his emotion by the poet has the effect at secondhand of making it easier for the reader to manage his

own emotions. (Why certain sounds and rhythms gratify us more than others, and how they are connected with the themes and ideas that they are chosen as appropriate for conveying, are questions that may be passed on to the scientist.)

And this brings us back again to the historical point of view. The experience of mankind on the earth is always changing as man develops and has to deal with new combinations of elements; and the writer who is to be anything more than an echo of his predecessors must always find expression for something which has never yet been expressed, must master a new set of phenomena which has never yet been mastered. With each such victory of the human intellect, whether in history, in philosophy or in poetry, we experience a deep satisfaction: we have been cured of some ache of disorder, relieved of some oppressive burden of uncomprehended events.

This relief that brings the sense of power, and, with the sense of power, joy, is the positive emotion which tells us that we have encountered a first-rate piece of literature. But stay! you may at this point warn: are not people often solaced and exhilarated by literature of the trashiest kind? They are: crude and limited people do certainly feel some such emotion in connection with work that is limited and crude. The man who is more highly organized and has a wider intellectual range will feel it in connection with work that is finer and more complex. The difference between the emotion of the more highly organized man and the emotion of the less highly organized one is a matter of mere gradation. You sometimes discover books—the novels of John Steinbeck, for example—that seem to mark precisely the borderline between work that is definitely superior and work that is definitely bad. When I was speaking a little while back of the genuine connoisseurs who establish the standards of taste, I meant, of course, the people who can distinguish Grade A and who prefer it to the other grades.

[1940]

DICKENS AND THE
MARSHALSEA PRISON

1

The father of Charles Dickens's father was head butler in the house of John Crewe (later Lord Crewe) of Crewe Hall, Member of Parliament for Chester; and the mother of his father was a servant in the house of the Marquess of Blandford in Grosvenor Square, who was Lord Chamberlain to the Household of George III. This grandmother, after her marriage, became housekeeper at Crewe Hall, and it is assumed that it was through the patronage of her employer that her son John Dickens was given a clerkship in the Navy Pay Office.

John Dickens began at £70 a year and was in time increased to £350. But he had always had the tastes of a gentleman. He was an amiable fellow, with an elegant manner and a flowery vein of talk, who liked to entertain his friends and who could not help creating the impression of a way of life beyond his means. He was always in trouble over bills.

When Charles, who had been born (February 7, 1812) at Portsmouth and had spent most of his childhood out of London at Portsmouth, Portsea and Chatham, who had had a chance to go to the theater and to read the *Arabian Nights* and the eighteenth-century novelists, and had been taught by a tutor from Oxford, came up to London at the age of nine to join his parents, who had been obliged to return there, he was terribly shocked to find them, as a consequence of his father's debts, now living in a little back garret in one of the poorest streets of Camden Town. On February 20, 1824, when Charles was twelve, John Dickens was arrested for debt and taken to the Marshalsea Prison, announcing, as he left the house: "The sun has set upon me forever!" At home the food began to run low; and they had to pawn the household belongings till all but two rooms were bare. Charles even had to carry his books, one by one, to the pawnshop. It was presently decided that the boy should go to work at six shillings a week for a cousin who manufactured blacking; and through six months, in a rickety old house by the river, full of dirt and infested with rats, he pasted labels on blacking bottles, in the company of riverside boys who called him "the little gentleman." He wanted terribly to go on with his schooling, and couldn't grasp what had happened to him. The whole of the rest of the family moved into the Marshalsea with his father; and Charles, who had a lodging near them, went to the jail after work every evening and ate breakfast with them every morning. He was so ashamed of the situation that he would never allow his companion at the blacking warehouse, whose name was Bob Fagin, to go with him to the door of the prison, but would take leave of him and walk up the steps of a strange house and pretend to be going in. He had had a kind of nervous fits in his earlier childhood, and now these began to recur. One day at work he was seized with such an acute spasm that he had to lie down on some straw on the floor, and the boys who worked with him spent half the day applying blacking bottles of hot water to his side.

John Dickens inherited a legacy in May and got out of jail the twenty-eighth; but he let Charles keep on working in the warehouse. The little boys did their pasting next to the window in order to get the light, and people used to stop to look in at them because they had become so quick and skillful at it. This was an added humiliation for Charles; and one day when John Dickens came there, he wondered how his father could bear it. At last—perhaps, Dickens thought, as a result of what he had seen on this visit—John quarreled with Charles's employer, and took the boy out of the warehouse and sent him to school.

These experiences produced in Charles Dickens a trauma from which he suffered all his life. It has been charged by some of Dickens's critics that he indulged himself excessively in self-pity in connection with these hardships of his childhood; it has been pointed out that, after all, he had only worked in the blacking warehouse six months. But one must realize that during those months he was in a state of complete despair. For the adult in desperate straits, it is almost always possible to imagine, if not to contrive, some way out; for the child, from whom love and freedom have inexplicably been taken away, no relief or release can be projected. Dickens's seizures in his blacking-bottle days were obviously neurotic symptoms; and the psychologists have lately been telling us that lasting depressions and terrors may be caused by such cuttings-short of the natural development of childhood. For an imaginative and active boy of twelve, six months of despair are quite enough. "No words can express," Dickens wrote of his first introduction to the warehouse, in a document he gave to Forster, "the secret agony of my soul as I sunk into this companionship; compared these every day associates with those of my happier childhood; and felt my early hopes of growing up to be a learned and distinguished man crushed in my breast. The deep remembrance of the sense I had of being utterly neglected and hopeless; of the shame I felt in my position; of the misery it was to my young heart to believe that, day by day, what I had learned, and thought, and delighted in, and raised my fancy and my emulation up by, was passing away from me, never to be brought back any more; cannot be written. My whole nature was so penetrated with the grief and humiliation of such considerations, that even now, famous and caressed and happy, I often forget in my dreams that I have a dear wife and children; even that I am a man; and wander desolately back to that time of my life."

He never understood how his father could have abandoned him to such a situation. "I know my father," he once told Forster, "to be as kind-hearted and generous a man as ever lived in the world. Everything that I can remember of his conduct to his wife, or children, or friends, in sickness or affliction is beyond all praise. By me, as a sick child, he has watched night and day, unweariedly and patiently, many nights and days. He never undertook any business, charge or trust that he did not zealously, conscientiously, punctually, honorably discharge. His industry has always been untiring. He was proud of me, in his way, and had a great admiration of [my] comic singing. But, in the case of his temper, and the straitness of his means, he appeared to have lost utterly at this time the idea of educating me at all, and to have utterly put from him the notion that I had any claim upon him, in that regard, whatever." And Charles never forgave his mother for having wanted to keep him working in the warehouse even after his father had decided to take him out. "I never afterwards forgot," he wrote of her attitude at this time. "I never shall forget, I never can forget."

Of those months he had never been able to bring himself to speak till, just before conceiving *David Copperfield*, he wrote the fragment of autobiography he sent to Forster; and, even after he had incorporated this material in an altered form in the novel, even his wife and children were never to learn about the realities of his childhood till they read about it after his death in Forster's *Life*. But the work of Dickens's whole career was an attempt to digest these early shocks and hardships, to explain them to himself, to justify himself in relation to them, to give an intelligible and tolerable picture of a world in which such things could occur.

Behind the misfortune which had humiliated Charles was the misfortune which had humiliated his father. John Dickens was a good and affectionate man, who had done the best he was able within the limits of his personality and who had not deserved to be broken. But behind these undeserved misfortunes were sources of humiliation perhaps more disturbing still. The father of Charles Dickens's mother, also a £350-a-year clerk in the Navy Pay Office, with the title of Conductor of Money, had systematically, by returning false balances, embezzled funds to the amount of £5689 3s.3d. over a period of seven years; and when the fraud was discovered, had fled. And the background of domestic service was for an Englishman of the nineteenth century probably felt as more disgraceful than embezzlement. Certainly the facts about Dickens's ancestry were kept hidden by Dickens himself and have, so far as I know, only been fully revealed in the memoir by Miss Gladys Storey, based on interviews with Mrs. Perugini, Dickens's last surviving daughter, which was published in England in the summer of 1939.

But all these circumstances are worth knowing and bearing in mind, because they help us to understand what Dickens was trying to say. He was less given to false moral attitudes or to fear of respectable opinion than most of the great Victorians; but just as through the offices of his friends and admirers his personal life has been screened from the public even up to our own day, in a way that would have been thought unjustified in the case of a Keats or a Byron of the earlier nineteenth century, so the meaning of Dickens's work has been obscured by that element of the conventional which Dickens himself never quite outgrew. It is necessary to see him as a man in order to appreciate him as an artist—to exorcise the spell which has bewitched him into a stuffy piece of household furniture and to give him his proper rank as the poet of that portièred and upholstered world who saw clearest through the coverings and the curtains.

2

If one approaches his first novel, *Pickwick Papers*, with these facts of Dickens's biography in mind, one is struck by certain features of the book which one may not have noticed before.

Here the subject has been set for Dickens. He was supposed to provide some sort of text for a series of comic sporting plates by Seymour—something in the vein of Surtees's *Jorrocks*. As soon, however, as Dickens's scheme gives him a chance to get away from the sporting plates and to indulge his own preoccupations, the work takes a different turn.

There are in *Pickwick Papers*, especially in the early part, a whole set of interpolated short stories which make a contrast with the narrative proper. These stories are mostly pretty bad and deserve from the literary point of view no more attention than they usually get; but, even allowing here also for an element of the conventional and popular, of the still-thriving school of Gothic horror, we are surprised to find rising to the surface already the themes which were to dominate his later work.

The first of these interludes in *Pickwick* deals with the death of a pantomime clown, reduced through drink to the direst misery, who, in the delirium of his fever, imagines that he is about to be murdered by the wife whom he has been beating. In the second story, a worthless husband also beats his wife and sets an example of bad conduct to his son; the boy commits a robbery, gets caught and convicted—in prison remains obdurate to his mother's attempts to soften his sullen heart; she dies, he repents, it is too late; he is transported, returns after seventeen years and finds no one to love or greet him; he stumbles at last upon his father, now a sodden old man in the workhouse; a scene of hatred and violence ensues: the father, filled with terror, strikes the son across the face with a stick, the son seizes the father by the throat, and the old man bursts a blood-vessel and falls dead. The third story is a document by a madman, which, like the delirium of the dying clown, gives Dickens an opportunity to exploit that vein of hysterical fancy which was to find fuller scope in *Barnaby Rudge* and which was there to figure for him the life of the imagination itself. The narrator has lived in the knowledge that he is to be the victim of hereditary insanity. At last he feels that he is going mad, but at the same moment he inherits money: men fawn upon him and praise him now, but he secretly rejoices in the sense that he is not one of them, that he is fooling them. He marries a girl who loves another but who has been sold to him by her father and brothers; seeing his wife languish away and coming to understand the situation, fearing also lest she may hand on the family curse, he tries to kill her in her sleep with a razor; she wakes up but dies of the shock. When one of her brothers comes to reproach him, the madman throws him down and chokes him; runs amuck and is finally caught.

But it is in "The Old Man's Tale About the Queer Client" (Chapter XXI) that Dickens's obsessions appear most plainly. Here at the threshold of Dickens's work we are confronted with the Marshalsea Prison. A prisoner for debt, a "healthy, strong-made man, who could have borne almost any fatigue of active exertion," wastes away in his confinement and sees his wife and child die of grief and want. He swears to revenge their deaths on the man who has put him there. We have another long passage of delirium, at the end of which the prisoner comes to, to learn that he has inherited his father's money. At a seaside resort where he has been living, he sees a man drowning one evening: the father of the drowning man stands by and begs the ex-prisoner to save his son. But when the wronged man recognizes his father-in-law, the scoundrel who sent him to prison and who allowed his own daughter and grandson to die, he retaliates by letting the boy drown; then, not content with this, he buys up, at "treble and quadruple their nominal value," a number of loans which have been made to the old man. These loans have been arranged on the understanding that they are renewable up to a certain date; but the wronged man, taking advantage of the fact that the agreement has never been put on paper, proceeds to call them in at a time when his father-in-law has "sustained many losses." The old man is dispossessed of all his property and finally runs away in order to escape prison; but his persecutor tracks him down to a "wretched lodging"—note well: "in Camden Town" —and there finally reveals himself and announces his implacable intention of sending his persecutor to jail.

The old man falls dead from shock, and the revenger disappears.

In the meantime, the same theme has been getting under way in the main current of the comic novel. Mr. Pickwick has been framed by Dodson and Fogg, and very soon—another wronged man—he will land in the debtors' prison, where a good many of the other characters will join him and where the whole book will deepen with a new dimension of seriousness. The hilarity of the scene in court, in which Mr. Pickwick is convicted of trifling with Mrs. Bardell's affections—a scene openly borrowed from *Jorrocks* but wonderfully transformed by Dickens, and as brilliant as the story of the fiendish revenge on the fiendish father-in-law is bathetic—may disguise from the reader the significance which this episode had for Dickens. Here Dickens is one of the greatest of humorists: it is a laughter which is never vulgar but which discloses the vulgarity of the revered—a laughter of human ecstasy that rises like the phoenix from the cinders to which the dismal denizens of the tribunals have attempted to reduce decent human beings. It represents, like the laughter of Aristophanes, a real escape from institutions.

I shall make no attempt to discuss at length the humor of the early Dickens. This is the aspect of his work that is best known, the only aspect that some people know. In praise of Dickens's humor, there is hardly anything new to say. The only point I want to make is that the humor of Dickens does differ from such humor as that of Aristophanes in being unable forever to inhabit an empyrean of blithe intellectual play, of charming fancies and biting good sense. Dickens's laughter is an exhilaration which already shows a trace of the hysterical. It leaps free of the prison of life; but gloom and soreness must always drag it back. Before he has finished *Pickwick* and even while he is getting him out of jail and preparing to unite the lovers, the prison will close in again on Dickens. While he is still on the last instalments of *Pickwick*, he will begin writing *Oliver Twist*—the story of a disinherited boy, consigned to a workhouse which is virtually a jail and getting away only to fall into the hands of a gang of burglars, pickpockets and prostitutes.

And now we must identify the attitudes with which Dickens's origins and his early experiences had caused him to meet mankind. The ideal of *Pickwick Papers* is a kindly retired businessman, piloted through a tough and treacherous world by a shrewd servant of watchful fidelity, who perfectly knows his place: Mr. Pickwick and Sam Weller. But this picture, though real enough to its creator, soon gives way to the figure of a parentless and helpless child—a figure of which the pathos will itself be eclipsed by the horror of the last night in the condemned cell of a betrayer of others to the gallows, and by the headlong descent into hell of a brute who clubs his girl to death and who, treed like a cat by the pursuing mob, hangs himself in trying to escape.

3

Edmund Yates described Dickens's expression as "blunt" and "pleasant," but "rather defiant."

For the man of spirit whose childhood has been crushed by the cruelty of organized society, one of two attitudes is natural: that of the criminal or that of the rebel. Charles Dickens, in imagination, was to play the roles of both, and to continue up to his death to put into them all that was most passionate in his feeling.

His interest in prisons and prisoners is evident from the very beginning. In his first book, *Sketches by Boz*, he tells how he used to gaze at Newgate with "mingled feelings of awe and respect"; and he sketches an imaginary picture of a condemned man's last night alive, which he is soon to elaborate in *Oliver Twist*. Almost the only passage in *American Notes* which shows any real readiness on Dickens's part to enter into the minds and feelings of the people among whom he is traveling is the fantasy in which he imagines the effects of a sentence of solitary confinement in a Philadelphia jail. He visited prisons wherever he went, and he later found this cruel system imitated in the jail at Lausanne. Dickens was very much gratified when the system was finally abandoned as the result of the prisoners' going mad just as he had predicted they would. He also wrote a great deal about executions. One of the vividest things in *Pictures from Italy* is a description of a guillotining; and one of the most impressive episodes in *Barnaby Rudge* is the narration—developed on a formidable scale—of the hanging of the leaders of the riots. In 1846, Dickens wrote letters to the press in protest against capital punishment for murderers, on the ground among other grounds that this created sympathy for the culprits; in 1849, after attending some executions in London with Forster, he started by writing to *The Times* an agitation which had the effect of getting public hangings abolished, Even in 1867, in the course of his second visit to America, "I have been tempted out," Dickens wrote Forster, "at three in the morning to visit one of the large police station-houses, and was so fascinated by the study of a horrible photograph-book of thieves' portraits that I couldn't put it down."

His interest in the fate of prisoners thus went a good deal farther than simple memories of the debtors' prison or notes of a court reporter. He identified himself readily with the thief, and even more readily with the murderer. The man of powerful will who finds himself opposed to society must, if he cannot upset it or if his impulse to do so is blocked, feel a compulsion to commit what society regards as one of the capital crimes against itself. With the antisocial heroes of Dostoevsky, this crime is usually murder or rape; with Dickens, it is usually murder. His obsession with murderers is attested by his topical pieces for *Household Words;* by his remarkable letter to Forster on the performance of the French actor Lemaître in a play in which he impersonated a murderer; by his expedition, on his second visit to America, to the Cambridge Medical School for the purpose of going over the ground where

Professor Webster had committed a murder in his laboratory and had continued to meet his courses with parts of the body under the lid of his lecture-table. In Dickens's novels, this theme recurs with a probing of the psychology of the murderer which becomes ever more convincing and intimate. Leaving the murderers of the later Dickens till we come to his later books, we may, however, point out here that the crime and flight of Jonas Chuzzlewit already show a striking development beyond the cruder crime and flight of Sikes. The fantasies and fears of Jonas are really, as Taine remarked, the picture of a mind on the edge of insanity. What is valid and impressive in this episode is the insight into the consciousness of a man who has put himself outside human fellowship—the moment, for example, after the murder when Jonas is "not only fearful *for* himself but *of* himself" and half-expects, when he returns to his bedroom, to find himself asleep in the bed.

At times the two themes—the criminal and the rebel— are combined in a peculiar way. *Barnaby Rudge*—which from the point of view of Dickens's comedy and character-drawing is the least satisfactory of his early books—is, up to *Martin Chuzzlewit,* the most interesting from the point of view of his deeper artistic intentions. It is the only one of these earlier novels which is not more or less picaresque and, correspondingly, more or less of an improvisation (though there is a certain amount of organization discernible in that other somber book, *Oliver Twist*); it was the only novel up to that time which Dickens had been planning and reflecting on for a long time before he wrote it: it is first mentioned in 1837, but was not written till 1841. Its immediate predecessor, *The Old Curiosity Shop,* had been simply an impromptu yarn, spun out— when Dickens discovered that the original scheme of *Master Humphrey's Clock* was not going over with his readers—from what was to have been merely a short story; but *Barnaby Rudge* was a deliberate attempt to find expression for the emotions and ideas that possessed him.

The ostensible subject of the novel is the anti-Catholic

insurrection known as the "Gordon riots" which took place in London in 1780. But what is obviously in Dickens's mind is the Chartist agitation for universal suffrage and working-class representation in Parliament which, as a result of the industrial depression of those years, came to a crisis in 1840. In Manchester the cotton mills were idle, and the streets were full of threatening jobless men. In the summer of 1840 there was a strike of the whole North of England, which the authorities found it possible to put down only by firing into the working-class crowds; this was followed the next year by a brick-makers' strike, which ended in bloody riots. Now the immediate occasion for the Gordon riots had been a protest against a bill which was to remove from the English Catholics such penalties and disabilities as the sentence of life imprisonment for priests who should educate children as Catholics and the disqualifications of Catholics from inheriting property; but the real causes behind the demonstration have always remained rather obscure. It seems to indicate an indignation more violent than it is possible to account for by mere anti-Catholic feeling that churches and houses should have been burnt wholesale, all the prisons of London broken open, and even the Bank of England attacked, and that the authorities should for several days have done so little to restrain the rioters; and it has been supposed that public impatience at the prolongation of the American War, with a general desire to get rid of George III, if not of the monarchy itself, must have contributed to the fury behind the uprising.

This obscurity, at any rate, allowed Dickens to handle the whole episode in an equivocal way. On the surface he reprobates Lord George Gordon and the rioters for their fanatical or brutal intolerance; but implicitly he is exploiting to the limit certain legitimate grievances of the people: the neglect of the lower classes by a cynical eighteenth-century aristocracy, and especially the penal laws which made innumerable minor offenses punishable by death. The really important theme of the book—as Dickens shows in his preface, when he is discussing one of the actual occurrences on which the story is based—is the hanging under the Shop-lifting Act of a woman who has been dropped by her aristocratic lover and who has forged notes to provide for her child. This theme lies concealed, but it makes itself felt from beginning to end of the book. And as *Pickwick,* from the moment it gets really under way, heads by instinct and, as it were, unconsciously straight for the Fleet prison, so *Barnaby Rudge* is deliberately directed toward Newgate, where, as in *Pickwick* again, a group of characters will be brought together; and the principal climax of the story will be the orgiastic burning of the prison. This incident not only has nothing to do with the climax of the plot, it goes in spirit quite against the attitude which Dickens has begun by announcing. The satisfaction he obviously feels in demolishing the sinister old prison, which, rebuilt, had oppressed him in childhood, completely obliterates the effect of his right-minded references in his preface to "those shameful tumults," which "reflect indelible disgrace upon the time in which they occurred, and all who had act or part in them." In the end, the rioters are shot down and their supposed instigators hanged; but here Dickens's *parti pris* emerges plainly: "Those who suffered as rioters were, for the most part, the weakest, meanest and most miserable among them." The son of the woman hanged for stealing, who has been one of the most violent of the mob and whose fashionable father will do nothing to save him, goes to the scaffold with courage and dignity, cursing his father and "that black tree, of which I am the ripened fruit."

Dickens has here, under the stimulus of the Chartist agitation, tried to give his own emotions an outlet through an historical novel of insurrection; but the historical episode, the contemporary moral, and the author's emotional pattern do not always coincide very well. Indeed, perhaps the best thing in the book is the creation that most runs away with the general scheme that Dickens has attempted. Dennis the hangman, although too macabre to be one of Dickens's most popular characters, is really one of his best comic inventions, and has more interesting symbolic implications than Barnaby Rudge himself. Dennis is a professional executioner, who has taken an active part in the revolt, apparently from simple motives of sadism. Knowing the unpopularity of the hangman, he makes an effort to keep his identity a secret; but he has found this rather difficult to do, because he sincerely loves his profession and cannot restrain himself from talking about it. When the mob invades Newgate, which Dennis knows so well, he directs the liberation of the prisoners; but in the end he slips away to the condemned cells, locks them against the mob and stands guard over the clamoring inmates, cracking them harshly over the knuckles when they reach their hands out over the doors. The condemned are his vested interest, which he cannot allow the rebels to touch. But the momentum of the mob forces the issue, breaks through and turns the criminals loose. When we next encounter Dennis, he is a stool pigeon, turning his former companions in to the police. But he is unable to buy immunity in this way; and he is finally hanged himself. Thus this hangman has a complex value: he is primarily a sadist who likes to kill. Yet he figures as a violator as well as a protector of prisons. In his role of insurgent, he attacks authority; in his role of hangman, makes it odious. Either way he represents on Dickens's part a blow at those institutions which the writer is pretending to endorse. There is not, except in a minor way, any other symbol of authority in the book.

The formula of *Barnaby Rudge* is more or less reproduced in the other two novels of Dickens that deal with revolutionary subjects—which, though they belong to later periods of Dickens's work, it is appropriate to consider here. In *Hard Times* (1854), he manages in much the same way to deal sympathetically with the working-class protest against intolerable industrial conditions at the same time that he lets himself out from supporting the trade-union movement. In order to be able to do this, he is obliged to resort to a special and rather implausible device. Stephen Blackpool, the honest old textile worker, who is made to argue the cause of the workers before the vulgar manufacturer Bounderby, refuses to join the union because he has promised the woman he loves that he will do nothing to get himself into trouble. He thus finds himself in the singular position of being both a victim of the blacklist and a scab. The trade-union leadership is represented only—although with a comic fidelity, recognizable even today, to a certain type of labor organizer—by an unscrupulous spell-binder whose single aim is to get hold of the workers' pennies. Old Stephen, wandering away to look for a job somewhere else, falls into a disused coal-pit which has already cost the lives of many miners, and thus becomes a martyr simultaneously to the employers and to the trade-union movement. In *A Tale of Two Cities* (1859), the moral of history is not juggled as it is in *Barnaby Rudge*, but the conflict is made to seem of less immediate reality by locating it out of England. The French people, in Dickens's picture, have been given ample provocation for breaking loose in the French Revolution; but once in revolt, they are fiends and vandals. The vengeful Madame Defarge is a creature whom—as Dickens implies—one would not find in England, and she is worsted by an Englishwoman. The immediate motive behind *A Tale of Two Cities* is no doubt, as has been suggested and as is intimated at the beginning of the last chapter, the English fear of the Second Empire after Napoleon III's Italian campaign of 1859: Dickens's impulse to write the book closely followed the attempt by Orsini to assassinate Napoleon III in the January of '58. But there is in this book as in the other two—though less angrily expressed—a threat. If the British upper classes, Dickens seems to say, will not deal with the problem of providing for the health and education of the people, they will fall victims to the brutal mob. This mob Dickens both sympathizes with and fears.

* * *

Through the whole of his early period, Dickens appears to have regarded himself as a respectable middle-class man. If Sam Weller, for all his outspokenness, never over-steps his role of valet, Kit in *The Old Curiosity Shop* is a model of deference toward his betters who becomes even a little disgusting.

When Dickens first visited America, in 1842, he seems to have had hopes of finding here something in the nature of that classless society which the foreign "fellow travelers" of yesterday went to seek in the Soviet Union; but, for reasons both bad and good, Dickens was driven back by what he did find into the attitude of an English gentleman, who resented the American lack of ceremony, was annoyed by the American publicity, and was pretty well put to rout by the discomfort, the poverty and the tobacco-juice which he had braved on his trip to the West. Maladjusted to the hierarchy at home, he did not fit in in the United States even so well as he did in England: some of the Americans patronized him, and others were much too familiar. The mixed attitude—here seen at its most favorable to us—which was produced when his British ideas intervened to rein in the sympathy which he tended to feel for American innovations, is well indicated by the passage in *American Notes* in which he discusses the factory-girls of Lowell. These girls have pianos in their boarding houses and subscribe to circulating libraries, and they publish a periodical. "How very preposterous!" the writer imagines an English reader exclaiming. "These things are above their station." But what is their station? asks Dickens. "It is their station to work," he answers. "And they *do* work. . . . For myself, I know no station in which, the occupation of today cheerfully done and the occupation of tomorrow cheerfully looked to, any one of these pursuits is not most humanizing and laudable. I know no station which is rendered more endurable to the person in it, or more safe to the person out of it, by having ignorance for its associate. I know no station which has a right to monopolize the means of mutual instruction, improvement and rational entertainment; or which has even continued to be a station very long after seeking to do so." But he remarks that "it is pleasant to find that many of [the] Tales [in the library] are of the Mills, and of those who work in them; that they inculcate habits of self-denial and contentment, and teach good doctrines of enlarged benevolence." The main theme of *Nicholas Nickleby* is the efforts of Nicholas and his sister to vindicate their position as gentlefolk.

But there is also another reason why these political novels of Dickens are unclear and unsatisfactory. Fundamentally, he was not interested in politics. As a reporter, he had seen a good deal of Parliament, and he had formed a contemptuous opinion of it which was never to change to the end of his life. The Eatanswill elections in *Pickwick* remain the type of political activity for Dickens; the seating of Mr. Veneering in Parliament in the last of his finished novels is hardly different. The point of view is stated satirically in Chapter XII of *Bleak House*, in which a governing-class group at a country house are made to discuss the fate of the country in terms of the political activities of Lord Coodle, Sir Thomas Doodle, the Duke of Foodle, the Right Honorable William Buffy, M.P., with his associates and opponents Cuffy, Duffy, Fuffy, etc., while their constituents are taken for granted as "a certain large number of supernumeraries, who are to be occasionally addressed, and relied upon for shouts and choruses, as on the theatrical stage." A little later (September 30, 1855), he expresses himself explicitly in the course of a letter to Forster: "I really am serious in thinking—and I have given as painful consideration to the subject as a man with children to live and suffer after him can honestly give to it— that representative government is become altogether a failure with us, that the English gentilities and subserviences render the people unfit for it, and that the whole thing has broken down since that great seventeenth-century time, and has no hope in it."

In his novels from beginning to end, Dickens is making the same point always: that to the English governing classes the people they govern are not real. It is one of the great purposes of Dickens to show you these human actualities who figure for Parliament as strategical counters and for Political Economy as statistics; who can as a rule appear only even in histories in a generalized or idealized form. What does a workhouse under the Poor Laws look like? What does it feel like, taste like, smell like? How does the holder of a post in the government look? How does he talk? what does he talk about? how will he treat you? What is the aspect of the British middle class at each of the various stages of its progress? What are the good ones like and what are the bad ones like? How do they affect you, not merely to meet at dinner, but to travel with, to work under, to live with? All these things Dickens can tell us. It has been one of the principal functions of the modern novel and drama to establish this kind of record; but few writers have been able to do it with any range at all extensive. None has surpassed Dickens.

No doubt this concrete way of looking at society may have serious limitations. Dickens was sometimes actually stupid about politics. His lack of interest in political tactics led him, it has sometimes been claimed, to mistake the actual significance of the legislation he was so prompt to criticize. Mr. T. A. Jackson has pointed out a characteristic example of Dickens's inattention to politics in his report of his first trip to America. Visiting Washington in 1842, he registers an impression of Congress very similar to his impressions of Parliament ("I may be of a cold and insensible temperament, amounting in iciness, in such matters"); and he indulges in one of his gushings of sentiment over "an aged, gray-haired man, a lasting honor to the land that gave him birth, who has done good service to his country, as his forefathers did, and who will be remembered scores upon scores of years after the worms bred in its corruption are so many grains of dust—it was but a week since this old man had stood for days upon his trial before this very body, charged with having dared to assert the infamy of that traffic which has for its accursed merchandise men and women, and their unborn children." Now this aged gray-haired man, Mr. Jackson reminds us, was none other than John Quincy Adams, who, far from being on his trial, was actually on the verge of winning in his long fight against a House resolution which had excluded petitions against slavery, and who was deliberately provoking his adversaries for purposes of propaganda. Dickens did not know that the antislavery cause, far from being hopeless, was achieving its first step toward victory. (So on his second visit to America—when, however, he was ill and exhausted—his interest in the impeachment of Andrew Johnson seems to have been limited to "a misgiving lest the great excitement . . . will damage our receipts" from his readings.) Yet his picture of the United States in 1842, at a period of brave boastings and often squalid or meager realities, has a unique and permanent value. Macaulay complained that Dickens did not understand the Manchester school of utilitarian economics which he criticized in *Hard Times*. But Dickens's criticism does not pretend to be theoretical: all he is undertaking to do is to tell us how practicing believers in Manchester utilitarianism behave and how their families are likely to fare with them. His picture is strikingly collaborated by the autobiography of John Stuart Mill, who was brought up at the fountainhead of the school, in the shadow of Bentham himself. In Mill, choked with learning from his childhood, overtrained on the logical side of the mind, and collapsing into illogical despair when the lack began to make itself felt of the elements his education had neglected, the tragic moral of the system of Gradgrind is pointed with a sensational obviousness which would be regarded as exaggeration in Dickens.

This very distrust of politics, however, is a part of the rebellious aspect of Dickens. Dickens is almost invariably *against* institutions: in spite of his allegiance to Church and State, in spite of the lip-service he occasionally pays them, whenever he comes to deal with Parliament and its laws, the courts and the public officials, the creeds of Protestant dissenters and of Church of England alike, he makes them either ridiculous or cruel, or both at the same time.

4

In the work of Dickens's middle period—after the murder in *Martin Chuzzlewit*—the rebel bulks larger than the criminal.

Of all the great Victorian writers, he was probably the most antagonistic to the Victorian Age itself. He had grown up under the Regency and George IV; had been twenty-five at the accession of Victoria. His early novels are freshened by breezes from an England of coaching and village taverns, where the countryside lay just outside London; of an England where jokes and songs and hot brandy were always in order, where every city clerk aimed to dress finely and drink freely, to give an impression of open-handedness and gallantry. The young Dickens of the earliest preserved letters, who invites his friends to partake of "the rosy," sounds not unlike Dick Swiveller. When Little Nell and her grandfather on their wanderings spend a night in an iron foundry, it only has the effect of a sort of Nibelungen interlude, rather like one of those surprise grottoes that you float through when you take the little boat that threads the tunnel of the "Old Mill" in an amusement park—a luridly lighted glimpse on the same level, in Dickens's novel, with the waxworks, the performing dogs, the dwarfs and giants, the village church. From this point it is impossible, as it was impossible for Dickens, to foresee the full-length industrial town depicted in *Hard Times*. In that age the industrial-commercial civilization had not yet got to be the norm; it seemed a disease which had broken out in spots but which a sincere and cheerful treatment would cure. The typical reformers of the period had been Shelley and Robert

Owen, the latter so logical a crank, a philanthropist so much all of a piece, that he seems to have been invented by Dickens—who insisted that his Cheeryble brothers, the philanthropic merchants of *Nicholas Nickleby*, had been taken from living originals.

But when Dickens begins to write novels again after his return from his American trip, a new kind of character appears in them, who, starting as an amusing buffoon, grows steadily more unpleasant and more formidable. On the threshold of *Martin Chuzzlewit* (1843–45: the dates of its appearance in monthly numbers), you find Pecksniff, the provincial architect; on the threshold of *Dombey and Son* (1846–48), we find Dombey, the big London merchant; and before you have got very far with the idyllic *David Copperfield* (1849–50), you find Murdstone, of Murdstone and Grimby, wine merchants. All these figures stand for the same thing. Dickens had at first imagined that he was pillorying abstract faults in the manner of the comedy of humors: Selfishness in *Chuzzlewit*, Pride in *Dombey*. But the truth was that he had already begun an indictment against a specific society: the self-important and moralizing middle class who had been making such rapid progress in England and coming down like a damper on the bright fires of English life—that is, on the spontaneity and gaiety, the frankness and independence, the instinctive human virtues, which Dickens admired and trusted. The new age had brought a new kind of virtues to cover up the flourishing vices of cold avarice and harsh exploitation; and Dickens detested these virtues.

The curmudgeons of the early Dickens—Ralph Nickleby and Arthur Gride, Anthony and Jonas Chuzzlewit (for *Martin Chuzzlewit* just marks the transition from the early to the middle Dickens)—are old-fashioned moneylenders and misers of a type that must have been serving for decades in the melodramas of the English stage. In Dickens their wholehearted and outspoken meanness gives them a certain cynical charm. They are the bad uncles in the Christmas pantomime who set off the jolly clowns and the good fairy, and who, as everybody knows from the beginning, are doomed to be exposed and extinguished. But Mr. Pecksniff, in the same novel with the Chuzzlewits, already represents something different. It is to be characteristic of Pecksniff, as it is of Dombey and Murdstone, that he does evil while pretending to do good. As intent on the main chance as Jonas himself, he pretends to be a kindly father, an affectionate relative, a pious churchgoer; he is the pillar of a cathedral town. Yet Pecksniff is still something of a pantomime comic whom it will be easy enough to unmask. Mr. Dombey is a more difficult problem. His virtues, as far as they go, are real: though he is stupid enough to let his business get into the hands of Carker, he does lead an exemplary life of a kind in the interests of the tradition of his house. He makes his wife and his children miserable in his devotion to his mercantile ideal, but that ideal is at least for him serious. With Murdstone the ideal has turned sour: the respectable London merchant now represents something sinister. Murdstone is not funny like Pecksniff; he is not merely a buffoon who masquerades: he is a hypocrite who believes in himself. And where Dombey is made to recognize his error and turn kindly and humble in the end, Mr. Murdstone and his grim sister are allowed to persist in their course of working mischief as a matter of duty.

In such a world of mercenary ruthlessness, always justified by rigorous morality, it is natural that the exploiter of others should wish to dissociate himself from the exploited, and to delegate the face-to-face encounters to someone else who is paid to take the odium. Karl Marx, at that time living in London, was demonstrating through these middle years of the century that this system, with its falsifying of human relations and its wholesale encouragement of cant, was an inherent and irremediable feature of the economic structure itself. In Dickens, the Mr. Spenlow of *David Copperfield*, who is always blaming his mean exactions on his supposedly implacable partner, Mr. Jorkins, develops into the Casby of *Little Dorrit*, the benignant and white-haired patriarch who turns over the rackrenting of Bleeding Heart Yard to his bull-terrier of an agent, Pancks, while he basks in the admiration of his tenants; and in *Our Mutual Friend*, into Fledgeby, the moneylender who makes his way into society while the harmless old Jew Riah is compelled to play the cruel creditor.

With Dickens's mounting dislike and distrust of the top layers of that middle-class society with which he had begun by identifying himself, his ideal of middle-class virtue was driven down to the lower layers. In his earlier novels, this ideal had been embodied in such patrons and benefactors as Mr. Pickwick, the retired business man; the substantial and warm-hearted Mr. Brownlow, who rescued Oliver Twist; and the charming old gentleman, Mr. Garland, who took Kit Nubbles into his service. In *David Copperfield* the lawyer Wickfield, who plays a role in relation to the hero somewhat similar to those of Brownlow and Garland, becomes demoralized by too much port and falls a victim to Uriah Heep, the upstart Pecksniff of a lower social level. The ideal—the domestic unit which preserves the sound values of England—is located by Dickens through this period in the small middle-class household: Ruth Pinch and her brother in *Martin Chuzzlewit*; the bright hearths and holiday dinners of the *Christmas Books*; the modest home to which Florence Dombey descends from the great house near Portland Place, in happy wedlock with the nephew of Sol Gills, the ships'-instrument-maker.

It is at the end of *Dombey and Son*, when the house of Dombey goes bankrupt, that Dickens for the first time expresses himself explicitly on the age that has come to remain:

"The world was very busy now, in sooth, and had a deal to say. It was an innocently credulous and a much ill-used world. It was a world in which there was no other sort of bankruptcy whatever. There were no conspicuous people in it, trading far and wide on rotten banks of religion, patriotism, virtue, honor. There was no amount worth mentioning of mere paper in circulation, on which anybody lived pretty handsomely, promising to pay great sums of goodness with no effects. There were no short-comings anywhere, in anything but money. The world was very angry indeed; and the people especially who, in a worse world, might have been supposed to be bankrupt traders themselves in shows and pretences, were observed to be mightily indignant."

And now—working always through the observed inter-relations between highly individualized human beings rather than through political or economic analysis—Dickens sets out to trace an anatomy of that society. *Dombey* has been the first attempt; *Bleak House* (1852–53) is to realize this intention to perfection; *Hard Times*, on a smaller scale, is to conduct the same kind of inquiry.

For this purpose Dickens invents a new literary *genre* (unless the whole mass of Balzac is to be taken as some-thing of the sort): the novel of the social group. The young Dickens had summed up, developed and finally outgrown the two traditions in English fiction he had found: the picaresque tradition of Defoe, Fielding and Smollett, and the sentimental tradition of Goldsmith and Sterne. People like George Henry Lewes have com-plained of Dickens's little reading; but no artist has ever absorbed his predecessors—he had read most of them in his early boyhood—more completely than Dickens did. There is something of all these writers in Dickens and, using them, he has gone beyond them all. In the historical novel *Barnaby Rudge*—a detour in Dickens's fiction—he had got out of Scott all that Scott had to give him. He was to profit in *Hard Times* by Mrs. Gaskell's industrial stud-ies. But in the meantime it was Dickens's business to cre-ate a new tradition himself.

His novels even through *Martin Chuzzlewit* had had a good deal of the looseness of the picaresque school of *Gil*

Blas, where the episodes get their only unity from being hung on the same hero, as well as the multiple parallel plots, purely mechanical combinations, that he had acquired from the old plays—though he seems to have been trying more intensively for a unity of atmosphere and feeling. But now he is to organize his stories as wholes, to plan all the characters as symbols, and to invest all the details with significance. *Dombey and Son* derives a new kind of coherence from the fact that the whole novel is made to center around the big London business house: you have the family of the man who owns it, the manager and his family, the clerks, the men dependent on the ships that export its goods, down to Sol Gills and Captain Cuttle (so *Hard Times* is to get its coherence from the organism of an industrial town).

In *Bleak House,* the masterpiece of this middle period, Dickens discovers a new use of plot, which makes possible a tighter organization. (And we must remember that he is always working against the difficulties, of which he often complains, of writing for monthly instalments, where everything has to be planned beforehand and it is impossible, as he says, to "try back" and change anything, once it has been printed.) He creates the detective story which is also a social fable. It is a *genre* which has lapsed since Dickens. The detective story—though Dickens's friend Wilkie Collins preserved a certain amount of social satire—has dropped out the Dickensian social content; and the continuators of the social novel have dropped the detective story. These continuators—Shaw, Galsworthy, Wells—have of course gone further than Dickens in the realistic presentation of emotion; but from the point of view of dramatizing social issues, they have hardly improved upon *Bleak House.* In Shaw's case, the Marxist analysis, with which Dickens was not equipped, has helped him to the tighter organization which Dickens got from his complex plot. But in the meantime it is one of Dickens's victories in his rapid development as an artist that he should succeed in transforming his melodramatic intrigues of stolen inheritances, lost heirs and ruined maidens—with their denunciatory confrontations that always evoke the sound of fiddling in the orchestra—into devices of artistic dignity. Henceforth the solution of the mystery is to be also the moral of the story and the last word of Dickens's social "message."

Bleak House begins in the London fog, and the whole book is permeated with fog and rain. In *Dombey* the railway locomotive—first when Mr. Dombey takes his trip to Leamington, and later when it pulls into the station just at the moment of Dombey's arrival and runs over the fugitive Carker as he steps back to avoid his master—figures as a symbol of that progress of commerce which Dombey himself represents; in *Hard Times* the uncovered coal-pit into which Stephen Blackpool falls is a symbol for the abyss of the industrial system, which swallows up lives in its darkness. In *Bleak House* the fog stands for Chancery, and Chancery stands for the whole web of clotted antiquated institutions in which England stifles and decays. All the principal elements in the story—the young people, the proud Lady Dedlock, the philanthropic gentleman John Jarndyce, and Tom-all-Alone's, the rotting London slum—are involved in the exasperating Chancery suit, which, with the fog-bank of precedent looming behind it like the Great Boyg in *Peer Gynt*, obscures and impedes at every point the attempts of men and women to live natural lives. Old Krook, which his legal junkshop, is Dickens's symbol for the Lord Chancellor himself; the cat that sits on his shoulder watches like the Chancery lawyers the caged birds in Miss Flite's lodging; Krook's death by spontaneous combustion is Dickens's prophecy of the fate of Chancery and all that it represents.

I go over the old ground of the symbolism, up to this point perfectly obvious, of a book which must be still, by the general public, one of the most read of Dickens's novels, because the people who like to talk about the symbols of Kafka and Mann and Joyce have been discouraged from looking for anything of the kind in Dickens, and usually have not read him, at least with mature minds. But even when we think we do know Dickens, we may be surprised to return to him and find in him a symbolism of a more complicated reference and a deeper implication than these metaphors that hang as emblems over the door. The Russians themselves, in this respect, appear to have learned from Dickens.

Thus it is not at first that we recognize all the meaning of the people that thrive or survive in the dense atmosphere of *Bleak House*—an atmosphere so opaque that the somnolent ease at the top cannot see down to the filth at the bottom. And it is an atmosphere where nobody sees clearly what kind of race of beings is flourishing between the bottom and the top. Among the middle ranks of this society we find persons who appear with the pretension of representing Law or Art, Social Elegance, Philanthropy, or Religion—Mr. Kenge and Mr. Vholes, Harold Skimpole, Mr. Turveydrop, Mrs. Pardiggle and Mrs. Jellyby, and Mr. and Mrs. Chadband—side by side with such a sordid nest of goblins as the family of the moneylender Smallweed. But presently we see that all these people are as single-mindedly intent on selfish interests as Grandfather Smallweed himself. This gallery is one of the best things in Dickens. The Smallweeds themselves are artistically an improvement on the similar characters in the early Dickens: they represent, not a theatrical convention, but a real study of the stunted and degraded products of the underworld of commercial London. And the two opposite types of philanthropist: the moony Mrs. Jellyby, who miserably neglects her children in order to dream of doing good in Africa, and Mrs. Pardiggle, who bullies both her children and the poor in order to give herself a feeling of power; Harold Skimpole, with the graceful fancy and the talk about music and art that ripples a shimmering veil over his systematic sponging; and Turveydrop, the Master of Deportment, that parody of the magnificence of the Regency, behind his rouge and his padded coat and his gallantry as cold and as inconsiderate as the Chadbands behind their gaseous preachments. Friedrich Engels, visiting London in the early forties, had written of the people in the streets that they seemed to "crowd by one another as if they had nothing in common, nothing to do with one another, and as if their only agreement were the tacit one that each shall keep to his own side of the pavement, in order not to delay the opposing streams of the crowd, while it never occurs to anyone to honor his fellow with so much as a glance. The brutal indifference, the unfeeling isolation of each in his private interest, becomes the more repellent the more these individuals are herded together within a limited space." This is the world that Dickens is describing.

Here he makes but one important exception: Mr. Rouncewell, the ironmaster. Mr. Rouncewell is an ambitious son of the housekeeper at Chesney Wold, Sir Leicester Dedlock's country house, who has made himself a place in the world which Sir Leicester regards as beyond his station. One of the remarkable scenes of the novel is that in which Rouncewell comes back, quietly compels Sir Leicester to receive him like a gentleman and asks him to release one of the maids from his service so that she may marry Rouncewell's son, a young man whom he has christened Watt. When Lady Dedlock refuses to release the maid, Rouncewell respectfully abandons the project, but goes away and has the insolence to run against Sir Leicester's candidate in the next parliamentary election. (This theme of the intervention of the Industrial Revolution in the relations between master and servant has already appeared in *Dombey and Son* in the admirable interview between Dombey and Polly Toodles, whom he is employing as a wet-nurse for his motherless child. Polly's husband, who is present, is a locomotive stoker and already represents something anomalous in the hierarchy of British society. When the Dombeys, who cannot accept her real name, suggest calling Polly "Richards," she replies that if she is to be called out of her name, she ought to be paid extra. Later, when Dombey makes his railway journey, he runs into Polly's husband, who is working on the engine. Toodles speaks to him and engages him in conversation, and Dombey resents this, feeling that Toodles is somehow intruding outside his own class.)

But in general the magnanimous, the simple of heart, the amiable, the loving and the honest are frustrated, subdued, or destroyed. At the bottom of the whole gloomy edifice is the body of Lady Dedlock's lover and Esther Summerson's father, Captain Hawdon, the reckless soldier, adored by his men, beloved by women, the image of the old life-loving England, whose epitaph Dickens is now writing. Captain Hawdon has failed in that world, has perished as a friendless and penniless man, and has been buried in the pauper's graveyard in one of the foulest quarters of London, but the loyalties felt for him by the living will endure and prove so strong after his death that they will pull that world apart. Esther Summerson has been frightened and made submissive by being treated as the respectable middle class thought it proper to treat an illegitimate child, by one of those puritanical females whom Dickens so roundly detests. Richard Carstone has been demoralized and ruined; Miss Flite has been driven insane. George Rouncewell, the brother of the ironmaster, who has escaped from Sir Leicester's service to become a solider instead of a manufacturer and who is treated by Dickens with the sympathy which he usually feels for his military and nautical characters, the men who are doing the hard work of the Empire, is helpless in the hands of moneylenders and lawyers. Caddy Jellyby and her husband, young Turveydrop, who have struggled for a decent life in a poverty partly imposed by the necessity of keeping up old Turveydrop's pretenses, can only produce, in that society where nature is so mutilated and thwarted, a sickly defective child. Mr. Jarndyce himself, the wise and generous, who plays in *Bleak House* a role very similar to that of Captain Shotover in Bernard Shaw's *Heartbreak House* (which evidently owes a good deal to *Bleak House*), is an eccentric at odds with his environment, who, in his efforts to help the unfortunate, falls a prey to the harpies of philanthropy.

With this indifference and egoism of the middle class, the social structure must buckle in the end. The infection from the poverty of Tom-all-Alone's will ravage the mansions of country gentlemen. Lady Dedlock will inevitably be dragged down from her niche of aristocratic idleness to the graveyard in the slum where her lover lies. The idea that the highest and the lowest in that English society of shocking contrasts are inextricably tied together has already appeared in the early Dickens—in Ralph Nickleby and Smike, for example, and in Sir John Chester and Hugh—as a sort of submerged motif which is never given its full expression. Here it has been chosen deliberately and is handled with immense skill so as to provide the main moral of the fable. And bound up with it is another motif which has already emerged sharply in Dickens. Dickens had evidently in the course of his astonishing rise, found himself up against the blank and chilling loftiness—what the French call *la morgue anglaise*—of the English upper classes: as we shall see, he developed a pride of his own, with which he fought it to his dying day. Pride was to have been the theme of *Dombey*: the pride of Edith Dombey outdoes the pride of Dombey and levels him to the ground. But in *Bleak House*, the pride of Lady Dedlock, who has married Sir Leicester Dedlock for position, ultimately rebounds on herself. Her behavior toward the French maid Hortense is the cause of her own debasement. For where it is a question of pride, a high-tempered girl from the South of France can outplay Lady Dedlock: Hortense will not stop at the murder which is the logical upshot of the course of action dictated by her wounded feelings. Dickens is criticizing here one of the most unassailable moral props of the English hierarchical system.

Between *Dombey and Son* and *Bleak House*, Dickens published *David Copperfield*. It is a departure from the series of his social novels. Setting out to write the autobi-

ography of which the fragments appear in Forster's *Life*,
Dickens soon changed his mind and transposed this material into fiction. In the first half of *David Copperfield*, at
any rate, Dickens strikes an enchanting vein which he had
never quite found before and which he was never to find
again. It is the poem of an idealized version of the loves
and fears and wonders of childhood; and the confrontation
of Betsey Trotwood with the Murdstones is one of
Dickens's most successful stagings of the struggle between
the human and the anti-human, because it takes place on
the plane of comedy rather than on that of melodrama.
But *Copperfield* is not one of Dickens's deepest books: it is
something in the nature of a holiday. David is too candid
and simple to represent Dickens himself; and though the
blacking warehouse episode is utilized, all the other bitter
circumstances of Dickens's youth were dropped out when
he abandoned the autobiography.

5

With *Little Dorrit* (1855-57), Dickens's next novel after
Bleak House and *Hard Times*, we enter a new phase of his
work. To understand it, we must go back to his life.

Dickens at forty had won everything that a writer could
expect to obtain through his writings: his genius was universally recognized; he was fêted wherever he went; his
books were immensely popular; and they had made him
sufficiently rich to have anything that money can procure.
He had partly made up for the education he had missed
by traveling and living on the Continent and by learning
to speak Italian and French. (Dickens's commentary on
the Continental countries is usually not remarkably penetrating; but he did profit very much from his travels
abroad in his criticism of things in England. Perhaps no
other of the great Victorian writers had so much the consciousness that the phenomena he was describing were of
a character distinctively English.) Yet from the time of his
first summer at Boulogne in 1853, he had shown signs of

profound discontent and unappeasable restlessness; he suffered severely from insomnia and, for the first time in his life, apparently, worried seriously about his work. He began to fear that his vein was drying up.

I believe that Forster's diagnosis—though it may not go to the root of the trouble—must here be accepted as correct. There were, he intimates, two things wrong with Dickens: a marriage which exasperated and cramped him and from which he had not been able to find relief, and a social maladjustment which his success had never straightened out.

The opportunities of the young Dickens to meet eligible young women had evidently been rather limited. That he was impatient to get married, nevertheless, is proved by his announcing his serious intentions to three girls in close succession. The second of these was Maria Beadnell, the original of Dora in *David Copperfield* and, one supposes, of Dolly Varden, too, with whom he fell furiously in love, when he was eighteen and she nineteen. Her father worked in a bank and regarded Charles Dickens, the stenographer, as a young man of shabby background and doubtful prospects; Maria, who seems to have been rather frivolous and silly, was persuaded to drop her suitor—with the result for him which may be read in the letters, painful in their wounded pride and their backfiring of a thwarted will, which he wrote her after the break. This was one of the great humiliations of Dickens's early life (he was at that time twenty-one) and, even after he had liquidated it in a sense by depicting the futilities of David's marriage with Dora, the disappointment still seems to have troubled him and Maria to have remained at the back of his mind as the Ideal of which he had been cheated.

He lost very little time, however, in getting himself a wife. Two years after his rejection by Maria Beadnell, he was engaged to the daughter of George Hogarth, a Scotchman, who, as the law agent of Walter Scott and from having been mentioned in the *Noctes Ambrosianae*, was invested with the prestige of having figured on the fringes of the Edinburgh literary world. He asked Dickens to write for the newspaper which he was editing at that time in London, and invited the young man to his house. There Dickens found two attractive daughters, and he married the elder, Catherine, who was twenty. But the other daughter, Mary, though too young for him to marry—she was only fifteen when he met her—had a strange hold on Dickens's emotions. When, after living with the Dickenses for a year after their marriage, she suddenly died in Dickens's arms, he was so overcome by grief that he stopped writing *Pickwick* for two months and insisted in an obsessed and morbid way on his desire to be buried beside her: "I can't think there ever was love like I bear her. . . . I have never had her ring off my finger day or night, except for an instant at a time, to wash my hands, since she died. I have never had her sweetness and excellence absent from my mind so long." In *The Old Curiosity Shop*, he apotheosized her as Little Nell. What basis this emotion may have had in the fashionable romanticism of the period or in some peculiar psychological pattern of Dickens's, it is impossible on the evidence to say. But this passion for an innocent young girl is to recur in Dickens's life; and in the meantime his feeling for Mary Hogarth seems to indicate pretty clearly that even during the early years of his marriage he did not identify the Ideal with Catherine.

Catherine had big blue eyes, a rather receding chin and a sleepy and languorous look. Beyond this, it is rather difficult to get a definite impression of her. Dickens's terrible gallery of shrews who browbeat their amiable husbands suggests that she may have been a scold; but surely Dickens himself was no Joe Gargery or Gabriel Varden. We do not know much about Dickens's marriage. We know that, with the exception of his sister-in-law Georgina, Dickens grew to loathe the Hogarths, who evidently lived on him to a considerable extent; and we must assume that poor Catherine, in both intellect and energy, was a good deal inferior to her husband. He lived with her, however, twenty years, and, although it becomes clear toward the end that they were no longer particularly welcome, he gave her during that time ten children.

And if Dickens was lonely in his household, he was lonely in society, also. He had, as Forster indicates, attained a pinnacle of affluence and fame which made him one of the most admired and most sought-after persons in Europe without his really ever having created for himself a social position in England, that society *par excellence* where everybody had to have a definite one and where there was no rank reserved for the artist. He had gone straight, at the very first throw, from the poor tenement, the prison, the press table, to a position of imperial supremacy over the imaginations of practically the whole literate world; but in his personal associations, he cultivated the companionshp of inferiors rather than—save, perhaps, for Carlyle—of intellectual equals. His behavior toward Society, in the capitalized sense, was rebarbative to the verge of truculence; he refused to learn its patter and its manners; and his satire on the fashionable world comes to figure more and more prominently in his novels. Dickens is one of the very small group of British intellectuals to whom the opportunity has been offered to be taken up by the governing class and who have actually declined that honor.

His attitude—which in the period we have been discussing was still that of the middle-class "Radical" opposing feudal precedent and privilege: Mr. Rouncewell, the ironmaster, backed against Sir Leicester Dedlock—is illustrated by the curious story of his relations with Queen Victoria. In 1857, Dickens got up a benefit for the family of Douglas Jerrold, in which he and his daughters acted. The Queen was asked to be one of the sponsors; and, since she was obliged to refuse any such request for fear of being obliged to grant them all, she invited Dickens to put on the play at the palace. He replied that he "did not feel easy as to the social position of my daughters, etc., at a

Court under those circumstances," and suggested that the Queen might attend a performance which should be given for her alone. She accepted, and sent backstage between the acts asking Dickens to come and speak to her. "I replied that I was in my Farce dress, and must beg to be excused. Whereupon she sent again, saying that the dress 'could not be so ridiculous as that,' and repeating the request. I sent my duty in reply, but again hoped Her Majesty would have the kindness to excuse my presenting myself in a costume and appearance that were not my own. I was mighty glad to think, when I woke this morning, that I had carried the point." The next year he was approached on behalf of the Queen, who wanted to hear him read the *Christmas Carol;* but he expressed his "hope that she would indulge me by making one of some audience or other—for I thought an audience necessary to the effect." It was only in the last year of his life—and then only on what seems to have been the pretext on the Queen's part that she wanted to look at some photographs of the battlefields of the Civil War which Dickens had brought back from America—that an interview was finally arranged. Here the record of Dickens's lecture manager, George Dolby, supplements the account given by Forster. Dickens told Dolby that "Her Majesty had received him most graciously, and that, as Court etiquette requires that no one, in an ordinary interview with the sovereign, should be seated, Her Majesty had remained the whole time leaning over the head of a sofa. There was a little shyness on both sides at the commencement, but this wore away as the conversation proceeded." When Victoria regretted that it had not been possible for her ever to hear Dickens read, he replied that he had made his farewell to the platform; when she said that she understood this, but intimated that it would be gracious on Dickens's part so far to forget his resolve as to give her the pleasure of hearing him, he insisted that this would be impossible. Not impossible, perhaps, said the Queen, but inconsistent, no doubt—and she knew that he was the most consistent of men. Yet they parted on very good terms: she invited him to her next levee and his daughter to the drawing-room that followed. If there is some stickling for his dignity on Dickens's part here, there is evidently also some scruple on the Queen's.

To be caught between two social classes in a society of strict stratifications—like being caught between two civilizations, as James was, or between two racial groups, like Proust—is an excellent thing for a novelist from the point of view of his art, becuse it enables him to dramatize contrasts and to study interrelations which the dweller in one world cannot know. Perhaps something of the sort was true even of Shakespeare, between the provincial bourgeoisie and the Court. Dostoevsky, who had a good deal in common with Dickens and whose career somewhat parallels his, is a conspicuous example of a writer who owes his dramatic scope at least partly to a social maladjustment. The elder Dostoevsky was a doctor and his family origins were obscure, so that his social position was poor in a Russia still predominantly feudal; yet he bought a country estate and sent his sons to a school for the children of the nobility. But the family went to pieces after the mother's death: the father took to drink and was murdered by his serfs for his cruelty. Dostoevsky was left with almost nothing, and he slipped down into that foul and stagnant underworld of the Raskolnikovs and Stavrogins of his novels. Dickens's case had been equally anomalous: he had grown up in an uncomfortable position between the upper and the lower middle classes, with a dip into the proletariat and a glimpse of the aristocracy through their trusted upper servants. But this position, which had been useful to him as a writer, was to leave him rather isolated in English society. In a sense, there was no place for him to go and belong; he had to have people come to him.

And in the long run all that he had achieved could not make up for what he lacked. *Little Dorrit* and *Great Expectations* (1860–61), which follows it after *A Tale of Two Cities*, are full of the disillusion and discomfort of this period of Dickens's life. The treatment of social situations and the treatment of individual psychology have both taken turns distinctly new.

Dickens now tackles the Marshalsea again, but on a larger scale and in a more serious way. It is as if he were determined once for all to get the prison out of his system. The figure of his father hitherto has always haunted Dickens's novels, but he has never known quite how to handle it. In Micawber, he made him comic and lovable; in Skimpole, he made him comic and unpleasant—for, after all, the vagaries of Micawber always left somebody out of pocket, and there is another aspect of Micawber— the Skimpole aspect he presented to his creditors. But what kind of person, really, had John Dickens been in himself? How had the father of Charles Dickens come to be what he was? Even after it had become possible for Charles to provide for his father, the old man continued to be a problem up to his death in 1851. He got himself arrested again, as the result of running up a wine bill; and he would try to get money out of his son's publishers without the knowledge of Charles. Yet Dickens said to Forster, after his father's death: "The longer I live, the better man I think him"; and *Little Dorrit* is something in the nature of a justification of John.

Mr. Dorrit is "a very amiable and very helpless middle-aged gentleman ... a shy, retiring man, well-looking, though in an effeminate style, with a mild voice, curling hair, and irresolute hands—rings upon the fingers in those days—which nervously wandered to his trembling lip a hundred times in the first half-hour of his acquaintance with the jail." The arrival of the Dorrit family in prison and their gradual habituation to it are done with a restraint and sobriety never displayed by Dickens up to now. The incident in which Mr. Dorrit, after getting used to accepting tips in his role of the Father of the Marshalsea, suddenly becomes insulted when he is offered copper halfpence by a workman, has a delicacy which makes up in these later books for the ebb of Dickens's bursting exuberance. If it is complained that the comic characters in these novels, the specifically "Dickens characters," are sometimes mechanical and boring, this is partly, perhaps, for the reason that they stick out in an unnatural relief from a surface that is more quietly realistic. And there are moments when one feels that Dickens might be willing to abandon the "Dickens character" altogether if it were not what the public expected of him. In any case, the story of Dorrit is a closer and more thoughtful study than any that has gone before of what bad institutions make of men.

But there is also in *Little Dorrit* something different from social criticism. Dickens is no longer satisfied to anatomize the organism of society. The main symbol here is the prison (in this connection, Mr. Jackson's chapter is the best thing that has been written on *Little Dorrit*); but this symbol is developed in a way that takes it beyond the satirical application of the symbol of the fog in *Bleak House* and gives it a significance more subjective. In the opening chapter, we are introduced, not to the debtors' prison, but to an ordinary jail for criminals, which, in the case of Rigaud and Cavalletto, will not make the bad man any better or the good man any worse. A little later, we are shown an English business man who has come back from many years in China and who finds himself in a London—the shut-up London of Sunday evening—more frightening, because more oppressive, than the thieves' London of *Oliver Twist*. " 'Heaven forgive me,' said he, 'and those who trained me. How I have hated this day!' There was the dreary Sunday of his childhood, when he sat with his hands before him, scared out of his senses by a horrible tract which commenced business with the poor child by asking him, in its title, why he was going to Perdition?" At last he gets himself to the point of going to see his mother, whom he finds as lacking in affection and as gloomy as he could have expected. She lives in a dark and funereal house with the old offices on the bottom floor, one of the strongholds of that harsh Calvinism plus hard business which made one of the mainstays of the Victorian Age; she lies paralyzed on "a black bier-like sofa," punishing herself and everyone else for some guilt of which he cannot discover the nature. The Clennam house is a jail, and they are in prison, too. So are the people in Bleeding Heart Yard, small tenement-dwelling shopkeepers and artisans, rackrented by the patriarchal Casby; so is Merdle, the great swindler-financier, imprisoned, like Kreuger or Insull, in the vast scaffolding of fraud he has contrived, who wanders about in his expensive house—itself, for all its crimson and gold, as suffocating and dark as the Clennams'—afraid of his servants, unloved by his wife, almost unknown by his guests, till on the eve of the collapse of the edifice he quietly opens his veins in his bath.

At last, after twenty-five years of jail, Mr. Dorrit inherits a fortune and is able to get out of the Marshalsea. He is rich enough to go into Society; but all the Dorrits, with the exception of the youngest, known as "Little Dorrit," who has been born in the Marshalsea itself and has never made any pretensions, have been demoralized or distorted by the effort to remain genteel while tied to the ignominy of the prison. They cannot behave like the people outside. And yet that outside world is itself insecure. It is dominated by Mr. Merdle, who comes, as the story goes on, to be universally believed and admired—is taken up by the governing class, sent to Parliament, courted by lords. The Dorrits, accepted by Society, still find themselves in prison. The moral is driven home when old Dorrit, at a fashionable dinner, loses control of his wits and slips back into his character at the Marshalsea: " 'Born here,' he repeated, shedding tears. 'Bred here. Ladies and gentlemen, my daughter. Child of an unfortunate father, but—ha—always a gentleman. Poor, no doubt, but—hum—proud.' " He asks the company for "Testimonials," which had been what he had used to call his tips. (Dr. Manette, in *A Tale of Two Cities*, repeats this pattern with his amnesic relapses into the shoemaking he has learned in prison.) Arthur Clennam, ruined by the failure of Merdle, finally goes to the Marshalsea himself; and there at last he and Little Dorrit arrive at an understanding. The implication is that, prison for prison, a simple incarceration is an excellent school of character compared to the dungeons of Puritan theology, of modern business, of money-ruled Society, or of the poor people of Bleeding Heart Yard who are swindled and bled by all of these.

The whole book is much gloomier than *Bleak House*, where the fog is external to the characters and represents something removable, the obfuscatory elements of the past. The murk of *Little Dorrit* permeates the souls of the people, and we see more of their souls than in *Bleak House*. Arthur Clennam, with his broodings on his unloving mother, who turns out not to be his real mother (a poor doomed child of natural impulse, like Lady Dedlock's lover), is both more real and more depressing than Lady Dedlock. Old Dorrit has been spoiled beyond repair: he can never be rehabilitated like Micawber. There is not even a villain like Tulkinghorn to throw the odium on a predatory class: the official villain Blandois has no organic connection with the story save as a caricature of social pretense. (Though the illustrations suggest that he may have been intended as a sort of cartoon of Napoleon III, whose régime Dickens loathed—in which case the tie-up between Blandois and the Clennams may figure a close relationship between the shady financial interests disguised by the flashy façade of the Second Empire and the respectable business interests of British merchants, so inhuman behind their mask of morality. Blandois is crushed in the end by the collapse of the Clennams' house, as people were already predicting that Napoleon would be by that of his own.) The role of the Court of Chancery is more or less played by the Circumlocution Office and the governing-class family of Barnacles—perhaps the most brilliant thing of its kind in Dickens: that great satire on all aristocratic bureaucracies, and indeed on all bureaucracies, with its repertoire of the variations possible within the bureaucratic type and its desolating picture of the emotions of a man being passed on from one door to another. But the Circumlocution Office, after all, only influences the action in a negative way.

The important thing to note in *Little Dorrit*—which was originally to have been called *Nobody's Fault*—is that the fable is here presented from the point of view of imprisoning states of mind as much as from that of oppressive institutions. This is illustrated in a startling way by "The History of a Self-Tormentor," which we find toward the end of the book. Here Dickens, with a remarkable pre-Freudian insight, gives a sort of case history of a woman imprisoned in a neurosis which has condemned her to the delusion that she can never be loved. There is still, to be sure, the social implication that her orphaned childhood and her sense of being slighted have been imposed on her by the Victorian attitude toward her illegitimate birth. But her handicap is now simply a thought-pattern, and from that thought-pattern she is never to be liberated.

Dickens's personal difficulties make themselves felt like an ache at the back of *Little Dorrit*—in which he represents his hero as reflecting: "Who has not thought for a moment, sometimes?—that it might be better to flow away monotonously, like the river, and to compound for its insensibility to happiness with its insensibility to pain." The strain of his situation with his wife had become particularly acute the year that the book was begun. Dickens had been very much excited that February to get a letter from Maria Beadnell, now married. The readiness and warmth of his response shows how the old Ideal had lighted up again. He was on the point of leaving for Paris, and during his absence he looked forward eagerly to seeing her: he arranged to meet her alone. The drop in the tone of his letters after this meeting has taken place is blighting to poor Mrs. Winter. He had found her banal and silly, with the good looks of her girlhood gone. He put her into his new novel as Flora Finching, a sort of Dora

Spenlow vulgarized and transmogrified into a kind of Mrs. Nickleby—that is, into another version of Dickens's unforgiven mother. It seems clear that the type of woman that Dickens is chiefly glorifying during the years from *Martin Chuzzlewit* through *Little Dorrit:* the devoted and self-effacing little mouse, who hardly aspires to be loved, derives from Georgina Hogarth, his sister-in-law. Georgina, who had been eight when Dickens was married, had come to womanhood in the Dickens household. Dickens grew fond of her, explaining that his affection was due partly to her resemblance to her dead sister. She gradually took over the care of the children, whom Dickens complained of their mother's neglecting; and became the real head of the household—creating a situation which is reflected in these heroines of the novels. The virtues of Ruth Pinch are brought out mainly through her relation to her brother Tom; Esther Summerson, who keeps house for Mr. Jarndyce but does not suspect that he wants to marry her, is suspended through most of *Bleak House* in a relation to him that is semi-filial; Little Dorrit is shown throughout in a sisterly and filial relation, and Arthur Clennam, before he figures as a lover, plays simply, like Mr. Jarndyce, the role of a protective and elderly friend. In the love of Little Dorrit and Clennam, there seems to be little passion, but a sobriety of resignation, almost a note of sadness: they "went down," Dickens says at the end, "into a modest life of usefulness and happiness," one of the objects of which was to be "to give a mother's care . . . to Fanny's [her sister's] neglected children no less than to their own."

These children of Dickens's—he now had nine—were evidently giving him anxiety. He used to grumble about their lack of enterprise; and it would appear from Mrs. Perugini's story, which trails off in a depressing record of their failures and follies and untimely deaths, that in general they did not turn out well. The ill-bred daughter and worthless son of Dorrit probably caricature Dickens's

fears. Surely the Dorrits' travels on the Continent caricature the progress of the Dickenses. Old Dorrit's rise in
the world is no rescue at the end of a fairy tale, as it
would have been in one of the early novels. The point
of the story is that this rise can be only a mockery: the
Dorrits will always be what the Marshalsea has made
them.

[1941]

HEMINGWAY:
GAUGE OF MORALE

1

Ernest Hemingway's *In Our Time* was an odd and original book. It had the appearance of a miscellany of stories
and fragments; but actually the parts hung together and
produced a definite effect. There were two distinct series
of pieces which alternated with one another: one a set of
brief and brutal sketches of police shootings, bullfight
crises, hangings of criminals and incidents of the war; and
the other a set of short stories dealing in its principal sequence with the growing-up of an American boy against a
landscape of idyllic Michigan, but interspersed also with
glimpses of American soldiers returning home. It seems to
have been Hemingway's intention—*"In Our Time"*—
that the war should set the key for the whole. The cold-
bloodedness of the battles and executions strikes a discord
with the sensitiveness and candor of the boy at home in
the States; and presently the boy turns up in Europe in
one of the intermediate vignettes as a soldier in the Italian
army, hit in the spine by machine-gun fire and trying to
talk to a dying Italian: *"Senta*, Rinaldi. *Senta,"* he says,
"you and me, we've made a separate peace."

But there is a more fundamental relationship between the two series. The shooting of Nick in the war does not really connect two different worlds: has he not found in the butchery abroad the same world that he knew back in Michigan? Was not life in the Michigan woods equally destructive and cruel? He had gone once with his father, the doctor, when he had performed a Caesarean operation on an Indian squaw with a jackknife and no anaesthetic and had sewed her up with fishing leaders, while the Indian hadn't been able to bear it and had cut his throat in his bunk. Another time, when the doctor had saved the life of a squaw, her Indian had picked a quarrel with him rather than pay him in work. And Nick himself had sent his girl about her business when he had found out how terrible her mother was. Even fishing in Big Two-Hearted River—away and free in the woods—he had been conscious in a curious way of the cruelty inflicted on the fish, even of the silent agonies endured by the live bait, the grasshoppers kicking on the hook.

Not that life isn't enjoyable. Talking and drinking with one's friends is great fun; fishing in Big Two-Hearted River is a tranquil exhilaration. But the brutality of life is always there, and it is somehow bound up with the enjoyment. Bullfights are especially enjoyable. It is even exhilarating to build a simply priceless barricade and pot the enemy as they are trying to get over it. The condition of life is pain; and the joys of the most innocent surface are somehow tied to its stifled pangs.

The resolution of this dissonance in art made the beauty of Hemingway's stories. He had in the process tuned a marvelous prose. Out of the colloquial American speech, with its simple declarative sentences and its strings of Nordic monosyllables, he got effects of the utmost subtlety. F. M. Ford has found the perfect simile for the impression produced by this writing: "Hemingway's words strike you, each one, as if they were pebbles fetched fresh from a brook. They live and shine, each in its place.

So one of his pages has the effect of a brook-bottom into which you look down through the flowing water. The words form a tesellation, each in order beside the other."

Looking back we can see how this style was already being refined and developed at a time—fifty years before—when it was regarded in most literary quarters as hopelessly non-literary and vulgar. Had there not been the nineteenth chapter of *Huckleberry Finn?*—"Two or three nights went by; I reckon I might say they swum by; they slid along so quick and smooth and lovely. Here is the way we put in the time. It was a monstrous big river down there—sometimes a mile and a half wide," and so forth. These pages, when we happen to meet them in Carl Van Doren's anthology of world literature, stand up in a striking way beside a passage of description from Turgenev; and the pages which Hemingway was later to write about American wood and water are equivalents to the transcriptions by Turgenev—the *Sportsman's Notebook* is much admired by Hemingway—of Russian forests and fields. Each has brought to an immense and wild country the freshness of a new speech and a sensibility not yet conventionalized by literary associations. Yet it *is* the European sensibility which has come to Big Two-Hearted River, where the Indians are now obsolescent; in those solitudes it feels for the first time the cold current, the hot morning sun, sees the pine stumps, smells the sweet fern. And along with the mottled trout, with its "clear water-over-gravel color," the boy from the American Middle West fishes up a nice little masterpiece.

In the meantime there had been also Ring Lardner, Sherwood Anderson, Gertrude Stein, using this American language for irony, lyric poetry or psychological insight. Hemingway seems to have learned from them all. But he is now able to charge this naïve accent with a new complexity of emotion, a new shade of emotion: a malaise. The wholesale shattering of human beings in which he has taken part has given the boy a touch of panic.

2

The next fishing trip is strikingly different. Perhaps the first had been an idealization. Is it possible to attain to such sensuous bliss merely through going alone into the woods: smoking, fishing, and eating, with no thought about anyone else or about anything one has ever done or will ever be obliged to do? At any rate, today, in *The Sun Also Rises*, all the things that are wrong with human life are there on the holiday, too—though one tries to keep them back out of the foreground and to occupy one's mind with the trout, caught now in a stream of the Pyrenees, and with the kidding of the friend from the States. The feeling of insecurity has deepened. The young American now appears in a seriously damaged condition: he has somehow been incapacitated sexually through wounds received in the war. He is in love with one of those international sirens who flourished in the cafés of the post-war period and whose ruthless and uncontrollable infidelities, in such a circle as that depicted by Hemingway, have made any sort of security impossible for the relations between women and men. The lovers of such a woman turn upon and rend one another because they are powerless to make themselves felt by *her*.

The casualties of the bullfight at Pamplona, to which these young people have gone for the fiesta, only reflect the blows and betrayals of demoralized human beings out of hand. What is the tiresome lover with whom the lady has just been off on a casual escapade, and who is unable to understand that he has been discarded, but the man who, on his way to the bull ring, has been accidentally gored by the bull? The young American who tells the story is the only character who keeps up standards of conduct, and he is prevented by his disability from dominating and directing the woman, who otherwise, it is intimated, might love him. Here the membrane of the style has been stretched taut to convey the vibrations of these qualms. The dry sunlight and the green summer landscapes have been invested with a sinister quality which must be new in literature. One enjoys the sun and the green as one enjoys suckling pigs and Spanish wine, but the uneasiness and apprehension are undruggable.

Yet one can catch hold of a code in all the drunkenness and the social chaos. "Perhaps as you went along you did learn something," Jake, the hero, reflects at one point. "I did not care what it was all about. All I wanted to know was how to live in it. Maybe if you found out how to live in it you learned from that what it was all about." "Everybody behaves badly. Give them the proper chance," he says later to Lady Brett.

" 'You wouldn't behave badly.' Brett looked at me." In the end, she sends for Jake, who finds her alone in a hotel. She has left her regular lover for a young bullfighter, and this boy has for the first time inspired her with a respect which has restrained her from "ruining" him: "You know it makes one feel rather good deciding not to be a bitch." We suffer and we make suffer, and everybody loses out in the long run; but in the meantime we can lose with honor.

This code still markedly figures, still supplies a dependable moral backbone, in Hemingway's next book of short stories, *Men Without Women*. Here Hemingway has mastered his method of economy in apparent casualness and relevance in apparent indirection, and has turned his sense of what happens and the way in which it happens into something as hard and clear as a crystal but as disturbing as a great lyric. Yet it is usually some principle of courage, of honor, of pity—that is, some principle of sportsmanship in its largest human sense—upon which the drama hinges. The old bullfighter in "The Undefeated" is defeated in everything except the spirit which will not accept defeat. You get the bull or he gets you: if you die, you can die game; there are certain things you cannot do. The burlesque show manager in "A Pursuit Race" refrains from waking his advance publicity agent when he overtakes him and realizes that the man has just lost a long struggle against whatever anguish it is that has driven him to drink and dope. "They got a cure for that," the manager had said to him before he went to sleep; " 'No,' William Campbell said, 'they haven't got a cure for anything.' " The burned major in "A Simple Enquiry"— that strange picture of the bed-rock stoicism compatible with the abasement of war—has the decency not to dismiss the orderly who has rejected his proposition. The brutalized Alpine peasant who has been in the habit of hanging a lantern in the jaws of the stiffened corpse of his wife, stood in the corner of the woodshed till the spring will make it possible to bury her, is ashamed to drink with the sexton after the latter has found out what he has done. And there is a little sketch of Roman soldiers just after the Crucifixion: "You see me slip the old spear into him?— You'll get into trouble doing that some day.— It was the least I could do for him. I'll tell you he looked pretty good to me in there today."

This Hemingway of the middle twenties—*The Sun Also Rises* came out in '26—expressed the romantic disillusion and set the favorite pose for the period. It was the moment of gallantry in heartbreak, grim and nonchalant banter, and heroic dissipation. The great watchword was "Have a drink"; and in the bars of New York and Paris the young people were getting to talk like Hemingway.

3

The novel, *A Farewell to Arms*, which followed *Men Without Women*, is in a sense not so serious an affair. Beautifully written and quite moving of course it is. Probably no other book has caught so well the strangeness of life in the army for an American in Europe during the War. The new places to which one was sent of which one had never heard, and the things that turned out to be

in them; the ordinary people of foreign countries as one
saw them when one was quartered among them or obliged
to perform some common work with them; the pleasures
of which one managed to cheat the War, intensified by the
uncertainty and horror—and the uncertainty, nevertheless, almost become a constant, the horror almost taken for
granted; the love affairs, always subject to being suddenly
broken up and yet carried on while they lasted in a spirit
of irresponsible freedom which derived from one's having
forfeited control of all one's other actions—this Hemingway got into his book, written long enough after the
events for them to present themselves under an aspect
fully idyllic.

But *A Farewell to Arms* is a tragedy, and the lovers are
shown as innocent victims with no relation to the forces
that torment them. They themselves are not tormented
within by that dissonance between personal satisfaction
and the suffering one shares with others which it has been
Hemingway's triumph to handle. *A Farewell to Arms,* as
the author once said, is a *Romeo and Juliet.* And when
Catherine and her lover emerge from the stream of action—the account of the Caporetto retreat is Hemingway's best sustained piece of narrative—when they escape
from the alien necessities of which their romance has been
merely an accident, which have been writing their story
for them, then we see that they are not in themselves convincing as human personalities. And we are confronted
with the paradox that Hemingway, who possesses so remarkable a mimetic gift in getting the tone of social and
national types and in making his people talk appropri-
ately, has not shown any very solid sense of character, or,
indeed, any real interest in it. The people in his short
stories are satisfactory because he has only to hit them off:
the point of the story does not lie in personalities, but in
the emotion to which a situation gives rise. This is true
even in *The Sun Also Rises,* where the characters are
sketched with wonderful cleverness. But in *A Farewell to
Arms,* as soon as we are brought into real intimacy with

the lovers, as soon as the author is obliged to see them through a searching personal experience, we find merely an idealized relationship, the abstraction of a lyric emotion.

With *Death in the Afternoon*, three years later, a new development for Hemingway commences. He writes a book not merely in the first person, but in the first person in his own character as Hemingway, and the results are unexpected and disconcerting. *Death in the Afternoon* has its value as an exposition of bullfighting; and Hemingway is able to use the subject as a text for an explicit statement of his conception of man eternally pitting himself—he thinks the bullfight a ritual of this—against animal force and the odds of death. But the book is partly infected by a queer kind of maudlin emotion, which sounds at once neurotic and drunken. He overdoes his glorification of the bravery and martyrdom of the bullfighter. No doubt the professional expert at risking his life single-handed is impressive in contrast to the flatness and unreality of much of the business of the modern world; but this admirable miniaturist in prose has already made the point perhaps more tellingly in the little prose poem called "Banal Story." Now he offsets the virility of the bull-fighters by anecdotes of the male homosexuals that frequent the Paris cafés, at the same time that he puts his chief celebration of the voluptuous excitement of the spectacle into the mouth of an imaginary old lady. The whole thing becomes a little hysterical.

The master of that precise and clean style now indulges in purple patches which go on spreading for pages. I am not one of those who admire the last chapter of *Death in the Afternoon*, with its rich, all too rich, unrollings of memories of good times in Spain, and with its what seem to me irrelevant reminiscences of the soliloquy of Mrs. Bloom in *Ulysses*. Also, there are interludes of kidding of a kind which Hemingway handles with skill when he assigns them to characters in his stories, but in connection with which he seems to become incapable of exercising good sense or good taste as soon as he undertakes them in his own person (the burlesque *Torrents of Spring* was an early omen of this). In short, we are compelled to recognize that, as soon as Hemingway drops the burning-glass of the disciplined and objective art with which he has learned to concentrate in a story the light of the emotions that flood in on him, he straightaway becomes befuddled, slops over.

This befuddlement is later to go further, but in the meantime he publishes another volume of stories—*Winner Take Nothing*—which is almost up to its predecessor. In this collection he deals much more effectively than in *Death in the Afternoon* with that theme of contemporary decadence which is implied in his panegyric of the bull-fighter. The first of these stories, "After the Storm," is another of his variations—and one of the finest—on the theme of keeping up a code of decency among the hazards and pains of life. A fisherman goes out to plunder a wreck: he dives down to break in through a porthole, but inside he sees a woman with rings on her hands and her hair floating loose in the water, and he thinks about the passengers and crew being suddenly plunged to their deaths (he has almost been killed himself in a drunken fight the night before). He sees the cloud of sea birds screaming around, and he finds that he is unable to break the glass with his wrench and that he loses the anchor grapple with which he next tries to attack it. So he finally goes away and leaves the job to the Greeks, who blow the boat open and clean her out.

But in general the emotions of insecurity here obtrude themselves and dominate the book. Two of the stories deal with the hysteria of soldiers falling off the brink of their nerves under the strain of the experiences of the War, which here no longer presents an idyllic aspect; another deals with a group of patients in a hospital, at the same time crippled and hopeless; still another (a five-page masterpiece) with an old man who has tried to commit suicide although he is known to have plenty of money, and who now creeps into a café in search of "a clean well-lighted place": "After all, he said to himself, it is probably only insomnia. Many must have it." Another story, like *The Sun Also Rises*, centers around a castration; and four of the fourteen are concerned more or less with male or female homosexuality. In the last story, "Fathers and Sons," Hemingway reverts to the Michigan woods, as if to take the curse off the rest: young Nick had once enjoyed a nice Indian girl with plump legs and hard little breasts on the needles of the hemlock woods.

These stories and the interludes in *Death in the Afternoon* must have been written during the years that followed the stock market crash. They are full of the apprehension of losing control of oneself which is aroused by the getting out of hand of a social-economic system, as well as of the fear of impotence which seems to accompany the loss of social mastery. And there is in such a story as "A Clean Well-Lighted Place" the feeling of having got to the end of everything, of having given up heroic attitudes and wanting only the illusion of peace.

4

And now, in proportion as the characters in his stories run out of fortitude and bravado, he passes into a phase where he is occupied with building up his public personality. He had already now become a legend, as Mencken was in the twenties; he is the Hemingway of the handsome photographs with the sportsman's tan and the outdoor grin, with the ominous resemblance to Clark Gable, who poses with giant marlin which he has just hauled in off Key West. And unluckily—but for an American inevitably—the opportunity soon presents itself to exploit this personality for profit: he turns up delivering Hemingway monologues in well-paying and trashy magazines; and the Hemingway of these loose disquisitions, arrogant, belligerent and boastful, is certainly the worst-invented character to be found in the author's work. If he is obnoxious, the effect is somewhat mitigated by the fact that he is intrinsically incredible.

There would be no point in mentioning this journalism at all, if it did not seem somewhat to have contributed to the writing of certain unsatisfactory books. *Green Hills of Africa* (1935) owes its failure to falling between the two genres of personal exhibitionism and fiction. "The writer has attempted," says Hemingway, "to write an absolutely true book to see whether the shape of a country and the pattern of a month's action can, if truly presented, compete with a work of the imagination." He does try to present his own role objectively, and there is a genuine Hemingway theme—the connection between success at big-game hunting and sexual self-respect—involved in his adventures as he presents them. But the sophisticated technique of the fiction writer comes to look artificial when it is applied to a series of real happenings; and the necessity of sticking to what really happened makes impossible the typical characters and incidents which give point to a work of fiction. The monologues by the false, the publicity, Hemingway with which the narrative is interspersed are almost as bad as the ones that he has been writing for the magazines. He inveighs with much scorn against the literary life and against the professional literary man of the cities; and then manages to give the impression that he himself is a professional literary man of the touchiest and most self-conscious kind. He delivers a self-confident lecture on the high possibilities of prose writing; and then produces such a sentence as the following: "Going downhill steeply made these Spanish shooting boots too short in the toe and there was an old argument, about this length of boot and whether the bootmaker, whose part I had taken, unwittingly first, only as interpreter, and finally embraced his theory patriotically as a whole and, I believed, by logic, had overcome it by adding onto the heel." As soon as Hemingway begins speaking in the first person, he seems to lose his bearings, not merely as a critic of life, but even as a craftsman.

In another and significant way, *Green Hills of Africa* is disappointing. *Death in the Afternoon* did provide a lot of data on bullfighting and build up for us the bullfighting world; but its successor tells us little about Africa. Hemingway keeps affirming—as if in accents of defiance against those who would engage his attention for social problems—his passionate enthusiasm for the African country and his perfect satisfaction with the hunter's life; but he has produced what must be one of the only books ever written which make Africa and its animals seem dull. Almost the only thing we learn about the animals is that Hemingway wants to kill them. And as for the natives, though there is one fine description of a tribe of marvelous trained runners, the principal impression we get of them is that they were simple and inferior people who enormously admired Hemingway.

It is not only that, as his critics of the Left had been complaining, he shows no interest in political issues, but that his interest in his fellow beings seems actually to be drying up. It is as if he were throwing himself on African hunting as something to live for and believe in, as something through which to realize himself; and as if, expecting of it too much, he had got out of it abnormally little, less than he is willing to admit. The disquiet of the Hemingway of the twenties had been, as I have said, undruggable—that is, in his books themselves, he had tried to express it, not drug it, had given it an appeasement in art; but now there sets in, in the Hemingway of the thirties, what seems to be a deliberate self-drugging. The situation is indicated objectively in "The Gambler, the Nun and the Radio," one of the short stories of 1933, in which everything from daily bread to "a belief in any new form of government" is characterized as "the opium of the people" by an empty-hearted cripple in a hospital.

But at last there did rush into this vacuum the blast of the social issue, which had been roaring in the wind like a forest fire.

Out of a series of short stories that Hemingway had written about a Florida waterside character he decided to make a little epic. The result was *To Have and Have Not*, which seems to me the poorest of all his stories. Certainly some deep agitation is working upon Hemingway the artist. Craftsmanship and style, taste and sense, have all alike gone by the board. The negative attitude toward human beings has here become definitely malignant: the hero is like a wooden-headed Punch, always knocking people on the head (inferiors—Chinamen or Cubans); or, rather, he combines the characteristics of Punch with those of Popeye the Sailor in the animated cartoon in the movies. As the climax to a series of prodigies, this stupendous pirate-smuggler named Harry Morgan succeeds, alone, unarmed, and with only a hook for one hand—though at the cost of a mortal wound—in outwitting and destroying with their own weapons four men carrying revolvers and a machine gun, by whom he has been shanghaied in a launch. The only way in which Hemingway's outlaw suffers by comparison with Popeye is that his creator has not tried to make him plausible by explaining that he does it all on spinach.

The impotence of a decadent society has here been exploited deliberately, but less successfully than in the earlier short stories. Against a background of homosexuality, impotence and masturbation among the wealthy holiday-makers in Florida, Popeye-Morgan is shown gratifying his wife with the same indefatigable dexterity which he has displayed in his other feats; and there is a choral refrain of praise of his *cojones*, which wells up in the last pages of the book when the abandoned Mrs. Popeye regurgitates Molly Bloom's soliloquy.

To be a man in such a world of maggots is noble, but it is not enough. Besides the maggots, there are double-crossing rats, who will get you if they are given the slightest chance. What is most valid in *To Have and Have Not* is the idea—conveyed better, perhaps, in the first of the series of episodes than in the final scenes of massacre and agony—that in an atmosphere (here revolutionary Cuba) in which man has been set against man, in which it is always a question whether your companion is not preparing to cut your throat, the most sturdy and straightforward American will turn suspicious and cruel. Harry Morgan is made to realize as he dies that to fight this bad world alone is hopeless. Again Hemingway, with his barometric accuracy, has rendered a moral atmosphere that was prevalent at the moment he was writing—a moment when social relations were subjected to severe tensions, when they seemed sometimes already disintegrating. But the heroic Hemingway legend has at this point invaded his fiction and, inflaming and inflating his symbols, has produced an implausible hybrid, half Hemingway character, half nature myth.

Hemingway had not himself particularly labored this moral of individualism *versus* solidarity, but the critics of the Left labored it for him and received his least creditable piece of fiction as the delivery of a new revelation. The progress of the Communist faith among our writers since the beginning of the Depression has followed a peculiar course. That the aims and beliefs of Marx and Lenin should have come through to the minds of intellectuals who had been educated in the bourgeois tradition as great awakeners of conscience, a great light, was quite natural and entirely desirable. But the conception of the dynamic Marxist will, the exaltation of the Marxian religion, seized the members of the professional classes like a capricious contagion or hurricane, which shakes one and leaves his neighbor standing, then returns to lay hold on the second after the first has become quiet again. In the moment of seizure, each one of them saw a scroll unrolled from the heavens, on which Marx and Lenin and Stalin, the Bolsheviks of 1917, the Soviets of the Five-Year Plan, and the GPU of the Moscow trials were all a part of the same great purpose. Later the convert, if he were capable of it, would get over his first phase of snow blindness and learn to see real people and conditions, would study the development of Marxism in terms of nations, periods, personalities, instead of logical deductions from abstract propositions or—as in the case of the more naïve or dishonest—of simple incantatory slogans. But for many there was at least a moment when the key to all the mysteries of human history seemed suddenly to have been placed in their hands, when an infallible guide to thought and behavior seemed to have been given them in a few easy formulas.

Hemingway was hit pretty late. He was still in *Death in the Afternoon* telling the "world-savers," sensibly enough, that they should "get to see" the world "clear and as a whole. Then any part you make will represent the whole, if it's made truly. The thing to do is work and learn to make it." Later he jibed at the literary radicals, who talked but couldn't take it; and one finds even in *To Have and Have Not* a crack about a "highly paid Hollywood director, whose brain is in the process of outlasting his liver so that he will end up calling himself a Communist, to save his soul." Then the challenge of the fight itself—Hemingway never could resist a physical challenge—the natural impulse to dedicate oneself to something bigger than big-game hunting and bullfighting, and the fact that the class war had broken out in a country to which he was romantically attached, seem to have combined to make him align himself with the Communists as well as the Spanish Loyalists at a time when the Marxist philosophy had been pretty completely shelved by the Kremlin, now reactionary as well as corrupt, and when the Russians were lending the Loyalists only help enough to preserve, as they imagined would be possible, the balance of power against Fascism while they acted at the same time as a police force to beat down the real social revolution.

Hemingway raised money for the Loyalists, reported the battle fronts. He even went so far as to make a speech at a congress of the League of American Writers, an organization rigged by the supporters of the Stalinist regime in Russia and full of precisely the type of literary revolutionists that he had been ridiculing a little while before. Soon

the Stalinists had taken him in tow, and he was feverishly
denouncing as Fascists other writers who criticized the
Kremlin. It has been one of the expedients of the Stalin
administration in maintaining its power and covering up
its crimes to condemn on trumped-up charges of Fascist
conspiracy, and even to kidnap and murder, its political
opponents of the Left; and, along with the food and muni-
tions, the Russians had brought to the war in Spain what
the Austrian journalist Willi Schlamm called that diversion of doubtful value for the working class: "Herr Vy-
shinsky's Grand Guignol."

The result of this was a play, *The Fifth Column*,
which, though it is good reading for the way the characters talk, is an exceedingly silly production. The hero,
though an Anglo-American, is an agent of the Communist
secret police, engaged in catching Fascist spies in Spain;
and his principal exploit in the course of the play is clearing out, with the aid of a single Communist, an artillery
post manned by seven Fascists. The scene is like a push-
over and getaway from one of the cruder Hollywood
Westerns. It is in the nature of a small boy's fantasy, and
would probably be considered extravagant by most writers of books for boys.

The tendency on Hemingway's part to indulge himself
in these boyish daydreams seems to begin to get the better
of his realism at the end of *A Farewell to Arms*, where the
hero, after many adventures of fighting, escaping, love-
making and drinking, rows his lady thirty-five kilometers
on a cold and rainy night; and we have seen what it could
do for Harry Morgan. Now, as if with the conviction that
the cause and the efficiency of the GPU have added several cubits to his stature, he has let this tendency loose;
and he has also found in the GPU's grim duty a pretext to
give rein to the appetite for describing scenes of killing
which has always been a feature of his work. He has progressed from grasshoppers and trout through bulls and
lions and kudus to Chinamen and Cubans, and now to
Fascists. Hitherto the act of destruction has given rise for

him to complex emotions: he has identified himself not merely with the injurer but also with the injured; there has been a masochistic complement to the sadism. But now this paradox which splits our natures, and which has instigated some of Hemingway's best stories, need no longer present perplexities to his mind. The Fascists are dirty bastards, and to kill them is a righteous act. He who had made a separate peace, who had said farewell to arms, has found a reason for taking them up again in a spirit of rabietic fury unpleasantly reminiscent of the spy mania and the sacred anti-German rage which took possession of so many civilians and staff officers under the stimulus of the last war.

Not that the compensatory trauma of the typical Hemingway protagonist is totally absent even here. The main episode is the hero's brief love affair and voluntary breaking off with a beautiful and adoring girl whose acquaintance he has made in Spain. As a member of the Junior League and a graduate of Vassar, she represents for him—it seems a little hard on her—that leisure-class playworld from which he is trying to get away. But in view of the fact that from the very first scenes he treats her with more or less open contempt, the action is rather lacking in suspense as the sacrifice is rather feeble in moral value. One takes no stock at all in the intimation that Mr. Philip may later be sent to mortify himself in a camp for training Young Pioneers. And in the meantime he has fun killing Fascists.

In *The Fifth Column*, the drugging process has been carried further still: the hero, who has become finally indistinguishable from the false or publicity Hemingway, has here dosed himself not only with whiskey, but with a seductive and desirous woman, for whom he has the most admirable reasons for not taking any responsibility, with sacred rage, with the excitement of a bombardment, and with indulgence in that headiest of sports, for which he has now the same excellent reasons: the bagging of human beings.

5

You may fear, after reading *The Fifth Column*, that Hemingway will never sober up; but as you go on to his short stories of this period, you find that your apprehensions were unfounded. Three of these stories have a great deal more body—they are longer and more complex—than the comparatively meager anecdotes collected in *Winner Take Nothing*. And here are his real artistic successes with the material of his adventures in Africa, which make up for the miscarried "Green Hills: The Short Happy Life of Francis Macomber" and "The Snows of Kilimanjaro," which disengage, by dramatizing them objectively, the themes he had attempted in the earlier book but that had never really got themselves presented. And here is at least a beginning of a real artistic utilization of Hemingway's experience in Spain: an incident of the war in two pages which outweighs the whole of *The Fifth Column* and all his Spanish dispatches, a glimpse of an old man, "without politics," who has so far occupied his life in taking care of eight pigeons, two goats and a cat, but who has now been dislodged and separated from his pets by the advance of the Fascist armies. It is a story which takes its place among the war prints of Callot and Goya, artists whose union of elegance with sharpness has already been recalled by Hemingway in his earlier battle pieces: a story which might have been written about almost any war.

And here—what is very remarkable—is a story, "The Capital of the World," which finds an objective symbol for, precisely, what is wrong with *The Fifth Column*. A young boy who has come up from the country and waits on table in a pension in Madrid gets accidentally stabbed with a meat knife while playing at bullfighting with the dishwasher. This is the simple anecdote, but Hemingway has built in behind it all the life of the pension and the city: the priesthood, the working-class movement, the grown-up bullfighters who have broken down or missed out. "The boy Paco," Hemingway concludes, "had never known about any of this nor about what all these people would be doing on the next day and on other days to come. He had no idea how they really lived nor how they ended. He did not realize they ended. He died, as the Spanish phrase has it, full of illusions. He had not had time in his life to lose any of them, or even, at the end, to complete an act of contrition." So he registers in this very fine piece the discrepancy between the fantasies of boyhood and the realities of the grown-up world. Hemingway the artist, who feels things truly and cannot help recording what he feels, has actually said goodbye to these fantasies at a time when the war correspondent is making himself ridiculous by attempting to hang on to them still.

The emotion which principally comes through in "Francis Macomber" and "The Snows of Kilimanjaro"—as it figures also in *The Fifth Column*—is a growing antagonism to women. Looking back, one can see at this point that the tendency has been there all along. In "The Doctor and the Doctor's Wife," the boy Nick goes out squirrel-hunting with his father instead of obeying the summons of his mother; in "Cross Country Snow," he regretfully says farewell to male companionship on a skiing expedition in Switzerland, when he is obliged to go back to the States so that his wife can have her baby. The young man in "Hills Like White Elephants" compels his girl to have an abortion contrary to her wish; another story, "A Canary for One," bites almost unbearably but exquisitely on the loneliness to be endured by a wife after she and her husband shall have separated; the peasant of "An Alpine Idyll" abuses the corpse of his wife (these last three appear under the general title *Men Without Women*). Brett in *The Sun Also Rises* is an exclusively destructive force: she might be a better woman if she were mated with Jake, the American; but actually he is protected against her and is in a sense revenging his own sex through being unable to do anything for her sexually. Even the hero of *A Farewell to Arms* eventually destroys Catherine—after enjoying her abject devotion—by giving her a baby, itself born dead. The only women with whom Nick Adams's relations are perfectly satisfactory are the little Indian girls of his boyhood who are in a position of hopeless social disadvantage and have no power over the behavior of the white male—so that he can get rid of them the moment he has done with them. Thus in *The Fifth Column* Mr. Philip brutally breaks off with Dorothy—he has been rescued from her demoralizing influence by his enlistment in the Communist crusade, just as the hero of *The Sun Also Rises* has been saved by his physical disability—to revert to a little Moorish whore. Even Harry Morgan who is represented as satisfying his wife on the scale of a Paul Bunyan, deserts her in the end by dying and leaves her racked by the cruelest desire.*

And now this instinct to get the woman down presents itself frankly as a fear that the woman will get the man down. The men in both these African stories are married to American bitches of the most soul-destroying sort. The hero of "The Snows of Kilimanjaro" loses his soul and dies of futility on a hunting expedition in Africa, out of which he has failed to get what he had hoped. The story is not quite stripped clean of the trashy moral attitudes which have been coming to disfigure the author's work:

---

* There would probably be a chapter to write on the relation between Hemingway and Kipling, and certain assumptions about society which they share. They had much the same split attitude toward women. Kipling anticipates Hemingway in his beliefs that "he travels the fastest that travels alone" and that "the female of the species is more deadly than the male"; and Hemingway seems to reflect Kipling in the submissive infra-Anglo-Saxon women that make his heroes such perfect mistresses. The most striking example of this is the amoeba-like little Spanish girl, Maria, in *For Whom the Bell Tolls*. Like the docile native "wives" of English officials in the early stories of Kipling, she lives only to serve her lord and to merge her identity with his; and this love affair with a woman in a sleeping-bag, lacking completely the kind of give and take that goes on between real men and women, has the all-too-perfect felicity of a youthful erotic dream. One suspects that "Without Benefit of Clergy" was read very early by Hemingway and that it made on him a lasting impression. The pathetic conclusion of this story of Kipling's seems unmistakably to be echoed at the end of *A Farewell to Arms*.

the hero, a seriously intentioned and apparently promising writer, goes on a little sloppily over the dear early days
in Paris when he was earnest, happy and poor, and blames
a little hysterically the rich woman whom he has married
and who has debased him. Yet it is one of Hemingway's
remarkable stories. There is a wonderful piece of writing
at the end when the reader is made to realize that what has
seemed to be an escape by plane, with the sick man looking down on Africa, is only the dream of a dying man.
The other story, "Francis Macomber," perfectly realizes
its purpose. Here the male saves his soul at the last minute, and then is actually shot down by his woman, who
does not want him to have a soul. Here Hemingway has at
last got what Thurber calls the war between men and
women right out into the open and has written a terrific
fable of the impossible civilized woman who despises the
civilized man for his failure in initiative and nerve and
then jealously tries to break him down as soon as he
begins to exhibit any. (It ought to be noted, also, that
whereas in *Green Hills of Africa* the descriptions tended
to weigh down the narrative with their excessive circum-
stantiality, the landscapes and animals of "Francis Macomber" are alive and unfalteringly proportioned.)

Going back over Hemingway's books today, we can see
clearly what an error of the politicos it was to accuse
him of an indifference to society. His whole work is a criticism of society: he has responded to every pressure of the
moral atmosphere of the time, as it is felt at the roots of
human relations, with a sensitivity almost unrivaled. Even
his preoccupation with licking the gang in the next block
and being known as the best basketball player in high
school has its meaning in the present epoch. After all,
whatever is done in the world, political as well as athletic,
depends on personal courage and strength. With Hemingway, courage and strength are always thought of in physical terms, so that he tends to give the impression that the
bullfighter who can take it and dish it out is more of a man

than any other kind of man, and that the sole duty of the revolutionary socialist is to get the counter-revolutionary gang before they get him.

But ideas, however correct, will never prevail by themselves: there must be people who are prepared to stand or fall with them, and the ability to act on principle is still subject to the same competitive laws which operate in sporting contests and sexual relations. Hemingway has expressed with genius the terrors of the modern man at the danger of losing control of his world, and he has also, within his scope, provided his own kind of antidote. This antidote, paradoxically, is almost entirely moral. Despite Hemingway's preoccupation with physical contests, his heroes are almost always defeated physically, nervously, practically: their victories are moral ones. He himself, when he trained himself stubbornly in his unconventional unmarketable art in a Paris which had other fashions, gave the prime example of such a victory; and if he has sometimes, under the menace of the general panic, seemed on the point of going to pieces as an artist, he has always pulled himself together the next moment. The principle of the Bourdon gauge, which is used to measure the pressure of liquids, is that a tube which has been curved into a coil will tend to straighten out in proportion as the liquid inside it is subjected to an increasing pressure.

The appearance of *For Whom the Bell Tolls* since this essay was written in 1939 carries the straightening process further. Here Hemingway has largely sloughed off his Stalinism and has reverted to seeing events in terms of individuals pitted against specific odds. His hero, an American teacher of Spanish who has enlisted on the side of the Loyalists, gives his life to what he regards as the cause of human liberation; but he is frustrated in the task that has been assigned him by the confusion of forces at cross-purposes that are throttling the Loyalist campaign. By the time that he comes to die, he has little to sustain him but the memory of his grandfather's record as a soldier in the

American Civil War. The psychology of this young man is presented with a certain sobriety and detachment in comparison with Hemingway's other full-length heroes; and the author has here succeeded as in none of his earlier books in externalizing in plausible characters the elements of his own complex personality. With all this, there is an historical point of view which he has learned from his political adventures: he has aimed to reflect in this episode the whole course of the Spanish War and the tangle of tendencies involved in it.

The weaknesses of the book are its diffuseness—a shape that lacks the concision of his short stories, that sometimes sags and sometimes bulges; and a sort of exploitation of the material, an infusion of the operatic, that lends itself all too readily to the movies.

[1941]

PHILOCTETES:
THE WOUND AND THE BOW

The *Philoctetes* of Sophocles is far from being his most popular play. The myth itself has not been one of those which have excited the modern imagination. The idea of Philoctetes' long illness and his banishment to the bleak island is dreary or distasteful to the young, who like to identify themselves with men of action—with Heracles or Perseus or Achilles; and for adults the story told by Sophocles fails to set off such emotional charges as are liberated by the crimes of the Atreidai and the tragedies of the siege of Troy. Whatever may have been dashing in the legend has been lost with the other plays and poems that dealt with it. Philoctetes is hardly mentioned in Homer; and we have only an incomplete account of the plays by Aeschylus and Euripides, which hinged on a critical moment of the campaign of the Greeks at Troy and which seem to have exploited the emotions of Greek patriotism. We have only a few scattered lines and phrases from that other play by Sophocles on the subject, the *Philoctetes at Troy,* in which the humiliated hero was presumably to be cured of his ulcer and to proceed to his victory over Paris.

There survives only this one curious drama which presents Philoctetes in exile—a drama which does not supply us at all with what we ordinarily expect of Greek tragedy, since it culminates in no catastrophe, and which indeed resembles rather our modern idea of a comedy (though the record of the lost plays of Sophocles show that there must have been others like it). Its interest depends almost as much on the latent interplay of character, on a gradual psychological conflict, as that of *Le Misanthrope.* And it assigns itself, also, to a category even more special and less generally appealing through the fact (though this, again, was a feature not uncommon with Sophocles) that the conflict is not even allowed to take place between a man and a woman. Nor does it even put before us the spectacle—which may be made exceedingly thrilling—of the individual in conflict with his social group, which we get in such plays devoid of feminine interest as *Coriolanus* and *An Enemy of the People.* Nor is the conflict even a dual one, as most dramatic conflicts are—so that our emotions seesaw up and down between two opposed persons or groups: though Philoctetes and Odysseus struggle for the loyalty of Neoptolemus, he himself emerges more and more distinctly as representing an independent point of view, so that the contrast becomes a triple affair which makes more complicated demands on our sympathies.

A French dramatist of the seventeenth century, Chateaubrun, found the subject so inconceivable that, in trying to concoct an adaptation which would be acceptable to the taste of his time, he provided Philoctetes with a daughter named Sophie with whom Neoptolemus was to fall in love and thus bring the drama back to the reliable and eternal formula of Romeo and Juliet and the organizer

who loves the factory-owner's daughter. And if we look
for the imprint of the play on literature since the Renaissance, we shall find a very meager record: a chapter of
Fénelon's *Télémache,* a discussion in Lessing's *Laocoön,* a
sonnet of Wordsworth's, a little play by André Gide, an
adaptation by John Jay Chapman—this is all, so far as I
know, that has any claim to interest.

And yet the play itself *is* most interesting, as some of
these writers have felt; and it is certainly one of Sophocles'
masterpieces. If we come upon it in the course of reading
him, without having heard it praised, we are surprised to
be so charmed, so moved—to find ourselves in the presence of something that is so much less crude in its subtlety
than either a three-cornered modern comedy like *Candida*
or *La Parisienne* or an underplayed affair of male loyalty
in a story by Ernest Hemingway, to both of which it has
some similarity. It is as if having the three men on the
lonely island has enabled the highly sophisticated Sophocles to get further away from the framework of the old
myths on which he has to depend and whose barbari-
ties, anomalies and absurdities, tactfully and realistically
though he handles them, seem sometimes almost as
much out of place as they would in a dialogue by Plato.
The people of the *Philoctetes* seem to us more familiar
than they do in most of the other Greek tragedies;* and
they take on for us a more intimate meaning. Philoctetes remains in our mind, and his incurable wound
and his invincible bow recur to us with a special
insistence. But what is it they mean? How is it possible for Sophocles to make us accept them so naturally?
Why do we enter with scarcely a stumble into the
situation of people who are preoccupied with a snake-

---

* "Apropos of the rare occasions when the ancients seem just like us,
it always has seemed to me that a wonderful example was the repentance of the lad in the (*Philoctetes?*) play of Sophocles over his de-
ceit, and the restoration of the bow."—Mr. Justice Holmes to Sir
Frederick Pollock, October 2, 1921.

bite that lasts forever and a weapon that cannot fail?

Let us first take account of the peculiar twist which Sophocles seems to have given the legend, as it had come to him from the old epics and the dramatists who had used it before him.

The main outline of the story ran as follows: The demigod Heracles had been given by Apollo a bow that never missed its mark. When, poisoned by Deianeira's robe, he had had himself burned on Mount Oeta, he had persuaded Philoctetes to light the pyre and had rewarded him by bequeathing to him this weapon. Philoctetes had thus been formidably equipped when he had later set forth against Troy with Agamemnon and Menelaus. But on the way they had to stop off at the tiny island of Chrysè to sacrifice to the local deity. Philoctetes approached the shrine first, and he was bitten in the foot by a snake. The infection became peculiarly virulent; and the groans of Philoctetes made it impossible to perform the sacrifice, which would be spoiled by ill-omened sounds; the bite began to suppurate with so horrible a smell that his companions could not bear to have him near them. They removed him to Lemnos, a neighboring island which was much larger than Chrysè and inhabited, and sailed away to Troy without him.

Philoctetes remained there ten years. The mysterious wound never healed. In the meantime, the Greeks, hard put to it at Troy after the deaths of Achilles and Ajax and baffled by the confession of their soothsayer that he was unable to advise them further, had kidnapped the soothsayer of the Trojans and had forced him to reveal to them that they could never win till they had sent for Neoptolemus, the son of Achilles, and given him his father's armor, and till they had brought Philoctetes and his bow.

Both these things were done. Philoctetes was healed at Troy by the son of the physician Asclepius; and he fought Paris in single combat and killed him. Philoctetes and Neoptolemus became the heroes of the taking of Troy.

Both Aeschylus and Euripides wrote plays on this subject long before Sophocles did; and we know something about them from a comparison of the treatments by the three different dramatists which was written by Dion Chrysostom, a rhetorician of the first century A.D. Both these versions would seem to have been mainly concerned with the relation of Philoctetes to the success of the Greek campaign. All three of the plays dealt with the same episode: the visit of Odysseus to Lemnos for the purpose of getting the bow; and all represented Odysseus as particularly hateful to Philoctetes (because he had been one of those responsible for abandoning him on the island), and obliged to resort to cunning. But the emphasis of Sophocles' treatment appears fundamentally to have differed from that of the other two. In the drama of Aeschylus, we are told, Odysseus was not recognized by Philoctetes, and he seems simply to have stolen the bow. In Euripides, he was disguised by Athena in the likeness of another person, and he pretended that he had been wronged by the Greeks as Philoctetes had been. He had to compete with a delegation of Trojans, who had been sent to get the bow for their side and who arrived at the same time as he; and we do not know precisely what happened. But Dion Chrysostom regarded the play as "a masterpiece of declamation" and " a model of ingenious debate," and Jebb thinks it probable that Odysseus won the contest by an appeal to Philoctetes' patriotism. Since Odysseus was pretending to have been wronged by the Greeks, he could point to his own behavior in suppressing his personal resentments in the interests of saving Greek honor. The moral theme thus established by Aeschylus and Euripides both would have been simply, like the theme of the wrath of Achilles, the conflict between the passions of an individual—in this case, an individual suffering from a genuine wrong—and the demands of duty to a common cause.

This conflict appears also in Sophocles; but it takes on a peculiar aspect. Sophocles, in the plays of his we have, shows himself particularly successful with people whose natures have been poisoned by narrow fanatical hatreds.

Even allowing for the tendency of Greek heroes, in legend
and history both, to fly into rather childish rages, we still
feel on Sophocles' part some sort of special point of view,
some sort of special sympathy, for these cases. Such
people—Electra and the embittered old Oedipus—suffer
as much as they hate: it is because they suffer that they
hate. They horrify, but they waken pity. Philoctetes is
such another: a man obsessed by a grievance, which in his
case he is to be kept from forgetting by an agonizing physical ailment; and for Sophocles his pain and hatred have a
dignity and an interest. Just as it is by no means plain to
Sophocles that in the affair of Antigone *versus* Creon it is
the official point of view of Creon, representing the interests of his victorious faction, which should have the last
word against Antigone, infuriated by a personal wrong; so
it is by no means plain to him that the morality of Odysseus, who is lying and stealing for the fatherland, necessarily deserves to prevail over the animus of the stricken
Philoctetes.

The contribution of Sophocles to the story is a third
person who will sympathize with Philoctetes. This new
character is Neoptolemus, the young son of Achilles, who,
along with Philoctetes, is indispensable to the victory of
the Greeks and who has just been summoned to Troy.
Odysseus is made to bring him to Lemnos for the purpose
of deceiving Philoctetes and shanghai-ing him aboard the
ship.

The play opens with a scene between Odysseus and the
boy, in which the former explains the purpose of their
trip. Odysseus will remain in hiding in order not to be recognized by Philoctetes, and Neoptolemus will go up to
the cave in which Philoctetes lives and win his confidence
by pretending that the Greeks have robbed him of his father's armor, so that he, too, has a grievance against them.
The youth in his innocence and candor objects when he is
told what his role is to be, but Odysseus persuades him by
reminding him that they can only take Troy through his
obedience and that once they have taken Troy, he will be

glorified for his bravery and wisdom. "As soon as we have won," Odysseus assures him, "we shall conduct ourselves with perfect honesty. But for one short day of dishonesty, allow me to direct you what to do—and then forever after you will be known as the most righteous of men." The line of argument adopted by Odysseus is one with which the politics of our time have made us very familiar. "Isn't it base, then, to tell falsehoods?" Neoptolemus asks. "Not," Odysseus replies, "when a falsehood will bring our salvation."

Neoptolemus goes to talk to Philoctetes. He finds him in the wretched cave—described by Sophocles with characteristic realism: the bed of leaves, the crude wooden bowl, the filthy bandages drying in the sun—where he has been living in rags for ten years, limping out from time to time to shoot wild birds or to get himself wood and water. The boy hears the harrowing story of Philoctetes' desertion by the Greeks and listens to his indignation. The ruined captain begs Neoptolemus to take him back to his native land, and the young man pretends to consent. (Here and elsewhere I am telescoping the scenes and simplifying a more complex development.) But just as they are leaving for the ship, the ulcer on Philoctetes' foot sets up an ominous throbbing in preparation for one of its periodical burstings: "She returns from time to time," says the invalid, "as if she were sated with her wanderings." In a moment he is stretched on the ground, writhing in abject anguish and begging the young man to cut off his foot. He gives Neoptolemus the bow, telling him to take care of it till the seizure is over. A second spasm, worse than the first, reduces him to imploring the boy to throw him into the crater of the Lemnian volcano: so he himself, he says, had lit the fire which consumed the tormented Heracles and had got in return these arms, which he is now handing on to Neoptolemus. The pain abates a little; "It comes and goes," says Philoctetes; and he entreats the young man not to leave him. "Don't worry about that. We'll stay." "I shan't even make you swear it, my son." "It would not be right to leave you" (it would not be right, of course, even from the Greeks' point of view). They shake hands on it. A third paroxysm twists the cripple; now he asks Neoptolemus to carry him to the cave, but shrinks from his grasp and struggles. At last the abscess bursts, the dark blood begins to flow. Philoctetes, faint and sweating, falls asleep.

The sailors who have come with Neoptolemus urge him to make off with the bow. "No," the young man replies. "He cannot hear us; but I am sure that it will not be enough for us to recapture the bow without him. It is he who is to have the glory—it was he the god told us to bring."

While they are arguing, Philoctetes awakes and thanks the young man with emotion: "Agamemnon and Menelaus were not so patient and loyal." But now they must get him to the ship, and the boy will have to see him undeceived and endure his bitter reproaches. "The men will carry you down," says Neoptolemus. "Don't trouble them: just help me up," Philoctetes replies. "It would be too disagreeable for them to take me all the way to the ship." The smell of the suppuration has been sickening. The young man begins to hesitate. The other sees that he is in doubt about something: "You're not so overcome with disgust at my disease that you don't think you can have me on the ship with you?"—

> οὐ δή σε δυσχέρεια τοῦ νοσήματος
> ἔπεισεν ὥστε μή μ' ἄγειν ναύτην ἔτι;

The answer is one of the most effective of those swift and brief speeches of Sophocles which for the first time make a situation explicit (my attempts to render this dialogue colloquially do no justice to the feeling and point of the verse):

> ἅπαντα δυσχέρεια, τὴν αὑτοῦ φύσιν
> ὅταν λιπών τις δρᾷ τὰ μὴ προσεικότα.

"Everything becomes disgusting when you are false to your own nature and behave in an unbecoming way."

He confesses his real intentions; and a painful scene occurs. Philoctetes denounces the boy in terms that would be appropriate for Odysseus; he sees himself robbed of his bow and left to starve on the island. The young man is deeply worried: "Why did I ever leave Scyros?" he asks himself. "Comrades, what shall I do?"

At this moment, Odysseus, who has been listening, pops out from his hiding place. With a lash of abuse at Neoptolemus, he orders him to hand over the arms. The young man's spirit flares up: when Odysseus invokes the will of Zeus, he tells him that he is degrading the gods by lending them his own lies. Philoctetes turns on Odysseus with an invective which cannot fail to impress the generous Neoptolemus: Why have they come for him now? he demands. Is he not still just as ill-omened and loathsome as he had been when they made him an outcast? They have only come back to get him because the gods have told them they must.

The young man now defies his mentor and takes his stand with Philoctetes. Odysseus threatens him: if he persists, he will have the whole Greek army against him, and they will see to it that he is punished for his treason. Neoptolemus declares his intention of taking Philoctetes home; he gives him back his bow. Odysseus tries to intervene; but Philoctetes has got the bow and aims an arrow at him. Neoptolemus seizes his hand and restrains him. Odysseus, always prudent, beats a quiet retreat.

Now the boy tries to persuade the angry man that he should, nevertheless, rescue the Greeks. "I have proved my good faith," says Neoptolemus; "you know that I am not going to coerce you. Why be so wrong-headed? When the gods afflict us, we are obliged to bear our misfortunes; but must people pity a man who suffers through his own choice? The snake that bit you was an agent of the gods, it was the guardian of the goddess's shrine, and I swear to you by Zeus that the sons of Asclepius will cure you if you let us take you to Troy." Philoctetes is incredulous, refuses. "Since you gave me your word," he says, "take me home again." "The Greeks will attack me and ruin me." "I'll defend you." "How can you?" "With my bow." Neoptolemus is forced to consent.

But now Heracles suddenly appears from the skies and declares to Philoctetes that what the young man says is true, and that it is right for him to go to Troy. He and the son of Achilles shall stand together like lions and shall gloriously carry the day.— The *deus ex machina* here may of course figure a change of heart which has taken place in Philoctetes as the result of his having found a man who recognizes the wrong that has been done him and who is willing to champion his cause in defiance of all the Greek forces. His patron, the chivalrous Heracles, who had himself performed so many generous exploits, asserts his influence over his heir. The long hatred is finally exorcised.

In a fine lyric utterance which ends the play, Philoctetes says farewell to the cavern, where he has lain through so many nights listening to the deep-voiced waves as they crashed against the headland, and wetted by the rain and the spray blown in by the winter gales. A favorable wind has sprung up; and he sails away to Troy.

It is possible to guess at several motivations behind the writing of the *Philoctetes*. The play was produced in 409, when—if the tradition of his longevity be true— Sophocles would have been eighty-seven; and it is supposed to have been followed by the *Oedipus Coloneus*, which is assigned to 405 or 406. The latter deals directly with old age; but it would appear that the *Philoctetes* anticipates this theme in another form. Philoctetes, like the outlawed Oedipus, is impoverished, humbled, abandoned by his people, exacerbated by hardship and chagrin. He is accursed: Philoctetes' ulcer is an equivalent for the abhorrent sins of Oedipus, parricide and incest together, which have made of the ruler a pariah. And yet somehow both are sacred persons who have acquired superhuman

powers, and who are destined to be purged of their guilt.
One passage from the earlier play is even strikingly repeated in the later. The conception of the wave-beaten
promontory and the sick man lying in his cave assailed by
the wind and rain turns up in the *Oedipus Coloneus* (Coloneus was Sophocles' native deme) with a figurative
moral value. So the ills of old age assail Oedipus. Here are
the lines, in A. E. Housman's translation:

> This man, as me, even so,
> Have the evil days overtaken;
> And like as a cape sea-shaken
> With tempest at earth's last verges
> And shock of all winds that blow,
> His head the seas of woe,
> The thunders of awful surges
> Ruining overflow:
>
> Blown from the fall of even,
>   Blown from the dayspring forth,
> Blown from the noon in heaven,
>   Blown from night and the North.

But Oedipus has endured as Philoctetes has endured in
the teeth of all the cold and the darkness, the screaming
winds and the bellowing breakers: the blind old man is
here in his own person the headland that stands against
the storm.

We may remember a widely current story about the
creator of these two figures. It is said that one of Sophocles' sons brought him into court in his advanced old age
on the complaint that he was no longer competent to
manage his property. The old poet is supposed to have recited a passage from the play which he had been writing:
the chorus in praise of Coloneus, with its clear song of
nightingales, its wine-dark ivy, its crocus glowing golden
and its narcissus moist with dew, where the stainless
stream of the Cephisus wanders through the broad-swell-
ing plain and where the gray-leaved olive grows of itself
beneath the gaze of the gray-eyed Athena—shining Co-

lonus, breeder of horses and of oarsmen whom the Nereids lead. The scene had been represented on the stage and Sophocles had been made to declare: "If I am Sophocles, I am not mentally incapable; if I am mentally incapable, I am not Sophocles." In any case, the story was that the tribunal, composed of his fellow clansmen, applauded and acquitted the poet and censored the litigating son. The ruined and humiliated heroes of Sophocles' later plays are still persons of mysterious virtue, whom their fellows are forced to respect.

There is also a possibility, even a strong probability, that Sophocles intended Philoctetes to be identified with Alcibiades. This brilliant and unique individual, one of the great military leaders of the Athenians, had been accused by political opponents of damaging the sacred statues of Hermes and burlesquing the Eleusinian mysteries, and had been summoned to stand trial at Athens while he was away on his campaign against Sicily. He had at once gone over to the Spartans, commencing that insolent career of shifting allegiances which ended with his returning to the Athenian side. At a moment of extreme danger, he had taken over a part of the Athenian fleet and had defeated the Spartans in two sensational battles in 411 and 410, thus sweeping them out of the eastern Aegean and enabling the Athenians to dominate the Hellespont. The *Philoctetes* was produced in 409, when the Athenians already wanted him back and were ready to cancel the charges against him and to restore him to citizenship. Alcibiades was a startling example of a bad character who was indispensable. Plutarch says that Aristophanes well describes the Athenian feeling about Alcibiades when he writes: "They miss him and hate him and long to have him back." And the malady of Philoctetes may have figured his moral defects: the unruly and unscrupulous nature which, even though he seems to have been innocent of the charges brought against him, had given them a certain plausibility. It must have looked to the Athenians, too, after the victories of Abydos and Cyzicus, as if he possessed an invincible bow. Plutarch says that the men who had served under him at the taking of Cyzicus did actually come to regard themselves as undefeatable and refused to share quarters with other soldiers who had fought in less successful engagements.

Yet behind both the picture of old age and the line in regard to Alcibiades, one feels in the *Philoctetes* a more general and fundamental idea: the conception of superior strength as inseparable from disability.

For the superiority of Philoctetes does not reside merely in the enchanted bow. When Lessing replied to Winckelmann, who had referred to Sophocles' cripple as if he were an example of the conventional idea of impassive classical fortitude, he pointed out that, far from exemplifying impassivity, Philoctetes becomes completely demoralized every time he has one of his seizures, and yet that this only heightens our admiration for the pride which prevents him from escaping at the expense of helping those who have deserted him. "We despise," say the objectors, "any man from whom bodily pain extorts a shriek. Ay, but not always; not for the first time, nor if we see that the sufferer strains every nerve to stifle the expression of his pain; not if we know him otherwise to be a man of firmness; still less if we witness evidences of his firmness in the very midst of his sufferings, and observe that, although pain may have extorted a shriek, it has extorted nothing else from him, but that on the contrary he submits to the prolongation of his pain rather than renounce one iota of his resolutions, even where such a concession would promise him the termination of his misery."

For André Gide, in his *Philoctète*, the obstinacy of the invalid hermit takes on a character almost mystical. By persisting in his bleak and lonely life, the Philoctetes of Gide wins the love of a more childlike Neoptolemus and even compels the respect of a less hard-boiled Odysseus. He is practicing a kind of virtue superior not only to the virtue of the latter, with his code of obedience to the demands of the group, but also to that of the former, who forgets his patriotic obligations for those of a personal attachment. There is something above the gods, says the Philoctetes of Gide; and it is virtue to devote oneself to this. But what is it? asks Neoptolemus. I do not know, he answers; oneself! The misfortune of his exile on the island has enabled him to perfect himself: "I have learned to express myself better," he tells them, "now that I am no longer with men. Between hunting and sleeping, I occupy myself with thinking. My ideas, since I have been alone so that nothing, not even suffering, disturbs them, have taken a subtle course which sometimes I can hardly follow. I have come to know more of the secrets of life than my masters had ever revealed to me. And I took to telling the story of my sufferings, and if the phrase was very beautiful, I was by so much consoled; I even sometimes forgot my sadness by uttering it. I came to understand that words inevitably become more beautiful from the moment they are no longer put together in response to the demands of others. . . ." The Philoctetes of Gide is, in fact, a literary man: at once a moralist and an artist, whose genius becomes purer and deeper in ratio to his isolation and outlawry. In the end, he lets the intruders steal the bow after satisfying himself that Neoptolemus can handle it, and subsides into a blissful tranquillity, much relieved that there is no longer any reason for people to seek him out.

With Gide we come close to a further implication, which even Gide does not fully develop but which must occur to the modern reader: the idea that genius and disease, like strength and mutilation, may be inextricably bound up together. It is significant that the only two writers of our time who have especially interested themselves in Philoctetes—André Gide and John Jay Chapman*— should both be persons who have not only, like the hero of the play, stood at an angle to the morality of society and

---

* See page xxvi. [L.M.D.]

defended their position with stubbornness, but who have suffered from psychological disorders which have made them, in Gide's case, ill-regarded by his fellows; in Chapman's case, excessively difficult. Nor is it perhaps accidental that Charles Lamb, with his experience of his sister's insanity, should in his essay on "The Convalescent" choose the figure of Philoctetes as a symbol for his own "nervous fever."

And we must even, I believe, grant Sophocles some special insight into morbid psychology. The tragic themes of all three of the great dramatists—the madnesses, the murders and the incests—may seem to us sufficiently morbid. The hero with an incurable wound was even a stock subject of myth not confined to the Philoctetes legend: there was also the story of Telephus, also wounded and also indispensable, about which both Sophocles and Euripides wrote plays. But there is a difference between the treatment that Sophocles gives to these conventional epic subjects and the treatments of the other writers. Aeschylus is more religious and philosophical; Euripides more romantic and sentimental. Sophocles by comparison is clinical. Arthur Platt, who had a special interest in the scientific aspect of the classics, says that Sophocles was scrupulously up-to-date in the physical science of his time. He was himself closely associated by tradition with the cult of the healer Asclepius, whose son is to cure Philoctetes: Lucian had read a poem which he had dedicated to the doctor-god; and Plutarch reports that Asclepius was supposed to have visited his hearth. He is said also to have been actually a priest of another of the medical cults. Platt speaks particularly of his medical knowledge—which is illustrated by the naturalism and precision of his description of Philoctetes' infected bite.

But there is also in Sophocles a cool observation of the behavior of psychological derangements. The madness of Ajax is a genuine madness, from which he recovers to be horrified at the realization of what he has done. And it was not without good reason that Freud laid Sophocles under contribution for the naming of the Oedipus complex—since Sophocles had not only dramatized the myth that dwelt with the violation of the incest taboo, but had exhibited the suppressed impulse behind it in the speech in which he makes Jocasta attempt to reassure Oedipus by reminding him that it was not uncommon for men to dream about sleeping with their mothers—"and he who thinks nothing of this gets through his life most easily." Those who do not get through life so easily are presented by Sophocles with a very firm grasp on the springs of their abnormal conduct. Electra is what we should call nowadays schizophrenic: the woman who weeps over the urn which is supposed to contain her brother's ashes is not "integrated," as we say, with the fury who prepares her mother's murder. And certainly the fanaticism of Antigone—"fixated," like Electra, on her brother—is intended to be abnormal, too. The banishment by Jebb from Sophocles' text of the passage in which Antigone explains the unique importance of a brother and his juggling of the dialogue in the scene in which she betrays her indifference to the feelings of the man she is supposed to marry are certainly among the curiosities of Victorian scholarship—though he was taking his cue from the complaint of Goethe that Antigone had been shown by Sophocles as acting from trivial motives and Goethe's hope that her speech about her brother might some day be shown to be spurious. Aristotle had cited this speech of Antigone's as an outstanding example of the principle that if anything peculiar occurs in a play the cause must be shown by the dramatist. It was admitted by Jebb that his rewriting of these passages had no real textual justification; and in one case he violates glaringly the convention of the one-line dialogue. To accept his emendation would involve the assumption that Aristotle did not know what the original text had been and was incapable of criticizing the corrupted version. No: Antigone forgets her fiancé and kills herself for her brother. Her timid sister (like Electra's timid sister) represents the normal feminine point of view. Antigone's point of view is peculiar, as Aristotle says. (The real motivation of the Antigone has been retraced with unmistakable accuracy by Professor Walter R. Agard in *Classical Philology* of July, 1937.)

These insane or obsessed people of Sophocles all display a perverse kind of nobility. I have spoken of the authority of expiation which emanates from the blasted Oedipus. Even the virulence of Electra's revenge conditions the intensity of her tenderness for Orestes. And so the maniacal fury which makes Ajax run amok, the frenzy of Heracles in the Nessus robe, terribly though they transform their victims, can never destroy their virtue of heroes. The poor disgraced Ajax will receive his due of honor after his suicide and will come to stand higher in our sympathies than Menelaus and Agamemnon, those obtuse and brutal captains, who here as in the *Philoctetes* are obviously no favorites of Sophocles'. Heracles in his final moments bids his spirit curb his lips with steel to keep him from crying out, and carry him through his self-destructive duty as a thing that is to be desired.

Some of these maladies are physical in origin, others are psychological; but they link themselves with one another. The case of Ajax connects psychological disorder as we get it in Electra, for example, with the access of pain and rage that causes Heracles to kill the herald Lichas; the case of Heracles connects a poisoning that produces a murderous fury with an infection that, though it distorts the personality, does not actually render the victim demented: the wound of Philoctetes, whose agony comes in spasms like that of Heracles. All these cases seem intimately related.

It has been the misfortune of Sophocles to figure in academic tradition as the model of those qualities of coolness and restraint which that tradition regards as classical. Those who have never read him—remembering the familiar statue—are likely to conceive something hollow and marmoreal. Actually, as C. M. Bowra says, Sophocles is "passionate and profound." Almost everything that we are told about him by the tradition of the ancient world suggests equanimity and amiability and the enjoyment of unusual good fortune. But there is one important exception: the anecdote in Plato's *Republic* in which Sophocles is represented as saying that the release from amorous desire which had come to him in his old age had been like a liberation from an insane and cruel master. He *has* balance and logic, of course: those qualities that the classicists admire; but these qualities only count because they master so much savagery and madness. Somewhere even in the fortunate Sophocles there had been a sick and raving Philoctetes.

And now let us go back to the *Philoctetes* as a parable of human character. I should interpret the fable as follows. The victim of a malodorous disease which renders him abhorrent to society and periodically degrades him and makes him helpless is also the master of a superhuman art which everybody has to respect and which the normal man finds he needs. A practical man like Odysseus, at the same time coarse-grained and clever, imagines that he can somehow get the bow without having Philoctetes on his hands or that he can kidnap Philoctetes the bowman without regard for Philoctetes the invalid. But the young son of Achilles knows better. It is at the moment when his sympathy for Philoctetes would naturally inhibit his cheating him—so the supernatural influences in Sophocles are often made with infinite delicacy to shade into subjective motivations—it is at this moment of his natural shrinking that it becomes clear to him that the words of the seer had meant that the bow would be useless without Philoctetes himself. It is in the nature of things—of this world where the divine and the human fuse—that they cannot have the irresistible weapons without its loathsome owner, who upsets the processes of normal life by his curses and his cries, and who in any case refuses to work for men who have exiled him from their fellowship.

It is quite right that Philoctetes should refuse to come to Troy. Yet it is also decreed that he shall be cured when he shall have been able to forget his grievance and to devote his divine gifts to the service of his own people. It is right that he should refuse to submit to the purposes of Odysseus, whose only idea is to exploit him. How then is the gulf to be got over between the ineffective plight of the bowman and his proper use of his bow, between his ignominy and his destined glory? Only by the intervention of one who is guileless enough and human enough to treat him, not as a monster, nor yet as a mere magical property which is wanted for accomplishing some end, but simply as another man, whose sufferings elicit his sympathy and whose courage and pride he admires. When this human relation has been realized, it seems at first that it is to have the consequence of frustrating the purpose of the expedition and ruining the Greek campaign. Instead of winning over the outlaw, Neoptolemus has outlawed himself as well, at a time when both the boy and the cripple are desperately needed by the Greeks. Yet in taking the risk to his cause which is involved in the recognition of his common humanity with the sick man, in refusing to break his word, he dissolves Philoctetes' stubbornness, and thus cures him and sets him free, and saves the campaign as well.

[1941]

V
Patriotic Gore

~~~~~~

EDITOR'S NOTE

Like the portraits in *To the Finland Station*, Wilson's Civil War portraits have the appeal both of biography and of a historical perspective in which past and present are organically connected. In *Patriotic Gore* pride in the American character is reconciled with skepticism of the mythology of the Civil War, the great crusade. Only through such a rejection of manifest destiny could a modern American writer give the national epic convincing heroes. "The drama has already been staged by characters who have written their own parts," Wilson states in the role of an interpreter of the documents. This book, however, also illustrates his enjoyment of what he called "the theater of glove puppets—not the kind on wires but the kind that you put your hands in." The characters are animated by the author's imagination, which seizes on a trait and heightens it, bringing his own experience and values to the material.

A humanist who sees history as the work not of economic or institutional forces but of men, Wilson broadens this view to include women and do justice to the role of private life in public affairs. Through the letters of Harriet Beecher Stowe and her husband he documents the personal energy and discontent behind *Uncle Tom's Cabin*,

showing what the book owes to a New England Calvinism
that was losing its doctrinal hold. The account of *Uncle
Tom's Cabin* included here is followed in *Patriotic Gore*
by a thorough study of the themes and milieus of her subsequent novels. Wilson admires Stowe's vigorous character more than her prose, but has no such reservations
about the journal of Mary Chesnut. He discerns Mrs.
Chesnut's consciously artistic purpose and some of her
central concerns, as these have since been amplified in
C. Vann Woodward's edition of the journal. Posted at the
center of the South's plantation aristocracy, she saw in
the petted independence of the men of a slaveholding
caste, in the moral frustration of the women, weaknesses
that undercut the success of her country in the field.

Although unimpressed by the myth of the lost cause,
the critic admired the individualism and intense personal
loyalties of the Confederates, just as he enjoyed his
Southern relatives. His vignettes of the fatalistic, determined Jackson and of Lee, a republican Roman who modeled himself on Washington, confirm the hold these men
maintain on the national imagination. He knows the
Union leaders better, however. The Grant portrait has
been a favorite of readers, interweaving the testimony of
contemporaries with the effect of the *Personal Memoirs* to
retrieve the man's reputation from his failures as a President. General Grant's humaneness, modesty, and lack of
illusions about his historical role are as impressive as the
objectivity and concision of the book which, in the fashion
of Wilson's nineteenth-century literary heroes, he completed when dying. Grant's prose exemplifies the new
"war style," which Wilson sees replacing the inflated eloquence of prewar literature and oratory.

When Americans look for greatness in their public men,
the portrait of Holmes will provide a standard against the
image-making of the pollsters and the media. The Justice
is not sentimentalized, despite the dissenting opinions on
labor and free speech which have endeared him to liberals.
Wilson shows Holmes as bleakly self-centered and dem-

onstrates how the Civil War destroyed his social ideals
along with his religion, leaving a Hobbesian view of state
power to sustain his philosophy of law. The spiritual energy of Calvinism survived in the work in which this
skeptic aimed to "touch the superlative." On the subject
of Holmes's patriotism, *A Piece of My Mind* is less ambiguous than are the last paragraphs of this study, and of *Patriotic Gore*. "Justice Holmes felt a stake in the United
States of a kind which his friend Henry James did not
feel," Wilson explains in defining those he calls the "serious republicans." "Holmes had, as James had not, *identified* his own interests with those of the American
Republic [Wilson's italics]." This is what Wilson does
through Holmes. His own father was almost on the Supreme Court, and in an essay on the Holmes-Laski correspondence he had shown the ·socialist Laski finding a
spiritual father in the old Justice. Now the critic does
much the same thing, as he ends the epic history on a heroic note, showing how the republican idealism which,
like Holmes himself, was battered by the war, and driven
in on itself during the gilded age, survived to help sustain
the country into the age of Franklin Roosevelt.

The accounts of Stowe and Chesnut, of the Southern
soldiers and of Grant's memoirs, are sections of Wilson's
large, portmanteau chapters, and three of these titles are
mine. A Southern soldier not included is the colorful, determined guerrilla commander Mosby. While all this material was first tried out in *The New Yorker*, the portrait
of Justice Holmes appeared only in *Patriotic Gore*, and is
here for the first time reprinted.

HARRIET BEECHER STOWE

Let us begin with *Uncle Tom's Cabin.*

This novel by Harriet Beecher Stowe was one of the greatest successes of American publishing history as well as one of the most influential books—immediately influential, at any rate—that have ever appeared in the United States. A year after its publication on March 20, 1852, it had sold 305,000 copies in America and something like two million and a half copies in English and in translation all over the world. As for its influence, it is enough to remember the greeting of Lincoln to Mrs. Stowe when she was taken to call on him at the White House: "So this is the little lady who made this big war." Yet, in the period after the war, the novel's popularity steadily declined. Mrs. Stowe's royalty statements for the second half of 1887 showed a sale of only 12,225, and eventually *Uncle Tom* went out of print. Up to the time when it was reprinted, in 1948, in the Modern Library Series, it was actually unavailable except secondhand.

What were the reasons for this eclipse? It is often assumed in the United States that *Uncle Tom* was a mere propaganda novel which disappeared when it had accomplished its purpose and did not, on its merits, deserve to live. Yet it continued to be read in Europe, and, up to the great Revolution, at any rate, it was a popular book in Russia. If we come to *Uncle Tom* for the first time today, we are likely to be surprised at not finding it what we imagined it and to conclude that the post-war neglect of it has been due to the strained situation between the North and the South. The Northerners, embarrassed by the memory of the war and not without feelings of guilt, did not care to be reminded of the issue which had given rise to so much bitterness. In the South, where before the war any public discussion of slavery had by general tacit agreement been banned, nothing afterwards was wanted less than Northern criticism of pre-war conditions. It was still possible at the beginning of this century for a South Carolina teacher to make his pupils hold up their right hands and swear that they would never read *Uncle Tom*. Both sides, after the terrible years of the war, were glad to disregard the famous novel. The characters did still remain bywords, but they were mostly kept alive by the dramatizations, in which Mrs. Stowe had had no hand and which had exploited its more obviously comic and its more melodramatic elements. These versions for the stage kept at first relatively close to the novel, but in the course of half a century they grotesquely departed from it. By the late seventies, *Uncle Tom's Cabin* was half a minstrel show and half a circus. The live bloodhounds that were supposed to pursue Eliza as she was crossing the ice with her baby—which did not occur in the novel—began to figure in 1879, and were typical of this phase of the play. The original characters were now sometimes doubled: you had two Topsys, two Lawyer Markses, two Uncle Toms. Topsy sang comic songs, and Uncle Tom was given minstrel interludes, in which he would do a shuffle and breakdown. In the meantime, on account of sectional feeling, the book could not be read in schools as the New England classics were, and it even disappeared from the home. It may be said that by the early nineteen-hundreds few young people had any at all clear idea of what *Uncle Tom's Cabin* contained. One could in fact grow up in the United States without ever having seen a copy.

To expose oneself in maturity to *Uncle Tom* may therefore prove a startling experience. It is a much more impressive work than one has ever been allowed to suspect. The first thing that strikes one about it is a certain eruptive force. This is partly explained by the author in a preface to a late edition, in which she tells of the oppressive silence that hung over the whole question of slavery before she published her book. "It was a general saying," she explains, "among conservative and sagacious people that this subject was a dangerous one to investigate, and that nobody could begin to read and think upon it without becoming practically insane; moreover, that it was a subject of such delicacy that no discussion of it could be held in the free states without impinging upon the sensibilities of the slave states, to whom alone the management of the matter belonged." The story came so suddenly to Mrs. Stowe and seemed so irresistibly to write itself that she felt as if some power beyond her had laid hold of her to deliver its message, and she said sometimes that the book had been written by God. This is actually a little the impression that the novel makes on the reader. Out of a background of undistinguished narrative, inelegantly and carelessly written, the characters leap into being with a vitality that is all the more striking for the ineptitude of the prose that presents them. These characters—like those of Dickens, at least in his early phase—express themselves a good deal better than the author expresses herself. The Shelbys and George Harris and Eliza and Aunt Chloe and Uncle Tom project themselves out of the void. They come before us arguing and struggling, like real people who cannot be quiet. We feel that the dams of discretion of which Mrs. Stowe has spoken have been burst by a passionate force that, compressed, has been mounting behind them, and which, liberated, has taken the form of a flock of lamenting and ranting, prattling and preaching characters, in a drama that demands to be played to the end.

Not, however, that it is merely a question of a troubled imagination and an inhibited emotional impulse finding vent in a waking fantasy. What is most unexpected is that, the farther one reads in *Uncle Tom*, the more one becomes aware that a critical mind is at work, which has the complex situation in a very firm grip and which, no matter how vehement the characters become, is controlling and coordinating their interrelations. Though there is much that is exciting in *Uncle Tom's Cabin*, it is never the crude melodrama of the decadent phase of the play; and though we find some old-fashioned moralizing and a couple of

Dickensian deathbeds, there is a good deal less sentimentality than we may have been prepared for by our memories of the once celebrated stage apotheosis—if we are old enough to have seen it: *Little Eva in the Realms of Gold.* We may even be surprised to discover that the novel is by no means an indictment drawn up by New England against the South. Mrs. Stowe has, on the contrary, been careful to contrive her story in such a way that the Southern states and New England shall be shown as involved to an equal degree in the kidnapping into slavery of the Negroes and the subsequent maltreatment of them, and that the emphasis shall all be laid on the impracticability of slavery as a permanent institution. The author, if anything, leans over backwards in trying to make it plain that the New Englanders are as much to blame as the South and to exhibit the Southerners in a favorable light; for St. Clare and Miss Ophelia, intended as typical products of, respectively, Louisiana and Vermont, are, after all, first cousins; they are the children of two New England brothers, both of whom are described as "upright, energetic, noble-minded, with an iron will," but one of whom had "settled down in New England, to rule over rocks and stones, and to force an existence out of Nature," while the other had "settled in Louisiana, to rule over men and women, and force existence out of *them.*" The difference between the two cousins is, then, chiefly a difference of habitat: the result of the diverse effects of a society in which you have to do things for yourself and of a society in which everything is done for you. And as for Simon Legree—a plantation owner, not an overseer, as many people imagine him to be (due, no doubt, to some telescoping of episodes, in the later productions of the play, which would have made him an employee of St. Clare's)—Simon Legree is not a Southerner: he is a Yankee, and his harsh inhumanity as well as his morbid solitude are evidently regarded by Mrs. Stowe as characteristic of his native New England. Nor are these regional characterizations—though later, by the public, turned into clichés—of an easy or obvious kind. The contrasted types of the book, through their conflicts, precipitate real tragedy, and even, in some episodes, high comedy—the Sisyphean efforts, for example, of the visitor from Vermont, Miss Ophelia, to bring system into the St. Clare household, and her bafflement by the Negro-run kitchen, a place of confusion and mystery, out of which she is unable to understand how the magnificent meals are produced. There is, in fact, in *Uncle Tom*, as well as in its successor *Dred*, a whole drama of manners and morals and intellectual points of view which corresponds somewhat to the kind of thing that was then being done by Dickens, and was soon to be continued by Zola, for the relations of the social classes, and which anticipates such later studies of two sharply contrasting peoples uncomfortably involved with one another as the *John Bull's Other Island* of Bernard Shaw or E. M. Forster's *A Passage to India*.

But such a writer as Forster or Shaw is a well-balanced man of letters contriving a fable at his leisure. Mrs. Stowe's objectivity is taut, intent. She has nothing of the partisan mentality that was to become so inflamed in the fifties; and Lord Palmerston, who had read the book three times, was evidently quite sincere in complimenting her on the "statesmanship" of *Uncle Tom's Cabin*. She is national, never regional, but her consciousness that the national ideal is in danger gave her book a desperate candor that shook South and North alike, and a dramatic reverberation that, perpetuated by the run of the play, has outlasted the analysis of the novel. In what terms this ideal of the United States was conceived by Harriet Beecher Stowe appears very clearly from a passage in her autobiographical notes: "There was one of my father's books that proved a mine of wealth to me. It was a happy hour when he brought home and set up in his bookcase Cotton Mather's *Magnalia*, in a new edition of two volumes. What wonderful stories those! Stories, too, about my own country. Stories that made me feel the very ground I trod on to be consecrated by some special dealing of God's providence." And she tells of her emotions, in her childhood, on hearing the Declaration of Independence read: "I had never heard it before," wrote Mrs. Stowe, "and even now had but a vague idea of what was meant by some parts of it. Still I gathered enough from the recital of the abuses and injuries that had driven my nation to this course to feel myself swelling with indignation, and ready with all my little mind and strength to applaud the concluding passage, which Colonel Talmadge rendered with resounding majesty. I was as ready as any of them to pledge my life, fortune, and sacred honor for such a cause. The heroic element was strong in me, having come down by ordinary generation from a long line of Puritan ancestry, and just now it made me long to do something, I knew not what: to fight for my country, or to make some declaration on my own account." Her assumption, in writing *Uncle Tom*, is that every worthy person in the United States must desire to preserve the integrity of our unprecedented republic; and she tries to show how Negro slavery must disrupt and degrade this common ideal by tempting the North to the moral indifference, the half-deliberate ignorance, which encourages inhuman practices, and by weakening the character of the South through the luxury and the irresponsibility that the institution of slavery breeds. For Harriet Beecher Stowe, besides, the American Union had been founded under the auspices of the Christian God, and she could not accept institutions that did such violence to Christian teaching. One of the strongest things in the novel is the role played by Uncle Tom—another value that was debased in the play. The Quakers who shelter Eliza are, of course, presented as Christians; but not one of the other white groups that figure in *Uncle Tom's Cabin* is living in accordance with the principles of the religion they all profess. It is only the black Uncle Tom who has taken the white man's religion seriously and who—standing up bravely, in the final scene, for the dignity of his own soul but at the same

time pardoning Simon Legree—attempts to live up to it literally. The sharp irony as well as the pathos is that the
recompense he wins from the Christians, as he is gradually put through their mill, is to be separated from his
family and exiled; tormented, imprisoned and done to
death.

Another feature of the stage melodrama that is misleading in regard to the novel is the unity, or effect of unity,
imposed on its locale and chronology. The play is made to
center on New Orleans, and one sensational scene is made
to follow another so fast that we do not have any idea of
the actual passage of time. The two distinct strands of the
story have, furthermore, to be tied up together in a way
that they are not in the book. The novel has a quite different pattern, for in it the Negro characters—Uncle Tom
and his family, on the one hand; George Harris and Eliza,
on the other—are involved in a series of wanderings
which progressively and excitingly reveal, like the visits of
Chíchikov in Gogol's *Dead Souls*, the traits of a whole society. One of the main sources of interest, as in Gogol, is
the variety of Southern households to which, one after the
other, we are introduced; first, the bourgeois Kentuckian
Shelbys, who are naturally decent and kindly, but also essentially conventional and very much attached to their
comfort; then the homelier Ohio Quakers, with their
kitchen-centered existence and their language based on
the Bible; then the St. Clares, in their villa on Lake Pont-
chartrain—their wastefulness and laxness and charm, the
whole family languishing with maladies that are real or
imaginary, full of bad conscience, baffled affections and
unfulfillable longings; then, finally—in the lowest circle—
the nightmare plantation of Simon Legree, a prison and a
place of torture, with its Negroes set to flog other Negroes
and its tensions of venomous hatred between Simon Legree and his mistress—where, amidst the black moss and
the broken stumps of the muddy and rank Red River, the
intractable New England soul is delivered to its deepest
damnation. The creator of this long sequence, with its in-

terconnecting episodes of riverboat, tavern and slave market, was no contemptible novelist. Even Henry James, that expert professional, is obliged to pay her his tribute when he tells us, in *A Small Boy and Others*, of a performance of the play that had been for him in childhood a thrilling "aesthetic adventure," which had first, he says, awakened his critical sense, and admits that the novel constitutes a perhaps unique literary case of a book which has made its impression without the author's ever having concerned herself with literary problems at all, "as if," as he says, "a fish, a wonderful 'leaping' fish, had simply flown through the air." One hardly knows, in this connection, to what other book of its period one can properly compare *Uncle Tom's Cabin*. Turgenev's *A Sportsman's Sketches*, exactly contemporary with it, which is supposed to have had some effect in expediting the abolition of serfdom and which has sometimes been spoken of as "the Russian *Uncle Tom's Cabin*," belongs so much more to the level of sophisticated literary art that it is difficult today to realize how subversive its implications once were. The Brontës have something in common with Harriet Beecher Stowe, but even they belong more to belles lettres, and their subjects are not social problems but passionate feminine daydreams. *Uncle Tom* is more closely akin to some such early novel of Dickens as *Oliver Twist*, and Dickens, who admired the book, was correct in detecting his own influence.

Uncle Tom was an explosive that had been shot into the world by a whole combination of pressures, personal as well as historical. Harriet Beecher had been born in Litchfield, Connecticut, but she had gone to live in Cincinnati, Ohio, in 1832, when her father Lyman Beecher, a then famous Presbyterian preacher, had founded in that Western city Lane Theological Seminary. Four years later, when she was twenty-five, she married Calvin Ellis Stowe, the professor of Biblical literature at Lane, and, with widely spaced visits to New England, which were evidently blessed escapes, she remained eighteen years in

Ohio. Cincinnati was then a pork-packing center, and the streets were obstructed with pigs; it was also a river-town, and the bar-rooms were full of bad characters. The situation across the state line was a constant source of disturbance. There were always desperate slaves fleeing from over the river, and some Ohioans wanted to help them while others wanted to hunt them down. Lyman Beecher was opposed to slavery but had not been converted to Abolition. On this subject, as in his theology, he tried to steer a politic course; but at the time of his absence one summer, the trustees of his new theological school provoked an Abolitionist movement by suppressing an Anti-Slavery Society and forbidding discussion of the subject "in any public room of the Seminary." A self-confident and brilliant student rallied and led a sedition of the whole student body, who left their buildings and encamped in a suburb, and eventually, in 1835, he carried away a large part of the seminary, students and faculty both, to Oberlin College, also in Ohio, which had just received an endowment for a theological department that was to be open to colored students. In the summer of 1836, a mob in Cincinnati wrecked the press of an Abolitionist paper, and this was followed by further riots, in the course of which Harriet Stowe, going into the kitchen one day, found her brother Henry Ward Beecher pouring melted lead into a mold. When she asked, "What on earth are you doing, Henry?" he answered, "Making bullets to kill men with." He faced the streets with two guns in his pockets. Both Harriet and Henry, as a result of this experience, seem secretly to have become Abolitionists. The Stowes a little later took into their household a colored girl who said she was free but who was presently claimed by her master; Calvin Stowe and Henry Beecher, armed with pistols, arranged her escape at night. This girl was the original of Eliza Harris. In the meantime, another of Harriet's brothers, Edward, now the head of Illinois College, had encouraged Elijah Lovejoy, one of the most zealous of the Abolitionists, who had been publishing a paper in St.

Louis and was threatened by the pro-slavery element, to transfer his operations to Alton, Illinois. In the November of 1837, the year after the Cincinnati riots, Lovejoy was shot to death while defending his printing press, which had just been unloaded from a Mississippi steamboat, and it was reported—though this turned out to be false—that Edward Beecher had also been murdered.

In this period, the issue of slavery was becoming involved with church politics. An exacerbated controversy was going on between the Princeton Theological Seminary and the Yale Divinity School, with Princeton on the unyieldingly conservative and Yale on the relatively liberal side. Lyman Beecher, who had studied at Yale, had found in Cincinnati a bitter opponent, a certain Dr. Joshua Wilson, the pastor of the First Presbyterian Church, a Calvinist fanatic so uncompromising that he refused to have pictures in his house on the ground that they were graven images. Dr. Wilson had occupied unchallenged the position of leader of the Church in the West, and he seems to have been jealous of Beecher. He succeeded— taking his cue, it is said, from Princeton—in having Lyman Beecher tried for heresy in 1835, first before the Presbytery, then before the Synod, but in both cases his victim had been acquitted. Though rugged and open in manner, Lyman Beecher was a very astute politician. It is wonderful to find him declaring that he is sound on infant depravity by putting into solemn language his conviction that young children were badly behaved, exhibiting, as he says, "selfishness, self-will, malignant anger, envy and revenge," the evidence of "a depraved state of mind, voluntary and sinful in its character and qualities." (His denial that infant damnation had ever been an article of the Calvinist creed was evidently derived from Calvin's reservation in favor of children who belonged to the Elect.) When his son Henry Ward Beecher was about to be examined for ordination at Fort Wayne, Indiana—to which the old man rode seventy miles, arriving "besplashed and bespattered," as another of

his sons has written, "with smoking steed and his saddle-
bags crusted with mud"—the father admonished him as
follows: "Preach little doctrine except what is of moldy
orthodoxy; keep all your improved breeds, your short-
horned Durhams, your Berkshires, etc., away off to
pasture. They will get fatter and nobody will be scared.
Take hold of the most practical subjects; popularize
your sermons. I do not ask you to change yourself;
but, for a time, while captious critics are lurking, adapt
your mode so as to insure that you shall be rightly under—
stood." Yet a split in the Church now took place. "The
South," said Dr. Beecher in later years, "had generally
stood neutral. They had opposed going to extremes in
theology either way. Rice, of Virginia, was a noble fellow, and held all steady. It was Rice who said, after my
trial, that I ought to be tried once in five years, to keep up
the orthodoxy of the church. He was full of good humor,
and did so much good. But they got scared about abolition. Rice got his head full of that thing, and others. John
C. Calhoun was at the bottom of it. I know of his doing
things—writing to ministers, and telling them to do this
and do that. The South finally took the Old School side. It
was a cruel thing—it was a cursed thing, and 'twas slavery
that did it."

At the General Assembly in Philadelphia in 1838, Dr.
Wilson had Beecher and Calvin Stowe read out of the
Presbyterian Church. That same day in Philadelphia, a
new building called Liberty Hall, which had just been
dedicated to Abolition and to which white Quaker women
had been seen going arm and arm with Negro men, was
burned down by a mob, with the firemen refusing to put
out the blaze. Dr. Beecher set out in the autumn on a kind
of marauding expedition and persuaded several students
from other colleges to transfer to Lane Seminary. In
Louisville, he ran into a man he knew who was keeping a
store in the city, and he induced him to give up his business and study for the ministry at Lane. When Beecher
got back to the seminary, he found that his son-in-law,

Calvin Stowe, who was a periodic hypochondriac, had succumbed to discouragement and taken to his bed. "Wake up!" cried Dr. Beecher. "I've brought ye twelve students. Get up and wash, and eat bread, and prepare to have a good class."

The Stowes had by this time four children—the first two of which were twins—and Harriet began to write stories in order to bring in some money. In the summer of 1841, several incidents of violence occurred. A man who was hiding a slave that had run away from Kentucky went so far as to attack the owner when the latter attempted to search his house; and at about the same time a local farmer was murdered by Negroes who were stealing his berries, and in the city a white woman was raped. In September, there were race riots that lasted a week, with several persons killed and wounded. A farmer with a Dutch name, who was to turn up in *Uncle Tom's Cabin* as Old John Van Trompe, made an effort to rescue nine slaves, only one of whom succeeded in getting away; but for the loss of this slave he was sued by the owner. He was defended by Salmon P. Chase, at that time a young lawyer in Cincinnati, who had played a courageous part in the 1836 riots and who was later to defend Dr. Beecher when the relentless Old School Presbyterians tried to oust him from the presidency of his seminary in order to take it over themselves. In Beecher's case, Chase was successful, but he failed in his defense of the farmer. He took it up to the Supreme Court at his own expense, but he lost on every decision. His client was finally ruined by having to pay the costs as well as fines and damages. A third brother of Harriet's, Charles, who was also to have entered the ministry, had been shaken in his faith at college by a treatise of Jonathan Edwards's, in which Edwards appeared to be arguing that man was completely deprived of the power of moral choice and yet that God held him accountable. Though Charles's resourceful father found it possible to interpret Edwards in a less discouraging way, the boy abandoned religion and became what he called a fatalist.

Eventually, however, to Lyman's great joy, he emerged from this state of mind and, like his brothers, went into the ministry; but in the meantime he had been working as a clerk in New Orleans and, returning to Cincinnati at the time when mob violence was running high, he brought stories of plantation life in Louisiana that were later to be used by Harriet for the episode of Simon Legree. During the winter of 1842–43, there was a typhoid epidemic in the Seminary, and everybody turned out to nurse the sick. In July, just as Harriet Stowe was on the point of having another baby, her brother George, also a minister, accidentally shot himself. She was an invalid for months after the birth of the child; nor did the baby seem likely to live, and yet the little girl did survive. The Stowes, with their growing family, had no other means than Calvin's meager salary, and their life became rather sordid. A letter of Harriet's to Calvin, written on June 16, 1845, when Calvin is away at a ministers' convention, strikes the note of this dismal period:

"My dear Husband,—It is a dark, sloppy, rainy, muddy, disagreeable day, and I have been working hard (for me) all day in the kitchen, washing dishes, looking into closets, and seeing a great deal of that dark side of domestic life which a housekeeper may who will investigate too curiously into minutiae in warm, damp weather, especially after a girl who keeps all clean on the *outside* of cup and platter, and is very apt to make good the rest of the text in the *inside* of things.

"I am sick of the smell of sour milk, and sour meat, and sour everything, and then the clothes *will* not dry, and no wet thing does, and everything smells moldy; and altogether I feel as if I never wanted to eat again.

"Your letter, which was neither sour nor moldy, formed a very agreeable contrast to all these things; the more so for being unexpected. I am much obliged to you for it. As to my health, it gives me very little solicitude, although it is bad enough and daily growing worse. I feel no life, no energy, no appetite, or rather a growing distaste for food;

in fact, I am becoming quite ethereal. Upon reflection I perceive that it pleases my Father to keep me in the fire, for my whole situation is excessively harassing and painful. I suffer with sensible distress in the brain, as I have done more or less since my sickness last winter, a distress which some days takes from me all power of planning or executing anything; and you know that, except this poor head, my unfortunate household has no mainspring, for nobody feels any kind of responsibility to do a thing in time, place, or manner, except as I oversee it.

"Georgiana is so excessively weak, nervous, cross, and fretful, night and day, that she takes all Anna's strength and time with her; and then the children are, like other little sons and daughters of Adam, full of all kinds of absurdity and folly.

"When the brain gives out, as mine often does, and one cannot think or remember anything, then what is to be done? All common fatigue, sickness, and exhaustion is nothing to this distress. Yet do I rejoice in my God, and know in whom I believe, and only pray that the fire may consume the dross; as to the gold, that is imperishable. No real evil can happen to me, so I fear nothing for the future, and only suffer in the present tense.

"God, the mighty God, is mine, of that I am sure, and I know He knows that though flesh and heart fail, I am all the while desiring and trying for His will alone. As to a journey, I need not ask a physician to see that it is needful to me as far as health is concerned, that is to say, all human appearances are that way, but I feel no particular choice about it. If God wills I go, He can easily find means. Money, I suppose, is as plenty with Him now as it always has been, and if He sees it is really best, He will doubtless help me."

It was a very hard summer for both of them. Calvin, who was supposed to be raising money for the Seminary, stayed away till the beginning of October. He detested this money-raising, for which he was entirely unfitted.

"This work," he writes Harriet on June 30, "is beyond measure irksome and trying to me, and the long absence from you and the children almost insupportable. And after all, it is not going to result in any immediate pecuniary *affluence* I can assure you. At most it will just enable us to struggle through another year, and give us hope that we shall not be obliged through excessive poverty to quit our post." And in September: "I am so nervous that any attempt to preach on the subject of raising money brings on neuralgic pains that are intolerable and lay me aside for a week or two. . . . If I cannot live without begging money, I must die; the sooner the better." He is passing, besides, through a serious crisis. He fears that he is losing his faith, and he has been frightened by recent scandals created in the clerical world by certain "licentious hypocrites" into wondering whether it might not be possible for him, too, to disgrace his calling.

"I long to be with you once more," he writes in the letter first quoted. "I am a miserable creature without a wife, and having been blessed with such a wife as you are, it is the harder to be alone so much and so long, and in an employment so essentially disagreeable to me. Let me have a competent salary, let me be permitted to study and teach and lecture everyday, let me have my dear little children around me every evening, and let me sleep in my own bed with my own good wife every night, and Prince Albert himself is not so happy a man as I. Though I have, as you well know, a most enthusiastic admiration of fresh, youthful female beauty; yet it never comes anywhere near the kind of feeling I have for you. With you, every desire I have, mental and physical, is completely satisfied and filled up, and leaves me nothing more to ask for. My enjoyment with you is not weakened by time nor blunted by age, and every reunion after separation is just as much of a honey-moon as was the first month after the wedding. Is not your own experience and observation a proof of what I say? Does it not always *seem to be* just as I represent it? Just as it seems, so it is in reality. No man can love and respect his wife more than I do mine. Yet we are not as happy as we might be. I have many faults, and you have some failings, and Anna [the Stowes' maid and nurse], with all her good qualities, is rather aggravating sometimes—but the grace of God can mend all.

"I have thought much of our domestic happiness lately in connection with the melancholy licentiousness, recently detected, of several clergymen of high reputation in the east."

A bishop in Philadelphia, whom Calvin has admired as a writer for his effective refutation of the "historical argument against Christianity," "it now appears has long been addicted to intoxication, and while half boozled has caught young ladies who were so unfortunate to meet him alone, and pawed them over in the most disgusting manner, and actually attempted to do them physical violence. This has been going on for years until it could be borne no longer, and now it all comes out against him, to the dishonor of religion, his own unspeakable shame and anguish, and the distress unutterable of his wife and children." And: "Another distinguished high church episcopalian clergyman in Philadelphia, nearly 60 years old, is said to be in precisely the same predicament as his bishop. Bless the Lord, O my soul, that with all my strong relish for brandy and wine, and all my indescribable admiration and most overflowing delight in handsome young ladies, no offences of this kind have yet been written down against me in God's book. Next comes the most melancholy case of N. E. Johnson, lately editor of the N.Y. evangelists and recently pastor of the Meth. Church in Bloomfield, N.J., though he has been admired as an evangelical, spiritual, revival preacher of great talent and concentrated piety, and married to an intelligent, amiable and pious woman who has borne him children, though associating without suspicion with the most pious men and the most accomplished and Christian women, it now appears that for 8 or 9 years past he has been in the habit of not only visiting the theaters ... but also the brothels and bawdy houses of the city of N.Y. where he would get beastly drunk and revel and swelter with the vilest harlots. . . .

"Last in this dreadful catalogue, J. H. Fairchild, formerly pastor of the Orthodox church in South Boston, and lately of Exeter N.H. a man 55 years old, twice married, and whose daughters are mothers. Circumstances have recently occurred, which show that he has for years been licentious, that while elder he seduced one of his own kitchen girls, committed adultery with a member of his own church; and lately he has cut his throat and killed himself in the agony of his shame, while pastor of one of the most respectable churches in Exeter. . . .

"Now what shall we think of all these horrid disclosures? Is there anybody we can trust? Are all ministers brutes? I confess I feel almost ashamed to go into a pulpit or ask anyone to contribute a cent for ministerial education. . . ."

Harriet's answer is prompt and firm: she takes the situation seriously, and that she and Calvin were quite right in doing so was to be proved by the later justification of a "presentiment" she speaks of here, in connection with a visit from her younger brother, Henry Ward Beecher, who was eventually to become involved in a similar, if less sordid, scandal: ". . . Yesterday Henry came from Crawfordsville uncommonly depressed and sober and spoke in church meeting of unexpected falls among high places in the church and the need of prayer for Christians. He seemed so depressed that a horrible presentiment crept over me. I thought of all my brothers and of you—and could it be, that the great Enemy has prevailed against any of you, and as I am gifted with a most horrible vivid imagination, in a moment I imagined—nay saw as in a vision all the distress and despair that would follow a fall on your part. I felt weak and sick—I took a book and lay down on the bed, but it pursued me like a nightmare—and something seemed to ask Is your husband any better *seeming* than so and so!—I looked in the glass and my face which since spring has been something of the palest was so haggard that it frightened me. The illusion lasted a whole forenoon and then evaporated like a poisonous mist—but God knows how I pity those heart wrung women—wives worse than widows, who are called to lament that the grave has *not* covered their husband—the father of their children! Good and merciful God—why are such agonies reserved for the children of men! I can conceive now of misery which in one night would change the hair to grey and shrivel the whole frame to premature decrepitude!— misery to which all other agony is as a mocking sound! What terrible temptations lie in the way of your sex—till now I never realised it—for tho I did love you with an almost *insane* love before I married you I never knew yet or felt the pulsation which showed me that I could be tempted in that way—there never was a moment when I felt anything by which you could have drawn me astray—for I loved you as I now love God—and I can conceive of no higher love—and as I have no passion—-I have no jealousy,—the most beautiful woman in the world could not make me jealous so long as she only *dazzled the senses*—but still my dear, you must not wonder if I want to warn you not to look or *think* too freely on womankind. If your sex would guard the outworks of *thought*, you would never fall—and when so dizzying so astounding are the advantages which Satan takes it scarce is implying a doubt to say 'be cautious'. . . ."

But Calvin's religious difficulties he confides to his father-in-law rather than to Harriet. "I wanted to tell you something of the state of my soul," he writes to Lyman Beecher on July 17. "Since I left Cleaveland I have suffered a great deal of mental agony, partly no doubt from physical causes. I feel that my heart is not right in the sight of God, that I do not yet know Christ as I ought to know him. I have been exceedingly distressed with skeptical doubts as to the reality of experimental religion, and whether the whole Bible is not after all a humbug; or at least merely the most simple and touching development of the religious sensibilities natural to man, which the human mind has yet been able to produce and whether in this state of things I ought not to leave the ministry and all studies connected with it, and devote myself to education, which is always a good, let the truth of religion stand as it may. I think with excessive pain of the great amount of exaggeration and humbug that exists in the so-called benevolent movement of the day, and of the great amount of selfishness and sectarianism in religious movements. I pray, and it is speaking to a dead wall and not to God—I call upon Christ, and he is a dead man who was buried 18 centuries ago—I try to be spiritually-minded, and find in myself a most exquisite relish, and deadly longing for all kinds of sensual gratification—I think of the revival ministers who have lived long in licentiousness with good reputation, and then been detested,—and ask myself, who knows whether there be any real piety on earth? O wretched man that I am! Who shall deliver me? . . . You are near the close of a long life spent in spreading the Gospel. Is the veil rent, and can you see through it into the holy of holies? Oh happy man if you can, and God grant me the same privilege, even at the expense of my life, O happy day when I and my wife and children are all in the quiet grave!"

To Harriet he writes three days later: "Though I can cheerfully trust the final salvation of my soul to Christ; yet I cannot now trust him for the temporal wants of my family and the institution. A strange inconsistency! Like Melanchthon, I have an unshaken hope of being forgiven and getting to heaven at last but everything else distresses me to death almost." He reproaches her on the 29th for not writing to strengthen his faith, to support his "feeble and tottering steps." "*My soul is weary of my life*, and I feel it would be the greatest of mercies to take me out of the world. . . . Still I have felt that I could have some hold on Christ through you, and I have longed for your letters to come that I might stay myself on those thrilling paragraphs with which they at first abounded—but there are

lately no special religious views in them—no more than
what I or any ordinary professor of religion might write.
Perhaps it is because my letters have had so little of the
spirit of Christ in them that they have chilled and discouraged you. Lean and barren they have been I do not
doubt but I hope you will not allow my deathfulness to
deprive you of life when you are capable of living and I
am not." He did feel, however, that his paralyzing despair
might prove to be merely a test, "a process of spiritual
purification" through which the Lord was leading him;
and by August 17, he seems to have emerged and recovered his faith: "My mind is now free," he writes from
Portland, Maine, "and I can commune with my God and
Saviour, but my nervous system has received such a shock
that I am incapable of any serious exertion. My nerves in
every part of my body feel sore, and there is danger of universal neuralgia unless I keep quiet. . . . I had a grand sail
the other day all around the harbor, and while some of the
company were profane and rebellious enough to amuse
themselves with catching fish which they did not want,
and knew nothing what to do with them after they had got
them, I left the boat and scrambled around on the rocks,
and let the waves roar and dash all over me, and felt quite
delighted." When he had spoken in the earlier letter of not
being able to rely on Christ "for the temporal wants of my
family and the institution," he meant that he was unsuccessful in raising funds for the Seminary; and Harriet—
September 3—tries heartily to reassure him that he can
perfectly rely both on God and her: "My love you do
wrong to worry so much about temporal matters—you
really *do wrong:* You treat your Saviour *ungenerously*
and you ought not to do it—Every letter of yours contains
such unbelieving doubts 'Who will take care of us and
keep us out of debt?'—My love if you were *dead* this
day—and I feeble as I am with five little children I would
not doubt nor despond nor expect to starve—tho *if* I *did*
expect to starve I could bear it very well since Heaven is
eternal. . . . It is all humbug—got up by Satan—this fuss-

ing about a temporal future—if you will put the affairs all into my hands and let me manage them my own way and not give a thought during winter only to be good and grow in grace *I'l engage* to bring things out right in spring . . .—Now do take me up on this—"

In Calvin's two last letters to Harriet—of September 29 and 30—as the end of their separation draws near, we get for the first time a glimpse of what their life together had been. He is not looking forward now to a reunion which will be "just as much of a honey-moon as was the first month after the wedding." With a sudden return to the practical and a dropping of his valetudinarian tone, he explains to her all her faults, though admitting certain faults on his own part. She is slack and forbearing, he tells her, while he is methodical and irritable. He likes to have morning prayers and meals on time; she doesn't care when they have them. He likes to have the things in the house assigned to their places and left there; but it "seems to be your special delight to keep everything . . . on the move." He likes to have his newspapers "properly folded"; but she and Anna have vexed him "beyond all endurance" by "dropping them sprawling on the floor, or wabbling them all up in one wabble, and squashing them on the table like an old hen with her guts and gizzard squashed out."

But the next day a pang of compunction compels him to write her again: "The last letter I wrote you does not satisfy me, because it does not do you justice on a point on which you have seldom had justice done you, I mean your earnest and successful endeavour for self-improvement. In all respects in which both nature and an exceedingly defective or one-sided education have made you imperfect, I recognise and admire in you an earnest and Christian-like purpose to amend. Nature and bad education have done me great injury, and I know by my own experience how hard it is to get the better of such defects; and you have succeeded on your part far better than I have on mine." He cannot, however, refrain from enlarging on her shortcomings further: "Naturally thoughtless of expense and inclined to purchase whatever strikes your eye, without much reflection on the proportion of expenditure to be devoted to such objects, this propensity was indulged and greatly increased by your relations with Kate [her sister Catharine]. It can be corrected only by a rigid habit of keeping strict written accounts of all available income, of all absolute wants, and of all actual expense. . . . But there is another matter which needs care. When your mind is on any particular point, it is your nature to feel and act as if that were the only thing in the world; and you drive at it and make every thing bend to it, to the manifest injury of other interests. For instance, when you are intent on raising flowers, you are sure to visit them and inspect them very carefully every morning; but your kitchen would go for two or three days without any inspection at all, you would be quite ignorant of what there was in the house to be cooked, or the way in which the work was done. Your oversight of the flowers would be systematic and regular; of the kitchen, at haphazard, and now and then. You should be as regular in the kitchen as in the garden.— Again, you seldom hesitate to make a promise, whether you have ability to perform it or not, like your father and Kate, only not quite so bad; and promises so easily made are very easily broken. On this point Kate has no conscience at all, your father very little; and you have enough to keep you from making such promises, if you would only think beforehand whether you could fulfill them or not. . . .

"Well, no more on this subject at present. I got your flower seeds and a pound of the guano. An ounce of the guano is to be dissolved in a gallon of water and applied to the plant once a week. This is the scientific direction so that a pound of guano will last a long time. I hope you will be content this winter with keeping a very few choice plants—for *labor* is a great article in our family; and we must adopt some plan to save labor and fuel. By the way, there is one other thing I will mention, because it has often vexed and irritated me intolerably. I must clean the stable, wash the carriage, grease the wheels, black my boots, etc. etc. but you scorn to sweep the carriage, you must always call your servant to do it, and not stoop yourself to so menial an act. This makes me mad, for you are not too good to do in your line what I am everyday obliged to do in mine. Now I believe I have opened my whole budget, and in these two letters given you all my grievances. I pray the Lord to strengthen me on my return to treat you with uniform tenderness, kindness, and love. I suffer amazingly every day I live. I hardly know what to make of it, unless it be the Lord's penance of our sin. You have suffered a great deal, but I doubt whether you have ever suffered as I have this summer.

"I will try to come home cheerful and confiding in God. By the good hand of God upon me I expect to be in Pittsburg Wednesday night, and then in Cincinnati as soon as I can get there—Probably I shall not write you again. Forgive me all the wrong I have ever done you, and give me credit for sincere endeavours to do better. I cannot tell you what admiration I have heard expressed of you wherever I have been, and not always in a way at all calculated to sooth my vanity. Good bye.

"affectionately C.E.S."

Harriet succeeded, the following spring, in getting away to Brattleboro, Vermont, where she took "the water cure" and remained for almost a year. But soon after she returned to the West, she found that she was pregnant again. And now Calvin, who, in Harriet's absence, had relapsed into hypochondria, decided that he, too, required a cure. He, too, had recourse to Brattleboro and remained away fifteen months. The completeness, during such absences, of Calvin's eclipse and the extent to which he unloaded on Harriet all the responsibility for the family may be gauged from a letter of July 29, 1855, written during another long absence: "I shall return as soon as possible after the meeting in N. York in Sept.—and until then you must manage all household matters in your own way— just as you would if I were dead, and you had never anything more to expect from me. Indeed, to all practical purposes I am dead for the present and know not when I shall live again. If I have the ability to do it, I will by and by write you a letter about household matters the coming season." A series of cholera epidemics had been added, in the years of their residence, to the other nerve-taxing elements of Cincinnati life; and while Harriet was handling the household alone, this series reached a terrible climax. At the peak of the new epidemic, a thousand people a week were dying. The city was filled with the fumes of the soft coal that was burned as a disinfectant, and everything was black with soot. There was general demoralization, and many people less austere than the Beechers and Stowes did their best to stay drunk all the time. Harriet wrote to her husband that he must not think of coming back. The Stowe children's pet dog died; then their old colored laundress died—the twins helped to make her a shroud. Then Harriet's most recent baby began to have convulsions, and in four days it, too, was dead. Harriet herself was attacked by cramps, and the doctor assumed she was dying; but her father, who had been away attending the Yale Commencement, was back now to give her support. The indomitable old preacher, now seventy, rubbed Harriet's hands, as he writes his wife, "with perseverance and vigor"; and he always remained by her side, spending the night "on a settee in the dining room, hot as an oven and thronged with mosquitoes, sleepless from their annoyance, and conscious of every noise and movement." He gave Harriet a dose of brandy, which made her at first delirious, but he seems to think it pulled her through. "The night of suspense passed safely, and she was better in the morning." "I am not sick," he adds, to reassure his wife, "—never was better in my life, though last week I had to diet and abstain from corn and succotash; but this week I have studied and worked like Jehu

every day, trimming up the trees, hoeing in the garden till
my face was bathed and my shirt soaked, and yet I have
not felt so well for a year past—so much like being young
again."

So one's picture of this phase of Harriet's life is not
really one of unrelieved horror. Such clerical New
England families had a heritage of hearty vitality as well
as of moral fortitude that prevented them from becoming
pathetic. Yet, in the first sixteen years of her marriage,
poor Harriet was suffering from miseries that must have
been as little avowed—such complaints as the one I have
quoted are rare—as the ever-rankling anxieties of slavery.
Uncle Tom, with its lowering threats and its harassing
persecutions, its impotence of well-meaning people, its
outbreaks of violence and its sudden bereavements, had
been lived in the Beecher home, where the trials and tribulations, as they used to be called, of the small family
world inside were involved with, were merged in, the tra-
vail of the nation to which it belonged. This obscure personal anguish of Harriet Stowe went to energize her
famous novel which had so strong an impact on public affairs, as did also the courage and faith, the conviction that
God, after all, was just. And finally a turn does come in
the fortunes of Calvin and Harriet Stowe: God does at last
provide; a door of escape is unlocked; He is now at last
giving them something which will offset their doubt, their
ordeal, their self-imposed obligations, their self-control
under His difficult exactions; the world will at last yield
them something for what they have done and are. In the
autumn of 1849, Bowdoin College in Maine offers Calvin a
professorship, and though he knows that the chair is the
worst-paid in the college—a thousand dollars a year—he
is only too glad to accept. The Seminary tries to keep him
by offering him fifteen hundred, and, immediately after
this, the Theological Seminary at Andover makes him an
even better offer. But he is definitely committed to Bowdoin, and the next spring the Stowes move to Maine.
When they arrive, it is still very cold, and the house they

are going to live in is shabby and bare and forlorn, but they light up a fire and set to work. Harriet spreads a long table on which the family can eat and she can write, and she repaints the woodwork and repapers the walls, and this is the end of their long testing: they will never be so poor or so racked again.

At the end of the year 1850, the Fugitive Slave Bill became a law. Non-Southerners were now held responsible for Negroes who had fled from the South, and, as an inducement to the local officials who decided on the claims of ownership, a premium was put on returning them. When Harriet got a letter from a sister-in-law which said: "Hattie, if I could use a pen as you can, I would write something that will make this whole nation feel what an accursed thing slavery is," she read the letter to her children, then, crumpling it in her hand, stood up and said, "I will if I live." When her brother Henry Ward Beecher came to see her a little later, they talked about the odious law. He was now preaching Abolition from his pulpit in Plymouth Church, Brooklyn, and holding benevolent "auctions," in which he brought before his congregation slaves that had escaped from the South, and called for contributions in order to buy their freedom. He, too, urged Harriet to write a book. She had met, a short time before, at the house of her brother Edward, who now had a church in Boston, a Negro preacher who had once been a slave and both of whose arms had been crippled by flogging, but who had succeeded in escaping to Canada and getting himself an education there; and one Sunday, when she had just taken Communion, the death of Uncle Tom was revealed to her "almost as a tangible vision." Scarcely able to restrain her emotion, she went home and wrote it down; and now the rest of Uncle Tom's story "rushed upon her with a vividness and importunity that would not be denied." She poured it out late in the evenings, after the demands of the household had been dealt with. She does not seem to have planned the story in advance, yet the course that it was taking imposed itself as something uncontrollable, unalterable. The novel appeared first as a serial in an anti-slavery weekly which was published in Washington, and it ran to such length—it continued from June 8, 1851, to April 1, 1852—that the editor begged her to cut it short; but the story had taken possession of its readers as well as of Mrs. Stowe, and when the editor published a note suggesting that the public might have had enough, this elicited a violent protest, and Uncle Tom was spared none of the stages which were to lead him to the final scene which had come to Mrs. Stowe in church.

THE JOURNAL OF MARY CHESNUT

[One of] Mrs. Chesnut's main subjects [in her journal] is the plantation of her husband's parents at Camden, South Carolina, where she is sometimes obliged to stay and where she suffers acutely from boredom. She suffers also from the irking constraint imposed upon her by her ninety-year-old father-in-law, an opinionated austere old man who, even when deaf and blind, still keeps such a strong hand on his immense domain that he never has trouble with his slaves. This household of the old-world Chesnuts reminds one of the Bolkónskys of *War and Peace* (comparisons with Russia seem inevitable when one is writing about the old South). The father, presiding at dinner, as "absolute a tyrant as the Tsar of Russia," with his constantly repeated axioms and his authoritarian tone, is a less piquant Bolkónsky *père*. James Jr. is an equally distinguished and equally conscientious, if not equally dashing, André; Miss Chesnut, his sister, may figure as a cool-headed and penurious, a less sympathetic Princess Marie. But there is also a dowager Mrs. Chesnut, originally from Philadelphia, who was married in 1796 and falls easily into telling people about "stiff stern old Martha Washington" and describing the Washingtons' drawing room. The younger Mrs. Chesnut likes her mother-in-law, who has evidently more human warmth than the other members of the family and who, though never buying books herself, borrows them from other people and reads them in enormous quantities; but, in general, the younger woman finds Mulberry, the Chesnut estate, both oppressive and melancholy. "My sleeping apartment is large and airy, with windows opening on the lawn east and south. In those deep window seats, idly looking out, I spend much time. A part of the yard which was once a deer park has the appearance of the primeval forest; the forest trees have been unmolested and are now of immense size. In the spring, the air is laden with perfumes, violets, jasmine, crab apple blossoms, roses. Araby the blest never was sweeter in perfume. And yet there hangs here as on every Southern landscape the saddest pall. There are browsing on the lawn, where Kentucky bluegrass flourishes, Devon cows and sheep, horses, mares and colts. It helps to enliven it. Carriages are coming up to the door and driving away incessantly."

The Chesnut Negroes are faithful; they have been well trained and well treated. Yet everyone is rather uneasy. Mrs. Chesnut the younger herself has, like Kate Stone, a horror of slavery. When she sees a mulatto girl sold at auction in March, 1861, "My very soul sickened," she writes, and a few days later, when, with a visiting Englishwoman, she is again passing the auction block, "If you can stand that," she says to her companion, "no other Southern thing need choke you." And "I wonder," she is soon reflecting, "if it be a sin to think slavery a curse to any land. Men and women are punished when their masters and mistresses are brutes, not when they do wrong. Under slavery, we live surrounded by prostitutes, yet an abandoned woman [a white one, she means] is sent out of a decent house. Who thinks any worse of a Negro or mulatto woman for being a thing we can't name? God forgive us, but ours is a monstrous system, a wrong and an iniquity! Like the patriarchs of old, our men live all in one

house with their wives and their concubines; and the mu-
lattoes one sees in every family partly resemble the white
children. Any lady is ready to tell you who is the father of
all the mulatto children in everybody's household but her
own."

This problem of the mixture of white and black blood,
so systematically suppressed by Southern writers—"the
ostrich game," Mrs. Chesnut calls this—she treats with
remarkable frankness and exclaims at the hypocrisy of the
Chesnuts in locking up the novels of Eugène Sue, and
even a Gothic romance by the Carolinian Washington
Allston, when the colored girls of the household are more
or less openly promiscuous. "I hate slavery," she writes at
the beginning of the war. "You say there are no more
fallen women on a plantation than in London, in proportion to numbers; but what do you say to this? A magnate
who runs a hideous black harem with its consequences
under the same roof with his lovely white wife, and his
beautiful and accomplished daughters? He holds his head
as high and poses as the model of all human virtues to
these poor women whom God and the laws have given
him. From the height of his awful majesty, he scolds and
thunders at them as if he never did wrong in his life.
Fancy such a man finding his daughter reading *Don Juan*.
'You with that immoral book!' And he orders her out of
his sight. You see, Mrs. Stowe did not hit the sorest spot.
She makes Legree a bachelor."

Encountering such passages, we wonder whether the
prudery of Buck Preston with her fiancé may not be
something more than a curious local development of the
nineteenth-century proprieties, something more than a
romantic convention derived from the age of chivalry.
That Buck Preston was not unusual in her reluctance to
let men see her feet is shown by another anecdote, this
time about James Chesnut's young nephew: "Today he
was taking me to see Minnie Hayne's foot. He said it was
the smallest, the most perfect thing in America! Now, I
will go anywhere to see anything which can move the cool

Captain to the smallest ripple of enthusiasm. He says Julia Rutledge knew his weakness, and would not show him her foot. His Uncle James had told him of its arched instep and symmetrical beauty. So he followed her trail like a wild Indian, and when she stepped in the mud, he took a paper pattern of her track, or a plaster cast; something that amazed Miss Rutledge at his sagacity." And Mrs. Chesnut herself, though she is not disinclined to flirt as the younger ladies do and occasionally provokes jealous scenes on the part of Mr. Chesnut, is offended by risqué stories and horrified by current French novels (which, nevertheless, she continues to read); will not allow legs to be mentioned; and cannot digest the news, brought back by a traveler from Europe, that the sternly moralistic George Eliot has been living in sin with George Henry Lewes.

One is forced to the conclusion that the pedestalled purity which the Southerners assigned to their ladies, the shrinking of these ladies themselves from any suggestion of freedom, were partly a "polarization" produced by the uninhibited ease with which their men could go to bed with the black girls. There is an atmosphere of tittering sex all through Mrs. Chesnut's chronicle, yet behind it is a pride that is based on fear and that sometimes results in coldness. Mrs. Chesnut, who was married at seventeen, has obviously no passionate interest in her husband, yet though Chesnut has, we gather, amused himself with occasional love affairs—not, so far as one is told, with blacks but with white women of inferior social status—she has never dared to take a lover. To allow oneself to weaken in this direction would be to associate oneself with the despised and dreaded slave girls who were bearing their masters' half-breeds, to surrender one's white prestige. The gaiety and ease of these ladies must have always masked a fundamental, a never-relaxing tension.

Mrs. Chesnut, in this intimate record, drops the mask and expresses herself with more candor than was usual for Southern ladies, even, as one imagines, in the working of their own minds. Her attitude toward Harriet Beecher

Stowe is strikingly different, for example, from that of most Southerners of Mrs. Chesnut's own day or, indeed, of any day. Grace King, the New Orleans historian and novelist, born in 1852, writes in her autobiography of the "hideous, black, dragonlike book that hovered on the horizon of every Southern child" but which in her own family was never allowed to be mentioned. Mrs. Chesnut takes this horror more coolly and shows a strong interest in *Uncle Tom's Cabin.* In March of 1862 she rereads it, and at any instance of cruelty to slaves she is likely to mention that Mrs. Stowe would be delighted to hear of it. "I met our lovely relative," she writes in May, 1864, "the woman who might have sat for Eva's mother in *Uncle Tom's Cabin.* Beautifully dressed, graceful, languid, making eyes at all comers, she was softly and in dulcet accents regretting the necessity of sending out a sable Topsy to her sabler parent, to be switched for some misdemeanor. I declined to hear her regrets as I fled in haste." She says of the grandfather of one of her friends that he used to "put Negroes in hogsheads, with nails driven in all round, and roll the poor things downhill."

Her own point of view is vigorously expressed in November, 1861, in an outburst against Mrs. Stowe. Mrs. Stowe, she declares, and Greeley and Thoreau and Emerson and Sumner "live in nice New England homes, clean, sweet-smelling, shut up in libraries, writing books which ease their hearts of their bitterness against us. What self-denial they do practice is to tell John Brown to come down here and cut our throats in Christ's name. Now consider what I have seen of my mother's life, my grandmother's, my mother-in-law's. These people were educated at Northern schools, they read the same books as their Northern contemporaries, the same daily papers, the same Bible. They have the same ideas of right and wrong," while they of the South are doomed to "live in Negro villages," the inhabitants of which "walk through their houses whenever they see fit, dirty, slatternly, idle, ill-smelling by nature. These women I love have less chance to live their own lives in peace than if they were African missionaries. They have a swarm of blacks about them like children under their care, not as Mrs. Stowe's fancy painted them, and they hate slavery worse than Mrs. Stowe does.... The Mrs. Stowes have the plaudits of crowned heads; we take our chances, doing our duty as best we may among the woolly heads. My husband supported his plantation by his law practice. Now it is running him in debt. Our people have never earned their own bread. Take this estate, what does it do, actually? It all goes back in some shape to what are called slaves here, called operatives or tenants or peasantry elsewhere. I doubt if ten thousand in money ever comes to this old gentleman's hands. When Mrs. Chesnut married South, her husband was as wealthy as her brothers-in-law. How is it now? Their money has accumulated for their children. This old man's goes to support a horde of idle dirty Africans, while he is abused as a cruel slave-owner."

In this she is unfair to the New Englanders: she forgets that Elijah Lovejoy has been murdered for his Abolitionist agitation, that Garrison has been dragged through the streets of Boston and Whittier stoned by a mob in New Hampshire, and that Sumner has had his head broken and been incapacitated for two years by a furious South Carolinian; and she of course had not the least idea of the years of anxiety and hardship which, in the case of Harriet Beecher Stowe, had produced her explosive book. Yet there is plenty of evidence in Mrs. Chesnut's diary that slavery had become to the Southerners a handicap and a burden. At one point she makes the assertion that "not one third of our volunteer army are slave-owners" and that "not one third of that third fail to dislike slavery as much as Mrs. Stowe or Horace Greeley."

Mrs. Chesnut notes again and again the apparent impassivity of the Negroes in relation to what is going on. "We have no reason to suppose a Negro knows there is a war," she is still able to write in November, 1861. "I do not speak of the war to them; on that subject, they do not be-

lieve a word you say. A genuine slave-owner, born and
bred, will not be afraid of Negroes. Here we are mild as
the moonbeams, and as serene; nothing but Negroes
around us, white men all gone to the army." Yet one of
their neighbors, a Cousin Betsey, has been murdered only
a few weeks before. This old lady, whose domestic servants are said to have been "pampered" and "insubordi-
nate," has been smothered in her bed by two of them after
her son has promised them a thrashing. The elder Mrs.
Chesnut, a Northerner, had been frightened in her youth
by the stories of the Haiti rebellion, and, as a result, now
treats every Negro "as if they were a black Prince Albert
or Queen Victoria." She makes her daughter-in-law uneasy by incessantly dwelling, as the younger woman says,
"upon the transcendent virtues of her colored household,
in full hearing of the innumerable Negro women who literally swarm over this house," then by suddenly saying to
the family at dinner, " 'I warn you, don't touch that soup!
It is bitter. There is something wrong about it!' The men
who waited at table looked on without a change of face."
But the staff of the Chesnut household finally begins to
crack in an unexpected place. James Chesnut is very much
dependent on his Negro valet Lawrence, who is always at
his side, always, says Mrs. Chesnut, with "the same
bronze mask," who darns socks and has made Mrs. Chesnut a sacque, who is miraculous in his resourcefulness at
producing, despite wartime shortages, whatever is wanted
in the way of food—even to that special rarity, ice for mint
juleps and sherry cobblers. But in February, 1864, while
the Chesnuts are living in Richmond, Lawrence turns up
at breakfast drunk. When he is ordered to move a chair, he
raises it over his head and smashes the chandelier. His
master, whose self-control is always perfect, turns to his
wife and says, "Mary, do tell Lawrence to go home. I am
too angry to speak to him!" But Lawrence "will soon be
back," Mrs. Chesnut confides to her diary, "and when he
comes he will say: 'Shoo! I knew Mars' Jeems could not do
without me!' And indeed he cannot."

In the meantime Colonel Higginson and his fellow Yankees were exploring the abandoned plantations of the South Carolinian Sea Islands. We hear something from Mrs. Chesnut of the families to which these had belonged. Of the Middletons, on whose place Charlotte Forten had admired the magnolia tree and from whose house she had taken the bathtub, Mrs. Chesnut writes as follows: "Poor Mrs. Middleton has paralysis. Has she not had trouble enough? . . . Their plantation and house at Edisto destroyed [it had actually been plundered but not destroyed], their house in Charleston burned, her children scattered, starvation in Lincolnton, and all as nothing to the one dreadful blow—her only son killed in Virginia. Their lives are washed away in a tide of blood. There is nothing to show they were ever on earth." And of another expropriated family from the coastland taken over by the Northerners: "Captain Barnwell came to see us," she writes. "We had a dinner for them at Mulberry. Stephen Elliott was there. He gave us an account of his father's plantation at Beaufort, from which he has just returned: 'Our Negroes are living in great comfort. They were delighted to see me, and treated me with overflowing affection. They waited on me as before, gave me beautiful breakfasts and splendid dinners; but they firmly and respectfully informed me: "We own this land now. Put it out of your head that it will ever be yours again." ' "

The Negroes on the Chesnut plantation, with the exception of one boy who goes off with the Yankees, all, however, remain loyal to the family when Sherman's army comes through Camden. This has not always been the case with the slaves of their neighbors, and an annoying problem presents itself when the black women run away and drop off their children beside the road. It is with somewhat mixed feelings that their former owners greet the efforts of a well-meaning person who has collected these abandoned babies and brought them back in a cart. The soldiers of the Northern Army have bayoneted the runaway women if they proved to be an encumbrance;

eighteen corpses are found. And the Chesnuts have been fortunate, also, in that their house has not been burned down. Neither James nor his wife was then at home. He had sent her to North Carolina to be out of the line of Sherman's march, and they had been fully prepared to lose everything. But when at last they make their way back to Camden, through a countryside with no sign of habitation except the "tall, blackened chimneys," they find that the house is still standing, though the horses have all been driven off and the road to Charleston is strewn with their books and letters and papers. One side of the house has been badly damaged: every window broken, every bell torn down, every door smashed in, and every piece of furniture demolished. But this wreckage had been arrested when Sherman, in one of his relentings, decided that it had gone far enough. "It was a sin," he had told his soldiers, "to destroy a fine old house like this, whose owner was over ninety years old." Miss Chesnut has behaved splendidly. When a Yankee officer entered and sat down at the fire to warm himself, she said to him "politely," " 'Rebels have no rights. But I suppose you have come to rob us. Please do so and go. Your presence agitates my blind old father.' The man had jumped up in a rage: 'What do you take me for? A thief?' " Miss Chesnut is proud of the fact that they have lost, aside from the horses, the smashed furniture and the scattered books, only two gold-headed canes and two bottles of champagne.

The old man survived everything with dignity. His wife, also over ninety, had died before the final disaster. His daughter-in-law remembers having seen him in the mornings sauntering down the wide corridor from his own to his wife's bedroom, with a large hairbrush in his hand. He would take his stand on the rug before the fire in her room and, as he brushed his few remaining white locks, would roar out to her his morning compliments so loudly that it shook the panes in the windows of the room above. One morning, after her mother-in-law's death, Mary Chesnut, passing the door of Mrs. Chesnut's room, saw her father-in-law kneeling and sobbing beside the empty bed. When we hear of him last, he is ninety-three, but "apparently as strong as ever and certainly as resolute of will." His Negro servant Scipio has never deserted old Chesnut: "six feet two, a black Hercules and as gentle as a dove in all his dealings with the blind old master, who boldly strides forward, striking with his stick to feel where he is going." "Partly patriarch, partly *grand seigneur,*" his daughter-in-law sums him up, "this old man is of a species that we will see no more; the last of the lordly planters who ruled this Southern world. His manners are unequalled still, but underneath this smooth exterior lies the grip of a tyrant whose will has never been crossed."

On the eve of Lee's surrender, when Mary Chesnut has taken refuge in North Carolina, her husband comes to see her and tells her that many of their own fellow Southerners are rejoicing over the ruin of the planter class. "They will have no Negroes now to lord it over!" he says he has heard one of them say. "They can swell and peacock about and tyrannize now over only a small parcel of women and children, those only who are their very own family."

SOUTHERN SOLDIERS: TAYLOR, JACKSON, LEE

Near the end of Mrs. Chesnut's chronicle we find the following entry (May 10, 1865): "Said Henrietta: 'That old fool Dick Taylor will not disband and let his nasty Confederacy smash and be done with it.' I rose. 'Excuse me. I cannot sit at table with anybody abusing my country.' So I went out on the piazza, but from the windows came loud screams of vituperation and insult. 'Jeff Davis's stupidity, Joe Johnston's magnanimity, Bragg's insanity.' So I fled. Next day she flew at me again, and raved until I was led out in hysterics, and then I was very ill. They thought I was dying, and I wish I had died."

This Dick Taylor was General Richard Taylor, the son of Zachary Taylor, one of the heroes of the Mexican War, who had been elected President in 1848 but had died in his second year of office. Richard Taylor wrote a volume of memoirs called *Destruction and Reconstruction: Personal Experiences of the Late War*, first published in 1879, which is perhaps the masculine document that, from the point of view of realistic intelligence, is most nearly comparable to Mary Chesnut's diary.

Richard Taylor was a handsome, high-mettled young man—thirty-five at the beginning of the war—who had had, for a Southerner of the period, an exceptionally good education: he had studied at Edinburgh and Paris and had been graduated from Yale. He had never before been a soldier, and had had only a glimpse of the Mexican War, when he had visited his father's camp. His first occupation after college had been managing his father's Mississippi plantation; later, after Zachary's death, he bought a larger one in Louisiana. He collected a considerable library and was famous for the success of his race horses and the brilliance of his conversation. He had been more or less active in politics and, though not a strong defender of the Southern system, had voted for secession in the senate of his state. He was bitter about the carpetbaggers, after the war, and excoriated the Grant regime, but declared that "the extinction of slavery was expected by all and regretted by none." As a soldier, he was full of audacity, sharp-tongued and rather arrogant with his equals, with his men rather undemocratic. He was evidently feared by the latter, and on one occasion had several shot in order to correct their slack discipline, but he trained them to a degree of efficiency that seems to have been rare among the Confederate forces. He criticizes what he regards as "the vicious system of election of officers [by the ranks]," which, he says, "struck at the very root of that stern discipline without which raw men cannot be converted into soldiers," and he later makes a similar point when he says that the difficulty of this—"converting raw men into soldiers"—is greatly increased when the men are mounted: "Living on horseback, fearless and dashing, the men of the South afforded the best possible material for cavalry. They had every quality but discipline, and resembled Prince Charming, whose manifold gifts, bestowed by her sisters, were rendered useless by the malignant fairy."

Better educated than most of his fellow officers and with more experience of the world, he sees everything in a larger context. His book is full of allusions to "the witty Dean," "honest Dick Steele," Rabelais's *mauvais quart d'heure* and Walpole's correspondence with Mme. du Deffand, as well as comparisons of recent events with French, English and German military history, that show a wide range of reading. Like Mrs. Chesnut, not approving of slavery and not much believing in victory, he is not intellectually committed to the struggle in which his pride—as a vindicator of Southern honor—has spurred him to take so active a part, and the effect of this is rather peculiar. Richard Taylor is conscious, and a little vain, of being a *rara avis;* he is a connoisseur of soldiers and battles; he plays his fine role with a shade of disdain, even, perhaps, with a shade of enjoyment—vain, also, and almost perverse—of its gratuitousness and ultimate futility.

When Dick Taylor was early promoted to the rank of brigadier general, he tried at first to decline this honor on the ground that there were several colonels who deserved it through right of seniority; but, persuaded to accept it by his fellow officers, he took part with this rank under Stonewall Jackson in the Shenandoah Valley campaign of the spring of 1862. Jackson came to think highly of Taylor and Taylor to admire Jackson—though they could hardly have been, temperamentally, more unlike and more uncongenial; and this mixture of esteem with unlikeness makes Dick Taylor's portrait of Jackson, as it is gradually filled in, stroke by stroke, a unique and a piquant one. The only thing the two men had in common was that both of them inspired in their troops a respect that was tinged with fear. But Jackson was more alien to his people than his dashing young brigadier general; he had nothing of the spirit of chivalry or of playing the game for the game's sake. "He impressed me always," said Grant of him, "as a man of the Cromwell stamp, a Puritan—much more of the New Englander than the Virginian. If any man believed in the rebellion, he did."

The son of a bankrupt lawyer from Virginia beyond the Alleghenies, Jackson had been left an orphan at three; he had had to work hard for an education and had become at fourteen a devout attendant at the Presbyterian church. He was close to those types of the North, those single-track embodiments of will, whom these gentlemanly Southerners dreaded: the impassive indefatigable Grant, the Jehovah-led avenger John Brown. Thomas Jackson (not yet called "Stonewall") seems indeed to have had some fellow feeling with Brown when he presided as major of militia at Brown's hanging at Charlestown. He had prayed for the mad Brown's soul the night before the execution, and when it was over had written his wife that the fanatic "had behaved with unflinching firmness. . . . I was much impressed with the thought that before me stood a man in the full vigor of health, who must in a few moments enter eternity. I sent up the petition that he might be saved. Awful was the thought that he might in a few minutes receive the sentence, 'Depart, ye wicked, into everlasting fire!' I hope that he was prepared to die, but I am doubtful. He refused to have a minister with him." Thomas Jackson himself was sometimes thought a little mad.

Mrs. Chesnut had listened with interest to a character-ization of Jackson by one of his generals: "Jackson's men had gone half a day's march before Pete Longstreet waked and breakfasted. . . . I think there is a popular delusion about the amount of praying Jackson did. He certainly preferred a fight on Sunday to a sermon. Failing to manage a fight, he loved next best a long Presbyterian sermon, Calvinistic to the core. He had no sympathy with human infirmity. He was a one-idea man. . . . He classed all who were weak and weary, who fainted by the wayside, as men wanting in patriotism. If a man's face was white as cotton and his pulse so low that you could not feel it, he merely looked upon him impatiently as an inefficient soldier, and rode off out of patience. He was the true type of all great soldiers. He did not value human life where he had an object to accomplish. He could order men to their death as a matter of course. Napoleon's French conscription could not have kept him supplied with men, he used up his command so rapidly. Hence, while he was alive there was more pride than truth in the talk of his soldiers' love for him. They feared him, and obeyed him to the death; faith they had in him. . . . But I doubt if he had their love. . . . Be ye sure, it was bitter hard work to keep up with Stonewall Jackson, as all know who ever served with him. He gave orders rapidly and distinctly, and rode away without allowing answer or remonstrance. When you failed, you were apt to be put under arrest. When you succeeded, he only said 'good.' " His certainty that his army was the instrument of God was as strong as that of any Northerner. "General Lee is very kind," he said when his commanding general had congratulated him on a victory, "but he should give the praise to God"; and, concluding that one of his operations had been blocked by divine interference, on account of its having been attempted on Sunday, he forbade any use, for a second attempt, of powder procured on the Sabbath. Jackson accepted slavery, says his sister-in-law in a memoir, "as it existed in the Southern States, not as a thing desirable in itself, but as allowed by Providence for ends which it was not his business to determine." Distressed by the ignorance of the Negroes, he had established, "by much personal effort and under some obloquy, a Sunday school for them in Lexington, which he kept up with assiduous diligence till the breaking out of the war."

But Richard Taylor, incapable of hero worship, was not at all frightened of Jackson and observed him with a critical eye. "An ungraceful horseman," he writes, "mounted on a sorry chestnut with a shambling gait, his huge feet with out-turned toes thrust into his stirrups, and such parts of his countenance as the low visor of his stocking cap failed to conceal wearing a wooden look, our new commander was not prepossessing." Jackson was taciturn, implacable, unable to joke; he lived on hardtack and water and was always sucking a lemon—this seems to have been his only indulgence. He was as obstinate a Spartan as any New Englander. Mrs. Chesnut reports him as having said, "in his quaint way: 'I like strong drink, so I never touch it.' " On one occasion, Taylor tells us, when some of his Creole soldiers were waltzing to the music of their band, General Jackson remarked "after a contemplative suck at a lemon, 'Thoughtless fellows for serious work!' " and once, when Taylor swore at his troops, "he placed his hand on my shoulder" and "said in a gentle voice, 'I am afraid you are a wicked fellow.' " The only moment, says Taylor, when Jackson appeared to brighten was at a battle in which his own troops were being shot up by the enemy at a time when they "were advancing steadily, with banners flying and arms gleaming in the sun. . . . Jackson was on the road, a little in advance of his line, where the fire was hottest, with reins on his horse's neck, seemingly in prayer. Attracted by my approach, he said, in his usual voice, 'Delightful excitement.' I replied that it was pleasant to learn he was enjoying himself, but thought he might have an indigestion of such fun if the six-gun battery was not silenced." Later on, Taylor made an attempt to intervene with his formidable chief in behalf of a General Winder, who had asked leave to go to Richmond, had been refused by Jackson and in pique had resigned from the service. "Holding Winder in high esteem, I hoped to save

him to the army, and went to Jackson, to whose magnanimity I appealed, and to arouse this dwelt on the rich
harvest of glory he had reaped in his brilliant campaign.
Observing him closely, I caught a glimpse of the man's
inner nature. It was but a glimpse. The curtain closed, and
he was absorbed in prayer. Yet in that moment I saw an
ambition boundless as Cromwell's, and as merciless. . . . I
have written that he was ambitious; and his ambition was
vast, all-absorbing. . . . He loathed it, perhaps feared it;
but he could not escape it. . . . He fought it with prayer,
constant and earnest—Apolyon and Christian in ceaseless
combat."

This last observation of Taylor's and his tone in regard
to this trait of his chief's brings out an important difference. The Southerners, as a rule, did not entertain this
kind of ambition. Though touchy and competitive among
themselves, they were defending an ancient ideal, a traditional kind of society, in which each wanted merely to
maintain his place; the roles they aimed to play were
knightly. Even Lee, the idol of his people, when his fortune had been lost in the war, made no effort to enrich
himself or to exercise political influence, but accepted,
with the utmost modesty, the presidency of Washington
College, once a "classical school" of distinction, but by
that time left a ruin by the Federal troops, with a student
body of forty and a faculty of four. Elsewhere than in the
South the men who had got to be public figures were
looking forward to a dynamic future. The Union was
strong and could now move ahead, and the Northerners
plunged after money and power.

Stonewall Jackson was killed by accident in May, 1863,
at the battle of Chancellorsville, in which he had defeated
the Unionists; he was shot by his own men, who had mistaken him, in the moonlight, for a Yankee. Mrs. Chesnut
went to see him lying in state in the Confederate Capitol
in Richmond—"Shall I ever forget," she asks, "the pain
and fear of it all?"; and at the time that Grant is carrying
all before him, she continually utters such cries as

"Stonewall, if he could only come back to us here!"; "One year more of Stonewall would have saved us!"; "If we had Stonewall or Albert Sidney Johnson where Joe Johnston and Polk are, I would not give a fig for Sherman's chances"; "Chickamauga is the only battle we gained since Stonewall was shot by Malone's brigade." Richard Taylor, writing of Jackson after the war, exhibits a characteristic detachment: "Fortunate in his death, he fell at the summit of his glory, before the sun of the Confederacy had set, ere defeat and suffering and selfishness could turn their fangs upon him." In a less romantic and rhetorical vein, Grant doubted whether Jackson would have been equally successful in the later phase of the war. Such "sudden daring raids" as his "might do against raw troops and inexperienced commanders, such as we had at the beginning of the war, but not against drilled troops and a commander like Sheridan."

That other effective and untypical Southern general, Nathan Bedford Forrest of Tennessee, who "got there fustest with the mostest," is not mentioned by Mrs. Chesnut. He was liked and respected by Taylor, who saw him often in the final weeks of the war. Taylor notes that Forrest "read with difficulty" and that his father had been "a poor trader in Negroes and mules." With Taylor and with Mrs. Chesnut, we are always in the world of the Confederate gentry, and the weakness of its situation is brought out for us all the more vividly by the brilliance of the minds that describe it.

It is true that such exciting figures as Dick Taylor and Jeb Stuart and Mosby are typical of one element of the Confederate Army. Its most celebrated soldier, however— though popular romance has extended to him something of the glamor of the Southern legend—really represents a different tradition. Robert E. Lee has left no apologia. Though his records were mostly destroyed by his clerks on the retreat from Petersburg or burnt up in the fire when Richmond fell, he was collecting in his later years the materials for a book on his Virginia campaigns; but he did not live to write it. We can only come at all close to Lee through the volume of personal documents compiled by his son, Captain Robert E. Lee: *Recollections and Letters of General Robert E. Lee*, which shows him in his relations with his family and as president of Washington College. As a letter-writer, Lee is monotonous. Though occasionally playful with his children, when he is talking of their love affairs or the family pets, his tone is extremely sober, and these letters have in common with his military dispatches that they are occupied mainly with practical arrangements, about which he issues the most precise instructions. During the period after the war, he exercises an admirable restraint—in view of the policies of the Reconstruction—in not commenting on current events. These injustices, he says, must be left to time: the animosity of the North will subside; and, in the meantime, agreeing with intelligent critics in the South as well as in the North that what the South most needs is education, he is quietly and conscientiously devoting himself to this end.

As always, his life is an exemplification of principles rarely expressed—among which are fundamental the assumptions of the Church of England, hardly altered by transplantation, which have little in common with the religion of New England, the agonies of sin and salvation. Nor does Lee speak directly with God, irrespective of time or place, as Stonewall Jackson had done. He is punctilious in going to church, where he sits in the family pew, humble before his Maker but the cornerstone of the congregation. He respectfully trusts in God; there is no drama in his intercourse with Heaven. "You will, however, learn before this reaches you that our success at Gettysburg was not so great as reported—in fact, that we failed to drive the enemy from his position, and that our army withdrew to the Potomac. Had the river not unexpectedly risen, all would have been well with us; but God, in His all-wise providence, willed otherwise, and our communications

have been interrupted and almost cut off. The waters have
subsided to about four feet, and, if they continue, by tomorrow, I hope, our communications will be open. I trust
that a merciful God, our only hope and refuge, will not
desert us in this hour of need, and will deliver us by His
almighty hand, that the whole world may recognize His
power and all hearts be lifted up in adoration and praise of
His unbounded loving-kindness. We must, however, submit to His almighty will, whatever that may be. May God
guide and protect us all is my constant prayer." And
everything that happens in his family is confidently referred to the divine authority. "I am so grieved, my dear
daughter," he writes to his daughter-in-law, "to send
Fitzhugh to you wounded. But I am so grateful that his
wound is of a character to give us full hope of a speedy recovery. . . . I know that you will unite with me in thanks
to Almighty God, who has so often sheltered him in the
hour of danger, for his recent deliverance, and lift up your
whole heart in praise to Him for sparing a life so dear to
us, while enabling him to do his duty in the station in
which He has placed him." When he learns that this
daughter-in-law has died, he writes his wife of their eventual reunion: "What a glorious thought it is that she has
joined the little cherubs and our angel Annie in Heaven.
Thus is link by link the strong chain broken that binds me
to earth, and our passage soothed to another world." To
his wife, on a wedding anniversary, not long after the end
of the war: "Do you recollect what a happy day thirty-
three years ago this was? How many hopes and pleasures
it gave birth to! God has been very merciful and kind to
us, and how thankless and sinful I have been. I pray that
He may continue his mercies and blessings to us, and give
us a little peace and rest together in this world, and finally
gather us and all He has given us around His throne in
the world to come."

There is nothing about Lee that is at all picturesque,
but his dignity and distinction are impressive, and this
memoir helps us better to understand the reasons for his

lasting prestige in the North as well as the South—why a New Englander who had served in the Union Army like the younger Charles Francis Adams should have wanted to have a statue of him in Washington. The point is that Lee belongs, as does no other public figure of his generation, to the Roman phase of the Republic; he prolongs it in a curious way which, irrelevant and anachronistic though his activities to a Northerner may seem to be, cannot fail to bring some sympathetic response that derives from the experience of the Revolution. The Lees had been among the prime workers in our operations against the British and the founding of the United States. Robert's father, "Light-Horse Harry," had been one of the most brilliant heroes of our war against the Crown, a favorite of George Washington, with the privilege of direct communication with him, and afterwards Governor of Virginia for three successive terms. Robert Lee himself had married the daughter of a grandson of Martha Washington, which grandson had been adopted by the Washingtons, and she and Robert, after they married, went to live in the old Custis mansion at Arlington, which was full of Washington relics. To say the American Revolution was always present in the Lee background would be perhaps to understate the situation: the Lees had never really emerged from the world of the Thirteen Colonies. Robert was born on the Lee estate at Stratford in Westmoreland County, in a huge old H-shaped brick house, built in 1730, which, with its widely spaced double pair of chimneys, its broad floor-beams, its great kitchen, great attic, great hall, its accounting room, its farmyard, its stables that made it supreme in its countryside, unneighbored and self-sustaining, was a profoundly serious place, a headquarters of responsibility. That the Lees' responsibility somewhat lapsed when Light-Horse Harry returned from the wars and ruined himself in grandiose speculations and when the Henry Lee who was Robert's half-brother and inherited the family place ruined his political career by creating a scandal with his wife's sister and getting himself into such financial difficulties that he was eventually obliged to sell Stratford, undoubtedly acted on Robert—who had neither his father's extravagance nor his brilliance—as a stimulus to return to the Roman ideal. He was under an obligation to restore the slipping status of the Lees, and the sense of responsibility, displaced later not merely from Stratford but also from the Arlington mansion, which the Federals took over in the Civil War (including the Washington relics the return of which the Radical Congress forbade in 1869 and which were only given back to the family in the early nineteen-hundreds)—this sense of responsibility is evident in everything he does: both in the field during the Civil War and afterwards, when the cause was lost, in his patient administration of Washington College, his supervision of the care of his invalid wife, his advice to his son about running a farm.

What is especially interesting and of fundamental importance is the transference by Lee of the spirit that accomplished the Revolution from the earlier crisis to the later. It is likely to seem strange to the Northerner that this upright and scrupulous man who had taken the oath to the United States and had served as superintendent of West Point, who wanted to abolish slavery, who did "not believe in secession as a constitutional right, nor that there is sufficient cause for revolution," who detested the boasting of the "Cotton States," their habitual truculent arrogance and their threats against the "Border States" for their reluctance to go along with them, should have become the commander of the Confederate Army and have led it through four years of the bitterest fighting when he did not even hope that the South could win: "I have never believed," he told General Pendleton, a day or two before his surrender, that "we could, against the gigantic combination for our subjugation, make good in the long run our independence unless foreign powers should, directly or indirectly, assist us [he had made it clear at an early stage that no such intervention was to be expected].... But such considerations really made with me no difference. We had, I was satisfied, sacred principles to maintain and rights to defend, for which we were in duty bound to do our best, even if we perished in the endeavor." Nor was Lee the only Southern soldier who did not expect to win: such paladins were too proud to need hope. This was partly, as has been said, in the spirit of the traditional gentlemen's duel, their heritage from the eighteenth century; but in Lee's case, as to some extent in theirs, it was an instinctive emulation of his ancestors, the manifestation of a regional patriotism more deeply rooted than loyalty to the United States. Virginians regarded Virginia as itself an autonomous country, which, with the help of certain New Englanders and certain Philadelphians, had expelled the monarchical forces and established in America a republican society, and it was not going to be interfered with by those now rather unfamiliar elements inhabiting the rest of the country to whom Lee, who had not sat with them in Congress, always referred as "those people." The same sense of honor and independence which stimulated Virginia to stand up to the Crown later spurred them to stand up to the Yankees. With Lee this was almost automatic: he had no real understanding of politics, no interest in economics. He had only the ancient valor and the tradition of a certain sort of role which the Lees were appointed to play.

His biographer Douglas Southall Freeman has shown that just before Lee's decision to resign from the Union Army, he had been reading a life of Washington, and his comment in a letter home is significant and characteristic: "How his spirit [Washington's] would be grieved could he see the wreck of his mighty labors! I will not, however, permit myself to believe till all ground of hope is gone that the work of his noble deeds will be destroyed, and that his precious advice and virtuous example will so soon be forgotten by his countrymen. As far as I can judge by the papers, we are between a state of anarchy and Civil War. May God avert us from both. It has been evident for years that the country was doomed to run the full length of democracy. To what a fearful pass it has brought us. I fear that mankind will not for years be sufficiently Christianized to bear the absence of restraint and force." Washington was a great Virginian, the enemy of disorder and anarchy; he had tried to save America from this, but when the structure he had founded broke down, one naturally remained with Virginia. The classical antique virtue, at once aristocratic and republican, had become a national legend, and its late incarnation in Lee was to command a certain awed admiration among Northerners as well as Southerners.

THE PERSONAL MEMOIRS OF
U. S. GRANT

When Mark Twain, in 1881, first met ex-President Grant, he tried to persuade him to write his memoirs. Grant, says Mark Twain, "wouldn't listen to the suggestion. He had no confidence in his ability to write well; whereas we all know now that he possessed an admirable literary gift and style. He was also sure that the book would have no sale, and of course that would be a humility, too. I argued that the book would have an enormous sale, and that out of my experience I could save him from making unwise contracts with publishers, and would have the contract arranged in such a way that they could not swindle him, but he said he had no necessity for any addition to his income."

Three years later, however, Grant was ruined by the colossal swindle in which he had lost almost all his money as well as that of several of his relatives and a large loan that William H. Vanderbilt had made him; and he agreed to write a book for the Century Company. When Mark Twain heard about this, he went to talk to Grant about it.

He discovered that the Century people had been telling Grant that they expected to sell only from five to ten thousand copies, and that they were offering him only ten percent royalties. The successful humorist insisted to Grant that he ought to try for better terms elsewhere. The old general had been made the victim, both as President and in his recent speculation, of a whole ghastly series of confidence games, but he had still so little head for business that, since the Century Company had asked him first, he did not want to take the book to another publisher. Mark Twain replied that, in that case, Grant ought to give the book to him—he was at that time himself a publisher—since it was he who had suggested it first. Grant was struck by the justice of this, but thought Mark Twain was going too far, taking far too great a risk out of kindness, in offering him twenty percent on the list price or seventy percent of the net returns. The first of these arrangements he would not allow, but he was finally persuaded to accept the second. If the book made no money, he said, Mark Twain would not owe him anything. And he set out to write the memoirs under handicaps as serious as any that he had faced in the Civil War. Grant was ill: he was suffering from cancer of the throat. But he dictated the first part of the manuscript, and when it became impossible to use his voice—in increasing discomfort or pain, which, alleviated by doses of cocaine, he bore with his usual fortitude—he wrote out the rest of the story. He finished it in eleven months, and died about a week later, July 23, 1885. The book sold three hundred thousand copies in the first two years after publication, a little less than half as many as *Uncle Tom's Cabin*, and made $450,-000 for Grant's impoverished family. The thick pair of volumes of the *Personal Memoirs* used to stand, like a solid attestation of the victory of the Union forces, on the shelves of every pro-Union home. Today, like *Uncle Tom*, they are seldom read by anyone save students of the Civil War; yet this record of Grant's campaigns may well rank, as Mark Twain believed, as the most remarkable work of its kind since the *Commentaries* of Julius Caesar. It is also, in its way—like Herndon's *Lincoln* or like *Walden* or *Leaves of Grass*—a unique expression of the national character.

Owen Wister has said truly, in his little book on Grant, that Grant's was an even odder case than Lincoln's. For Lincoln had been always ambitious: he had passionately desired to distinguish himself as a political figure, he had a "call" to lead the country in its crisis. Even during his years of obscurity, he had always been hardworking, effective; there are in Lincoln's career no real slumps. But Grant—the son of a tanner, born in Ohio in a two-room cabin—had never given people the impression that he had any very high ambition. He did not want to work in his father's tannery, and he said that he much preferred farming to any other occupation. When his father shipped him off to West Point, he went there without enthusiasm. "If I could have escaped West Point without bringing myself into disgrace at home," he once told John Russell Young, his companion on his journey around the world, "I would have done so. I remember about the time I entered the academy there were debates in Congress over a proposal to abolish West Point. I used to look over the papers, and read the Congress reports with eagerness to see the progress the bill made, and hoping that the school had been abolished." When he graduated, he tells us in his *Memoirs*, he had had no idea of remaining in the army and had wanted to prepare himself for a professorship of mathematics "in some college." He was, however, ordered off to the Mexican War, of which he did not approve. "I do not think," he said to Young, in his later years, "there was ever a more wicked war than that waged by the United States on Mexico. I thought so at the time, when I was a youngster, only I had not moral courage enough to resign: I had taken an oath to serve eight years, unless sooner discharged, and I considered my supreme duty was to my flag. I had a horror of the Mexican War, and I have always believed that it was on our part most unjust." He served in the quartermaster department, and when the war was over, he spent six years in a succession of dreary posts. He eventually took to drink and was made to resign from the army. The seven years that followed were equally depressing; he tried several occupations—selling real estate, clerking in a custom house, running for county engineer—and failed in every one. He was regarded at one point, in St. Louis, as so hopeless a down-and-outer that, fearing they would be asked for a loan, people sometimes crossed the street in order not to meet him. He ended by working in a leather store—in Galena, Illinois—which was run by his two younger brothers.

But it was characteristic of Grant that a period of moral collapse should have been followed by a period of intense concentration. When Fort Sumter was fired upon, he immediately volunteered. He was at that time thirty-nine. I shall not retrace his campaigns nor show how, through the exercise of this power of concentration, he came to be assigned by Lincoln to the top leadership of the Union armies. But since he does not in his *Personal Memoirs* either emphasize his own exceptional qualities or celebrate his own achievements, one must cite, in connection with the *Memoirs*, the testimony of such close associates as his military secretary Adam Badeau and his aide-de-camp Horace Porter to Grant's poise and detachment in the field—the qualities which also distinguish his writing. Badeau says of Grant that he "never braved danger unnecessarily; he was not excited by it, but was simply indifferent to it, was calm when others were aroused. I have often seen him sit erect in his saddle when everyone else instinctively shrank as a shell burst in the neighborhood. Once he sat on the ground writing a dispatch in a fort just captured from the enemy, but still commanded by another near. A shell burst immediately over him, but his hand never shook, he did not look up, and continued the dispatch as calmly as if he had been in camp." Horace Porter tells similar stories. "Ulysses don't scare worth a damn," was said of him by one of his soldiers. When he was writing dispatches at Petersburg, exposed to the enemy's fire, and this fire "became hotter and hotter, several of the officers, apprehensive for the general's safety, urged him to move to some less conspicuous position; but he kept on writing and talking, without the least interruption from the shots falling around him, and apparently not noticing what a target the place was becoming or paying any heed to the gentle reminders to 'move on.' After he had finished his dispatches he got up, took a view of the situation, and as he started toward the other side of the farmhouse said with a quizzical look at the group around him: 'Well, they do seem to have the range on us.' " "This calmness was the same," says Badeau, "in the greatest moral emergencies. At the surrender of Lee, he was as impassive as on the most ordinary occasion; and until some of us congratulated him, he seemed scarcely to have realized that he had accomplished one of the greatest achievements in modern history."

But this constant attentiveness and self-control put Grant under a terrible strain, and whenever there was a break in the tension of war, he was likely to revert to the bottle. During the winter of 1862–63, when he was waiting to capture Vicksburg, he indulged in a private spree on a boat on the Mississippi. The facts about these aberrations had always been kept rather dark and very little had been known about them till the recent publication of a memoir—*Three Years with Grant*—by a man named Sylvanus Cadwallader, a correspondent for the New York *Herald,* who had been very close to the General and come to occupy a kind of privileged position. He could not bring himself to put these memories on paper till he was seventy years old, in the middle nineties—"To speak the whole truth," he writes, "concerning General Grant's periodical fits of intemperance has required all the courage I could summon"—and the Illinois State Historical Library, which had acquired the manuscript, did not get to the point of publishing it till 1955. Cadwallader was, it seems, on the boat with Grant at the time of his Vicksburg debauch. He says that Grant—making no concealment—simply stupefied himself with whiskey. Cadwallader first made an effort to induce the officers aboard to do something to restrain the General, but they felt that this would amount to insubordination, and it developed upon the civilian Cadwallader to "take the General in hand." "I . . . enticed him into his stateroom, locked myself in the room with him, and commenced throwing bottles of whiskey . . . through the windows . . . into the river. Grant soon ordered me out of the room, but I refused to go . . . I said to him that I was the best friend he had in the Army of the Tennessee; that I was doing for him what I hoped someone would do for me, should I ever be in his condition." Eventually, "after much resistance," he got Grant to take off his clothes and lie down, and "soon fanned him to sleep." The next day they landed, and the General, having had too much whiskey again, began putting the spurs to his horse "the moment he was in the saddle, and the horse darted away at full speed before anyone was ready to follow. The road was crooked and tortuous, following the firmest ground between the sloughs and bayous. . . . Each bridge had one or more guards stationed at it, to prevent fast riding or driving over it; but Grant paid no attention to roads or sentries. He went at about full speed through camps and corrals, heading only for the bridges, and literally tore through and over everything in his way. The air was full of dust, ashes, and embers from campfires; and shouts and curses from those he rode down in his race." Cadwallader pursued him, caught up with him, and again had to get him to sleep, this time "on the grass, with the saddle for a pillow." The next day he dreaded seeing Grant, thinking he would be embarrassed, and "purposely kept out of his way," but when he did meet the General again, Grant did not, to Cadwallader's surprise, "make the most distant allusion" to the incident. "But there was a perceptible change in his bearing towards me. I was always recognized and spoken to as if I had been regularly gazetted as a member of his staff. My comfort and convenience was considered; a tent pitched and struck for me whenever and wherever I chose to occupy it."

It was difficult, Cadwallader says, for people who had only seen Grant in the aspect he usually wore to credit these dissipations. Unlike a Sherman or a Sheridan, he never used profanity or betrayed excitement; his habitual coolness and self-restraint were always an important factor in keeping up the morale of his men. Cadwallader adds a notable instance to the many already recorded. Grant, he says, at the siege of Vicksburg, "had gone into the cramped exposed redoubt to see how the work was progressing and, noticing the reluctance with which the men could be brought to the open embrasure, deliberately clambered on top of the embankment in plain view of the sharpshooters, and directed the men in moving and placing the guns. The bullets zipped through the air by dozens, but strangely none of them touched his person or his clothing. He paid no attention to appeals or expostulations, acting as though they were not heard; and smoked quietly and serenely all the time, except when he removed his cigar to speak to the men at work. His example shamed the men into making a show of courage; but several were wounded before he left the place."

There occurred, as Sherman tells us, after Vicksburg, "a general relaxation of effort, a desire to escape the hard drudgery of camp: officers sought leaves of absence to visit their homes, and soldiers obtained furloughs and discharges on the most slender pretexts"; and Grant himself was not proof against this. He was drunk on dress parade in New Orleans and afterwards fell off his horse. He spent twenty-one days in bed and had to go limping to Chattanooga, the scene of the next of his victories.

But when the effort of the war was over, he did not again go to pieces. His wife was now constantly with him, and she always had a stabilizing effect on him. Detached from the troops that he manipulated as well as from his fellow officers, living alone with his responsibility, he had required a close human relationship, and Julia Grant had been brought on, when possible, in the lulls of her husband's campaigning.

Before one goes on to the *Personal Memoirs*, it is worthwhile to call attention to one of Grant's notes to his doctor, written just before his death when he could not speak: "If I live long enough I will become a sort of specialist in the use of certain medicines, if not in the treatment of disease. It seems that man's destiny in this world is quite as much a mystery as it is likely to be in the next. I never thought of acquiring rank in the profession I was educated for; yet it came with two grades higher prefixed to the rank of General officer for me. I certainly never had either ambition or taste for political life; yet I was twice President of the United States. If anyone had suggested the idea of my becoming an author, as they frequently did, I was not sure whether they were making sport of me or not. I have now written a book which is in the hands of the manufacturers. I ask that you keep these notes very private lest I become an authority on the treatment of diseases, I have already too many trades to be proficient in any. Of course I feel very much better for your application of cocaine, the first in three days, or I should never have thought of saying what I have said above."

But the book that Grant had written turned out to be another of his victories. The *Personal Memoirs of U. S. Grant* has had a number of distinguished admirers who were primarily interested in literature rather than war. I have spoken of Mark Twain's appreciation. Matthew Arnold devoted a long essay to the *Memoirs* in his *Civilization in the United States*, written after his trip to America. "I found in [the *Personal Memoirs*]," he says, in his lofty way, after explaining that when he had met Grant in England, he had thought him a dull fellow: "a man, strong, resolute and business-like, as Grant had appeared to me when I first saw him; a man with no magical personality, touched by no divine light and giving out none. I found a language all astray it its use of *will* and *shall*, *should* and *would*, an English employing the verb *to con-*

script and the participle *conscripting,* and speaking in a dispatch to the Secretary of War of having *badly whipped* the enemy; an English without charm and without high breeding. But at the same time I found a man of sterling good-sense as well as of the firmest resolution; a man, withal, humane, simple, modest; from all restless self-consciousness and desire for display perfectly free; never boastful where he himself was concerned, and where his nation was concerned seldom boastful, boastful only in circumstances where nothing but high genius or high training, I suppose, can save an American from being boastful. I found a language straightforward, nervous, firm, possessing in general the high merit of saying clearly in the fewest possible words what had to be said, and saying it, frequently, with shrewd and unexpected turns of expression."

It may perhaps seem stranger that the *Personal Memoirs* should have been one of the favorite books of Gertrude Stein, and that, in her volume called *Four in America,* she should have written about the author at length. But it is not really difficult to understand what Gertrude Stein admired in Grant, what she must have felt she had in common with him; his impassivity, his imperturbability, his persistence in a prosaic tone combined with a certain abstractness which she regarded as essentially American and which was also, I think, one of the reasons for her enjoyment of Frank Stockton and Henry James. She must have found in him a majestical phlegm, an alienation in the midst of action, a capacity for watching in silence and commanding without excitement. The impression produced by her curious portrait is that Miss Stein has been led by this aloof side of Grant to fancy that in other circumstances he might have become a religious leader, or rather, perhaps, that there was an aspect of Grant which had something in common with the leaders of religions. Grant did certainly present like Miss Stein a mask that was hard to penetrate, did share with her some quality that was not of this world but which yet did not seem to relate itself to the other world of the mystic. It is interesting in this connection to note a passage in a letter to Gertrude Stein by Lloyd Lewis, one of Grant's biographers: "My mind harps on Grant and religion ever since I began reading your MS. . . . Morale was stiffened upon his every advent. This is not much different than a conviction of salvation. People didn't star him as a savior, nor perhaps as the worker of miracles at all. But they did begin to believe in themselves . . . He could do this without sermons or oratory of any kind. I don't know how he did it . . . Your religious concepts of the situation are the best I have read on this puzzling point." Yet in any literal sense Grant was not religious at all. Though he thoroughly believed in the Union cause as he had not in our war with Mexico, it is evident that the war did not wear for him that aspect of Armageddon, the heritage of the older Puritanism, that excited the Abolitionists and that came to influence Lincoln. Only rarely did Grant express himself in terms of the New England mythology, as when, for example, on one occasion, he said to John Russell Young that "it was only after Donelson that I began to see how important was the work that Providence devolved upon me," or to Lincoln, in his speech of acceptance of his commission of lieutenant general: "I feel the full weight of the responsibilities now devolving on me, and I know that if they are met it will be due to those armies, above all, to the favor of that Providence which leads both nations and men." When a clergyman complained to Grant that too many battles were taking place on Sunday, he replied: "You see, a commander, when he can control his own movements, usually intends to start out early in the week so as not to bring on an engagement on Sunday; but delays occur often at the last moment, and it may be the middle of the week before he gets his troops in action. Then more time is spent than anticipated in manœuvring for position, and when the fighting actually begins it is the end of the week, and the battle, particularly if it continues a couple of days, runs into Sunday." "It is unfortunate," commented the

clergyman. "Yes, very unfortunate," admitted Grant.
"Every effort should be made to respect the Sabbath day,
and it is very gratifying to know that it is observed so
generally throughout our country." On his deathbed,
when a preacher came to pray with him, Grant said he did
not mind how much praying he did if it made his wife and
children feel better. And yet in what Grant did and in
what he wrote, it is true that there is something of the
driving force, the exalted moral certainty, of Lincoln and
Mrs. Stowe. The completely non-religious Sherman once
paid him the very strange compliment of writing to Grant
that his feeling about him, at the time when he had been
fighting under the General's command, could be likened
"to nothing else than the faith a Christian has in his Savior." Alexander H. Stephens, the Vice-President of the
Confederacy, whose remark about Lincoln I have already
quoted, said of Grant when he had seen him, near the end
of the war, at the time of the Confederate peace mission:
"He is one of the most remarkable men I have ever met.
He does not seem to be aware of his powers."

This capacity for inspiring confidence, this impression
Grant gave of reserves of force, comes through in the *Personal Memoirs* without pose or premeditation. Grant faltered a little in the later chapters—sometimes repeating
himself—when his sufferings blur the text; but, in general,
the writing of the *Memoirs* is perfect in concision and
clearness, in its propriety and purity of language. Every
word that Grant writes has its purpose, yet everything
seems understated. We see the reason for his special admiration for the style of Zachary Taylor: "He knew how
to express what he wanted to say in the fewest well-
chosen words, but would not sacrifice meaning to the
construction of high-sounding sentences." That no one
can have tampered much with the original text of the
Memoirs—it was rumored that Mark Twain had ghosted
it and Badeau, after Grant's death, made a claim to have
written most of it—is proved by the complete uniformity
of their style with that of Grant's dispatches, his letters

and his recorded conversations. "In conversation," says Young, "he talks his theme directly out with care, avoiding no detail, correcting himself if he slips in a detail, exceedingly accurate in statement, always talking well, because he never talks about what he does not know." "His voice," says Horace Porter, "was exceedingly musical, and one of the clearest in sound and most distinct in utterance that I have ever heard. It had a singular power of penetration, and sentences spoken by him in an ordinary tone in camp could be heard at a distance which was surprising.... In his writing, his style was vigorous and terse, with little of ornament; its most conspicuous characteristic was perspicuity. General Meade's chief of staff once said: 'There is one striking thing about Grant's orders: no matter how hurriedly he may write them on the field, no one ever had the slightest doubt as to their meaning, or ever had to read them over a second time to understand them....' He rarely indulged in metaphor, but when he did employ a figure of speech, it was always expressive and graphic.... His style inclined to be epigrammatic without his being aware of it." Even Henry James, reviewing a volume of Grant's letters, speaks of "a ray of the hard limpidity of the writer's strong and simple Autobiography."

These literary qualities, so unobtrusive, are evidence of a natural fineness of character, mind and taste; and the *Memoirs* convey also Grant's dynamic force and the definiteness of his personality. Perhaps never has a book so objective in form seemed so personal in every line, and though the tempo is never increased, the narrative, once we get into the war, seems to move with the increasing momentum that the soldier must have felt in the field. What distinguished Grant's story from the records of campaigns that are usually produced by generals is that somehow, despite its sobriety, it communicates the spirit of the battles themselves and makes it possible to understand how Grant won them. Humiliated, bankrupt and voiceless, on the very threshold of death, sleeping at night sitting up in a chair as if he were still in the field and could not risk losing touch with developments, he relived his old campaigns; and one finds confirmed in these memoirs everything that has been said about Grant by those who were associated with him. One is impressed by the clairvoyance, coolness, the consistency of purpose, the endurance that, subject to occasional relapses, were able to sustain themselves in a kind of dissociation from ordinary life and yet to marshal men, to take cities and to break down the enemy's strength. The magnitude of Grant's command, which, says Porter, has "seldom been equalled in history," his will, which "was almost supreme in all purely military questions," his authority, which "was usually unquestioned," are reflected in the scope and the sureness of his descriptions of his complicated operations; and he has also, without conscious art, conveyed the suspense which was felt by himself and his army and by all who believed in the Union cause. The reader finds himself involved—he is actually on edge to know how the Civil War is coming out. We grow anxious, we imagine the anxiety of Lincoln, we are aware of the quick intensity with which he must be watching the dispatches. At the moment when the drop in morale that preceded Lincoln's second election seems endangering the cause of the Union, the pressure on Grant in the field, the desperate need for victories, make the early months of 1864 seem a turning-point in the destiny of the United States. Then with spring we get the hardly hoped successes. Retracing in his narrative the steps of his movements, Grant carries the reader along with his army—as it were, almost without impediment. A fiasco like the Petersburg mine, which Horace Porter, in his book *Campaigning with Grant,* describes as so horrible and so daunting a disaster, is noted by Grant as "a stupendous failure" but is made to seem an obstacle quickly surmounted. We are here with a plan and a power which do not admit serious obstacles.

The action of the *Memoirs* mounts up to two climaxes: the taking of Vicksburg and Lee's surrender. The same moral is pointed by both. "The enemy had been suffering," writes Grant, "particularly towards the last. I myself saw our men taking bread from their haversacks and giving it to the enemy they had so recently been engaged in starving out." And later: "The prisoners were allowed to occupy their old camps behind the intrenchments. No restraint was put upon them, except by their own commanders. They were rationed about as our own men, and from our supplies. The men of the two armies fraternized as if they had been fighting for the same cause. When they passed out of the works they had so long and so gallantly defended, between the lines of their late antagonists, not a cheer went up, not a remark was made that would give pain. Really, I believe there was a feeling of sadness just then in the breasts of most of the Union soldiers at seeing the dejection of their late antagonists.

"The day before the departure the following order was issued: 'Paroled prisoners will be sent out of here tomorrow. They will be authorized to cross at the railroad bridge, and move from there to Edward's Ferry, and on by way of Raymond. Instruct the commands to be orderly and quiet as these prisoners pass, to make no offensive remarks, and not to harbor any who fall out of ranks after they have passed.' "

Grant had not then met Lincoln and was not to do so till March of the following year, when he received his commission as lieutenant-general. I believe, as I shall presently explain, that he was strongly influenced by reasons of his own in the direction of generosity toward the enemy; but, once he had talked with Lincoln, his understanding with him seems to have been complete, and their frequent conversations together must have strengthened him in this disposition. "Lincoln, I may almost say," John Russell Young reports Grant's telling him, "spent the last days of his life with me. I often recall those days. He came down to City Point in the last days of the war, and was with me the whole time. . . . He was a great man, a very great man.

The more I saw of him, the more this impressed me. He was incontestably the greatest man I ever knew." At the surrender at Appomattox, it is obvious that Grant is doing his best to carry out the Lincolnian policy of no bitterness and no reprisals, a policy for which Lincoln had had to contend with those powerful elements in his own party who wanted to reduce the South to the status of a subjugated province.

In connection with the Civil War, in general, it is astonishing to what extent the romantic popular legend has been substituted for the so much more interesting and easily accessible reality. It is not, of course, true that Robert E. Lee surrendered underneath an apple tree, and that he presented his sword to Grant, who immediately handed it back to him. Grant himself makes a point of explaining that none of this ever happened, yet many people still think it did. The reality was far more dramatic and more characteristic of the actors. The pursuit of Lee, in Grant's *Memoirs*, creates from its beginning a peculiar interest. I do not want to add to the bizarre interpretations already offered for *Moby-Dick* by suggesting that it anticipates the Civil War, but there are moments, in reading the *Memoirs*, when one is reminded of Captain Ahab's quest. Grant had served with Lee in Mexico and, as he says, knew that Lee was mortal. He makes it plain that for him the Virginian had never had the same prestige that he did for a good many Northerners as well as for his fellow Southerners; and he afterwards told John Russell Young that he had been far more afraid of Joe Johnston. Yet we cannot help feeling that Lee represents for Grant a challenge that is always at the back of his mind. "His praise," Grant tells us, "was sounded throughout the entire North after every action he was engaged in: the number of his forces was always lowered and that of the National forces exaggerated. He was a large, austere man, and I judge difficult of approach to his subordinates. To be extolled by the entire press of the South after every engagement, and by a portion of the press of the North with equal vehe-

mence, was calculated to give him the entire confidence of
his troops and to make him feared by his antagonists. It
was not an uncommon thing for my staff-officers to hear
from Eastern officers, 'Well, Grant has never met Bobby
Lee yet.' " It would seem that the Confederate leader, too,
felt something of a personal challenge. He regretted the
dismissal of McClellan and the substitution of Grant because, as he said, he had always understood pretty well
how McClellan was going to act but he could not be sure
of Grant. At the end of the war, he declared, "There is
nothing left for me to do but go and see General Grant,
and I would rather die a thousand deaths." He would
hardly have spoken thus of McClellan. We look forward to
the eventual encounter as to the final scene of a drama—as
we wait for the moment when Ahab, stubborn, intent and
tough, crippled by his wooden leg as Grant had sometimes
been by his alcoholic habits, will confront the smooth and
shimmering foe, who has so far eluded all hunters—and
the meeting does at last take place. The great Southerner
appears with his jewelled sword, presented by some ladies
in England; his handsomely spurred new boots, stitched at
the top with red silk; his new uniform, buttoned to the
throat; his silver-gray hair and beard and his long gray
buckskin gauntlets; while Grant, not expecting to meet
him so soon, has arrived in an unbuttoned blue flannel
blouse, swordless and spattered with mud and with nothing but his lieutenant-general's shoulder-straps to show
that he is not a private. "I remember now," he said to
Young, "that I was concerned about my personal appearance. . . . I was afraid Lee might think I meant to show
him studied discourtesy by so coming—at least I thought
so. But I had no other clothes within reach, as Lee's letter
found me away from my base of supplies." Yet the sim-
plicity of Grant's costume is not only characteristic but
significant. His indifference to the badges of rank has already been brought out, in the *Memoirs*, by his comments
on other generals who cared more about such things than
he did; and this ideal of the powerful leader, with no

glamor and no pretensions, who is equally accessible to everybody and who almost disclaims his official rank, though never explicit with Grant, is implicit in his story of Lee's surrender. It is an ideal that he shared with Lincoln, and that was perhaps something new in the world. It was to reappear in Russia with Lenin, and in the young Red Army in its Leninist phase, before the restoration of epaulettes. And in Grant there was a genuine diffidence. His state of mind at Appomattox was not in the least exultant, but, he tells us, "sad and depressed. I felt like anything rather than rejoicing at the downfall of a foe who had fought so long and valiantly, and had suffered so much for a cause."

It is impossible to summarize this scene. One would have to quote it entire. The note of the whole encounter is struck by the unexpected beginning:

"We soon fell into a conversation about old army times. He remarked that he remembered me very well in the old army, and I told him that as a matter of course I remembered him perfectly, but from the difference in our ranks and years (there being about sixteen years' difference in our ages), I had thought it very likely that I had not attracted his attention sufficiently to be remembered by him after such a long interval." Horace Porter, who was present at the interview, says that Lee replied, "Yes, I met you on that occasion, and I have often thought of it, and tried to recollect how you looked, but I have never been able to recall a single feature." "Our conversation," Grant continues, "grew so pleasant that I almost forgot the object of our meeting. After the conversation had run on in this style for some time, General Lee called my attention to the object of our meeting, and said that he had asked for this interview, for the purpose of getting from me the terms I proposed to give his army. I said that I meant merely that his army should lay down their arms, not to take them up again during the continuance of the war unless duly and properly exchanged. He said that he had so understood my letter. Then we gradually fell off again into conversation about matters foreign to the subject which had brought us together."

What follows is still, I believe, not too well known to be quoted. Grant had written out brief terms of surrender: the Confederates to give their paroles and turn over their army, artillery and public property, with the exception of the officers' sidearms and their private horses and baggage; then to return to their homes, where they were "not to be disturbed by United States Authority" so long as they observed their paroles and the laws in force where they might reside.

"When I put my pen to the paper I did not know the first word that I should make use of in writing the terms. I only knew what was in my mind, and I wished to express it clearly, so that there could be no mistaking it. As I wrote on, the thought occurred to me that the officers had their own private horses and effects, which were important to them, but of no value to us; also that it would be an unnecessary humiliation to call upon them to deliver their side arms.

"No conversation, not one word, passed between General Lee and myself, either about private property, side arms, or kindred subjects. He appeared to have no objections to the terms first proposed; or if he had a point to make against them he wished to wait until they were in writing to make it. When he read over that part of the terms about side arms, horses and private property of the officers, he remarked, with some feeling, I thought, that this would have a happy effect upon his army.

"Then, after a little further conversation, General Lee remarked to me again that their army was organized a little differently from the army of the United States (still maintaining by implication that we were two countries); that in their army the cavalrymen and artillerists owned their own horses; and he asked if he was to understand that the men who so owned their horses were to be permitted to retain them. I told him that as the terms were written they would not; that only the officers were per-

mitted to take their private property. He then, after reading over the terms a second time, remarked that that was
clear.

"I then said to him that I thought this would be about
the last battle of the war—I sincerely hoped so; and I said
further I took it that most of the men in the ranks were
small farmers. The whole country had been so raided by
the two armies that it was doubtful whether they would
be able to put in a crop to carry themselves and their families through the next winter without the aid of the horses
they were then riding. The United States did not want
them and I would, therefore, instruct the officers I left behind to receive the paroles of his troops to let every man of
the Confederate Army who claimed to own a horse or
mule take the animal to his home."

This scene has the same effect as the quick easing-off
after the capture of Vicksburg. The long effort for victory
at last succeeds, but the victory itself is presented with
complete and deliberate flatness. (It is amusing that an
English review should have said of the *Personal Memoirs*
that they did not contain "a battle piece worth quoting.")
Grant hated the kind of vindictiveness exhibited by Andrew Johnson in the early months of his presidency,
when, as Grant tells us, he was always denouncing the
South and saying, "Treason is a crime and must be made
odious." Though Grant's own policy had largely been
directed by Lincoln, it is plain from his handling of his
subordinates that he disliked to humiliate people. He had
himself known humiliation, in the days after the Mexican
War when his drinking had cost him discharge from the
army. He had known it again after Shiloh, that uncoor-
dinated free-for-all scrimmage at an early stage of the war,
when neither officers nor men had yet learned their business. Grant's strange unreadiness here—perhaps due, as
Lew Wallace, who was present, suggests, to the ineptitude
and jealousy of Halleck, who had more or less tied his
hands—had given Halleck a pretext to shelve him. At that
time, it had been only the confidence of Lincoln which

had prevented Grant's being removed from command and only the exhortations of Sherman which had prevented him from resigning. Sherman, in his own memoirs, has recorded how Grant had suffered from "the indignity, if not insult, heaped upon him" then. (The rumor was quick to spread that Grant had been drinking again, but everyone who was at Shiloh and has written about it says that Grant was completely in control of himself. "He spoke," says Lew Wallace, "in an ordinary tone, cheerful and wholly free from excitement. From his look and manner, no one could have inferred that he had been beaten in a great battle only the day before. If he had studied to be undramatic, he could not have succeeded better.") The fact was, I think, that Grant did not care to pass humiliation on.

JUSTICE OLIVER WENDELL HOLMES

With the Oliver Wendell Holmeses, father and son, the theology of Calvinism has faded, but its habits of mind persist. The father of Dr. Holmes was Abiel Holmes, a Connecticut preacher, who came to occupy in Cambridge, Massachusetts, the pulpit of the First Congregational Church. He had been educated at the Yale Divinity School, which at that time stood somewhat to the left of the fundamentalist Princeton Theological Seminary but still kept closer to Calvinist orthodoxy than the Harvard Divinity School, already infected in the twenties with the fashionable Unitarianism. Abiel Holmes was himself not severe in the matter of doctrine: he appears in the novels of his son in the characters of the Congregational ministers who are surreptitiously humanizing their creed. But he found himself, in his Cambridge church, between a new liberalizing party and the still powerful old orthodox

Calvinists. Under pressure of an orthodox newspaper and especially, among the clergy, of Lyman Beecher, the father of Harriet Beecher Stowe, he abandoned the now common practice of exchanging Sunday pulpits with other Congregationalist ministers, regardless of their theological views. But his parish was attainted with liberalism and did not care to have Dr. Beecher, with whom Holmes had been led to exchange, assailing them from the pulpit with the menace that if they should yield to the Unitarian heresy, a "moral desolation" would "sweep over the land." Dr. Holmes in his novels made his kindly old ministers escape from the pressures of orthodoxy, but the contrary had been true in the case of his father, who barred liberal preachers from his pulpit and was forced to resign by his congregation and to set up a Second Congregational Church.

The effect of this on Abiel's son, at that time a student at Harvard, was to stir in him a strong opposition to the traditional Puritan theology, which he came to feel was wholly monstrous and a hindrance to human progress. He said that his whole conception of the place of man in the universe had been upset at some point in his childhood by seeing the planet Venus through a telescope. Through the study and practice of medicine, he tried to substitute the discipline of science for the discipline of the old morality. I have spoken of his *One-Hoss Shay* as a parable of the break-up of Calvinism; and his novels are intended to show that destructive or peculiar tendencies on the part of an individual are due not to Original Sin but to "prenatal influence" (at that time taken seriously even by the medical profession), special heredity or early trauma. The first of these novels, *Elsie Venner*, published in 1861, so outraged the Protestant clergy that one religious paper as far away as Chicago made a point of denouncing each instalment as the story came out in *The Atlantic Monthly*. Yet Holmes himself, as he tells us, was never to succeed completely in freeing himself from the Calvinist inculcations: he could never, to the end of his life, allow himself to read novels till sundown on the Sabbath, and there always went on in his mind a dialogue between the inherited doctrine and the new scientific point of view.

The young Wendell, who could start from the point to which his father had succeeded in advancing, was not troubled by these hauntings from the past and put the old New England God behind him—though, as we shall see, in his temperament and his type of mind, he was much closer to the Puritan breed than his father. He had read Herbert Spencer at Harvard and had incurred a rebuke from the president for answering back a professor who was teaching a course on the Evidences of Religion. But during his service in the Civil War, he was subjected to a desperate ordeal, which, instead of having the effect, as such ordeals sometimes do, of impelling him to turn to God, caused him definitely to dismiss this Deity. He had enlisted when he was only just twenty, in April, 1861, and he had been badly wounded in the chest at the Battle of Ball's Bluff in October. "I thought I was a gone coon," he wrote to Frederick Pollock long afterwards, and he was actually not expected to live. "I happened to have a bottle of laudanum in my pocket and resolved if the anguish became unbearable to do the needful. A doctor (I suppose) removed the bottle and in the morning I resolved to live." But in the meantime the crisis had occurred. Here is his own account of it, written down almost immediately afterwards, an effort at self-observation—very remarkable on the part of so young a man—which shows his courage and the strength of his intellect:

"Much more vivid [than his recollection of what was actually happening] is my memory of my thoughts and state of mind for though I may have been light-headed my reason was working—even if through a cloud. Of course when I thought I was dying the reflection that the majority vote of the civilized world declared that with my opinions I was *en route* for Hell came up with painful distinctness—Perhaps the first impulse was tremulous—but then I said—by Jove, I die like a soldier anyhow—I

was shot in the breast doing my duty up to the hub—
afraid? No, I am proud—then I thought I couldn't be
guilty of a deathbed recantation—father and I had talked
of that and were agreed that it generally meant nothing
but a cowardly giving way to fear—Besides, thought I,
can I recant if I want to, has the approach of death
changed my beliefs much? & to this I answered—No—
Then came in my Philosophy—I am to take a leap in the
dark—but now as ever I believe that whatever shall happen is best—for it is in accordance with a general law—
and *good & universal* (or *general law*) are synonymous
terms in the universe—(I can now add that our phrase
good only means certain general truths seen through the
heart & will instead of being merely contemplated intellectually—I doubt if the intellect accepts or recognizes
that classification of good and bad). Would the complex
forces which made a still more complex unit in *Me* resolve
themselves back into simpler forms or would my angel be
still winging his way onward when eternities had passed?
I could not tell—But all was doubtless well—and so with a
'God forgive me if I'm wrong' I slept—But while I was
debating with myself Harry Sturgis bulged upon the
scene—I don't remember what I said—I know what I
wanted—it was the cool opinion of an outsider—a looker-
on—as a *point d'appui* for resistance or a που στω from
which to spring aloft, as the case might be; at any rate a
foreign substance round which my thoughts could crys-
tallize—Sturge I hear says I was very profane, to this effect—'Well Harry I'm dying but I'll be G. d'd if I know
where I'm going'—But I doubt it although a little later I
swore frightfully—to the great horror of John O'S. who
tried to stop me thinking I was booking myself for Hell
rapidly. Sturge thereat with about his usual tact, begun
'Why—Homey—you believe in Christ, don't you' etc.
with a brief exposition of doctrine argumentatively set
forth—I gave him my love for Pen whom I'd not yet seen,
& the same message home which I subsequently gave the
Fire Zouave Surgeon and Sturge departed." He had de-

nied God and still survived, and that was the end of God in the cosmogony of Oliver Wendell Holmes, who was never again tempted to believe and who lived to be over ninety.

The young Holmes's experience of the Civil War, besides settling for him the problem of faith, also cured him, and cured him for life, of apocalpytic social illusions. Perhaps no one had enlisted at the beginning of the war with a more devoted ardor then Holmes. "It is almost impossible here," says Higginson in his *Cheerful Yesterdays,* "to produce the emotions of that period of early war enlistments. . . . To call it a sense of novelty was nothing; it was as if one had learned to swim in air, and were striking out for some new planet. All the methods, standards, habits, and aims of ordinary life were reversed, and the intrinsic and traditional charm of the soldier's life was mingled in my own case with the firm faith that the death-knell of slavery itself was being sounded." The memory of that early exaltation was to remain with Holmes all his life. He had been almost as much carried away by the novels of Walter Scott as any of his Southern contemporaries, and, as late as 1911 we find him writing to the Baroness Moncheur, wife of the Belgian ambassador: "Just now I am having one of my periodic wallows in Scott. He also is dear to most people, I suppose—but the old order in which the sword and the gentleman were beliefs, is near enough to me to make this their last voice enchanting in spite of the common sense of commerce. The same belief was what gave interest to the South, but they paid for it by their ignorance of all the ideas that make life worth living to us. But when you see it in costume, with people who could not have heard of evolution, belated but in its last and therefore articulate moment, Oh what a delight it is." This spirit of romantic chivalry he brought to the Abolitionist cause, by which he afterwards said he was "moved . . . so deeply that a Negro minstrel show shocked me and the morality of *Pickwick* seemed to me painfully blunt," and he had acted as a bodyguard to Wendell Phillips when there was a threat of his being mobbed at an anti-slavery meeting. He had left college in his senior year and forfeited graduation in order at once to enlist.

He thus accepted the war as a crusade, and, even in the April of 1864, when he had been through some of the worst of the fighting, he forced himself to continue to do so. "I have long wanted to know more of Joinville's *Chronicle* than I did," he writes to Charles Eliot Norton apropos of an article of his, "but the story seems to come up most opportunely now when we need all the examples of chivalry to help us bind our rebellious desires to steadfastness in the Christian Crusade of the 19th century. If one didn't believe that this was such a crusade, in the cause of the whole civilized world, it would be hard indeed to keep the hand to the sword; and one who is rather compelled unwillingly to the work by abstract conviction than borne along on the flood of some passionate enthusiasm, must feel his ardor rekindled by stories like this."

For this cause and in this crusade, the young Oliver Wendell Holmes, as we have already seen, had faced death at the very beginning: "It is curious," he wrote in the account of his wounding from which I have already quoted, "how rapidly the mind adjusts itself under some circumstances to entirely new relations—I thought for a while that I was dying, and it seemed the most natural thing in the world—the moment the hope of life returned it seemed as abhorrent to nature as ever that I should die." He went home on leave to recover, but returned to his regiment the following March (in the second year of the war). He was wounded again at Antietam in September: the bullet went through his neck and just missed his windpipe and jugular vein. He was shipped home again for six weeks; then, in the middle of November, was ordered back. He had a moment of extreme discouragement. From Virginia, three days later, he writes: ". . . with the crack brained Dreher & obstinate ignoramus Shepherd as act'g Col & Lt. Col. the Regt is going to H——L as fast as ever it can or at least no thanks to them if it isn't—I wouldn't trust it under them for a brass tuppence in a fight—They'd send it to the devil quicker even than Gen. Sumner and I've pretty much made up my mind that the South have achieved their independence & I am almost ready to hope spring will see an end—I prefer intervention to save our credit but believe me, we never shall lick 'em.—The Army is tired with its hard [work?], and its terrible experience & still more with its mismanagement & I think before long the majority will say that we are vainly working to effect what never happens—the subjugation (for that is it) of a great civilized nation. We shan't do it—at least the Army can't—" In December he writes to his father: "... —I never I believe have shown, as you seemed to hint, any wavering in my belief in the right of our cause—it is my disbelief in our success by arms in wh. I differ from you. ... —I think in that matter I have better chances of judging than you—and I believe I represent the conviction of the army—& not the least of the most intelligent part of it—The successes of wh. you spoke were to be anticipated as necessary if we entered into the struggle—But I see no farther progress—I don't think either of you realize the unity or the determination of the South. I think you are hopeful because (excuse me) you are ignorant. But if it is true that we represent civilization wh. is in its nature, as well as slavery, diffusive & aggressive, and if civ. & progress are the better things why they will conquer in the long run, we may be sure, and will stand a better chance in their proper province—peace—than in war, the brother of slavery—brother—it is slavery's parent, child and sustainer at once—At any rate dear Father don't because I say these things imply or think that I am the meaner for saying them—I am, to be sure, heartily tired and half worn out body and mind by this life, but I believe I am as ready as ever to do my duty—" He had dysentery that winter and was wounded in the heel at Fredericksburg on May 1 of the following year.

The young soldier now spent ten months at home; but

he returned to the army again in January, 1864. He had become a lieutenant-colonel and was made aide-de-camp to Major General Horatio Wright, who was stationed above the Rapidan. In Wright's corps there were only the remnants of Holmes's Massachusetts Twentieth Regiment. The friends with whom he had graduated from Harvard, the officers he had fought beside, were mostly dead. Some thought that he himself was not fit to serve; but he went through the terrible battles of the Wilderness: Spottsylvania, North Anna, Cold Harbor. In May, he performed an exploit of which he was rather proud. He describes it as follows in a letter to his parents: "The afternoon of the 29th I had my narrowest escape—Dispatch to carry—important—don't spare y'r horse—gallop—1 mile—small boy (one well known as Col Upton's scout) retreating at a run—reports fired at 2 reb. cav^y—looked round for forces—one straggler (infty) one (unarmed) man on mule, one sick officer— & boy—I spy 4 of our cav^y foraging dismiss former forces & order them with me—trot—when boy was shot at gallop—bend in road—woods cease—bang—bang—whiz—whiz—about 20 reb^s in line—'Halt. Surrender' I pulled up & sung out 'friends' deceived by number and darkness of their clothes—They keep on shooting then I saw & put in licks for straight ahead—Anon a fellow comes riding down the road—I think I'll gobble him—he to me 'Halt Surrender' I see others on R. of road—he is unslinging his carbine as I get to him, I put my pistol to his breast & pull—enclosed cap snaps—then I run the gauntlet—bang—whiz—Halt—Surrender lying along the neck of my horse—Got my dispatch through & return in triumph to find myself given over for lost—" But in spite of a certain exuberance here, we have come a long way from the boyish exhibitionism of the days just before Ball's Bluff. His diaries and letters, both, become more and more confused and disjointed. The action is moving so fast that we hardly know where we are: yells and firing, shells bursting, brains spattering.

The dead are piled in trenches at the edge of the wood, and the trees have been shot to splinters.

"Before you get this," he writes to his parents on May 16, 1864, "you will know how immense the butchers bill has been—And the labor has been incessant—I have not been & am not likely to be in the mood for writing details. I have kept brief notes in my diary wh. I hope you may see some day—Enough, that these nearly two weeks have contained all of fatigue & horror that war can furnish— The advantage has been on our side but nothing decisive has occurred & the enemy is in front of us strongly in-trenched—I doubt if the decisive battle is to be fought be-tween here and Richmond—nearly every Regimental off—I knew or cared for is dead or wounded—

"I have made up my mind to stay on the staff if possible till the end of the campaign & then if I am alive, I shall re-sign—I have felt for some time that I didn't any longer believe in this being a duty & so I mean to leave at the end of the campaign as I said if I'm not killed before."

He was later annoyed with his father—the natural an-noyance of the man in the field with the immoderate bel-ligerence of the people at home—for misunderstanding this letter. He had long ago, however, grown used to the slaughter. "It's odd," he had written fifteen months be-fore, "how indifferent one gets to the sight of death—per-haps, because one gets aristocratic and don't value much a common life. Then they are apt to be so dirty it seems nat-ural—'Dust to Dust'—I would do anything that lay in my power but it doesn't much affect my feelings." But he has just been through much of the worst of the war. He has constantly expected to be killed, and we gather that he wrote notes to his parents before he went into battle, and no doubt, as many soldiers at Cold Harbor did, pinned them onto his clothes. He seems to have destroyed them later when he was going over these papers. But in the meantime, he writes as follows: "rec^d y'r letters of 21d 22d the latter fr. dad, stupid—I wish you'd take the trouble to read my letters before answering—I am sure I cannot have conveyed the idea, rightfully, that I intended resigning before the campaign was over (i.e. next winter just near the end of my term of service)—then I probably shall for reasons satisfactory to myself—I must say I dislike such a misunderstanding, so discreditable to my feeling of soldierly honor, when I don't believe there was a necessity for it—I shall stay on the staff and wish you'd notify the Governor to commission new field officers to the 20th I waive promotion—I am convinced from my late experience that if I can stand the wear and tear (body & mind) of regimental duty that it is a greater strain on both than I am called on to endure—If I am satisfied I don't really see that anyone else has a call to be otherwise—I talked with Hayward the mentor of the Regt & told him my views on the matter—I am not the same man (may not have quite the same ideas) & certainly am not so elastic as I was and I *will not acknowledge the same claims upon me under those circumstances* that existed formerly—a day & a half have passed since I wrote last word—it is quarter to 12 between May 31 & June 1 I have just been riding through black woods after some H^dQrs—and we are going to have another of those killing night marches as soon as we can start out of a country worse than the wilderness if possible—I have hardly known what a good night's sleep was since the campaign opened—constantly having, as tonight, to be up all night—" "I started in this thing a boy," he later—in June—wrote his parents. "I am now a man and I have been coming to the conclusion for the last six months that my duty has changed." In July he was mustered out: his three years' enlistment was over.

The conclusions to which Holmes had been brought under pressure of his service in the Civil War were to affect in fundamental ways the whole of his subsequent thinking. But his relation to the war was peculiar. He did not like to refight its battles; he did not care to read about it. Over and over to his correspondents, he reiterates this reluctance to revert to the years of the war, making exceptions only for Lord Charnwood's *Lincoln* and for John S. Mosby's memoirs, which had been sent him by "old Mosby," as he calls him, "the famous guerilla man on the Southern side." He even extends this disinclination to Thucydides, of which, when he gets around to it at the age of eighty-three, he writes to Sir Frederick Pollock: "It isn't the kind of thing I like to read—just as I hate to read of our Civil War." Nor is he concerned with the consequences of the war. By that summer of 1864, he had had quite enough of the army and was eager to embark on a learned career. He started in at Harvard Law School that autumn and graduated in 1866. By this time Lincoln was dead, and there had died with him any possibility of a clear and decent policy toward the South. The struggle had commenced in Congress which was to culminate in the attempt on the part of the Radical Republicans to drive President Andrew Johnson from office. During the years when Holmes was first practicing law in Boston and editing the *American Law Review,* the exposures of the squalid scandals of the Grant administrations were being one after another exposed in the papers. But Holmes, who was later deliberately to make a practice of not reading the newspapers seems already to have adopted the policy of dissociating himself from current events. An account of the impeachment of Andrew Johnson confines itself, says his biographer Mr. Mark De Wolfe Howe, to the purely legal aspects of the trial without giving any intimation of approval or disapproval. Holmes was solely intent on his own success, a success for which he was quite prepared to pay any cost in effort it demanded.

The young Holmes had brought out of the war a tough character, purposive, disciplined and not a little hard, a clearly defined personality, of which his humor and affable manners, his air of being a man of the world and the ready susceptibility to feminine attraction which he some-

times a little paraded,* could never quite embellish the
bleakness. His concentration on his work, his grim industry, were astonishing to those who knew him at the time
when his career was still to make. It was said of him by
one friend that he knew more law than anybody else in
Boston and by another that he, the friend, had "never
known of anyone in the law who studied anything as hard
as Wendell." He had been worried at first by a feeling that
this profession was unrewarding and sterile. Like his father, he had always had a strong taste for literature and
had even once thought of becoming a poet. A sonnet that
he wrote in the army has a throb of the emotional power
of which I have spoken above as redeeming in that period
the verse of the amateur in contrast to the rhymed editorial. He was to speak of his early forebodings in regard to
the career he had chosen in an address to a college audience in 1897: "There were few," he says, "of the charts
and lights for which one longed when I began. One found
oneself plunged in a thick fog of details—in a black and
frozen night, in which were no flowers, no spring, no easy
joys. Voices of authority warned that in the crush of that
ice any craft might sink. One heard Burke saying that law
sharpens the mind by narrowing it. One heard in Thackeray of a lawyer bending all the powers of a great mind to
a mean profession. One saw that artists and poets shrank
from it as from an alien world. One doubted oneself how
it could be worthy of the interest of an intelligent mind.
And yet one said to oneself, law is human—it is a part of
man, and of one world with all the rest." And working
hard and working uphill, stubborn tension of the will and
the intellect, were natural, even necessary, for Holmes;
they were a part of his Puritan heritage. He produced his
great book *The Common Law*—in 1880, when he was
thirty-nine—by dint of dogged application in the evenings. "I can assure you," he wrote his friend Pollock, "it

---

* "Oh, to be eighty again!" he is said to have exclaimed at ninety
when passing a pretty woman on the street.

takes courage and perseverance to keep at a task which has to be performed at night and after making one's living by day." He told a friend that he hoped by this book to supersede Blackstone and Kent and that he aimed to become, first, Chief Justice of the Supreme Court of Massachusetts, then Justice of the Supreme Court of the United States.

This ambition and his relentless pursuit of it were dismaying to some of his friends. A man who knew him well, James Bradley Thayer, a partner in the law firm for which Holmes first worked, said of him that, in spite of his "attractive qualities and solid merits," he was "wanting sadly in the noblest region of human character,—selfish, vain, thoughtless of others"; and one of his ex-secretaries, not himself a New Englander, once said to me that Holmes had a streak of "the mean Yankee."

His relations with William and Henry James are, in this connection, particularly significant. Holmes and William, as young men, were extremely close. Holmes's mind was fundamentally philosophical, rather than either legal or literary, and they had discussed the great problems together; but Holmes, in his later years, when, in spite of his professions of skepticism, his negative convictions had become quite rigid, felt that James had gone rather soft, that he was giving in to religion and leaving a loophole for the supernatural. Their sympathies became more and more imperfect, and William James, in his letters to Henry, makes his own feelings almost ferociously clear: "The more I live in the world," he wrote in 1869, "the more the cold-blooded, conscious egotism and conceit of people afflict me. . . . All the noble qualities of Wendell Holmes, for instance, are poisoned by them, and friendly as I want to be towards him, as yet the good he has done me is more in presenting me something to kick away from or react against than to follow and embrace." And years later (1876), when he has been to visit the Holmeses at Mattapoisett, he writes Henry that Wendell "is a powerful battery, formed like a planing machine to gouge a deep

self-beneficial groove through life; and his virtues and his
faults," James adds, "were thrown into singular relief by
the lonesomeness of the shore, which as it makes every
object, rock or shrub, stand out so vividly, seemed also to
put him and his wife under a sort of lens for you. . . ."

In the case of Henry James, I have been told on good
authority that when Holmes went to see him on his visits
to England, he was in the habit rather brutally of baiting
him on account of his expatriation, as if he were shrinking
from the dust and heat of life in his native country; and it
is evident from James's correspondence with Holmes that
when the former revisited the United States in 1910–11,
the latter was not quite sure that the former would want
to see him. The intimation of this in a letter brought out
all that was most feminine in Henry James, and one is reminded of James's story "Poor Richard," published forty-
four years before, and evidently inspired by the holiday
that he and Holmes and another ex-soldier had spent in
North Conway, New Hampshire, with James's cousin
Minnie Temple. "I ask myself frankly today, dear Wendell—or rather, still more frankly, ask *you*—why you
should 'feel a doubt' as to whether I should care to see
you again and what ground I ever for a moment gave you
for the supposition that the 'difference in the sphere of our
dominant interests' might have made 'a gulf that we cannot cross.' As I look back at any moment of our contact—
which began so long ago—I find myself crossing and
crossing with a devotedness that took no smallest account
of gulfs, or, more truly, hovering and circling and sitting
on your side of the chasm altogether (if chasm there
were!)—with a complete suspension, as far as you were
concerned, of the question of any other side. Such was my
pleasure and my affection and my homage—and when and
where in the world did you ever see any symptom of anything else?" But Henry James, too, had his reservations.
When Holmes had sent him a Memorial Day address delivered at Harvard in 1895, he wrote William: "It must
have been rarely beautiful as delivered. It is ever so fine to

read, but with the always strange something unreal or meager his things have for me—unreal in connection with his own remainder, as it were, and not *wholly* artful in expression. But they are 'very unique'—and I shall write to him in a high key about this one."

This address—*The Soldier's Faith*—illustrates in a striking way the paradox of Holmes's attitude toward the Civil War. Though he did not want to hear about it, though he seems to have felt little interest in it as an episode in American history, he had it with him, nevertheless, all his life. That he has managed to survive his regiment has become for him a source of pride, and in writing to correspondents, even to those whom he does not know well and even as late as 1927, he rarely fails to signalize the dates of the Battles of Ball's Bluff and Antietam, at both of which he had been wounded, by some such note as "31 years and one day after Antietam," "Antietam was 65 years ago yesterday," "We are celebrating Antietam, where if a bullet had gone one eighth of an inch differently the chances are that I should not be writing to you." It is as if he were preening on paper his formidable military mustaches, for the trimming of which, he mentions to Pollock, he depends upon a favorite Washington barber. (John De Forest wore a similar pair, and Ambrose Bierce's, although not of the handlebar type, had also the military bristle. Neither of these, however, was at all on the scale of Holmes's.) "It may well be," says Mr. Howe, "that of the two wars, the war in fact and the war in retrospect, it was the latter which was dominantly formative of [Holmes's] philosophy." He seems now to have completely lost sight of the angry young man who had once rebelled against the butcheries of Cold Harbor and the Wilderness. He comes finally to insist on the dignity of war as an exercise in personal virtue. "I do not know what is true," he wrote in *The Soldier's Faith*. "I do not know the meaning of the universe. But in the midst of doubt, in the collapse of creeds, there is one thing I do not doubt, that no man who lives in the same world with most of us can doubt, and that is that the faith is true and adorable which leads a soldier to throw away his life in obedience to a blindly accepted duty, in a cause which he little understands, in a plan of campaign of which he has no notion, under tactics of which he does not see the use."

He seems now to approve of all wars—at least those in which the English-speaking peoples take part. At the time of our war with Spain, he writes Pollock that the sound of a military band recalls to him "old days": "It gives one a certain ache. It always seems to me that if one's body moved parallel to one's soul, one would mind campaigning less as an elderly man than as a young man"; and he "confesses to pleasure" in hearing, on the part of his friend Brooks Adams, "some rattling jingo talk after the self-righteous and preaching discourse, which has prevailed to some extent at Harvard College and elsewhere." Writing to Pollock when the Boer War is going on, he wishes the British "a speedy success"; and writing to Harold Laski in 1916, he assures him of the ancient Romans that, "It did those chaps a lot of good to live expecting some day to die by the sword." When Pollock, after World War I, visiting France in 1928, writes Holmes of his indignation at the idea of "preaching to the French" that they ought to forget what the Germans have done to them, he replies, "I agree with your condemnation of armchair pacifists on the general ground that until the world has got farther along war not only is not absurd but is inevitable and rational—although of course I would make great sacrifices to avoid one." A saying of Rufus Choate's about John Quincy Adams that the latter "had the instinct for the jugular"—Holmes's own having been barely missed when he was shot through the neck at Antietam—was to become one of his favorite phrases.

These evidences of abiding pugnacity, when piled up as I have done with them above, may give the impression that Holmes was a tiresome old professional veteran, always ready to rattle his saber; but actually he was much too well-bred and much too serious-minded ever to let himself become boring or ridiculous. With his essentially philosophic mind, which was speculative but also very rigorous, he must account for the war and his part in it in terms of a general philosophy, and it is here that his honesty as a thinker is to be seen at its most impressive. There is no cant about the war in Holmes; for a Northerner of his generation, he permits himself a minimum indulgence in conventional special pleading and obscuration of actuality by myth. It is true that although at one point in the war he had come to believe that the Union was aiming at "the subjugation . . . of a great civilized nation," he was to become, when the war was over, distinctly contemptuous of the Southerners and to write to Senator Albert J. Beveridge: "I hope that time will explode the humbug of the Southern Gentleman in your mind—not that there weren't a few—and not that their comparatively primitive intellectual condition didn't sometimes give a sort of religious purity of type, rarer in the more civilized and therefore more sceptical northerner. But the southern gentlemen generally were an arrogant crew who knew nothing of the ideas that make the life of the few thousands that may be called civilized." Elsewhere he goes even further and declares that he has never known a Southerner whom he considered to be a gentleman. But he always accepts realistically and indeed makes the basis of his system—legal as well as historical, since law, in Holmes's conception, is always molded by history—the action of the Union and its consequences.

He has repudiated the gospel of the militant God; he thinks that God has had nothing to do with it. The New England theocracy is gone forever. "I can't help an occasional semi-shudder," he says in a letter to Laski of May 8, 1918, "as I remember that millions of intelligent men think that I am barred from the face of God unless I change. But how can one pretend to believe what seems to him childish and devoid alike of historical and rational foundations? I suppose such thoughts would be as likely to occur to you about Valhalla or the Mahometan hell as

about this. Felix [Frankfurter] said so himself the other
night—but I was brought up in Boston—and though I
didn't get Hell talk from my parents it was in the air.
Oh—the *ennui* of those Sunday morning church bells,
and hymn tunes, and the sound of the citizen's feet on the
pavement—not heard on other days. I hardly have recovered from it now. I am glad to remember that when I was
dying after Ball's Bluff I remembered my father's saying
that death-bed repentances generally meant only that the
man was scared and reflected that if I wanted to I couldn't,
because I still thought the same."

That Holmes had begun to think early about the problem of moral relativity and actually to formulate the conceptions which were to govern his thinking in later life we
have seen from his reflections on his escape from death
after his wounding at Ball's Bluff. He had decided already
at twenty that "good" and "general law" were "synonymous terms in the universe," that "good only means certain general truths seen through the heart and will instead
of being merely contemplated intellectually," and that he
doubted "if the intellect accepts or recognizes that classification of good and bad."

What is left, without God's direction, is simply a con-
flict of forces, in which the party that wins rules the roost.
Mr. Howe, in his searching biography, has shown how
Holmes's point of view owed a good deal to Darwin's theory of the survival of the fittest and to the positivism of
Auguste Comte, as well as to the pragmatism of Charles S.
Peirce, who had been one of Holmes's circle in Boston.
Such thinkers as Peirce had rejected the authority of both
divine and "natural" law. Moral values could not be decided in any objective way, and if two sets of values con-
flicted, the question of which should prevail could only be
decisively settled by one side's suppressing the other.
"Pleasures are ultimates," Holmes writes to Laski on August 5, 1926, "and in cases of difference between ourself
and another there is nothing to do except in unimportant
matters to think ill of him and in important ones to kill

him. Until you have remade the world I can class as important only those that have an international sanction in war." It is amusing but very characteristic that this dictum about fundamentals should have been prompted by a difference of opinion between Holmes and his British correspondent as to the merits of Jane Austen's novels, for which Holmes, like Mark Twain, did not care; but it was none the less a serious expression of the Justice's fundamental ideas. The question of the dullness of Jane Austen leads him to argue his pragmatic position, and this pragmatic position implies his attitude toward the Civil War. The Unionists and the Southern secessionists had had, from Holmes's point of view, a serious difference of opinion about matters sufficiently important to warrant their resorting to arms. The Northerners had had to kill the Southerners in order to keep the South in the Union. And thus, at least, Holmes is never misleading. He does not idealize Lincoln; he does not shed tears about slavery. He does not call the planters wicked; he merely says that they are not truly "civilized." In his opinions on cases in the South in which the court has been intimidated by a mob, he will censor its legal procedure, but he never, even off the bench, gives way to moral indignation.

The rights, then, in any society, are determined, after a struggle to the death, by the group that comes out on top. Holmes is always insisting on the right to kill, to establish authority by violent means, to suppress in a crisis, as Lincoln did, subversive or obstructive speech. In peacetime, the sovereign power has the right to impose its policies, and the function of the laws that it passes is to see that these are carried out.

Quotations from Holmes could be multiplied to demonstrate his philosophy of *force majeure*—as they could be on any other point of his thinking, for in his papers and correspondence he repeated his opinions again and again, often in the same words. One may quote from his letters to Laski and Pollock such passages as the following. To Laski, October 26, 1919: "I fear we have less freedom of speech here than they have in England. Little as I believe in it as a theory, I hope I would die for it and I go as far as anyone whom I regard as competent to form an opinion in favor of it. Of course when I say I don't believe in it as a theory I don't mean that I do believe the opposite as a theory. But on their premises it seems to me logical in the Catholic Church to kill heretics and [for] the Puritans to whip Quakers—and I see nothing more wrong in it from our ultimate standards than I do in killing Germans when we are at war. When you are thoroughly convinced that you are right—wholeheartedly desire an end—and have no doubt of your power to accomplish it—I see nothing but municipal regulations to interfere with your using your power to accomplish it. The sacredness of human life is a formula that is good only inside a system of law." There is of course on Holmes's part a certain inconsistency here, to which we shall return in a moment. To Laski, January 14, 1920: "I repeat my old aphorism that everything is founded on the death of men—society, which only changes the modes of killing—romance, to which centuries, that is generations, of dead, on the memorial tablets of a great war, are necessary." And on the following February 1, he expressed the same idea to Frederick Pollock: "I loathe war—which I described when at home with a wound in our Civil War as an organized bore—to the scandal of the young women of the day who thought that Captain Holmes was wanting in patriotism. But I do think that man at present is a predatory animal. I think that the sacredness of human life is a purely municipal ideal of no validity outside the jurisdiction. I believe that force, mitigated so far as may be by good manners, is the *ultima ratio,* and between two groups that want to make inconsistent kinds of world I see no remedy except force. I may add what I no doubt have said often enough, that it seems to me that every society rests on the death of men . . ." And to Laski on May 20 of the same year: "Perhaps you respect the self-assertion a little more than I do," he writes apropos of Randolph Bourne, who had opposed our intervention in the First World War. "If I may quote my favorite author (as Thackeray says) with regard to his objections to treating a man as a thing—a means—and not as an end in himself, 'If a man lives in society, he is liable to find himself so treated!' I have no scruples about a draft or the death penalty."

I do not mean at all to depreciate Holmes by pointing out the special emphasis that he put upon killing. This was the heritage of the Civil War. Ambrose Bierce, as we have seen, after a similar experience, was obsessed by the idea of death, and he succumbed to its morbidity as Holmes did not. Holmes's long and hard service as a soldier had, besides, given him something else which was to become excessively rare in the period after the war, when most Northerners wanted to forget or to disguise what had happened. For a young man who has always lived comfortably and accepted the security of convention, it may be an educational advantage for him to see his society with the bottom knocked out, its most honored institutions threatened and its members, irrespective of class, thrown together in conflict to the death or in obligatory cooperation. The law had broken down in America; the Constitution had gone to pieces. It was impossible for an honest man of Holmes's probing intelligence to pretend that the law was a sacred code, which had simply to be read correctly. He always saw it as a complex accretion, a varied assortment of rules that had been drawn up through more than a thousand years and which represented the needs and demands of people existing in particular places at particular periods of history. He was not the first writer to examine the law from an historical point of view, and he must have been influenced by *Ancient Law*, the pioneering book by Sir Henry Maine, which was published in 1861. But in his treatise on *The Common Law* he, too, was a pioneer in examining our legal code in the light of its historical origins. The book begins with a statement of the attitude and method of the author which has now become a classical formulation: "The life of the law has not been logic: it has been experience. The felt necessities of the time, the prevalent moral and political theories, intuitions of public policy, avowed or unconscious, even the prejudices which judges share with their fellow-men, have had a good deal more to do than the syllogism in determining the rules by which men should be governed. The law embodies the story of a nation's development through many centuries, and it cannot be dealt with as if it contained only the axioms and corollaries of a book of mathematics." He unravels with subtlety and coolness many curious misunderstandings by which antiquated statutes have been carried along and have been made to mean something quite different from what they did in their remote beginnings. He shows, also, how ancient ideas of morality still color the language of modern law and how modern ideas of morality are read back into language where they do not belong. Holmes's interest in the law, as he often says, is anthropological and sociological as well as philosophical. He likes to treat tradition lightly, to insist that a law's long existence is no reason for not repealing it tomorrow; yet, skeptical though he is, he believes in the general validity of any corpus of law as the expression of the dominant will of any considerable social group.

How, then in view of this philosophy, was it possible for Oliver Wendell Holmes to become, in the nineteen-twenties, a great hero of the American "liberals," who were intent upon social reforms and who leaned sometimes pretty far to the Left?

There was a certain element of comedy in this situation. Besides believing that might made "rights," Holmes could not, in his economic views, have been further from Harold Laski and the editors of *The New Republic*, and he was as contemptuous of what he called "the upward and onward" as H. L. Mencken was of what he called "the uplift." He was actually, in certain ways, intellectually closer to Mencken than to his favorite young friend Laski, to whom he writes (February 10, 1920): "I took malevolent pleasure in Mencken's *Prejudices,* which devotes a chapter to speaking ill of [Thorstein Veblen]. Do you know that writer [Mencken]? With various foibles, he has a sense of reality and most of his prejudices I share." The economic views of Holmes did not admit of redistribution of wealth, and they had never, as has been said by Mr. Francis Biddle, changed at all since he was twenty-five. "On the economic side," he writes to Laski on January 8, 1917, "I am mighty skeptical of hours of labor and minimum wages regulation, but it may be that a somewhat monotonous standardized mode of life is coming. Of course it only means shifting the burden to a different point of incidence, if I be right, as I think I be, that every community rests on the death of men. If the people who can't get the minimum are to be supported, you take out of one pocket to put into the other. I think the courageous thing to say to the crowd, though perhaps the Brandeis school don't believe it, is, you now have all there is—and you'd better face it instead of trying to lift yourselves by the slack of your own breeches. But all our present teaching is hate and envy for those who have any luxury, as social wrongdoers." He had a conception of "the stream of products," as he called it, as something with which one should not try to tamper. "For instance, take taxation—," he writes Laski, May 17, 1917, "if you stop with preliminary machinery you think of breaking up great estates and old families by an inheritance tax or of cutting down great profits by an income tax—if you pass by means to ends you see that any form of considerable taxation means withdrawing so much of the stream to feed, clothe, and house those whom the Government elects to feed, clothe, and house—and that the rest of the crowd must have so much less." And he had been permanently influenced by Malthus. "To my mind," he says in a letter of May 24, 1919, "the notion that any rearrangement of property, while any part of the world propagates freely, will prevent civilization from killing its weaker members, is absurd. I

think that the crowd now has substantially all there is—
and that every mitigation of the lot of any body of men
has to be paid for by some other or the same body of
men—and I don't think that cutting off the luxuries of the
few would make an appreciable difference in the situation."

The only possibility for human improvement that he
seems to have been able to envisage is some process of
breeding a "selected race." He mentions this in a letter to
Pollock of February 1, 1920; and he seems to be referring
to a theory which he has already rather remotely invoked
without elaborating upon it in a paper of five years before,
"Ideals and Doubts" (reprinted in *Collected Legal
Papers*): "I believe that the wholesale social regeneration
which so many now seem to expect, if it can be helped by
conscious, coordinated human effort, cannot be affected
appreciably by tinkering with the institution of property,
but only by taking in hand life and trying to build a race."
This last reference to building a race is illuminated by
passages in unpublished letters. To Lady Leslie Scott he
had written in 1912: "As to eugenics I don't exactly know
what your government could undertake if they wanted to
tackle it. But, as you probably know, I have thought from
before the days of Galton that it was the true beginning,
theoretically, of all improvement. The folly, to my mind,
of socialism is that it begins with property instead of with
life. I remember saying to Arthur McLellan in the
Army—the day will come when the boss will say we shall
be wanting some statesmen (artists, manufacturers or
whatnot) in thirty years—John A376 and M2—which I
think embodied the principles in sufficiently concrete
form." And to another correspondent, in 1917, he pro-
fesses a profound contempt for any variety of socialism
which does not try to remold life rather than rearrange
property and to put to death all the people who do not
come up to a certain standard. But he does not, so far as I
have been able to find, enlarge on this proposed solution.

One cannot be sure whether Holmes is thinking of eugenics or education.

There were, however, two important matters as to which the opinions of Holmes seemed to be often on the same side as those of the liberals: labor and free speech. In the course of his twenty years—1882–1902—as a judge of the Massachusetts Supreme Court (and Chief Justice from 1899), he had sometimes dissented in cases where the right to strike or to picket was being denied by his colleagues, and this had horrified conservative Boston and gained him the reputation of being rather a dangerous man, a reputation which provoked some strong protests when in 1902 he was appointed by Theodore Roosevelt to the Supreme Court of the United States. "They don't know much more," he wrote Pollock, "than that I took the labor side of *Vegelahn v. Gunther* and as that frightened some money interests, and as such interests count for a good deal as soon as one gets out of the cloister, it is easy to suggest that the judge has partial views, is brilliant but not very sound. . . ." In the United States Supreme Court itself, he continued to pursue this policy of not hesitating to decide against the "money interests." He dissented, for example, with Louis Brandeis, from a majority decision which declared unconstitutional an Act of Congress that prohibited the transportation from one state to another of the products of factories in which children were employed, contending that if Congress had the power to regulate interstate commerce in such matters as fraudulent drugs and the transportation of girls for purposes of prostitution, it had also the power to prohibit the transportation of "the product of ruined lives." In writing this dissenting opinion, he evidently feels some sympathy for the children; but he had no special feeling for labor. He seems instinctively to have turned away from the dingy industrial world with which these opinions dealt. He said once that his only firsthand contact with Massachusetts industrial life had been occasionally taking out, in his youth, the girls from the Lawrence factories. It is true that his long friendship with Louis D. Brandeis, whom he had known when the latter taught at Harvard Law School and with whom he was later associated when Brandeis, in 1916, was appointed to the Supreme Court by Wilson, did something to call his attention to the badness of working conditions and the odds against which labor was struggling. He writes at the same time to Pollock and to Laski, in May, 1919, when he is already seventy-eight years old—using in both cases the same murderous metaphor—that "Brandeis the other day [I quote from the letter to Pollock] drove a harpoon into my midriff with reference to my summer occupations. He said you talk about improving your mind, you only exercise it on the subjects with which you are familiar. Why don't you try something new, study some domain of fact. Take up the textile industries in Massachusetts and after reading the reports sufficiently you can go to Lawrence and get a human notion of how it really is." But, Holmes goes on to say, "I hate facts. I always say the chief end of man is to form general propositions—adding that no general proposition is worth a damn. Of course a general proposition is simply a string of facts and I have little doubt that it would be good for my immortal soul to plunge into them, good also for the performance of my duties, but I shrink from the bore—or rather I hate to give up the chance to read this and that, that a gentleman should have read before he dies. I don't remember that I ever read Machiavelli's *Prince*— and I think of the day of Judgment." And to Laski, in June of the following year: "In consideration of my age and moral infirmities he [Brandeis] absolved me from facts for the vacation and allowed me my customary sport with ideas." In his attitude toward any dispute at law between working class and "money interests," Holmes felt himself so incomparably superior to the common run of either that it cost him no struggle of conscience to announce what he thought was just, and, in writing certain opinions, he even felt, I think, a certain lofty relish, *"le plaisir aris-tocratique de déplaire."*

In the matter of free speech, he was perhaps somewhat inconsistent, in philosophy, if not in practice. We have seen this in one of the quotations above. He does not like to hear people talk about the "class war" in the United States, and he is reluctant to extend to a dominant group *inside* an established society the same authority that he willingly assumes for a conquering over a conquered nation: "When I talk of law I talk as a cynic," he writes Laski (December 3, 1917). "I don't care a damn if twenty professors tell me that a decision is not law if I know that the courts will enforce it. . . . And I understand by human rights what a given crowd will fight for (successfully)." He had already expressed similar opinions in a letter of September 15, 1916, but had added: "All my life I had sneered at the natural rights of man—and at times I have thought that the bills of rights in Constitutions were over-worked—but these chaps [Faguet and Hazlitt, whom he has just been reading] remind me, if I needed it . . . that they embody principles that men have died for, and that it is well not to forget in our haste to secure our notion of general welfare." (Note that what justifies these principles is that men have allowed themselves to be killed for them.)

It may be that the influence of his new friends the liberals counted for something with Holmes in his opinions after the First World War in cases in which the issue of free speech was involved. In the cases of Schenck and Debs, he had upheld, under the wartime Espionage Act, convictions for obstructing the draft. But he had reacted to the wartime intolerance against any sort of expression of radical opinion, as he invariably did, after the Civil War, to fanaticism of the Left or the Right. He writes Laski in connection with Debs on March 16, 1919: "The federal judges seem to me (again between ourselves) to have got hysterical about the war. I should think that the

President when he gets through with his present amuse-
ments [Wilson's visit to Europe in the interests of the
League of Nations] might do a little pardoning." And to
Pollock on April 5: "I am beginning to get stupid letters of
protest against a decision that Debs, a noted agitator, was
rightly convicted of obstructing the recruiting service so
far as the law was concerned. I wondered that the Government should press the case to a hearing before us, as the
inevitable result was that fools, knaves, and ignorant persons were bound to say he was convicted because he was a
dangerous agitator and that obstructing the draft was
a pretence. How it was with the Jury of course I don't
know, but of course the talk is silly as to us." In the
Abrams case, which followed in the same year, dissenting
with Brandeis from the majority opinion, Holmes took a
strong line in favor of Civil Rights and tried to square the
right to free speech with his philosophy of the rights of
power. Russian immigrants had scattered some leaflets in
which—though the authors made plain that they were not
opposed to the war against Germany—the munition
workers were urged to strike against the armed intervention by the United States in opposition to the Russian
Revolution. Holmes held that even this exhortation did
not constitute "resistance to the United States." "In this
case," he goes on, "sentences of twenty years' imprisonment have been imposed for the publishing of two leaflets
that I believe the defendants had as much right to publish
as the Government has to publish the Constitution of the
United States now vainly invoked by them. Even if I am
technically wrong and enough can be squeezed from these
poor and puny anonymities to turn the color of legal lit-
mus paper—I will add, even if what I think the necessary
intent were shown—the most nominal punishment seems
to me all that possibly could be inflicted, unless the defendants are to be made to suffer not for what the indictment
alleges but for the creed that they avow—a creed that I
believe to be the creed of ignorance and immaturity when
honestly held, as I see no reason to doubt that it was held

here, but which, although made the subject of examination at the trial, no one has a right even to consider in dealing with the charges before the Court." He now, in his final paragraph, reverts to his theory that repression is the prerogative of established power: "Persecution for the expression of opinions seems to me perfectly logical. If you have no doubt of your premises or your power and want a certain result with all your heart you naturally express your wishes in law and sweep away all opposition. . . . But when men have realized that time has upset many fighting faiths, they may come to believe even more than they believe the very foundations of their own conduct that the ultimate good desired is better reached by free trade in ideas—that the best test of truth is the power of the thought to get itself accepted in the competition of the market, and that truth is the only ground upon which their wishes can safely be carried out. That, at any rate, is the theory of our Constitution. It is an experiment, as all life is an experiment. Every year if not every day we have to wager our salvation upon some prophecy based upon imperfect knowledge. While that experiment is part of our system I think that we should be eternally vigilant against attempts to check the expression of opinions that we loathe and believe to be fraught with death, unless they so imminently threaten immediate interference with the lawful and pressing purposes of the law that an immediate check is required to save the country. I wholly disagree with the argument of the Government that the First Amendment left the common law as to seditious libel in force. History seems to me against the notion. I had conceived that the United States through many years had shown its repentance for the Sedition Act of 1798 by repaying fines that it imposed. Only the emergency that makes it immediately dangerous to leave the correction of evil counsels to time warrants making any exception to the sweeping command, 'Congress shall make no law . . . abridging the freedom of speech.' Of course I am speaking only of expressions of opinion and exhortations, which were all that were uttered here, but I regret that I cannot put into more impressive words my belief that in their conviction upon this indictment the defendants were deprived of their rights under the Constitution of the United States."

The important point here is that, in firm disregard of the panic created by the Russian Revolution, he is giving the foreign radicals the benefit of a doubt. This opinion provoked a fierce outburst on the part of John Henry Wigmore, the Dean of Northwestern Law School, which Holmes characterized as "bosh," but it brought from Harold Laski a paean of praise. It may be that in the climate of appreciation provided by the liberal group the spirit of Puritan protest was coming to life in Holmes after the paralyzing stroke to his idealism administered by the Civil War, in which the Abolitionist protest against slavery had been discredited by his practical experience, and his incipient sympathy with the protest of the South had been killed by the victory of the North and by a realistic recognition of the power of the latter to impose its will. But the liberals of the post–World War period were now slaking Holmes's thirst for intercourse with men of ideas. They stimulated and entertained him as well as gave him the admiration he craved. He had always been rather lonely, since the days of the Harvard philosophers, for the intellectual companionship of equals. His long correspondence with Sir Frederick Pollock, a sort of English opposite number, like Holmes a great legal scholar with wide-ranging historical and literary interests—which began in the middle seventies and continued to the end of Holmes's life—shows how eager he was for this. "I . . . must vent a line of unreasoning—rage I was going to say—dissatisfaction is nearer. . . ." he writes to Pollock of the newspaper comments on his appointment to the United States Supreme Court. "They are so favorable that they make my nomination a popular success but they have the flabbiness of American ignorance. I had to get appreciation for my book in England before they dared say anything here except in one or two quarters. . . . It makes one sick when he has broken his heart in trying to make every word living and real to see a lot of duffers, generally I think not even lawyers, talking with the sanctity of print in a way that at once discloses to the knowing eye that literally they don't know anything about it. . . . If I haven't done my share in the way of putting in new and remodeling old thought for the last 20 years then I delude myself. Occasionally some one has a glimpse—but in the main damn the lot of them." Later on, in 1917, he writes enthusiastically about Laski, the brilliant young Jew from Manchester then lecturing on politics and history at Harvard: "He goes with some of the younger men like Frankfurter and the *New Republic* lot, who make much of your venerable uncle and not only so, but by bringing an atmosphere of intellectual freedom in which one can breathe, make life to him a good deal more pleasant."

But the further these liberals incline toward the Left, the less can Holmes accept their conclusions. "I have begun Karl Marx's book," he had written Pollock in 1893, "but although he strikes me as a great man I can't imagine a combination less to my taste than Hegel and political economy"; and he writes later, in 1912, that Proudhon was "a man of insights, who ends by boring you as all men with issues and panaceas in their head do, especially if you think you know the answer," and that "I liked to have him walk into Karl Marx as a plagiarist and a humbug, after K.M.'s bullying everybody else as a bourgeois intelligence." Of "the accursed Trotsky's" autobiography he writes to Laski (July 10, 1930): "I am interested enough not to throw the book aside but I shall be glad when I am done with it. I don't like him and the book seems to have a dominant purpose to blow his own horn at the expense of Stalin. I feel the tone that I became familiar with in my youth among the abolitionists. He to be sure takes his principles for granted. I should like to see them stated. If he still believes in Marx I thought that *Capital* showed chasms of unconscious error and sophistries that might be conscious." The certainty of one's moral rightness, the absolute confidence in one's system always set up in him the old antagonism. "He seems to me," he writes Harold Laski in September, 1918, of the pacifist activities of Bertrand Russell, "in the emotional state not unlike that of the abolitionists in former days, which then I shared and now much dislike—as it catches postulates like the influenza"; and in October, 1930, when he has been reading Maurice Hindus's *Humanity Uprooted,* "His account of the Communists shows in the most extreme form what I came to loathe in the abolitionists—the conviction that anyone who did not agree with them was a knave or a fool. You see the same in some Catholics and some of the 'Drys' apropos of the 18th amendment. I detest a man who knows that he knows." The agitation over the Sacco-Vanzetti case had the same effect on Holmes. He received an appeal by counsel for the defendants for a writ of habeas corpus on August 10, 1927, in the week when the two Italian anarchists were condemned to be executed for a supposed murder, and ten days later an appeal for an extension of time in order to apply to the Supreme Court for writs of *certiorari* and for a stay of execution while the application was pending. Both of these Holmes denied on the ground, in the first instance, that he "had no authority to take the prisoners out of the custody of a State Court having jurisdiction over the persons and dealing with the crime under a State law," and in the second, because, as he says, he "thought no shadow of a ground could be shown on which the writ could be granted." These appeals had been made in the hope that the Justice would recognize an analogy between the Sacco-Vanzetti case and a Southern Negro case of a few years before in which he had formulated the majority decision in granting a writ of habeas corpus for five men convicted of murder in a court which, as Holmes says, was dominated by a mob, "ready to lynch the prisoner, jury, counsel and possibly the judges if they did not convict"; but he declined to accept this analogy: the prejudices alleged in the Massachusetts court were not really the same thing; in any trial some prejudice could be alleged. And why so much fuss over Sacco and Vanzetti when "a thousand-fold worse cases of Negroes come up form time to time, but the world does not worry about them." The demonstrations at home and abroad, a shower of denunciatory or pleading letters and the blowing-up of the house of one of the jurors had the effect of getting the old Justice's back up. "My prejudices," he writes Laski, after the executions, "are against the convictions, but they are still stronger against the run of the shriekers.... *The New Republic* had an article that seemed to me hysterical.... So far as one who has not read the evidence has a right to an opinion I think the row that has been made idiotical, if considered on its merits, but of course it is not on the merits that the row is made, but because it gives the extremists a chance to yell." In December of the following year: "[Felix Frankfurter] is convinced of their innocence—but I was not convinced that too much talk had not been made on the theme. *The New Republic* recurs to it from time to time. But *The New Republic* strikes me as having becoming partisan in tone of late judging from an occasional glance. It seemed to nag at Coolidge—and I rather think believes a number of things that I don't. I come nearer to reading it than I do reading any other newspaper—but I can't be said to read that."

The extent to which Holmes was a "liberal" has therefore been considerably exaggerated; but it is true that the "American Renascence," which began first to stir under Theodore Roosevelt, which was manifesting itself quite vividly when our armies got back from France and which reached in the course of the twenties at least almost the dignity of an Enlightenment, did make Holmes a conspicuous figure and cause him to be generally recognized in the intellectual world as the truly great man he was. His prestige at the Harvard Law School seems steadily to have increased with the years, and in the same year, 1914, that *The New Republic* was founded, Felix Frankfurter, a sort of disciple of Holmes, or at least in certain respects a continuator of the Holmes tradition, became a professor there. Holmes had always been fond of young people—he had no children of his own, and he was now much sought after and honored by younger men of congenial tastes. Every year he was supplied with a secretary who had graduated from Harvard Law School—a post for which the qualifications were not only special competence in legal studies but historical and cultural interests which would make him a companion for Holmes. The old Justice begins to appear—as he has never in his life done before—in the light of an established sage, a god of the national pantheon. His books are reprinted and read; his minor papers collected and published. In following his correspondence, one feels that he smiles more and growls less. He knows, and the public knows, that Justice Holmes has become a classic. In the reaction against the gentility, the timidity, the sentimentality of American cultural life, he is seen to have been a humanist, a realist, a bold and independent thinker, who has required of himself from the first to meet the highest intellectual standards and who had even, with little public encouragement, succeeded in training himself to become also a distinguished writer. *The Common Law,* though lucid in intention, is so compact and so closely reasoned that it is sometimes opaque to the layman, and one is relieved to hear even from lawyers that they sometimes find it difficult reading. But in general Holmes's legal studies are so elegantly and clearly presented, so free from the cumbersome formulas and the obsolete jargon of jurists, that, though only an expert can judge them, they may profitably be read by the layman.

As for the speeches and non-legal essays, they ought to be read by everyone. One guesses that it is only Holmes's atheism, his lack of conventional patriotism and his complete incapacity for the optimism which, in that period of national self-congratulation, had become almost obligatory for public figures—Holmes thought that even William James was too open-minded and exuberant—which have kept them out of school and college textbooks. The younger Holmes was not, like his father, a fluently felicitous writer; but his literary sense was developed in a remarkable, if limited, way. One feels sometimes that this sense is quite subtle, as when, in a letter to Owen Wister, he compares the effects of light on light in Dante's *Paradiso* with Andrew Marvell's "green thought in a green shade," or when he comments, in a letter to Laski, on Alfred de Musset's stories: "He is like the flowering of an apple tree and hardly lives beyond the moment of copulation, but I can't believe that knowing but essentially second-rate Remy de Gourmont that we now know that A. de M's phrase is empty. Charm is one of the few things that survive." But there is also a certain unwillingness to let himself go with the poets. He firmly maintains that Macbeth, on hearing of the death of his lady, would hardly have been likely to soar into the "Out, out, brief candle" speech; and, having put himself through the *Odyssey* in Greek, he doubts whether it has been really worth while. He is torn between a moral obligation to make himself acquainted with the classics and a feeling that they are out of date, that it is more profitable to read something modern. But he developed, for his occasional pieces, a literary style of his own which conforms to the same austere ideal as his professional legal papers. He worked very hard over writing, and he gave to these short pieces a crystalline form as hard and bright as Pater's flame. They are perfect, and they are undoubtedly enduring—since their value lies not merely in the style, by means of which he "makes every word tell": it is almost impossible for Holmes even to touch upon any problem of legal interpretation or to compose a brief memorial for some old colleague of the Boston bench or bar without assigning it or him to a place in a larger scheme.

It is Holmes's special distinction—which perhaps

makes him unique among judges—that he never dissociates himself from the great world of thought and art, and that all his decisions are written with awareness of both their wider implications and the importance of their literary form. He was not merely a cultivated judge who enjoyed dipping into belles lettres or amusing himself with speculation: he was a real concentrator of thought who had specialized in the law but who was trying to determine man's place, to define his satisfactions and duties, to try to understand what humanity is. It is this that makes Holmes's correspondence, as well as his more formal writings, so absorbing and so fortifying and a very important part of his "*œuvre.*" In spite of his strong negative predispositions, he will not relinquish a fundamental skepticism as to human convictions and systems, and he is always alert and attentive, always inquiring and searching, to find out some further answers. "The book is pretty thick with suggestions. . . ." he writes Pollock when he is reading Spengler. "I don't value his conclusion, but do his *aperçus.* Isn't that so of all theorists and system makers. . . . Yet when one suspects that a man knows something about life that one hasn't heard before one is uneasy until one has found out what he has to say." Through his long lifetime—Holmes died at ninety-four—he seems never to falter or to become fatigued in the discharge of his professional duties or in the eager intellectual life which occupied him beyond his profession. Among the sequences of correspondence so far published, Holmes is to be seen at his best in his long exchange of letters with Pollock. With Laski, a much younger man, whom he did not know till 1916, there is never the same intimate relationship; and Laski sometimes falsifies his side, in his effort to keep the old man amused, by resorting to a certain amount of flim-flam. But in the correspondence with Pollock, in which both are as free as was possible for men of their generation from common nineteenth-century prejudices, as they discuss their professional interests and boundlessly range beyond them—Frederick Pollock was a great linguist and traveler—through a friendship that lasted six decades, we see Holmes on his highest level.

Of his generation that fought in the Civil War and among the really gifted men whose characters and subsequent careers were profoundly modified by it, Holmes the younger perhaps stands alone as one who was never corrupted, never discouraged or broken, by the alien conditions that the war had prepared. How was it that he managed to survive, to function as a first-rate intellect, to escape the democratic erosion?

He was indeed a very special case. It is plain that his unshakable self-confidence, his carapace of impenetrable indifference to current pressures and public opinion was due partly to the impregnable security of belonging to the Boston "Brahmin" caste. This term had been invented by Dr. Holmes, and the peculiar position of the caste, its conception of its own special function, is explained in the opening chapters of his novel *Elsie Venner*. The Boston Brahmins, says Dr. Holmes, are not only distinct from any other group in New England, they differ from any other aristocracy in the world. There are, to be sure, in New England, families who seem to rise by suddenly making money, but they lose it in the third generation, and they cannot become Brahmins. The distinguishing mark of the Brahmin is that, from generation to generation, he maintains a high tradition of scholarship: the Brahmins are all preachers, lawyers, doctors, professors and men of letters. Some rough ambitious young boy may come to college from the New England countryside and prove able to compete with a Brahmin, but this is rather an exceptional event, and if one finds a young man with an unknown name, not "coarse" and "uncouth" like the countryman, but slender, with a face smooth and pallid, features "regular and of a certain delicacy," whose eye is "bright and quick," whose lips "play over the thought he utters as a pianist's fingers dance over their music," whose "whole air, though it may be timid, and even awkward, has nothing clownish," you may be sure that his mother was a Brahmin. There must of course at some point have been money to supplement the aptitude for learning. The author of *Elsie Venner* does not say this in so many words, but he admits that it is sometimes possible for a Brahmin to become impoverished and that in that case he may marry property. Now, Oliver Wendell Holmes the elder had himself married the daughter of a Jackson, a justice of the Massachusetts Supreme Court, whose family, successful merchants, owned most of the large town of Pittsfield (where Oliver Jr. spent his boyhood summers), and the son married Fanny Bowditch Dixwell, the granddaughter of the celebrated author of that Bible of the New England sea trade, the *Practical Navigator*, and the daughter of Epes Sargent Dixwell, who had read law in Judge Jackson's office and later, with a reputation as the best classical scholar in Boston, been headmaster of the Boston Latin School, at which Oliver Jr. had studied.

It would be easy, by appropriate quotation, to create the impression that Holmes was an egregious social snob of a peculiarly provincial kind. His contempt for the common run of men had come out very strongly at the time of the war, when for the first time he had had to have some contact with it. "While I'm living *en aristocrate*," he had written his sister on his way back from furlough to rejoin his regiment, "I'm an out-and outer of a democrat in theory, but for contact, except at the polls, I loathe the thick-fingered clowns we call the people—especially as the beasts are represented at political centres—vulgar, selfish and base." We have seen his opinion of Southerners and their pretensions to be considered gentlemen. Of even the Philadelphians he writes Pollock that, "While not infrequently having the manners of the great world," they have "somehow ... always ... struck me as hopelessly injected with the second rate, when I have seen them in their law, on which they pride themselves— but I would not breathe this aloud." He hardly ever mentions the Jameses without referring to the fact that they are Irish, with, in Henry's case, an intimation of underbreeding in comparison to the Anglo-Saxon and, in William's, an implication that, though lively and full of eloquence, he is not quite to be taken seriously. (His attitude toward the Jews is quite different. Through his intelligence and his love of learning, his sharpness of mind and his humor, he has obviously more in common with certain of his Jewish colleagues than with most of his Gentile ones; and there is also no doubt the traditional prestige which the Jews have had in New England, due to the self-identification of the Puritans with the Old Testament Israelites. Holmes is said to have believed that the Wendells were Jewish—they were originally Vondals from Holland; and he seems to have regarded the intellectual Jew as a special variety of Brahmin.)

Holmes's attitude toward the ablest of the Presidents under whom, as a soldier or a judge, he had served was invariably patronizing. He was not at first impressed by Lincoln: "Few men in baggy pants and bad hats," he wrote to one correspondent, "are recognized as great by those who see them." And to Beveridge: "Until I was middle-aged I never doubted that I was witnessing the growth of a myth. Then the revelation of some facts and the greatness of some of his speeches—helped perhaps by the environing conviction of the later world—led me to accept the popular judgment—which I do, without a great deal of ardor or very great interest in the man." Of Theodore Roosevelt, by whom he had been appointed to the Supreme Court, he writes Pollock that he "was very likeable, a big figure, a rather ordinary intellect, with extraordinary gifts, a shrewd and I think pretty unscrupulous politician. He played all his cards—if not more." Roosevelt had apparently expected Holmes, in return for his appointment to the Court, to vote in support of the President's measures, and when Holmes had soon failed to do this in dissenting from a majority decision, in the Northern Securities case, which held that this company had violated the Sherman Anti-Trust Act, the President—by way of third parties—emphatically expressed his displeasure. The response of the Brahmin judge to such an explosion of pique on the part of a successful New York politician was a lofty New England contempt. In the same letter quoted above, he tells Pollock that "a Senator in his [Roosevelt's] day" had said that "What the boys like about Roosevelt is that he doesn't care a damn for the law." Holmes continues, "It broke up our incipient friendship . . . as he looked on my dissent to the *Northern Securities Case* as a political departure (or, I suspect, more truly, couldn't forgive anyone who stood in his way). We talked freely later but it never was the same after that, and if he had not been restrained by his friends, I am told that he would have made a fool of himself and would have excluded me from the White House—and as in his case about the law, so in mine about that, I never cared a damn whether I went there or not." It is amusing, in view of this, to remember the acute sensitivity—the Coolidges being an old Massachusetts family—of his suspicion that *The New Republic* is "nagging" at the pygmy Coolidge. It has been thought that his reluctance to intervene in the Sacco-Vanzetti case was due to a stubborn unwillingness to impugn the Massachusetts bench, on which he himself no longer sat—a reluctance which he had not felt, in the Negro and the Leo Frank cases, in regard to the Southern judiciary.

It will, however, be seen that there runs all through this the special ideal of the Brahmin, whose superiority is not merely social. The Philadelphians, though sometimes good-mannered, are decidedly second-rate at law; the Irish, though gifted, lack rigor; Lincoln, though he wore baggy trousers and though he could hardly be interesting to a Brahmin, did in his speeches have moments of greatness. And it is greatness, not a polished complacency—though, to be sure, a better turned-out greatness than that of which Lincoln was capable—at which Holmes himself always aims. When he says—it is a favorite phrase—that someone is "a great swell," he never means that he is socially brilliant but always that he is preeminent intellectually—a top expert in some departments or a profound and original thinker. When he speaks of "touching the superlative"—another favorite phrase—he always means excelling in one's work. After the funeral of Mahlon Pitney, one of his Supreme Court colleagues, he writes Pollock, "He could not touch the superlative, and when he first came to the bench riled me by excessive discourse. But he took his work seriously, was untiring in industry, had had some experience of life, and as Brandeis always said and, I came to think, truly had intellectual honesty that sometimes brought him out against his prejudices and first judgment." And elsewhere in a letter to Pollock: "I am looking forward with curiosity to the new Chief Justice [William Howard Taft]. He marked a fundamental difference in our way of thinking by saying that this office always had been his ambition. I don't understand ambition for an office. The only one that I feel is to believe when the end comes, for till then it is always in doubt, that one has touched the superlative. No outsider can give you that, although the judgment of the competent, of course, helps to confidence—or at least to hope. Between ourselves I doubt if Mr. T. can do that."

It was not true, as we have seen, that Holmes had never been ambitious for office; but it *was* true that, having attained it, he wanted to feel that he stood in the highest rank of a non-official scale of values. How eager he was for assurance of this appears in a letter to Pollock just after his eighty-first birthday: "I have had some letters and one or two notices in the paper that have touched me deeply. They have said what I longed to hear said and would almost willingly have died to hear twenty years ago"—that is, in 1902, when Roosevelt had appointed him to the Supreme Court and when Holmes had complained to Pollock of the lack of recognition of his merits, as he was later sometimes to complain that he was not fully accepted as "a great judge." "The only thing an internal man cares for," he writes Dean Wigmore in 1910, "is to believe he is

taking the right track for intellectual mastery. Only a few
men in this world . . . can do anything to assure one's
ever-doubting soul about that." There is surely something
of Calvinism in this: the anxiety, the undermining doubt
as to whether one has really been Elected. Holmes is Calvinist in his concentration on making certain of his own
elite status, as well as in his almost complete lack of interest in other people as individuals. There is no gossip in
Holmes's letters, very little discussion of personalities;
when he expresses an opinion of somebody, it is always in
terms of his abilities, that is, of his eligibility to be counted
among the Elect. He read a good many novels—he seems
to have had a special liking for French ones—and in
Washington he and his wife went to the theater every
Thursday night; but he did not care much for biographies.
His reading is dominated by a sense of duty and a Puritanical fear of idleness. He feels that he must grapple with
certain works, quite apart from any pleasure they give
him, and, once having begun a book, no matter how dull
or verbose it is, he must read every word to the end. He is
always imagining—this is humorous, of course, but it
shows a habit of mind—that God, at the Judgment Day,
will ask him to report on the books which he ought to have
read but hasn't. Yet in all this he shows a humility which
redeems a certain narcissism. He likes to believe of others,
whatever their reputations, that they have not really
touched the superlative, and his biographer says that he is
grudging in acknowledging his debt to his predecessors;
but of certain people—Pollock, for example—he seems
somewhat to stand in awe, and he is always confessing his
deficiencies. One feels that he is not very far from Calvin's
conception of "the Communion of Saints." Calvin readily
admitted that his clergy on the earth were not free from
non-Elect elements; but this alloy did not impair the true
church, which consisted of those who were saved,
whether living or already in Heaven, and who constituted
a kind of club from which everyone not saved was excluded. So Holmes finds his only solidarity with the clas-

sical "great swells" of the past and with the few possible "great swells" of the present and future.

Now, despite the fact that Holmes as a judge is dealing constantly with concrete cases of men in relation to men and in spite of his insistence that "the life of the law" has been not logic but historical experience, in spite of the common sense that he brings to the application of his principles—in spite of all this, it would seem that dedication to an ideal of excellence which is not to save others but to justify oneself must cut one off from the rest of society. He had no children to bring to his notice the problems of the contemporary world, and is said not to have wanted any, since he feared they would distract him from his great objective. In Holmes's effort to touch the superlative by practicing his juristic profession with all its drudgery and its hard limitations, he evolves the conception of the "jobbist" and even forms a kind of jobbists' club, which, however, except by correspondence, may not involve personal contacts. The jobbist is one who works at his job without trying to improve the world or to make a public impression. He tries to accomplish this professional job as well as it can be accomplished, to give it everything of which he is capable. The jobbist is alone with his job and with the ideal of touching the superlative—which in his grandfather Abiel Holmes's time would have been called being chosen for salvation.

The extent to which the grandson succeeded, after his service in the Civil War, in remaining aloof and detached from the life of the United States was a phenomenon of a very uncommon kind. He is at first, when appointed to the Supreme Court, as he writes Pollock, "more absorbed, interested and impressed than ever I had dreamed I might be. The work of the past seems a finished book—locked up far away, and a new and solemn volume opens. The variety and novelty to me of the questions, the remote spaces from which they come, the amount of work they require, all help the effect. I have written on the constitutionality of part of the Constitution of California, on the powers of the Railroad Commissioners of Arkansas, on the question whether a law of Wisconsin impairs the obligation of the plaintiff's contract. I have to consider a question between a grant of the U.S. in aid of a military road and an Indian reservation on the Pacific coast. I have heard conflicting mining claims in Arizona and whether a granite quarry is 'Minerals' within an exception in a Railway land grant and fifty other things as remote from each other as these." But though the Holmeses had made one trip to the Coast in 1888 and spent two weeks at Niagara Falls, it would never have occurred to the Justice to pay a visit to any of these places or even to read them up. And not only does he resist the suggestion that he look into the conditions of American labor, he even makes it a rule not to see the papers, which he feels are a waste of time. "I don't read the papers," he writes Pollock, in 1905, "or otherwise feel the pulse of the machine." It was mainly through Mrs. Holmes that he acquired any knowledge of current events. Of American business he knew almost nothing, only as much as his cases compelled him to learn. "We are sitting and having cases that I dislike about rates and the Interstate Commission. I listen with respect but without envy to questions by Brandeis and Butler using the words of railroading that I imperfectly understand" (to Laski, 1929). But he tried to give the business man his due, and he cherished a strange idealization of James J. Hill, the Western railroad magnate, against whose monopolistic operations the government had intervened in the Northern Securities suit and whose case had been supported by Holmes in the dissent which had infuriated Roosevelt. "I regard a man like Hill," he tells Pollock in 1910, "as representing one of the greatest forms of human power, an immense mastery of economic details, an equal grasp of general principles, and ability and courage to put his conclusions into practice with brilliant success when all the knowing ones said he would fail. Yet the intense external activity that calls for such powers does not especially delight me." And to Laski in 1923: "I . . . don't sympathize with your artist friends in their loathing for business men. It seems to me merely an illustration of the inability of men to appreciate other forms of energy than that which is natural to them. I am not, and I fear could not be a business man—but the types that I have in mind seem to me among the greatest. This is a disinterested appreciation of what generally is disagreeable to me." He had been in fact almost as little prepared as Lincoln or Grant or Lee to understand the social-economic developments that followed the Civil War, and he seems to have had as little to do personally with the tycoons whom he tries to praise as with the factory workers of Lawrence. If he *had* known them from personal contact, as had that other Boston Brahmin, the younger Charles Francis Adams, who became an expert on railroads and eventually president of the Union Pacific, Holmes would no doubt have agreed with him when he said, in his testy New England way: "A less interesting crowd I do not care to encounter. Not one that I have ever known would I care to meet again, either in this world or the next; nor is one of them associated in my mind with the idea of humor, thought or refinement." (This reference to the next world would seem to have something to do with the New England assimilation of the Communion of Saints to a kind of superior club.)

The real key to Holmes's attitude to business, as to many other aspects of life, is to be found in the distaste for facts and the preference for "general propositions" which he expresses, in the quotation above, in connection with Brandeis's efforts to interest him in factory conditions. This is one of his recurrent themes. He tells Laski, in a letter of January 16, 1918: "My difficulty in writing about business is that all my interest is in theory and that I care a damn sight more for ideas than for facts." And so he further confesses to the same correspondent (October 9, 1921) that his conception of Jim Hill as his "favorite" man of action has been derived "not from knowledge of Hill but from a theoretic construction of what he might have been." To Pollock he writes in 1904: "I never knew any facts about anything and always am gravelled when your countrymen ask some informal intelligent question about our institutions or the state of politics or anything else. My intellectual furniture consists of an assortment of general propositions which grow fewer and more general as I grow older. I always say that the chief end of man is to frame them and that no general proposition is worth a damn." He repeats this in a letter to Pollock seventeen years later, adding, "We are not sure of many things and those are not so."

Though he is still always inquiring into the destiny of man, he can no longer believe that the human race is necessarily of any importance. He writes to Pollock when he is seventy-eight: "I have just read Marvin, *The Century of Hope*, an interesting conspectus of the modern period inspired by a rather deeper belief in the spiritual significance of man than I am able to entertain and a consequently greater faith in the upward and onward destiny of the race." This readiness to conceive of the human race as an insignificant detail of the universe seems also to be traceable to Calvin, who believed that mankind was nothing in comparison with the omnipotence and infinity of God. In the letter just quoted and another that follows, Holmes even allows himself the concession of using the word *God*: "I only don't believe, i.e. have no affirmative belief, that man was necessary to God, in order to find out that he existed (if the cosmos wears a beard, as to which I have no opinion). It seems to me probable that the only cosmic significance of man is that he is part of the cosmos, but that seems to me enough. . . . It strikes me that these philosophers [such as Ralph Barton Perry of Harvard] have gone round the globe to get to the spot close to which they stood before they began to philosophise—also that they still show their theological inheritance by assuming the special cosmic importance of man. I see no reason to believe that God needed him otherwise than as he may need all that is." But he usually speaks in terms of a beardless universe, and it is one of his recurring contentions that it is foolish to revolt against this universe—in the manner of the angry romantics—because man is a part of this universe and cannot differentiate himself from it in such a way as to create an issue as between himself and it.

As for transforming human society, the old Justice— having lost in the war the high hopes of the Northern crusade and fallen back on a Calvinist position which will not admit the realization of the Kingdom of God on earth—must simply, as a jurist and a jobbist, submit to the dominant will of the society he has sworn to serve. He sometimes detested the laws that this society made him enforce and would, as we have seen, sometimes seize upon the benefit of a doubt to declare himself in the opposite sense. He did not approve of the Sherman Anti-Trust Act and had no sympathy with the Volstead Act, which deprived him of the bottle of champagne which it had always been his ritual to drink with his wife on the occasion of their wedding anniversary. If the business men made the laws, he would have to accept their authority; if the people should decide to vote for socialism, he would have to accept that, too—and it was always from the point of view of assessing this latter possibility that he did his occasional reading in the literature of socialism.

So Holmes achieved isolation, remaining unperturbed and lucid, through the whole turbid blatant period that followed the Civil War—with its miseries of an industrial life that was reducing white factory workers to the slavery which George Fitzhugh had predicted, with its millionaires as arrogant and brutal as any Carolina planters, with the violent clashes between them as bloody as Nat Turner's rebellion or John Brown's raid upon Kansas, with its wars in Cuba and Europe that were our next uncontrollable moves after the war by which we had wrested California from the Mexicans and the war by which we had compelled the South to submit to the Washington government. These events touched him only at second hand in the cases that came up before his tribunal and which elicited his crystalline opinions. His Brahminism,

his high-minded egoism and his philosophic temper of
mind had equipped him with an impenetrable integument.

Eventually the country at large came to join Holmes's
colleagues in the law and his later-coming liberal admirers
in assigning to him a consecrated authoritative role,
though certainly the public in general knew as little about
his work and ideas as they had when he was appointed to
the Supreme Court. It was partly, no doubt, the prestige
of longevity when the ancient has retained his faculties,
partly the feeeling of awe—of which I have spoken in
connection with Lee—inspired by the rare survival of the
type of the republican Roman, irrespective of what he
now stands for: Justice Holmes was perhaps the last
Roman. But there was also, I think, something more
which was not inconsistent with these. The popular feeling about Holmes was illustrated in a striking and touching way in the reception by Eastern audiences, sixteen
years after Holmes's death (in 1951), of a rubbishy film
about him with the title *The Magnificent Yankee*. It was
significant that what most moved these audiences were
not the parts that were personal and sentimental but the
scenes, all too few and inept, in which the hero's moral
courage was shown. They seemed to be responding to
these with a special enthusiasm of reassurance because
they were made to feel—at a moment of the national life
particularly uncertain and uncomfortable: the end of Tru-
man's second administration—the Korean War, the Hiss
trial, the rise of McCarthy—that here was a just man, a
man of the old America who, having proved himself early
in the Civil War, had persisted and continued to function
through everything that had happened since, and had
triumphed in remaining faithful to some kind of traditional ideal. But what *was* this ideal they applauded? I
have tried to make out what Holmes meant to them. Independence and fair-dealing, no doubt; rectitude and courage as a public official; and a conviction that the United

States had a special meaning and mission to devote one's whole life to which was a sufficient dedication for the highest gifts.

Was this Holmes's own understanding of the "job" to which he found himself committed? When he died in 1935 at the age of ninety-four, it appeared that he had left all his small fortune—something over $270,000—to the government of the United States. There was much speculation over this. It was true that his wife was dead, that, childless, he had not even any relatives to whom such a sum might have been useful. But why had he not bequeathed it to Harvard Law School or some other institution to be used for some specific purpose? I have heard two quite different explanations, both suggested by younger men who had seen a good deal of Holmes. One felt that his failure to do this was due simply to a lack of imagination. Having rarely, so far as is known, given a penny to a cause or a charity, indifferent to the improvement of others while preoccupied with the improvement of himself, it never came into Holmes's head to contribute to the usefulness of an institution. The other of Holmes's friends believed that, on the contrary, there was a definite point in Holmes's disposal of his money. He had fought for the Union; he had mastered its laws; he had served in its highest court through a period of three decades. The American Constitution was, as he came to declare, an "experiment"—what was to come of our democratic society it was impossible for a philosopher to tell—but he had taken responsibility for its working, he had subsisted and achieved his fame through his tenure of the place it had given him; and he returned to the treasury of the Union the little that he had to leave.

VI
Credos and
Characterizations

~~~~~~~~~~~~~~~~~~~~~~~~~~~~~~~~~~

EDITOR'S NOTE

Throughout his life, like the old-time religionists he some-times ridiculed, Wilson testified to his values wherever he discovered them, in situations, places, people, or their writing. His work is full of the nuances of his experience, the excitement of his discoveries and affirmations. His let-ters to friends expound his aesthetic and moral principles. The young Fitzgerald, an exuberant nationalist to whom Europe seemed "of merely antiquarian interest," is lec-tured on the need of Americans for a Continental stan-dard. On the other hand, when writing to Allen Tate a few years later, Wilson insists that intellectuals should know their country better, a theme in the Dos Passos and Eliot reviews included in Part II of this book. His letter to Dos Passos illustrates his criticism of his contemporaries, always direct and detailed, characteristically relieved by a compliment or an invitation for the weekend. In the role of spokesman for the Sacred Vocation he tries to fortify Louise Bogan's morale and to protect Fitzgerald's reputa-tion after his death, urging a biographer to separate fact from legend. He argues with Thornton Wilder about Joyce, and for Elena Wilson he movingly sketches Max Beerbohm in old age.

His generous praise of *The Real Life of Sebastian*

Knight derives from the early phase of his correspondence with Nabokov, when Wilson was helping the Russian establish himself in this country. Nonetheless, one can see that their egos will clash, and readers of their whole correspondence will enjoy their arguments about everything from diction and versification to Dostoevsky, Greek drama, Lenin, and Freud. The critic could not persuade his friend to take James, Malraux, or Faulkner seriously. In the face of Nabokov's assorted prejudice "against all women writers" Wilson promoted the classic objectivity of Jane Austen, placing her "among the half dozen greatest English writers (the others being Shakespeare, Milton, Swift, Keats, and Dickens)."

In the passages included in "On Writers and Cultures" the critic characteristically defines his standards not directly but in the Boswellian role of an appreciator of others, from Austen to Audubon. As in his essays, the people he admires often resemble the many-sided man of the Renaissance, and this ideal is implicit when he writes of the versatility and range of Michelet, John Jay Chapman's self-reliance, "the intelligence of the civilized human race" in Santayana. He finds the same civilized intelligence in Peacock's comedy and Shaw's music of ideas, without extending his love for these British minds to English society. Unlike T. S. Eliot, with his deference to the mother country, Wilson regularly redeclares his independence and enjoys debunking British snobberies. In an eloquent passage from *Patriotic Gore* he makes the old republic of Jefferson and Audubon his spiritual home. He adopts a self-consciously Western stance in his sensitive account of the Russian literary landscape. Not wanting to see American criticism politicized in the Russian mold, in the thirties he made useful distinctions between short- and long-range writing, between the writer's obligation to his craft and to an ideology or cause. Writing "for the immediate interest or a group or a class" will not yield a generalized picture of human life.

"The Dante who wrote the *Divine Comedy* in exile is something quite different from the Dante who was so active in politics in Florence." The nature of Wilson's literary commitment made him equally skeptical of writing based on an entertainment formula. His jocular assault on detective stories in *The New Yorker* was a product of investigating the genre and caused readers to write in insisting on examples that would prove him wrong.

In his later, more intellectually isolated years he tells us as much about what matters to him in his reporting as in his letters and his criticism. Remaining untempted by the Christian faith, he investigated other traditions and rituals as he sought out the strengths of minority civilizations, able to resist standardization and the imperial state. Less well known than his report on the Little Water Ceremony of the Iroquois is that on the Zuni Shálako, a spectacular fusion of magic, theater, and sustained physical energy, through which the morale of the tribe is annually renewed. This satisfied Wilson's wish for a symbolic illusion of transcendence. Characteristically, after an account of its color and meaning that is praised by students of the rite—which has never been filmed—he resisted the impulse of worship this "principle of bounding a soaring life" evoked. "One did not want to rejoin the Zunis in their primitive Nature cult; and it was hardly worthwhile for a Protestant to have stripped off the mummeries of Rome in order to fall victim to an agile young man in a ten-foot mask."

The intellectual and moral authority that Wilson saw in Freud, Marx, Trotsky, as well as the part-Jewish Proust, drew him to Judaism in "On First Reading Genesis." His impressionistic account of the ancient Hebrew tongue is half anthropology, half a bookman's relish of language, a scholar's pleasure in the text itself—the "dance of accents" which articulates the chant of the verse, and "the vowel-pointings [that] hang like motes, as if they were the molecules the consonants breathed." This language seemed to mirror and sustain the moral vitality of the Jewish people. Wilson next reported on their homeland for *The New Yorker,* and his tour in Israel was something of a skeptic's pilgrimage, a return to the Hebraic root of the Western cultural tradition. In "Jerusalem the Golden" (the title of an old hymn) the pilgrim senses in the landscape and light of the holy city the power of the religious ideals which it has given to the world, even as the skeptic reacts against the competing faiths and churches, the whole history of religious warfare. Wilson inspects the Church of the Holy Sepulcher, with its Mohammedan doorman and its relics of opposed Christian sects, with somewhat the attitude that Gibbon had in Rome when, Henry Adams reminds us, the Englishman "darted a contemptuous look upon the stately monuments of superstition." At a time when the future status of Jerusalem is of international concern, readers may well return to an essay that concludes, "the Jews made Jerusalem the high place of God and thus gave it to the whole human race."

All the letters here are from *Letters on Literature and Politics,* edited by Elena Wilson in 1977. I have preserved Mrs. Wilson's cuts, which are marked by ellipses. The Nabokov-Wilson correspondence, edited by Simon Karlinsky for Harper and Row, was recently featured in a dramatic dialogue, performed at the centenary symposium in Wilson's honor in New York. The titles for the excerpts from the essays and letters in "On Writers and Cultures" are mine. I have abbreviated the attack on detective stories—which was followed by a second such—and there are several omissions from Wilson's account of Zuni. His survey of the anthropological literature, and a side trip to vist the Navaho, may be found in *Red, Black, Blond and Olive,* along with the discursive retelling of the Biblical stories which follows his essay on the language of *Genesis.* The whole Israel section of this book, including "On First Reading Genesis" and "Jerusalem the Golden," was reprinted by Farrar, Straus and Giroux in a paperback, *Israel and the Dead Sea Scrolls*, along with Wilson's studies of the Scrolls from 1954 through 1969.

The Nabokov-Wilson correspondence is available from Harper and Row. The titles for the excerpts from the essays and letters in "On Writers and Cultures" are mine. There are several omissions from Wilson's account of Zuni, including a survey of the anthropological literature and a side trip to visit the Navaho. These sections are found in *Red, Black, Blond and Olive*, along with the discursive retelling of the Biblical stories which follows his essay on the language of *Genesis*. The whole Israel section of this book, including "On First Reading Genesis" and "Jerusalem the Golden," was reprinted by Farrar, Straus in a paperback, *Israel and the Dead Sea Scrolls*, along with Wilson's studies of the Scrolls from 1954 through 1969.

LETTERS

Dear Scott: It was terrible that we didn't meet. I never knew you had been here until John Wyeth told me—I think, the day you left. But you should have left a note at the American Express. I called there, expecting something from you.

Your reaction to the Continent is only what most Americans go through when they come over for the first time as late in life as you. It is due, I suppose, first, to the fact that they can't understand the language and, consequently, assume both that there is nothing doing and that there is something inherently hateful about a people who, not being able to make themselves understood, present such a blank façade to a foreigner, and second, to the fact that, having been a part of one civilization all their lives, it is difficult for them to adjust themselves to another, whether superior or inferior, as it is for any other kind of animal to learn to live in a different environment. The lower animals frequently die, when transplanted; Fitzgerald denounces European civilization and returns at once to God's country. The truth is that you are so saturated with twentieth-century America, bad as well as good—you are so used to hotels, plumbing, drugstores, aesthetic ideals, and vast commercial prosperity of the country—that you can't appreciate those institutions of France, for example, which are really superior to American ones. If you had only given it a chance to sink it! I wish that I could have seen you and tried to induct you a little into the amenities of France. Paris seems to me an ideal place to live: it combines all the attractions and conveniences of a large city with all the freedom, beauty, and regard for the arts and pleasures of a place like Princeton. I find myself more contented and at ease here than anywhere else I know. Take my advice, cancel your passage and come to Paris for the summer! Settle down and learn French and apply a little French leisure and measure to that restless and jumpy nervous system. It would be a service to American letters: your novels would never be the same afterwards. That's one reason I came to France, by the way: in America I feel so superior and culturally sophisticated in comparison to the rest of the intellectual and artistic life of the country that I am in danger of regarding my present attainments as an absolute standard and am obliged to save my soul by emigrating into a country which humiliates me intellectually and artistically by surrounding me with a solid prefection of a standard arrived at by way of Racine, Molière, La Bruyère, Pascal, Voltaire, Vigny, Renan, Taine, Flaubert, Maupassant, and Anatole France. I don't mean to say, of course, that I can actually do better work than anybody else in America; I simply mean that I feel as if I had higher critical standards and that, since in America all standards are let down, I am afraid mine will drop, too; it is too easy to be a highbrow or an artist in America these days; every American savant and artist should beware of falling a victim to the ease with which a traditionless and half-educated public (I mean the growing public for really good stuff) can be impressed, delighted, and satisfied; the Messrs. Mencken, Nathan, Cabell, Dreiser, Anderson, Lewis, Dell, Lippmann, Rosenfeld, Fitzgerald, etc., etc., should all beware of this; let them remember that, like John Stuart Mill, they all owe a good deal of their eminence "to the flatness of the surrounding country"! I do think seriously that there is a great hope for New York as a cultural center; it seems to me that there is a lot doing intellectually in America just now—America seems to be actually beginning to express herself in something like an idiom of her own. But, believe me, she has a long way to go. The commercialism and industrialism, with no older and more civilized civilization behind except one layer of eighteenth-century civilization on the East Coast, impose a terrific handicap upon any other sort of endeavor: the intellectual and aesthetic manifestations have to crowd their way up and out from between the crevices left by the factories, the office buildings, the apartment houses, and the banks; the country was simply not built for them and, if they escape with their lives, they can thank God, but would better not think they are 100 percent elect, attired in authentic and untarnished vestments of light, because they have obviously been stunted and deformed at birth and afterwards greatly battered and contaminated in their struggle to get out. Cabell seems to me a great instance of this: it is not the fact that he is a first-rate writer (I don't think, on the whole, that he is) which has won him the first place in public (enlightened public) estimation; it is the fact that he makes serious artistic pretensions and has labored long and conscientiously (and not altogether without success) to make them good. We haven't any Anatole France, or any of the classic literature which made Anatole France possible; consequently, Cabell looks good to us.

When I began this letter I intended to write only a page, but your strictures upon poor old France demanded a complete explanation of practically everything from the beginning of the world. I don't hope to persuade you to stay in Europe and I suppose you haven't time to come back to France. It's a great pity. (Have you ever tried the Paris–London airline, by the way? I think I shall, if I go to England.)

Mencken's letter went somewhat as follows (I haven't it with me):

"Dear Mr. Wilson: It would be needless to thank you. No one has ever done me before on so lavish a scale, or with so persuasive an eloquence. A little more and you would have persuaded even me. But what engages me more particularly as a practical critic is the critical penetration of the second half of your article. Here, I think, you have told the truth. The beer cellar, these days, has become as impossible as the ivory tower. One is irresistibly impelled to rush out and crack a head or two—that is, to do something or other for the sake of common decency. God knows what can be done. But, at any rate, it is easier to do with such a fellow as you in the grandstand.

"You must come down to Baltimore sometime. I pledge you in a large Humpen of malt. Yours sincerely, H. L. Mencken."

I am sending you *The Bookman:* I happen to have a copy.

Yours always, E.W.

To ALLEN TATE   May 20, 1929

Dear Allen: I was awfully sorry to hear that you had been sick, and I hope you are well now. Checks for both of your reviews have been put through. The Hergesheimer one is first-rate, I think.

As for the American problem, "American consciousness" is a phrase which you seem to have invented yourself, and doesn't quite express what I mean. Of course everybody, as you say, has to have something to lean on outside himself, but my point about the "fantasies" I was discussing was that they had been allowed to become a means of getting away from the probabilities of the future. I always distrust the *laudator temporis acti* when he seems to have no hope or faith in the future, and the American social revolutionaries who look forward to a clean sweep of American bourgeois civilization seem to me in the same class as the peoples whose eyes are turned toward the past, because they are looking forward to something which seems to be extremely unlikely, if not impossible. I think it is true, as you say, that the only thing possible in the present situation is for the individual to save his own integrity. As a matter of fact, this has al-

ways been true in America—in the North, at least—but I
begin to wonder whether the time hasn't arrived for the
intellectuals, etc., to identify themselves a little more with
the general life of the country. This is pretty difficult, God
knows, and it may be that the United States will develop
into a great imperialistic power with all its artists, critics,
and philosophers as ineffective and as easily extinguished
as the German ones were in 1914. But this is a gloomy vision, and I do not want to see it become actual. The people
with social-revolutionary leanings like Dos Passos and
Rob Wolf talk as if they did. I did not think that you, on
the basis of your writings, could be convicted of the kind
of point of view in respect to the old South which I was
talking about in the Eliot article. Otherwise I should have
named you. But I have met a number of Southerners, even
among the ablest, who have seemed to me to have their
eyes turned backward in this way, and I am sure you must
have had such moods and moments yourself, though you
are now distinguished from many of your fellow Southerners and from most Americans of all kinds by your curiosity about and interest in the whole country and in the
world in general. I have leaned heavily on backward-
looking fantasies myself in my time, and will sometime
describe them to you. Naturally we fortify our own souls
by looking backward, but it is surely mistaken to talk as
some people do, as if the future were to contain the realization of some ideal conditions of the past, or as if the future could never, under any circumstances, come up to the
past.

I saw Raymond [Holden] and Louise [Bogan] the
other night for the first time since last summer. Raymond
has had an appendicitis and has been quite sick. Louise
has been working on her book of poems, which is coming
out in the fall. She looks fine and is all full of Thoreau. I
had a party last Saturday night to which they came along
with the Humphrieses and some other people. About
midnight the guests began very slowly breaking phono-

graph records over each other's heads. It was like a slowed-up moving picture. I don't know what the significance of this is.

Yours as ever, Edmund

To Louise Bogan   April 1931

Dear Louise: I'm terribly sorry you've been in a bad state—I sympathize profoundly, having been there myself. But it is an excellent thing to go to bed on these occasions, and McKinney is really an awfully good man. Remember me to him.

I'm sorry that I haven't seen more of you and that we haven't had more chance to talk lately. My affection and admiration for you are deep—have been from way back, as you know. You are one of the people that I value most and count most on. I didn't realize how upset you were lately, though I suppose I ought to have. I always think of you as fundamentally such a strong and wise individual that I discount your anxieties and things.

These are times of pretty severe strain for anybody, to lapse into a vein of editorial generalization. Everything is changing so fast and we are all more or less in a position of having been brought up in one kind of world and having to adjust muscles, socially, sexually, morally, etc., to another which is itself in a state of flux. Still, we have to carry on, and people like you with remarkable abilities, even though they're more highly organized nervously than other people, are under a peculiar obligation not to let this sick society down. We have to take life—society and human relations—more or less as we find them—and there is no doubt that they leave much to be desired. The only thing that we can really make is our work. And deliberate work of the mind, imagination, and hand, done, as Nietzsche said, "notwithstanding," in the long run remakes the world.

I don't know if these edifying remarks may not be en-

tirely beside the point in your case. If they are, please forgive them. I am appending a little poem in a different vein,
which, however, points the same high moral.*

Margaret is writing you. We called you up on the phone
a lot of times before we knew where you were and never
could get an answer at the apartment. We'll come up to
see you as soon as you can see people.

In the meantime, my dear, my best sympathy and love
are radiating at a high rate of vibration in the direction of
the neurological.

Edmund

By the way, here is the title of my forthcoming book:
Jitters of 1930–31
A Record of Happenings between October and March
with some records on American Idealism
What do you think of it?

To John Dos Passos   July 16, 1939
                          The University of Chicago

Dear Dos: To begin with, I don't think your account of
what you are doing in your books is accurate. You don't
merely "generate the insides of your characters by external description." Actually, you do tell a good deal about
what they think and feel. "Behavioristic" only applies
properly to the behavior of rats in mazes, etc.—that is, to
animals whose minds we can't enter into, so that we can
only take account of their actions. Maupassant, in the
preface to *Pierre et Jean,* announced his intention of abol-
ishing "psychology" and using something like this method
for human beings; but even he, as I remember, cheated;
and in any case, how much or how little (in point of
quantity) a writer chooses to tell you about his characters,
or how directly or indirectly, is purely a technical matter.

_____
* "The Extravert of Walden Pond," in *Night Thought.*"
[L.M.D.]

What has to be gotten over is what life was like for the characters (unless you're trying to give the effect of their being flies). You yourself in your books themselves make no pretense of not going inside your people whenever it suits you to do so. As for Defoe, he is so close to his people that you can't always tell whether he isn't merely ghostwriting them (since they tell their stories in the first person, he, too, gives you what they think and feel)— certainly, there isn't much criticism of them, in reference to moral standards, let alone social ideals, implied; whereas what you are doing is intensely critical and much closer to Stendhal-Flaubert-Tolstoy than to Defoe and the eighteenth-century novelists.

My idea about *Adventures of a Young Man* was that you hadn't conveyed—it doesn't matter by what means— the insides of Glen Spottwood. The sour picture of his experiences in New York is like *Manhattan Transfer* but off the track, it seemed to me, because the object of *M.T.* was to give a special kind of impression of New York, whereas in *Y.M.* you are concerned with the youthful years of an idealistic young man. You make all the ideas seem phony, all the women obvious bitches, etc.—you don't make the reader understand what people could ever have gotten out of those ideas and women—or even what they expected to get out of them. (In general, I've never understood why you give so grim a picture of life as it seems in the living—aside from the ultimate destinies of people. You yourself seem to enjoy life more than most people and are by way of being a brilliant talker; but you tend to make your characters talk clichés, and they always get a bad egg for breakfast. I sometimes think you consider this a duty of some kind.) And it seems to me that you have substituted for the hopes, loves, wounds, exhilarations, and depressions of Glen a great load of reporting of externals which have no organic connection with your subject. I never know what you are trying to do with such descriptions as those of the New Hampshire lake, of the

New York streets, of Glen's arrival in Spain, etc. I feel that you ought to be showing these things in some particular way which would reveal his personality and state of mind or which would at least imply some criticism on your part of the whole situation. (You have sometimes done this admirably elsewhere—as when the Harvard boy in *U.S.A.* sees the façade of Notre-Dame in the twilight looking—I think—as if it were made of crumbly cigarette ashes.) Do you mean, for example, to suggest a contrast between the grandeur and beauty of the lake and the ignoble behavior of the man who runs the camp, to which the boys are subjected? I can't tell, because it seems to me that the descriptions are written exactly as you yourself might have written them in your notebook. And as for New York—though this may partly be due to my own rather moony tendencies—I believe that people get used to this kind of surroundings, so that they don't notice them but, as they are going from place to place, see their own thoughts instead. You don't spare Glen a single delicatessen store.

I must say, though, that the more I thought about the book, the better it has seemed from the point of view of the idea itself, which, as one looks back on it, disengages itself and takes on life. But I don't think you quite wrote it. I take it, for example, that the critical moment is when Glen declares in court that he doesn't believe in lying, because he believes in the dignity of man; but most readers, I find in talking to people, don't notice this at all, because you haven't built it up. You haven't told them enough about Glen's soul (or whatever it is). He seems too much on the plane of banality of the other characters— the reader tends to think that you mean to make him banal, too. (About the best review I have seen, by the way, is one in—I think—the English *New Statesman*, which regards the book as a sort of *Pilgrim's Progress*. Of course, the political issue has somewhat obscured it for people over here. They don't have the Trotsky-

Stalin controversies in the same acute way in England.)

We've been having an awfully good time out here. The situation at the university is something fantastic—I can't do justice to it in a letter; but the faculty are much more lively and up-to-date and the students much more serious-minded than they've seemed to me in general in the East. The professors at least have the feeling that education has new possibilities and that they're really trying to do something in their work. At Princeton, they're resigned to stagnation, and make a point of being old fogies. It's ironical that at a time when at Princeton, which has always had so much to say about humanistic studies, the study of Greek is totally dead, they should be teaching the language here to quite a large number of students, who start in as beginners in college and are reading the *Symposium* at the end of the first year. I have students in my courses of all races, religions, nationalities, and colors—including a German Catholic nun. Some of them are very bright.

We've seen a great variety of people—including Gerry Allard and his colleagues, who have really made me feel a little that what the intellectuals write in New York has importance for the labor movement. Robert Morss Lovett got off to the Virgin Islands yesterday, looking very debonair and cheerful in a new Panama hat.

I don't suppose there's any chance of your getting out here? I may stay on till the first of October, as I like it and am paying a rent for our apartment that covers the whole season. The Midway and the lake front up here beat anything in the way of a park in New York. The people are better-looking, too. It is a great sight to see them, over the weekends, in the water and on the grass ... Mary sends love. She has written about your book for *Partisan Review*, so that if you don't know how to write the next one, it won't be our fault ...

Love to Katy—and all the Provincetown incumbents.

As ever, Bunny W.

To Thornton Wilder   June 20, 1940
                                           Wellfleet

Dear Wilder: I was very much interested in your letter, but I think you're exaggerating the importance of the anal element—which has always been present in Joyce (Bloom's preoccupation with Molly Bloom's rear). Don't you think, after all, that he means to present it as merely mixed up with all the other elements of the human situation? I think you're probably right about AACB (though this would be only one aspect of 1132—I agreed with your earlier idea that it represented the Earwicker family, and this seems to me the fundamental symbol). But I'm not so sure about *the keys to my heart*, or the *Arkglow's seafire*—why should some of it go according to Grimm's law, and some not, and why should *K* be used twice? Nor does it seem to me quite legitimate to get *arse* out of *heart*. Have you ever read any of those books about Baconian ciphers in Shakespeare? Those theories can sometimes be made to seem quite plausible. And I once examined a book of Walter Arensberg which attempted to show by anagrams that Dante had an Oedipus complex. One of his points was that the recurrence of the word *Poi* at the beginning of lines in the *Divina Commedia* was dictated by the requirements of the cipher. After all, there are only a very limited number of letters in the alphabet, and the combinations in any one language are limited—certain combinations are bound to recur. If you read the words backward, you can make them recur more often; if you bring in Grimm's law, you can make them recur oftener still. You say yourself that you can do more or less the same thing by applying the same method to the *Boston Transcript*.

I still feel that the central thing in *Finnegans Wake* is the family situation, which is to be regarded as one of a series of such situations presented in Joyce's books. This is really, it seems to me, the thing that ought to be fully worked out. If you go through the book from *this* point of view, you will find it in almost every paragraph—and there is some kind of a little imbroglio (about the letter and the woman who wrote it) that has never been disentangled.

I've looked for the deadly sins in *Anna Livia Plurabelle*—but can't seem to find them. Where do they begin?

I found *Our Town* up here at the newsstand in that cheap edition the other day, and read it—it still seemed to me awfully good. It's certainly one of the few really first-rate American plays. You were going to send me *The Merchant of Yonkers*, which I haven't seen.

I do hope you turn up here later. There are a number of things I'd like to talk to you about. For one thing, I'm going to be back on *The New Republic*, for a few months anyway, in the fall, and was hoping I could get you to write something about *F.W.* for it.

Cordially, Edmund Wilson

To Vladimir Nabokov   October 20, 1941
                                                                          Wellfleet

Dear Vladimir: I've just read *Sebastian Knight*, of which Laughlin has sent me proofs, and it's absolutely enchanting. It's amazing that you should write such fine English prose and not sound like any other English writer. You and Conrad must be the only examples of foreigners succeeding in English in this field. The whole book is brilliant and beautifully done, but I liked particularly the part where he is looking up the various Russian women, the description of the book about death, and the final dreamlike train ride (as well as the narrator's long dream). It makes me eager to read your Russian books, and I am going to tackle them when my русский язык* is a little stronger.

---

* Russian (language).

I hope you will get somebody at Wellesley to read your proofs—because there are a few, though not many, mistakes in English. You tend to lean over backward using *as* instead of *like* and sometimes use it incorrectly. The critic's remark about Sebastian's being a dull man writing broken English, etc., is not a pun, but rather a *bon mot.* If the conjuror with the accent is supposed to be American, he would never say *I fancy,* but probably *I guess.* I am sure that your phonetic method of transliterating Russian words is one of those things that you are particularly stubborn about: but I really think it's a mistake. It looks outlandish to people who don't know Russian and is confusing to people who do. I boggled for some time over your version of a А у ней на шейку паук.* Combinations like *neigh* and *sheik* (and do these really represent the Russian vowels?), into which I fear you have been led by your lamentable weakness for punning, are not the logical phonetic way of representing these sounds; they introduce irrelevant ideas. You were right in thinking I should object to *smuggled smugness,* though in other cases your sensitivity to words provides you with some admirable observations and effects. I agree about the word *sex*—it is an awful word. But what about *Geschlecht—das Geschlecht!*

Now, can't you and your family come up here and spend Thanksgiving (the third Thursday of November) with us, staying on afterwards? We'd love to have you and have plenty of room for you all. If you're tied up for the holiday at Wellesley or otherwise, perhaps you could come up some weekend—almost any after the first of November? In the meantime, we may be in Boston some weekend before then, and we might have lunch or something . . .

I haven't really told you why I like your book so much. It is all on a high *poetic* level, and you have succeeded in being a first-rate poet in English. It has delighted and

---

* Ah-oo-neigh na sheiku pah-ook: There is a spider on her neck.

stimulated me more than any new book I have read since I
don't know what.

Our best regards to you both.

As ever, Edmund Wilson

To Arthur Mizener   April 4, 1950
Wellfleet

Dear Arthur: I have badgered you enough about the Fitzgerald book but I had been thinking of sending you some
general tips and your last letter encourages me to do so.

It is important, in writing a biography, to remember
that you are telling a story and that the problems of presenting the material are in many ways just the same as
those of presenting a subject of fiction. You cannot take
for granted, on the part of the reader, any knowledge
whatever of your particular subject. You have to introduce it to him so that he will understand it every step of
the way, and you have to create your characters and background and situations just as you would those of fiction.
You must put yourself in the reader's place. *The Kenyon
Review* and the rest of them are not a particularly good
school for this, because they are always making allusions
to writers and movements and books without explaining
what these things mean to them (very often they don't
quite know). They assume that the reader will have read
the same books and made the same assumptions as themselves.

And the biographer has not only to choose and place
every detail of his picture, but to calculate the tone
of every sentence. It is quite obvious that, in dealing with
Scott, you have produced, by not hitting the tone, an effect you didn't intend. This has sometimes happened to
me when some completely irrelevant feeling has got into
something I was writing. To correct it, you have to approach the thing in a perfectly objective way and readjust
it step by step, systematically, so as to put it in a different
light. In spite of the fact that the biographer is given his

materials in the shape of letters, memoirs, etc., he is just as much responsible for the portrait that emerges as Scott was for the Great Gatsby.

But, in dealing with the given data, you do have a different problem from the writer of sheer fiction, because you have to have some principles for deciding what constitutes evidence. Biographers, of course, have dealt with this problem in a variety of different ways. It is always a lot of trouble to check on facts, and in the case of an amusing or romantic character, anecdotes grow rapidly into legends. I recommend, in this connection, that book about Henry James called *The Legend of the Master,* in which the author tries to run down the truth about some of the most famous James anecdotes. When I was writing about Lenin in the *Finland Station,* I tended to accept the memoirs published in the Soviet Union. I hadn't realized how early the deliberate mythmaking had been begun. Now I am not at all sure that some of my details of his return to Russia were not made up out of the whole cloth for the purposes of a volume of eulogies, of the authenticity of which I was convinced by the proletarian status of the supposed witnesses, but by which I may well have been taken in. Trotsky, whose first volume of a life of Lenin is one of the best things on the subject, does not even believe in the memoir published by Lenin's sister, which I decided to accept. You don't have any such baffling problem in finding out about Scott, but it is always an awful nuisance to try to get at the truth behind conflicting accounts, and though you are scrupulous and scholarly with texts, you have not had any occasion before to train yourself in examining evidence. In regard to the nut-kicking incident, for example (if it was nuts: I thought it was something else, which shows how legends vary), I suggest that you write to John Dos Passos ... explaining that you have heard several versions and asking him exactly what happened. He was there and he is an accurate observer and is likely to tell you the truth.

Well, I seem to be having a field day as an Elder Biographer giving advice. Don't feel, by the way, that you are bound to accept all my or anybody else's suggestions about the MS.

As ever, Edmund W.

To Elena Wilson   March 15, 1954
                                                      Rapallo

. . . We went to Max [Beerbohm]'s villa this afternoon. It is pretty, looks right down on the sea, has a pleasant sunny terrace. He has just recovered from flu and received us in a bathrobe, sitting up in a chair. He makes an extraordinarily distinguished impression, and his head and face have more weight and strength than I had gathered from photographs of him and from his caricatures of himself. He talked extremely well and is not in the least gaga, remembered with perfect accuracy every detail of his own and other people's work. He gave us a long physical description of Bernard Shaw as he had looked when Max had first known him in London that showed how minute his observation of people is. He hadn't cared for Virginia Woolf's diary, had been struck, as I was, by her preoccupation with her own worries and her lack of consideration for other people—but then he doesn't in the least appreciate the things that are good about her, can't see anything in her books. He said a lot of amusing things; but there is a mischievous-small-boy side of him that finally becomes a little tiresome—not in his conversation, but in the innumerable books (of other people) that he has doctored in various comic ways, and too many of which we were shown, not at his instance, but by the faithful Mme Jungmann (a very able, amiable, and well-read German, who came to his rescue after his wife's death—she had before that taken care of [Gerhardt] Hauptmann). He has lived here for forty-four years, lately on a diminishing scale— Sam [Behrman] says that he is now very poor, and that it is hard to do anything for him: he has refused a large fee to appear on television, etc. I felt that it had been worthwhile to come here to see him (may go back tomorrow if she phones that he is up to it). He is certainly a remarkable person, more continental than English (he has charming portraits of his grandparents that make them look like idealized characters in eighteenth-century operas, the eye in both cases *espiègle* and the mouth as if it were just about to smile). Seeing him out here makes you feel that he is independent and self-sufficing, quietly and scrupulously devoted to his own ideals. He said that most caricaturing nowadays was ugly, whereas "though I am not the person to say it—and I had half a mind to leave it unsaid—my drawings are pretty and agreeable to have around." He showed us a little watercolor in pink and blue that he had lately made of Edward VII and said, "Now, you see that's a pretty little drawing." He told us that he had stopped doing caricatures when he came to the time of life at which he realized that what he was producing were simply painstaking likenesses that showed pity for their subjects instead of making them amusing. "Pathos," he said, "is no quality for a caricaturist." He was interesting about Walter Sickert, whose painting he does not think successful: he had too much theory, would have made perhaps a good critic: "A painter ought not to be too clever in that way. He should be a passionate gaze, putting down what he sees or what he thinks he sees". . .

ON WRITERS AND CULTURES
Jane Austen

There have been several revolutions of taste during the last century and a quarter of English literature, and through them all perhaps only two reputations have never been affected by the shifts of fashion: Shakespeare's and Jane Austen's. We still agree with Scott about Jane Austen, just as we agree with Ben Jonson about Shakespeare. From Scott, Southey, Coleridge and Macaulay (to say nothing of the Prince Regent, who kept a set of her works "in every one of his residences") to Kipling and George Moore, Virginia Woolf and E. M. Forster, she has compelled the amazed admiration of writers of the most diverse kinds, and I should say that Jane Austen and Dickens rather queerly present themselves today as the only two English novelists (though not quite the only novelists in English) who belong in the very top rank with the great fiction writers of Russia and France. Jane Austen, as Mr. Stark Young once said, is perhaps the only English example of that spirit of classical comedy that is more natural to the Latin people than to ours and that Molière represents for the French. That this spirit should have embodied itself in England in the mind of a well-bred spinster, the daughter of a country clergyman, who never saw any more of the world than was made possible by short visits to London and a residence of a few years in Bath and who found her subjects mainly in the problems of young provincial girls looking for husbands, seems one of the most freakish of the many anomalies of English literary history.

T. S. Eliot: The Poet and the Public Figure

There is a scoundrel and actor in Eliot. It was the young scoundrel who wrote the good poetry and it is now the old scoundrel who is putting on the public performance. In private, he is humorous and disarming about his reputation, but the performance still goes on; and just as his poems are all dramatic monologues, so all of his public utterances, except when he is writing about literature—and sometimes even then—are in the main merely speeches for one or other of his dramatic "personae." When he is writing for clerical papers or addressing a Conservative dinner, he allows himself reactionary audacities which he rarely hazards with his larger audience. (He did let some of these loose in the lectures collected in *After Strange Gods*—delivered at the University of Virginia, where I suppose he thought it was safe to let his snobberies and antiquated loyalties rip—but when hostile repercussions reached his sensitive ear, he did his best to suppress the volume.) But these dramatically slanted opinions are so dim and make so little sense that I don't see how they can do much damage. l was talking about this just now with Arthur Schlesinger, usually an up-in-arms liberal, and—rather to my surprise—he anticipated my opinion by saying that all this side of Eliot didn't matter. In his poetry and in his personal relations, he is sensitive, gentle, and rather touching. In spite of his assertion to the contrary when I talked to him years ago, he is ready to converse with unbelievers, and he is not disagreeable to Jews; and he makes fun of all the old gentilities that he otherwise pretends to represent. The shrewd Yankee operator who always remains discreet but gets away with murder is balanced by the Yankee idealist who—in literature, the only thing about which he feels intensely—is able to stand by his convictions and, on occasion, without sticking his neck out (as Lewis and Pound habitually did), to show a firm courage. In his tiresome performances as the humble great man, he is more and more betraying his vanity: he talks about his own work in far too many of this last collection of essays. He is absurd in his pretensions to pontificate—did you know that he has recently announced that it is proper not entirely to despise Longfellow? But the literary and academic worlds are apparently full of people who want nothing better than to follow his directives. He enjoys his conspicuous position, and I imagine that this has been one of the few compensations in a life of which the sufferings and conflicts have been finely and frankly expressed in his poetry.

> To Van Wyck Brooks,
> *Letters on Literature and Politics*

George Santayana

It would not be precisely true to say that Santayana is narcissistic, but he is interested in his own thought as a personal self-contained system, and in his life as a work of art which owes its integrity and harmony partly to a rigorous avoidance of indiscriminate human relationships. The objective materials with which his mind works have been the systems of other thinkers and the assumptions underlying civilizations. It is easy to see, when one meets him, how his attitude toward the world has derived from his personal characteristics and from the circumstances of his life. A pure Latin of small stature, with fastidious taste and a subtle mind, it was his fate to spend most of his formative years living among Anglo-Saxons. In another man this position might have produced an alternation of the defiant with the propitiatory; but Santayana has subjected himself to a self-discipline which has kept him both firm and, as he said to me of his relations with the English, "discreet." The discretion is self-protective, the mockery a tempering of insolence. I felt occasionally, in his tone about other people a suggestion of something feline which was perhaps not quite congruous with the true Socratic irony; and he seems always to have found it difficult to resist a display of virility. Unsympathetic with the Germans, he yet admired the officers in uniform that he saw in his student days; and his weakness for Mussolini may partly have been due to a similar reaction.

But to say this is merely to say that the books of George Santayana have been written by a human being; and one is, if anything, even more impressed by him after meeting him than one had been in reading these books. The image of him came back to me afterwards in the course of the solitary evenings that I spent when I was first in Rome: alone, with his plain table and his narrow bed, so far from Spain and from Harvard, yet with all the philosophies, the religions and the poetry through which he had passed making about him an iridescent integument, the manners of all the societies in which he had sojourned awhile supplying him with pictures and phrases; a shell of faded skin and frail bone, in which the power of intellect, the colors of imagination, still burned and gave out, through his books and his gentle-voiced conversation, their steady pulsations and rays, of which the intensity seems even to increase as the generator is more worn by use. I do not imagine he is troubled by the thought of death or that it even impinges as a shadow: his present so triumphant functioning appears to absorb and enchant him. Nor is he really alone in the sense that the ordinary person would be. He is still in the world of men, conversing with them through reading and writing, a section of the human plasm that, insulated by convent walls and by exceptional resistances of character, still registers the remotest tremors. He has grown, it seems, almost immune to physical or emotional shock. While others, in these years of the war, have been shaken by the downfall of moralities or have shuddered under the impact of disaster, while they have been following the conflict with excitement, his glass has scarcely clouded or brightened; but the intelligence that has persisted in him has been that of the civilized human race—so how can he be lonely or old? He still loves to share in its thoughts, to try on its points of view. He has made it his business to extend himself into every kind of human consciousness with which he can establish contact, and he reposes on his shabby chaise longue like a monad in the universal mind.

"Roman Diary: A Visit to Santayana,"
Europe without Baedeker

John Jay Chapman

To Chapman, the great writers of the past were neither a pantheon nor a vested interest. He approached them open-mindedly and boldly, very much as he did living persons who he thought might entertain or instruct him. Not that he judged them by contemporary standards; but he would go straight to them across the ages in the role of an independent traveler, who was willing to pay his toll to the people that kept the roads but wished to linger with them as little as possible. He sometimes committed blunders: he got the relationships mixed up in the *Antigone*, and he never grasped the simple enough principles which govern, in the *Divine Comedy*, the assignment of the souls to the different worlds—complaining that Dante's arrangements involved a good deal of injustice. "You know," he says in a letter, "I've never known the literature of the subjects I wrote on. I never knew the Emerson literature—except Emerson himself." But Chapman has at least always got there and had a good look at the man; and he can always tell you about him something that you have not heard before.

"John Jay Chapman,"
The Triple Thinkers

Jules Michelet

The mature Michelet is a strange phenomenon. He is in many ways more comparable to a novelist like Balzac than to the ordinary historian. He had the novelist's social interest and grasp of character, the poet's imagination and passion. All this, by some unique combination of chances, instead of exercising itself freely on contemporary life, had been turned backward upon history and was united with a scientific appetite for facts which drove him into arduous researches.

The impression he makes on us is quite different from that of the ordinary modern scholar who has specialized in some narrowly delimited subject and gotten it up in a graduate school: we feel that Michelet has read all the books, been to look at all the monuments and pictures, interviewed personally all the authorities, and explored all the libraries and archives of Europe; and that he has it all under his hat. The Goncourts said that Michelet's attractiveness lay in the fact that his works "seem to be written by hand. They are free from the banality and impersonality which the printed thing has; they are like the autograph of a thought." But what Michelet really goes back to is an earlier stage of printing before either the journalistic or the academic formulas had come between first-hand knowledge and us. He is simply a man going to the sources and trying to get down on record what can be learned from them; and this role, which claims for itself, on the one hand, no academic sanctions, involves, on the other hand, a more direct responsibility to the reader.

"Michelet and the Revolution,"
To the Finland Station

Thomas Love Peacock

The fact that Peacock's *imagination* is not vigorous, varied or rich has, I believe, rather kept people from realizing how exquisite his effects sometimes are. It is usual to treat him as a satirist whose power is more or less weakened by his scoring off both sides of every question; but the truth is that Peacock is an artist the aim of whose art is to achieve not merely a weaving of ideas but also an atmosphere—an aroma, a flavor, a harmony. You get closer to what Peacock is trying to do by approaching him through his admiration for Mozart—"There is," he wrote, "nothing perfect in this world except Mozart's music"—than by assimilating him to Lucian or Voltaire. His books are more like light operas than novels (it was quite natural that *Maid Marian* should have been made into one) and the elements of fantasy with which they play—the civilized orangutan of *Melincourt*, who is chivalrous with the ladies, the seven lovely maidens of *Gryll Grange* who keep house for the young man in the tower—as well as the landscapes of mountain streams, the drives and rides in the New Forest, the boating and skating parties, are as important as the conversations. It all makes a delicious music, at the same time sober and gay, in which the words fall like notes from a flute, like progressions on an old-fashioned pianoforte, lighted by slim white candles. In *Gryll Grange*, when we come to the snowstorm, we almost have the illusion that these pale and sifted words of Peacock's are dropping on the page like snowflakes and that they melt away as we read. Even the openings of Peacock's unfinished novels—so sure is his touch on the keyboard to convey us at once to his realm—may be enjoyed as little works in themselves, like the "preludes" of Debussy or Chopin.

"The Musical Glasses of Peacock,"
Classics and Commercials

Shaw's Music

Bernard Shaw has had the further advantage of a musical education. "Do not suppose for a moment," he writes, "that I learnt my art from English men of letters. True, they showed me how to handle English words; but if I had known no more than that, my works would never have crossed the Channel. My masters were the masters of a universal language; they were, to go from summit to summit, Bach, Handel, Haydn, Mozart, Beethoven and Wagner. . . . For their sakes, Germany stands consecrated as the Holy Land of the capitalistic age." Einstein has said that Shaw's plays remind him of Mozart's music: every word has its place in the development. And if we allow for some nineteenth-century prolixity, we can see in Shaw's dramatic work a logic and grace, a formal precision, like that of the eighteenth-century composers.

Take *The Apple Cart*, for example. The fact that Shaw is here working exclusively with economic and political materials has caused its art to be insufficiently appreciated. If it had been a sentimental comedy by Molnar, the critics would have applauded its deftness; yet Shaw is a finer artist than any of the Molnars or Schnitzlers. The first act of *The Apple Cart* is an exercise in the scoring for small orchestra at which Shaw is particularly skillful. After what he has himself called the overture before the curtain of the conversation between the two secretaries, in which the music of King Magnus is foreshadowed, the urbane and intelligent King and the "bull-roarer Boanerges" play a duet against one another. Then the King plays a single instrument against the whole nine of the cabinet. The themes emerge: the King's disinterestedness and the labor government's sordid self-interest. The development is lively: the music is tossed from one instrument to another, with, to use the old cliché, a combination of inevitableness and surprise. Finally, the King's theme gets a full and splendid statement in the long speech in which he declares his principles: "I stand for the great abstractions: for conscience and virtue; for the eternal against the expedient; for the evolutionary appetite against the day's gluttony," etc. This silver voice of the King lifts the movement to a poignant climax; and now a dramatic reversal carries the climax further and rounds out and balances the harmony. Unexpectedly, one of the brasses of the ministry takes up the theme of the King and repeats it more passionately and loudly: "Just so! . . . Listen to me, sir," bursts out the Powermistress, "and judge whether I have not reason to feel everything you have just said to the very marrow of my bones. Here am I, the Powermistress Royal. I have to organize and administer all the motor power in the country for the good of the country. I have to harness the winds and the tides, the oils and the coal seams." And she launches into an extraordinary tirade in which the idea of political disinterestedness is taken out of the realm of elegant abstraction in which it has hitherto remained with the King and reiterated in terms of engineering: "every little sewing machine in the Hebrides, every dentist's drill in Shetland, every carpet sweeper in Margate," etc. This ends on crashing chords, but immediately the music of the cabinet snarlingly reasserts itself. The act ends on the light note of the secretaries.

This music is a music of ideas—or rather, perhaps, it is a music of moralities. Bernard Shaw is a writer of the same kind as Plato. There are not many such writers in literature—the *Drames philosophiques* of Renan would supply another example—and they are likely to puzzle the critics. Shaw, like Plato, repudiates as a dangerous form of drunkenness the indulgence in literature for its own sake; but, like Plato, he then proceeds, not simply to expound a useful morality, but himself to indulge in an art in which moralities are used as the motifs. It is partly on this account, certainly, that Bernard Shaw has been underrated as an artist. Whether people admire or dislike him, whether they find his plays didactically boring or morally stimulating, they fail to take account of the fact that it is the enchantment of a highly accomplished art which has brought them to and kept them in the playhouse. It is an art that has even had the power to preserve such pieces as *Getting Married*, of which the 1908 heresies already seemed out of date twenty or thirty years later but of which the symphonic development still remains brilliant and fresh. So far from being relentlessly didactic, Shaw's mind has reflected in all its complexity the intellectual life of his time; and his great achievement is to have reflected it with remarkable fidelity. He has *not* imposed a cogent system, but he has worked out a vivid picture. It is, to be sure, not a passive picture, like that of Santayana or Proust: it is a picture in which action plays a prominent part. But it does not play a consistent part: the dynamic principle in Shaw is made to animate a variety of forces.

> "Bernard Shaw at Eighty,"
> *The Triple Thinkers*

British Manners

I had never before fully grasped what was meant by "British rudeness." The point about it is that what we consider rudeness is their form of good manners. In other countries, manners are intended to diminish social friction, to show people consideration and to make them feel at ease. In England it is the other way: good breeding is something you exhibit by snubbing and scoring off people. This is of course closely connected with their class system, and it is partly a question of accent, vocabulary and general style, which your inferior cannot acquire. I have been told that, when a way of talking begins to pass into common use, the higher people evolve something new which will again fence them off from the lower. Certainly I heard interchanges in London of which I could hardly understand a word. But their competitiveness is also involved: it is a game to put your opponent at a disadvantage, and if you succeed in saying something blighting in a way which makes it impossible for him to retaliate without a loss of dignity more serious than that which he incurs by accepting it, you are considered to have won the encounter. You have the status of King of the Castle till somebody else comes to pull you down.

> "Notes on London at the
> End of the War,"
> *Europe without Baedeker*

Audubon and the American Scene

In the world of the early America just after the Revolution—loose settlements and pleasant towns growing up on the banks of great rivers, in the span of enormous landscapes and on the edge of mysterious wilds—it was occasionally possible for the arts to take seed and quietly to flower in a purer and freer form than was easy at a later date. In Albemarle County, Virginia, it is marvelous to see with how sure a touch Thomas Jefferson has situated his charming creations on the hospitable little hills in such a way as to involve the landscape in a personal work of art. The bubble domes, the candid façades, the variety of the classical cornices in the "pavilions" that enclose the university "lawn" and in which the professors live, the delightful white octagon rooms, with French windows that open on level vistas, have humanized the Palladian style into something eclectic and lovely; and the very imperfections of these buildings—the big clock at Monticello which has to be off-center in the portico in order to be centered in the hall, the slight irregularity of the number and spacing of the pillars in the college colonnade—only make them blend more pleasantly with nature.

So the marvelous plates of John James Audubon—the animals and birds of a continent—have come to life among the forests and wastes, the vast plains and the inland waterways, where their recently discovered originals had been living on equal terms with the Indians. The animating power of this artist is seen perhaps even better in his "quadrupeds" than in his birds. His larger animals—his bison and bears and bull moose—sometimes take him beyond his range, but his spermophiles and rodents and moles and other of the smaller animals—which do not exceed the scale of the birds but do not meet the artist halfway by providing so much gay color and obvious grace—are delightful illustrations of his genius for personalizing and dramatizing his subjects and, by the imaginative use of landscape, embodying them in balanced compositions: the black fox with his silver-sleek coat and the bright points of light in his alert yellow eyes; the magnificent striped plume of the mother skunk defending from the vantage of a hollow log her still groping babies inside it; the huge paws and topaz eyes of the staring Canadian lynx; the tusked snouts of Richardson's meadow mice pursuing their obstinate path through the gray bristling winter woodland; the cotton rats of the South, sleazy and blue-eyed poor whites, with their imbecile mouths agape, as, with a primitive log shack in the background, they feed on a prostrate yam; the violet rosettes of the star-nosed moles that delicately vibrate to their prey in the darkness of the burrows or streams where they hunt: a strange contrast with the free-skimming sails on the river in the distance behind them; the scampering family of Sciuridae in their apparently innumerable variety: the purposive snakelike black squirrel, the kittenlike downy squirrel, the pleased and admiring female of the Oregon flying squirrel, as, seated among the acorns, she watches her mate take off, the well-contained long-haired squirrel tenaciously clutching his nut among yellow-brown autumn leaves that harmonize with his belly's burnt-orange, the red-bellied squirrels with their plum-like blend of rose-orange and purple-gray, one prudently hugging its birch branch while the other, jauntily poised, stands up on its hind legs and leans forward, with forepaws flung wide, as if it saw something of special interest.

The stories and poems of Poe do not, of course, have much in common with this outdoor American world, and, yet they are also products of this early thinly-populated America. In those neighborly old-fashioned towns there were also close and lonely frame-houses in which isolated morbid relationships, under the influence of alcohol or laudanum, could give rise to visions and hallucinations that had as little relation to society as the animals and birds of Audubon. The vague background of velvet and silk, heavy portières and plush-covered furniture, remembered or longed-for grandeur, only serves to give sharper focus to those images, at once burning and cold— the pangs of horror or pain, bridled hatred or ingrown desire—which are excreted, in the provincial solitude, under pressure of the narrow rooms. And if these hard compulsive pieces of Poe's are thus crystallized like precious gems, the melodies of Stephen Foster flow as naturally as the dews of evening or the amber of maple sap. From the wistful lament of the slave, the jingle of the minstrel refrain, the romantic piano ballad with which the young ladies of that era were in the habit of charming their beaux, he condensed little drops of emotion that have never lost their freshness and felicity. (Here a trimming of barbershop chords which was added by Foster's "arrangers" sometimes figures as a period equivalent to Poe's rustling curtains and irrelevant plush.)

Now, Audubon and Foster and Poe were all of them to become very popular, yet they did not find much steady support in the loose-strewn communities among which they lived. Poe and Foster, though they found a certain market, were never able to make their earnings keep pace with their living expenses; both took to the bottle and died relatively young, wretchedly and almost anonymously. Audubon, closer to the earth and a scientist absorbed in his subject, lived to be sixty-nine, but he was so little broken to society that, on his visit to Scotland, his sponsors and friends had to make him shear off the primeval growth of his long and bad-smelling hair before they would let him go to London: "This day My Hairs were sacrificed," he wrote in his diary, "and the will of God usurped by the wishes of Man." Yet in their work all these artists had had more spontaneity than was usual with the accepted celebrities who followed them. There was in literature still something of this brightness and freshness in the poems and notebooks of Emerson, in the liquidities and densities of *Walden*, in the vividness of Melville's voyages; but all these writers inhabit the natural world—the countryside, the village, the open sea—and as the cities of the East expand, with their tightening reticulation of railroads, their landscape-annihilating factories, this quality comes to seem more and more a choked leak through the cracks of a hardening surface.

"The Poetry of the Civil War,"
Patriotic Gore

Russian Language and Culture

Though I personally like Russians extremely—sharing with them a certain indifference to the mechanical efficiency of the West as well as their intellectual appetite—and though I greatly admire their art, there are moments, nevertheless—after a prolonged immersion, say, in Mussorgsky's music or in one of the nineteenth century novelists—when I feel, like M. De Vogüé, a kind of disgust and revulsion. *Boris Godunov,* one of the greatest of operas, perhaps the greatest opera of its century—with its idiot, its sinister bells, its story of the bloodstained Tsar, demoralized by the threat of a claimant who is himself an audacious impostor, the barbaric palace: a prison of guilt, the horror that hangs over its nursery—in the end, it makes us want to refresh ourselves with the bell-clear melodies of Mozart or even with Wagner's heroics. And the swinish back-country of Gogol, full of overeaten landowners and overgrown orchards, wretched slaveys and maniacal masters; the old nests of gentlefolks of Turgenev, with their messiness of family relations and their herds of ill-treated serfs—one may be glad to get away to Jane Austen. Lenin, of course, declared war on all this, and the Communists have made efforts to clear it away. But they are Russians, and must work in the Russian tongue, with the habits and the mentality that have made it. Their language, so brilliantly expressive, so rich in vocabulary and idiom, so varied in verbal nuances, so wonderful for poetry and drama, is less suited to practical uses. In the hands of its great writers, it never becomes formal or dry: it lives wherever you touch it. Yet it is clumsy for the clear presentation of summarized data or logical analysis, for arguments, transactions, reports. How to construct a precision instrument out of the rank and tangled materials of one of those old Russian gardens—full of creepers and ferns and moss, where nothing has been pruned or trimmed, where the paths have not been smoothed with gravel, where the flower beds do not make patterns— which merge with a forest of birch-trees? And add to this unkempt, untended, this grammatically anarchical Russian tongue the jargon of German Marxism: no simile can cope with the situation! You have a medium that acts by itself as a block to communication, that itself makes an iron curtain.

"Russia,"
A Piece of My Mind

Literature and Politics

There are a great many different kinds of writing varying between what may be called long-range writing, on the one hand, and close-range writing, on the other. Long-range writing (in fiction) gives a comprehensive picture of human life over an extended period of time, as Dante or Balzac does, or gives pictures of human beings generalized from wide areas and periods (Sophocles, Shakespeare, etc.). The type of short-range writing is the editorial, the public speech, the advertisement. Now for long-range writing to be possible, it is necessary to have a more or less established society in which the writer will be able to get leisure and have firm enough ground to stand on so that he will be able to look around. Some periods (more or less stabilized periods) make this easier than others; but it is no use pretending that it does not always mean a considerable amount of struggle to extricate oneself from the demands of the social complex to which one belongs or that it does not involve a good deal of spiritual solitude. It will be the same under socialism and will be so for more generations than we are able to imagine. And there is no use pretending that periods of genuinely anarchic social upheaval promote anything but the shortest-range writing; where everybody is trying to save his skin, there is no chance for the necessary *recueillement*. The literature of the French Revolution was the oratory of Danton, the journalism of Camille Desmoulins, the Marseillaise, and the few poems on current events that André Chénier got a chance to write before they cut off his head. And what is true of practically everybody when a revolution is on is true in ordinary times of all the people who are writing for the immediate interests of a party or a group or a class. Of course, a writer may work sometimes on the long-range plane and other times write for immediate interests. The Dante who wrote the *Divine Comedy* in exile is something quite different from the Dante who was so active in politics in Florence. There is a lot about politics in the *Divine Comedy*, but Dante has treated himself and his adventures just as objectively as he has treated some historical political figure like Hugh Capet, merely as an actor in a larger drama. His real subject is a thousand years of Christendom, and the Dante who wrote the drama is the Dante who had become convinced, as he says, that the "honorable" thing to do was to "make a party by himself"—the party we all have to belong to when we are aiming at the kind of thing that Dante was aiming at. And the Shakespeare who wrote patriotic propaganda in *Henry V* and celebrated Queen Elizabeth in *Henry VIII* is something quite different from the Shakespeare who wrote the magnificent long-range political plays, *Coriolanus* and *Antony and Cleopatra*. (Swift, whom you mention, is a queer case. The bulk of his work looks like close-range writing, but he is really a long-range writer. His will to power was stronger than his interest in any cause. When he missed his advancement in London, where he had hoped to get an important preferment, he went back to Dublin with the utmost reluctance but so furious with the English court that he was driven to identify himself with the Irish. The passion behind his Irish pamphleteering is in a sense irrelevant to the subject: he did the Irish a good turn when he roused them to rebel against Wood's halfpence; but he was afterwards just as savage on what was really the reactionary side as soon as the interests of the clergy were threatened. His great work of this period was *Gulliver's Travels*, which is one of the longest-range books ever written.) The important thing is to know what kind of writing one is doing and to take the necessary steps to do it properly.

To John Dos Passos,
Letters on Literature and Politics

The Writer's Responsibility

The times, it is true. are confusing. It is not always easy to know what to do. But one thing that is certainly not worth doing is formulating theoretical positions. One has to make up one's mind in what capacity one is going to function. And from the moment one is not trying to function as an organizer or an active politician (and agitational literature is politics), one must work in good faith in one's own field. A conviction that is genuine will always come through—that is, if one's work is sound. You may say, This is no time for art or science: the enemy is at the gate! But in that case you should be at the gate: in the Spanish International Brigade, for example, rather than engaged in literary work. There is no sense in pursuing a literary career under the impression that one is operating a bombing-plane. On the one hand, imaginary bombs kill no actual enemies; and, on the other, the development of a war psychology prevents one's real work from having value. When you "relax the aesthetic and ethical standards," you abandon the discipline itself of your craft.

"Communist Criticism,"
The Shores of Light

WHY DO PEOPLE READ DETECTIVE STORIES?

For years I have been hearing about detective stories. Almost everybody I know seems to read them, and they have long conversations about them in which I am unable to take part. I am always being reminded that the most serious public figures of our time, from Woodrow Wilson to W. B. Yeats, have been addicts of this form of fiction. Now, except for a few stories by Chesterton, for which I did not much care, I have not read any detective stories since one of the earliest, if not the earliest, of the imitators of Sherlock Holmes—a writer named Jacques Futrelle, now dead, who invented a character called the Thinking Machine and published his first volume of stories about him in 1907. Enchanted though I had been with Sherlock Holmes, I got bored with the Thinking Machine and dropped him, beginning to feel, at the age of twelve, that I was outgrowing that form of literature.

Since, however, I have recently been sampling the various types of popular merchandise, I have decided that I ought to take a look at some specimens of this kind of fiction, which has grown so tremendously popular and which is now being produced on such a scale that the book departments of magazines have had to employ special editors to cope with it. To be sure of getting something above the average, I waited for new novels by writers who are particularly esteemed by connoisseurs. I started in with the latest volume of Rex Stout's Nero Wolfe stories: *Not Quite Dead Enough.*

What I found rather surprised me and discouraged my curiosity. Here was simply the old Sherlock Holmes formula reproduced with a fidelity even more complete than it had been by Jacques Futrelle almost forty years ago. Here was the incomparable private detective, ironic and ceremonious, with a superior mind and eccentric habits, addicted to overeating and orchid-raising, as Holmes had his enervated indulgence in his cocaine and his violin, yet always prepared to revive for prodigies of intellectual alertness; and here were the admiring stooge, adoring and slightly dense, and Inspector Lestrade of Scotland Yard, energetic but entirely at sea, under the new name of Inspector Cramer of Police Headquarters. Almost the only difference was that Nero Wolfe was fat and lethargic instead of lean and active like Holmes, and that he liked to make the villains commit suicide instead of handing them over to justice. But I rather enjoyed Wolfe himself, with his rich dinners and quiet evenings in his house in farthest West Thirty-fifth Street, where he savors an armchair sadism that is always accompanied by beer. The two stories that made up this new book—*Not Quite Dead Enough* and *Booby Trap*—I found rather disappointing; but, as they were both under the usual length and presented the great detective partly distracted from his regular profession by a rigorous course of training for the Army, I concluded that they might not be first-rate examples of what the author could do in this line and read also *The Nero Wolfe Omnibus*, which contains two earlier book-length stories: *The Red Box* and *The League of Frightened Men*. But neither did these supply the excitement I was hoping for. If the later stories were sketchy and skimpy, these seemed to have been somewhat padded, for they were full of long episodes that led nowhere and had no real business in the story. It was only when I looked up Sherlock Holmes that I realized how much Nero Wolfe was a dim and distant copy of an original. The old stories of Conan Doyle had a wit and a fairytale poetry of hansom cabs, gloomy London lodgings and lonely country estates that Rex Stout could hardly duplicate with his backgrounds of modern New York; and the surprises were much more entertaining: you at least got a room with a descending ceiling or a snake trained to climb down the bellrope, whereas with Nero Wolfe— though *The League of Frightened Men* makes use of a clever psychological idea—the solution of the mystery was not usually either fanciful or unexpected. I finally got to feel that I had to unpack large crates by swallowing the excelsior in order to find at the bottom a few bent and rusty nails, and I began to nurse a rankling conviction that detective stories in general are able to profit by an unfair advantage in the code which forbids the reviewer to give away the secret to the public—a custom which results in the concealment of the pointlessness of a good deal of this fiction and affords a protection to the authors which no other department of writing enjoys.

I have been told by the experts, however, that this endless carrying on of the Doyle tradition does not represent all or the best that has been done with the detective story during the decades of its proliferation. There has been also the puzzle mystery, and this, I was assured, had been brought to a high pitch of ingenuity in the stories of Agatha Christie. So I have read also the new Agatha Christie, *Death Comes as the End*, and I confess that I have been had by Mrs. Christie. I did not guess who the murderer was, I was incited to keep on and find out, and when I did finally find out, I was surprised. Yet I did not care for Agatha Christie and I hope never to read another of her books. I ought, perhaps, to discount the fact that *Death Comes as the End* is supposed to take place in Egypt two thousand years before Christ, so that the book has a flavor of Lloyd C. Douglas not, I understand, quite typical of the author. ("No more Khay in this world to sail on the Nile and catch fish and laugh up into the sun whilst she, stretched out in the boat with little Teti on her lap, laughed back at him"); but her writing is of a mawkishness and banality which seem to me literally impossible to read. You cannot *read* such a book, you run through it to see the problem worked out; and you cannot become interested in the characters, because they never can be allowed an existence of their own even in a flat two dimensions but have always to be contrived so that they can seem either reliable or sinister, depending on which quarter, at the moment, is to be baited for the reader's suspicion.

It is all like a sleight-of-hand trick, in which the magician diverts your attention from the awkward or irrelevant movements that conceal the manipulation of the cards, and it may mildly entertain and astonish you, as such a sleight-of-hand performance may. But in a performance like *Death Comes as the End*, the patter is a constant bore and the properties lack the elegance of playing cards.

ZUNI: SHÁLAKO

I started for the first night of the Shálako festival (December 16 this year), with a small party of other visitors, at about four in the afternoon. All cars going down the hill were stopped by the police and searched for liquor. This, I was later told, failed almost completely in its purpose, since the Zunis, by way of their grapevine, would send the word back to Gallup for their bootleggers to come in around the hills.

We arrived at the pueblo just in time for the advent of the Council of the Gods, a group in which the Shálakos are not included. A fording place of mud and stones had been built across the Zuni River, and the gods, coming down from a stone formation known as the White Rocks, made their entrance over it into the town. The young Fire God comes first—a boy in his early teens, his nude body painted black and spotted with red, yellow, white and blue, wearing a black spotted mask, like a helmet, that covers the whole of his head, and carrying a smoldering brand. We missed his arrival, however, and did not see him till later. The main procession, which was now approaching, produced an uncanny impression. First comes the high god of the festival, Sáyatasha, the Rain God of the North; and behind him his deputy, Hútutu, the Rain God of the South. Sáyatasha, in his mask, has what looks from a distance like a blank black-and-white Pierrot face, between a black banged wig and a black-and-white-striped ruff, and he is dressed in a white gown. He stalks pompously in a long slow stride, accompanied by a short sharp rattle, made by shaking a cluster of deer scapulae every time he puts down his foot. It is the rhythm of authority and dignity which is reserved for him alone and—like the music for Wotan in the *Ring*—accompanies him all through the ceremonies. As he comes closer, we make out his accoutrements. A long flat horn, in place of an ear, sticks out from the right side of his mask, like an upcurved turquoise pennon; it has a heavy black fringe on its underside and a white feather dangling at the end. This horn presages long life for the Zuni people; and the left eye, a long black streak prolonged through an outstanding wooden ear, also heavily fringed, invokes a special long life for the "people of one heart." The right eye, not extended beyond the face, is intended to threaten short life to those who practice witchcraft. Sáyatasha has a bow and arrows, and "prayer plumes"—that is, sticks with feathers attached that are supposed to give wings to the prayers. His follower Hútutu is much the same, except that he has two ears and no horn, and that his eyes are set in a single black stripe which stretches across his mask, and from the tip of one ear to that of the other. Each is followed by a Yámuhakto, or Wood Carrier, who comes to pray for the trees, so that the people may have firewood and beams for their houses. The masks of the Yámuhakto are turquoise and bell-glass-shaped, with expressionless holes for the eyes and mouth, and each of these masks is surmounted with an untrimmed black wig, a tuft of yellow macaw feathers, and a kind of long green wand, from which hang down toward the shoulders long tassels of many-colored yarns. The Yámuhakto are wearing white buckskin skirts, and the naked upper parts of their bodies are painted a kind of purple and festooned with great garlands of beads. They carry deer antlers and bunches of feathers. All four of these principal divinities are wearing enormous round collars—shaped like life preservers and striped black-on-white like peppermints—that extend far beyond their faces and conceal the joint made by the mask. The two whippers, the Sálimopiya, come last, carrying yucca switches. Both have bell-glass-shaped masks, noses like long pipes, eyeholes that are connected like spectacles, yellow topknots of feathers that stick out behind like weather vanes, and huge ruffs of black raven feathers. Both are nude except for a loincloth and wear spruce wreaths on wrists and ankles; but they are decorated in different ways: one, the Warrior of the Zenith, has a mask that is checkered in bright squares of color, with much yellow and red, which represents a spectrum of the midday sun, and red sunbursts where the ears would be. The other, the Warrior of the Nadir, is wearing a black mask with blue eyes and a blue snout.

All these figures proceed at a rhythm that is set by Sáyatasha's rattle, but involves at least three different gaits. Hútutu paces at a shorter stride then Sáyatasha, and the Sálimopiyas move with a quicker, a running step. All the time one hears a soft lively whistling that resembles the calling of birds. One cannot tell which of the figures is making these sounds, because one cannot see their faces; and, arising from no visible human source, scanning no human chant, yet filling the quiet air, the song seems the genuine voice of deities that are part of Nature. So they pass, while the people wait in silence, across the little dwindled river, where a dead dog lies on the bank and old tin cans and paper boxes have been caught here and there on the mud flats; they march up between the rude corrals, in one of which a big sow is grunting.

The Council now blesses the village, proceeding to six different points, where small holes have been dug in the ground. The people come out of the houses and sprinkle the divinities with sacred meal, and the Council, at every excavation, plants prayer plumes and sprinkles meal and performs some solemn maneuvers. Sáyatasha and Hútutu, each with his Yámuhakto, make two units that parade back and forth, while the Sálimopiya mark time, never slackening their running pace but turning around in one spot. The climax of the ceremony comes when Sáyatasha and Hútutu walk up to one another and stop. Sáyatasha cries "Hu-u-u," and his vis-à-vis answers "Hu-tu-tu. Hu-tu-tu." The livelier calls, one decides, must be made by the Sálimopiya, since they seem to match the brisker tempo. It is evident that all these calls have been imitated directly from bird-cries—one remembers the expertness at this of Fenimore Cooper's Indians—bird-cries, perhaps, heard at dusk or at night and attributed to elemental beings.

Though owls, with the Indians, have a bad reputation, being usually connected with witchcraft, Hútutu is obviously an owl. I assumed at first that the voices were whistles in the snouts of the Sálimopiyas, but learned that they were produced by the throat and lips. I was told of a conversation in English in which one Zuni had said to another, "Gee, you make that noise good!" At one year's Shálako, Miss Bunzel says, the Sálimopiyas were severely criticized for not being sufficiently handsome, for not showing sufficient animation, and for not giving loud enough calls. Yet the whistling is never shrill, it is always under perfect control; and the confrontation of Sáyatasha and Hútutu is performed with an unearthly impressiveness. At last, with much ceremonial, they enter the house prepared for them—it has a cozy, brand-new, suburban look. Though we whites have been behaving with discretion, the Indians are afraid we may go too close and warn us to keep our distance.

In the meantime, the six Shálakos, the guests of honor, have been sitting out in front of a cabin, in which the actors put on their costumes, in a field back of one of the trading posts. These creatures are gigantic birds, the messengers of the rain gods, which, erect, stand ten or twelve feet tall. They have cylindrical turquoise faces with protruding eyes that roll up and down, long wooden beaks that snap, and upcurving tapering turquoise horns on either side of their heads. They wear big ruffs of raven feathers, black banged wigs and towering fan-shaped crests of black-and-white eagle tail-feathers. But their entrance into the village is arranged to take place just at the moment when twilight is falling, and one can now see them only dimly as, proceeding in single file and escorted by men in black blankets, they make their way to the river and, with a rhythmic jingle of bells fastened around their ankles, come slowly across the ford. The dark is blotting them out at the moment they arrive on the hither side; they squat in a row of six on the road by which the Council came. Now, with night, it grows very cold. The visitors hang around for a time—there is a group of young men and women, anthropological students from the University of New Mexico—afraid to ask the Zunis what is going to happen next or when it is going to happen. We lean on the egg-shaped ovens, and one of the girls gets a present of a loaf of white Zuni bread, made from sour dough, which she breaks up and offers around: it is still warm and tastes delicious. But the last orange-yellow light has faded out of the sky to our left, and still the birds do not move. The Zunis have gone indoors, and the whites drift away, too. Only the Indian Agent and I remain.

An hour and a half pass. We walk up and down to un-freeze our feet. The Shálakos utter from time to time a single reiterated bird-note, which sounds as if it came, not from close at hand, but from the other side of the river; and at intervals they clack their beaks—which we can hear with remarkable distinctness—not at random, but one at a time, like counting-off in the army. At one point, while they are making this sound, the bell in one of the churches, with a strange irrelevance, begins to ring. The men, wrapped in black blankets, go back and forth silently with flashlights, which are never allowed to play on the birds. They are only revealed now and then for a second by the swerve of an occasional Zuni car. An airplane passes above us, winking green and red. The Indians begin to emerge and line up along the road; we assume that the show is starting, but we still have a long time to wait. At last, with other blanket-swathed figures, a group of twelve men arrives, jingling bells on their ankles; surprisingly, they seem costumed like characters in a production of *Romeo and Juliet.* These are the Shálako impersonators. (The birds, during the interval of waiting, have apparently been worked by "managers," who ac-company and supervise them.) For each bird there are two dancers, who will alternate through the night. These twelve dancers, appointed a year ago, have been in training for their work ever since. Their roles, which bring much prestige, are exacting and responsible ones. Besides learning the difficult dances and memorizing endless speeches, they have had to build the Shálako houses. Though they begin by impersonating the gods, these latter, the night of the festival, will actually enter into them, and the men, with their masks, become sacred objects. If anyone touches a Shálako, or if the Shálako stumbles or falls—as it seems one of them did last year—the dancer is supposed to be struck dead by the god. A mistake on the part of the impersonator means either that someone has seen his mask while it was still in the dressing room and has not been whipped for impiety or that he himself has been making love to somebody else's wife and is unworthy to play the role. When a disaster of this kind occurs, the crowd must at once go away: the Sálimopiya drive them off with whips. The dancer, of course, does not actually die, but his family go into mourning and behave as if he had. And though the Shálako actor must pull the cords that control the beak and the eyes, he is never—on pain of instant death—allowed to look up toward the top of the mask to watch the mystery in operation. Nobody except the manager may understand the Shálako's mechanics. These, then, were the dancers whom we now heard returning from six different points of the pueblo. We counted the jingling groups till the sixth had disappeared in the shadow where the birds were sitting.

Then suddenly, at some signal, a chorus of voices was raised. The Shálakos were on their feet. They came up from the road to the river and filed past us with their escort and choir; and the effect of this was thrilling and lovely in a way that it would be hard to imagine. The great birds, not rigidly erect but bent forward with the dignity of their kingly crests and their beardlike feathery ruffs, as if they were intent on their errand and knew each its destination, did not, in the frosty night, the pale moonlight and the window lamplight, appear in the least comic, as they had in the pictures that one had seen; they hardly seemed even grotesque. And the welcoming hymns that accompanied them, in a harmony one did not understand but with the voices intertangled and singing against one another, had a beauty one could not have expected— not wild but both solemn and joyful—not entirely unlike our own anthems. Each of the Shálako birds is brought to the house prepared for it, and when it has come, it kneels down in front of the door, while prayer meal is sprinkled before it. The warm yellow light from inside gives comfort and life in the winter dark. The chants of reception are sung, and the bird, curt and proud in acceptance, snaps its beak in response to the welcome. Then the Shálako goes into the house and takes its seat before a turquoise altar. The impersonator comes out from inside, while a blanket is held up to screen him, and he and his alternate make offerings of seeds. Then they take seats beside the host, who hands them a cigarette, which he and they pass back and forth as they smoke it. The host addresses as "Father!" that one of the impersonators who is supposed to speak for the Shálako, and the latter replies, "Son!" They exchange other terms of relationship; then the host asks it, "How have you prayed for us? If you will tell us that, we shall be very glad to know it."

"I have come," says the Shálako, "from the sacred lake, and I have come by all the springs." He enumerates all the springs that the Zunis in their wanderings passed, when they were looking for a site for their town. "I have come to see my people. For many years I have heard of my people living here at Ítiwana [the Middle], and for long I have wanted to come. I want them to be happy, and I have been praying for them; and especially I want the women to be fortunate with their babies. I bring my people all kinds of seeds, all the different kinds of corn, and all the different kinds of fruit and wild green things. I have been praying for my people to have long life; and whoever has an evil heart should stand up in the daylight. I have been praying that my people may have all different kinds of seeds and that their rooms may be full of corn of all colors and beans of all colors and pumpkins and water gourds, and that they may have plenty of fresh water, so that they may look well and be healthy because of the pumpkins and the beans and the corn. I want to see them healthy. . . . Yes, I have worked hard and prayed for all my people. I do not want any of the roots to rot. I do not want anyone to sicken and die, but I want everyone to stand up firmly on his feet all year. This is how I have prayed for you."

The first Shálako house I visited, when, later, the dancing began, made upon me a tremendous impression. The rooms where the dances are held are dazzling with electric light and blazing with decorations. The walls are completely covered with brilliant blankets and shawls, pale buckskins and queer blue or green hangings, made by the Navahos, on which square-headed elongated figures represent the Navaho gods. At one end of the room is a turquoise altar, ornamented with eagle feathers. A group of fetishistic animals, carved from stone, is set out in a row before it. In the audience, most of the men, having discarded their modern clothes, are wrapped in their best black blankets, and the women wear over their heads their best green or red or flowered shawls, and sometimes a kind of black apron, made of silk with fancy designs.

Against this background and before this audience, a Shálako and his alternate are dancing, balancing one another in a bizarre moving composition that seems to fill and charge the whole room. The unmasked dancer here is putting on such an extraordinary performance that he distracts attention from the bird. His costume has a suggestion of the Renaissance that may have been derived from the Spaniards. He wears a tight-fitting white buckskin cap with a curtain that hangs down behind, like the headwear of Giotto's Dante, and a fillet of red ribbon with silver bells. His black shirt is trimmed at the shoulders and sleeves with ribbons of many colors; his black kilts are embroidered in blue and circled with embroidered sashes.

His knees are painted red, and the lower part of his legs is yellow, and he has tassels of blue yarn tied below the knees. With his brown bare feet he treads up and down— at a rate, as one observer has calculated, of about four times as many steps a minute as a marathon runner takes—in a quick, sharp, unflagging rhythm. This rhythm is also marked with a pointed yucca wand held before him in the right hand at an unwavering phallic angle. His eyelids are dropped, his eyes seem closed; the firm line of his mouth is drawn down—as if, in dedicating himself to his role, he has achieved a solemn sublimation and is shut off from the rest of the world. His whole demeanor is perfectly disciplined as he slowly moves thus back and forth from one end of the room to the other. And the Shálako, towering above him, actually seems lighter than he and dancing to an easier rhythm, as it turns in place or marks time or—astonishing in its swiftness and grace—swoops the length of the floor in a birdlike flight, never butting into the wall or ceiling and never so much as brushing the spectators, who sit close on either side.

These spectators rarely move, they are receptive, quiet and calm; and the white visitor, too, becomes rapt. He, too, feels the thrill and the awe at the elemental power summoned. It seems as if the dancer, by his pounding, were really generating energy for the Zunis; by his discipline, strengthening their fortitude; by his endurance, guaranteeing their permanence. These people who sit here in silence, without ever applauding or commenting, are sustained and invigorated by watching this. It makes the high point of their year, at which the moral standard is set. If the Zunis can still perform the Shálako dances, keeping it up all night, with one or other of the performers always dancing and sometimes both dancing at once, they know that their honor and their stamina, their favor with the gods, are unimpaired. The whole complicated society of Zuni in some sense depends on this dance. Our ideas of energy and power have tended to become, in the modern world, identified with the natural forces—electricity, combustion, etc.—which we manipulate mechanically for our benefit, and it is startling to see human energy invoked and adored as a force that is at once conceived as a loan from the non-human natural forces and as a rival pitted against them; or rather, to put it in terms that are closer to the Zuni point of view, to see all the life of the animal world and the power of the natural elements made continuous with human vitality and endowed with semi-human form.

Here, too, one finds theater and worship before they have become dissociated, and the spectacle suggests comparisons in the fields of both religion and art. In the theatrical connection, it seems curious at first to be reminded of the Russian ballet, but the reason soon becomes quite plain. It must have been true that Dyághilev brought into the conventional ballet, with its formal routines and patterns, something that was genuinely primitive. He had really opened the way for an infusion of old Russia—by giving new life to the music of Rimsky and Borodín, who had already returned to folk material; through the Mongolian wildness of Nizhínsky; through the barbaric splendors of Bakst; through the atavistic stridencies and iterative beat of the Stravinsky of *Le Sacre du Printemps*. The kind of thing one sees in the Shálako dance must be something like the kind of thing that was revived by the Russian ballet—not brought to the point of refinement to which Dyághilev was able to carry it, but, in its color and variety and style, in the thoroughness of the training involved and the scrupulous care for detail, a great deal more accomplished and calculated than one could easily conceive without seeing it. In the other, the religious, connection, one comes quite to understand the student of comparative religions quoted by Erna Fergusson, who said that it was "no wonder missionaries have had no luck in converting these people to Christianity. It will never be done. The essential mental rhythm of the two races is too far apart. You could imagine reducing that Shálako figure two feet or even four; you could not possibly turn it into Christ on the Cross." The difficulty, one sees, would be to induce the flourishing Zunis—who have maintained their community for centuries, as sound and as tough as a nut, by a religion that is also a festive art—to interest themselves in a religion that has its origin in poverty and anguish. The Zunis, moreover, have no sense of sin; they do not feel that they need to be pardoned. What the Shálako bird brings is not pardon, but good cheer and fecundity. It is formidable; the children hide from it the day it comes into town, and if anybody falls asleep, it leans over and wakes him by snapping its beak. But the great bird loves the people, and the people love the bird. They build a house for it and spread it a feast, and it dances before them all night to show them its satisfaction.

In each of the other two Shálako houses, two Shálakos were dancing together, occasionally assisted by Mudheads. At one place, where I looked in through a window, I saw people holding a blanket while the Shálako sat down in a corner, and the alternate changed places with the weary man who had just been performing his role. In the house of Sáyatasha, the Council of the Gods, with their masks off, were performing stately evolutions, accompanied by the adolescent Fire God, who—slim and handsome in his speckled nudity—danced with the dropped eyelids and resolute lips of the Shálako impersonator. But the great success of the evening was a Shálako who danced alone. It was marvelous what this dancer could do, as he balanced his huge bird-body. He would slowly pavane across the floor; he would pirouette and teeter; he would glide in one flight the whole length of the room as smoothly as a bird alighting. The masks are constructed like crinolines; there are hoops sewn inside a long cylinder that diminishes toward the top; and the whole thing hangs from a slender pole attached to the dancer's belt. So the movements are never stiff. The Shálakos, ungainly though they may seem at first when one watches them from afar by daylight, are created in the dance as live beings; and this one was animated from top to toe, vibrating as if with excitement—gleaming with its turquoise face, flashing its white embroidered skirt, while its fox-skins flapped like wings at the shoulders. The dance conveyed both delicacy and ecstasy, and the music—produced by a small group of men who sat, as if in a huddle, facing one another, as they chanted, beat a drum and shook rattles—exercised a peculiar enchantment. There are many different songs for the dances, and they vary in mood and pace; but each consists of a single theme repeated over and over, with a rest after so many bars and occasional changes in tempo, which momentarily relieve the dancer. In this case, the recurrent lapses—during which the Shálako, poised for flight, marked time and snapped his beak at the end of his room-long runway—would be followed by brisk pickings-up, when the bird would skim across the floor; and this reprise always had about it an element of the miraculous, of the miracle of the inexhaustible energy, leaping up after every subsidence with the same self-assertive joy. Carried along by the rhythm yourself, alternately let down and lulled, then awakened and stimulated, in a sequence that never faltered, you were held by a kind of spell. The great blue-and-white creature irresistibly took on for you, too, an extra-human personality, became a thing you could not help watching, a principle of bounding and soaring life that you could not help venerating. A white woman who had once seen the dance told me that it had given her a shudder and thrill, in her chair at the end of the room, to feel the eaglelike bird swooping down on her. And I found that it was only with effort that I, too, could withstand its hypnotic effect. I had finally to take myself in hand in order to turn my attention and to direct myself out of the house. For something in me began to fight the Shálako, to reject and repulse its influence just at the moment when it was most compelling. One did not want to rejoin the Zunis in their primitive Nature cult; and it was hardly worth while for a Protestant to have stripped off the mummeries of Rome in order to fall a victim to an agile young man in a ten-foot mask.

Yet the effect of it lingered and haunted me even after I was back in my guest-house. Kept wakeful as I was with coffee, the monotonously repetitive music, the indefatigable glowing bird that had dominated the crowded room, drawn toward it all upward-turned eyes, suspended in a trance all wills, stayed with me and continued to trouble me. I was glad to find a letter in my room which recalled me to my own urban world and which annoyed me, when I read it, so much that I was distracted from the vision of the Shálako.

[1947]

ON FIRST READING GENESIS

I discovered a few years ago, in going through the attic of my mother's house, an old Hebrew Bible that had belonged to my grandfather, a Presbyterian minister, as well as a Hebrew dictionary and a Hebrew grammar. I had always had a certain curiosity about Hebrew, and I was perhaps piqued a little at the thought that my grandfather could read something that I couldn't, so, finding myself one autumn in Princeton, with the prospect of spending the winter, I enrolled in a Hebrew course at the Theological Seminary, from which my grandfather had graduated in 1846. I have thus acquired a smattering that has enabled me to work through Genesis, with constant reference to the English translation and the notes of the Westminster Commentaries, and this first acquaintance with the Hebrew text has, in several ways, been to me a revelation. In the first place, the study of a Semitic language gives one insights into a whole point of view, a system of mental habits, that differs radically from those of the West. But, besides this, I had never read Genesis before. In college I had taken the second half year of a course in Old Testament literature, so I did have some familiarity with the prophets and the later phases of Biblical history, but the Pentateuch and the earlier historical books were known to me only in patches or through simplified versions of Bible stories that had been read to me when I was a child. I came to them in the original for the first time rather late in life, when I had already read many other books, and since such an experience is probably rare— Hebrew being studied mainly by Christian seminarists and orthodox Jews, both of whom come to it early and with definite religious predispositions—I am going to give a report on it. I am myself neither a Jew nor a Christian, and I propose to disregard, in doing so, the little I know of the tons of theological commentary that have been written by the various churches. I do not propose to take for granted—as, from recent conversations on this subject with even well-educated people, I conclude I am warranted in not doing—that the reader is any better acquainted with even the most famous Bible stories than I was when I recently began to explore them.

First of all, the surprises of the language. The Bible in Hebrew is far more a different thing from the Bible in any translation than the original Homer, say, is from the best of the translations of Homer, because the language in which it is written is more different from English than Greek is. To speak merely from the point of view of style, the writing of the earliest books is a good deal tighter and tougher—Renan calls it a twisted cable—than is easy to imitate with the relatively loose weave of English. It is also much more poetic, or, rather, perhaps—since the King James Version does partly take care of this with its seventeenth-century rhythms—poetic in a more primitive way. Certain passages are composed in a kind of verse, and even the prose has a metrical basis. The first verse of Genesis, for instance, almost corresponds to a classical hexameter, and we soon feel we are reading an epic or a saga or something of the sort. The progress of the chronicle is interspersed with old prophecies and fragments of ballads that have evidently been handed down by word of mouth and that stand out from the background of the narrative by reason of their oracular obscurity and their "parallelistic" form. There are many plays on words and jingles that disappear in our solemn translations, and the language itself is extremely expressive, full of onomatopoetic effects. The word for "to laugh" is *tsakháq* ("kh" as in "Chekhov"), and thus Isaac is called Isaac (*Yitskháq*) because Sarah, in her delightful scene with God, cannot refrain from laughing when He tells her she shall yet bear a child; a light rain is called *matár*, a heavier downpour *géshem* (it was a *géshem* that caused the Deluge). The words for the emotions are likely to come from the physical states that accompany them. The verbs for "to love" and "to hate" are both based on heavy breathing: *aháv* and *ayáv*. Patience and impatience are rendered as the taking of long or short breaths.

The Hebrew language is also emphatic to a degree with which our language can hardly compete. The device for affirming something strongly is to repeat the important word, and God's warning to Adam that he will "dying, die," if he disobeys His orders, seems weakened in our verison—"thou shalt surely die"—as does Joseph's assertion that "stolen, I was stolen out of the land of the Hebrews" by "indeed I was stolen." Nor can we match the vehement expression of the violent Hebrew emotions. When Jehovah, about to invoke the Flood, has become disgusted with man, it is not adequate to say that the thoughts of man's heart were "only evil continually"; in the *"raq ra kol hayyóm"* of the text, we seem to hear the Creator actually spitting on his unworthy creation. "And Isaac trembled very exceedingly" is the rendering of the King James Version of the passage in which Isaac discovers that Jacob has deceived him, which falls short of "Isaac trembled mightily a great trembling," and in the next verse we read that Esau "cried mightily a great and bitter cry." This violence and vehemence of the Hebrews is implicit in the structure of the language itself. They did not conjugate their verbs for tenses, as the modern Western languages do, since our modern conception of time was something at which they had not yet arrived—a significant feature of the language that I want, in a later section of this essay, to discuss by itself at length. What the Hebrews had instead of tenses were two fundamental conjugations for perfect and imperfect—that is, for action completed and action uncompleted. And both of these two "aspects" theoretically exist in seven variations for every verb (though actually the complete set is rare) that have nothing to do with time. The primary form of the verb is known as the "light" or simple form, and the second is the passive of this. So much seems plain enough sailing, but what follow are three intensive forms—active, passive and reflexive—and two causatives—active and passive.

These verbs, which take little account of time, are the instruments, then, of a people who, at the period when this language was formed, must have been both passionate and energetic. It is not a question of *when* something happens, but whether the thing is completed or certain to be completed. There are special forms, the causatives, for getting things done: "I will multiply your descendants," "They made Joseph take off his coat." The intensives are unexpected to the non-Semitic reader, who has difficulty in getting the hang of them, but feels a dynamic element in the very bone of the language, and soon begins to find them fascinating. The translator of these strange verb forms, which double the middle consonant and vary the pattern of vowels, is obliged to resort to an adverb or a stronger verb. The intensive form of one of the words for "to kill," the paradigm verb that the student learns, is given in the grammars as "kill brutally." So you have "break" and "break to pieces," "grow" and "grow luxuriantly." A curious example, which occurs in Genesis 24:21, illustrates the problems of translators. When the emissary of Abraham meets Rebecca at the well and watches her attentively in silence, to see whether she will behave in the way by which he has proposed to God that the wife appointed for Isaac may be made to reveal herself, a verb that means "to look at" is put in the intensive form. The old Revised Version made it "And the man looked steadfastly on her"; the new Revised Version has it "gazed at her"—the first of these, that is, adds an adverb, the second tries to find an appropriate verb, and the nuances conveyed are different.

These intensives are sometimes baffling. It is not always easy to see what is implied in a given context. The forms may, in certain cases, turn intransitive into transitive verbs; the intensive of "to learn" may mean "to teach," or indicate multiplicity or frequency. The student soon finds himself groping amid modes of being and acting that cannot be accommodated to our Western categories, and of which the simplified descriptions supplied by his beginner's grammar do not really give him much grasp. The intensive reflexive, for example, has uses that are puzzling to render or even to understand. It seems to imply behavior that ranges from what Henry James, borrowing from the French, meant by "abounding in one's own sense" to what we mean by "throwing one's weight around." When Enoch or Noah "walks with God," he does so in this form of the verb "to walk," and nobody has ever known how to render it. Yet one gets from the Hebrew original the impression that the walking of these patriarchs was of a very special kind, that it had the effect of making them both more important and more highly charged. This expression, in the Old Testament, says Dr. John Skinner, the author of the volume on Genesis in the International Critical Commentary series, in general "signifies intimate companionship, and here denotes a fellowship with God morally and religiously perfect. . . . We shall see, however, that originally it included the idea of initiation into divine mysteries." I have looked Enoch up in a number of translations, and the only attempts I have found to give the verb form its special force are in the independent modern translations by James Moffatt and Monsignor Knox, the former of whom says that Enoch "lived close to God," the latter that he was "the close friend of God." The flaming sword set by God at the gate of the Garden of Eden is made to "turn" in the intensive reflexive, and the English translations, from the King James Version to the Revised Standard Version, render this as "turned every way." I imagine something a little more spectacular. Gesenius's standard lexicon seems to bear me out in suggesting "brandished, glittering." Yet as soon as you are beginning to pride yourself on seizing the force of the intensive reflexive, you are pulled up by finding that this variation of the verb that means "to shave" implies, in the hygienic prescriptions of Leviticus, nothing more interesting than "to shave oneself" or "to get oneself shaved."

When Abraham, foreseeing that the beauty of Sarah will cause Pharaoh to want her for his harem, has passed her off as his sister, in order that Pharaoh may not be impelled to put him out of the way, and when Pharaoh, afflicted by God for a sin he has committed unknowingly, learns at last what is causing the trouble and sends Abraham about his business, he says, "Here is your wife. Take her and go!" We are amused, when we first read this incident, to find "send" in the intensive form and to hear the brusque snap of *"qakh valékh!"* Yet we later on find that these words are more or less a conventional formula that does not necessarily imply irritation and that "send" in the intensive occurs when the sending is not necessarily ejective. There is something, we become aware, peremptory in the language itself. You have drawn-out "cohortative" forms that express, for the first person, exhortation, strong intention or earnest entreaty, along with clipped jussive forms for other people or things, as when God says, "Let this or that happen." The whole language is intensely purposeful, full of the determination to survive by force or by wit, to accomplish certain objectives, to lay down laws that will stabilize life and ensure its perpetuation, to fix the future by postive prophecies.

As this will of the ancient Hebrew finds expression in the dynamic verb forms, so the perdurability of the people is manifested in what may be called the physical aspects of the language. The prime unit of Hebrew is a group of three consonants. Nearly every verb consists of such a trinity. The values may be modified—the consonant may be doubled or be altered to a kindred sound, as "f" to "p," "v" to "b"—by a dot written inside the letter, and the intervening vowels may be indicated by a system of dots and dashes written above and below, but they were not so originally written and are not—except in poetry and in a single daily paper—so written today in Israel. The Hebrew alphabet thus differs from our alphabet in not including characters for the vowels, or even, in every case, different characters for kindred consonantal sounds. It is a system of twenty-two integers, a set of unsupplantable blocks, and each Hebrew word makes a shell into which a varying content of vowel sounds may be poured. The verbs are modified by prefixes and endings, and some of the conjugations take prefixes, but, to a Westerner, the most striking feature of the Hebrew conjugations is the way in which a shift of meaning (from active to passive, for example) is effected by a vowel change inside this consonantal shell—the kind of thing that we do on a lesser scale in inflecting our so-called strong verbs: e.g., "sing, sang, sung." We may put in an "o" for the noun and get "song," and the Jews, too, can use the same shell, with a different vowel content, for a noun. What impresses is the hardness of this shell.

Our first look at the text of the Bible, when we have mastered the alphabet, is likely to give us the feeling that this system is extremely impractical. It requires what must seem to the beginner an annoying and easily avoidable effort to coordinate with the heavy consonants the elusive little dashes and dots that hover about them like midges, especially since two of the former are not consonants in our sense at all but gutterals, no longer pronounced, which have to be regarded as blanks and read with the sounds of the vowels that are indicated above or below them. Even the printing of these signs is difficult, impossible for a linotype machine, since they appear in innumerable combinations. The result is that, even in learned books, the consonants are, if possible, written without "pointings," and what you get is a kind of shorthand. You must already know the words extremely well in order to be able to recognize them. Yet some further acquaintance induces respect, and a perception that this method is appropriate, an inalienable element of the Jewish tradition. The characters themselves are impressive—not so fluent as the Roman and Greek, and retaining even more than these the look of having been once cut in stone.* To write out Hebrew vocabulary, with black ink and a stub pen, affords a satisfaction that may give one a faint idea of the pleasures of Chinese calligraphy, as well as a feeling of vicarious authority as one traces the portentous syllables. One remembers the hand of Jehovah writing on Belshazzar's wall (though He had to write Aramaic in order to be understood by that alien and uninstructed king). These twenty-two signs that Moses was believed to have brought back from Egypt graven on the Tables of the Law, and from which, in their early Phoenician form, all our European alphabets have been derived, have, austere in their vowelless terseness, been steadily proceeding from right to left, over a period of two thousand years, among people that read from left to right; and in the Bible they take on an aspect exalted and somewhat mysterious: the square letters holding their course, with no capitals for proper names and no punctuation save the firm double diamond that marks the end of a verse, compact in form as in meaning, stamped on the page like a woodcut, solid verse linked to solid verse with the ever recurrent "and,"

---

* The movement from right to left is supposed to have been determined by the engraver's having held the chisel in his left hand and the hammer in his right, and thus naturally having worked from the right.

the sound of which is modulated by changes of vowel, while above and below them a dance of accents shows the pattern of the metrical structure and the rise and fall of the chanting, and, above and below, inside and out, the vowel pointings hang like motes, as if they were the molecules the consonants breathed. Difficult for the foreigner to penetrate and completely indifferent to this, they have withstood even the drive toward assimilation—to their Spanish and Germanic neighbors—of the Jews of the Middle Ages; and in the dialect of German that is Yiddish, in newspapers spread in the subway, they still march in the direction opposite to that of all the other subway newspapers, English or Spanish or Italian, Hungarian or Russian or Greek, with only a light sprinkling of points to indicate Germanic vowels. And we have seen them reassemble in Israel, reconstituting their proper language— not embarrassed in the least by the fear that the newspaper reader of our century, even knowing Hebrew perfectly, may have difficulty in distinguishing, in the British reports, a vowelless Bevan from a vowelless Bevin. They march on through our modern events as if they were invulnerable, eternal.

[1952]

JERUSALEM THE GOLDEN

Waked up every morning early by the bright, firm and even light, looking out on translucent clouds that hung in a pellucid heaven, far below which Mount Zion, a modest mound in the bosom of the high barren hills, just outside the walls of the ancient city, was crowned with the diadem of its monastery. I grew to be fond of Jerusalem, of which much of the attraction resides in its combining luminosity with bareness. This is said to be the best time of the year—late March and early April: the steep and yet rounded hills, studded with little gray boulders, striated with narrow ledges, are now freshened for a brief time with green, and in the country, where the mixed flocks of goats and sheep graze on the fenceless slopes, there is a sprinkling of wild red poppies and little yellow daisies. In a few weeks, they tell me, the landscape becomes parched, with only the deep-green oases created by irrigation. It is a mild and monotonous country, and this is what is unexpected. Did the Prophets, in their gloom of foreboding, flash their lightning of conviction from these quiet hills, where everything is open to the sky? Were the savage wars of Scripture fought here? Did its paeans first sound from these pastures? The prejudice of the Jews against images may be partly explained by these contours which do not suggest shapes, by these colors which do not compose pictures. The little old villages of the Arabs were almost like boulders themselves; Stephen Spender has truly said of them that they fit into the mountainsides like teeth in a jawbone. The new settlements of the Israelis are equally unostentatious—neat groupings of low white houses that give an effect of ease; I saw one with pale pink roofs that was charming. Modern Israel, on the whole, has kept to the old Jewish severity. There are no pictures in orthodox homes, and the pictures in other houses, even where the books are good, are likely to be not well chosen. It is strange to reflect that from here came those legends that inspired so much of the art of the Renaissance, all that blazing of color, that teeming of flesh—Pharaoh's daughter in her gorgeous silks, surrounded by the ladies of an Italian court, as she comes upon Moses in the bulrushes; the rippling and wistful Botticellian Judith, exhaling a delicate charm after cutting off the head of Holofernes; the beautiful blue madonnas, the heaven-cracking crucifixions; Michelangelo's romantic Moses, his full-bodied Adams and Davids; all the coffers of the Roman churches overflowing with jewels and fabrics, all the Florentine miles of paint. How very unlikely it seems that they sprouted from the history of these calm little hills, dotted with stones and flocks, under pale and transparent skies.

The emotion and the drama of the Bible not only no longer seem present in Palestine; they have left no real monuments behind them. The Acropolis and the Forum are still there to see, but Solomon's Temple and Palace are not. It is only that the site of Jerusalem has in itself an arresting grandeur. No great city of Europe stands so high, and it is wonderful and almost terrifying to look out on the valley of Kidron and across at the opposite hillside littered with the tombs attributed to Absalom and other ancients as well as with the stones of a cemetery of modern Jewish graves which the Arabs have thrown on their faces, or to gaze up the precipitous slope at the wall that still circles the city. But of Jewish pre-Christian Jerusalem, little today survives; the fragment of wall to which the Jews used to come to weep for their lost kingdom, the tombs of the Sanhedrin in the hillside, with their high and imposing façades and their narrow rectangular doors, designed to make looting difficult, that give glimpses of large square chambers, plundered long ago and empty now. The foundations of the present old wall are supposed to have been laid by Herod, but the rest of it was probably built by the Byzantines and Suleiman the Magnificent. If the wide paved expanse of the sanctuary in which the Mosque of Omar stands on what has always been accepted as the site of the Temple was actually laid out by Herod, it was done under the influence of the Romans. Below it lies the only construction that impresses like those of Rome: the great pillared subterranean vaults that are known as Solomon's Stables. Here the Jews took refuge from Titus, come to destroy their Temple; here, more than a thousand years later, come to rescue the Holy Sepulcher, the Knights Templar put up their horses. One can see their hitching holes in the columns. These grim and enormous piers that stretch away in endless long rows, lit only by one set of windows, on the side that forms part of the precipice, make a kind of gray underground forest that is dreadful and troubling today, with its air of an abode of power that no power has permanently possessed or has stamped with its peculiar identity, neither Herod nor Rome nor Christendom. But, for the rest, what could be less suggestive than those dreary grottoes and caves and rocks, sheltered mostly by rubbishy churches, that are shown you as Calvary, the Sepulcher, the place of the Annunciation, the house of Jesus at Nazareth, the Fountain of the Virgin, the Tomb of the Virgin, the place where the Virgin died. They are none of them considered authentic, and would not be any better if they were. Only Galilee, the Lake of Tiberias, as you come down to it from the mountains above—softly misted, with its blues and greens, the far bank a wall of wrinkled yellow rock, and its waters blue, still and dull—has something of idyllic mystery. At Capernaum, on the far bank, is a synagogue in which Jesus is supposed to have taught, and one passes a church on a little hill that is said to mark the setting of the Sermon on the Mount. Yet, even discounting the miracles, it is hard to imagine what happened here in any very lively or concrete way. I found it easier, when I was traveling through Italy and passing the Lago di Garda, on which I could see from the train the little peninsula of Sirmio, to imagine the poet Catullus coming back from his Bithynian exile and, as he puts off the cares of his journey, finding peace in his longed-for bed. For Garda was concrete to Catullus, it was solidly and pleasantly a part of his life. He has left a description of it, by which we can recognize it. But the Gospels do not describe Galilee. Sirmio is still there in Italy, but in a sense the Holy Places are not there.

What you find in Palestine instead is a kind of debris of the three great religions that have sprung from and flourished there. Side by side and mutually exclusive, you have the synagogue, the church and the mosque, as well as the many varieties of the Christian church in both its Eastern and Western, its Catholic and its Protestant forms. They have for so long been practicing dissension in the name of the single God whom they all derive from the ancient Jews that one has almost forgotten the irony of their bitterness or contempt for one another. But the non-religious visitor, in entering these places of worship, bewildered by the constant necessity of remembering whether to keep on his hat, take off his hat or take off his shoes at the door, may become a little impatient with the outward forms of religion. On Mount Zion—which has given its name to Heaven—he discovers a state of affairs, a squalor, confusion and strife, at the same time digusting and comic. I climbed up there with a guide, by a long flight of steps, to inspect the so-called tomb of David. You see, first, inscribed on a wall in bold and clear Hebrew lettering, the familiar quotation from Isaiah—"For from Zion will go forth the Law, and the word of the Lord from Jerusalem." But Mount Zion, just outside the old wall, is a corner of the Old City that has remained in Jewish hands. The frontier, with its barbed-wire spite-fence, runs right between it and the wall, and you are obliged to enter the tomb by a narrow path lined with barbed wire and hung with signs in Hebrew and English that warn you, DANGER MINES. Beyond the barbed wire are an empty Arab house and little fields that must once have been lawns but are all grown up now with long grass. The red poppies and yellow daisies remind you of that passage from Edgar Quinet that Joyce likes to play with in *Finnegans Wake*: the wild flowers that go on blooming through the wreckage of civilizations and come down to us through the ages, *"fraîches et riantes comme aux jours des batailles."*

Inside the supposed tomb, you find a Jewish house of prayer, dedicated to David, with a display of silver vessels and sacred red cloths, presided over by pale bearded custodians. This a few years ago was a Moslem house of prayer, before the Jews captured it from the Arabs. Up against it is a Benedictine monastery, the Church and Convent of the Dormition, which is supposed to mark the spot where the Virgin died, or rather, where she fell asleep

just before her ascension to Heaven. I succeeded in persuading this man to come with me to see the monastery,
though he showed a certain reluctance—I do not know
whether because he was hesitant about getting too close to
the Arabs or because he was afraid that the monks might
not want him in their Christian cathedral; and another
Jewish visitor, who heard us talking, hooked on to us and
decided to go with us. He said that he ought not to go—an
Orthodox Jew, it seems, is forbidden to enter a Christian
church—but that he didn't want to miss the opportunity.
Most of the monks had been withdrawn since the war, but
we found a German brother who took us around. It was
not a very beautiful place; it had been built fifty years
before, under the patronage of the late Kaiser, on the
foundations of a Crusaders' church. There was an altar
contributed by German Catholics for somebody murdered
by the Nazis, and Hungarian chapels with frescoes in
horned-toad Hungarian style. The monk took us down to
the crypt and lit candles to show us the monument over
the spot where the Virgin is supposed, not to have died,
but to have made her departure from earth: she lies rigid,
with an ivory face and mantled in dried-blood marble.
The two Jews were quiet, a little shy. Emerging, we explored apprehensively the deserted stone paths of the
monastery that led us between high walls and ended in
barbed-wire cul-de-sacs. There is no neutral ground here,
and where the two sides are close together, the inhabitants
of the two cities like sometimes to take potshots at one another. We returned to the valley, keeping carefully to the
path that makes the right-of-way to Zion and crosses
the neutral strip which separates Israel from Jordan. This
is mined and fenced off with barbed wire. Occasionally a
dog or a child strays over and steps on a mine. Not far off,
an extension of this valley was the ill-famed ancient Ge-
henna, where the Hebrews relapsed into the primitive cult
of sacrificing their children to Moloch. On your way to
and from Zion, you pass the Jerusalem Animal Hospital,
which is just over the line on the Israeli side. The barking

of the dogs in this hospital had been keeping me awake at night, and, before I found out what it was, I had almost imagined that the dogs on both sides took up at night the quarrel of their masters and yapped at each other till morning. (At the time of certain shootings in this part of the city that have taken place since I left, the veterinary hospital, I learn from the *Times,* was isolated from food supplies, but the "matron" stood by her charges and has received a citation from the S.P.C.A., with a bronze medal of the kind "usually awarded to an animal for bravery," as well as one from the American Feline Society.)

The presence of this valley of hatred, though rarely referred to in Israel, is constantly felt and inflicts constraint. For the Eastertide pilgrims who cross the line on their way to the Mount of Olives and the other places associated with Jesus, it should heighten their respect for his teaching. The passage from Israeli to Jordanian Jerusalem has been made by the Arabs, in their fear of the Israelis and their somewhat childish desire to behave as unpleasantly as possible, to seem almost as difficult and perilous as gaining admission to Lhasa. If you come with an Israeli passport, they do their best to make it impossible, and travelers are driven to such farcical devices as double passports and detachable visas. One visitor who had been in Israel and who, just as he was leaving Jordan, inadvertently thanked the authorities in Hebrew was held up for several hours. I had found this same atmosphere of suspicion when I applied for a visa in London: the doorman at the Jordan Legation had held the door open on a crack and directed me to the rear of the buiding, where I climbed up a kind of fire-escape to some rooms on the top floor, apparently closed off from the rest, in which an anxious official, alarmed at my having written "None" after the question about my "Religion"—I had previously been questioned as to whether I was Jewish—suggested in a feeble way that he might forward my request to his capital and convinced me that my case was hopeless. When I did succeed finally, through the efforts of our consul—who functions in both the Jerusalems—in crossing the inflamed frontier, I happened to arrive in Old Jerusalem at the moment when the Israelis were changing the guard at the Hebrew University on Mount Scopus. This institution was founded by Weizmann in 1925 and has a library of a million volumes, but it is an enclave now in Arab territory, under the protection of the United Nations and not available for use by the Israelis, who have thus lost their scholarly equipment and are obliged to house their college where they can. There is also a Mount Scopus hospital which the Israelis had also to abandon when the Arabs, shooting into their convoys, killed several doctors and nurses. The Israeli guard on these buildings is changed every two weeks, and there at the Mandelbaum Gate, in front of the gashed and gutted houses that have been left as they were at the armistice, with their gaping arched Arab windows that so much suggest a life of ease, stood a squad of Arab soldiers at attention, while the gray Israeli trucks, which were blinded so that the inmates could not see out, had their oil drums and food supplies searched.

The medley of sects and religions is seen at its most fantastic in the shrines of the Old City. The so-called Mosque of Omar is a pretty little Moslem rotunda, gracefully arched and domed, and covered with charming blue tiles contributed by Suleiman the Magnificent, that shelters a large yellowish old bumpy rock believed by the Jews to have been, first, the rude altar to which Abraham came with Isaac, then the threshing floor of Araunah the Jebusite, on which David was ordered by God to build the altar that later became that of the Temple. It is surrounded by an iron grille contributed by the Crusaders. This monument is now in the hands of the Arabs, and it is the Moslems who worship there at the consecrated rock of the Jews. The Church of the Holy Sepulcher, which shelters two other rocks, supposedly Calvary and Jesus' Tomb, is guarded by a Mohammedan doorman, who always has charge of the keys, but it is otherwise occupied by Christians. This confused and uncomforting building—on the site of which, according to legend, Hadrian erected a Temple of Venus, in order to keep Christians away from it—now houses five Christian churches, cathedrals within a cathedral: the Greek Orthodox, the Roman Catholic, the Syrian, the Armenian and the Coptic, the services of which overlap, interrupting and blurring one another.

The Church of the Holy Sepulcher is badly in need of repairs—is, in fact, on the point of collapse and only propped by a precarious scaffolding—but the five cults responsible for it can never agree as to what is to be done. When I inquired what was going to happen to it, I was given the cynical answer that the very next earthquake would shake it down and that no one then would have to worry. It is a macabre claustrophobic place, and probably contains more bad taste, certainly more kinds of bad taste, than any other church in the world. You enter the imprisoned parvis through the wall of the Arab street by apertures inconveniently narrow, and are confronted by a great cage of braces that almost conceals the façade: a metal structure trimmed with barbed wire, which makes it resemble a station of the old New York elevated railway. Going in, you see first, on your left, an Oriental bed in an alcove, on which, when he is not on his feet, the Mohammedan caretaker reclines. (There are services that take place at night, when visitors are locked in the church.) Before you, flanked by monstrous candles that almost reach to the ceiling, that look as if they were made of celluloid and are painted like postcards or greeting cards with miniature views of Jerusalem and little bows of blue ribbon, lies the smooth flat red Unction Stone, where the body of Jesus is supposed to have lain and which the pilgrims get down on their knees to kiss, the more fastidious ladies wiping it first with a handkerchief. Exploring the cramped and cluttered, the labyrinthine and closetlike interior, among blue and red balls, tinsel stars and bulbous brass lamps and thuribles that hang from the ceiling like Christmas-tree ornaments, you come upon the Sepulcher itself, which stands like a kind of tower in the center of a gloomy rotunda, the paint of whose dome was peeled off by a fire in 1808 (caused by a drunken Greek monk) and whose paintings are masked by the scaffolds that hold the pillars erect. On the bases of these pillars are fixed strips of glass that will break if a crack occurs. In your efforts to get the hang of this dark and disorganized interior, you may look in on a kind of exhibition room where reliquaries of gold and silver are lit up in a long glass showcase, and where little old women in black are circulating and kissing the part of the glass that is opposite each of the relics. In a chamber of the Russian church, hung with embroidered pictures that are heavy with Byzantine gold, and portraits of the prelates of the Orthodox Church, half fancy, half photographic, you come upon a bearded old priest, sitting behind a table and competently answering in various languages the questions of a crowd of visitors, who are writing their names in a book. Climbing narrow and high stone stairs, you arrive at a giddying gallery, one corner of which is scribbled with names and addresses from all over the world, among the scrawled scripts of which the word "DUBLIN" stands out, printed. Here you find dreadful modern mosaics—of Abraham and Isaac, and other Old Testament subjects—the gift of the presiding Franciscans. Descending to the crypt by a broad flight of steps, you are handed a candle and penetrate, in the darkness, to the spot where the True Cross is supposed to have been found, in Constantine's time, by the Empress Helena. Above it looms a faceless statue, bulky and spooky in the darkness, that the flame of the candle falls short of.

At the Tenebræ services of Holy Week, the Church of the Holy Sepulcher is jammed by what is, I suppose, one of the most international congregations and one of the most variegated to be seen anywhere in the world. There are excursions of nuns from all over Europe, accompanied by shepherding and ciceroning priests. The white-gowned choristers, the brown-robed Franciscans, the Greek priests in their flat-topped black hats are all in their best clothes. The Latin Patriarch, in a little red cap and a richly embroidered coat, is conducting the Tenebræ office from a throne that faces the Sepulcher. Christianized Arab women, with white headdresses and Arab robes, kneel on the floor with their children. A black nun in a big starched white cap with corners that stick out like wings is praying by herself in a niche so dark that only the bonnet is visible above the huddled figure. Catholic priests and Anglican clergymen stand about in black clothes and British boots. There are whiffs of urine and incense. What if the whole stale and rickety place, fissured by some piercing note, should come down on our heads and bury us! There is also a claustrophobia brought on by the vulgarity and the scrambled cults. One recalls that, at the ceremony of the Holy Fire in 1834, the tension, the heat, and the crowding produced a terrible panic. When the moment has come for this yearly miracle, a specialty of the Eastern rite, the Greek Patriarch passes into the Sepulcher, in which, the day before, Good Friday, the holy flame has been extinguished, and hands out a bunch of candles, bound together in a cage-topped torch, which are supposed to have been ignited without human intervention. The pilgrims and other worshippers, who have often been standing there all night, now press forward to light their own candles—for the fire, rekindled by a miracle, is supposed to ensure salvation. This results in a mad and remorseless scramble.

At the ceremony on Holy Saturday, 1834, the candle smoke became so stifling that three people fell out of the galleries and were killed on the heads of the crowd below. "One poor Armenian lady, seventeen years of age," writes the Honorable Robert Curzon,* who was present, "died where she sat, of heat, thirst and fatigue." On his way out of the church, he continues, "I got as far as the place where the Virgin is said to have stood during the crucifix-

---

* *Visits to the Monasteries of the Levant,* London, 1849.

ion, when I saw a number of people one on another . . . [stretching] as far as I could see towards the door. I made my way between them as well as I could, till they were so thick that there was actually a great heap of bodies on which I trod. It then suddenly struck me they were all dead! . . I . . . saw that sharp hard appearance of the face that is never to be mistaken. Many of them were quite black with suffocation, and further on were others all bloody and covered with the brains and entrails of those who had been trodden to pieces by the crowd." Farther on, he found the crowd trying to get out the great door. "The guards outside [Mohammedans], frightened at the rush from within, thought that the Christians wished to attack them, and the confusion soon grew into a battle. The soldiers with their bayonets killed numbers of fainting wretches, and the walls were spattered with blood and brains of men who had been felled, like oxen, with the butt-ends of the soldiers' muskets. Everyone struggled to defend himself or to get away, and in the melee all who fell were immediately trampled to death by the rest. So desperate and savage did the fight become that even the panic-struck and frightened pilgrims appeared at last to have been more intent upon the destruction of each other than desirous to save themselves." Curzon himself escaped only by fighting his way back into the body of the church across the dead and dying. He noticed that the Unction Stone was piled with corpses. At least five hundred people were killed. And even in 1918, Sir Ronald Storrs was forced, at this ceremony, to protect from the blows of the jealous Armenians a visiting Greek archbishop, "as he passed in glittering tiara from the Tomb to the 'Golgotha Chamber.' "* Not many years before, the Franciscans and Greeks had come to blows over the right to sweep certain stairs, and bystanders were hurt by the flying stones.

It is a relief to get out of the place and catch a glimpse of

---

* *Orientations*, London, 1937.

a courtly kaváss—one of those red-fezzed and bright-jacketed attendants who walk before important personages, pounding the pave with their staffs—engaged in exchanging amenities with a lady who had just left the church.

Yet the lasting significance of Jerusalem is not in the least diminished by the scandal and grotesquerie of the Holy Sepulcher, by the fact that the Temple has been destroyed and that its site is in the hands of the Moslems, who will not let a Jew come near it, that the city is now split across by the quarrel of the Israelis and Arabs. It has been always of the essence of the Jewish genius that it works through the spirit and the intellect, that, in spite of the importance to the Jews of such names as Jerusalem and Zion, it does not need a habitation other than the souls of men. It is a paradox of Jewish history that a moral force, an inspiration, which has leapt geographical boundaries and been felt by so many minds, regardless of race or class, should have been generated and transmitted by a people who have carried exclusiveness to fantastic lengths, who have manifested the extremes of intolerance and who have suffered from equal intolerance on the part of the champions of other religions which have taken their cue from the Scriptures. (It is strange to think that even the Feeneyites, shrieking against the Jews on Boston Common—the disciples of a heretic priest, who has taught them that only Catholics can be saved—should be doing it in the name of a God whom they owe to the Jewish Bible.) One cannot, of course, blame the Jews for all the horrors of Mohammedan and Christian history; bigotry and cruelty are universal. Yet the Bible, on one of its sides, does tend to encourage both. Julius Caesar, who dispassionately and ruthlessly cut off the hands of the Gauls, who slaughtered them and sold them into slavery, did not do so in the name of God; and the Greeks, who looked down on the "barbarians" and who fought them when the necessity arose, did not preach their extermination on account of their worship of alien gods. This has been the regrettable side of the influence of the religious ideas of the Jews: the impulse to fanaticism. The life-giving positive side—often involved with the other, though certain of the great Jewish teachers have embodied it in its purest form—is the faith in, the affirmation of, the power of the human spirit, in touch with its divine source and independent of place or condition. This paradox, this contradiction, is illustrated in a striking way by Jesus' conversation with the woman of Samaria. On my trip to Mount Gerízim to attend the Samaritan Passover, I stopped off at Jacob's Well, at which this conversation is supposed to have taken place and which is apparently one of the very few Holy Places that have any chance of being real, and I reread the scene in John 4. The purely sectarian issue between the Samaritans and the Jews is brought up in the most typical way. (Jesus himself—to the Jews a heretic— was accused by them of being a Samaritan.) "Our fathers," says the woman to Jesus, "worshipped on this mountain [Gerízim], and you say that in Jerusalem is the place where men ought to worship." The reply that Jesus is reported to have made is a curious combination of the old point of view of the Jews, and the claim to an exclusive and literal correctness, with the intense religious instinct that accompanies this and transcends it. "Woman, believe me," He answers, "the hour is coming when neither on this mountain nor in Jerusalem will you worship the Father. You worship what you do not know; we worship what we know, for salvation is from the Jews. But the hour is coming, and now is, when the true worshippers will worship the Father in spirit and truth, for such the Father seeks to worship Him. God is spirit, and those who worship Him must worship in spirit and truth."

For the Christian, the center of worship was no longer to be Jerusalem, and the second destruction of the Temple was to compel even the most orthodox Jews (if not the Samaritans) to dissociate the spirit of God from any particular place. Even the later Zionists, returning to the earthly Jerusalem, were loyal to a vision that was hardly of earth. How implausible it seems that Protestants in Britain and the United States should be singing their hymns about Israel, Zion and Jerusalem the Golden, without—for the most part, certainly—attaching to them very much meaning of an historical or geographical kind! How implausible that English poets should have written of the "Traffic of Jacob's ladder/ Pitched betwixt Heaven and Charing Cross," and of fighting to "build Jerusalem/ In England's green and pleasant land"!

I thought, when I returned to the modern Jerusalem, that the bright light, the high bare hills, were more surely the Jerusalem of the Psalms and the Prophets than even the best-documented relics of the Temple and the ancient wall. This was the Jerusalem of which Jesus said that not one stone should be left upon another, that it was destined to be "trodden down of the Gentiles." The substantial tomb built by Herod for the family that he murdered and for whose murder he tried thus to atone is still standing, just behind my hotel. It was right on the firing line during the war and is still snarled about with barbed wire. During the period of hardship that followed the war, it was lived in by a destitute family and is full of tin cans and turds; it has never been cleaned out for tourists. Nation has risen against nation, as Jesus predicted they would, and kingdom against kingdom; there is little now to be read of in the papers save "wars and rumors of wars." Through this city, among these mountains, have passed, in the course of some twenty-five centuries, the Hebrews, the Babylonians, the Greeks, the Persians, the Romans, the Byzantines, the Arabs, the Turkomans, the Franks, the Moslems, the Crusaders, the Mongolians, the Mamelukes, the Turks, the British, the Israelis. Jerusalem has been ruled or governed by—to name only a few, the most notable—David, Solomon, Nebuchadnezzar, Nehemiah, Antiochus Epiphanes, the Maccabees, Pompey, the Herods, Pontius Pilate, Bar Kochba, Chosroes II, Godefroy de Bouillon, Saladin, Suleiman the Magnificent, El-Jazzar, Sir Ronald Storrs and Ben-Gurion. One can hardly grasp all these vicissitudes—the peoples and nations and causes, the policies and personalities. Their history becomes unimaginable, and they all seem to recompose, like the sequence of colors of the spectrum, in this tranquil luminous sky. The Jews made Jerusalem the high place of God and thus gave it to the whole human race.

[1954]

VII
Fiction

EDITOR'S NOTE

As a young man Wilson had high hopes for his fiction. In *I Thought of Daisy* (1929) he attempted to synthesize his intellectual vision with his life in the bohemia of Greenwich Village. In the early '30s he planned a novel derived from his journals, but put this aside in his urgency to tell the human story of the development of revolutionary Marxism. At the decade's end he outlined a possible novel which was to unfold in three stages, the first part of which will be belatedly published as *The Higher Jazz*. He abandoned the project for the stories that became *Memoirs of Hecate County* (1946). Though he would recall this as "my favorite among my books," the commercial success of *Hecate County* was soon dampened when it was banned as pornographic. Wilson's novelistic imagination fulfilled itself in the large canvasses of *To the Finland Station*, *Patriotic Gore*, and his literary portraiture.

Two pieces of fiction are presented here, each as sustained and polished as his best historical portraits. The first is social commentary with an irony moving toward satire, the second macabre and fanciful. "The Men from Rumpelmayer's" sprang directly from personal experience, recorded in a long journal entry about a weekend he spent partying in Boston not long before the executions of Sacco and Vanzetti. Though never entirely sure of the innocence of the two men—Vanzetti's testament was convincing in its moral fervor, yet time would establish that Sacco owned the murder weapon—he was ashamed of the ineffectuality and irresponsibilty which the narrator of this story discovers link him to a decaying bourgeoisie. The analogy between the prisoners and the lobsters in a paper bag, the stench of the condemned clams, and other such details darken the story for the reader, as they presumably did when Wilson looked back on them.

"Ellen Terhune," from *Memoirs of Hecate County*, presents much more sympathetic characters, its central figure a near-great woman composer struggling for a creative breakthrough. The narrator, responding to her nervous strain, is drawn back into her life and family history at a series of turning-points, each progressively further in the past. The phantasmagorical transformation of experience echoes Gogol, Poe, and Henry James, with anticipations of magical realism. Wilson forces us to accept the paranormal, providing a degree of rational explanation, for it is as though she has summoned this man to witness her story and undertand its tragic end. The machinery of moving back in time may sometimes creak, but the writing is often brilliant, as in Wilson's description of the music that conveys the cry of her soul—music she was never able to write that reaches the world only through his conceptual reconstruction. "Ellen Terhune" is a fictional enactment of the theme of the wound and the bow, the major chord of Wilson's work at the end of the thirties. It draws on the mixed emotions of excitement and unease that thinking about Edna Millay and her poetry continued to evoke in him. A historical *tour-de-force*, it locates readers in the cultural life of the turn-of-the century, looking back to his own boyhood in a "house of the 'eighties" not unlike Vallombrosa.

THE MEN FROM RUMPELMAYER'S

I woke up in a country club. When I got out of bed, it was rather late, and there was a tennis match going on below my window. I saw the dimmed and mist-dampened tennis courts, from which the sounds of the game came subdued and sparse. Slender Boston girls, in gray or brown coats, stood with their backs to me, looking on— they were smart and, in that boyish way, graceful. Beyond, there were people on benches; I was able to tell the girls from the men only by their whitish crossed legs. It was one of those moist murky days past mid-August when one can already feel the fall, and as I dreamily made my toilet in the bathroom, I derived from the fields and dark trees, seen from the window through the haze-thickened air, a quiet enjoyment as I first caught the flavor of that rich lapsing of the long autumn which makes us taste a kind of freshness even in the beginnings of luxurious decay. There was no one in the dining-room when I at last went down, but I enjoyed having breakfast alone: the brightly sprig-flowered curtains and the light slender-runged chairs seemed pleasantly clean like my hands, which, I reflected, had not been so clean since I had gone up to camp for the summer. I noted the headline of the Boston paper: "Supreme Court Decides Sacco Appeal Today"—then I read the meager paragraphs which followed, and, as there seemed to be nothing else except syndicated comic features and advertisements, I turned to a copy of *Life*, which had a cover by John Held, Jr., in blue and red.

Afterwards, I idly lolled on a large dark porch enclosed in glass, and presently Ralph appeared with both the girls. "Do you feel testy this morning?" said Julia. "We're all feeling pretty testy." "Not a bit," I said. "Good-natured to a fault." "That might get on my nerves this morning." "Well, you're *looking* extremely fresh." And so they always did—they were not Boston girls, but Californians and had the well-grown figures and strong color of the West. Julia wore white straw shoes with interwoven strands of red, light straw-colored stockings, a pretty straw-colored skirt flowered in blue and red, a close-fitting light blue jersey and a scarf of a pinkish violet which echoed and complemented both the red in her shoes and the blue of the jersey. I reflected that Julia and Lynn had a great gift of dressing attractively: they had also that amusing vocabulary, something entirely their own—such as their use of "testy" just now. "When I look at those white teeth," I said, "that clear skin—that clear tanned ruddy skin—and those brown eyes and wide eyebrows—I realize that you are two of the handsomest girls that this country has ever produced!" "That's just the inclemency of the weather," said Lynn. "It makes us come like bright rays." Julia and I laughed, but Ralph only smiled by stretching his mouth: his eyes behind his rimless spectacles were already more or less slits and could be little narrowed by laughter. The things that the girls said always seemed to be just beyond him: either such things as he wouldn't have thought worth saying or as he wouldn't have cared to hear said so quickly—at any rate, such things as made a kind of conversation in which he could not take a real part. Yet he evidently derived gratification from possessing a wife and a sister-in-law who pleased people as much and amused them as much as Lynn and Julia did. And he tried, in his way, to keep up with them. "Well, what shall we order?" propounded Lynn, who had just caught sight of a waiter. "Sarsaparilla with cream?—Four sarsaparillas with cream?" "I don't know whether I could stand that," I said. "It's nourishing," explained Julia. "You can dispense with luncheon entirely." "Yes," said Lynn. "It's not only nourishing, it makes the idea of food seem repulsive." "Oh, all right!" I yielded.

Ralph picked up the paper and read the headlines about Sacco and Vanzetti. I had tactfully refrained, the evening before, from mentioning this explosive subject. "Some of your friends were up here," he said. "Bill Morris came rushing over to Hoppner and Post to get us to cash a hundred-dollar check for him to bail the others out." "What do you think about it all?" I asked. "I think it's a shame," he said, "to arrest people like Powers Hapgood for speaking on Boston Common—he was making a perfectly law-abiding speech. The Common has been supposed to be a public forum ever since the Revolution." I thought he was going to draw some conclusion from this, but he did not pursue the subject. "What do you think about the merits of the case?" I inquired. "I think they ought to have a new trial," he answered, "but they haven't got a chance in the world. Fuller is a hard-boiled politician. They never had a prayer with that committee: Grant is *non compos mentis*, and of all the prejudiced people in Boston—and everybody in Boston is more or less prejudiced—Lowell is probably the most so. He's successful at raising endowments for Harvard— he has a wonderful way with millionaires—but it would be hard to find anyone less suitable for conducting an impartial investigation into something like this where the men accused are attackers of authority and property. I've given up saying anything about it, though—when I try to argue at the club, everybody jumps on my neck." The New Englanders did, after all, I noted, express themselves in a plain-spoken fashion. I had not myself assumed that the Governor's Committee was a farce: I had supposed that Lowell, Stratton and Grant were more or less intelligent men, and I had been imagining something like one of those plays by Galsworthy in which everyone does the wrong thing from the most conscientious motives. "I've been absolutely sure they were innocent," said Julia, "ever since I read how Vanzetti said, 'I am innocent of these two harms!' I'm sure that nobody who would say that could have done anything really bad—do you think so? 'I am innocent of these two harms.'"

The sarsaparilla and cream arrived. "They call things like this 'tonic' here," said Lynn. "It makes it sound bitter and bracing." But nothing could have been sweeter than this beverage—it did make me feel slightly sick. Then they began to debate what we should do. Lynn suggested going for dinner—we had had breakfast too late for lunch—to a place called the Bass Point House; but Ralph disapproved of this—though, it seemed, he had been in the habit of taking her there before they were married. "As long as he's got to take the seven-thirty train," he said, "—that is, eight-thirty daylight-saving—we'd better have dinner in town." "Let's go to the Squamscott Club!" said Lynn. "That takes a long time, too," he objected. "Let's go to Mother's apartment and have a regular lobster supper!" "Sea food," said Julia. "Shore dinner," said Lynn. They were being ironic in their Western way, but Ralph was only partly aware of it. "I'll cook them myself," he said. "I'll give you a superb dinner!" It occurred to me that he might be afraid that, if he took us to the Squamscott Club, I might try to make a speech about Sacco and Vanzetti. So we presently started off in the car: it was quite a long ride to Boston. "Well," Lynn demanded, "where's that snack?" "It's in that side pocket," said Ralph, who was driving. She got out a ginger-ale bottle, which Ralph, in his neat careful way, had wrapped up in newspaper and tied with a string, and a set of paper cups. "We brought along a little snack," she explained. It was alcohol and ginger ale. "Well, it's a relief to have the ginger ale famine over," I said. "I hope that drink I concocted last night didn't make you ill." When the ginger ale had given out, I had tried mixing lime juice and alcohol. "What an awful drink that was," said Lynn. "It tasted like turpentine!" "You did put a flower in it, though," said Julia. "You put a snapdragon petal in each one—so, while it may not have been a very good drink, it was really awfully pretty. I'd like to have a dress like that," she added. "Sort of a deep garnet on a sort of acidulous yellow—I've never seen anything like it." "You'd have to have green eyes to wear that color," said Lynn. "Green eyes and reddish hair.—Do you smell the condemned clams?" A stench that was rank and stagnant reached us from the mud of the shallow beach, where the water looked dull, thick and cold. "What do you mean?" I inquired. "Are the clams here really condemned?" "Yes," she said, "all the clams are condemned between Nahant and Revere Beach. You can smell them." "That smell hasn't got anything to do with the clams," said Ralph. "It's just the way the water smells." "No," said Lynn. "I'm sure it's the clams." "Well, you're absolutely crazy," said Ralph, in his insistent even-tempered way. "That smell has nothing to do with the clams. It's always smelt like that in summer." "There are two people clamming," said Lynn, indicating two distant figures. "Two condemned people clamming for condemned clams." "Only condemned people are allowed to go clamming here," supplemented Julia. We didn't, however, pursue this joke. "Well," said Ralph, "if you insist on having it that Revere Beach smells of condemned clams, you're at liberty to cherish that delusion. But it's silly to tell people that." We presently began to sing. The girls had been singing together all their lives, and I always found them delightful. They first gave us, "I can be happy, I can be glad, It all depends on you—"; and then, at my request, one of their most successful numbers, which they had learned on a cruise to the West Indies and which always reminded them, they said, of the wonderful nights on deck: "Forsaken—forsaken—forsaken I lie—Like a stone by the roadside, while men pass me by." This song did not move me with its pathos, but it brought before me the beauty of a southern night, the wide air of some white clean ship, and the voices of those young girls, with their dear American clearness, their American freedom and gaiety. Ralph sang *Flamin' Marnie the Sure-Fire*

Vamp, of which, as it were in competition with the girls, he had learned all the words, all the stanzas, and which he rendered with complacency but without expression. I followed with an old nonsense college song, so different from the modern kind that it had something of the strangeness of folk poetry. "Do you want to go past the prison where Sacco and Vanzetti are?" Julia asked me. "We can go around that way." "You can't go past," said Ralph. "The road is closed: they won't let cars go by."

We crossed the Charles and went up Beacon Hill. I looked out at the narrow old streets, with their British-looking chimney-pots and their walls of well-laid red bricks that now wore an impressive dinginess of antiquity; those silver-nobbed doorways of Bulfinch that melt on the eye like music: white panels and Ionic columns, under fanlights as clear as crystal and flanked by white-curtained panes. Then we turned off into less elegant streets, and Ralph apologized: "You may think I'm taking you slumming, but I know where to get the best lobsters." We stopped in front of a fish market, and while Ralph was inside, I bought a paper, but there was nothing about the case in it yet. "Be careful of that," said Ralph, handing Lynn in the back seat a paper-bag. "Oh, are those lobsters?" asked Lynn, taking it rather gingerly. "Those are lobsters," said Ralph. There were little holes for them to breathe through. She put them away on the floor of the car.

When we drew up at Ralph's mother's apartment, he produced from under a lap-robe one of those great glass gallon jugs in which they sell alcohol. "Great Scott!" I said. "Is that alcohol? I thought we drank that all up last night!" "It's a magic jug," said Ralph, his eyes narrowing with pleased satisfaction. "It's full again every morning." "The Hoppner wonder-jug," said Lynn. "The old oaken bucket," said Julia.

The apartment was old-fashioned and pleasant. Sitting on a couch, while Ralph mixed the drinks, among the bare floors and the shrouded furniture, I was glad to breathe the odor of an old city house. It made me think at first of New York, but then I took account of the fact that there was another American city in which the houses had that old-fashioned smell. That fragrance of the city interior, which I used to catch deliciously as a child when I came up from the country during the holidays to visit my New York relatives, now spoke to my mind through my nostrils in terms, not of odor, but of interest: it seemed to me that life was interesting where dark libraries and drawing rooms smelt like that, and I had, for the first time since my arrival, a vision of how interesting Boston had been. I remembered with something like a feeling of guilt how little I had been in touch with it—to the degree that when, the day before, I had got off the train at the South Station, I had not said to myself, "This is Boston!" but had thought more of the Santa Barbara which I was to find in Lynn and Julia than of the Boston I was to find in Ralph. There were an engraving from Raphael; some photographs of Italy; a painting of Roman ruins enveloped in that blue-green haze which seems so to preserve the atmosphere, at once romantic and stuffy, of the culture of the nineteenth century; and a picture of Apollo and the Muses. I had once met Ralph's grandmother: she was a very old lady, with a green eyeshade that concealed her eyes, and it had surprised me that, in spite of the eyeshade, she should seem to be so sharply aware of what was going on about her, or that so dowdily dressed an old lady should talk with such style and precision. She had known Sumner, Emerson, Lowell, and it was said that she had had something like a flirtation with Dickens when he had stayed with her family in Boston. Her father had been Thomas Hoppner of Hoppner and Post, the publishers, in whose office Ralph was now working. It had, I thought, shown a great deal of courage for him to marry an Irish girl—

though, of course, her coming from California and her not being a Catholic made it somewhat different.

Ralph soon reappeared with a round of drinks and handed them around unsmilingly, but with his usual self-satisfaction—and we found ourselves grateful to get them. He presently began to sing: "I can be happy, I can be glad, It all depends on gin!"; and we gave him a smile on this. Then he unlocked the glass doors of the bookcase and showed me some of the first editions—they were mostly brownish yellow and had inscriptions in faded yellow ink—as well as a volume that recorded the proceedings of a Porcellian Club dinner, in which the name of the elder Holmes appeared along with that of Hoppner. "Well," suggested Lynn, "how about something to eat?" "Yes: something to eat," said Julia. "Have the men from Rumpelmayer's come? That's my prize line," she explained to me. "I got it out of an English novel." Ralph held up the bag of lobsters: "Here they are, all alive!" he announced. "Would you like to see them? Would it whet your appetite?" "Oh, no: don't!" said Lynn. "I hate them!" So Ralph carried them off in the bag. "Well, I hate to do this," he said. "But I love to eat 'em!" "Do they boil them alive?" asked Julia. "Yes: I guess so," I answered. "Oh, how awful!" she said.

"Oh, I meant to ask you," I switched, following an association of shore dinners. "What's become of Lois and Ed? Did you see them when you were in Santa Barbara?" "Oh, it's so terrible!" she answered. "Lynn and I are so depressed about it! She's in love with somebody else, and he doesn't want to give her a divorce because he's still so in love with her. He finally disappeared, you know, and went on a terrible bender—he went up to San Francisco—and nobody knew where he was—and Lois thought he'd killed himself. And then finally he turned up, looking haggard and wan and as if he hadn't changed his clothes for weeks—you know how spick and span he always used to be! He just came into the house and asked where the goldfish with the black tail was— they'd had a goldfish with a black tail that he'd been particularly fond of. And the goldfish had been killed by the earthquake that had happened while he was away— but Lois said when she told him she felt like a lying wretch, because it seemed so improbable that one should have been killed and the rest be all right—and she knew that he believed that his favorite had perished through her neglect. And then afterwards he slammed a glass door, you know, and it broke and cut her arm. And after that, he was just in the depths, and they've both been sunk ever since. Lynn and I have been brokenhearted over it—we try not to talk about it! We can't think of anything to do. They both write us letters separately. We've invited them to come on and visit us separately— that's the only thing we can think of to do." "And Ed's really such a nice fellow," I said. Julia took up the tale: "When we remember how cute he used to be—how he used to come cavorting into the house, shouting, 'Hey! Hey! And how!' But Lois says he gets on her nerves, and I can perfectly see how he would." Looking out into the dim wet dusk, I reflected on how darling the girls were: their humanity and generosity; they were scarcely even jealous of one another!

Ralph summoned us into the dining-room for the sup-per which he was proud to have prepared alone. He had produced tomato soup, canned succotash, and the lob-sters with melted butter. There were big thick slices of bread. We enjoyed it all very much. "Don't you want me to break that claw?" he asked Lynn. "No, thanks: you eat it," she said. "I will if you really don't want it." He took it into the kitchen, and we heard him hammering. When he returned, he brought a gallon of alcohol, which he manipulated against his biceps, with his thumb in the little round hole in the handle. He had discovered a bot-tle of grenadine. "It's not as pretty as yours," Julia said to me. "I mean the drinks that you made last night."

Ralph rather bored us by singing all the stanzas of "Oh, landlord, fill the flowing bowl Until it cloth run over!" Before I reached the point of not caring, I was beginning to wonder whether college wasn't going on a little too long.

On the train, I read with cocktail-dazed eyes that the Massachusetts Supreme Court had refused, on technical grounds, to accept the appeal for Sacco and Vanzetti. The next day, when I had gone back to camp from Boston, two telegrams reached me. One—signed "Forsaken"—said, "Come back at once. The men from Rumpelmayer's are draining the old oaken bucket"; the other was from a friend connected with the Sacco-Vanzetti Defense Committee and told me that "picketers and speakers were needed for last protest." But I had used up my extra money, so I couldn't answer either summons.

ELLEN TERHUNE

I always felt, when I went to the Terhune house, that I was getting back into the past—or rather, perhaps, that an atmosphere which had first been established at the beginning of the eighties, when the house in which she lived had been built, had been preserved there as a vital medium down into the nineteen twenties. Most of the places in Hecate County seemed either newer or older—modern households or old-fashioned farms; but the moment I entered the gate in the high green picket-fence, which was matted with honeysuckle in summer, and caught sight of the white obelisk of the windmill, dismantled though it was of its sails, towering behind the trees, I felt that I had come back into something which had definitely vanished with the war but which was perfectly familiar from my childhood.

There was a drive, always covered with gravel, that swept around in a beautiful curve and brought you up under a big *porte-cochère*, which reminded you of horses with fly-nets, and shiny and black closed carriages; and the house, which was yellow and covered with shingles that overlapped with rounded ends like scales, was an impressive though rather formless mass of cupolas with foolscap tops, dormers with diamond panes, balconies with little white railings and porches with Ionic columns, all pointing in different directions. It had been built or bought by Ellen Terhune's grandfather, a brilliant and highly successful doctor. Dr. Bristead, even in that period when doctors were more "humanistic" and had wider interests than now, had been a man of remarkable cultivation, and the house was richly lined with the evidences of his pastimes, his studies and his travels. One found in the downstairs rooms such treasures and curiosities as signed photographs of or framed letters from Theodore Roosevelt, Kipling, Pierre Loti, Mark Twain, Adelina Patti, Paderewski, Mechnikov and Pasteur, all of whom had been patients or correspondents of his; a statue of Hebe by Canova, a Daubigny and a couple of Corots; a hookah, which Ellen told me her grandfather had actually smoked; a group of Chinese gongs, with which dinner was still announced; a regal set of carved ivory chessmen, brought back from a trip to the Orient, which had elephants instead of bishops; an Australian bushman's boomerang; a Stradivarius and an eighteenth-century clavichord.

The Bristeads had especially been musical. The doctor had mastered several instruments; and he had organized a family trio in which he had played the cello, his daughter the violin, and Mrs. Bristead the piano. Later, when the doctor's wife had died and his daughter had come with Ellen to live with them, they had had the trio again, with Ellen, at the age of twelve, taking over the cello. When her mother had died a few years later and she was living there alone with her grandfather, they had played an immense amount of music; they had gone right through Beethoven and Brahms, both of whom her grandfather had ended by detesting; had then escaped backward into the eighteenth century, with Ellen learning Boccherini's cello sonatas and the doctor getting special transcriptions made of Pergolesi's trios for violins and bass; and had from there, in obedience to one of her grandfather's peculiarly indomitable manias, gone right back through the history of music. Ellen had been forced to retrace the elegance and restraint of Corelli at an age when she would much rather, she told me, have been pounding out Schubert and Schumann; and the doctor had had a small organ installed and relentlessly insisted on their deciphering the intricate masses of Palestrina, thence exploring mediaeval motets, troubadour songs and Gregorian chants, and, finally, reconstructing ancient Greek modes.

Ellen had thus had the advantage of an exceptional musical training, and she had begun to compose early. By the time she got out of the Conservatoire, where she had started in at eighteen, she was producing work of real merit. She had been influenced in Paris by Debussy; but, working with the whole-tone scale, she had developed an impressionism distinctly her own. She was, in fact, probably the first woman composer who had ever contributed to music anything of authentic value. It is strange that, though women have excelled as novelists and lyric poets, and though there are a few women painters of interest, there should be no important music by women. That is unless Ellen Terhune be an exception, and I have always thought her work first-rate, though it somehow seems incommensurable with masculine compositions of even the same school. It would be foolish to compare her with Chaminade, with whom she has nothing in common; but, on the other hand, even Ravel and Debussy were builders on a bigger scale than Ellen. Her talent in the best of her work, her songs and piano pieces, is as personal as Georgia O'Keeffe's pictures or Marianne Moore's poems: a woman's sharp and ready reactions to people and things encountered and a woman's emotions of quick challenge, of a kind of dark resigned despair or of a clear and rapt exaltation.

I called on Ellen one afternoon in the summer of 1926. It was August, and I had assumed she was in Maine, where she usually went at that time of year; but I ran into her one day at the post office and she asked me to come to see her. I was delighted, because I always liked to talk to her—her comment on the musical world was wonderful—and, though some considered her arrogant and forbidding, I found her personality sympathetic. It would be especially a relief to get away from the Hecate County summer life, which had involved a great many parties with people who were only made tolerable by summer sports and drinking. I went to see her that same afternoon.

But I found her much disturbed and distressed. She had three highballs in rapid succession, which I had never known her to do before, and which made me a little disappointed, as it associated her to my mind with the summer people, great publishers of their emotions over drinks, so that her house seemed less the haven I had hoped for.

It turned out that Ellen like everyone else was going through a domestic crisis. She had married a man somewhat younger than herself, the conductor Sigismund Soblianski. He had genuinely admired her abilities, had done more perhaps than anyone else to have her work performed; and he had profoundly respected her character as only the matriarchal Jew can respect the austerity of a woman who is set firmly on her own moral base; but the fact that she was also an artist—she had married too late to have children, which might have done something to fuse them—had stimulated a fatal competition. Sigismund, before he married, had worked rather seriously at composing, but Ellen was so much better than he was that he must have become ashamed of his productions, for he ceased to write anything at all. Instead, he had begun to develop a hair-raising professional exhibitionism. A brilliant and resourceful musician with a special gift for dramatizing effects, he had gradually come to abandon the playing of new or native music, which, partly at the instance of Ellen, he had originally attempted to encourage, and to go in for great quantities of Chaikovsky and Strauss, Sibelius, Beethoven and Wagner, overcoloring and overacting, and posing to a public who adored him while the serious musicians gave him up.

It was a long time, however, since Ellen and he had seemed to be living together—though I did still run into him sometimes in the country. He had always had his rehearsals in town and Ellen did not like the city; and he had had, also, during the last two or three years, a whole series of love affairs which everybody knew about and which Ellen appeared to accept. He had even adopted the practice of bringing out his protégée of the moment—serious-minded little Russian dancer or black-eyed Hungarian violinist—to spend the day with Ellen; but this, though she took it coolly, I am sure Ellen did not like. The truth was, I always thought, that they were still much involved with one another, and that Sigismund did such things in a kind of defiance of Ellen for making him feel second-rate.

But he now, she told me, wanted a divorce; he wanted to get married again. And I could see that Ellen was profoundly upset—though she ascribed her reluctance to the fear that he was making a fool of himself. The woman that he proposed to marry was a much- and long-publicized actress, and Ellen was inclined to believe that Sigismund's interest in her was merely a part of his own self-publicizing activity. Frances Fielding was one of those figures who took the place, during the twenties and thirties, of the old-fashioned male matinee idol. She was adored by a following mainly feminine, and she was supposed not to care much about men. But in her pictures and plays she was invariably subdued, at the end of much high-spirited rebellion, by a stubborn and combative lover; and it was obvious that there would be for the public a wonderful double story about Frances at last meeting her fate at the same time that Sigismund Soblianski had found a creature as dashing as himself. It was particularly disturbing to Ellen, who had tolerated the little protégées, because she was herself the type of the serious professional woman of an earlier generation and was losing to a formidable competitor.

"I always thought she was hard as nails," she said, "but she does have a certain—shall I say, style and brilliance?—I can't bear to call it glamor. She and Sigismund are both what the Russians call 'firebirds,' I suppose—they like to show their plumage in an atmosphere of bright lights and admiration. They're only able really to express themselves by creating for themselves characters that are two-thirds fictitious. And I don't shine in that way—I'm naturally quiet and drab. I can't bear to go to night clubs and places, and I long ago ceased to enjoy staying up all night over musical suppers where people get intoxicated and take off Shalyapin and play Viennese waltzes. I'd rather be home in bed reading. I don't like to travel the way Sigismund does, and I hate triumphant tours. I'd rather stay right here with my house and my piano and my furniture and my daily routine. Sigismund is younger than I am and he's temperamentally quite different. I suppose I was always a wet blanket for him, and I can't blame him if he wants somebody gayer. Only I'd like him to have somebody who would be good for him. I can't imagine she really cares about him. I'm afraid he'll end up in Hollywood."

Ellen was, of course, not drab, but there *was* something in her that didn't give. As I looked around the room, I reflected that, though Sigismund had spent much of his time here during the early years of their marriage, though the house had been supposed to be *their* house, he had left little or no imprint upon it. Dr.

Bristead and his daughter and Ellen—both Ellen and her mother were only children—had assembled the things in that room. The low couch on which I was sitting was comfortable but there was something rather stale about it. It had been ministering for too many years to the comfort of too much the same people; the upholstery and the cushions had become almost as personal as a bed, and the pattern of flowers was faded. The effect of the whole room, in fact, seemed somehow a little tinged with the yellow of the discoloring photographs; and, though there were beautiful old dark cabinets and tiptop tables and one of the finest of those convex mirrors, with a still glowing round gold frame and an American eagle on top, the room had never quite been purged of the bad taste of preceding generations; and the delicate crepuscular paintings were thrown into deeper shadow by larger canvases, also French, of picturesque Moorish scenes that made patches of rather messy color, just as the orange-pink gladioluses and the deep maroon double dahlias had, the former a touch of Victorian china, the latter a touch of upholstery. Still there was something about it I liked, and I was glad it had remained the same.

And now Ellen was telling me about her girlhood. She had been terribly homely, she said, and she had had an awful time at dances: she always knew that, if a boy asked her to dance, it was only because his mother had made him. "I was a sight," she said. "I had crooked teeth and my head was too big for my body. Even Mother was discouraged about me." She was certainly not bad-looking now and she could never have been so homely as she imagined; but she was short and did have rather a large square head on a neck that was a little too small for it—physically, she resembled the doctor—and I could see that, with her precocious intelligence, she might not have been a belle. But her magnificent agate-green eyes must at any age have been arresting: they seemed to concentrate the light of the intellect as a powerful lens

does the sun, and in this intellectual quality they suggested the eyes of a remarkable man; yet they were also
extremely feminine and responded to everything that
met them as the eyes of men seldom do. The rest of Ellen's features were neither so striking nor so mobile: her
mouth was small and her nose a little owl-like, and her
face with its square jawbones was too broad for them.
But the effect of her eyes was mesmeric.

She involved you in her concentration, and as she went
on describing her childhood, I was forced to see it all as
she did. Her parents should never have married, she
said—though I tried to point out that it was silly to imply
that she should never have existed. They had never had
anything in common. Her father, before his marriage, had
been a man about town and a sportsman—she showed me
a photograph with a handsome mustache, hair amiably
parted in the middle, and some kind of small chrysanthe-
mum in the buttonhole. He had done a great deal of
drinking, and they had belonged, in the first years of their
marriage, to a rich and rather fast set. He had had no intellectual or artistic tastes, and for her mother, brought up by
Dr. Bristead, this life must have been deeply uncongenial,
even, she thought, disgusting. Ellen's father, a Wall Street
man with a seat on the Stock Exchange, had been ruined,
the year before Ellen was born, by the crash of 1884; and
after that he had always done badly. They had gone to live
with Ellen's grandfather, and her father was always in
town. Sometimes he was brought home in very bad
shape—which she gradually learned was due to drinking—and had to stay in bed for weeks. He had killed himself when Ellen was eleven in a cheap little New York
hotel, of which he had been ashamed to let her mother
know the address.

Those tragedies of the turn of the century! I thought;
it was one thing to die or be broken for a political ideal
or a social order as had happened to both Southerners
and Northerners in the years of the Civil War; but to

die, to be crushed, to be shattered, through the overpowering progress of big business, through the unrestrained greed of speculation, seemed hard on those men and women whom we remember as gentle and bright and who look at us, in such photographs as those which Ellen produced from a drawer, with the American friendliness and candor.

She could hardly remember anything pleasant in the relations between her father and mother. Her mother had studied violin and had wanted a professional career; her marrying Ellen's father had put an end to this, and she had never forgiven him for it. She would complain that she had given up her music and then been left without resources for the social life in which he had involved her. "She might have had," said Ellen, "a quite different life. Technically, she was very good. I don't think she was meant for marriage." They had used to have long dreadful controlled quarrels, which Ellen would sometimes overhear: her mother's cold voice would go on and on, pretending to appeal to him in a reasonable way—What was she to think? What was she to expect? when he didn't keep his promises to her, when he didn't even care any more whether he humiliated her in public or not. He would be sorry, try to reassure her about his conduct and prospects for the future. It was heartbreaking, Ellen said: though not at all intellectual, he had really been a lovable man, and he had a distinction of feeling quite different from her mother's hard dignity. After he had lost his money, he had never been willing to borrow from friends—though there were plenty who would have been glad to help him. But he had never had to work before, and he had never in his career as a ladies' man been up against anyone like Ellen's mother. "It must have been wretched beyond words," she said. "You say that I ought to be glad I came out of it—but, even assuming that I'm worth anything, how does that make it better for Mother and Father, who died without getting what they wanted themselves when I was still an ugly little girl?"—"They must have been happier than you think," I said. "All married people have those conversations, and then they go to bed and forget it."—"There was something about Mother that chilled people," she went on, disregarding my attempt to be helpful and forcing me to follow her vision of the unrelieved hopelessness of her parents' situation. "She was sensitive on her musical side, but I suppose that what she presented to Father was a surface of solid whalebone.—And I do the same thing!—I know it. I chill people and put them in the wrong. That's what I did with Sigismund. He always said I made him feel guilty. But it's really because I always feel guilty. Mother made *me* feel guilty, too. I can't help thinking that I oughtn't to make claims on people, that I oughtn't to expect them to care about me. I behave as if I took this for granted, and then I reproach them for neglecting me. I know myself all too well!"

"You can't still think you're not good-looking," I said. "It isn't merely a question of that: Mother had a special and distressing reason for not liking the way I looked. It seems that she had a terribly bad time when I was born on account of my head's being so big, and I don't think she ever really recovered from it. I suppose it was what she died of. She used to talk about it sometimes in my presence. She may have thought I didn't understand, but she must have wanted people to pity her for having produced such a little monstrosity, and I think she also wanted me to feel that she had suffered and sacrificed herself for me." She was casual enough in tone; she was not herself laying it on; but, under the compulsion of her serious eyes, I felt the pain of the situation penetrate me and pin me to the spot. "I imagine, though, that she didn't exaggerate," she relentlessly and steadily went on. "I'm not sure I can't remember it myself. I've been subject all my life to peculiar spells when I think that I can't move or do anything. . . . I get it when I'm nervously exhausted," she explained in reply to my question, "and sometimes in my sleep. It's a perfectly horrible feeling—it's a kind of overpowering inertia that seems all to be located in my head—as if I were weighed down by a millstone, as if my head were a great stone ball. I suppose, though, that it's only an intensified form of a tendency I have all the time—I'm an extremely inert person. I think my difficulties in getting born may have made it more difficult for me to live. I hate so to move or make serious changes. That's one reason I'm so tiresome for Sigismund." "I've always thought of you, Ellen," I said, "as a very dynamic person." "Some of the most dynamic people," she insisted, "can't move at all, you know. They try to make up by a lot of loud talking and rushing around from place to place for their fear that they're really static." "You don't do that," I assured her. "No: I sit like a fire hydrant—that can always be tapped for cold water.—I've been trying to face my immobility lately and to do something with it in music. I've always been a little bit scared by these states that I was telling you about, and I thought it might be a good thing to take hold of them and deliberately exploit them—to try to put them outside myself."

I was afraid that she had been suffering from them lately: there were circles about her eyes, and her face, even for her, seemed pale. I thought the drinks were making her run on in a way that was not characteristic of her and that I probably oughtn't to encourage, and I was glad to shift the conversation from her parents to her artistic problems. "What are you working on now?" I asked. "I've been trying to do a sonata," she said, "just an old-fashioned sonata." Was any of it in shape to play? "I've been having rather a struggle with it," she said, "but I'll play you the part I mean." She put out her cigarette, and we went into the next room to the piano.

There were no leaves to turn—she had it in her head—and I sat in a low carved armchair which reminded me vaguely of Abbotsford, and contemplated the curious shape of a "nun's trumpet" or *tromba marina* which was hung on the opposite wall. This obsolete instrument, which the doctor had acquired and even more or less managed to play, producing, as Ellen had told me, rather unpleasant hoarse and squawking sounds, looked more like an oar or a cricket bat than a member of the violin family, whose curves it completely lacked. It seemed to me pathetically mistaken; and so did Ellen's music. This piece, which she said was the second movement, began with a four-note theme that sounded simple and conventional enough, and I was prepared for something genuinely classic; but the theme was not given the development one expects in the sonata form nor did it even get the kind of variation that one finds in a passacaglia. She did not even retard or speed it up: she simply played it over and over. It was as if she did not know what to do with it, and the listener was constantly subjected to the embarrassment of fearing that the pianist had got stuck like a phonograph which stutters. There was at moments a suggestion of a second theme that seemed to play about the first in a flimsy and trivial manner, but this would fade off in atmospheric chords and leave the field to the original four notes, as boring and inexpressive as ever. It was like a perverse child, compelled to practice on a summer day, and deliberately annoying the household. At the end, the ghost of a second theme limped off and dropped away in irremediable speciousness and impotence, and we were back with the same confounded phrase, which was never satisfactorily resolved, but simply repeated eight times at precisely the same loudness and tempo.

It sounded a little insane; I felt more worried about Ellen than before. I sat constrained, almost scared, when she stopped, and did not know what to say. Of course it was rather remarkable to have carried off this monotony musically—if she had done so, of which I was not very sure—and that was the line that I took with her. I saw that she was vibrating with tension, that the music had excited her in a way which seemed to be almost unbearable for her and was rather embarrassing for me. She was perspiring in the August heat, and I began to perspire, too. "I'm afraid you're not well," I said.

I remembered with uneasiness that she had sometimes been subject to a kind of epileptic seizure, which was preceded by nervous headaches. I had seen her in one of these fits one evening when I had taken her to a concert where a concerto of hers was to be done and where Sigismund had to conduct. She had usually played her own things; but she was not a very accomplished pianist, and on this occasion Sigismund had believed that it would be better to get a pianist who was accustomed to playing with orchestra. This performer had, however, not much liked the piece and had been antagonized by Sigismund's vehement coaching, and, in spite of a house packed with friends and admirers, who gave it the expected ovation, Ellen knew that it had not been right. I do not think, as a matter of fact, that it was one of her good things, and I imagine that the dutiful applause made her feel worse about it At any rate, she withdrew to the ladies' room and stayed there so long that I was worried. I went in and found her rigid on a couch, with an anxious attendant bending over her and trying to get her to speak. As soon as the concert was finished, her husband and I took her back to the hotel. He told me that she had had such fits before, and that they sometimes lasted for hours. On this occasion, however, she came to and got into a cab, though I did not hear her speak again.

I was afraid this afternoon that the question of divorce might be bringing on another such seizure. But she smiled and tried to reassure me. "It makes me nervous to play that thing," she said. "I wish I could get it finished. The last part has been driving me crazy, and even this part isn't right yet.—I can see that you're thoroughly depressed by it." "Oh, no," I untruthfully answered: "I think it's remarkably interesting." She smiled at the conventional evasion, and I disliked having to talk so to Ellen.

I asked her before I left whether there was somebody there in the house with her, and she told me that she had a maid. I didn't like to remind her of the concert: she was the kind of self-managing woman that it is hard to do anything for. I told her that she must let me know if there was any way in which I could help her; and she apologized for boring me with her own affairs—"But you're one of the few people I can talk to. Out here you're the only one—I don't really know any more even who the people are who live here, though we used to know everybody."

It was all pretty awful, I thought, as I walked along the drive toward the gate, between the lawns which the late sun was gilding and the magnificent collection of trees (a true collection, planted by the doctor and including many exotics and rarities), with the vision of Ellen's wide sweating forehead under her none-too-abundant brown hair and of her eyes which I had thought, toward the end of my visit, were beginning to get a little out of touch with me till, at the moment when I was saying good-by, they had come back to responsive life. She did not know even who lived about here; and there had been a few seconds just now, while I was talking about her music and she had seemed to hesitate in replying and to stare and go into herself, when I had not been quite sure she knew me.

I turned away my mind, I confess, with a certain complacent relief to a big party I looked forward to that evening: one of those gatherings where great quantities of tan-backed girls and scarlet-faced men, with highballs fizzing in their hands, lift laughing and strident voices among glass-topped cocktail tables and lamps that give indirect lighting.

II

I dropped in on her again in September when I came back from a short summer trip. I noticed that Ellen's place showed signs of restoration and refreshment. The honeysuckle on the fence had been trimmed, and the name on the gates, "Vallombrosa," had evidently been recently repainted. I had the impression that the trees and the shrubbery had also been lately pruned; and the sails had been put back on the windmill, which was turning in a chilly wind that came up suddenly as I entered the driveway.

Ellen herself I found rejuvenated in a most surprising way. She no longer had rings under her eyes, and she displayed a kind of nervous vitality which I thought at first was overwrought but which I presently came to feel as natural. The rather recessive attitude which had grown on her with her alienation from Sigismund seemed to have given way to a readiness to meet and taste life. It seemed to me that the definite break with him, which I noticed she never mentioned, had had the effect of releasing her to revert to her own personality, which, I thought, must have suffered and shrunk in the course of her relationship with Sigismund; and it seemed to be a symbol of this that she had completely changed her style of dressing and her way of doing her hair. The last time I had seen her she had been wearing the short skirt of 1926, and she had at one time bobbed her hair, which had made her head a little too mannish; but now she had been letting it grow, and, parting it in the middle and brushing it over her ears, had coiled it at the back of her head and stuck a comb at an angle behind it, and she was wearing a white shirt-waist with full sleeves and a long green-and-black plaid skirt, which were old-fashioned but very becoming to her. She looked somehow smarter than she had before. I complimented her on her appearance, but said nothing about the antiquity of the costume. I thought at first that she had got it out of some trunk and that it must be at least twenty years

old; but as I looked at it, it seemed to me new, and I concluded that she had had it made to order. It was an affecta-
tion, of course, perhaps a self-conscious protest against
Sigismund; but I rather enjoyed it for the emphasis it gave
to the non-fashionable character of her work: it was a joke
on the cult of jazz and the professional lost generation that
one of the most original of American artists should have
the aspect of a period piece.

My relation with Ellen today seemed somehow a little
less intimate. She was not alienated as I had felt her to be
at the end of my last visit, as if she were losing the outside
world; but her perceptions appeared to have been dimmed
by her intentness on her musical interests. She looked at
me for a moment when I first came in as if she were not
quite sure that she recognized me, replying rather formally to my greeting; and at one point she seemed to assume that I had personally known Dr. Bristead. She was
more obviously excited about her music than I had ever
seen her before and talked as if she had been composing
with a new gust of creative energy. She told me about
playing some piano pieces—a suite which she had just
written—at the invitation of Arthur Whiting, at an informal concert in his studio, at which the Schirmers and the
Damrosches had been present, and on a program with
D'Indy and Loefller. Though she always maintained the
attitude of the advanced and self-confident woman who is
not afraid of conventions and who knows that she can
compete with men in fields which they have largely monopolized, she was obviously gratified by this; and I was
at first a little puzzled at her pleasure in recognition from
so stuffy a quarter; but I felt that she was perhaps, as
sometimes happens, falling back for reassurance in her
new personal loneliness on public appreciation of her work
from anywhere and by anybody. "Well, that makes you a
classic!"—I smiled. "They don't really approve of me at
all," Ellen said. "They think I'm a freak like Carrie Nation. Arthur Whiting made one of his sly jokes about my

being more masculine than Debussy. But Whiting at least is no fool. Some of the people there were still sure that Debussy was a lunatic, and they thought that my use of the whole-tone scale had something to do with Max Nordau's *Degeneration*—and that the whole thing was mixed up with woman suffrage. I don't know why American musicians have to be such a lot of old women!"

Yet she seemed to me herself today unmistakably and agreeably feminine. The very outspokenness and challenge to men which the young ladies of that generation had cultivated when they set out on professional careers characterized her as a woman more vividly than the sexually neutralized role of the business girl or bar companion did the women of my own generation; and she had also a pretty keen instinct to make her attractiveness felt: she talked with a certain flashing play of her proud and arresting eyes. So she must have appeared, I imagined, in the days when she had been wholly independent and after her grandfather's death.

By this time our old understanding had completely been reestablished, and she was letting herself go. She was very amusing and ruthless about the older American composers—the fancy-dress costumes from Italy and France and the mythological insipidities which played so large a part in their work: the reveries at Carcassonne and the tone poems on *Pippa Passes*, the Icaruses and Daphnes and Psyches, the sarabands of satyrs and nymphs. "David Emery Nickerson's *Semiramis*," she said, "is simply Mrs. Wentworth of Boston. In the first part you see her in her Brookline house surrounded by obedient Nubians; in the second, she has a conversation with David Emery Nickerson and he reads her some sonnets by Rossetti; in the third, she regrets that she can never be married to David Emery Nickerson and goes in for social work."

I was rather surprised, however, when she told me that the pieces of her own which she had played at the Whiting concert had titles that seemed to connect them with the impressionism of an earlier period and that did not seem characteristic of the harder and more formal style in which she had been lately working. They were *Gulls off the Coast of Nantucket*, *The Lighthouse*, and *The Island Cemetery*—the products, she said, of her vacation. I forbore to ask about the sonata which had seemed to worry her so. She had evidently been to Nantucket since the time when I had seen her in August, and managed to come back refreshed.

I begged her to play her new suite, and she consented with a frankness and grace which seemed youthful and contrasted with the professional matter-of-factness, that matter-of-factness of the middle-aged artist that has almost become grim, with which she had taken me into her workshop before. We went again into the adjoining music room, where the cellos and violins, even the old dark cracked box of the clavichord, looked ripe in the September light, which made things inside seem the ruddier for the turn for the colder outside. It was pleasant to watch Ellen's straight back, her sure and energetic features, as she took command of the keyboard. And the pieces were lucid and lovely—at moments they were even thrilling. They did seem to me a lapse into the past: they were so much like other things she had written in a vein I thought she had put behind her. But then, why shouldn't she escape into the past? It was better than going to pieces. I noticed, however, in the last one an insistent reiterated phrase which recalled the obsessive monotony of the movement from the sonata she had played me. "I like the one about the cemetery particularly," I said, wanting to reassure her after our rather painful conversation in connection with the other piece. "I think you've handled that heavy recurrent effect perfectly successfully there." "It returns to solemnity and deadness," she said, playing the last bars again. "I wanted to give the effect of the whole thing being anchored by the graveyard. In a place like that, it's the

dead, the men who have died at sea, that give life its
price, its importance. You feel them under the ground,
just lying there and never moving. The cemetery doesn't
speak aloud, but everybody knows what it means. Even
the lighthouse implies the cemetery—and the gulls can
fly around above the graves, they can fly ever so high up
above them—but the gulls are just light irresponsible
spirits that haven't anything to lose from the sea—the
thing that's really serious is the human dead, and the living who are pledged to the dead. The islanders who are
dead are lying there like the part of the island that's submerged—all the part that's above water is based on
them.—You see I've got suggestions of the same effect in
the other pieces, too." She showed me how the flight of
the gulls would fall back into the shadow of the earth
and how the graveyard returned a deep echo to the peal-
ing of the Lisbon bell.

"Are you sure that that belongs with the gulls and the
bell?" I felt that it tarnished the clearness. "No: it *doesn't*
belong with them, of course: it's supposed *not* to belong—but it has to be there just the same.—Oh, I know
it: it's flat, flat, flat!" she said suddenly, flinging over the
leaf and getting up from the piano. "It's the David Emery Nickerson in all of us—or should I say, the Mrs.
Wentworth of Brookline?" She smiled and was amusing
again.

She had said it as the French would say, *"C'est plat,
plat, plat!"* and I had noticed during our conversation an
addiction to French gestures and phrases. She had had
"toute une histoire" over a manuscript which she had sent
to a music competition, and she had shrugged over the
inefficiency of the old fuddiduds who made the awards.
There was a certain fluidity and elegance that might
have been brought back from Paris about her hair and
the green silk bow that she wore in her starched white
collar and that softened the squareness of her face. That
was one curious thing, I reflected as I was walking away

from the house, about the effect on American artists of going to study abroad. They got in Europe a kind of inoculation with the cultures of alien races which might give them the illusion for a time that they were part of European culture, that, carried along by its current, they had actually been merged in its waters. But in ninety-nine cases this had never affected in any at all vital way the native American base. If this base had no principle of growth of its own, the inoculation simply wore off and left something that was flat, flat, flat.

I found that I was thinking of Ellen as if she had just come back from Paris. In her case, of course, when France had worn off, she *had* had a base that sent up shoots. Yet there was something about those iterated phrases—which suggested a stubborn child's question or the insurmountable image of a mad person—that wasn't right, wasn't good.

I thought about Ellen often; I hoped she wasn't herself going mad. I tried to call her a few weeks later, and they told me the phone was out of order.

I walked over that afternoon. The trees of Vallombrosa were quite transformed with reds that were blazing or paling, deep orange, or lemon-yellow, made richer by a slight autumn mist; and they were so much in advance of the trees outside, which were only just beginning to turn, that I wondered whether the doctor's rare species were particularly sensitive to frost.

When I had almost arrived at the house, a girl on a bicycle shot by me, coasting along the drive. She looked toward me when she had set her bicycle against the latticed base of the piazza, and I felt that she expected me to speak to her. But something in her face disconcerted me, and, instead of inquiring for Mrs. Soblianski, I asked—perhaps because Sigismund seemed now so remote from that house in the presence of what I took to be a relative and because at the same time it was incorrect to refer to Ellen as "Miss"—whether "Mrs. Terhune" were at home. "Mrs. Terhune is in the city," said the girl. She had green eyes that reminded me of Ellen's and a rather pale indoor face. She wore a bang over her forehead and short hair fluffed out behind, and she had on a white dress with a long skirt and long sleeves and an enormous folded-over collar that completely enveloped her shoulders. I had been startled to note as she rode by me that she was also wearing long black stockings. Just the wrong thing for bike-riding— what an archaizing family they were! (I assumed this was some cousin of Ellen's): it made me a little impatient.

"Won't you come in?" she said, as I stood searching her face rather queerly. It was a serious intelligent face, and her manner was so mature that it was difficult to tell her age, though she could not have been more than thirteen or fourteen. I replied that I wouldn't come in but would sit down on the porch for a moment. There were a pair of white wicker-backed rockers, and we settled ourselves in them side by side. "How has Mrs. Terhune been?" I inquired, conscious that I had said it again. "She had to go to the hospital," replied the girl. "Grandfather took her up today." I was startled and troubled to hear it; I hoped it wasn't anything serious. "Grandfather says it isn't serious." I was glad that there had been someone to take care of her. "She may have to have a slight operation—they won't be able to decide for a few days." She had a reasonable and earnest tone and the language of an experienced head nurse; but I saw that she was distressed and keyed up: she had a nervous little trick like a tic of tossing her bang aside. I wondered about the operation and asked for the name of the hospital, which turned out to be, not, as I expected, the Neurological Institute or anything of the sort, but a gynecological place.

I didn't want to inquire further and presently remarked on the beauty of the trees. She explained to me the different species, of which she knew all the Latin names, with the same peculiar poise and precision, which seemed to mask an uncomfortable tenseness. "Haven't you been doing a lot to the place lately?" I asked. She thought a moment and tossed her bang: "We've planted a new copper beech. It was almost the only thing we didn't have. I hope it gets to be as gorgeous as the ones on the place across the road. They look as if they were made of bronze. You could play them on the cello." She did not smile and was not trying to be clever: that was the way they evidently talked in that family. "We have a new birdhouse, too." "Have you really?" I expressed an interest. "It's a summer hotel for martins. Would you like to see it?" she asked.

She led me by steps down a terrace that smelt rankly of grass in the autumn damp and past large symmetrical maples that had dropped their leaves in round golden rugs, to a cluster of cedars and firs where I did not remember to have been. I noticed that Sigismund's studio, which ought to have been visible from there, had been taken down since summer. There was not a trace of it left; and I was shocked at the thought that Ellen had had it removed out of bitterness. I was amused, when we came to the birdhouse, to see that it had been designed in the same ornamental and obsolete style as Dr. Bristead's house itself. There were three stories perforated by windows and numerous cupolas and towers. The young cousin explained to me about purple martins, which, she said, were really steel-blue and opened and shut like scissors. She talked about other birds, too, and I saw that she not only knew their habits and names, but had a kind of poetic perception of their qualities. It occurred to me that Ellen in her girlhood must have perceived things in the same quaint and personal way. She had once composed, I remembered, a whole suite of little pieces on objects and creatures about the place: the cupola, the stained-glass window, the garden, the pedigreed collie—and yes, there had been a birdhouse.

There was a squirrel cage not far away, and I went over to see what was in it. It was built around the trunk of an oak and had one of those wheels that they turn. When we came up, there was a squirrel inside it, madly making it spin. I have always disliked these wheels, which I regard as an imposture on the squirrels. "Do you think they like to do that?" I asked. "I don't know," the girl seriously answered. "They don't have to go in there, you know. But I suppose it must be rather discouraging for them when they stop and the wheel begins to carry them back. It always makes them start working again even when they must be tired. They're afraid of going backwards, I guess. Yes: I don't think that can be at all pleasant." She gave her bang a twitch. "Some people are sorry they were born, but everyone has a right to his life, don't you think? People just have to go ahead and realize their own possibilities."

I thought I caught an echo here of old plays by Bernard Shaw or other writings of the live-your-own-life era, which she must have got hold of in her grandfather's house and which had made an impression on her. But it reminded me also of Ellen and her talk about her mother and father. The girl, of course, was perfectly right: you did have to go ahead and do your best with whatever you had. I felt a little disgusted at Ellen's attempt to undo her own past by having Sigismund's studio removed. After all, he had studied and composed there in the most creditable phase of his career. They had worked together, been something together, even though they had later pulled apart. And now she had struck it out as if it had never been.

As we were watching, the squirrel in the cage stopped running against its treadmill. But it did not behave as the girl had described: it allowed itself to be carried around tail-first for several revolutions, then darted out of the wheel and began rushing up and down and from one corner of the cage to the other, as if it were trying to find a breach.

"Do you like them shut up in cages," I asked as we were walking away, "or running around wild?" "When they're wild," she readily answered, "they aren't really any more free than they are when they're kept in cages, if you take the different conditions into account. They can only live in certain places where they can get certain kinds of things to eat, and in the cage they don't have to worry about food because we give them lots of nuts and things—and they're safer than they are outside, because they're protected from the red squirrels. The red squirrels bite the gray squirrels and try to drive them out." She was a formidable little pedant—perhaps a little prig. She could never have been much with other children. It was appalling to think of the figure she would cut among boys and girls of her own age in that dress and those long black stockings and with those metal bands on her teeth. I felt, in fact, a certain nervous self-consciousness involved with her precocious complacency.

"I shouldn't mind living in a cage," she went on, "if I were sure I'd get out someday. I *am* in a sort of cage out here." These shifts of hers disconcerted me, and I didn't know how to reply. "Young people often feel they're caged," I said in a tone of lightness and kindness but with a feeling that I was being sententious. "But, as you say, they find the way out." "Grandfather doesn't want me to go away to school, because he says that he and the governess can teach me a great deal better, and when I went to school in New York last winter it did make it rather embarrassing because I was so far ahead of all the other girls. But I think that there are other reasons for a girl's going away to school." "Yes, of course there are," I assented—I found myself siding against her grandfather. "I wish you would tell Grandfather that," she said in her sedate way. She evidently assumed I was a friend of her family's, or was it merely that we had somehow established a sympa-

thetic understanding? "I will if the occasion presents itself," I found myself naturally replying. "Oh, please do!
won't you?—It might help, you know,"—she became for a
moment quite girlish; then returned to her judicious tone:
"Of course, if anything happened to Mother, I'd have to
stay here with Grandfather. I shouldn't be justified in going away."

We had reached the front steps, and I said good-by.
She invited me to come again in her most mature manner and hoped, with a twitch of her bang, that her
mother would soon be back. I hoped—getting the name
right with an effort, as if I were obliged to struggle with
some false conception that bulked in my mind without
my being able to see it—I hoped that Miss Terhune
would soon be better. The effect that this had on the girl
I was unable to understand and yet it gave me a queer
sort of qualm as if I knew that I had said the wrong
thing. She suddenly seemed embarrassed, but she handled it with her usual self-possession: "Oh, I'm not really
sick. Mother worries about me, but Grandfather says it's
not important. It's silly, of course, to have fainting-fits,
but I'm not really sick at all!" I saw that she had taken
my remark to herself: she must be some sort of niece of
Ellen's father. "Well, I hope," I said, "that everybody's
better."

As I left her alone on the steps, with the darkened
house behind her, in that countryside of deserted residences, the colors of the trees fading in the day-end and
the thickening mist, I was visited by a doubt, a pang, by
a feeling almost dolorous that lingered, as if I almost
knew something about her which I could not remember
to have learned, as if I wanted to save her from something. Though I had never quite recognized the fact in
the past, I could see now that that house was an unhappy one. I thought about the girl mounting the steps,
passing the chairs in which nobody sat, swinging open
the large front door with its paneling of varnished oak

and its upper and lower parts that were separate—going back into that lampless interior, so full of an American past which I felt to be even at its best rather cluttered, middle-class and banal. I had left the place so quiet and dark that it seemed to me even improbable that anyone would come out of the kitchen to drum on the Chinese gongs and summon her in to dinner.

III

When the summer people in Hecate County go away after the first of September, the people who stay on through the winter are more thrown in on themselves and on one another. New contours of the community emerge; you distinguish a new scale of values. You gradually become interested in neighbors of whom you would never have seen anything at the time when there was more going on; and you meditate on the lives of persons who mean absolutely nothing to you.

I brooded a good deal on Ellen. I sent flowers and a note to the hospital, but I never had any reply. Her phone was still out of order, and I thought I ought to call at her house and find out what had happened to her; yet for days I was inhibited from doing so by the brake of some instinctive reluctance which would divert me into town to buy papers or make me call upon some other neighbor when I had intended to go to Ellen's.

This reluctance was due partly to an unpleasant reaction which I had had after my last two visits. One of the symptoms of certain neurotic states is an irrational drop of morale, a depression that may suddenly descend on you and absolutely flatten you out, from some stimulus that seems irrelevant or trifling—a passing sarcasm in conversation directed at someone else, a child ducking a cat in the gutter, a memory drifting into your head of something clumsy you once did in your childhood. I had had a touch of this at one time, and I found that my visits to Ellen's renewed it. This was only, I told myself, vicarious: I was merely being affected accidentally by things that in reality were experienced by others; but it was enough to give me disagreeable sinkings, living as I then did alone, in the evening or even the next afternoon after I had been at Vallombrosa with Ellen. It was a revival of my old morbidity; but it took a peculiar turn. I would feel suddenly after lunch or dinner that living in the country was hopeless, that I had no communication with other people, and that nothing I was doing meant anything; yet on the other hand I could not see any hope in living in the city or traveling: I knew what human beings were—they might be more or less picturesque in their various environments and climates, and to the young this was a source of excitement; but to me, on the verge of thirty, it was desolatingly, incontrovertibly evident that people under any conditions were the same wry pathetic freaks, and why should I go to the trouble of moving about among them in order to observe the shapes which their defects and distortions could take?

I had had something like this feeling before, though the emphasis on deformity, I believed, was new; but in the past it had led to an impulse which was vaguely directed toward suicide. Now the impulse was aimed at an act that would be absolutely immediate and definite: to go back to Ellen's house. This seemed a good deal less serious than suicide; yet there was something about it that scared me. For one thing, it presented itself as a compulsion imposed from outside as to which I had not even the option of yielding on my own terms; and, for another, I had a definite conviction that, in revisiting Ellen's house, I was getting into something very queer that I didn't know how to handle. I did my best to resist this compulsion, and I did not allow myself to go till the impulse was no longer felt as morbid and I could put it to myself that I was merely dropping in to inquire about the illness of a friend. But, nevertheless, I went: I could only choose one way.

I did, however, semi-consciously, make a point of going early in the afternoon so that I should not have to be there at nightfall. I tried to insist to myself that I could not really be afraid because the day itself was overcast and dull. Yet when I entered the gates of Vallombrosa, the sky became suddenly clear. I looked up: it was almost cloudless; before me the thinning branches and the angles of the slate-covered roof were distinct and a little bleak in the emptied October light; and I recognized, against my intelligence, that each of my last entrances there had been marked by some discontinuity of weather or of the appearance of things on the grounds.

Discomfited, I became self-conscious: like an explorer in an unknown terrain, I scanned the place carefully for changes, without, I told myself, noticing any; then I dropped my eyes to the driveway and I saw that the ground was wet: though it had not rained yet outside, it had recently been raining on the Bristead place. There were hoofmarks in the muddy gravel, and what looked like the tracks of a carriage.

I rang the bell at the paneled front door and observed, as I stood on the porch, a croquet set in a long wooden box which I noted that I did not remember. I felt a little dizzy for a moment, but told myself it was perfectly natural that the visiting girl cousin should have brought it out.—Then a brisk and definite step; an accurate hand on the latch; the door opened, and I found myself confronted with a woman I had never seen—the mother of the girl, no doubt. She bore some resemblance to Ellen: her long nose was a little beakish and her jawbones, like Ellen's, stood out; but she was blonder and rather taller. Her sharp eyes were not green but blue-gray, and they were not so intelligent as Ellen's.

"Oh, how do you do," she said in a cordial but formal manner, as if, though she did not know me, she knew about me and had expected my visit. I came into the familiar hallway. "Won't you leave your coat and hat here?" she said. I noticed, as I was taking off my coat, that she gave a keen glance at my clothes—the glance of a woman who is certain that she knows what is correct and what is not, who is severely and unremittingly critical of everyone with whom she has to do and who is not in the habit of hesitating to make her disapproval felt. But any surprise that I may have caused her by the unconventionality of *my* clothes could have been nothing to the shock I received when she turned to lead me into the living room. She was wearing a kind of bustle, a built-out ruffle at the back of her skirt that looked like one of the scalloped crests on that elaborate and poisonous jellyfish called the Portuguese man-of-war. She had also a jacket buttoned closely in front, with two little tails that stuck out above the ruffle; and on her dress, which was silk and mauve, there were several fringes of lace: at the bottom of the skirt, at the throat, and on the sleeves that came just beyond her elbows. It must have been the kind of thing that was in fashion in the middle of the eighties; but the dress was so handsome and so naturally worn that it did not seem obsolete. Her hair was done up high toward the back of her head, and she was wearing black onyx earrings.

The smell of the living room, though this had been different before, seemed curiously natural, too. It emanated from the fumes of a hot coal-grate red-glowing in the white marble fireplace, from the stuff of the garnet curtains muffling the windows with balances and loops, and from the pinkish flowered thick-napped carpeting which I told myself was not really suffocating and which caused me to say to myself "Brussels carpet" in the moment before I sat down. But I had been at first so stunned by the whole situation that I had not been able to look at things calmly, and I subsided into it now in a way that seemed to be depriving me of the power to examine them closely and take account of what had happened to the house.

"It was kind of you to come," she said. "My father was extremely sorry that he had to go to town today. They telephoned him this morning that Mr. Schroeder's condition was worse. It's such a deeply distressing tragedy! He was deceived by the people he trusted, and my father says the shock has almost killed him." "Yes: I'm sorry not to see your father," I fell readily into replying. "He told me to tell you you would hear from him," she said, and immediately addressed herself to what was evidently the business before us. "I don't know how far he has described to you my symptoms" . . . "Not in any great detail," I answered.

I told myself, suddenly relieved at discovering a clue to the strange situation, that the woman was obviously insane and that she was going to tell me about voices and about people who were working against her as they had against Mr. Schroeder. But, instead, she began giving me a very precise, a positively clinical, chronicle of fainting-fits, spells of nausea, and convulsive internal pains. I presently grasped that she was pregnant and, in my rather light-headed embarrassment, I was about to ask her whether she were the mother of the girl I had seen the other day, but I pulled myself up at the realization that such a question would be out of character with the role I was allowing myself to assume—since the physician I was supposed to be would undoubtedly know about her children and would probably not have been here when I had. Such a query, in fact, was impossible; I found that I was powerless to put it—I was powerless to say or do anything which would violate the logic of the scene. And now, with a beating of the heart, but inevitably and by clear recognition, I sank into the consciousness that the woman before me was Ellen's unfortunate mother and that her father was old Dr. Bristead; and I knew—had already known?—that it was Ellen herself in her girlhood whom I had seen on my previous visit: Ellen as she had been in her girlhood and just before her mother's death; and that the Ellen I had met on the visit before had been Ellen at some time in her twenties when she had just come back from Paris. And now here was her mother, a young woman—I saw it perfectly—just before Ellen's birth. As the picture became clear in my mind, I stiffened and sat perfectly still. I was kept tense by the anxiety to follow her, to say something that played in with the story. The queer thing was that it had now become impossible for me to set myself right with Time, because whenever I summoned to mind the order of my adventures in that house, they seemed to me perfectly normal: looking out on my series of glimpses from the point of my visit today, the first image I saw was of Ellen as a girl, and the next was of Ellen a young woman; further on she was middle-aged—and wasn't this the natural sequence? I beheld her growing older—of course: that was what people did. I had a feeling of unreality, yet I couldn't see it in any other way. Giddily and intently I listened, inquiring, when it seemed necessary for me to say something: "Did your father prescribe anything for that?" or "How often have you been having these attacks?"

But she needed no prompting to talk. I got the impression that she was rather hypochondriac and was gloating over the tale of her symptoms. She was not at all restrained by the prudery which might have gone with the upholstery of her costume: she was the daughter of an enlightened doctor and she had been taught not to shrink from such subjects. Though she was dignified and restrained in the extreme, the very patient objectivity and exactitude with which she described her disorders somehow made demands on the hearer for astonishment and commiseration, and I found myself evincing in my expression and tone a graver and graver concern. "I dare say," she continued, "that my condition has been aggravated by the domestic situation—I suppose my father has spoken to you about it." "A little," I replied: I was remembering what Ellen had told me about her parents. "I don't know," she went on with pretended detachment but deadly masochistic hatefulness, "whether a normal parturition is possible under circumstances of that kind: continual scenes that are deeply disturbing to a person in my condition and the uncertainty every night as to whether my husband is coming home." "Can't you stay down here?" I suggested. "I don't want to stay longer than two or three days: I'm afraid of what might happen to him without me. When one thinks how even men of fine character like Mr. Schroeder and General Grant—I don't mean that my husband isn't a man of fine character, but he is unstable and a little irresponsible—when one thinks how even men like that have been ruined and humiliated!"

She now went on to tell me in detail about a physical examination which had been given her by her regular obstetrician and which had disclosed certain structural conditions that he was afraid might make childbirth difficult. "What does your father say about it?" I asked. "He tells me that he doesn't think it's serious, but he wished to consult you." The idea was somehow conveyed to me that she had called me for the purpose of advising her that it would be dangerous for her to have a baby—not, I thought, that she wouldn't go through with it, but she wanted to make her husband suffer by continual complaint and reproach. I felt that I must bite off the interview and escape from that disquieting house. Ellen's mother's cold eye and her reasonable smile which masked the morbidity of her pregnancy were exercising upon me an influence that I had to struggle to break.

"Everything is so uncertain, isn't it?" Mrs. Terhune was saying—"with all these dreadful disasters. One doesn't know what kind of world one is bringing one's children into. People lose all their resources overnight, and one doesn't want to have one's child not have the things one has had oneself." I answered shortly, and got up brusquely—being a doctor gave me this right—and told her that she must come to my office: I would give

her an examination there. She seemed puzzled and a little displeased as if she had imagined that this was what I
had called for, and suggested that it would be a good
thing if I could examine her right away, since her symptoms were becoming worse. "I'll phone you tomorrow,"
I said—then feared I had slipped in my role; they had
certainly had telephones then—or now, but had they
talked about "phoning" people? I was frightened for a
second, then fortified by the thought that my instinct
had kept me straight—I was still in the actual world. I
almost smiled at the joke; but the woman would not allow it. She looked at me gravely, as if she were a trifle
dismayed and even not quite sure what I meant; and I
saw that she thought I had been speaking of some unfamiliar clinical technique. I seized the occasion to shake
hands and say good-by in a reassuring manner, and get
out of the house and outside the grounds.

All the way down the drive, however, I had the illusion that her insistence was attached to me, lengthening
out like a rubber band, whose pull I felt growing stiffer
as it was thinner and thinner drawn. At the gate I hoped
the pull would snap, but I awaited the moment with a
fear that it might not after all bring relief: it was as if I
were cheating on some perverse obligation, leaving unfinished some ugly task. Whatever I was leaving behind
me—and I did not quite know what it was—I was definitely involved in that thing.

I woke up in the night in a panic: a seizure of horror and
disgust which had projected itself in a nightmare. I had
thought I was in the hallway of Ellen's house, struggling
with the *tromba marina*, which I was trying to carry upstairs. It would catch in the mahogany-stained banisters in
such a way that it was difficult to extricate or it would get
between my legs and cause me to fall on all fours on the
heavily-carpeted stairs. And this was all bound up in some
way with the naked Canova Hebe, which I had noted the

day before in the hallway, though Ellen had always kept it
in a museum-like reception room. The statue in the
dream, I decided, had represented some ideal of nineteenth-century womanhood, symmetrical, smooth and
chaste, to which my clumsy mishaps with the obsolete instruments were somehow an impious affront. But then the
thing took a sinister turn. I had the bow of the *tromba marina* and I was trying to do something damaging to a modern violin: instead of using it to draw forth music, I was
jabbing it into the f-holes; I was compelled to do this, but
whenever I did, Mrs. Terhune would shriek out in a way
that I felt was overdone and malicious—it was all, as a
matter of fact, prearranged—yet which, none the less, convicted me of hideous guilt.

I turned on the light to make sure that that woman
was not with me there, and as I looked at my green-
stained woodwork and my rough-finished plastered
walls, of which the fine leaded folding windows opened
right on the trees and the grass, I was aware that a revelation had been pushing to the surface through sleep. In
that loneliness of the forest surrounding my house, the
meaning pressed in with the night. What the woman really wished me to do was to declare her unfit to have a
baby and to recommend a legal abortion. She wanted to
spite her husband, the child that was to be, life itself.
But why? I couldn't understand her. Was she human or a
specter of nightmare? She was real in the sense that I
had seen her, with her horrible well-cut mauve dress and
her cold and shallow eyes, and that I could not get her
out of my head; but in the dream there was somebody
behind her, she emanated from somebody else—at the
moment just before she began to scream, it had seemed
to me that her eyes were bright green, alive with intellect, and glaring not in hypocritical agony but in fixed
and unforgiving condemnation.

And now I seemed to see it quite clearly: the apparition
had come from Ellen. It was Ellen herself who had created

this monster in the image of her mother, who was forcing her to get rid of her baby, who was destroying her own existence before it had come out of the womb! And she was somehow forcing me to abet her. . . . I had, I felt, to make a moral effort to free myself from Ellen's influence, and I got myself to sleep with a book just as the windows were unblotting from night.

When I woke again, this certainty faded. The sun was quite brilliant and bracing: it sent a long pane of light across my breakfast and brought out the whites and yellows of my eggs with their sprinkling of salt and pepper; I talked to my soft-spoken colored maid about the movie she had seen the night before; and I stood outside for a moment and was delighted by the deep-orange zinnias, the pompon clusters of little lemon marigolds, the big scarlet daisies of cosmos on high and spidery stems that still were bright at the end of October. I decided that my explanation of my visit of the day before had been simply a part of the nightmare. What I had seen was not a woman of the eighties but a contemporary relation of Ellen's, completely insane no doubt but an actual human being, and I must not allow myself to be led by her into getting insane myself. I expelled the whole thing from my mind; read the papers, wrote several letters, and contemplated a trip to the city. I needed the city, I felt.

But when I went for a walk that afternoon, the sun had gone out for the day and the whole thing came back on me again. I saw the situation precisely as I had seen it in the middle of the night, and I could not see it in any other way—I could not seem to get outside it. And I now felt not merely an irrational pull toward the house in which Ellen lived; I had a fear it would come to find me—that the past might have its gangsters, too, who could wait for you and meet you on the autumn roads where so little traffic passed. I presently turned back, came home, and lay on a couch and brooded.

Yet I could not go to town, I now told myself: there was something I could not leave unfinished. I had to see it finished, and I had to do my best to see that it was finished as it should be. Precisely what this meant I did not know—except that it imposed upon me a duty to stand up to the Bristead-Terhunes. I must not be afraid to go out, I must not be afraid to pass the place; I must even be not afraid to go back there, but I must not go back in response to that pull which was itself a fear.

All the rest of the week and the week following, then, I took my afternoon walk every day, and I several times glanced in at Vallombrosa, where I could not see that anything was changed—though I believe I did not look very closely. I still had my bad moments at night after the painful importunings of dreams and during stretches of those solitary strolls which had now become daily trials. But by the end of the second week I was imagining that the pressure was lighter. I had had two untormented nights, and I set out on Saturday afternoon with something like ease and indifference.

I walked first along a little back-road that ran parallel with the regular motor-road on which the Bristead house faced: it passed behind the Bristeads', but there was somebody else's place between Ellen and it. Then I turned down a hedge-lined lane that connected with the larger road, admitting to myself humorously as I did so that I had lately never taken these lanes. I heard something drive in behind me and I drew over close to the hedge, but it was something that ran very lightly, and I did not glance round as it passed. A horse stopped in front of me: I looked up and saw a lady in a varnished yellow phaeton, who seemed to be speaking to me. "Oh, how do you do," I replied with an instinctive familiarity that preceded conscious recognition. "You ought to have let us know that you were coming today," she said as she reached down her gloved hand. She was slimmer and brisker and trimmer than when I had seen her before.

She was wearing a tight dress of a brown-and-green plaid, with a beautiful hourglass waist and no bustle or ruffle to encumber the skirt, and a pretty little straw bonnet, which was tied under her chin with a big green bow.

I got in at her invitation, as if it were a matter of course, and she drove on, sitting up very straight between the gracefully scrolling wicker fenders and behind the slim long-lashed whip that stood upright and smart in its socket. I was occupied for the first few minutes in fitting my story to my role. There was a passage in the conversation where she and I almost lost connections when I had to explain that I had walked instead of asking them to meet me at the train because I so much enjoyed walking, then found out that the railroad station was eight or nine miles away. I was forced to confess, laughing nervously, that I had only been boasting before, that a farmer had brought me part way. And I did not notice at first that we were driving through a landscape that seemed new to me. We had turned out of the lane to the right through a gate I had not known was there, and now were trotting along a driveway which should have led to the house next door to the Bristeads'; but, to my surprise, there was no house there: instead of a house, there was a wide expanse of lawn, unbroken by a hedge or fence, through which the long drive made a curve. We approached a yellow new-looking house and drew up under a *porte-cochère*. I realized suddenly and queerly that we were back at Vallombrosa again. I remarked that I hadn't known about this driveway which connected with the other road. "Yes: the drive runs right through," she replied. It came to me that the place next door was still a part of the Bristead estate: the doctor would later sell it. I had entered into the domain of the Bristeads as soon as I had turned into the lane.

"I don't know why Jerry didn't see me," she said when she had waited hardly a second. "Would you mind going into the house and telling Rosa to call him?—I think he's getting very lax," she said, as I climbed down from the phaeton. I opened the front door and went in. Should I bolt? No, I couldn't do that. I walked resolutely through the hallway—conscious, as I passed the Hebe, that I did not give it a thought. But when I got to the door to the kitchen, I knew there would be nobody there. I opened it, however, and looked in. There was a big black coal-range with a stovepipe, a bare clean wooden floor, a double row of copper pots and pans hanging along the wall. I called out, "Hello . . . Rosa . . ."; but nobody answered. I ought now, I said to myself, to go out the back door to the stable; but I was swayed by a half-dreamlike instinct that I should not find anyone there either; and my sense that I was not going to go there was strengthened by a voice from the hallway which told me that the coachman had come.

I joined her. She was removing her bonnet. "Well, the styles in men's clothes astonish me," she said, as I took off my overcoat. "Is that really what they're wearing now?" "I'm perhaps a little eccentric," I said. "I get to town so seldom," she continued, as we went into the living room, "that I don't even know the fashions—and I believe that the young men I see are rather conservative about their clothes."

The atmosphere, I felt, was relaxed. The room seemed to be largely unchanged. There were the curtains, the grate with its coals, the tables with low-hanging covers, the ornaments on a whatnot in the corner. I noticed a large bronze gas-chandelier with shades of pattern-frosted glass. I must have scrutinized these objects rather curiously because she glanced toward a group of swords and sabers, hung up so as to form a design, at which she evidently thought I was looking, and explained: "Those are oriental weapons. I don't think they have any place here—but Papa seems to consider them decorative. I tell him he ought to build a small armory.—Do sit down: take that comfortable chair."

I questioned her, still standing for a moment, about the various kinds of weapons; but she wasn't quite sure what they were and was obviously impatient with them. There was some matter that she wanted to get on to—so I finally took the comfortable chair. "I should like to talk to you quite frankly about something," she began almost as soon as we were seated, "and I want you to advise me frankly. You're the closest friend now that we have—though it's been such a long time since we've seen you." I was, then, an old family friend. "I have no brothers or uncles to turn to as most women have—I have nobody in the world but Papa, and you know how prejudiced he is about so many things, and how obstinately he sticks to his prejudices. I know that I can say that to you because you know that I love and admire him more than anyone else in the world—but—well, you know how sure he is about everything." I nodded and smiled in concurrence. "Well, I'd like to put my problem before you—if you don't mind being plunged into family affairs just the very minute you come. I know it's not a very cheerful welcome, but I think that if I'm going to talk about it, I'd better do it before Papa gets back. You know that he doesn't give people much chance to express opinions different from his own.—Well, here is my problem quite baldly. A young man has asked me to marry him—" "And your father doesn't approve of him," I put in, a little more at ease in the new situation than I had been in the role of physician. "—And Papa doesn't approve of him at all. In fact, he's violently opposed to my marrying him—and you know how he is when he's opposed to anything. He's even making it difficult now for Fred to come to the house." The young man, then—I half felt I had known it already, was Ellen's father, Fred Terhune, and this was Ellen's mother, younger than when I had seen her before and not yet come to a decision about marrying him.

"Why does he object to this young man?" I asked. "It's simply that he's in Wall Street," she answered. "I think that his attitude is very unreasonable. The financiers have done so much for this country and it's ridiculous to pretend that they're not as good as our best—Mr. Morgan, for example, who has just as much taste as Papa and is making such a wonderful collection. It isn't as if he were in business! Fred's family are Terhune Brothers, the bankers, and his position is perfectly unexceptionable. I am sure that his character is sound. He was a little wild in his younger days, but now he wants a home and an ordered life. That's hard for Papa to understand, because Papa has always been occupied with intellectual things, and he can't recognize that a man whom he regards as a mere man of fashion can be a proper person to marry. I really think he'd rather I married a musician—someone preferably who played the cello, so that we could have a family trio." I was aware of the prejudice against "business" on the part of the professional classes that had lasted in the United States till long after our national life had been actually dominated by businessmen; but this prejudice, I thought, as a rule, had not been extended to bankers, and I put down the doctor's opposition to distrust of the particular young man or to some special and personal crankiness. But she went on to indicate another cause which I guessed to be fundamental. "Of course, I understand, too, that Papa has been lonely since Mama's death, and that he doesn't want to have me leave him. But, after all, Papa has so many resources—his work and his music and his collections and his chess—and I can't go on like this forever. He doesn't understand that if I don't get married now, I may be left alone myself. And Fred needs me, too—he's told me so with all the feeling of which anyone is capable and I can see that his bachelor life is beginning to do him harm.—Now please tell me frankly and sincerely what you think I ought to do. Shall I just go ahead and marry Fred in spite of Papa's opposition? I feel that he's perfectly capable of refusing to give me anything and never having anything to do with me again. But if I do as Papa wants, I'll feel that I'm betraying Fred's trust in me. Now how would you advise me to act?"

This, then, was an earlier turning-point, another moment to determine the future; and again there was the curious effort to put off the decision on me.

This plea of Miss Bristead's, who I gathered was now in her latish twenties, reminded me of Ellen's appeal, at the time I had seen her in her girlhood, that I should put in a word with her grandfather to have her sent away to school. And I had now a very clear conviction of something that I had only felt without figuring it to myself before: that Dr. Bristead was an egregious old egoist, selfish in his relations with his family and oppressive in his opinionated omniscience. The daughter, too, in her turn, would want to get away from Dr. Bristead, and she would certainly have sympathized with her mother. I sympathized with her myself. Miss Bristead had a genuine distinction, she was handsome in her glamorless way; above all, as she leaned forward in her modish dress that reminded me of Ellen's plaid skirt when she had just come back from Paris, and threw out her very well-shaped hands that might have been reproduced in china for those vases that hold single flowers—above all, she was an eager young woman who wanted to escape from that house and marry an urgent suitor. Besides, there was a certain authority, a certain force of assertion she commanded, to which I could feel myself yielding. Why shouldn't she, I asked myself, be bored with ministering to her father's hobbies? Why shouldn't she want to live in town? Why shouldn't she yearn for and why shouldn't she share in that codified social life for which she was obviously well adapted and of which her father had undoubtedly skimped her? Why shouldn't she marry

Fred? He was doing no one any good—it seemed to me, as if I had known him—as a man about town past his prime. He could at least give her an independent position, help her to found a family. It was as if I could not foresee the future.

"I'm sure that it's right for you to marry him," I replied to her request for advice. "I do wish you would tell Papa that!"—she was grateful to me for recommending the thing that she wanted to do, though she must have been sure all along that I would follow the lead she had given. "If anyone could persuade him, you could. I don't want to do anything without his consent—it would be so distressing for everybody!" "I'll try," I assured her, smiling.

She looked away toward the adjoining music room, the door into which was open, but which I could not see from where I sat, as if she had just heard somebody enter it. Then she was turning to me again as if to go on talking when someone began to play the piano—ringing out, as imagined at random, the Don Juan theme from Strauss, which had not been quite accurately remembered. Miss Bristead looked up as if uncertain how to deal with the situation; but the music went on consecutively, developing and playing with the theme. We saw that it was an organized piece. "Oh, yes: do play it, dear!"—she looked toward the music room. "This is your new composition, isn't it? I want so very much to hear it!" She leaned over and said to me in a lowered voice, which was, however, it seemed to me, quite loud enough to carry clearly into the next room: "Our guest is playing something of her own. I hope you don't mind. It may not be very wonderful, and I don't think the middle of the afternoon is quite the best time to listen to music, do you?—but I don't want to stop her now that she's started. I wasn't sure whether she was going to be here and I hope she won't be in our way."

I nodded and gestured with my hand so that she would be still and I could listen to the music. It was amusing and very adroit. The composer had taken an echo of the blare of the Don Juan theme and subjected it to all kinds of transformations. After stating it at first in its full exultation, she had gone on to break its pace and to reduce it to a wavering whimper. Against this appeared a steadier theme, sober, distinct and insistent, which began by going along with Don Juan in a fairly orderly manner but ended by getting at odds with him in a jagged amalgamation that seemed to be jamming the movement. Miss Bristead gave me a look of ironic disapproving amazement when these cacophonies began to sound. She had listened before that rather thoughtfully, as if she did not know quite how to take it, with her cheek leaned against her fine fingers and her face partly turned toward the door; but now, as the music appeared to her to be getting more and more insane, she coughed toward me a dry little laugh as if it might all be supposed to be funny, and slightly shifted her pensive pose, self-consciously and pleasantly smiling. Don Juan had the last word of the contest that went on in the music, but in a triumph that verged, I thought, on the trashy. The whole thing had reminded me of Sigismund, who so loved to exploit the Strauss tone-poem, identifying himself with the hero and bringing down the house. "I *don't* know what you want to do to our ears," said Miss Bristead in the direction of the doorway: "That certainly doesn't lack vivacity—but it does sound a little like a couple of children letting *Chopsticks* run away with them."

There was no answer from the other room: after a moment the piano began again. Miss Bristead faintly raised her eyebrows at the pianist's bizarre rudeness—for this person whom I could not see had offered neither announcement nor excuse—and again became silent. And now, almost without astonishment, I recognized the slow movement of the sonata that Ellen had played me in August. Yes: I heard unmistakably that theme—that sullen

immovable impediment—which had worried me so at the
time and of which I had felt a premonition in the music of
Ellen's youth. I looked up toward the door with interest,
and Miss Bristead shot me a glance and threw out her
hands in a gesture of "Well, I give it up!" How horrible
Ellen's harmonics must sound to her mother, I thought:
they must be forty or fifty years beyond her. I smiled
faintly and nodded curtly and thereafter kept clear of her
eye. I listened to the music with attention. It was not now
so thudding and stunning: she had worked out devices to
vary it so that it no longer made one nervous with the fear
that she was simply getting stuck, and yet she had kept the
effect of monotony. Daring and disconcerting though it
was, I saw that it would be ultimately successful. Certainly, Ellen was an admirable musician!

When again there was a pause for a moment, Miss
Bristead sat and looked at her lap. But quickly she returned to the charge: "I suppose," she said humorously
to the doorway, "that the first section represented Baby
when he was just beginning to bang and that the second
is called *Five-Finger Exercises.*"

The piano picked up when the space had been made. I
listened for this movement with excitement. It began
with the theme of obstruction again, and, though this
had been sharpened and speeded up, I felt at first rather
disappointed. In a moment, I was almost terrified. The
four notes which had not let her move now in their way
became hysterically insistent. The thing seemed to be
getting out of hand and was beginning to sound absolutely hellish, a shrieking of desperation; and the horror
of the nightmare came back on me. Miss Bristead got up
and coughed slightly and went out through the door into
the hall as if she had to speak to the maid but at the
same time desired definitely to indicate that she was
done with the music. I continued to listen, and there
crept upon me a dark apprehension like that of those
days when I had dreaded to come to the house: the pi-

ano seemed to be carrying me, like the panic of my dreams, to some bad unintelligible goal. The awful accelerated movement had passed from the negative of inertia to a frenzied destructive denial. But now it met a new kind of theme, which it seemed to have thrown up itself and which was lifted like the human cry in the slow movement of Beethoven's last string quartet, shuddering and terror-stricken at first as it shrilled from the sinister harping that was beginning to tear like a beast at a carcass, then rising to a plangency, to a clarity, that, passing the conventional limits of this sort of affirmation in music, began to assail one's attention more recklessly, more compellingly, more triumphantly, just as the diabolic yapping of the other theme, becoming fiercer and fiercer, had forced itself beyond all limits. This cry, itself now reiterated, not only wrecked the bounds of the conventional, it seemed even to escape from the probable—anguished, appealing, pitying, recognizing all human discrepancy, debasement, self-disgust and self-accusal of the individual who knows his own nature and who yet cannot undo what he is; but reaching by the voice of music out of the brooding of deformity in solitude to speak to other beings of their solitudes and of the general human fate, declaring by its certainty of pain how much our nature wrongs us. The voice broke away: for that moment, becoming at once more complex and more ordered, it had been freed to a life of its own—something that shone and resounded and yet had a solid wholeness, something that had left all deformity behind and that nothing now could ever violate.

Miss Bristead came back into the room just as the final statement was struck, pulling up perhaps a little short of the development one might have expected and yet perfectly making its point. "That was immensely interesting!" she said to the person in the music room. "It must be extremely fatiguing playing such violent music." She sat down beside me on the couch and remarked in her inadequately lowered voice: "I don't think our friend in the next room has discovered the use of the soft pedal yet—as well as a number of other things! . . . I don't think she's entirely normal—one can see it by her over-sized head."

I realized then that it was not only in technique that Ellen's music was beyond Miss Bristead: musically trained though she was, she had no real feeling for music whatever. The daughter had been mistaken in her notion that her mother's marriage had shut her off from a musical career: Miss Bristead was conventional and worldly, she could not conceivably be anything else. And now Ellen, surmounting her own despair, had come back all the way through the years to justify her, to communicate her love, to show her that something fine had come out of her, something that might make all that—the coldness, the sickness, the quarreling, the bad birth and the ugly changeling—something that might make all that right. I wanted to tell Ellen that she had triumphed, that she had perhaps written a masterpiece. I wanted to assure her, confronted as we were by the Gorgon-like incomprehension of her mother, that I at least understood and applauded.

"I liked it very much," I said, and got up quickly and went into the music room. But Ellen had already escaped. There was nobody there: I looked around. Everything seemed perfectly familiar, unexpectedly and yet reassuringly: the mask of Beethoven, the old violins, Ellen's silver-framed photograph of Debussy. But the room, rather queerly, was much darker than the one from which I had come.

I had an impulse to go after Ellen and call to her that I was there. I was eager to see her again. But I knew that it would be better to return to Miss Bristead and ask her to make Ellen come in. I went back, then, into the living room; but it was empty: Miss Bristead had gone out again. This room had darkened, too—the weather must suddenly have clouded. I turned on the electric lamp on the little round table by the couch, and saw that the mahogany of the surface was dimmed by a film of dust. There was a pile of current magazines, current for 1926. I picked two or three of them up and noted the dates on the covers. Then I looked about the room. There it was just as I had seen it in August. All the shades were drawn. I picked up from another table a vase of faded flowers and got a whiff of a foul stink: they were gladioluses withered to a crisp yellow thinness. On the mantel were the shrunk mummies of dahlias. The house had been shut up in haste: the flowers had been forgotten.

I found my hat and coat in the hall, but the big front door was fast locked. I came back into the living room, threw up one of the front windows, and stepped out on the dark porch, where I saw that it had just been raining. I did not fear that Miss Bristead would catch me—I knew there was nobody there.

The next day I read in the paper that Ellen Terhune had died. She had gone, it turned out, to the city the night of my visit in August. She had taken a little suite—registering under her maiden name—in a little old hotel in the West Fifties which was frequented by musical people and where you could have a piano in your room. She had apparently made efforts to compose during the first two or three weeks she had been there; but later she would be found by the chambermaid lying on the couch or the bed in what seemed to be a kind of stupor, and the management became aware that she was never going out and not eating. They had decided that she was suffering from the sleeping sickness and got a doctor in. But Ellen had then revived and explained that she had come for a rest and did not want to be annoyed, and sent the doctor about his business.

She now reassured the hotel people by directing that a breakfast with two pots of coffee should be brought to her every morning; and she was heard at the piano again, pounding the same thing over and over in a way that made them fear she had gone insane. In the evening she would leave the hotel, but they did not know where she went.

One day, however, she had not got up but had stayed in bed till afternoon, and the maid had not been able to do the rooms. It was the day of my last call in the country, and at what must have been the same hour that I was listening to the playing of the sonata, the maid heard the piano and knocked. She had just started work on the bedroom when Ellen stopped and came in and put on her things to go out. She was tense and her hands, which had been strained over the keys, had difficulty adjusting themselves to manage her coat and hat. The chambermaid tried to help her, but Ellen paid no attention.

She went out quickly and rang for the elevator. On the trip down, the elevator boy said, he had stopped and gone back up a floor to get a passenger who had rung after they passed, and Ellen had "bawled him out," telling him he must never go back once he had passed a floor. This sudden scolding had so flustered the boy, who was new and rather inexpert with the old-fashioned elevator, that he had made the situation worse by stopping below the door and then jerking the car up just as the passenger was stepping down. Then, in an effort to make up for his delay, on the assumption that Ellen was in a hurry, he had shot abruptly down, in a drop which the passenger who had just got in said afterwards had given him an unpleasant shock. It must have shocked Ellen, too, for she was pale when they reached the bottom, and leaned against the side of the elevator for a moment before she got out. The boy was worried and tried to help her; but she stepped out by herself into the lobby, and there she fell dead. It was said that she had had a bad heart.

VIII
Verse

EDITOR'S NOTE

Wilson's poetry is quite removed from that of the modernists he promoted in *Axel's Castle*. The serious work of his youth keeps alive a tradition of concentrated, morally earnest English lyric poetry going back through Hardy and the nineties to Matthew Arnold. He ponders his experience and that of those closest to him in disciplined, perhaps overdisciplined, verse before he could do so in the matter-of-fact terms of prose. The elegant surroundings of a European leisure-class, as he saw them in Florence, made him more loyal to the stark beginnings of our literature in Puritan New England. His father's death touched him, he reflects in the second poem, as piling dead bodies in the basement of a hospital in France hadn't, though he did not fully understand his father's suffering till after his own nervous breakdown. That experience is also evoked in "The Voice," a piece which begins with the limits of life as represented in great literature, moving to a cousin's neurotic collapse, then Wilson's doomed marriage to Margaret Canby. His fine elegy on Fitzgerald, dated February 1942, remembers their shared youth in iambic pentameter couplets. Looking back from the seeming collapse of civilization during World War II, Wilson takes the novelist as one of his marked fictional heroes.

Much of the later poetry is satirical light verse. "The
Mass in the Parking Lot," with its clever summations of
major figures whom the critic knew, attacks what he
deemed a failure of nerve in the literary world after the
war, when religion was fashionable and his own dissent
from the cult of Kafka earned him the reputation of a
philistine. In the final short selection, the aging critic
turns his wit upon himself.

BOBOLI GARDENS

There were no gardens there like those
That, groomed for pleasure and for ease,
Rose-clouded with the laurel-rose,
Hung high above blue distances.

There were no fountains, dolphin-fed,
For idle eyes to drift upon,
Where gold-fish, flecking green with red,
Drift idle in the eternal sun;

No sloping alleys gliding smooth
Through velvet glooms or golden light,
Round-moulded like the marble youth
That stops the alley-way with white;

No naiad satyr-sprayed and pale;
No lap-dog lions poised in rank;
No Ganymede, demure and frail,
The satyr crouching at his flank;

No Homer smooth on creamy skin,
With green-blue-gold embroidery lined.
The black and dingy boards of Ginn
Your poets, like your God, confined.

In bare-swept houses, white and low;
High stony pastures never ploughed;
The pure thin air; the frozen snow;
And the sad autumn dark with cloud—

There, setting bare feet on bare wood,
They came who late in silks had gone;
Dim candor by your desks they stood,
Austere to wake the winter dawn.

WHEN ALL THE YOUNG WERE DYING

When all the young were dying, I dwelt among the
    dead—
Many I lifted from the homeless bed
And laid in that low chamber side by side,
But they were unknown men,
Nor told me youth had died.

But you—when all the years of honor and success—
Skill, courage, learning, and their fullest scope
Had brought but darkness, brooding, loneliness;
The solitary walk, the muffled door;
Scorn of that public life which once had been your
    hope—
When dead I saw you, silent, straight and lean,
The film of age's tarnishment effaced,
Life's heaviness refined—
Looking, I knew at last that I had seen
That man of whom old Princeton teachers told—
The wonder of the Halls, the generous, the bold—
That youth by age and honor left behind,
By manhood's melancholy languished for—
The face of that young Princeton orator,
Rejoined in death at last.

—I blamed the day, the place,
Where flesh was rotting where it seemed most
    smooth,

Propping with age's comfort and grave ways
The broken back of youth:
Bred to one world and wearied by this other,
From which youth's straight backbone still kept you
    out,
You had earned but isolation and decay.

—Now I, more arrogant in a wiser day,
But half my life behind me, son of that father,
Know what blind life, what tomb of solitude,
What doubt, what draining of the spirit's blood,
Were ended where you lay.

THE VOICE

On a Friend in a Sanitarium

All Virgil's idyls end in sunsets; pale
With death, the past of Dante opens deep;
The men of Shakespeare do not break, they fail;
And Joyce's dreamers always drift asleep.

—Her loved American laughter, male and clear,
That rang so young in London or in Rome—
A quarter-century gone, my fortieth year—
Is mute among those living ghosts at home.

And I who have been among them and who know
The spirit shrunken to its shuttered cell,
Now hear no laughter—only, piercing low,
This voice that always says, "Farewell! sleep well!"

———

I heard it, dulled with love against your breast,
I heard it in our peace of summer suns;
I heard it where the long waves of the West
Retard the dark with loud suspended guns;

And even in the white bark of that wood,
Those mountains roped and broken by our race,
Beside those high streams where the horses stood
And watched our strange and desperate embrace.

ON EDITING
SCOTT FITZGERALD'S PAPERS

Scott, your last fragments I arrange tonight,
Assigning commas, setting accents right,
As once I punctuated, spelled and trimmed
When, passing in a Princeton spring—how dimmed
By this damned quarter-century and more!—
You left your *Shadow Laurels* at my door.
That was a drama webbed of dreams: the scene
A shimmering beglamored bluish-green
Soiled Paris wineship; the sad hero one
Who loved applause but had his life alone;
Who fed on drink for weeks; forgot to eat,
"Worked feverishly," nourished on defeat
A lyric pride, and lent a lyric voice
To all the tongueless knavish tavern-boys,
The liquor-ridden, the illiterate;
Got stabbed one midnight by a tavern mate—
Betrayed, but self-betrayed by stealthy sins—
And faded to the sound of violins.

Tonight, in this dark long Atlantic gale,
I set in order such another tale,
While tons of wind that take the world for scope
Rock blackened waters where marauders grope
Our blue and bathed-in Massachusetts ocean;
The Cape shakes with the depth-bomb's dumbed
    concussion;

And guns can interrupt me in these rooms,
Where now I seek to breathe again the fumes
Of iridescent drinking-dens, retrace
The bright hotels, regain the eager pace
You tell of. . . . Scott, the bright hotels turn bleak;
The pace limps or stamps; the wines are weak;
The horns and violins come faint tonight.

A rim of darkness that devours light
Runs like the wall of flame that eats the land;
Blood, brain and labor pour into the sand;
And here, among our comrades of the trade,
Some buzz like husks, some stammer, much afraid,
Some mellowly give tongue and join the drag
Like hounds that bay the bounding anise-bag,
Some swallow darkness and sit hunched and dull,
The stunned beast's stupor in the monkey-skull.

I climbed, a quarter-century and more
Played out, my college steps, unlatched my door,
And, creature strange to college, found you there:
The pale skin, hard green eyes, and yellow hair—
Intently pinching out before a glass
Some pimples bred by parties at the Nass;
Nor did you stop abashed, thus pocked and blotched,
But kept on peering while I stood and watched.
Tonight, from days more distant now, we find,
Than holidays in France were, left behind,
Than spring of graduation from the fall
That saw us grubbing below City Hall,
Through storm and darkness, Time's contrary stream,
There glides amazingly your mirror's beam—
To bring before me still, glazed mirror-wise,
The glitter of the hard and emerald eyes.
The cornea tough, the aqueous chamber cold,
Those glassy optic bulbs that globe and hold—
They pass their image on to what they mint,
To blue ice or green buds attune their tint
And leave us, to turn over, iris-fired,
Not the great Ritz-sized diamond you desired
But jewels in a handful, lying loose:
Flawed amethysts; the moonstone's milky blues;
Chill blues of pale transparent tourmaline;
Opals of shifty yellow, chartreuse green,
Wherein a vein vermilion flees and flickers—

Tight phials of the spirit's light mixed liquors;
Some tinsel zircons, common turquoise; but
Two emeralds, green and lucid, one half-cut,
One cut consummately—both take their place
In Letters' most expensive Cartier case.
And there I have set them out for final show,
And come to the task's dead-end, and dread to know
Those eyes struck dark, dissolving in a wrecked
And darkened world, that gleam of intellect
That spilled into the spectrum of tune, taste,
Scent, color, living speech, is gone, is lost;
And we must dwell among the ragged stumps,
With owls digesting mice to dismal lumps
Of skin and gristle, monkeys scared by thunder,
Great buzzards that descend to grab the plunder.
And I, your scraps and sketches sifting yet,
Can never thus revive one sapphire jet,
However close I look, however late,
But only spell and point and punctuate.

THE MASS IN THE PARKING LOT

. . . And whom should we meet there, on the loose,
But André Gide in a big burnoose.
What were his words of wisdom? Damn it,
He was whooping it up for Dashiell Hammett.
More correctly garbed, we encountered later
T. S. Eliot, the Great Dictator.
Having just awakened from troubled sleep,
He told us Charles Williams was terribly deep.
And Wystan Auden, with rigorous views
But his necktie hanging around his shoes,
Expounded his taste for detective stories,
Which he reads to illumine the current mores.
But all—with the single exception of Gide,
Who prefers sailor Melville's more masculine breed—

Were exceedingly strong for Henry James,
With his stunningly high artistic aims.
"I've made a discovery! Isn't it thrilling?
He's as good as Stendhal," cried Lionel Trilling.
With a rumble-de-bum and a pifka-pafka
Came the fife-and-drum corps parading for Kafka.
Full of multiple meanings and *sotto voce's*,
They had more and more grown to resemble roaches:
Thus debasing themselves, they drew close to the
     Master,
And could crawl into cracks to avoid disaster.

The scene was a desolate parking lot,
In an undetermined suburban spot,
Though few of us had any cars to park,
And the air was bad and the day was dark.
And most were agreed they must hold a mass
To bring some poignant epiphka to pass;
But the problem was who should officiate,
Who lead the choir, who pass the plate.
Roman Catholics, cheek by jaw,
Sat Graham Greene and Evelyn Waugh;
But Waugh, with his wiles and his wicked jokes,
Was keen to bring in the county folks,
While Graham, a child of the Scots and the Picts,
Liked the richer and riper derelicts.
Eliot and Auden, Anglo-Caths,
Amateur clergymen, lean as laths,
Morally snobbish but madly self-humbling,
Made an almost inaudible mumbling bumbling.
And Huxley was brewing a new brand of Yogi
To banish the bestial sexual bogey,
While Isherwood, lately a Quaker nudist,
Had turned Anglo-American Babist-Buddhist.
And that gentleman-caterer Somerset Maugham,
Whom they amiably praised since he couldn't awe
     'em,

The prince of chain-restaurant pastry-cooks,
Had been dashing a flavor of God in his books
—Though what flavor it was I shall never know,
For I cannot get down his unleavened dough.

So they argued with moderate animation
And well-planted accents of abnegation,
Till somebody said, "It won't be so hard
If we all concentrate on Kierkegaard."
And they fixed up a flimsy receiving set,
Over which, with some fussing, they managed to
  get—
Through a cracked screech of Marxism, still fanatic,
And a rattle of Existentialist static—
A Voice that said, "Fellows, I've got a new sponsor.
If you're sending Me prayers and you want an answer.,
Turn to Alpha Omega XYZ
At nine-thirty tonight for a load of Me.
You've already discovered the wonderful fun it
Affords to find God in a dim who-dun-it—
How *The Trial, The Castle, The Ambassadors*
Ooze purest religion from all their pores.
Well, boys, you must see Me on television,
Where I wallop my point with appalling precision.
I'm the brains of a flickering comic-strip
That lets all the most hideous instincts rip.
On the one hand, the treacherous heretics
Are implacably conked with brutal bricks;
While the saint is popped off, an exploded zero—
Though to you boys, perhaps, an inferior hero.
It's only the sinner with faith who wins,
For he's saved by his faith, and you're thrilled by his
  sins:
He's a beautiful bum who always escapes,
Just gasping a prayer when perdition gapes.
You may find this a little bit crude—but I doubt it:
I believe that you boys will be mad about it!"

And I watched it begin—a wavering splotch
Made a big comic rabbit—I had to watch,
In a clamp of compulsion I couldn't shake,
Till, choking and groaning, I burst awake.
The lights were on and the windows closed,
Just as they had been when I dozed;
And below me lay flaccidly sprawling near
An avant-garde quarterly (well in the rear)
That had slumped to the floor with unheeded flop
When my slackening fingers had let it drop.

SOMETHING ABOUT THE AUTHOR

There was an old werewolf named Wilson
Whose jaws were as strong as a Stillson;
   But when wanted one day
   To go after his prey,
They found he was sleeping off Pilsen.

IX
From the Journals

~~~~~~

EDITOR'S NOTE

Wilson's journals are autobiography in documentary form, as well as a repository for scholars. Sometimes likened to *The Education of Henry Adams*, they appeared posthumously over almost twenty years, helping to support his family as planned. He first created *A Prelude* out of his notebooks from age thirteen through World War I, filling them out with retrospective interpolations. *The Twenties* chronicles his beginnings in New York City after the war, as interpreted by young Wilson and the older man looking over his shoulder. Able partly to edit this journal before his death, he shaped a series of snapshots into the story of a youth's initiation. The selections presented here describe friends and fellow writers, the nature of literature, and the emotional experience through which he finally comes of age with the Ukrainian waitress from Brooklyn, Frances Menihan.

The Thirties, *Forties*, and *Fifties* were edited by Leon Edel, who finished the editing of *The Twenties*. *The Thirties*, largely given over to the first six years of the decade, dramatizes the social crisis and Wilson's intense though fragmented private life. In some respects it is the richest of the journals. These selections take him from the beginning of his marriage to Margaret Canby at Cape Cod through his yearning, guilty remembrances after her death, and from the powerful field-notes behind his Depression reporting to a humorous interlude in his sometimes baffling 1935 visit to the Soviet Union.

In the passages from *The Forties*, the dehumanizing of the Japanese and Germans by American propaganda reinforces Wilson's awareness of the tragedy of the war for the human race, but he regains his equilibrium on the road in postwar Europe as the scenes with Evelyn Waugh and others show. A short section introduces the Haitian novelist and anthropologist Phito Marcelin, a close friend of Wilson's later years. His profound appreciation of Elena Thornton helps us understand why she would remain a loyal helpmate despite his deficiencies as a husband. His vision of life is also crystalized in the reflections on the death of Katy Dos Passos and the aging Edna Millay.

He wrote *The Fifties* and *The Sixties* in more finished form, knowing that he wouldn't be transforming them into anything else. In the early '50s he reclaimed the family house in the exhilarating open country of northern New York, and it became a literary symbol of sorts, with the poems his friends carved into the old window glass. The continued intellectual vigor conveyed by the birthday list included here is evident in the scene with one of the scholars studying the Dead Sea Scrolls and the sketches of Auden and Whitehead, the observations on the integration of sophisticated Englishmen into American culture. Readers may correlate his account of the Iroquois ceremony with that of the Zuni Shálako.

The Sixties, which I edited, is a rounded and complete evocation both of literary fulfillment and of the struggle to maintain one's energies in the face of old age. These selections place Wilson in the glitter of a party for Stravinsky in New York and of the Kennedy White House, where he is at ease and very much himself with the president. Hemingway's suicide makes him feel as if he has had "a prop knocked out." As "a man of the twenties," however, he travels, savors his memories, enjoys the personalities of rural neighbors as well as the illustrious. When overwhelmed by maladies, he seeks a sense of renewed vitality with younger women who look up to him intellectually. He continues to respond to the beauty of the upstate countryside and the sense it imparts of life's transience.

THE TWENTIES

Bank Street. The darkening sky of a June day, where the air still seems clear below and the houses, the windows, the trees maintain all their distinctness. —The remote unmenacing rumble of thunder—it will rain a little or pass off. —The pianist playing the music of some impressionist composer— wandering, seriously disporting himself in the treble in some light lingering in water or some wind-ruffled garden of Debussy—the metallic wavering and shimmer.

Morning after; plying to and from New Republic. A broken phonograph record and ashes on the floor—warm day, messy sweaty feeling of feet not in shoes, vagueness and inadequacy to life—the shifting and chuting of a load of bricks on Twentieth Street, the air gritty with brick dust— babies lying as if dead in their baby carriages, asleep in the heat—little burned or syphilitic girl always playing on Twenty-first Street—pretty and healthy black-haired Italian girl sitting reading in a doorway.

Great Neck, mid-April. Fitz said he was going abroad because his reputation was diminishing in America, and he wanted to stay away till he had accomplished something important and then come back and have people give him dinners. There was great talk on Lardner's part of going to the Red Lion or some other roadhouse, but when we did leave—all the liquor now gone—we simply went on to Lardner's, where we drank Grand Marnier—he insisted on presenting us each with a little bottle—and more Scotch.

Zelda had gone to sleep in an armchair and covered herself with a shawl—she was bored by Scott's chart of the Middle Ages and had made herself very disagreeable about it. Scott was sore because we had crabbed his revelation. "You pronounce too many words wrong," Lardner had said. Lardner read the golf rules aloud.

(This was a little book put out by the local golf club. Lardner read these rules at length with a cold and somber scorn that was funny yet really conveyed his disgust with his successful suburban life.)—Then we went back to the Fitzgeralds'. Lardner and I started talking about the oil scandal, and Fitz fell asleep in his chair. Lardner and I went on talking about baseball, Heywood Broun, Lardner's writing, the Americanized *Carmen*, the Rascoes, etc. Deep blue patches appeared at the windows. I couldn't think at first what they were—then I realized it was the dawn. The birds tuned up one at a time. It grew light. It was seven o'clock. Scott asked what we had been talking about. Lardner said we had been talking about him.—"I suppose you analyzed me ruthlessly."

When we were talking about his own work, Lardner said that the trouble was he couldn't write straight English. I asked him what he meant, and he said: "I can't write a sentence like 'We were sitting in the Fitzgeralds' house, and the fire was burning brightly.'"

e.e. cummings on the failure of the committee headed by A. Lawrence Lowell, the president of Harvard, to recommend clemency for Sacco and Vanzetti. I asked him what A. Lawrence Lowell was like: "Well, he was one of my father's greatest friends!—he goes around everywhere with a little poodle whose balls trail on the ground and make the letter H.— that's what he's like!—I've known several of these young men who are being groomed—groomed is the word!—for big positions—First, their teeth go—then they wear glasses—then, you mightn't believe it, but it's really so!— they have to be seen at certain places on Fifth Avenue, at certain times, with a silk hat!—and if they do that and are always on hand and make calls and suck pricks—after a while somebody dies, and they stand up and put on their silk hats and take out their pricks, and, if they've been good, they get the job.—When Henry dies, you get to be Lee, and when Lee dies, you become Higginson! There's a kind of

collar he [Lowell] wears that's part of the tradition—my father was supposed to be part of the tradition, too, but he
dressed like a gentleman—he wore a wing collar—but Lowell wears a kind of thing that's just wrapped around his neck,
and there's a kind of little black bow tie that they have to
wear with it that gets way up on one side under their coat—
so they wrap this old dried condom around their necks—
and their Adam's apple falls out."

Literature is merely the result of our rude collisions with
reality, whose repercussions, when we have withdrawn
into the shelter of ourselves, we try to explain, justify, harmonize, spin into an orderly pattern in the smooth resum-
ing current of a thought which for a moment has been
shattered and torn by them.

Men and women writers so closely identified, each with
its separate sex, that it is almost impossible to judge them
together—each functions, even as an artist, so completely
within the sphere of influence of its sex—tied to that stake
and only circulating about it within a narrow radius—so
that I hardly knew how to estimate the merits of Christina
Rossetti, in relation, say, to Yeats, or those of Jane Austen
to Turgenev.

Examples of authors: Housman putting all his sensitive
and affectionate heart into sixty or seventy slight lyrics
and spending all the rest of his intellect on the reconstruction of the Latin text of a poet inferior to himself and all
the rest of his passion upon the excoriation of obscure
scholars who have happened not to distinguish themselves
in his own field.

And writers who were noted for *sober judgment!*—I remembered that such small reputation as I had achieved

was apparently based on the supposed sober judgment of
a few literary articles and reviews—yet, except when I
was writing about literature, nobody could have worse
judgment and I—I was invariably either treating occasions of importance either too casually or too flippantly
or extravagantly overdoing other occasions which were
intrinsically trivial—disgracefully underestimating or
grotesquely overstating—and the sober judgment which,
by an effort, I was sometimes able to muster in print was
nothing more than compensation for the disappointments
and humiliations of a life which never hit the mark or
suited the means to the end.

[I had got to know Anna at the Tango Gardens, a cheap
dance hall on Fourteenth Street.]
   Her pale little passionate face in the half light with that
mouth moist, and always ready, more like a sexual organ
than a mouth, felt the tongue plunging into it almost like
intercourse—liked to cuddle up at night—cuddled up with
her mother when she slept with her—her mother would
push her away—I don't know what I do to her.—Responds so easily with that rhythmic movement—quickly
catches rhythm—to any stimulation—("Well, do you want
me to bite it off?")

She was lying at the foot of the bed—I at the head—I
saw her eyes over her hips—soft-hard and round—like
cunning burs—burs like agate marbles—with their unexpected depth, especially when the rest of her face was
hidden.

—We slept uneasily, I continually turning from one side
to the other and switching over the pillow, and the mosquitoes harrying us.

In the morning, a capable young woman, in her green dress, ironing her apron on the card table.

The whole evening and night left me, through the following day, a memory of sweetness and dearness—affection, satisfaction.

She didn't think of writing as work—didn't think of me as working because I didn't work with my hands.

She looked chic and glowing, under the hall electric light, in her green dress coming downstairs to open the door for me—I loved to watch her movements as, sitting on a bed, she pulled on her sister's small gray galoshes— one knee lifted, back bent, arms pulling, head with reddish hair lowered.

She laughed.—"I'm going to get somebody who can do it eight or nine times."—When I told her that I was going to get married, she clung to me without saying anything. "So you were thinking about marrying somebody else all the time!"—I told her about everything and asked her if she understood and she said, "Yes."—Then she began to tell me the true story of her affairs since I had known her.

Last day. Narrow escapes from callers—pulled down shades (afternoon) and, after one prompt bout, lay quiet in each other's arms on the couch till our tender silence was broken by somebody, whom I didn't let in, ringing the doorbell— she seemed sad, but didn't say so—gray eyes brooding and desolate—she said, "Well, I'll have to look for another lover."—She told me not to cheat on Margaret—then when I dropped her with the taxi over on Second Avenue, she said, "Goodbye, be good to Margaret."

When all our ideas of honor and loyalty, derived from our social class, from our Renaissance education, from our foolish early fantasies of ourselves, have been broken up and carried off by the currents in which we find ourselves drowning, we are at a loss as to what to fall back on, but we are bound to fall back on something; and this is perhaps where the real conscious solidarity of the human race begins.

THE THIRTIES

[Cape Cod, 1930] August 17–18. From the window of the shack where I work, there is a little gap in the dune, where the path down to the beach goes, and above the white sand, against the not-dark blue sea, a sand grasshopper, white as bone, will flutter with a dry whir—and then a gull, the white of snow, will fly by on a longer more leisurely more noble rhythm.

—Then rougher weather, a terrific undertow—the first time that I've really felt it was formidable—and the waves rising toward you like elephants—deliberate, powerful, crushing. —There was a streaked red and orange sunset, wilder and more remote than any during the summer—it made the sea off Peaked Hill seem, no longer a highway and preserve of man's civilized New England life, where trawlers came and steamers passed, but a waste, uninhabited, almost unexplored.

The Storm. [The Peaked Hill building had been condemned because the sea was eating away the coast. We didn't know how close we were to losing the house in that storm. It went out the next January.] One morning the rusty metallic twisted fragments of the old wreck, of which the battered boiler still lay always at the edge of the tide, were exposed, some sticking out of the water and others lying closer to the shore—I investigated one and, in the strong undertow, cut myself on it.

Another morning the beach was covered with fish, cod-mouthed, brown-smeared haddock, fine-spiny-finned herring, limp squid, soft dog sharks (that rotted and made an awful stink), grinning skates (Callot's or Brueghel's devils)—the whole beach silver-scaled along a strip with sardine-looking spurling, which the bigger fish had lost their lives gobbling and pursuing till their bellies were hugely distended and sometimes the tail of a spurling was sticking out of one's mouth, the wrecked fragments—and enormous claw or sections of the carapace—of enormous lobsters lying among the wreckage of the farther shore; flounders.

Notes on suicides at San Diego. January–June 1930: 51; September–November 1930: 20; January–July 1931: 36.

January: insane—gas; despondency, no work or money—ch. [apparently E.W.'s abbreviation for children]; ill health, family troubles, no work—cutting arteries.

February: drunk and desperate—poison; desperate over ill health—shooting; desperate financial condition, worry—shooting; deranged—shooting; seeking sensation—bichloride of mercury; financial worry, illness—found in bay; cause unknown—cutting artery; deranged—gas.

March: shot self after shooting wife; no cause—gas; desperate over health—shooting.

April: cause unknown—gas; desperate over health—strangulation; desperate over health—sulfonal and Barbital; cause unknown—shooting; evidently ill health—gas; desperate and financial worry; cause unknown—strangulation; deranged—gas; deranged—gas.

May: desperate—Lysol.

June: deranged—drowning; no work—strangulation; deranged—shooting; health, and failure to collect money—cutting artery; rent due him from tenants—shooting; health—shooting; deranged—gas.

July: family trouble—ant paste; health—shooting; no work—gas; deranged—shooting; no work or money—drowning.

Chicago. Dark: great banks of square buildings carved out of soft darkness like swamp mud—or dark smoke solidified—all the vistas smoky—enormous black cubes of West Congress Street with snow and then a belt of light—black blind trucks all alike waiting in front of one of the factories—an occasional old one-story wooden house—a long wide deserted street with fairly low-power lights along only one side.

   —more of a feeling of latitude than New York, but dark

   —the cold bleak lake winds along the big streets

   —"Vote Red. The people are goofy."

Unemployed. In schools, factories, warehouses, old jails—whitewashed furniture—factory walls, yellow school walls soiled, blackboards punched through, thin blankets and a sheet, men in holey socks and slit union suits, tattooed with fancy designs and with the emblems of services they no longer served, with fallen arches taken out of their flattened shoes and done up with bandages of adhesive tape, or lying wrapped up in their blankets on their backs, their skin stretched tight over their cheek-bones and jawbones almost like the faces of the dead—the smell, peppery-sweetish stink: sulphur fumigations, cooking food, sweat, creosote disinfecting, urinals, one element or the other figuring more prominently from time to time but in the same inescapable fumes of humanity not living and functioning naturally but dying on its feet and being preserved as best one could, venereal disease, Negroes with t.b., lonely as a pet coon, men poisoned with wood alcohol—fifteen cents a pint—two sick and one to the psych hospital—benzine, kerosene, and milk—

I say, which will you have, your bottle or a bed? —and
they won't give up the bottle—I wouldn't be surprised if
a hearse drove up and a dead man got up and walked out
and asked for a flop—a crippled drunk again—one man
so lousy no one would go nearum and they puttum in the
stable with the horse and the horse tried to get away and
then the next morning they gaveum a shower and
scrubbedum with a long-handled brush. —They fumigate
the clothes and if they're moist it ruins them. Chicago is
probably doing as good a job as anybody. —Entertainments so that they won't hold meetings and get ideas of
revolt—the recreation hall (Hoover Hotel), thick with
smoke, men sitting on the steps of the platform and flop-
ping on the floor, newspapers lying around, people sitting
in the gallery waiting for the show to begin (Thurston the
magician, Tarzan, prize fights in gyms)—honest, good,
and capable faces—the floors covered with spit—don't let
them into the dormitories till five—humanity being reduced to the grayness or rather the colorlessness of the
monotonous streets.

[After Margaret's death] I felt for the first time how she'd
given me all my self-confidence, the courage that I had
before to say what I thought—all her natural smartness,
fine quality, taste—social self-confidence which I'd used
to repudiate conventional society and make her uncomfortable in doing so. —Your ideas have made one person
very unhappy—she had been ready to give up Jimmy for
me when she came East, I said I thought that was a horrible idea, I wouldn't have her do that for anything—but
that was the way I felt—we'd all be better off if she were
dead—she said I always had my base elsewhere: at Red
Bank—

Little hotel at Santa Barbara—remembered, as I took a
bath, how she used to notice my love of relaxing in a
warm bath and lying there indefinitely, in connection

with what Cummings had said about a warm bath representing the womb.

—Suppose I should say at the funeral that I'd, etc. — she'd had those impulses, too.

At Mrs. Waterman's house, when I began to cry, she said, I've never broken down. —Would look in her face in vain for Margaret's beauty, in Camilla's in vain for any trace of her—but Mrs. Waterman's voice was so sweet, like Margaret's, and her flurried way of saying things—simple abashed (at a loss) way of saying—when I told her to open letter containing will: But it's addressed to you! —so like Margaret—how Margaret would say, like a child, when I said I was going somewhere: Aren't you going to take me with you? —She'd said, You're a cold fishy leprous person, Bunny Wilson—had said, Well, then, you're a cad— All right then, I am—it was for being so thoroughbred I admired her—even the Scotch-Toronto sense of what was and wasn't done (it was mixed with Philadelphia sporting distinction)—would smoke her cigarette with perfect poise, saying nothing, serious-looking—this really put me at a disadvantage and drove me into asserting my intellectual advantage of her in satire on and comprehension of the social structure, sense of the futility of worldly privileges and distinctions—I had said that her ideal man was a top-hatted morning-coated Canadian walking down the streets of Toronto—she strongly denied it: No, it's not— we never wore morning coats.

[Odessa hospital] The doctor was an extremely genial man (in white trousers and white Russian shirt) who hadn't brought any thermometer—told me it was nothing—he and old international *femme de chambre.* Gay exit: *Je vous dis au revoir, monsieur.* One of his prescriptions impossible to get. *Femme de chambre* was going to do something about it, but turned out to be off-duty the next day. Half-Polish housewife who had only been working for Intourist a month: much disorder, they needed people who could

speak languages, Hotel orchestra, Gibbon. —Doctor's second visit: had been in every country but America—Scan-
dinavian countries, had even been to North Pole. My
temperature seemed to be way up, and we decided that I
had forgotten to shake the mercury down—but still up.
When he saw spot on my arm, his whole manner changed,
became intensely serious, told me it was scarlatina—when
I asked him what I ought to do, he shrugged his shoulders
and threw out his hands in supreme expression of being at
a loss—"Go to a hospital, I suppose"—he rushed out without goodbye or explanation, saying, "It's scarlatina! It's
scarlatina!" After that, nothing—(behavior of *femme de
chambre*, whom I finally got on the phone)—till little
woman with red-visored cap appeared and took me in am-
bulance to hospital. —Young doctor and pretty blond girl:
team of Jewish comedians—perfunctory bath by old
woman—did me up like mummy and put me on stretcher
on floor—the question of money and watch arose: comedy
by Jew, reaching out clawlike hands, till girl shut door on
him—I had to burst from my shroud to count the money. —
Jews carried me to another building, setting me down at one
point and discussing whether or not I had got a receipt for
my money. —They put me in doctors' and nurses' room: I
called attention to bedbug on tablecloth; nurse changed tablecloth. The young doctor had the windows opened at my
request, though nurse seemed to demur over opening second
one. The lights hadn't been turned out two minutes when I
became aware of the myriad teeming bed life. I summoned
nurse: two Russian types, sad one and cheerful one, both resigned, both taking all for granted—gave me new bed and
bedding. When I had got into this new bed, I remarked two
more bb's crawling along tablecloth on night table and evidently planning to drop on me. I showed them to sad old
woman and as she caught and killed them she made pathetic
deeply grief-stricken sounds of one who had seen many little
children die and who knew there was nothing to be done
about it. (While fixing up my new bed, she had knocked over

the wine bottle of gargle, and then the other nurse had knocked over the medicine glass). Then she began polishing the floor with her foot in that sort of dance they do: she would stop and rest, hand on her back—they seemed to pick on her—her eyes always looked if they had gone dry long ago. —I fell asleep and went into my fever dreams, I dreamed that I had written a play called *A Bit of the New,* which was about to be produced by some organization like the Guild as *Quite a Lot of the Old*—I was determined to go in on the second act (which took place on an old-fashioned American porch) made up as a stranger with side whiskers, bowler hat, watch chain and fob, etc., and deliver a long speech vitally affecting the plot, which I hoped would break up the play. I woke up repressing hysterical laughter and tears. I thought, "I mustn't let Russia get me: the Russians must have dreams like that!"

THE FORTIES

[World War II] It may be that one thing which is responsible for the war is simply the desire to use aviation destructively. It must be a temptation to humanity to blow up whole cities from the air without getting hit or burnt oneself, and while soaring serenely above them. Many must feel vicariously as I do the thrill of doing—I felt it when the Germans were bombing London before we had begun bombing them. It is the thrill of the liberation of some impulse to wreck and to kill on a gigantic scale without caring and while remaining invulnerable oneself. Boy with a slingshot shooting birds—can't help trying it out. This is true of mechanical warfare in general: the guns batter down at long distance, the tanks flatten out without feeling, the planes wipe out whole cities without one's having to picture what has happened. It is the gratification of the destructive spirit, as it were in a pure ab-

stract form: if the enemy does not get you, you are free as
a bird of the consequences. You are further removed from
your object by the intervention of the mechanical bomb-
sight: your end of the process is mathematical, the machinery sends the bomb to its target. Constraints of the
conventions and codes that we live under, and that we are
glad to see smashed.

Newsreel I saw, just after the publication of the Jap atroc-
ities in which you were shown dead or writhing Chinamen executed by the Japs. One of the American officers
who had brought back the stories said, in what was obviously a prepared dialogue, "No, I think that the Japanese
are animals." The Announcer: You hear what U.S. Captain says. He thinks that the J's are animals. And now we
must fight these *animals!* We must buy bonds to defeat
these *animals!* etc. This is precisely the kind of thing that
Goebbels used to instill into the Germans, the idea that
they could exterminate the Poles: The Poles were an inferior race—the blacks are not people, but animals.

[Evelyn Waugh] began by pretending to think that I was
a "simple man" from Boise, Idaho, and, alternatively, that
I was a Rhodes Scholar, preoccupied with Henry James.
Raved about Sergeant [Stuart] Preston, who had made
such an impression—he had been staying around Wind-
sor and they thought he was going to marry the Princess
Elizabeth. Later, in [Waugh's] rooms at the Hyde Park
Hotel (where I was also staying), I talked about the antagonism to Americans, and he acknowledged it with a
wicked gleeful grin in his bright little hard eyes, but went
on to say that it was really based on jealousy. He talked
about the opportunity for Americans of buying up fine
things cheap. At White's (to which he had asked me for a
drink), he said that England had better ruins than Italy.
When I said that they would have to put up an annex for

the overflow from Westminster Abbey, he said that he didn't think there were going to be any more distinguished men. (I said some derogatory things about *Brideshead Revisited,* and this really rocked him. When I quoted some absurd sentence, he said, "That doesn't sound like me, does it?" He handed me the book and said, "Find it.") I asked him when he talked of Europe as something different from England, whether he thought of England as not being Europe.

[Elena, 1946] Under the barely grizzled and frosted raspberry blanket, her hips, which had grown bigger at Minden, looked beautifully molded and her slender legs disappeared into the tail of a mermaid. —When I came back from the bathroom, I saw the light hit on her tail and the back of her instep—I seized it and she began to laugh—with her Russian V-shaped mouth and her green eyes and pointed nose like her mother (quite different from her German personality)—she had hidden the whiskey bottle but put it on the pillow next to her.

—Another night, while she was asleep in bed, she had brought her hand against her temple, with the flesh at her elbow brought squashed and round and the strength of her upper arm accented, and her face—unlike the other night—in repose and much stronger, with its full lips and wide-nostriled nose, and eyebrows alert and eyelids not stolidly dropped, and short brown hair over the clear blond forehead—her foreshortened arm looked stronger—with the sheet tucked back under her chin— wonderful curve of hip under the raspberry blanket, so much fuller (that is, just full enough) than when we had come on here—with her awkward gait, her praying-mantis head. —But she has always that beauty that shines like a light—the intelligence you can't get a grip on or wrestle with in an exchange of wisecracks, love that is tempered by intelligence and knows how and where to place itself.

[Katy Dos Passos's death] I felt, as I had not done before, that we (Givens, Shays, Chavchavadzes, Walkers, Dos Passoses, Susan, Matsons, Vorses, ourselves) had all become a group, a community, more closely bound up together than we had realized or perhaps wanted to be. It was already a whole life that we had lived there—since Dos—who had always scoffed at Provincetown as a middle-class artist colony—had come up there to court Katy and had first moved in to "Smooley Hall." All the parties, the days at the beach, the picnics, the flirtations, the drinking spells, the interims of work between trips, the moldy days of winter by stoves, the days of keeping going on a thin drip or trickle of income, stories and articles, bursts of prosperity, local property and cars, bibelots from Mexico or elsewhere, pictures and figures by local artists accumulated in P'town front rooms, walled in against the street—that was what our life had been when we had dedicated ourselves to the Cape, to the life of the silver harbor—and all the love and work that had gone with it, that we had come there to keep alive. The cemetery at Truro made me sad not only on account of Katy but because it reminded me of Mary—[brought] up our children together, long enough to feel grounded there and to have been molded to some solidarity. Musty foul smell of a dead rat associated with reading *War and Peace* in the evenings at the Walkers' house one spring, and later in my bathroom when we had lived in Polly Boyden's house and used to take walks up there—for me now, she was just as much gone, just as much destroyed, as Katy.

[Edna Millay, 1948] I felt a certain satisfaction in the idea that I was outlasting her, but at the same time was troubled and depressed at finding the metamorphosis she had undergone. She seemed to have ceased to care about her looks—one of the things that happens to the drinker, and I decided that the reason she did not like to go out was that she did not want to be seen. I kept looking away and out the window. —At the same time, the strength of her character and her genius overcame me, as the visit went on, just as it always had. One could not make any impression upon her—except occasionally by criticizing her poetry—any more now than in her youth. —I reflected in dismay, but not without some satisfaction, at my own relative competence and health, on the tendency of the writers of my generation to burn themselves out or break down: Scott and Zelda, John, Phelps Putnam (just dead), Paul Rosenfeld, Elinor Wylie, Edna. One didn't really believe till one saw it demonstrated that giving oneself up completely to art, to emotion, to enjoyment, without planning for the future or counting the cost, produced dreadful disabilities and bankruptcies later.

[Haiti, 1949] I was roused out of bed this morning by the arrival at eleven of the Marcelin brothers. They had breakfast with me and then came up here and talked till after two. I was very much interested in them. Pierre, who writes the novels with Phito, was different from what I had expected . . . He is in some ways much more attractive than Phito, has an almost feminine good looks, sensitiveness, and charm (without giving a pansy impression). I think that he is probably the more important of the two in their literary collaboration. My guess is that their collaboration is very close and I imagine that what will happen is that Pierre will join Phito in Washington and that they will write another novel together. Pierre speaks even more indistinctly than Phito, and when he is talking about anything at all delicate, absolutely whispers, so that the things I most want to hear are completely unintelligible to me. The other brother [Milo] attends the voodoo ceremonies and commits them all to memory without writing them down. He is publishing texts of all their rites. They talked about voodoo mythology. I think that they are rather *fin de race* and at the same time rather *déséquilibrés* between their French tradition and their African heritage. They have all three made a cult of *"le peu-ple"*—these two told me, as Phito had, that the peasants represented *"le meilleur de l'Haiti,"* and that their life is really richer than that of the bourgeoisie because they think they are surrounded by the spirits of the voodoo mythology and in constant communication with and possession by them. The Marcelin family is very distinguished here—there are a *rue* Marcelin and a *pont* Marcelin—but I am told that, with their considerable Negro admixture, they don't belong to the very top layer, which, it seems, consists entirely of people who are almost entirely white, who marry only whites or each other and who only engage in business, never politics.

THE FIFTIES

[Upstate New York]—At last you emerge into the country of Oneida and Lewis Counties—it was misty, just at sundown, and beautiful, the mist lying along the green silky fields, the green silky elms rising dimmed, the blurred orange light in the sky (the next day, clear, liquid and bright—white and yellow and orange)—it always gives rise in me to a kind of noble thought: dignity and beauty of the country which somehow has ennobled the lives of the people and all that old story of their immigration and living, away from New England, among the hills and the fields where they were all alone, but independent and free, flourishing—their human relationships and labors against the non-human grandeur of that setting—riding along those up and downhill roads, a man behind a horse in a buggy, a farm wagon or carriage, under the high heavens with fluid orange light or dark blue thunder clouds.

May 10. Birthday resolutions for my 58th year:
New Yorker articles
~~Mario Praz~~
~~Little Dickens Preface~~
from June 1 — ~~Gogol~~
~~Chekhov~~
~~Grant's Memoirs~~
Turgenev?
Edward Lear?
Owen Wister?

Frank Norris
The later T. R[oosevelt]
Read Lermontov and *Oblomov* and the rest of Pushkin
For Princeton—~~Harriet Beecher Stowe~~
~~Civil War Memoirs~~
~~Bierce~~ and Lanier
Finish the two more elegiac poems by Christmas. [In
time for spring 1954: Book containing Haiti, Zuñi, Rus-
sians, Edward Lear and Barham, and Genet.] For book to
be published January 1, 1953.

[London, 1954] I thoroughly enjoyed London, which
seemed almost its old comfortable self. Pleasure of getting
into the good soft yet solid English beds at the Basil Street
Hotel. All my English side has come out and felt at home on
this trip. I do not feel myself so much in a strange part of the
world as I did at the end of the war, when everything was actually strange, on account of the rockets, etc.—I have, I suppose, been trying to get back to the England of my
youth—1908 and 1914—of the Exposition at Shepherd's
Bush, the Dickensian waiter who amused my father at the
Metropole Hotel, of Maskelyne's Egyptian Temples, of *Pyg-
malion*, Gilbert the Filbert, our bicycle ride from Scotland
taking in all the cathedrals, of our teas in country inns, of our
comings and goings to and from the old Langham Hotel

(bombed in the last war, I went to look at it in '45), near which the vista of Portland Place used to remind me of *The Golden Bowl*, of the old music halls: Albert Chevalier, Vesta Victoria and Maria and Alice Lloyd. But I cannot get back to this, and the truth is that I have now lived long enough so that the series of my visits to London (and to other places in Europe) now form a sequence of memories each of which is still vivid and can easily be made to present itself as immediate yet of which the earlier ones are somehow so far in the past that I cannot hold them up, cannot anymore include them in any present functioning consciousness, and they seem to topple over at the end of the curve of the lengthened span of my life, even to be lost as actual. If that really means anything to me. I can remember them still with pleasure, yet they do not make part of my present life.

[Israel] *March 31.* Conversation with Flusser: he arrived with his briefcase, hatless. We sat down in the lobby as far away from the music as possible. Small and stocky, red hair, rimless spectacles. I said something about the controversy, and he said the important thing was not Zeitlin (this was what he thought I meant by the controversy), but the large question of what was implied by the scrolls. He is dynamic, imaginative, passionately interested—soon began talking French. He produced from his briefcase a Greek Testament and the text of the scrolls (hymns and *Manual of Discipline*), and showed me the parallels, sometimes translating the Hebrew into Greek (the holy spirit = רוח, purification by baptism, righteousness—*dikaiosune*)— the similarities, he pointed out, were all with the Epistles and John: the doctrine of the elect—predestination thus originated perhaps with this sect, and you had the succession: Dead Sea sect—St. Paul—Spinoza—Calvin—Marx. Horrible the doctrine of predestination! He would smile slyly and drily and laugh with dry harsh laugh. He thought that the Master of Righteousness had written all the thirty hymns (as Licht, who had been working on them, also thought possible), and spoke to me of him later over our drink, with positive and emphatic admiration—a strong and courageous soul.

—*Auden and Whitehead*, it seems to me, have been the two Englishmen of genius I have known who have embodied most authentically the strong creative English qualities— stout character, self-dependence, stubbornness in following their intuitions, combination of practicality with poetic and metaphysical thinking. And both have come to live in the United States. They have seemed of a different breed from the contemporary English don or London literary man. With Whitehead, coming to the States was partly due to logical positivism at Harvard and to his being made comfortable there, but partly perhaps to being old enough English to feel kinship with the old English on which were based the 17th-century Puritan and the 18th-century Revolutionary traditions. One felt in him the Englishman's awareness of his sturdiness, his special position in Europe but not the complacency, the paramount need to put down all the other peoples. In Auden's case, there was something of this, and something of the reaction of the middle-class Englishman who does not want to be a toady or even to succumb to the fashionable attitudes that defend literary London against the hierarchy of England. He did not, he made it clear, desire to be a member of the Connolly literary family. Such surpassingly gifted men are uncomfortable in the British class system—Dickens and Kipling are also examples, but they could not endure democratic habits and manners, and eventually went back home. Auden is the first such man who had succeeded in adapting himself—though he still, he was telling us the other night, can't reconcile himself to seeing certain kinds of people—especially wearing the gaudy ties that he loathes—eating in restaurants that he frequents: "I feel that they're not gentlemen—they oughtn't to be there." (Elena says that this is a regular second reaction of enthusiastic foreigners who become naturalized citizens.) He is certainly the first writer who has succeeded in making a language that combines American with English—he is a great master of language; and he has produced, in poetic form, a comprehensive description of the whole English-speaking industrial-ugly, democratic-leveling oppressive, urban and suburban world.

[The Old Stone House, 1957 (taken from *Upstate*)] Elena gave me a diamond-point pencil for Christmas, something I have long wanted, and I have been having my poet friends write verses with it on the panes of glass, sometimes directly on the windows here, sometimes on panes that I carry around. Those on the third floor, which look out on the sky and the tops of the trees, all deal with lofty missions or mythologies or the elements: by Saint-John Perse (Aléxis Léger) some lines from his *Vents*—

> *C'étaient de très grands vents*
> *Sur toutes faces de ce monde*

—his script is bold, clear and elegant, perfect for writing on glass; by Charley Walker, the well-known lines from *Prometheus*—in Greek and in his translation—about the winds and the waves and the innumerable laughter of the sea; a poem by Phito Thoby-Marcelin about a Haitian goddess:

> *Où est Caonabo?*
> *Caonabo n'est plus*
> *Qu'au sein d'une pensée . . .*

a passage from Isaiah in Hebrew (6.8.) by Isaiah Berlin: "And I heard the voice of the Lord, saying, Whom shall I send, and who will go for us? Then said I, Here am I, send me." (When he wrote this, he insisted that it was not at all his idea about himself; but I believe that it has been, a little.) On the second floor, passages about dreaming and sleep: John Wain, who came to see us here, in the bathroom, on the window, so I can read it from the tub, though it occurred to me afterwards that I should have had him inscribe it on the mirror:

> It tells you what you do but never why,
> Your image in the glass that watches you:
> You cannot catch it napping if you try . . .

Edwin Muir, in the little bedroom, though too high so that it is hidden by the shade, a translation from Hölderlin about a stag with agate eyes; Stephen Spender, on the window at the top of the stairs, where it comes out beautifully, shining, in the late afternoon light—I won't allow curtains to be hung over it: "I think continually of those who were truly great" . . . ; Louise Bogan in Helen's bedroom: "The landscape where I lie" . . . ; Wystan Auden in the back bedroom:

> Make this night loveable
> Moon, with eye single
> Looking down from up there
> Bless me, One especial
> And friends everywhere. . . .

On the door to the balcony Vladimir Nabokov's:

> бывают ночи только дягу
> в Россию попдывет кровать. . . .

all in the old spelling. I have not worked out for the first floor a satisfactory principle of selection, and there are not so many inscriptions as elsewhere. Alfred Bellinger and Stephen Spender composed for it special quatrains; Dorothy Parker, so far advanced in her afternoon drinking that I was surprised she was willing to do it at all, inscribed a rather undulant version of what she says is the only poem of hers she cares for:

> Whose love is given overwell
> Shall look on Helen's face in hell,
> Whilst they whose love is thin and wise
> May view John Knox in paradise.

[Iroquois: Little Water Ceremony] The third section is the climax of the symphony. Now the medicine at last is found. Each of the sections is opened and closed by Nick Bailey's "flourish of the flute." This is the whippoorwill, whose cry is thus imitated. It is a kind of leitmotif (like the bird in *Siegfried*), for it guides the questers to the medicine and it now for the first time (?) is heard in its pivotal role in the action. This section is more complicated and difficult to sing. The melody and shape of the songs of the two preceding sections has been uniform from beginning to end of each. But now the songs begin on unexpected notes and follow unconventional courses. This is magic, a force beyond nature is tearing itself free. There is a passage of reiteration that sounds as if some phenomena were being enumerated one by one, a litany of praise perhaps. A great structure is raised by the rattles that is neither the big shimmer, the express train, or the grand march. And a paean is let loose; it fills the room with its volume. One finds oneself surrounded, almost stunned, as if the four walls of the room had become the cylinder of a pipe organ and as if one were sitting inside it, immersed in a sustained diapason. How strange when the lights are turned on—strange apparently for the singers, too, who are blinking and dazed at first, having to bring themselves up short in this kitchen, in this new electric-lighted world—to find oneself there in the room with ten men who work during the day in the gypsum mines and plants, dressed in their unceremonious clothes; an assortment of physical types, some

handsome, some not so handsome, some young and some
old, some fat and some lean, some sallow, one almost
black, some with spectacles, some with their teeth gone,
who have just given body in the darkness to a projection
that absorbed them all. A car had driven up to the house;
its headlights had glared through the window. I saw the
profile against it of a man turning round to look; but the
singing was not interrupted, and the driver, who had
heard it, withdrew.

THE SIXTIES

At the reception [for Stravinsky] were Craft, Wystan and
Chester and other people that we did not know. The host
and hostess were fairly young, evidently fairly well off,
had collected some not absolutely first-rate modern pictures. The pianist and her father and I think other members of her family were there. Elena thought the Grafs
were in some way Swiss—Mrs. Graf talked French with a
very American accent. Mme Stravinsky had told them
that Str. would have something to eat immediately after
the concert. They had said they weren't sure that they had
enough plates: "Given him chicken à la king on an ashtray,
but he has to have something to eat." The result was ham,
crab meat salad, brownies and bread and cheese. As I was
filling my plate, Wystan appeared and said in a hushed
voice which was perhaps not quite hushed enough. "That
ham's too salt. The only excuse for rich people is that they
do things like that right." His face is now crisscrossed with
creases; it looks squarer than when I saw him last and like
some kind of technical map. He went early, leaving Chester, with whom, for the first time without Wystan, I had a
longish talk. He is gentle, not unintelligent, has to sur-
mount a not obstructive stammer.

The Russians made their own little nuclear group, in which we came to be included. I found out from the hostess later that it was the Stravinskys who had wanted us invited. Str. began by saying to me, "I read your lines" . . . I didn't understand this at first, and he explained *"vashi stroky,"* making lines in the air with his finger. I tried to tell him how much his music had meant to me—difficult in conversation: I said that it had been to me "an inspiration" when what I really meant was that, besides my enjoying it so much, it had helped to keep up my artistic morale. *"C'est réciproque, c'est réciproque,"* he said. He was jolly, amusing, even bubbling— quite frank and accessible, I thought, as we find with delight that such masters may be. I had not quite realized what a little wisp of a man he was—in France they used to call him "the insect." Even I seemed to have to bend over him, and I felt that his tiny stature, his in themselves unimpressive features, must in certain ways have made him shy, at the mercy of the world around him—I remembered *Petrushka* and *L'Histoire du Soldat.* Elena says he looks like a musical note: his legs and feet dwindle to tininess. But his opinions in conversation, like his music, are fearless and firm. Isaiah Berlin and some other friend had persuaded him to read *Doctor Zhivago,* which he had got through between rehearsals, but he had not liked it at all: he thought it a second-rate novel (comparing it, I imagine, with Turgenev, Tolstoy, etc.)—it was simply a collection of fragments, would have no lasting value—he had not even liked the poems, had never read any of Pasternak's poetry written before these. He adored— what seemed rather surprising—the writings of Harold Nicolson, thought they were very well written. His spoken English is not very good—his French a good deal better. With Elena he spoke mainly Russian.

He gave me to understand that he hoped that the Dead Sea scrolls had turned out not to be authentic: I remembered that he was very pious and said his prayers every day, so did not pursue the subject. He spoke of Schoenberg with less respect than he had seemed to in his published conversations: he was a man of considerable talent but *"désagréable"* and too romantic for him. I said that Schoenberg came out of Wagner. "Mahler—and Wagner, yes." It was Anton Webern that he really admired. I said that the English critics had been writing rave notices of *Moses und Aron* after the recent performance in Berlin. "The English critics are not very certain," he said, meaning not sure of what was what. He was depressing to Elena about Nicholas Nabokov—I had asked him about Nicholas's opera on Rasputin, which Virgil Thomson had told me was quite good. In the first place, the subject had shocked him: it was too early to write an opera about Rasputin. Then Nicholas was so unsatisfactory—half professional and half amateur. He said that Nicholas would bring him a piece and offer to dedicate it to him if he liked it; would play it and then Stravinsky would say nothing. He told us that if we ever came out to the Coast, we must visit him. He had his wife write their address and number and handed it to me, saying, "That's everything about Stravinsky!"

A hanger-on would bring him cheese and brownies. When offered a piece of cheese, he would lean forward and stick his tongue out. She called his attention to a plate at his side and induced him to put the cheese on it, rather than take it on his tongue. All this time, Elena tells me, the Russian ladies—Mme Str. and a woman whom E. already knew, a hanger-on of the musical world, of Stravinsky and the American ballet—were saying all kinds of "horrors" about the Swiss guests: "What *poshlost'* [crassness]! *Bogaty* [They're wealthy]." At last Mme Str. advised her husband, "You must congratulate *vashu shveitsarku* [your Swiss lady]," so he went to her with hands outstretched. "Who are all these people that we don't know?" said one of the ladies to the other. "*Esche shveitsary* [More Swiss]," with a shrug. When we left, we went down in the elevator with the Russians. "Now let's have a drink," said Str., with the mischievous smile of a small boy. I said that we wanted to go to his ballet—an all-Stravinsky evening, which would be only half over. As he was getting into his car, he faced us and said, "*Apploud!*" first making the motion of clapping, then throwing out his hands.

Death of Hemingway. This upset me very much. Absurd and insufferable though he often was, he was one of the foundation stones of my generation, and to have him commit suicide is to have a prop knocked out. I have now been told that his mind had been going and that he had had shock treatments in Rochester; I hear reports that he was quite demoralized and could sometimes hardly talk intelligently. But at the time I was depressed by the notion that, after encouraging writers "to last and get their work done," he should have died in such a panicky and undignified way as by blowing his head off with a shotgun. The desperation in his stories had always been real: his most convincing characters are always just a few jumps ahead of death. It is a wonder that this was not more noticed. Instead, the press and the public mainly took their cue for their conception of him from his show of full-blooded vitality. He was vain enough to fall in with this and to play up to the popular press. This phoney public *persona* begins to get into his work in the interludes of *Death in the Afternoon,* and it became after this quite rampant—though mostly in magazine and newspaper articles which he afterwards did not reprint—and one gets the impression that the serious artist had actually to struggle against it. The thing about the two bullfighters, parts of which came out in *Life,* looked to me perfectly awful; it was the only thing of his that I felt I could not read. *Life* was exploiting him for all he was worth, and he was collaborating. There was a picture of H. on every page: H. towering over the bullfighters. H. dining with Spanish friends who adored him, even the bull seemed to have his face. Something he said about this work in an interview or a statement printed by the editors made me think that he realized its badness and did not want to have it published as a book in that form. In any case, it did not appear.

As a character in one of Chekhov's plays says he's "a man of the eighties," so I find that I am a man of the twenties. I still expect something exciting: drinks, animated conversation, gaiety: an uninhibited exchange of ideas. Scott Fitzgerald's idea that somewhere things were "glimmering." I am managing to discipline myself now so that I shan't be silly in this way: diet and non-drinking, non-expectation of sprees. I believe that I am more or less succeeding in becoming a sedate old gentleman.

[White House, 1962] The dinner was in two large rooms, at tables of about ten people. Elena was at a table presided over by one of Kennedy's sisters and sat between "Chip" Bohlen and the director of the Metropolitan Museum. I found myself at Kennedy's table between Agnes de Mille and Geraldine Page. Kennedy had Mme Malraux, looking very beautiful, on his right, Mme Alphand on the other side, the wife of the French ambassador, a much less attractive lady. I didn't know then who Geraldine Page was, but she took it very well. She is handsome and seems intelligent; is not at all like an actress, has no public personality for off the stage. She told me that she had appeared in Tennessee Williams's *Summer and Smoke* and *Sweet Bird of Youth*. Agnes de Mille explained to me that she was a granddaughter of Henry George, and we talked about *Progress and Poverty*. She is apparently still a loyal Taxer.

Kennedy told me he had seen a review of *Patriotic Gore* and asked why I had called it that. He asked what conclusions I had come to about the Civil War. I answered that I couldn't very well tell him then and there and referred him to the Introduction. He said something about its being unusual for an author not to want to talk about his book. Later I asked him whether he ever saw Pat Jackson [Gardner Jackson, an old friend of mine, a well-to-do near-radical, who lived in Washington, served in the New Deal and once occupied Kennedy's apartment]. "Not for a year," he said. "He used to come and give me advice. He wanted me to help him get a plaque put up in Boston for Sacco and Vanzetti. I told him it wasn't time yet." I mentioned the monument in Boston to the Quaker who was executed by the Puritans. "That took them three hundred years," he said. "Those Puritans were brutal."

Irwin Shaw was on Mme Malraux's other side, talking vigorously to her in French. He has been living in Switzerland to avoid taxes, and had flown over especially for the dinner. The *New Yorker* people, who don't much like him, expressed surprise at his being there; but I found out from Alfred Kazin the probable reason: Kennedy has a friend who wants to make a play out of one of Shaw's stories, and he must have been asked at the President's instance. I said to Kennedy that he had certainly done a thorough job of entertaining the literary world: "Maybe they ought to entertain *me*." I told Mme Malraux that I had been surprised, as Camus said he had been, that Camus rather than Malraux should have been given the Nobel Prize. I said that I supposed that his past politics had had nothing to do with this. She said no, but I couldn't hear her explanation well enough to understand it. I had had, perhaps wrongly, the impression that Camus seemed to them safer than Malraux.

The President, who had had paper and pencil brought him and who had either been writing a message or making notes, now got up and introduced Malraux. He said, as he had at a previous such dinner, that there were more brains assembled that evening in the dining room of the White House than any time since Thomas Jefferson dined alone.

He said that this was one occasion in celebration of Franco-American amity at which mention of Lafayette was not going to be one of the main features. "Of course we all know that, after Washington, Lafayette was the greatest American of his time." He gave a brief description of Malraux as soldier, flier, explorer, writer and Minister of Culture under de Gaulle. Malraux replied by saying that he had been glad to come here and see our *"chef d'oeuvres"*—I couldn't imagine at first what masterpieces he meant, then realized that he was referring to the pictures in the National Gallery. [He had told me once in Paris that the Metropolitan was *"un musée de province,"* but that the National Gallery in Washington was a really important one.] He said that the United States was unlike the Roman Empire, unlike the Byzantine Empire, unlike any empire of the past. I cannot remember his words, so quote from a report of the speech that he made later on in New York, in which he said the same kind of thing: "The United States is the first nation to become the most powerful in the world without having sought to be so. Its exceptional energy and organization have never been oriented toward conquest." I said to Mme Malraux, as I certainly should not have done: *"Dites à Malraux que je n'en crois rien."* I didn't know that Kennedy understood French [I have learned since that he had been taking lessons] and was surprised when he took me up: "You don't tell us what you think." Malraux also in one of these speeches spoke of our having the most powerful weapon in the world and yet not wanting to use it. I was astonished at his going so far in diplomatic absurdities. After all, we had used it.

After dinner, there was a concert: Schubert's Trio in B Flat Major. The violinist was Isaac Stern. I had never heard it before—it was lovely, but I did not feel much like listening to music. Malraux, it seems, went to sleep. Marian Schlesinger said afterwards that he had had a little too much to drink; but I don't think this was necessarily true. He had been taking Jackie through the National Gallery and had had a long conference with Kennedy. He had evidently come over to try to iron out Kennedy's difficulties with de Gaulle. After the concert, Isaac Stern went to play the violin with a jazz orchestra. Elena had a talk with Balanchine, who, she said, seemed very depressed. He was going to Russia and didn't want to go. [He hated it when he got there and interrupted his stay by a trip back to New York].

When we said goodbye to the Kennedys, he said something again about my not wanting to tell him about my book: "I suppose I'll have to buy it." "I'm afraid so." I thought that it was better to say this than to tell him that Oxford had sent him a copy.

I spent all last winter in Cambridge finishing the Civil War book, did not even write in this journal. I got bored with dealing with political and literary history, bored with the limitations of the resources of my own vocabulary in dealing with this sort of thing, at which I don't think I am really at my best. It is a relief to get back to this journal.

[Paris, 1963] Helen arrived on Monday, and one afternoon we took her to Versailles: a gray day and a holiday with a flock of middle-class visitors. These French were small and dreary—you rarely nowadays see women dressed with chic—and they seemed so completely alien to the château, with its gardens and great galleries and huge portraits and gigantic historical episodes, that the latter had the appearance of having become disregarded and shopworn, no longer looked upon by the people with any vital relation to them and shoved away behind museum barriers. The glorious past was no longer there, though remotely and unreally it hovered in the background in the anachronistic figure of de Gaulle. The excitement of my

visits at the end of the First World War, when I stayed at
the American University Club in the rue de Richelieu and
went to the Guitry theater, or in 1922 (?) when Edna Millay was here and we had our little scene in the Bois de
Boulogne, or in the autumn of 1935, on my way back from
Russia, when I met Malraux and the Joyces, or even coming back with Elena and meeting her Russian relatives as
well as seeing Mamaine when she had just been divorced
from Koestler just before her death—I remembered all
these but they had now fallen back into the map of a much
flatter world, on which Boston and New York and Washington were other centers of more or less activity: France
and England comparatively supine while Washington
more energetic and aggressive. Prices in France are high,
and there is a good deal of unemployment.

Dinner with *Auden* Thursday night. He presented me
with bound sheets of his new collected poems. I thought
he was in very good form, and I had a very good time
with him. I asked him why he so had it in for Yeats, and
he answered that it was because at one time he had been
too much influenced by him. His own idea of poetry was
something much less rhetorical. His reaction against
Rilke was also due to his having been too much influenced by him. He quoted Erich Heller as having said that
Rilke was the greatest lesbian poet since Sappho. As
usual, the moment came—toward the end of the first bottle of wine—when he paid me extravagant compliments,
said that I was the only person he wrote for—he must
have meant in America—or something of the kind, that
he depended on me. I had managed, before dinner, to tell
him, without greatly arousing what Stephen Potter
rightly calls his masterly "lifemanship," that his anthology of minor nineteenth-century verse had been made a
mess of—he says that he has straightened it out for England—and that it seemed rather like another book of light
verse, with a few hymns stuck in. He seems to accept

these anthology jobs at the suggestion of publishers, and then, having compiled the material, not to pay any further attention to them. We had another bottle of wine in the lounge after dinner.

Highmarket [an abandoned crossroads village]: a well patterned old white door on a background of peeling asbestos shingles that imitated pale brownish bricks. —The vast gray capsizing barns, and the smaller ones settling askew. Huge carcasses of prostrate barns, mixed bones sticking out of the heavy hide; squalor of asbestos-shingled small house, with the front porches fallen through.

After so much drinking, I went to bed early; then woke up between 2 and 3 and finished Macaulay's history. Though he was dying, he more or less rounded it out by writing the deaths of James and Williams detached from where he dropped the main narrative. Quite fortifying to find him sustaining it, with the same high morality and thoroughness, through the parliamentary developments of the bills connected with the Irish forfeitures—same patience and eager interest.

When *Mary and I* got back in the late afternoon, we went to the Parquet for dinner. The conversation got rather sexy—she admitted to having read *Fanny Hill.* On the way back, I made her stop the car on the dark road across to 12A before you get to T'ville, and we did some enthusiastic kissing. "I don't know when you'll find me in this mood again." She came into the house with me here. I did not turn on the living-room light, and we did some more kissing on the sofa. I found out what her personality was like when she was excited and being made love to: "U-n-n-no! —It would make me feel guilty . . ." (when I told her that I wanted to see the rest of her body, she said

with conscious humor) "I'm perfectly beautiful, but no."
I took out my cock, and she felt it. It was gratifying to be
conscious that it was capable now of an erection. I kissed
her as long as it seemed rewarding, and in my pauses she
sometimes gave me little kisses on the cheek. She would
murmur little remarks so softly that, in my deafness, I
could not understand and would have to put my ear to
her mouth and ask her to repeat it. It was faintly comic
and out of key.

[Anne Miller, 1970] I gave her a good deal of Moselle
wine; criticized her poetry: she has no idea of rhyme or
meter. We agreed that writing poems is therapeutic—I
told her Edna Millay's saying, parodying the ad for apples: "A sonnet a day/Keeps the doctor away." She seems
to have been carrying on some kind of affair with someone for two years, trusted me to be discreet, showed me
one of his poems, which was just as undistinguished as
hers and sounded very much like them. I explained the
various kinds of metrical feet and suggested her trying a
sonnet. When she did, it didn't come out right—she said
that she didn't know why, but when she got to the last
lines, they always come out too long. I don't understand
her yen for me at my age, and I don't believe it was inspired by her finding that, according to that list in *Esquire*,
I was supposed to be one of the hundred most important
people in the world; she had already begun to show her
interest in me. She is very pretty, brisk, bright—flirta-
tious but also realistic and direct. I told her that all the
men in town must be in love with her—after a moment's
silence, "A few," as I had answered when Mary told me
that I must have had many beautiful women.

June 12. In the morning, went with Anne to the chasm on
Sugar River under the railroad bridge, which I don't seem
to have described in this journal before and which I

wanted to see again. Anne helped me through the stones—I could never have managed without her—she wore tennis shoes and a tennis dress; and when we got to the swimming hole and cataract, she went off from me and with her back to me took off her dress near the falls and went in swimming naked—I saw her slim brownish figure from behind, and she looked very pretty. Two tragedies occurred here: a boy was found drowned—it's not known whether or not he committed suicide—and two girls walking on the trestle were overtaken by the train: one lay down on the tie and let the train pass over; the other, the Erwin girl, I think, tried to hang on with her hands and fell off.

When you get beyond the broken stones, among which grow blue bugloss, buttercups and wood anemone—with a sprinkling of forget-me-nots and violets and occasionally the inevitable beer can, spearmint wrapper, black marks of picnic fires—you find yourself in a high-walled chasm of stratified limestone rock which is feathered with green fern and lined in the cracks with green moss. Birds flit back and forth between the walls. The river runs shallow here with moderate rapids. The cliffs where they overhang are dripping with springs, and across the river, the farther one goes, the more densely they are plumed, grown with trees: ash, feathery hemlock, elm—bushes of sumac. A dead tree droops down over the stream. The cascade is white, rather crooked and dragged. Below it, a brownish froth floats on the swimming hole, and this, and what she thought was a stagnancy of the water in a kind of inlet, made Anne think that it might be polluted and made her dubious about taking the children here. A stretch of primitive landscape invisible and little frequented just off the traffic of Route 12. Above the chasm, against the blue, the coverlet of small dappling clouds crawls slowly below the sky.

—Or else to imagine History as a crystalline sea-
anemone.

SHORT BIBLIOGRAPHY

Aaron, Daniel, "Introduction," Edmund Wilson, *Letters on Literature and Politics*. New York, 1977.

Castronovo, David. *Edmund Wilson*. New York, 1984.

Dabney, Lewis M., ed. *Edmund Wilson: Centennial Reflections*. Princeton, 1997. Commentary on Wilson by Daniel Aaron, David Bromwich, Andrew Delbanco, Jason Epstein, Louis Menaud, Jed Perl, and remembrances by Wilson's intellectual associates.

Dabney, Lewis M. "Introduction," *The Sixties*. New York, 1993.

Edel, Leon. "A Portrait of Edmund Wilson," *The Twenties*. New York, 1975.

French, Philip. *Three Honest Men: Edmund Wilson, F. R. Leavis, Lionel Trilling, a Critical Mosaic*. Manchester, England, 1980. Commentary on Wilson by Lionel Trilling, Stephen Spender, V. S. Pritchett, Jason Epstein, George Steiner, Yigael Yadin, and Gore Vidal.

Groth, Janet. *Edmund Wilson: A Critic for Our Time*. Athens, Ohio, 1989.

Meyers, Jeffrey, *Edmund Wilson: A Biography*. Boston and New York, 1995.

Schapiro, Meyer. "The Revolutionary Personality," *Partisan Review*. November–December 1940.

Wain, John, ed. *Edmund Wilson: The Man and His Work.* New York, 1978. Includes essays by Alfred Kazin, Larzer Ziff, Peter Sharett, Helen Muchnic, John Wain, and John Updike.

Warren, Robert Penn. "Edmund Wilson's Civil War," *Commentary.* August 1962.

Wellek, René. "Edmund Wilson (1895–1972)," *Comparative Literature Studies.* V, no. 1, March 1978.

ABOUT THE EDITOR

Lewis M. Dabney, Professor of English at the University of Wyoming, edited the last volume of Edmund Wilson's journal, *The Sixties*, and the forthcoming *Edmund Wilson: Centennial Reflections*. He is currently writing a biography of Wilson.

Other titles of interest

HERE AT THE NEW YORKER
Brendan Gill
New introd. by the author
428 pp., 131 illus.
80810-2 $15.95

**THE KINDNESS OF
STRANGERS**
The Life of Tennessee Williams
Donald Spoto
445 pp., 34 photos
80805-6 $15.95

ELIA KAZAN
A Life
Elia Kazan
864 pp., 130 photos
80804-8 $19.95

THE AMERICAN EARTHQUAKE
**A Chronicle of the Roaring
Twenties, the Great Depression,
and the Dawn of the New Deal**
Edmund Wilson
576 pp.
80696-7 $17.95

**BATTLE-PIECES AND
ASPECTS OF THE WAR**
Herman Melville
New introd. by Lee Rust Brown
282 pp.
80655-X $13.95

**THE COMPLETE HUMOROUS
SKETCHES AND TALES OF
MARK TWAIN**
Edited with an introduction
by Charles Neider
722 pp.
80702-5 $19.95

DISCRIMINATIONS
Essays and After-thoughts
Dwight Macdonald
New introd. by Norman Mailer
466 pp.   80252-X $11.95

FACES IN THE CROWD
**Musicians, Writers, Actors &
Filmmakers**
Gary Giddins
288 pp.
80705-X $13.95

FRANZ KAFKA
A Biography
Max Brod
295 pp., 8 photos,
3 pp of Kafka's sketches
80670-3 $13.95

GEORGE WASHINGTON
A Biography
Washington Irving
Edited and abridged with an
introduction by Charles Neider
790 pp., 3 illus, 5 maps
80593-6 $18.95

HARDBOILED AMERICA
Geoffrey O'Brien
216 pp., 137 illus. (8 pp. in color)
80773-4 $16.95

IN THE SPIRIT OF JAZZ
The Otis Ferguson Reader
Edited by Dorothy Chamberlain and
Robert Wilson
Foreword by Malcolm Cowley
327 pp., 1 photo
80744-0 $15.95

**THE LITERARY CRITICISM
OF JOHN RUSKIN**
Edited by Harold Bloom
430 pp.
80294-5 $12.95

**THE PAINTER OF MODERN
LIFE AND OTHER ESSAYS**
Charles Baudelaire
Edited by Jonathan Mayne
298 pp., 53 illus.
80279-1 $13.95

**REVOLUTION OF
THE MIND**
The Life of André Breton
Mark Polizzotti
784 pp., 48 photos, 1 line drawing
80772-6 $20.95

RICHARD WRIGHT READER
Edited by Ellen Wright and
Michel Fabre
910 pp., 66 photos
80774-2 $22.50

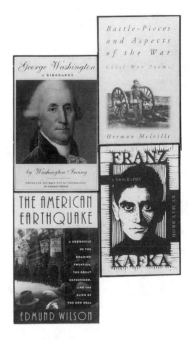